ITALIAN TREATISES ON FOIL, ÉPÉE, AND SABER

TRANSLATION FROM ITALIAN TO ENGLISH OF:

IL FIORETTO – DEI MAESTRI PIGNOTTI E PESSINA

LA SCIABOLA – DEI MASESTRI PIGNOTTI E PESSINA

LA SPADA – DEL MAESTRO GIUSEPPE MANGIAROTTI

LA SPADA – ESTRATTO DA: QUADERNI DI SCHERMA – MAESTRO TORAN

translation by

Brian A. Bacher

La pubblicazione è stata realizzata grazie alcontributo della Direzione generale Biblioteche e istituti culturali del Ministero della Cultura - volume di rilevante interesse culturale

EDITORE ACCADEMIA NAZIONALE DI SCHERMA
Napoli
2025

Published by Accademia Nazionale di Scherma
accademianazionalescherma@gmail.com
www.accademianazionaledischerma.it
Napoli
2025

INTRODUCTION

I am thankful and fortunate to have been invited into the Military Fencing Masters Program (later renamed Fencing Masters Program). Originally located within San Jose State University, California, USA. There I was able to further my understanding of fencing under Maestro Gaugler's teachings and instruction. Maestro was an animated storyteller, while remaining private. One of his many stories was his plan to go to Europe for just one semester. Time passed as he applied himself to his studies which took him to many different countries. He returned to California in 1969 with his Doctorate in Archeologic Classica all'Università di Firenze, Italy, eleven years after he left the states. Another story about how he and his wife were held at customs more than once while traveling back and forth across Europe as agents interrogated him about his fencing kit. One year the De Young Museum in San Francisco, California, USA held an exhibit of European Arms. Maestro gave us a personal tour delving into the depths of each important piece on display weaving together the history and development of the arms as we strolled through the halls of the museum. When we dined with Maestro, when he was offered Parmigiano with his pasta, he would say "make it swim in it" with a gleeful smile.

Maestro had an intensity about him. Fridays in the fencing room was a full afternoon of learning how to both fence and teach fencing. The class structure generally began with a lecture highlighting a fencing master from antiquity, followed by two and a half hours of foil, another hour and a half of saber and at least one hour of epee. Maestro Gaugler would then put on his white coach's plastron and give private lessons, and these were brutal. He would work as long as the student could manage, then more. Often the lesson would stretch beyond 45 minutes. If he did not like what he saw in preparation of an attack, he would rapidly beat the weapon away 3 or 4 times with such swiftness that there was no possibility of avoiding it. If the error continued, he would stop the lesson, raise his mask, press his lips together, looking right at you, saying, "let's try that again" then the lesson would resume. Maestro was always supportive and assured the student with measured positiveness about how well the lesson went and specific actions that he felt were best suited for the student's hand. Many of my lessons ended by marching forward, pointing in line at the correct distance, then disengaging in time with every ounce of strength remaining. Maestro would then free fence after the lessons, with either his preferred weapon, foil, or saber depending on who was in attendance that afternoon.

Maestro developed this level of intensity, focus, discipline, and supportive style of teaching during a lifetime of practice. His path began in his youth by watching fencing classes from a small hill that faced the only fencing club in Detroit, Michigan, USA. Later he found Aldo Nadi's book On Fencing, and from this book he knew fencing was a sport he wanted to become his passion. Maestro was determined to work with the best fencing teachers, which befit his proclivity as an accomplished artist and his growing interest in archeology. At his first opportunity, Maestro moved to Los Angles, California USA and became one of the last American students of the great Aldo Nadi.

Nadi encouraged Maestro to continue his studies in Europe, especially Italy. There he was pitted against other fencers who were steeped in the long tradition of fencing. Italians, being born into the birthplace of systematic swordplay, have a remarkable focus and determination when fencing on the strip while being fast friends off the strip. This personality trait I can attest is most true, having worked in Italy's fencing rooms.

Maestro obtained a faculty position in the Art and History department at San Jose State University in 1969. In 1979 Maestro founded the Military Fencing Masters Program at San Jose State University, the only university in the United States to have an internationally recognized preparatory school for fencing Masters, Provosts, and Instructors. His program closely followed the Italian system and pedagogy set by the Accademia Nazionale di Scherma. In 1987 Maestro introduced the first English version of his book Fencing Everyone to his program. Maestro instilled in his students the necessary richness, depth of tradition, and science of Italian fencing. He was able to manifest these traits from his years of experience in the fencing rooms across Italy, France, and Germany plus being of direct fencing lineage and last living link to Maestri: Radaelli, Pini, Barbasetti, Sestini, and Parise. Of Maestro's masters, Amilcare Angelini, Umberto Di Paola, Aldo Nadi, Giorgio Pessina, and Ettore Spezza, only Maestro Di Paola lived to see The Science of Fencing in print, and he was thrilled by its very existence.

The Military Fencing Masters Program was formerly reviewed in 1988 by Maestri Niccolo Perno, President of the Associazione Italiana Maestri di Scherma and Enzo Musumeci Greco, Member of the examining board of the Accademia Nazionale di Scherma. The Accademia is the very program Maestro Gaugler graduated from with his Maestro di Scherma in 1976. In 1998 his program was reviewed again, this time by Maestri Giancarlo Toran, President and Saverio Crisci, Vice President of the Associazione Italiana Maestri di Scherma and members of the examining board of the Accademia. Maestro Toran noted that the program "clearly bears the

Italian imprint and represents an island of Italian fencing methodology and tradition" following all the seriousness and rigor of the examinations found in Italy.

Maestro Gaugler wrote several books about fencing. Note, fencing was not his main advocation, being a professor of Etruscan Archeology was his professional focus. His works include:

- *Fechten für Anfänger und Fortgeschrittene Florett, Säbel, Degen* (München, Nymphenburger Verlagsbuchhandlung, 1983) [2nd ed. 1986; 3rd ed. Heyne, 2004]
- *Fencing Everyone* (Winston-Salem, N.C. : Hunter Textbooks, 1987)
- *The Science of Fencing: a Comprehensive Training Manual for Master and Student, Including Lesson Plans for Foil, Sabre, and Epée Instruction* (Bangor, Maine: Laureate Press, 1997) [2nd ed. 2004]
- *The History of Fencing: Foundations of Modern European Swordplay* (Bangor, Maine: Laureate Press, 1997)
- *A Dictionary of Universally Used Fencing Terminology: with approval of the Joint Board of Accreditation of the United States Fencing Association Coaches College and the San Jose State Univ. Fencing Masters Program* (Bangor, Maine: Laureate Press, 1997)

And

- *The Tomb of Lars Porsenna at Clusium and Its Religious and Political Implications* (Bangor, Maine: Laureate Press, 2002)
- Maestro Gaugler wrote as well numerous articles on fencing technique, history, and pedagogy. See bibliography maintained by the Accademia di Scherma Classica. http://www.clubscherma.org/ for additional references.

In January of 2011, Maestro was sadly notified he had only a few months to live. As proof to his tenacity and strength, he extended that date to early December before falling to cancer. He was survived by his wife Gladys whom he had fastidiously taken care of due to her own illness, and their daughter. During his last year I was fortunate enough to enjoy dinner on numerous occasions with him at his home in Sunnyvale, California, USA. Late that November was my last dinner with him. Maestro pulled me aside and encouraged me to continue my studies in Italy, and test for Maestro di Scherma. That was his last wish and conversation with me. His program continues under Maestra Janine Sahm. William Mathias Gaugler, born August 5th, 1931, passed December 10th, 2011.

Maestro, I fulfilled my promise.

Being set on this path to complete my studies, attending the national courses in Chianciano, Italy and to be tested by the commission of the Accademia was an enormous goal set before me.

My ability to attend classes in Italy, study, translate, and test would not have been possible without the help of the dear friend and mentor, Maestro di Scherma Igor Celli. To whom I am forever grateful.

The work presented herein is the English translation of the very theories Maestro studied and used as a foundation for his program. The authors of these treatises for foil and saber are Maestri Pignotti and Pessina, and epee by Giuseppe Mangiarotti. Plus, the notes and didactic updates found in the current volume, della Quaderni Scuola dello Sport Quaderni di Scherma, La Spada, complemento per la didattica, nasscita della moderna spada sprtiva, la prestazione schermistica by Maestro Toran, et al.

To Maestro Gaugler's Maestros: Amilcare Angelini, Umberto Di Paola, Aldo Nadi, Giorgio Pessina, and Ettore Spezza who shaped his skills. I humbly add my Maestros: William Gaugler, Igor Celli, Ralph Sahm, Giancarlo Toran, Davide Lazzaroni, and Paul Scherman for their invaluable contributions to my skills.

Brian A Bacher, Maestro di Scherma, Campbell, CA, USA January 2024

THE FOIL

IL FIORETTO

originally printed
ITALIAN FENCING FEDERATION - SCUOLA CENTRALE DELLO SPORT
ROME 1970

PREFACE

This treatise is the result of the work carried out by a Commission of renowned professionals and enthusiasts to whom the Federation requested their expertise as devoted practitioners of the art of fencing.

The members of the Commission are:

Masters Guido Comini, Umberto Lancia, Giuseppe Mangiarotti, Giorgio Pessina, Ugo Pignotti, and Messrs. Arturo De Vecchi, Edoardo Mangiarotti, and Alfredo Pezzana.

The Commission, thus constituted, after several working sessions, entrusted Masters Pessina and Pignotti with the task of preparing the final text based on the framework and spirit of the work conducted.

The purpose of this treatise is to provide those who wish to pursue a career as fencing masters with an official text from which they can learn the technique of foil fencing and subsequently pass it on to their students.

This treatise is therefore a theoretical-practical manual written primarily for pedagogical purposes, aimed at training new fencing masters.

Drawing parallels with other fields of human knowledge, our treatise serves the same purpose as grammar and syntax do for languages, laying out all the rules that must be learned by those who wish to write correctly in their language. Depending on how one learns to apply and use these rules in the creative process, they may become a masterful artist or remain a mediocre writer, even while strictly adhering to the most rigid norms of style.

Evidently, it is in the personal creative application that lies the secret of the success achieved by the true artist.

Similarly, the rules of this manual, conveyed through the ingenious teaching of the master, will form the necessary foundation for shaping a champion.

In our community, there is frequent discussion about treatises and their content, with many considering it necessary and useful for them to explain fencing actions that, in our view, are merely applications of basic actions.

For this reason, the text does not include applied actions that blur the lines between multiple fencing rules, leaving it to the intelligence and creative genius of the master to teach them using the method they deem most appropriate.

Firmly believing that the classical principles we learned from the great masters of our glorious fencing past, and which they spread throughout the world, remain today as they did yesterday, the foundation and essence of fencing, I express my hope — which is also a fervent wish — that this work of ours, rooted in the pure sources of our grand tradition, may make a meaningful contribution to the revival of Italian fencing.

I also extend heartfelt thanks to the members of the Commission for their significant contributions, especially to Masters Giorgio Pessina and Ugo Pignotti.

RENZO NOSTINI

ITALIAN FOIL

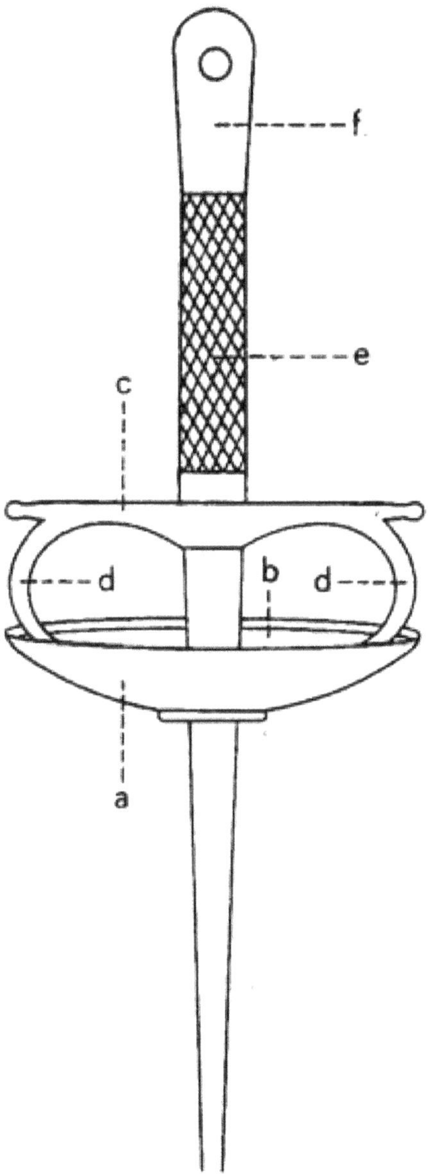

Fig. 1

CHAPTER I. ESSENTIAL ELEMENTS

(ELEMENTI ESSENZIALI)

The nomenclature of the foil's parts

The foil is composed of two main parts, the guard (*guardia*) and the blade (*lama*). The guard is made to protect the hand. The guard is made by the:

a. Bell guard (*coccia*), in iron or aluminum, in the shape of a spherical cap with a diameter of less than 120 mm, having a rectangular hole in the center to allow the passage to the threaded tang (*codolo*) and to the blade's (*ricasso*);

b. Pad (*cuscinetto*), in leather, rubber or fabric, also drilled in the center, which fits perfectly in the concave part of the bell guard;

c. Cross bar *(gavigliano)*, which is an iron bar of length equal to the diameter of the bell guard and perpendicular to the axis of the blade. at the center of the cross bar there is a hole, corresponding to the hole of the bell guard, in which passes only the threaded tang;

d. Two Arches (*due archetti*), also in iron, which support the cross bar and attached internally to the bell guard;

e. Handle (*manico*), generally of wood, drilled along the entire length of the axis to allow passage of the threaded tang;

f. Pommel (*pomolo*), cylindrical or truncated cone shape, made of iron, which screwed to the end of the threaded tang, it serves to keep the blade fixed to the guard and at the same time to give balance to the weapon (see fig. 1).

The blade, which is made of tempered steel, with a rectangular or square cross section, is composed of three main parts.

a. The tip (*bottone*), is an enlargement at the tip of the blade itself and has the purpose of preventing the blow from causing the least damage to the opponent;

b. The ricasso (*ricasso*) is the visible part of the blade between bell guard and the cross bar;

c. The threaded tang (*codolo*) is the part of the blade that passes through the grip and threads into the pommel.

The length of the blade is 900 mm, calculated from the convex part of the bell guard to the tip. The blade is divided imaginatively into three equal parts, which will take the name of "degrees", and precisely:

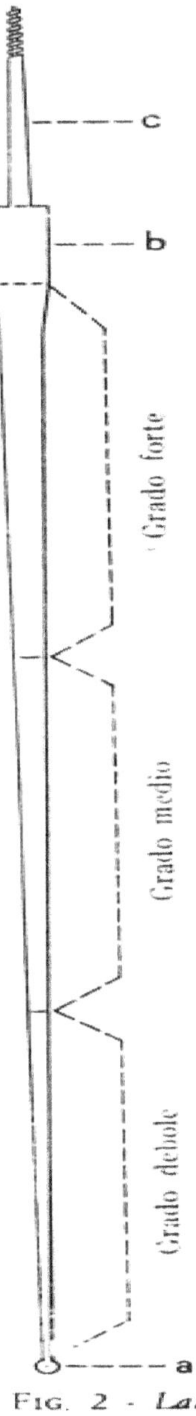

FIG. 2 - La

1.   **Strong** (*forte*), the part closest to the bell guard;
2.   **Medium** (*medio*) the section included between the other two;
3.   **Weak** (*debole*) neat the tip (Fig.2)

Note. — Only these foils can be considered the types of foil used today in Italy and perhaps in the world: the classic Italian model, of which we have described the nomenclature; the French one and the orthopedic (pistol grip) one. These models differ from each other only in the handle, since the blade or, better, the uncovered part of the blade (from the outside of the bell guard to the tip) or that part of the weapon destined to touch, block, provoke and suffer the contacts and the contrasts with the corresponding part of the adverse weapon, is the same for each type of foil. The Italian foil has, as it has been said before, the handle with the cross bar, which corresponds to the ancient cross of all the weapons of the past ages; the French foil has a handle with a long and completely smooth handle; the orthopedic foil, on the other hand, has a handle that allows the fingers (middle and the last two fingers) to find their fixed place marked by grooves resulting from the cast aluminum piece which is precisely the handle.

Since the classic Italian foil is the one used by the great majority of Italian fencers and that is, among other things, the foil composed of the greatest number of elements, it is pointless to describe the nomenclature of the French foil and orthopedic foil, because both are made only from   just   a   part   of   the   Italian   foil   described   above   (see   figs   3   and   4).

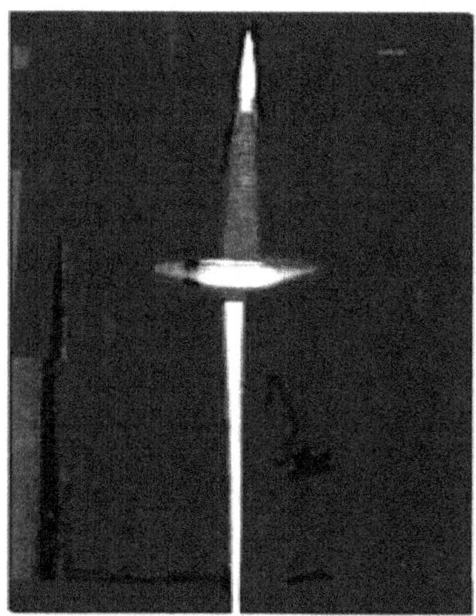

Fig. 3
Fioretto francese

Balance, weight, and total length of the foil *(Equilibrio, peso e lunghezza totale del fioretto)*

The balance of a weapon is felt as soon as it is handled. However, to establish exactly if a foil is well balanced, it is necessary that the center of gravity, which is found in the forte of the blade, is about 4 fingers width from the bell guard. Handling the foil with the four fingers placed under the blade, with the little finger close to the guard, it must remain in perfect balance on the index finger.

The weight of the foil must be less than 500 grams, while its length from the tip of the blade to the end of the pommel must be less than 110 centimeters.

Holding the foil *(Modo di impugnare il fioretto)*

Holding the Italian foil, put your index finger and the middle finger both between the ricasso and the left arch (if right-handed). The last digit of the index finger must stay under the ricasso and the fingernail touching the pad. The thumb passes over the cross bar to make pressure on the opposite side of the index finger on the top of the ricasso. The last two fingers hold the grip. The handle follows the concave part of the hand so that the pommel is always at the center of the wrist (see fig. 8).

It is very important to hold the foil properly because the success of each action depends on this.

The Fencing Master must therefore pay great care and attention so that the student does not neglect or modify the standards indicated above.

Hand positions *(Posizione di pugno)*

The positions of the armed hand that the fencer can take in different situations are called "hand positions". In the foil these positions are obtained by rotating the hand on the longitudinal axis of the forearm.

The positions of the hand are six, four primary and two intermediates, they are: position of first, second, third, fourth, second in third, third in fourth.

Holding the foil and placed in line (see fig. 12), the back of the hand is on the left and the crossbar is perfectly vertical: hand in second position *(di seconda)* when the back of the hand is at the top and the crossbar is horizontal: hand in third position: *(di terza)* when the back of the hand is on the right and the crossbar is vertical: hand in fourth position: *(di quarta)* when the back of the hand is at the bottom and the crossbar is horizontal: hand in second in third position: *(di seconda in terza)* when the hand is in the middle position between the second and the third and the crossbar in a diagonal line to the right: hand in third in fourth position: *(di terza in quarta)* when the hand is in the middle position between the third and fourth and the crossbar in a diagonal line to the left.

In foil, the hand in first position is only theoretical, and therefore we can disregard it. The other five all have a practical use in the execution of the various fencing movements.

The First Position *(La prima posizione)*

Holding the foil as shown before, the feet must be placed at 90-degree angle with the front foot pointing forward, (following the line of direction) on the fencing strip *(pedana)*. With the body perpendicular, with "open" and straight shoulders held at same level. Place the foil at hip level, hand in third position and the tip is facing down and back at a diagonal of 45 degrees. The non-weapon hand is on the hip holding the blade between thumb and index finger (see fig. 11)

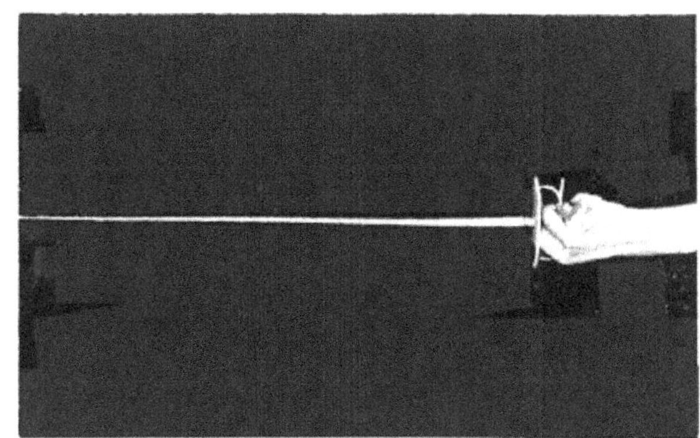

Fig. 5
Posizione di pugno
di prima

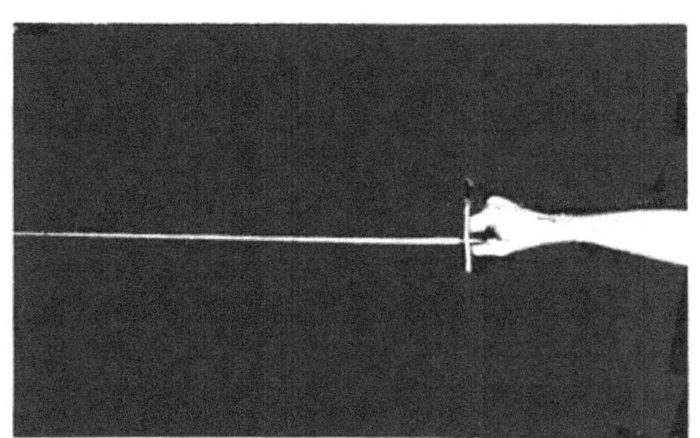

Fig. 6
Posizione di pugno
di seconda

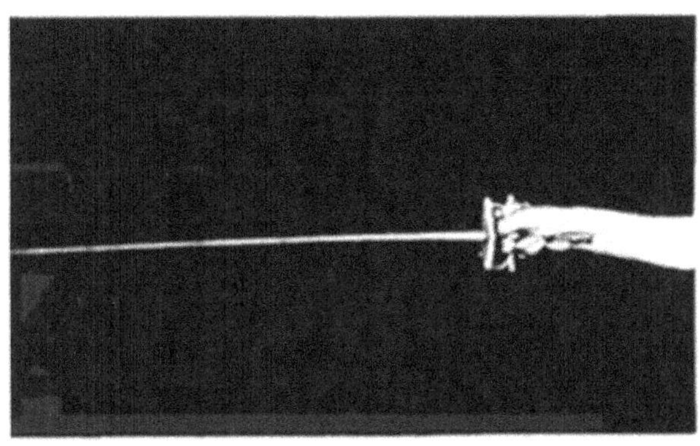

Fig. 7
Posizione di pugno
di terza

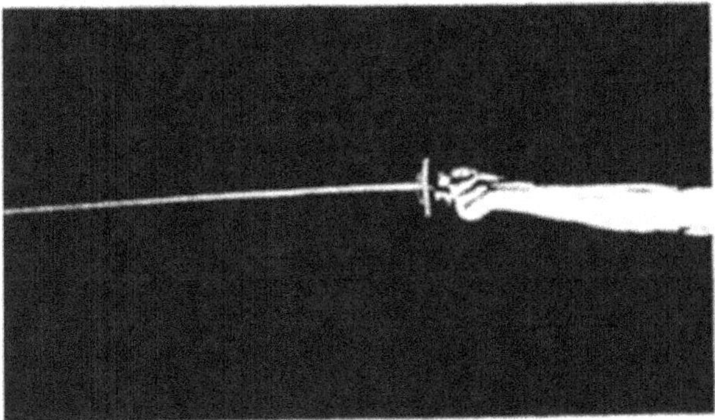

Fig. 8
Posizione di pugno
di quarta

Weapon in line *(L'arma in linea)*

The line made by the arms and weapon parallel to the fencing strip that point to the advisory's chest. Standing in first position, start the motion from the elbow, raising it to the shoulder and extending the forearm out level with the upper arm parallel with the fencing strip (see fig. 12).

The salute *(Il saluto)*

A dutiful act of courtesy to the opponent and to the audience that the fencer must never neglect at the beginning and end of every lesson or in the bout (1).

From the first position, bring the foil in line, then raise it, flexing the arm at the elbow, then bring it back in line with the hand in fourth position: in this way the opponent is greeted; then, once again flexing the arm at the elbow, it is stretched out not completely with the hand in third in fourth position to greet all those who will be on their inside, and finally, with the same procedure, but with the hand in second and third position, greet the bystanders on the inside.

Naturally the head should be rotated according to where the salute takes place, looking at those present.

---

(1) The salute has ancient origins and value of a symbolic gesture, because from the time of the barbarian invasions the Christian who went down to battle used to bring to his lips the hilt of the sword which, due to its cross shape, gave the gesture a high meaning.

Line of direction *(La linea direttrice).*

With both fencers in first position, facing one another with an imaginary line between them connecting one fencer to the other through the two heels and the front toe of each (see fig. 13).

This line indicates the path that the feet should normally follow during private lessons, exercises, or the assault.

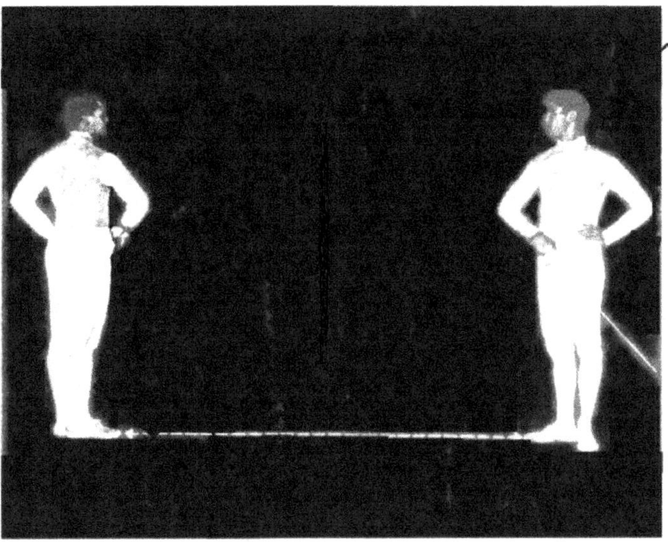

Fig. 13 - *Linea direttrice.*

The guard *(la guardia)*

The guard is the position that the fencer takes with the body, weapon in hand, to be ready for offensive, defensive, and counter offensive actions.

One comes down into the guard in two movements:

1) Describing and arc of a circle from bottom to top bring the foil in line while at the same time the unarmed arm comes into the same single line with the foil.
2) The front foot is brought forward by about 1 and ½ shoe lengths, bending at the same time the knees so that the knees are perpendicular to the toe of the corresponding foot and the front knee is centered over the corresponding foot. At the same time, the rear arm is bent at the elbow. The rear arm forming an arc with the elbow slightly higher than the shoulder with the fingers jointed, slightly pointing toward the head.

In guard position, the weight of the body must be broken down evenly between the legs with the head in a normal position, turned toward the opponent, arms on the same line of the shoulder, well in profile with the tip of the foil pointing to the chest of the opponent.

Weapon in line of offense *(L'arma in linea di offesa)*

With the tip of the foil threatening any part of the valid target and the arm naturally extended is weapon in line of offense. (1)

(1) This is the definition written in the "Reglement pour les épreuves de la F.I.E."

The lunge *(L'affondo)*

The lunge is the position of the body the fencer takes at the end of an offensive action, starting from the guard. This is performed in a single seamless coordinated movement beginning from the guard and without discontinuity ends in the lunge in perfect harmony.

Gradually, with absolute precedence of the tip of the foil and without giving any excess movement out of the guard, the completeness of the extended arm compels the body to thrust forward without the slightest break in the forward movement, one lifts the front foot, just verging on the strip and kicking out as far as extension permits, while the back leg violently drives out till the knee is locked. The front foot is positioned under and in line with the knee and the front thigh parallel with the strip. The back foot, acting as a brake, is held flat upon the strip.

The rear arm extends vigorously backwards stopping it almost parallel to the back leg. The head must remain fixed during the movement as well as the shoulders being relaxed and at the same level.

The chest is maintained erect throughout and, in the end, the front knee slightly forward in relation to the instep (see fig. 17, 18, 19).

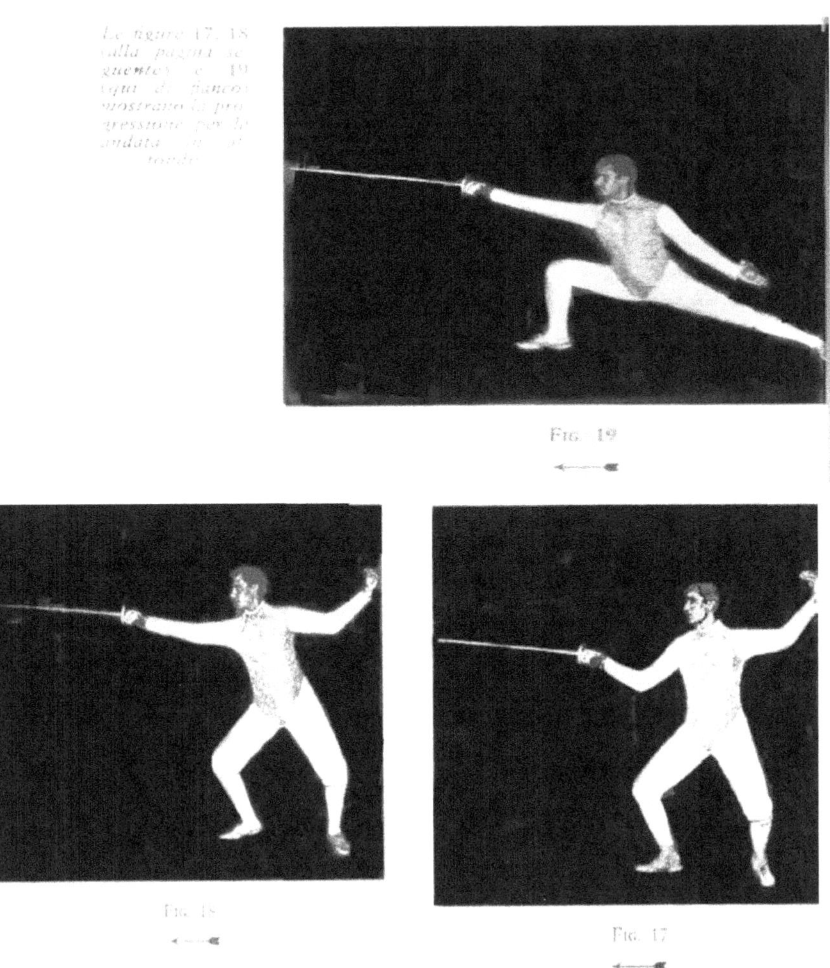

Fig. 19

Fig. 18

Fig. 17

Recover on guard *(Il ritorno in guardia)*

The recovery on guard is primarily the work of the legs while keeping balance of the torso by employing the back and abdominal muscles. Quick movement and composure are necessary. As with the lunge, the elements that make up the movement must be made without the slightest discontinuity and in harmony with each other.

From the lunge, push back rapidly with the front foot while simultaneously relaxing the back knee as one recovers the weight of the body back to center while the front foot recovers back to its original position in the guard, making sure the front heel does not lift from the strip any more than necessary. At the same time the rear arm is folded upwards with decisive movement.

Advance and Retreat *(Il passo avanti e il passo indietro)*

No fencing action is performed or even conceived if not for the function of keeping distance.

Therefore, being able to rightly advance and retreat are the most important means to which a fencer can control the appropriate distances for offense and defensive actions. The Advance means to decrease the distance from the opponent to the extent that he can be hit with the lunge.

From the guard the front foot is brought up from the ground just enough to glide forward one shoe length following the line of direction *(linea direttrice)* and the rear foot moving the same distance so that in the end of the step the distance between the feet is the same as the normal guard.

The retreat serves to take distance of greater breadth from the adversary in each moment so that they do not come to close. This is performed by retreating first with the rear foot followed immediately with the front foot.

On both advance and retreat, care must be taken that:

    a. The torso must be steady with no extraneous movement from the legs and the chest remains well profiled.
    b. The feet must remain in the line of direction.
    c. The distance between the heels, when the movement is complete, should be the same as before.
    d. These movements are made without rising out of the guard.
    e. The feet are always just grazing the surface of the strip.

Advance is said to tighten the distance or shorten the distance and the retreat to break or dissolve the distance.

Jump back *(Il salto indietro)*

The jump back is a leap backwards that brings you out of measure and is a set of coordinated movements that start with the front foot, bringing it back and to the outside of the rear foot. Then launching backward as far as possible with the rear foot. Where the feet will assume back into the normal guard.

The distance *(La misura)*

Measure refers to the distance between two fencers in the guard position, facing each other. Since the valid target in foil fencing is limited to the torso, this distance can be medium, long, or short. These correspond respectively to different types of measure, known as *correct measure or lunge measure, advancing measure, and close measure.*

Correct measure is when the opponent's target can be reached with a simple lunge; *advancing measure* is when reaching correct measure requires at least one forward step; *close measure* is when the opponent can be struck without the need for a lunge.

The practical method for assessing measure is as follows:

  – if two fencers are in the first position, facing each other with their weapons in line, they are at lunge measure if the tips of their weapons meet at the point where the weak part of the blade transitions to the middle; at advancing measure if the tips are just slightly in contact; at close measure if the tips meet at the point where the middle part of the blade transitions to the strong part.
  – if the two fencers are in guard, but still with their weapons in line, they are at lunge measure if the tips extend approximately four finger-widths beyond the respective guards; at advancing measure if the tips reach the point where the weak part of the blade transitions to the middle; at close measure if the tips touch each other's torsos.

It should be noted that these guidelines are relative and depend on the height and physical build of the individual fencer.

Advance-lunge *(Passo avanti-affondo)*

The advance-lunge is an uninterrupted sequence of movements consisting of the advance followed by the lunge and serves as the development of the attack by walking or marching. It is used when performing an offensive action that requires a step before reaching the target.

The advance-lunge consists of three continuous stages:

1 the advance of the front foot
2 the advance of the back foot
3 the lunge

Therefore, the execution of the marching actions that are composed of one or more movements of the foil is adjusted on the rhythm of the aforementioned three movements to obtain the whole harmonious, effective, coordinated, and fluent movement of the tip once the fencing action has begun. Continuously and uniformly accelerating motion forward without a discontinuity until its end.

This action, when performed while marching, requires a longer time than that performed with the lunge alone. Therefore, the study of such action is addressed as to the achievement of coordination between movements of the weapon and legs at speed.

If the distance to be covered is judged to be greater that what can be overcome with a normal advance it is advisable to fully advance the rear foot, thus meeting the heel of the front foot (*raddoppio*) or take suitable distance to carry out the action walking without exposing yourself to the opponent's counteroffensive action.

An action carried out by walking distance can be:

      a.   those that need keeping contact with the opponent's blade.
      b.   those so-called walking on the free blade (*ferro libero*).
      c.   those in which the contact between the two blades is only one shock point.

In the first and in the second case the attacker must take particular care in making the advance so as to not beat the strip causing movement in the body and the hand. (*attacco patinato*). (1)

In the third example the attacker can develop from the beginning all the power for the explosive movement so that the action is especially fast.

In the development of these, the latter action can be performed by a little leap or jump. This is accomplished by an imperceptible time gap replacing the step and just as the rear foot meets the strip the lunge will follow. *(di balestra o saltato)*

(1) Clarification, the Patinato is a rapid or accelerating step forward made with greater softness and without rising or causing jolts.

The gaining on the lunge *(Il raddoppio)*

The gaining on the lunge (*raddoppio*) begins from the guard, remaining bent over the legs, the fencer carries the rear foot forward until in contact with the heal of the front foot, and then lunging.

Therefore, by redoublement the distance can be exceeded by that of the advance-lunge. This movement can be performed from the lunge, this event assumes the name of "renewed attack with gaining on the lunge" (*ripresa d'attacco di raddoppio*).

Flèche *(La frecciata)* ***running attack or arrow***

Another kind of action, which we believe should be taught only when the fencer has acquired accuracy and mastery in the execution of the advance-lunge. For consideration and description this will be introduced on page 95.

Placements of the weapon *(Gli atteggiamenti con l'arma)*

The placement of the weapon refers to the position of the armed hand the fencer takes when they are on guard in relation to the advisory.

The development of the individual's offensive actions is directly subordinated to the placement in which it finds itself at the initial moment of the action itself. This must adapt to the conditions or placement offered by the adversary's weapon and to have the freedom and best possibility of implementation and success.

There are three placements of the weapon:

1. invitation (*invito*)
2. engagement (*legamento*)
3. blade in line (*arma in linea*)

The invitation is the placement of the weapon that one takes with the purpose of exposing a target.

The engagement is a contact that is established between the two blades so that one's own blade dominates the opposing steel diverting from the offensive line.

The blade in line is the placement of the weapon that has the weapon arm naturally extended with the tip of the foil in the direction of the adversary's chest.

Relationship between targets, invitations, and engagements *(Relazione tra bersalgi, inviti e legementi)*

As mentioned, the valid target of foil consists roughly of the torso. The limits that determine the exact surface of the target are the upper part of the neck up to the inguinal fold, excluding the arms up to the line that joins the tip of the respective humorous and armpit (1) (see fig 23, 24).

Both the invitation and engagement, when taken, determine the division of the aforementioned target, dividing it up into four distinct sectors taking the name of internal, (inside) external, (outside) above and below. (*interno, esterno, sopra e sotto).*

The line that runs through the tip of the foil directed to each of these sectors is called: internal line, external line, high line, and low line (*linea interna, esterna, alta e bassa).*

(1) after the introduction of electrical signaling in electric foil competitions, for technical reasons the ruff of the mask is not part of the valid target (at the time of this writing).

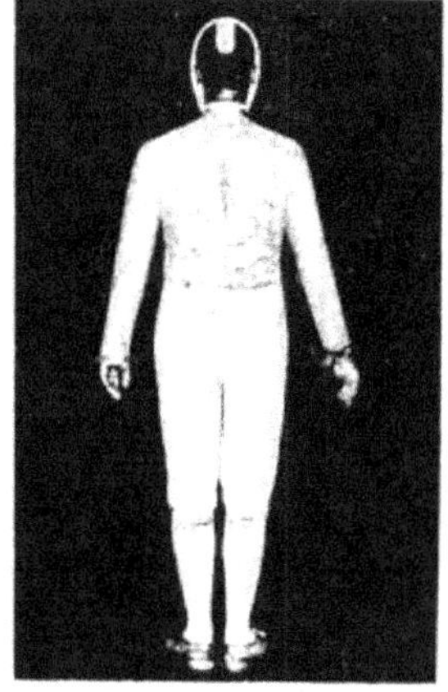

Bersaglio valevole

Fig. 23   Fig. 24

The invitations are four and are named: first (or half-circle), second, third, and fourth.

From the line engagement, in a single movement, the following invitations can be performed:

The **first invitation** (or half-circle) occurs when, by deviating the foil to the left with a forearm movement while simultaneously turning the wrist to the intermediate position between third and fourth, the tip of the weapon describes half of a circle. This places it a few centimeters outward from the opponent's right shoulder, forming a straight line with the slightly bent arm and the weapon. It exposes the flank or the low line (see figs. 25 and 31);

The **second invitation** occurs when, keeping the wrist in the fourth position (or turning it to the second position) and slightly bending the arm, the foil deviates to the right. The wrist is nearly at the level of the fencer's flank, with the weapon's tip slightly lower than the wrist and slightly away from the opponent's flank. It exposes the chest or the high line (see figs. 26, 27, and 32, 33);

the **third invitation** occurs when, keeping the wrist in the fourth position (or turning it to the intermediate position between second and third) and bending the arm, the foil is deviated a few centimeters to the right of the line, with the tip slightly outward and at approximately the height of the opponent's eye. It exposes the chest internally (see figs. 28, 29, and 34, 35);

The **fourth invitation** occurs when the arm is bent slightly, moving it along with the foil to the left, with the wrist turned to the intermediate position between third and fourth and at the level of the flank. The weapon's tip is almost at the level of the opponent's right eye and a few centimeters outward so that the blade follows a diagonal line to the left. It exposes the chest externally (see figs. 30, 36);

Engagements, like invitations, are four and take the same names: first or half-circle, second, third, and fourth. They involve the same arrangement of the arm, wrist, and weapon as invitations but dominate the opponent's blade, keeping it deviated from the line of offense rather than leaving it free, as in the case of invitations.

When performed correctly, engagements will place the strong part of the blade against the weak part of the opponent's blade if executed at lunge measure, or the middle of the blade against the weak part if executed at advancing measure.

Fig. 26 - Invito di seconda
con la posizione di pugno di 4ª

Invito visto di profilo

Fig. 25 - Invito di prima

Fig. 28 - Invito in seconda
con la posizione di pugno di 2ª

Fig. 29 - Invito in terza
con la posizione di pugno
di... in 3ª

Fig. 30 - Invito di quarta

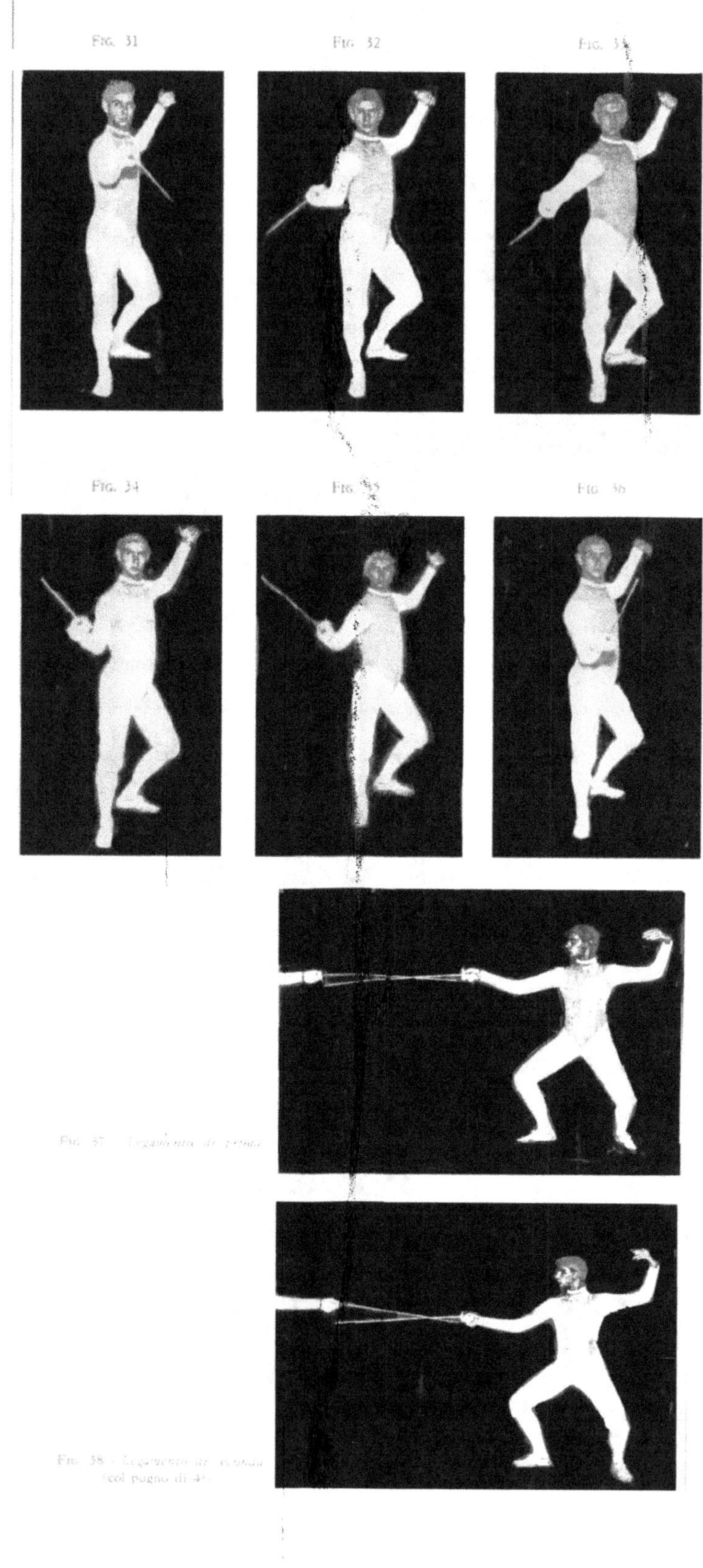

FIG. 31
FIG. 32
FIG. 33
FIG. 34
FIG. 35
FIG. 36

Change of engagements, transports, and envelopments *(Cambiamenti di legamento, transporti e riporti)*

Change of engagement (*cambiamenti di legamento*) is where the fencer changes from one engagement to the opposite one.

- From engagement in first to second and from second to first
- From engagement in third to fourth and from fourth to third

These changes are executed from one's own engagement by pivoting from the wrist, beginning with moving the point of the foil and releasing one's strength from the weak of the adversary's weapon and carrying it until the opposite engagement is assumed.

For one's own engagement, changes in the low lines the passage of the point takes place over the adversaries' blade and for changes in the high line the point travels under the blade.

Transports (*trasporti*) are the passage from one engagement to another engagement without separating the blade from the adversaries.

- From engagement in second to fourth and from fourth to second
- From engagement in first to third and from third to first

Envelopment (*riporto*) is a movement that wraps around the advisory's weak starting and ending in the same engagement.

They are called the envelopment in; first, second, third and fourth.

- Example: from the engagement in fourth, envelopment in fourth.

CHAPTER II. **THE OFFENSE** (*L'OFFESA*)

Definition of the simple offensive action *(azioni di offesa semplice)*

The definition of simple offensive action is any action whose development takes place without avoiding the adversary's parry.

The straight thrust *(Il colpo dritto o botta dritta)*

Any strike delivered in such a way that one's blade does not slide against the opponent's blade, and the tip of the blade follows a straight line, is called a "straight thrust" or "direct hit."

This action represents the fundamental offensive strike in response to the opponent's invitation and can be executed not only from the blade in line but also from one's invitation or engagement. It is performed from the guard at lunge distance, with the grip in the fourth position (or in the second if aimed at the flank line), proceeding as described for the lunge but with appropriate hand opposition (1).

(1) By hand opposition means the obtuse angle formed by the weapon and the arm, with its vertex at the wrist and aligned with the opponent's blade. This opposition serves to prevent the opponent's offense on the same line and is achieved by moving the arm laterally to the left or right, depending on the line to be covered. Therefore, at the conclusion of any action (simple or compound), the hand must maintain the appropriate opposition.

Disengagement *(La cavazione)*

Disengagement is the action where one releases their blade from the adversary's engagement.

Like the straight thrust (*botta dritta*) that is a fundamental offensive movement that is done in opposition to the invitation, the disengagement is not unlike the straight thrust and is the second fundamental offensive action that is done in opposition to the engagement made in a single fencing time.

From Lunging distance (*misura di allungo*), the movement starts by the fingers and the wrist, freeing your own blade from the opposing engagement, then describing with the tip an elongated spiral followed by the progressive extension of the arm leading to the line of the uncovered target and reducing the distance with the lunge, avoiding any discontinuity of movement.

In contrast to the engagement in first, second, third and fourth the disengage will be directed to the flank, above to the chest, inside and outside.

All the above-mentioned movements are completed with the hand in fourth position, and only the hit to the flank can the hand be in second.

With the straight thrust the adversary's movement can be perceived only with the eyes. The disengage can be seen this way as well with two of the five senses, by touch or feel through the blade or with the eyes when they make the action.

When releasing the tip of the foil it must be done with extreme lightness that is an unbroken spiral forward, without swings or extra movement that will alert the advisory of danger and allowing them to prepare their defense.

Fundamental glides *(Fili principali)*

The glide is an offensive action made from one's own engagement in opposition to the adversary's blade in line.

The glide can also be performed as a riposte following the parry.

The characteristic of the glide is an action that is based on the gaining of degrees and is determined by the skill of who performs it. Contact with the opposing blade must be maintained throughout the completion of the thrust (*stoccata*), this will serve as the guidance and support for who is making the action. The goal is to obtain a gradual deviation from the adversary's blade through the gaining of domination over the opponent's blade.

This action is difficult to describe with accuracy as the technique of this important and simple offensive action that can only be well learned after long practical study.

It requires great finesse of execution, rapidity, especially in the extension of the arm with a well centered hand being both soft and firm at the same time.

The glide, if executed from one's own engagement (*legamento*) consists of only one fencing time (*tempo*); if performed in opposition to the blade in line, it consists of two movements (two tempos) one for the engagement, and the second movement for the glide. In the latter case, the engagement is made gradually without discontinuity and a rapid arm extension after the gain of degrees has been established.

The glide takes its name from the engagement of its origin. Therefore, we have glide in first (*filo di prima or mezzo cerchio*), glide in second (*filo di seconda*), glide in third (*filo di terza*) and glide in fourth or external flanconade (*filo di quarta or fianconata esterna*).

Glide in first *(Filo di prima)*

From one's own engagement in first, gradually moving the hand to fourth hand position and moving it across to the right (outside) of the body and moving it slightly forward to deflect the opposing blade without any discontinuity or loss of contact with the opponent's blade, the thrust *(stoccata)* is made to the chest.

Glide in second *(Filo di seconda)*

From one's own engagement in second with the hand in fourth, or secondhand position, gradually slide the blade down the grade of that of the opponents with opposition to the outside of one's blade directing the touch to the flank.

Glide in third *(Filo di terza)*

From the proper engagement in third with hand in fourth position or second and third hand position, slide the blade over the opponent's blade while extending the arm rapidly and the tip of the foil is lead to the external target where, without losing contact the hit is delivered with the hand high and opposition to the outside.

Glide in fourth *(Filo di quatra o fianconata esterna)*

From one's own engagement of fourth, pivot on the point of contact of the engagement, turning the hand in fourth position, moving the tip in a slight helical movement. The hand is lowered slightly (and kept on the same line) to keep better domination over the opposing blade. The tip of the foil moves in the direction of the external target, without any pause or losing contact between the two blades complete the hit with opposition to the left (outside). This is done in one movement.

Note – Some feel that the execution of the glide in fourth and glide in first -as they are considered- when the thrust is to the internal target the glide *(filo)* on the adversary's blade with accentuated opposition to the inside. Such actions cannot be considered real glide because it is not always possible to keep in contact with the opposing blades.

Clarification of the glides at walking distance and pressure *(Precisazione sui fili eseguiti a misura camminando e sulle prese di ferro)*

When the bind originates directly from the engagement, its execution—like other single-motion actions (straight thrust, disengagement) —is only possible at lunge distance.

If we find ourselves at walking distance and wish to execute one of these simple actions, it is necessary first to move into the correct distance while maintaining the same blade posture as before beginning the advance, and then execute the strike as previously described. In such cases, however, it would not be correct to say that the bind, straight thrust, or disengagement was executed while advancing (as some treatises suggest). Instead, it should simply be referred to as "step-forward and bind," "step-forward and straight thrust," or "step-forward and disengagement," since during the advance, no movement of the blade should be indicated to avoid provoking the opponent to parry before the action is executed, that is, before initiating the lunge.

If, however, we find ourselves at walking distance and wish to execute the bind in opposition to the opponent's blade in line, the engagement is taken simultaneously with the forward step, and the bind is then completed with a lunge.

It is common practice to call this action "taking the blade and bind" or "taking the blade and straight thrust" when the engagement is followed by the straight thrust.

Glides preceded by transports *(fili preceduti da trasporti)*

Besides the four main *fili* described, which originate from the *legamenti* and take their name, others are possible, the execution of which takes place after performing a *trasporto*, that is, after a passage to another *legamento* without disengaging one's blade from the opponent's: these are understood as *fili* preceded by *trasporti*.

These *fili*, even if executed with harmonious, rapid, and continuous movement, consist of two phases.

It is essential to give great precedence to the point, gradually beginning the *trasporto* in a spiral motion until completing the *trasporto* itself together with the complete extension of the arm, and at the same time directing the point of the weapon at the target which will consequently be uncovered. They are: The *fianconata interna*, that is, *trasporto* from the third *legamento* to the first (low) *legamento* and *filo*; the *fianconata di seconda*, that is, *trasporto* from the fourth *legamento* to the second *legamento* and *filo*.

Here's how to proceed with their execution:

- **Fianconata interna:** Starting from the third *legamento*, maintaining or turning the fist in fourth position, the opponent's weapon is transferred from right to left in a spiral motion with gradual and complete extension of the arm, directing the point of one's own blade in the direction of the low inside target, on which, without pause and with opposition of the fist to the left, the blow is executed.
- **Fianconata di seconda:** Starting from the fourth *legamento*, turning the fist in fourth or second position, the opponent's weapon is transferred from low left to right in a spiral motion with gradual and complete extension of the arm, at the same time directing the point of the weapon in the direction of the flank, on which, without any discontinuity and with accentuated opposition of the fist to the right, the blow is executed.

Caution: We believe it is appropriate to point out that both the *fianconata di seconda* and the *fianconata interna* (improperly also called "false fourth cut") are not executable as a riposte, because during the *trasporto* it is very easy to bring the point of the opponent's weapon onto one's own low target (leg).

We also point out that the *filo di prima* and the *filo di seconda* are easier to execute when the opponent's weapon is held with the point lower than the fist, and the *filo di terza* and *filo di quarta*, instead, when the point is higher than the fist.

As before, it's important to understand the fencing terms for a full understanding of the text. I've left those terms in Italian, as a direct translation of them wouldn't be as useful as understanding their specific meaning in fencing.

Simple Beat (*Battute semplici*)

Even the simple beat and straight thrust, like the glide are fundamental actions that are in opposition to the opponent's blade in line, but its execution is quite different than the glide.

The beat is following the direction of the engagement and is performed more or less with a bent arm. The beat is performed by hitting with a dry sharp blow of measured violence using the strong of one's own blade against the medium of the opponent's blade. Thus, the result is diverting the blade from the line of offense with the straight thrust immediately following the beat, directing the hit to the unprotected target.

The beat can be executed from the opponent's blade in line (in this case we can execute from your own invitation or from one's own blade in line), this action can also be performed from one's own engagement. From your engagement, the principle of the beat is not to deviate the blade form the line of offense, but to distance it more than it already is with the same engagement, thus putting the advisory in a position to have a greater distance to perform the corresponding parry.

Note: this action can be performed by sliding one's own blade so that the strong increases pressure on the weak and medium grades of the opponent's blade. But this beat, named expulsion or power beat (*potenza*) today is rarely used.

Based on the three placements of the weapon beats can be simple or circular (*contro*). For now, we will only deal with the simple beat, that is deviating from the opponent's blade in the shortest path.

The beat, like the straight thrust, can be performed from any line and at either correct distance or walking distance (*allungo e camminando*) and always consists of two fencing times. However, it is considered a simple offensive action because like the straight thrust, disengage and glide it does not elude any parry.

Beat and straight thrust at right distance *(Battute e colpo dritto a misura di allungo)*

Beat in first (Battuta di prima):

first tempo — From one's invitation in second, hand in the intermediate position of third and fourth, the beat is given as an energetic and sharp impact on the opponent's blade from bottom to top to the left (inside) direction by means of the elasticity of the wrist subsidized by the forearm.

second tempo — Immediately complete the action by rapidly extending the arm while turning the hand to fourth hand position and the straight thrust is delivered to the internal target.

Beat in second (Battuta di seconda):

first tempo — From one's invitation in first with the hand in fourth or secondhand position, give a sharp dry blow diverting the opponents blade from left to right (inside to outside) diagonally or horizontally with elastic movement of the forearm;

second tempo — Immediately complete the extension of the arm and direct the hit to the chest with the hand in fourth position or direct the hit to the side (flank) with hand in second position.

Beat in third (Battuta di terza):

First tempo — From the invitation in fourth, turning the hand in fourth position give an energetic and dry strike on the opposing blade from left to right (inside to outside) using the elastic movement of the wrist and forearm;

second tempo — Immediately complete the extension of the arm directing the hit to the outside chest with hand in fourth position or to the side (flank) with the hand in second position. (1)

Beat in fourth (Battuta di quarta)

First tempo — From the invitation in third, hand in third and fourth position, give an energetic and dry strike on the opponent's blade from right to left by the elastic movement of the wrist and forearm;

second tempo — Immediately complete the extension of the arm with the hand turning in fourth position, direct the hit to the internal target.

(1) When the beat of third aims at executing the blow to the external target, it is advisable to execute it with the fist from second to third, gaining the degrees.

Beat and straight thrust at walking distance *(Battute e colpo dritto a misura camminando)*

Working with the step and lunge or walking distance, the four beats and straight thrust are coordinated as thus, the beat happens during the step forward and the rest of the action follows as prescribed before.

Note — it does not matter about the speed of execution, it is important that the two times are separate. The first tempo is for the beat and the second tempo is for the extension of the arm and thrust.

There is a moment during the beat when the arm is bent and the tip may be facing away from the target, the focus must be to extend rapidly after the beat because there is the chance the opponent will be able to regain the line.

For this reason, it can be helpful for the Maestro during first time of instruction to make this kind of exercise. Following the students' beat, have them extend the arm, then lunge. Incorporate tight on time so that the student when they beat the hand is tight, then relaxed, then tight again just before the hit (tight on time), and to give priority to the tip throughout the action.

As we say for the glides, the beat in first and second, it is easier to execute when the tip of the opponent is lower than their hand and, in the beat, and third or fourth having the tip above the opponent's hand.

Regarding the choice between the beat or the glide, because they are both done in opposition to the blade in line, it is suggested when we feel that the blade of the opponent is soft on line to execute the beat, and when the blade it tight the use of the glade is the better choice.

CHAPTER III. **THE DEFENSE** *(DELLA DIFESA)*

The defense in general *(Generalità sulla difesa)*

Defense is understood as any movement, executed with one's own weapon, aimed at deviating the opponent's weapon at the moment when the point of the latter is about to reach the target, or the removal of the target itself from the range of action of the opponent's offense, by retreating.

The first method is called: defense with the blade (or *defense col ferro*); the second: defense of measure (or *defense di misura*).

The latter does not allow the one who uses it to immediately transition to offense in turn, and therefore it does not conclude but prolongs the combat.

Defense with the blade (that is, the true parry), while offering not insignificant difficulties for its effective application at the right time, instead always gives the possibility to the one who executes it to immediately follow with their own offense.

Parries can be: simple, counter, half-counter, and yielding (*di ceduta*). For now, we will only deal with the simple ones, which, like all the others - with the exception, as we will see later, of the yielding ones - can be executed in two different ways, namely *di tasto* (by touch/opposition) and *di picco* (by beat/percussion): *di tasto*, when the deviation of the opponent's weapon is obtained by mere opposition of one's own weapon in such a way that, when the parry is concluded, the two blades will be in contact with each other; *di picco*, when the opposition on the opponent's blade, for the purpose of a greater deviation of the same, will conclude with a true and proper impact following which the two blades will be found distinctly disjoined.

Simple parries *(Parate semplici)*

When from an invitation or an engagement we defend the corresponding uncovered target with the parry moving along the shortest path, this is called simple parry (*parata semplice*). As well as when we move from one parry to another parry in a direct line.

The simple parries in foil are four, and they follow the four targets defined as: first (*mezzocerchio*), second, third and fourth. The parry follows the same provisions with the arm, hand and weapon already described for in the engagements, making sure to oppose the opponent's weak with one's own strong for utmost effectiveness.

Passage from one simple parry to another simple parry *(Passaggio da una parata semplice ad un'altra parata semplice)*

From the parry of first, or from the engagement or invitation of first, one passes to the parry of *second* in a single tempo: turning the fist into fourth or second position, one instantaneously brings one's own weapon diagonally from left to right so that the fist is almost at the height of the flank and the point of the weapon slightly lower.

From the second parry, or from the engagement or invitation in second position, transition to *the first* parry in a single motion: by turning the hand through the intermediate position of third into fourth, instantly move your weapon from right to left and upward, aligning the strong of your blade against the middle of the opponent's blade and deflecting its point away from the intended line.

From the third parry, or from the engagement or invitation in third position, transition to the *fourth parry* in a single motion: by turning the hand through the intermediate position of third into fourth, instantly move your weapon from right to left, aligning the strong of your blade against the middle of the opponent's blade and deflecting its point away from the intended line.

From the fourth parry, or from the engagement or invitation in fourth position, transition to the *third parry* in a single motion: by turning the hand into fourth position or through the intermediate position of second into third, instantly move your weapon from left to right, aligning the strong of your blade against the middle of the opponent's blade and deflecting its point away from the intended line.

Note — The transition from second to third and vice versa is also considered a simple parry.

Warning — The paths to follow and the positions of the arm and weapon established for the parries may need to be adjusted based on the more or less orthodox line formed by the opponent at the moment of executing the strike.

Fig. *Parata di prima*

Fig. *Parata di prima*

Fig – *Parata di seconda con il pugno di seconda*

Fig – Parata di terza con il pugno di quarta

Fig – Parata di terza con il pugno di seconda in terza

Fig – Parata di quarta

In fact, considering the valid target surface being threatened, and it is clear that to defend against the hit the attack that is lower or higher than the corresponding parry can defeat, one can

41

change the altitude to be lower or higher in order to oppose the incoming hit with the strong of your own blade against the middle of the opponent's blade to be effective.

Another important requirement for the maximum effectiveness of the parry is the selection of time, the exact moment to come to the contact of the advisories middle of their blade. Too late and the parry will be insufficient, too early or anticipated, the opponent will have time to change the line.

This being said, we can establish that in order to have the parry be accurate, the speed and choice of time are in direct relationship to the actual execution of the hit one wants to parry.

After a certain period of training, it will become very useful that the student become accustomed to the exact evaluation of the movement they will have to make with their blade in the different lines in order to adapt and limit the movement to the minimum needed for the various senses and planes of the hand, arm and of the foil in order to deflect the opponent from the plane of offense at the correct time of their shot, doing so with the needed degree of power exerted by the tight in time of the hand on the handle to overcome the resistance of the attacking blade.

Ceding parry *(Parata di ceduta)*

These parries are applicable in counter-opposition to some *filo* actions. There are two of them: the yielding parry of fourth (*ceduta di quarta*) and the yielding parry of third (*ceduta di terza*).

They are executed by yielding to the opponent's *filo* action, whether it is an attack or a riposte, giving the impression of wanting to give in to the pressure of the *filo* itself, and then assuming, almost at the completion of the action, the corresponding parry without ever interrupting the contact between the two blades.

The yielding parry of fourth (*ceduta di quarta*) is executed in counter-opposition to the *filo* and the *fianconata di seconda*, as well as to the *filo di quarta* (external *fianconata*); the yielding parry of third (*ceduta di terza*) is instead executed in counter-opposition to the *fianconata interna* (false *filo di quarta*).

Definition of the riposte *(Definizione della risposta)*

The riposte is the thrust that is immediately sent after parrying the offensive action of the opponent.

The riposte can be simple or compound. For now, we will only deal with the simple riposte.

Every parry, no matter which line defended, whether the parry is soft or sharp, the riposte has two simple variants: one by detachment (straight thrust) and the other by maintaining contact (glide).

Simple Ripostes *(Risposte semplici)*

From the parry of first, one can riposte with a straight thrust to the chest on the same line, or with a *filo* above the chest, superimposing one's own blade on the opponents.

From the parry of second, one can riposte above the chest, or with a *filo* to the flank.

From the parry of third, one can riposte below the flank or with a *filo* to the external target.

From the parry of fourth, one can riposte with a straight thrust to the inside of the chest, or with a *filo* to the flank externally.

CHAPTER IV. **COMPOUND ACTIONS** *(AZIONE COMPOSTE)*

Definition of the compound action *(Definizione delle azioni composte)*

Unlike the simple offensive actions (those whose development takes place without evading any parry, like all of those that we have described thus far) are compound actions that during their development, instead elude one or more parries. These actions follow the same first movements as the simple or fundamental actions, and as such also take place from the opponent's placement of the weapon, as in from invitation, engagement, or blade in line.

The feint in general *(Della finta in genere)*

Any movement with the weapon not followed by lunge but can induce the opponent to make parry is called "feint" *(finta)*. The feint, therefore, is nothing short of a simulation of the threat, with the ultimate goal to induce the opponent to parry as foresighted, this must have all the realism of the real attack, including the choice of time and only lacking the want of the final thrust. Generally, we resort to using the feint when we feel we are unable to overcome the opposing defense with a simple attack, or when despite having overcome the defense, it is deemed appropriate to not repeat the simple action. The feint can be more or less accentuated according to the lessor or greater impression it has on the opponent.

Consequently, we can assume that from the initial moment of the feint up to its maximum expression (in the latter case evading the parry becomes very difficult) there are many different moments (choice of time) to elude the corresponding parry to the defensive sensitivity of the opponent.

General Feint Actions in Relation to Simple Parries *(azione di finta in generein relazione alle parate semplici.*

The simulation of the thrust giving its fake action must be performed with such accent of truth as to induce the opponent to immediately move his own weapon to defend the presumed target in danger. Let's now move to the description of all the feint actions you can perform in opposition to simple parries. (1)

---

(1) Offensive actions, consisting of two movements and which evade a simple parry, are commonly called, by analogy, 'simple feint' actions.

Feint direct and disengage at lunging distance *(Finta dritta e cavazione a misura di allungo)*

The feint direct is the simulation of the simple attack by straight thrust followed by the disengagement, which, evading a simple parry it cannot be carried out other than on the target opposite to that of the feint and, like the straight thrust of which it is deriving is also carried out in opposition to an invitation or from one's own engagement. The execution consists of two stages: one for the feint, the other for the execution of the disengage as will be clearly seen below.

Feint and disengage from invitation in first.

FENCING MASTER	STUDENT
- Invitation in first. - Parry second. - He lets himself.	- As a first movement, he simulates the straight thrust by driving the tip of the blade on the flank line. - As a second movement, he immediately avoids the parry by performing the disengage above the chest.

Feint and disengage from invitation in second.

FENCING MASTER	STUDENT
- Invitation in second. - Parry first or third. - He lets himself be hit.	- He simulates the straight thrust by driving the tip of the blade on the chest line. - He immediately avoids the parry by performing the disengage to the flank or inside.

Feint and disengage from invitation in third.

FENCING MASTER	STUDENT
- Invitation in third. - Parry fourth. - He lets himself be hit.	- He simulates the straight thrust by driving the tip of the blade on the inside line. - He immediately avoids the parry by performing the disengage outside.

Feint and disengage from invitation in fourth

FENCING MASTER	STUDENT
- Invitation in fourth. - Parry first or third. - He lets himself be hit.	- He simulates the straight thrust by driving the tip of the blade on the outside line. - He immediately avoids the parry by performing the disengage inside.

Direct feint and disengage at walking distance *(Finta dritta e cavazione a misura camminando)*

It is executed in the same way as the straight feint from extension, with the only note that, along with the insinuation of the point to express the feint, a step forward is taken, keeping in mind that the initial movement of the weapon must take absolute precedence.

Feint by disengagement and disengage at lunging distance *(Finta di cavazione e cavazione a misura di allungo)*

The feint of the thrust is the simulation of the thrust. It is executed in the same way as the straight feint, but in opposition to an engagement rather than an invitation: the blade is disengaged from the engagement as if preparing to perform the thrust, and, immediately evading the opponent's corresponding simple parry, a thrust is delivered to the opposite target.

Feint of the thrust and thrust on the first engagement:
Feint by disengage and disengage from invitation in first

FENCING MASTER	STUDENT
- Engagement first. - Parry second. - He lets himself be hit.	- He simulates the disengage by driving the tip of the blade on the flank line. - He immediately avoids the parry by performing the disengage above to the chest.

Feint by disengage and disengage on invitation in second

FENCING MASTER	STUDENT
- Engagement in second. - Parry first or third. - He lets himself be hit.	- He simulates the disengage by driving the tip of the blade above on the chest. - He immediately avoids the parry by performing the disengage to the flank or inside.

Feint by disengage and disengage on invitation in third

FENCING MASTER	STUDENT
- Engagement in third. - Parry fourth. - He lets himself be hit.	- He simulates the disengage by driving the tip of the blade on the inside line. - He immediately avoids the parry by performing the disengage outside.

FENCING MASTER	STUDENT
- Engagement in fourth. - Parry third. - He lets himself be hit.	- He simulates the disengage by driving the tip of the blade on the outside line. - He immediately avoids the parry by performing the disengage inside.

Feint by disengage and disengage at walking distance *(Finta di cavazione e cavazione a misura camminando)*

The feint by disengage and disengage is executed as described above. You have to consider that, together with the feint, you have to make a step forward and must give priority to the tip of the foil.

Feint by glide and disengage at lunging distance *(Finta del filo e cavazione a misura allungo)*

The feint by glide is the simulation of the simple attack by glide itself, and like all other feint actions described so far this action is comprised of two movements, both if performed at lunge distance (right distance) or at walking distance.

Feint by glide of first and disengage

FENCING MASTER	STUDENT
- Parry third or first. - He lets himself be hit.	- From his own engagement in first, he simulates the glide to the external target as described above. - He immediately avoids the parry by performing the disengage to the chest inside or to the flank.

Feint by glide of second and disengage

FENCING MASTER	STUDENT
- Parry second. - He lets himself be hit.	- From his own engagement in second, he simulates the glide to the flank as described above. - He immediately avoids the parry by performing the disengage above to the chest.

Feint by glide of third and disengage

FENCING MASTER	STUDENT
- Parry first or third. - He lets himself be hit.	- From his own engagement in third, he simulates the glide to the external target as described above. - He immediately avoids the parry by performing the disengage to the flank or inside.

Feint by glide of fourth (or external flanconade) and disengage

FENCING MASTER	STUDENT
- Parry second. - He lets himself be hit.	- From his own engagement in fourth, he simulates the external flanconade as described above. - He immediately avoids the parry by performing the disengage above to the chest.

Feint by glide of second and disengage

FENCING MASTER	STUDENT
- Let's himself be engaged in fourth. - Parry second. - He lets himself be hit.	- From his own engagement in fourth, with harmonious movement to transport, he simulates the flanconade of second as described above for the simple action. - He immediately avoids the parry by performing the disengage above to the chest.

Feint by internal flanconade and disengage

FENCING MASTER	STUDENT
- Let's himself be engaged in third. - Parry first. - He lets himself be hit.	- From his own engagement in third, with harmonious movement to transport, he simulates the internal flanconade as described above for the simple action. - He immediately avoids the parry by performing the disengage above to the flank.

Feint by glide and disengage at walking distance *(Finta del filo e cavazione a misura camminando)*

This is carried out by combining the step forward with the feint by glide, then without pause the disengage. It must be clear that the initial movement of the weapon must take absolute precedence over the action.

Beat followed by feint at lunging distance *(Battute seguite da finta a misura di allungo)*

We have said the purpose of the beat is to divert the opponent's weapon from the offensive line in order to be able to carry out or pretend to make the straight thrust on the target which is uncovered with the beat. If the fencer who is performing the attack, after beating the opponent's blade executes a feint, the intention is to induce the opponent to parry, so that we must evade the parry by use of the disengage.

In practice, especially at lunging distance, who receives the beat (sharp and executed at the right timing), reacts immediately in defense, can be particularly useful especially with a beat in third or fourth, immediately disengaging to the inside or outside target to avoid the parry of the opponent so to not clash with the blade of the opponent.

In such cases the disengage is executed on the same spot as the beat without having to feint on the offensive line, and in the same moment as the reaction in third or fourth of the antagonist.

Beat of first, feint direct and disengage

FENCING MASTER	STUDENT
- Place his blade in line. - Parry fourth. - He lets himself be hit.	- As a first movement, he beats in first, as described above. - As second movement, he executes the feint to the internal target as described for the simple action. - He immediately avoids the parry by performing the disengage outside.

Beat of second, feint direct and disengage

FENCING MASTER	STUDENT
- Place his blade in line. - Parry second or third. - He lets himself be hit.	- He beats in second, as described above, immediately followed by the feint to the flank or above to the chest as described for the simple action. - He immediately avoids the parry by performing the disengage above or to the inside target.

FENCING MASTER	STUDENT
- Place his blade in line. - Parry fourth. - He lets himself be hit.	- He beats in third, as described above, immediately followed by the feint to the inside target as described for the simple action. - He immediately avoids the parry by performing the disengage above or to the outside target.

Beats followed by feint at walking distance *(Battuta seguite da finta a misura cammindando)*

The same rules apply for the actions performed with the step, coordinating the distance so that the beat is in time with the back foot and the final movement (the disengage) is completed with the lunge.

Grazing beat *(Battute di passaggio)*

The line that passes through one's own blade flows from the front to the back and above the advisories tip, releasing from obtaining a similar effect to that of a simple beat followed by a disengage in a single tempo.

Of these beats, given their particular characteristics, can be performed only in fourth with the hit to the flank and in third with the hit to the chest.

Of the two, the grazing beats in fourth is easier to execute.

Riposte by feint *(Riposta di finta)*

If after any parry the riposte hinted as simple, by following it with a disengage suitable to evade the opponents counter parry, this riposte is called by feint.

From the parry of first- you can riposte by feinting the thrust direct inside, then evading the counter parry of fourth, or feinting by glide above and disengage, eluding the counter parry of third.

From the parry of second - the riposte can be by feinting the thrust direct to the chest and disengage to the inside or flanconade evading the parry of third and first: or feint of glide of second and disengage over the blade eluding the counter parry of second.

From the parry of third- the riposte can be by feinting direct to the flank then disengage above to the chest eluding the counter parry of second or feinting by glide of third and disengage to the flank or inwards eluding the counter parry of first or third.

From the parry of fourth- the riposte can be by feinting direct (straight thrust) disengage inside (1) and counter parry of fourth or feinting to the flank and disengage over to the chest evading the counter parry of second.

(1) For the execution of this response, the same guidelines apply as those stated on page 55 for the fourth beat and thrust.

About double feint in general (*Della doppia finta in generale*)

If the second movement of any action of feint rather than make the thrust, pretend (feint) and add a third movement together with the lunge, you will have a double feint action. And this third movement is because we are still dealing with actions that are opposed to simple parry, that the second movement can only be a disengagement. The double feint takes its name from the first movement.

The double feint takes its name from the first movement; therefore, it can be called: double feint direct (*doppia finta dritta*), double feint by disengage (*doppia finta di cavazione*), double feint by glide (*doppia finta di filo*).

Like the feint direct, or disengagement or glide, they are derivatives coming from the straight thrust, of the disengage and the glide as opposed to a simple parry, so the corresponding double feint (*doppio finta*) are the resulting feinting action derivatives in opposition to two simple parries. And by analogy the common usage they also share the name of "simple double feint" (*doppia finta semplice*).

Note — when exercising the compound action especially in those with double feint it is very useful that the student know that the master will perform many parries and how the movements are made to make up the action the same minus one, the last parry, that is indispensable to defend themselves. The Fencing Master (*Maestro*) will also apply the last parry when he wants the student to exercise the counter-parry and riposte or experience this at speed of execution.

Double feint at lunging distance (*Doppia finta dritta a misura di allungo*)

In opposition to the opponent's invitation first (or rather: feint to the flank, feint of disengage above and disengage to the flank or inside)

FENCING MASTER	STUDENT
- Invite in first. - Parry second. - Parry first or third. - He lets himself be hit.	- He executes a feint to the flank. - He avoids the parry making the feint of disengage above. - He avoids even the second parry by performing the disengage to the flank or inside.

In opposition to the opponent's invitation second (or rather: feint above, feint of disengage to the flank or inside and disengage above or outside)

FENCING MASTER	STUDENT
- Invite in second. - Parry first or third. - Parry second or fourth. - He lets himself be hit.	-He executes a feint above. -He avoids the parry making the feint of disengage to the flank or inside. - He avoids even the second parry by performing the disengage above or outside.

In opposition to the opponent's invitation third
(or rather: feint inside, feint of disengage outside and disengage inside)

FENCING MASTER	STUDENT
- Invite in third. - Parry fourth. - Parry third. - He lets himself be hit.	- He executes a feint inside. He avoids the parry making the feint of disengage outside. He avoids even the second parry by performing the disengage above or outside.

In opposition to the opponent's invitation fourth
(or rather: feint outside, feint of disengage inside and disengage outside)

FENCING MASTER	STUDENT
- Invite in fourth. - Parry third. - Parry fourth. - He lets himself be hit.	- He executes a feint outside. - He avoids the parry making the feint of disengage inside. - He avoids even the second parry by performing the disengage above or outside.

Double feint at walking distance *(Doppia finta dritta a misura camminando)*

It is the methods indicated for the same action performed at walking distance (*misura camminando*) by coordinating the two feints with the step forward.

The first feint must therefore be joined with the first movement of the step, the next feint completion with the end of the step and the following disengagement together with the lunge.

Double feint by disengage (*Doppia finta di cavazione*)

This action both at the right distance (*allungo*) and walking distance (*camminando*) develops with the same rules indicated as above for the double feint (*doppia finta dritta*), because the latter eludes the parries.

It differs only from having originated from an engagement of the opponent rather than from an invitation and therefore the first movement of the action will be a feint of disengage instead of the feint direct.

Double feint by glide at right distance *(Doppia finta del filo a musiura di allungo)*

Double feint by glide of first (or rather: feint by glide of first, feint by disengage inside or to the flank and disengage outside or above to the chest)

FENCING MASTER	STUDENT
- Parry third or first. - Parry fourth or second. He lets himself be hit.	- He executes a feint of glide in first. - He avoids the parry making the feint of disengage inside or to the flank. - He avoids even the second parry by performing the disengage outside or above to the chest.

Double feint by glide of second
(or rather: feint by glide of second, feint by disengage above and disengage to the flank or inside)

FENCING MASTER	STUDENT
- Parry second. - Parry first or third. - He lets himself be hit.	- He executes a feint of glide in second. - He avoids the parry making the feint of disengage above to the chest. - He avoids even the second parry by performing the disengage to the flank or inside.

Double feint by glide of third (or rather: feint by glide of third, feint by disengage to the flank or inside and disengage above or outside)

FENCING MASTER	STUDENT
- Parry first or third. - Parry second or fourth. - He lets himself be hit.	- He executes a feint of glide in third. - He avoids the parry making the feint of disengage to the flank or inside. - He avoids even the second parry by performing the disengage above to the chest or outside.

Double feint by glide of fourth (or rather: feint by external flanconade, feint by disengage above and disengage to the flank or inside)

FENCING MASTER	STUDENT
- Parry second. - Parry first or third. - He lets himself be hit.	- He executes a feint of external flanconade. - He avoids the parry making the feint of disengage above to the chest. - He avoids even the second parry by performing the disengage to the flank or inside.

Double feint by internal flanconade (or rather: feint by internal flanconade, feint by disengage to the flank and disengage above)

FENCING MASTER	STUDENT
- Let himself engage in third. - Parry first. - Parry second. - He lets himself be hit.	- From his own engagement in third, with harmonious movement to transport, he simulates the internal flanconade. - He avoids the parry making the feint of disengage to the flank. - He avoids even the second parry by performing the disengage outside or above to the chest.

Double feint by flanconade of second (or rather: feint by flanconade of second, feint by disengage above to the chest and disengage to the flank or inside)

FENCING MASTER	STUDENT
- Let himself engage in fourth. - Parry second. - Parry first or third. - He lets himself be hit.	- From his own engagement in fourth, with harmonious movement to transport in second, he simulates the glide to the flank. - He avoids the parry making the feint of disengage above to the chest. - He avoids even the second parry by performing the disengage to the flank or inside.

Double feint by glide at walking distance (*Doppia finta del filo a misura cammindando*)

The same rule applies as for performing the same action at right distance (*allungo*), but the two movements must be well coordinated with the two movements of the step forward so that, without pause, one can perform the last disengage with the lunge.

Especially for any type of glide preceded by a transport, we must keep in mind that the movement of the weapon's point must have absolute precedence.

Conventional exercises

Conventional exercises consist of pre-set actions between two fencers and the actions that each of them must perform in relation to offense and defense, by attending scrupulously the detail serving the alternate execution of the actions themselves as established. These exercises complement the benefits in a valuable way to the lesson and constitute above all the first steps about the free application of the offense and its defense, without that is, that the fencing master asks for it to be executed each time.

They also serve to give greater senses of truth to the action learned in the lesson and to arouse in the student the first real reflections and considerations about the importance of the three fundamental elements of fencing have in building the action.

That is: distance, time and speed (*Misura, tempo and velocità*).

These exercises can be combined in many ways since any fencing combination of offense, defense and counter-offense can give rise to a certain conventional exercise. The ones we will cover below indicating exercise in reference to the sharing of offense and defense so far studied that is in reference to the feint and double feint action as opposed to simple parries.

All the other exercises can be combined as deemed useful for more complex training.

First Exercise: straight thrust (in opposition to the four invitations)

A	B
- Place himself on invitation. - Make a simple soft parry and riposte by detachment or by glide.	- Excutes the straight thrust to the correspondent target unprotected, trying to hit. - He lets himself be hit.

Second Exercise: disengage (in opposition to the four engagements)

A	B
- Make any the four engagements. - Make a simple soft parry of and risposte by detachment or by flide.	- Excutes the disengagement to the corresponding unprotected target, trying to hit. - He lets himself be hit.

Third Exercise: straight thrust or feint of straight thrust and disengage at lunging distance

This exercise is more difficult for the fencer who make the invitation because he doesn't know if the opponent will make a straight thrust or a feint.

This double possible solution makes the defense more difficult.

A	B
- Place himself on invitation. - Makes only one simple parry if the attack is by straight thrust, or double simple parry if the attack is by feint. - Execute the riposte as he wishes of (by detachment or by glide).	- Executes the straight thrust to the correspondent target unprotected, or executes the disengage to the correspondent target unprotected, trying to hit. - He lets himself be hit.

Fourth Exercise: disengage or feint of disengage and disengage at lunging distance

It is performed in opposition to any of the four engagements in the same way as described above for the exercise of the straight thrust.

Fifth Exercise: simple feint or double (in opposition to any of four invitations), at lunging distance first, then at walking distance.

Sixth Exercise: feint of disengagement or double (in opposition to any of four engagements), at lunging distance first, then at walking distance

In the fifth and sixth exercises even more are the difficulties that arise especially for those in defense, because they must choose to perform two or three parries.

To succeed, they will have to be careful not to lose control of the blade when passing from one parry to the other, because he needs to perform very tight and fast movements.

Regarding the fencer who is in attack, his attention must be particularly focused on not letting the blade to be intercepted during the feint movements, and to coordinate the feints with the movements of the legs when he takes the action while walking.

Note - completing with what is indicated for these six exercises can be composed of similar ones in reference to glides and beats (*fili e battute*).

CHAPTER V. **AUXILIARY ACTIONS** *(AZIONI AUSILIARE)*

Definition of the offensive auxiliary actions *(Definizione delle azione ausiliarie di offesa)*

The name itself clearly says that this group of actions are non-fundamental actions. However, this is not the case if you believe that they represent a negligible role of importance, since it is precisely through the application of these actions that increase the offensive and other possibilities while at the same time enriches one's own fencing repertoire.

Part of these are based on the imperfection of the placements assumed by the adversary, i.e., they originate on lines deemed to be covered and which are not completely so or on a weekly guarded line easily conquered by the antagonist.

We consider this explanation enough to understand what resources they offer in combat these so-called "auxiliary actions" and how useful they are, and therefore we have a detailed study for their application.

Thrust in lower fourth (*Tirare di quarta bassa*)

Against the opponent who usually invites, engages or parries in fourth with the hand at chest height and not near the abdomen, the attack can be directed to the target of the flank with the hand in fourth instead of the outside chest in order to surprise them on the line considered covered and thus to shorten the path of the same thrust, the hit is brought to the low line, thus the "lower fourth" ("*quarta bassa*"). (1)

(1) The "low fourth" strike, both as an attack and a response, can also be delivered with the third or third-to-fourth hand position, with the corresponding inward opposition.

Forced glides (*Fili sottomessi*)

Unlike the glade already described that originate from its own engagement, forced glides are executed instead when one's own blade is subject to improper engagement or a weak engagement of the opponent or however insufficient to guarantee the corresponding line to the engagement itself.

Therefore, making the forced glide means forcing the engagement, that is to completely regain the line that the antagonist had originally. Then, without losing the contact between the two blades and gaining the grade of the blade on the opponent through the extension of the arm, one glides without discontinuity and with the utmost decision, the hit is delivered on the target considered to be covered by the opponent.

The action must be performed quickly and above all it must start from absolute immobility to surprise and thus prevent the opponent from rectifying in time the engagement turning it into a parry.

From what has been described it is evident that the execution of the forced glide consists of a single movement. Therefore, this too, like the other glides, the straight thrust and the disengage, they can be executed only to the extent of lunging distance.

Forced glide from the engagement of first.

Maintaining contact of one's own blade with that of the opponents until the hit is executed with hand in fourth hand position, lowered and moved somewhat to your own inside, while at the same time the tip of the weapon, finds its way onto the internal target, where, without discontinuity and with opposition to the inside, the hit is delivered.

The forced glide on the engagement of second.

Preserving the contact of his own blade with that of the opponent until you can carry out the hit, keeping the hand in fourth hand position or turning it to second position, lowering the hand and moving it somewhat to the outside and glide at the same time with the point of the weapon on the flank where without any discontinuity and with marked opposition outside, the hit is delivered.

The forced glide of third.

Preserving the contact of his own blade with that of the opponent until the hit is carried out, and keeping the hand in fourth position, raising it somewhat and moving it to the inside, at the same time the point of the weapon is found to be on the external target, where without any discontinuity and with opposition to the outside, the thrust is delivered.

The forced glide of fourth.

Keeping contact on his own blade with that of the opponent up to the execution of the hit, raising the hand somewhat and moving it to the inside, glide at the same time with the tip of the weapon on the internal target where, without any discontinuity and with opposition inside, the blow is delivered.

Note - as we have said the forced glide consists of a single movement. But in learning it will be good to divide this into two fencing times: in the first time the setup of the line with the initial domination of the degrees on the opposing blade: in the second movement continue the hit with the lunge, maintaining the opposition owing of the hand.

As soon as the mechanics are learned, move quickly as possible to a single movement execution.

Feint of forced glide and disengage (*Finta del filo sottomesso e cavazione*)

The feint of forced glide, like all feint actions, are nothing but the simulation of the action and in this case the simulation in one of the four forced glides described.

This action is easy to carry out especially against the adversaries who being very sensitive to the pressures exerted on their blade, they have an immediate and defensive reaction such as to leave the opposite target widely uncovered than the threatened one. The action itself can be performed either as lunging or walking distance and in both cases consist of two tempos.

In fact, having to perform-for example-the forced glide in fourth at lunging distance, first we make the feint (observing all of the methods described for the respective forced glide minus the lunge) then, on the reaction of the opponent parrying fourth you disengage arriving to the external target with the lunge.

Instead of having to perform the same action at walking distance, first feint the forced glide together with the step forward, then in opposition to the defensive movement of the opponent, execute the disengage.

The same procedures will be observed for the execution of the forced glide in first, second, and third.

Double feint of forced glide (*Doppia finta del filo sottomesso*)

For the execution of the double feint of forced glide the same are valid for the right and walking distance as noted for the double feint actions in general. In the first tempo the feint by forced glide is performed, the second tempo the feint of disengage and in the third tempo the final disengage is completed in the same target where the first feint was performed.

False beat *(Battute false)*

These beats are performed, both in lunging and walking distance, when one's own blade is subject to the engagement of the opponent, beating the opposite direction to the engagement itself.

For the execution of the false beat followed by a feint, one proceeds with the same rules indicated in any of the four lines followed by a feint.

Expulsion and straight thrust *(Sforzo e colpo dritto)*

The similar beat named expulsion or "power" (sforzo or as noted earlier 'potenza') already noted on page 32 assumes the name of "expulsion" when performed from one of the four engagements without separating one's own blade from the opposing one.

The expulsion and straight thrust both in lunging and walking distance consist of two movements. The first, raising the tip somewhat and without losing contact on the blade slides down the opponent's iron following its degrees, the second movement turning the hand quickly to fourth position the hit is made as a direct thrust.

Note - the execution of this action makes it almost impossible for the opponent to disengage in time (*cavazione in tempo*) which we will see later in the chapter of counter offense (*uscite in tempo*).

Blade cover *(Copertino)*

The name of the "*copertino*" derives from the first movement of the action itself, where one covers over the opposing blade.

The *copertino* and straight thrust are done by exercising a light arm being almost completely extended on top of the opponent blade in order to divert it from the line of offense and then directing the hit to the chest.

From the lunging distance as well as walking distance, the blade cover and straight thrust are performed in two movements.

First movement - turning the hand to second hand position one slides over the opponent's blade starting with your own strong on their weak and ending on their medium grade, slightly deflecting the latter to ones left (inside) so that the tip of your weapon turns out and is slightly higher than one's hand and is pointed to the right (front) shoulder of the opponent.

Second movement - quickly turning the hand to fourth hand position and leaving the opponents blade the straight thrust to the chest is delivered on the same internal line.

Care must be taken to ensure that the action is successful to remove the tip of the adversary's weapon from the offensive line.

If one wishes to "feint of *copertino*" the primary two motions are carried out in the same manner deviating the tip of the weapon from the line of offense as mentioned above, but when the hand is quickly rotated back to fourth hand position it is in execution as a feint.

The change beat *(Intrecciata)*

The change beat is a beat that is performed from one's own engagement of either third or fourth or from the same engagement of the opponent.

It is performed by beating in the opposite direction to the above-mentioned engagement and therefore are preceded by a movement to release (one's blade) from the engagement.

The "*intrecciata*" and straight thrust, like the other beats are executable at both at lunging and walking distance and consist of two movements.

First movement: by releasing one's own blade from the engagement strike the opposite side of the advisories blade.

Second movement with maximum speed the straight thrust is made to the corresponding target.

To perform the change beat by lunging or walking distance, we will proceed with the same rules indicated for beats in general followed by a feint.

Beat of false fourth *(Battuta di quarta falsa)*

This beat is performed in both distances, lunging and walking, when the blade of the opponent is kept low on the flank line. The beat is made with the hand above the point of the weapon with a lateral movement right to left (outside to inside). Therefore, it is different from the beat of first (*mezzocerchio*) and assumes a different name.

It is also possible to execute the movement from one's own engagement in second or from the opponent's engagement. In such cases, having to perform a disengage movement before making the beat, the movement will be called change beat of false fourth (*"intrecciata di quatra falsa"*). For the execution of such a beat followed by a feint at lunging or walking distance, we proceed with the same rules indicated for the beats in general followed by a feint.

Disarmament *(Disarmo)*

Disarmament is an action performed on the blade of the opponent tending not to really disarm the opponent but to have him lose control of the weapon and therefore render him unable to defend. This can be achieved with the vertical disarm or with the spiral right or left.

The vertical disarm is applicable from one's own engagement or from the opponent's engagement of first or third.

The spiral disarm is applicable from one's own engagement in third or fourth or from the opponent's weapon in line, here is how it works.

Vertical disarmament (Disarmo verticale) — Turning the hand to third hand position and at the same time raising the tip of one's weapon with short arm flexion together with the lateral movement of the wrist, strongly sliding down the grade of the blade with energetic movement of the forearm and wrist moving in a vertically downward motion roughly to the middle degree of the opponent's blade with the strong of one's own and immediately direct the thrust to the chest with hand in fourth position.

Left spiral disarmament (Disarmo spirale a sinistra) — Whether in opposition to weapon in line or executed from the engagement of third, the movement is energetic with a spiral movement directed from right to left (outside to inside) so as to travel violently with the strength of one's own blade from the weak to the medium of the opponent's blade, then immediately delivering the thrust to the inner target with the hand in fourth hand position.

Right spiral disarmament (Disarmo spirale a destra) — Whether in opposition to the weapon in line or from one's own engagement in fourth, the disarm is made with an energetic effort in a spiral direction from left to down and to the right (inside to outside low) by using the strong of one's own blade traveling down the advisories blade from weak to medium degree. The thrust is directed to the flank with hand in second position or to the chest with hand in fourth position.

Note — the disarming actions described by us which in previous treaties were named *"Battuta atterrando"* (disarm vertical) or *"Guadagno"* (spiral disarm) are still theoretically valid, not that they are easy to implement. However, given the purpose for which they are tended, they must be followed only by the straight thrust at lunging distance.

Renewed attack *(Ripigliata o ripresa di attacco)*

The renewed attack (*ripigliata or ripresa di attacco*) is a second action of offense that starts from the lunge immediately after the negative outcome of the first attack. It is possible to execute the renewed attack if the opponent doesn't react after defending. This new action must then be performed in opposition to the opponent who has assumed or maintained defending himself with distance and depending on the distance in which he will find himself after having suffered the first attack, Therefore, as a result of the different situations that may occur, there are various ways to carry out the renewed attack, and each of them takes on a specific denomination. Here are the situations that can occur and how to proceed by applying the relative renewed attack.

1. The opponent, despite having regularly parried the attack, waits to respond, or does not respond at all. In that case, remaining in the lunge and raising the front foot to gain momentum replaced the point in the opposite line to the parry where the opponent had previously defended himself. This action is called second thrust (*secondo colpo*). (1)

(1) In some treatises the action described above is also called remise (rimessa), while in our opinion the real remittance is the second thrust with appropriate line adaptations under the parry of the opponent.

2. The opponent who proceeds similarly as in the case previous but favoring the parry with a step back, it is therefore advisable to return to the guard forward with the rear foot, and without any pause, thrust again with a lunge. This hit can be delivered with a single or double feint or an action on the blade if the opponent is receding with weapon in line. This action is called "renewed attack at lunging distance".

3. The opponent parrying of measure retreats much more than he needs to defend himself. In this case come back on guard forward, then in accordance with the attitude taken by the opponent, the step forward and lunge is taken (*passo avanti affondo*) this action is called "renewed attack walking".

This attack can also be coordinated with movement of redoublement or fleche either directly from the lunge or after coming back on guard with the left foot.

CHAPTER VI. **ABOUT CIRCULAR PARRY AND RELATED CIRCULAR OFFENSIVE ACTIONS** *(DELLE PARATE DI CONTRO E CONSEGUENTI AZIONE DI OFFESA CIRCOLATE)*

In general *(Generalità)*

In the previous chapters we talked about the actions of offense in relation to simple parries.

We are now going to describe the parries that are circular and the consequent offensive actions that may be put in place to evade such a defense.

As we will see, the defense is exercised in such a way and different from the simple parries. Consequently, the disengagement of the blade is just as different by the attacker for the execution of the compound action.

Circular parry *(Parata di contro)*

The parry can be assumed from either the invitation or engagement, and rather than moving one's own weapon to the opposite side to defend oneself from the straight thrust or disengagement by the opponent, pivot the hand, and describing with the tip of the weapon a circle around the opposing blade, returning to the same starting point.

The circular parry is carried out against either the weapon in line, or invitation or engagement, following a pressure or impact from the opponent on one's blade and followed by the straight thrust we perform the circular parry in the opposite direction to the simple parry.

Examples: when defending against the beat in fourth and straight thrust, rather than executing with the simple parry of fourth, we perform with its opposition, that is the circular parry of third. (*parata di contro di terza*).

When defending against the external flanconade (*fianconata esterna*) rather than using the simple parry of second (*parata semplice di seconda*), we will perform the opposite direction of circular parry of first.

When defending oneself from either the forced glide or beat in false fourth rather than execute with the simple parry of fourth, it can be defended with the circular parry of third. For as well in all other cases in which the parry can be made in the opposite direction by use of the circular parry.

Half circular parry *(Parate di mezza contro)*

The half circular parry can be executed from either the invitation (*invito*) or engagement (*legamento*) of the second or third, completing only half the circle needed to complete either the circular parry of the second or third. The same is done respectively for the half circular parry of fourth and first.

The half circular parry has the same defensive value as the circular parry and is evaded in the same way, i.e., with the deceive (*circolata*).

Note - it can be considered a half-circular (*mezza-contro*) when one passes from fourth to second defending oneself from a hit brought to the external target with accentuated angle.

Some consider half circular parry even from fourth to first and vice versa and someone else call simple parry "double parry". The definitions are not exact because in both cases they are carried out simple parry followed by half circular parry.

Circular beat *(Battute di contro)*

With a similar procedure to that described for counter parries, you can also perform "counter" strikes.

Starting from your own invitation, instead of striking by moving your blade to the opposite side as for simple strikes, you hit the center of the fist and, circling above or below the opponent's blade arranged in line, you execute the strike in the same direction as the invitation.

Thus, from your first invitation, you execute the first counter strike and a straight inside strike; from the second invitation, a second counter strike and a straight strike to the side or above the chest; from the third invitation, a third counter strike and a straight strike above or to the side; from the fourth invitation, a fourth counter strike and a straight inside strike.

These actions can be performed both at a stretch and while walking, keeping in mind that their effectiveness comes from knowing how to graduate the strike well and from immediately putting the weapon in line after the strike itself.

Nomenclature of circular offensive actions *(Nomenclatura delle azione di offesa circolate)*

- Feint, (whether the feint is made simple, disengage or glide), circular disengagement (eluding one circular parry).

-        Feint by (direct, disengage, or glide) circular disengagement and disengage (eludes one circular parry and one simple parry).

-        Double feint by (direct, disengage, glide) circular disengagement (evades one simple parry and one circular).

-        Feint by (direct, disengage, glide) and double circular disengagement (eludes two circular parries).

Note - by analogy with the criteria adopted for the primary offensive actions against simple parries, the nomenclature has been limited to the actions of the three simple attacks, otherwise the combinations would increase indefinitely.

However, from the above it appears clear that the direction to follow to release the tip of your own weapon in compound actions varies in relation to the type of the parry that opposes the opponent to defend himself: disengage and evade the simple parry, circular disengagement to evade the circular parry.

By increasing the number of movements, the procedure does not change, leaving the initial movement of the action unchanged, whatever it may be, since the offense is in relation to the defense.

Feint direct and circular disengagement *(Finta dritta circolata)*

It has already been said and demonstrated that when the feint direct as opposed to the simple parry the disengage ends in the reverse side to the feint. Thus, the resulting action is called feint direct and disengage *(finta dritta e cavazione)*.

Now if the same direct feint, if instead of the simple parry being used a circular or half circular parry is used, rather than disengaging and ending in the opposite target, follow the blade direction and end in the same position as started with the feint.

This action, which takes the name of feint direct and circular disengagement *(finta dritta e circolata)* consists of two movements, both can be performed either at lunging or walking distance.

Feint direct and circular disengagement on invitation of second (Finta dritta circolata sull'invito di seconda)

FENCING MASTER	STUDENT
- Invite in second. - Parry circular second or fourth (half circular). - He lets himself be hit.	- He executes the feint above to the chest. - He avoids the parry making the circular disengagement above to the chest.

Feint direct and circular disengagement on invitation of third (Finta dritta circolata sull'invito di terza)

FENCING MASTER	STUDENT
- Invite in third. - Parry circular third or first (half circular). - He lets himself be hit.	- He executes the feint inside. - He avoids the parry making the circular disengagement inside or to the flank.

Feint direct and circular disengagement on invitation of fourth (Finta dritta circolata sull'invito di quarta)

FENCING MASTER	STUDENT
- Invite in fourth. - Parry circular fourth. - He lets himself be hit.	- He executes the feint outside. - He avoids the parry making the circular disengagement outside.

Feint by disengagement circular disengagement *(Finta di cavazione circolata "controcavazione")*

Whether lunging or walking distance the execution of this action, which in common use is called "counter disengage" (*controcavazione*) we proceed in the way described for the feint direct and replacing the feint with the feint by disengagement, since the action originates from an engagement and not an invitation.

Feint direct circular disengagement and disengage *(Finta dritta circolata e cavazione) (also called finta dritta, finta di circolazione e cavazione)*

The execution of the action can be performed from lunging and walking distance. It is possible when the opponent, after having parried the first action with a circular parry, then defends the next successive feint with a simple parry, so it is possible to carry out the disengagement ending on the opposite target.

Feint direct circular disengagement and disengage on invitation of first (Finta dritta circolata e cavazione sull'invito di prima)

FENCING MASTER	STUDENT
- Invite in frist. - Parry circular first. - Parry second. - He lets himself be hit.	- Executes the feint to the falk. - He avoids the parry making the feint of circular disengagement to the falk. - He avoids event the second parry by performing the disengage above to the chest.

Feint direct circular disengagement and disengage on invitation of second (Finta dritta circolata e cavazione sull'invito di seconda)

FENCING MASTER	STUDENT
- Invite in second. - Parry circular second or fourth (half circular). - Parry first or third. - He lets himself be hit.	- Executes the feint above to the chest. -He avoids the parry making the feint of circular disengagement above to the chest or outside. -He avoids the second parry by performing the disengage to the flank or inside.

Feint direct circular disengagement and disengage on invitation of third
(Finta dritta circolata e cavazione sull'invito di terza)

FENCING MASTER	STUDENT
- Invite in third. - Parry circular third or first (half circular). - Parry fourth or second. - He lets himself be hit.	-Executes the feint inside. - He avoids the parry making the feint of circular disengagement inside or to the flank. - He avoids even the second parry by performing the disengage outside or above to the chest.

Feint direct circular disengagement and disengage on invitation of fourth
(Finta dritta circolata e cavazione sull'invito di quarta)

FENCING MASTER	STUDENT
- Invite in fourth. - Parry circular fourth. - Parry third - He lets himself be hit.	- Executes the feint to the outside target. - He avoids the parry making the feint of circular disengagement outside. - He avoids even the second parry by performing the disengage inside.

Feint by disengage circular disengagement and disengagement *(Finta di cavazione circolata e cavazione)*

The execution of this action can be done from both lunging and walking distance proceeded in the manner described above for that of the feint direct and disengage, replacing the first movement with the feint by disengagement, as the action originates in opposition to the engagement and not the invitation.

Double feint direct and circular disengagement *(Doppia finta dritta circolata)*

The execution of the action can be done from both lunging and walking distance. It is possible after the opponent having opposed the simple parry to the first feint and the contrasts that against the next feint with a circular movement ending on the same target as the second feint is directed.

Double feint direct circular disengagement on invitation of first
(Doppia finta dritta circolata sull'invito di prima)

FENCING MASTER	STUDENT

FENCING MASTER	STUDENT
- Invite in first. - Parry second. - Parry circular second or fourth (half circular). - He lets himself be hit.	- Executes the feint to the flank. - He avoids the parry making the feint above to the chest. - He avoids even the second parry by performing the circular disengage above to the chest or outside.

Double feint direct circular disengagement on invitation of second
(Doppia finta dritta circolata sull'invito di seconda)

FENCING MASTER	STUDENT
- Invite in second. - Parry first or third - Parry circular first or circular (half circular). - He lets himself be hit.	- Executes the feint above to the chest. - He avoids the parry making the feint to the flank or inside. - He avoids even the second parry by performing the circular disengage to the flank or inside or again to the flank.

Double feint direct circular disengagement on invitation of third
(Doppia finta dritta circolata sull'invito di terza)

FENCING MASTER	STUDENT
- Invite in third. - Parry fourth. - Parry circular fourth. - He lets himself be hit.	- Executes the feint inside. - He avoids the parry making the feint outside. - He avoids even the second parry by performing the circular disengage outside.

Double feint direct circular disengagement on invitation of fourth
(Doppia finta dritta circolata sull'invito di quarta)

FENCING MASTER	STUDENT
- Invite in fourth. - Parry third. - Parry circular third or first (half circular). - He lets himself be hit.	- Executes the feint outside. - He avoids the parry making the feint inside. - He avoids even the second parry by performing the circular disengage inside or to the flank.

Double feint by disengagement and circular disengagement *(Doppia finta di cavazione circolata)*

The execution of this action can be performed from both lunging and walking distance. We proceed in the manner described above for the execution of the double direct feint and circular disengagement *(doppia finta dritta e circolata)* remembering that the first movement of the action has its origin from the engagement and not the invitation, thus feint of disengage rather than direct feint.

Feint direct and double circular disengage *(Finta dritta e doppia circolata)*

This action can be performed by either lunging or walking distance, when the opponent, after having executed the circular parry against the first feint, repeats the same parry opposed to the second feint, allowing the execution of the attack to end in the same line where it began in, where the feints were pointing in.

Direct feint and double circular disengagement on invitation of first

(Finta dritta e doppia circolata sull'invito di prima)

FENCING MASTER	STUDENT
- Invite in first. - Parry circular first. - Parry again circular first. - He lets himself be hit.	- Executes the feint to the flank. - He avoids the parry making the circular feint to the flank. - He avoids even the second parry by performing the circular disengage to the same target, the flank.

Direct feint and double circular disengagement on invitation of second

(Finta dritta e doppia circolata sull'invito di seconda)

FENCING MASTER	STUDENT
- Invite in second. - Parry circular second or fourth (half circular). - Parry circular second or circular - Fourth. - He lets himself be hit.	- Executes the feint above to the chest. - He avoids the parry making the circular feint above to the chest or outside. - He avoids even the second parry by performing the circular disengage above to the chest or outside.

Direct feint and double circular disengagement on invitation of third

(Finta dritta e doppia circolata sull'invito di terza)

FENCING MASTER	STUDENT
- Invite in third. - Parry circular third or first (half circular). - Parry circular third or first. - He lets himself be hit.	- Executes the feint inside. - He avoids the parry making the circular feint inside or to the flank. - He avoids even the second parry by performing the circular disengage inside or to the flank.

Direct feint and double circular disengagement on invitation of fourth

(Finta dritta e doppia circolata sull'invito di quarta)

FENCING MASTER	STUDENT
- Invite in fourth. - Parry circular fourth. -Parry again circular fourth. - He lets himself be hit.	- Executes the feint outside. - He avoids the parry making the circular feint outside. He avoids even the second parry by performing the circular disengage outside.

**Feint by disengage and double circular disengagemen*t* (*Finta di cavazione e doppia circolata) (feint by disengagement, feint by circular disengagement and circular disengagement)*

This action can be executed from lunging and walking distance, proceeding in the way indicated for the feint direct and double circular disengagement (*finta di cavazione e doppia circolata*) bearing in mind that the first movement of the action having originated from the engagement and not an invitation, it will be a feint by disengage rather than direct.

Feint by glide and circular disengagement (*Finta del filo circolato*)

In the execution of this action can be done in both at lunging and walking distance, we proceed in the way described for the feint direct, only in the first movement rather than feinting direct, the glide will be the feint.

Feint by glide in first and circular disengagement
(Finta del filo di prima circolato)

FENCING MASTER	STUDENT
- Parry circular fourth. - He lets himself be hit.	- He executes the feint by glide in first (above to the chest) as known. - He avoids the parry making the circular disengagement outside.

Feint by glide in second and circular disengagement
(Finta del filo di seconda circolato)

FENCING MASTER	STUDENT
- Parry circular first. - He lets himself be hit.	- He executes the feint by glide in second. - He avoids the parry making the circular disengagement to the flank.

Feint by glide in third and circular disengagement
(Finta del filo di terza circolato)

FENCING MASTER	STUDENT
- Parry circular fourth. - He lets himself be hit.	- He executes the feint by glide in third. - He avoids the parry making the circular disengagement outside.

Feint by glide in fourth and circular disengagement
(Finta del filo di quarta circolato)

FENCING MASTER	STUDENT
- Parry circular first. - He lets himself be hit.	- He executes the feint by glide in fourth (external flanconade) as known. - He avoids the parry making the circular disengagement to the flank.

Feint by flanconade of second and circular disengagement
(Finta della fianconata di seconda circolata)

FENCING MASTER	STUDENT
- Let himself to be engaged in fourth. - Parry circular first. - He lets himself be hit.	-With the transport in second, he executes the feint by glide to the flank. - He avoids the parry making the circular disengagement to the flank.

Feint by internal flanconade and circular disengagement
(Finta della fianconata interna circolata)

FENCING MASTER	STUDENT
- Let himself to be engaged in third. - Parry circular first. - He lets himself be hit.	- With the transport in lower first, he executes the feint by glide to the internal target. - He avoids the parry making the circular disengagement above to the chest.

Double feint by glide and circular disengagement *(Doppia finta del filo circolato)*
(feint by glide, feint by disengagement and circular disengagement)

This action can be made at either at lunging or walking distance, proceeding in the way indicated for the double direct feint and circular disengagement, only in the first tempo, rather than feinting direct, the feint will be by glide.

Double feint by glide in first and circular disengagement
(Doppia finta del filo di prima circolato)

FENCING MASTER	STUDENT
- Parry third or first. - Parry circular third or circular first.	- He executes the feint by glide of first (above to the chest). - He avoids the parry making the feint of disengage to the flank. - He eludes even the second parry performing the circular disengagement inside or to the flank

Double feint by glide in second and circular disengagement
(Doppia finta del filo di seconda circolato)

FENCING MASTER	STUDENT
- Parry second. - Parry circular second or fourth (half circular). - He lets himself be hit.	- He executes the feint by glide of second. - He avoids the parry making the feint of disengage above to the chest. - He eludes even the second parry performing the circular disengagement above or outside.

Double feint by glide in thrid and circular disengagement
(Doppia finta del filo di terza circolato)

FENCING MASTER	STUDENT
- Parry first or third. - Parry circular first or circular third or first (half circular). - He lets himself be hit.	- He executes the feint by glide of third. - He avoids the parry making the feint of disengage to the flank or inside. - He eludes even the second parry performing the circular inside or to the flank or again inside.

Double feint by glide in fourth and circular disengagement
(Doppia finta del filo di quarta circolato)

FENCING MASTER	STUDENT
- Parry second. - Parry circular second or fourth (half circular). - He lets himself be hit.	- He executes the feint by glide of fourth (external flanconade). - He avoids the parry making the feint of disengage above to the chest. - He eludes even the second parry performing the circular disengagement above or outside.

Double feint by flanconade of second and circular disengagement
(Doppia finta della fianconata di seconda circolata)

FENCING MASTER	STUDENT
- Let himself to be engaged in fourth. - Parry second. - Parry circular second or fourth (half circular). - He lets himself be hit.	-With transport in second, He executes the feint by glide to the flank. - He avoids the parry making the feint of disengage above to the chest. - He eludes even the second parry performing the circular disengagement above or outside.

Double feint by internal flanconade and circular disengagement
(Doppia finta della fianconata di interna circolata)

FENCING MASTER	STUDENT
- Let himself to be engaged in third. - Parry first. - Parry circular first. - He lets himself be hit.	- With transport in lower first, he executes the feint by glide to the inside target. - He avoids the parry making the feint of disengage to the flank. - He eludes even the second parry performing the circular to the flank.

Feint by glide, circular disengagement and disengage *(Finta del filo circolato e cavazione) (feint by glide, feint by circular disengagement and disengage)*

If, instead of executing a simple parry followed by the circular parry, the order of parries is reversed, we will obtain the feint by glide, circular disengagement, and disengagement. Both actions can be done from lunging or walking distance, and they are carried out the same way described for the feint direct and disengage, executing, as first movement, the feint by glide instead of the feint direct.

Feint by glide and double circular disengagement *(Finta del filo e doppia circolata) (feint by glide, feint by circular disengagement and circular disengagement) (finta di filo, finta di circolata e circolata)*

For the execution of this action, it can be executed from both lunging and walking distance and proceeding in the same way as described for the feint direct *(finta dritta)* and double circular disengagement, only the first movement, rather than feinting the straight thrust, the glide will be the feint.

Warning - in the execution when using walking distance coordinated with all the circular actions as above described, maximum attention must be given to coordinate the feet and hand movements together as with the double feint with the step forward.

Beats followed by feint direct and circular disengagement *(Battute seguite da finta dritta circolata)*

For the execution of this action both from lunging and walking distance, executing the feint in the manner already known, it will proceed with the same rules indicated for the execution of the feint direct and circular disengagement *(finta dritta circolata)*. (1)

(1)Since in practice especially to the extent of lunging distance, the reaction in defense almost always takes place as soon as the beat is made, it follows that particularly in the beat of third or fourth immediately followed by the circular disengagement right or left, without performing the straight thrust immediately, to avoid being caught by the opponent.

Beat in first feint direct and circular disengagement
(Battuta di prima finta dritta e circolata)

FENCING MASTER	STUDENT
- Put the blade in line. - Parry circular third or first (half circle). - He lets himself be hit.	- Executes the beat and immediately make the feint to the inside target ad know. -He avoids the parry making the circular disengagement inside or the flank.

Beat in second feint direct and circular disengagement
(Battuta di seconda finta dritta e circolata)

FENCING MASTER	STUDENT
- Put the blade in line. - Parry circular first or fourth (half circle). - He lets himself be hit.	- Executes the beat and immediately make the feint to the flank or above to the chest as known. - He avoids the parry making the circular disengagement to the flank or to the chest outside.

Beat in third feint direct and circular disengagement
(Battuta di terza finta dritta e circolata)

FENCING MASTER	STUDENT
- Put the blade in line. - Parry circular first or circular fourth. - He lets himself be hit.	- Executes the beat and immediately make the feint to the flank or to the chest outside and known. - He avoids the parry making the circular disengagement to the flank or to the chest outside.

Beat in fourth feint direct and circular disengagement
(Battuta di quarta finta dritta e circolata)

FENCING MASTER	STUDENT
- Put the bade in line. - Parry circular third or first (half circular). - He lets himself be hit.	- Executes the beat and immediately make the feint to the inside target as known. - He avoids the parry making the circular inside to the chest or to the flank.

Feint by forced glide and circular disengagement *(Finta del filo sottomesso circolato)*

With the forced glide as we have seen when it is talked about when using auxiliary offensive actions, it runs in contrast to each of the four opposing engagements. Therefore, it will be possible to feint using the forced glide and circular disengagement at both lunging and walking distance when the feint of the glide itself contrasted with the circular parry.

Feint by forced glide from the engagement in first and circular disengagement

(Finta del filo sottomesso circolato sul legamento di prima)

FENCING MASTER	STUDENT
- Engage first. - Parry circular second. - He lets himself be hit.	- Executes the feint by forced glide to the inside target. - He avoids the parry making the circular disengagement above to the chest.

Feint by forced glide from the engagement in second and circular disengagement

(Finta del filo sottomesso circolato sul legamento di seconda)

FENCING MASTER	STUDENT
- Engage in second. - Parry circular first. - He lets himself be hit.	- Executes the feint by forced glide to the flank. - He avoids the parry making the circular disengagement to the flank.

Feint by forced glide from the engagement in third and circular disengagement

(Finta del filo sottomesso circolato sul legamento di terza)

FENCING MASTER	STUDENT
- Engage in third. - Parry circular fourth. - He lets himself be hit.	- Executes the feint by forced glide outside. - He avoids the parry making the circular disengagement outside.

Feint by forced glide from the engagement in fourth and circular disengagement

(Finta del filo sottomesso circolato sul legamento di quarta)

FENCING MASTER	STUDENT
- Engage in fourth. - Parry circular third or first (half circular). - He lets himself be hit.	- Executes the feint by forced glide inside. - He avoids the parry making the circular disengagement inside or to the flank.

Double feint by forced glide and circular disengagement *(Doppia finta del filo sottomesso circolato) (feint by forced glide, feint by disengagement and circular disengagement) (finta del filo sottomesso, finta di cavazione e circolazione)*

For the execution of this action, which requires avoiding a simple parry and one circular parry, can be made in both at lunging and walking distance, in the same way described for the double feint direct and circular disengagement, just in the first tempo of the action rather than feinting direct, one feints by forced glide *(filo sottomesso)*.

Feint by forced glide, circular disengagement and disengagement (Finta del filo sottomesso circolato e cavazione)

Rather than parrying simple and then circular as described for the double feint of the forced glide and circular disengagement, here we reverse the order of the parries, that is performing the circular parry first then the simple parry following the feint by forced glide.

This action can be executed from lunging and walking distance and is carried out in the same way as the feint direct and substituting the first feint with the forced glide (*filo sottomesso*)

Feint by forced glide and double circular disengagement *(Finta del filo sottomesso e doppia circolata)*

To perform this action that requires the avoidance of two circular parries, we proceed, whether executed at lunging and walking distance in the same way as for the feint direct and double circular disengagement, except in the first movement of fainting direct, the feint will be made with the forced glide.

False beat followed by direct feint and circular disengagement *(Battute false seguite da finta dritta circolata)*

The execution of this action, both to the extent of lunging or walking distance by the deviation of the opponent's weapon in line in the manner already known and then following the same procedure indicated for the execution of the straight thrust and circular disengagement (*botta dritta e circolata*).

Copertino followed by direct feint and circular disengagement *(Copertino seguito da finta dritta circolata)*

This action can be executed from both lunging and walking distance when carrying out the deviation of the opponent's weapon from the line of offense in the manner already known for the "*copertino*" and then following the same procedure indicated for the execution of the direct feint and circular disengagement.

Change beat followed by direct feint and circular disengagement *(Intrecciata seguite da finta dritta circolata)*

This action can be carried out from either lunging or walking distance. When the change beat (*intrecciata*) is made in a manner already known and followed by a feint direct (*finta dritta*) and circular disengagement (*circolata*).

Circular riposte *(Risposte circolate)*

The principal idea of the circular riposte follows the same criteria as the compound attack. If in a compound attack it is possible to avoid a simple parry with a disengagement or a circular parry with a circular disengagement, it is possible to do the same with the riposte following the parry, because, as we know, the riposte is the immediate offensive reaction after a parry.

CHAPTER VII. **THE FUNDAMENTAL ELEMENTS OF FENCING** *(GLI ELEMENTI FONDAMENTALI DELLA SCHERMA)*

Fencing time, speed, and distance *(Tempo, velocità e misura)*

We have said that fencing, for the attainment of its objectives, is based on three fundamental elements: time, speed, and measure (distance). But from what we are going to expose, it will be easy to understand that the time and measure are of greater importance than speed, although recognizing that the latter serves very well to complete the power of the fencer.

The "time" in fencing has many meanings and are distinct from one another. When we say that one fencer has a good choice of time it means to say that he possesses the gift of performing a certain action of offense in the best possible moment, as if he, reading the opponents brain or driven by a kind of inspiration, he could have guessed the right moment that the antagonist was in the most unfavorable condition and was determined their action would be ineffective, or in any case able to oppose it validly.

In other words, the choice of time consists in knowing when to take advantage of that moment in which the opponents reduced activity and concentration is at its lowest.

"Speed" is the minimum time that must be used in carrying out any offensive, defensive or counteroffensive action. It comes from muscular work, but it also enhanced by the choice of time.

"Measure" (or distance) properly means the useful distance to be able to reach the target in the execution of the thrust. A connoisseur of measure is therefore one who, when attacking perceives that the distance that separates the tip of his weapon from the opponent's target can be overcome by his offensive actions, which may be, as we already have said, be of measure lunging, step and lunge or arrow. (Correct, walking or fleche)

The fencing time *(Il Tempo schermistico)*

Fence time is the difference of time that must elapse between the offensive and counter offensive movement so that the latter can be judged valid.

A simple attack consists of only one movement. The feint direct and disengage consists of two movements, one is the feint and the other the disengagement, to perform the double feint direct there are three movements, one for the feint, one for the feint by disengagement and the third for the last disengagement.

For each of these movements it takes time and therefore three movements performed subsequently, without stopping or slowing down, there are three times.

However, if the executor of the action slows down or interrupts the action itself undergoing a moment of hesitation, they lose time (*tempo*) in the fencing meaning, by adding a time where not warranted, compared to the adversary who although left after him, therefore arriving before him one unit of time.

In common practice, if the attack is compound and each movement of the action itself is considered equal or corresponding to a time and he who counter-attacks to see that the counter action is valid, he must arrive on the target before the opponent begins his last movement.

That is: if the action of the attacker consists of two movements, the hit of the counter offensive movement must arrive before the second movement of the attacker begins.

Where it was a simple attack of one movement, the one who counter-attacks could be right (apart from the counter-offense of "time thrust" which is not part of this argument) when the attacker failed, as said later, in a defective execution, or slowed down, of a loss of time: this, however, should be considered as a case of absolute exception. The general rule for an action only made in one movement the counter offensive movement based on time does not exist.

Counter-offense (*Le uscite in tempo*)

The counter-offense (also called counterattack) (*uscite in tempo*) is nothing more, but an offensive action opposed to the attacking offensive action.

In other words, going out in time (*uscite in tempo, counterattack*) means canceling the offensive action by not parring as the response, but in an action equally blocking out the hit of the opponent with one's own thrust.

The counter-offenses are:

Arrest (or stop hit) (*colpo d'arresto*), the disengagement in time (*la cavazione in tempo*), *l'appuntata, l'imbroccata, la passata sotto, l'inquartata* (there is not an English term for these fencing actions, the Italian terms have remained), and the time thrust (*la contrazione*).

Generally, the exit in time is applied against the opponent who often falls into repetitions, or one guess their offensive intentions.

Arrest (or stop hit) *(Colpo d'arresto)*

This counter-offense serves to interrupt or, better, to stop the completion of a compound attack.

If it is a feint action the arrest must be made in the first tempo, and that is in the moment that the attacker is about to pass from one feint to the final thrust.

If the attacker is instead making a double feint action, the arrest is made also in the beginning of the second movement or after performing the parry in relation to the first movement, then execute the thrust.

Examples of arrest made on the first "time".

If in contrast to the invitation or engagement of first or third, the opponent attacks with a feint to the flank and disengage above or with a feint inside and disengage outside, at the moment of the feint, instead of parrying second or fourth, the blow is directed to the chest with the hand in fourth hand position and with opposition to the outside, thus preventing him from passing from the low line to the high line or from the internal line to the external line.

If in opposition to our invitation or engagement of second or fourth, the opponent attacks with a feint above and disengage to the flank or the feint to the inside and disengage to the outside, instead of parring first or third, direct the blow to the flank with the hand in fourth or second position with closure to the outside. This hit will block the passage from the high line to the low line or from the external line to the internal line.

Examples of the arrest in the second time.

From your own invitation or engagement of first or third, in opposition the double feint direct or by disengagement and direct respectively, either directing the blow to the flank or to the inside chest after having contrasted the first feint to the parry of second or fourth, remaining on guard, make for a direct thrust to the flank, with the hand in fourth or second hand position and with opposition to the outside, preventing the passage from the high line to the low line or from the outside to the inside.

From ones invitation or engagement of second or fourth, in opposition to the double feint direct or disengagement directed respectively over the chest or outside after having opposed the first feint with either a parry of first or third, the final feint is interrupted immediately, remaining in the guard direct the thrust above to the chest with the hand in fourth hand position and opposition to the outside, preventing the passage from the low line to the high line or that from the internal line to the outside. (1)

---

(1) With the arrest, when applied in the first tempo whether lunging or walking distance it is recommended that this action be performed with a small lunge.

Disengage in time *(La cavazione in tempo)*

The disengage in time is performed in contrast to the beginning of the opposing action where the opponent is tending to divert the blade from your line.

This disengage can take place even if, being at an invitation or engagement, the opponent starts his attack with a beat, change beat *(intrecciata)* or other pressure on your blade. (2)

---

(2) Unfortunately, in the latter cases by presidents of jury, doubts often arise about the validity of the disengage in time.

The Appuntata *(L'appuntata)*

This counter-offense is easy to apply against those who habitually, after having parried any offensive action, respond by a feint. Rather than countering or responding in opposition to the feint, remain in the lunge, and by way of an appeal (or call) to gain momentum, a new thrust will be fired with the appropriate opposition of the hand to the same target to which the original attack was directed.

The Imbroccata *(L'imbroccata)*

This counter-offense is used in opposition to gliding actions ending at the side i.e.: against the external flanconade or glide of fourth. If executed as an attack or riposte or in opposition to the flanconade of second carried out as an attack.

At the same time that the opponent makes one of the above actions, keep the hand in fourth hand position or rotating it to second hand position and gaining the degrees on the blade of the opponent and opposing the forte (strong) to the foible (weak), the thrust will be directed to the same line as the attack performed from the guard with opposition to the right.

The Inquartata *(L'inquartata)*

This counter-offense action is used in opposition to all actions of offense that end in the inside. For example when found to be in invitation or engagement in third, as soon as the opponent starts the direct attack or disengagement to the inside, the *inquartata* is executed by immediately shooting the hand toward the same target, putting opposition to the inside with the hand, then together with the momentum of the arm lay back the rear leg carrying the foot diagonally to the outside and profiling the shoulders well on the same line taken with the feet following the displacement of the leg, thus subtracting the target.

Wanting to perform, for example, the inquartata against a feint attack from the engagement or invitation of fourth, at the moment of the feint, parry third, and then hit direct inside as described as for the simple attack.

Fig. 49 - Inquartata

The *Passata sotto (La passata sotto)*

This counterattack is applicable instead, against all the offensive actions ending above to the chest or outside. Finding for example from the invitation or engagement of second or fourth, as soon as the opponent starts the straight thrust or disengagement respectively where the thrust was directed high or low, direct the hand to the outside and at the same time stretching the rear leg backward and lowering the body and your head so that it will be found below the opponent's weapon. In this position the chest adheres to the front thigh, while the left hand is placed on the floor as support beside the front foot.

Against the compound attack of the invitation or engagement of first or third, to the hint of the feint that is either going toward second or fourth and then the blow striking to the flankì as described in contrast to the simple action.

The time thrust *(La contrazione)*

The time thrust is the hit performed from the guard terminating on the final offensive movement and can be performed in all lines. (1)

This counterattack is used in opposition to the simple attack directly from the attitude of their own weapon on the same line to which the opposing offensive action is carried, preceding it and directing the thrust with opposition in order to obtain the complete deviation of the opponent's blade.

For the compound attack, first follow the parry or parries, then, on the last movement of the action thrust in the way described above.

(1) We consider it appropriate to point out that in foil fencing, where the valid target consists only of the trunk, to have a positive outcome from using the time thrust against a simple attack is very difficult indeed. To anticipate the final movement of the opposing action with another moving along the same distance, will succeed only to those who own the choice of time clearly superior to that of the attacker, or when the execution of the latter is very slow or in any case defective.

The counter-time (*Il controtempo*)

There is no fencing action to which cannot be applied its contrary, thus, to annul it.

Therefore, to all the counter attacks - with which like we have seen, the offensive action is annulled not by the parry and repost, but by a hit or thrust in opposition to the action itself - may in turn be canceled from the respective contrary, constituted by either the parry and riposte or from another countered attack.

This contrary is any of the aforementioned ways being applied take the generic name of "counter-time" (*controtempo*).

In general we act in counter-time when we have realized that the opponent is inclined to counterattack, In that case we will try to facilitate its implementation by showing him with clarity the action that could give rise to his counterattack, to deceive him, as if he really wanted to definitely develop the attack he expects while he is ready instead to apply the opposite as soon as he leaves in time (counter attacks).

From the above the execution of counter-time should be considered as comprising of one offensive simulation that is sufficiently clear and causes the counterattack of the opponent, allowing counter time (counterattack into the counterattack) by either an arrest or parry riposte in counter-time that neutralizes the opponent.

Example: the opponent being on the invitation or attempts to engage in either first or third and sensing that he wants to counterattack to the target above or to the outside, in opposition to our attack, direct your feint with a step to the low line and disengage above or feint inside and disengage outside, in order to draw the arrest to the highline. While he is counterattacking with the arrest to the chest, halt your advance and parry riposte in counter time from the guard.

Instead, finding the opponent in the invitation or engagement of second or fourth, you will advance by performing the feint to his high line clearly and thus prompting his arrest to the low line where you will halt your advance and oppose the arrest with a parry riposte in counter time from the guard thus annulling the advisories hit.

Consideration for counter attacks used in counter time. Counterattacks using the time thrust or *imbroccata* in counter-time consist basically of a parry and riposte.

The feint in time *(La finta in tempo)*

Against the opponent who is impressed by the counterattack and acts in counter time can be opposed with feint in time.

If the feint in time is from the arrest, it is a feint direct. If it is from the disengagement on time, it is a feint by disengagement.

The feint itself can be executed the same as the feint direct and disengagement (simple feint), or feint by disengagement and disengagement (controcavazione), Depending on whether the opponent, during his advance in counter-time, uses the simple parry or the circular parry.

The execution of the feint in time does not differ from the feint direct or the feint by disengagement actions performed as normal compound offense.

The feint in time, whatever it is. is carried out with the lunge, because the opponent at the moment of his parry has been eluded will be in the guard for counter time.

Arrest on the compound conter-offense *(Colpo d'arresto sull'uscita in tempo composta)*

In contrast to either the single or double feint in time, the resulting action is counter-time, by using the arrest against a compound attack with feint. The arresting action takes place on either the first or second movement depending on whether the feint is single or double.

The execution of this arrest in counter time is identical to the arrest as indicated before as a counterattack except it is used in opposition to the feint in time or double feint in time.

Example: your intuition that the opponent, in contrast to your beat in second or fourth, rather than performing the disengagement in time, he will perform the feint by disengagement in time, as soon as the feint is simulated, arrest to the flank or by flanconade of second.

Similarly, we proceed when the opponent executes the feint in time to either first or third, on contrast the arrests will be carried out as before in opposition to the feint the hit arrives above to the chest.

Success depends above all on knowing how to assess the measure. The distance between the two antagonists must be kept unaltered and the decision to arrest must be made without hesitation and keep the correct opposition of the hand as the hit arrives.

Probing action *(Lo scandaglio)*

For the probing actions *(scandaglio)* the intent is to conduct an investigation aimed at revealing the defensive or counter offensive intentions of the opponent. This is accomplished by simulating an attack with feints or working the blade to see their truthful response.

Concealing actions *(Il traccheggio)*

By concealing actions, we mean that the complex movements considered useful to prepare one's own determination or to stimulate a reaction from the antagonist, while disguising your own intentions.

The action of concealment can be completed by passing form one presentation of the blade to another, with feints, or transports and or changes of engagement, pressures or engagements exercised on the opposing blade with narrow and rapid passages of the point of the weapon around the opposing blade. And everything listed here, more often than not, are done in conjunction with small steps forward or backward.

The execution, albeit spontaneous, of the movements does not have to be simply mechanical, but implemented with intelligence and foresight, otherwise if this kind of movement the opponent will come to take advantage of it.

Actions performed at one's own choice of time and actions executed in time
(Azioni di attacco eseguite a propria scelta di tempo e azioni di attacco eseguite in tempo)

The attack is carried out at your own choice of time when the attack is carried out on your own determination as opposed to an already stated attitude of the adversary.

Instead, the attacks executed in time, when implemented in the precise instant that the opponent passes from one attitude to another (placement of the weapon).

As can be seen, the distinction between the two ways of performing an attack is characterized only by the instant of departure, since the "time" factor is always essential for the possible achievement of the hit.

- *First example* - if being engaged in fourth, we consider it appropriate, given the specific attitude, to go to the flank, we can certainly put in and taking note of our plan to attack starting from the moment that according to out intuitive sensitivity we consider it more prosperous. (our own initiative).

- *Second example* - we are still engaged by our opponent in fourth and we want to repeat the attack to the flank. But this time the offensive initiative is taken by the opponent who repeatedly mentions that they are disengaging to prepare a feint for which he tried to find out what will be the parry, whether simple or circular. Always resisting to this threat and never indulge the adversary with any parry as soon as he recalls the disengagement consequently placing the weapon online immediately to the flank will be made.

In the first example, we will have executed the attack to the flank from our own choice of time; in the second example we will have executed the attack in time, based on our opponent's choice of time.

With the same procedure as above, both offenses can be completed simply or compound and can be done frequently as desired one way or the other as indicated.

First and second intention actions *(Azione di prima e di seconda intenzione)*

Any offensive action, simple or compound, can be performed as first or second intention.

Of the first intention, if the action is executed with the intention of reaching the target directly with the action itself, i.e., with the intention of directly overcoming the opposing reaction.

The second intention, if the action is, instead, executed not with the aforementioned purpose, but with that of favoring and provoking the defensive or counteroffensive tendencies of the adversary and to apply to these the contrary actions considered most suitable.

While for the development of the actions of first intention all the time and speed skills are used to defeat the attacker, in those of second intention the performer - while giving the action all the features of truthfulness, so that the opponent's reaction is natural and spontaneous - will have to develop the attack in a manner contained on order not to find itself in the material impossibility to execute what was designed.

The second intention is very effective against those who usually, from a given parry, always respond to the same target.

Note - from what has been said above, it is largely evident between second intention and counter-time, so much so that it cannot be considered completely improper to also call the second intention counter-time. In fact, as we have previously seen, even with counter- time there is a tendency towards the realization of the hit not directly, but in contrast to one caused adverse reaction. However, not to generate confusion, the following distinction is commonly used: counter-time causes the exit in time or another counterattack, the second intention causes the parry and riposte, applying the counterpart to the opposite response.

Both the counter-time and second intention they constitute the most complex and difficult sector of all of fencing: in the field where, although possessing the indispensable technical framing, it is easy to get lost if they are not matched to it by profound observations and a lively intelligence: the field which the fencer is no longer ingenious, more acute can have the opportunity and chance to ensnare even a far more powerful and faster opponent.

Consideration about the cutover and fleche "running attack or arrow"
(Considerazione sulla cavazione angolata (coupè) e sulla frecciata)

We considered these two complementary actions appropriate to describe them last, not because we consider them to be secondary of importance, but only because their execution as we shall see, differs somewhat from that of all the other actions we have dealt with.

Performing the cutover *(L'esecuzione della cavzione angolata)*

While admitting the abuse (and not use, like many claim) of such action may lead to removal from classic and less risky fencing lines, however we cannot disregard the resources that it offers when it is used with moderation and prudence, and this can be used in the attack and of riposte.

The cutover, unlike the disengagement, is executable when contrasting only with the third and fourth engagements in the following way.

With a rapid hand movement and slight aid of the elbow joint, the tip of the foil is raised strictly necessary to pass over the tip of the opponent's weapon and to the opposite side of the engagement, verging on the opposing blade, immediately proceed with the execution of the thrust by having the tip of the weapon describe a parable.

The cutover is particularly useful against the opponent who, alternating simple parries, circle, or half circle parries, make it difficult to organize the plan of a compound attack.

In the case the execution of the cutover in addition to hitting the target of the chest (external or internal) may also arrive at the flank. It is equally useful if applied at a close distance as a riposte.

Note - It often occurs that even some strong fencers find themselves uncomfortable parrying such action. We believe that this depends on the fact that the masters, in general, teach the student to perform it well in the attack but not in defense of the cutover. In other words, we believe that they neglect to perform the cutover in turn against the student, who, not having studied the particular cadence that the cutover has compared to normal disengagements, it often incurs the error of parrying it in advance (empty parry) or late.

Performing the fleche *(L'eseuzione della frecciata)*

This is a particular attack which, especially when used with prudence, can be very effective.

Fleche (running attack) translates to arrow, the execution requires the maximum decision, since the slightest hint of hesitation can be enough to make it void or counterproductive.

Fig. 51   Fig. 52

The running attack stems from a set of movements that they bring the fencer to project themselves forward so that they pass from the guard to a position in which the body is assuredly leaning forward with the armed arm fully extended and the back arm lying backwards.

Indispensable for the success of this attack, it is the coordinated movement of the legs that must be triggered like in a fast race start. The back leg in the continuation of the movement, it will pass over the front leg and the fencer, once the distance to touch is reached will regain the balance finishing his run.

Note - unfortunately, many fencers set off as too often cause the melee attack. Need instead avoid this unsightly and dangerous inconvenience discarding from one side to the other of the line of direction, without leaving the piste and without colliding with the body of the opponent.

For the attacks using the fleche, in consideration of the rapidity with which the body must be thrown forward, it is advisable for the fencer to give preference to one or two movements in the action at most.

The defense against the attack of running is identical to that which is opposed to the other kinds of attack, parrying or counterattacking.

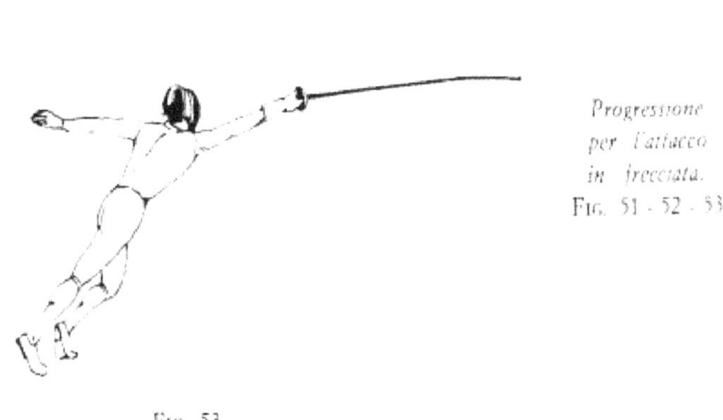

Fig. 53

To achieve an excellent execution of this particular attack, it will be good that the master, after having explained in detail the various movement sequences, let the student carry the free body running attack (fleche) up to when the student himself can execute the action without accuracy and mastery of execution with the point, that indispensable shot that the running attack requires.

CHAPTER VIII. **APPLICATION** *(APPLICAZIONE)*

Preparatory exercises for starting the bout *(Esercizi preparatori per l'avviamento all'assalto)*

Now that we have completed the study of all offense, defense and counteroffensive actions and perfecting their execution, we will now expose through which forms of exercises can be started to aid the student in the assault.

This without a doubt represents the most important and difficult period for the student and above all, the master, whom must be precise in this delicate part of his work, employing qualities of scrupulousness required and competence.

At least for the initial period, the student will have to perform the assault exercises together with the master who, adapting himself to the abilities and possibilities of the student in the alternate function of offense and defense, it will render in confidence while experimenting with their own skills in mechanical movement, time, and speed.

And even when the student, who has become more experienced, will pass to perform the same exercises with a teammate, it will be good that the master's control does not fail.

After this brief introduction, whose purpose is to recall on the important topic aiming particular attention on the part of the master, let us now deal with the various forms of these exercises summarized in the following groups:

- *First Group* - Execution of any pre-established fencing combination, performed employing their own choice of time, both from lunging or step and lunge distance. (l' *affondo e camminando*).

Example - the master establishes that the student will perform the feint by glide at step and lunge distance. The student only when he considers himself ready, will have to start with the decision, trying to score the action avoiding the simple parry of the master.

With a similar criterion, as opposed to the parry simple or otherwise, all the other corresponding actions can be studied.

- *Second Group* - Execution of any fencing combination with free choice of attack (simple or feint) without the attacker knowing what the defense will be.

Example - the master adopts a placement of the weapon (invitation, engagement, and weapon in line) the student must then adopt the appropriate probing action, and according to the master's reaction, apply the appropriate action in opposition to the master.

If the master does not want to react in defense, the student will have to resolve with the simple action.

-       *Third Group* - all actions included above in the two previous groups to be executed in time (in tempo).

Note - When the student has achieved the necessary confidence in the execution of the actions of attack, the "*Maestro*" will go on to let them perform the appropriate exercises for them to develop the correct response of parry and riposte.

Apprenticeship for the bout *(Tirocinio all'assalto)*

The free application of all fencing actions studied, it becomes concrete in the first assault exercises, which are of great importance for the formation of the fencer.

In the groups of preparatory exercises previously indicated, it is noted that the different functions have their own development subject to agreement on the initiative of the offense and defense, so that each of the two is fulfilled separately and distinct from the other: in the training of the assault, however, the same functions alternate and succeed watch other without any preventive agreement on the initiative of the attack, of the defense or of the counter offence.

Without doubt, it is precisely in this first real step towards the implementation of building fencing in this manner that presents the greatest difficulties, almost all the initiates the assault converge their attention exclusively or towards the attack or towards the defense, in a way that prolonged pauses or inactivity follow simultaneous attacks, which demonstrated how difficult it is for new fencers to pass with appropriate speed from one conception to the other.

Therefore, a rule of absolute rigor for the master will be that of carefully following the student in the first steps of the assault, both by pulling with them very much bland and convincing, both by making them meet opponents not very strong or otherwise suitable for performing a simple game, and that until the student himself will not have acquired sufficient ease in orientation, especially for regarding the rapid transition from conception offenses to defense or counter-offense.

The master, adapting himself to the student's abilities, for the first few times he will facilitate it by playing a game of maximum simplicity and opposing the defense with only parries simple, so that the student does not get lost in the construction of his offensive, defensive and counter-offensive movements. It will also use moderation in responses in order to facilitate the counterpart, refraining from the counter attacks because the student himself can develop his attacks with the utmost decision.

He will then progressively try to surprise him with some compound attack and will also include in the defense the counter-parries. And if progress will be satisfactory sometimes it will also apply the counterattack (counter-offensive) the second intention and counter- time, always recalling his attention each time the use of a specific movement correctly corresponding to the opportunity of the movement.

We consider this brief and summary discussion on the behavior of the master towards the student to understand how important and delicate his work is in the period that the student himself begins to free himself from ties of pure scholastic and gradually moving towards free and subjective construction.

This period can be more or less long, depending on the individual; for some it may last only a few weeks, for others however it may even be months.

However, it is always better to extend the time beyond what is necessary because it is very easy for the new fencer, abandoned to himself, to take on faults, which is then very difficult, if not impossible, to eliminate.

The bout *(L'assalto)*

The bout represents a fight between two fencers in which, through a rigorous and reasoned application of offensive, defensive and counteroffensive actions, each of the two antagonists' tires to prevail over the other.

Specifics are not enough to achieve success. Attitudes of mechanics, speed and time and measure are necessary, but these are governed by the prompt intelligence and quick determination.

It often happens that an excellent mechanical fencer is exceeded in the bout by the less technically gifted but shrewd and smarter fencer in applying its concepts with opportunity. This means that - regardless of any consideration of physical attitudes - the essential technical basis is not sufficient in its own to provide the elements to make each individual a strong fencer.

Each bout has always new features and different, infinite possibilities of play, reasoning and applications that find their implementation from time to time and depending on the intelligence and sensitivity of the individual fencers. This is why fencing is considered one of the more difficult sports/disciplines.

Given, as we have said, that the conduct of the combat varies with the opponent, being completely subjective fencing concepts would be absurd wanting to establish fixed rules to achieve the greatest result in an assault, However, experience allows us to provide some indications that, if applied, of course, case by case, they can be very useful:

1) Keep in mind that all movements must be based on maximum naturalness and spontaneity.
2) Use only those actions with caution that have been learned and perfected in the detailed study.
3) Pay the utmost attention to respecting the measure.
4) Search through the appropriate probing actions to learn of the offensive and defensive intentions of the opponent and apply the related and most suitable actions against it.
5) Do not lose your temper, but always stay present in the bout, against impetuous adversaries, since the precipitation and excitement not only do they not allow the necessary choice of time and distance- which, it is always should be remembered, they are the main factors for the success- but they don't even allow you to conceive what is most appropriate to perform.
6) Do not resolve to attack or counterattack in time without having first sufficiently investigated the intentions of the opponent.
7) Be quick and precise in your ripostes to avoid the remise by the opponent and vary the parries and ripostes so as to not allow the opponent to easily find his orientation and the understanding of your actions and employ the opposites.
8) Do not systematically fall victim to the initiative of the adversary who is inclined to attack but limit them by surprising them with actions carried out in time or with the appropriate counterattack.
9) Use counter-time and second intention respectively against the adversaries who favor counter attacks or show the same pattern in the riposte, bearing in mind that in fencing habits constitute a defect and therefore avoid incurring the same in yourself.

Note - through exercise with weaker opponents against which the concerns are limited, not only can you gain confidence in thrusting, be it carried out in the attack or riposte, but study is also made easier for the development and refinement of the various fencing concepts.

Instead, practicing with opponents of equal strength develops the sense of emulation with consequent strengthening of volitional faculties, given the natural desire that each of us has to overcome the antagonist.

Against the strongest adversaries one measures one's degree of progress in relation to the resistance and the contrast that one is able to oppose them.

About the simultaneous *(Dell'incontro)*

The principle behind the study of fencing is that of being able to hit the opponent and avoiding being hit. But during a bout it often occurs that the two fencers touch simultaneously, and what that happens is said that they have *"concurred"*. In that case it is the exclusive right of the person in charge of the management of the bout to examine or establish, based on the rules conventional fencing of for, which of the two, one be considered touched.

If, due to non-evaluable coincidences, the two fencers are each touched both attacking at the same moment, which is called "common time" (simultaneous) the fencing phrase must be considered void, i.e.: it must not be assigned the hit to either fencer, not being able to attribute precedence to one or the other. The same applies to remises that are simultaneous, in all other cases it always means one of the two fencers is in the wrong.

1) The fencer who, wanting to perform an attack acting on the blade, (whether online or not) the action continues, though not having beat the blade itself is wrong. He is equally wrong that, executing any counterattacks and is touched.
2) He is wrong who, as opposed to an action on compound attack, tries the parry and resolves to riposte without having found the blade.
3) He is wrong who, during the development of a compound action is made to find the blade in parry and ripostes immediately while the action itself is carried out despite the blade being met by a parry.

Note - it is not to be considered "simultaneous" if the attack and counterattack end in the same line, the counter attacker is wrong.

Fencing between two fencers with different weapon handed guard *(Dello schermire fra avversari di mano o guardia diversa)*

The reader, following what has been exposed so far, will have certainly noted that all the fencing technique of the foil and the consequent application have had been assumed for two right-handed opponents.

If this is to be considered rational, since normally they encounter right-handed fencers, however we cannot deny that the particular tendencies and skills acquired through this study and exercise, they come in part get frustrated with the right-handed fencer who meets an opponent who uses the weapon with his left hand and when he meets another left-handed fencer.

In such cases it occurs that all reactions, both in the offensive, defensive and counteroffensive, caused in contrasts that necessarily have the two antagonist blades during the fight, put in relation to the sensitivity acquired against the right-handed opponent, they manifest themselves inversely by shielding with left-handed.

Let's see for example what happens when the glide in fourth to the flank is executed on the right when the same glide is instead executed on the left-handed opponent.

In the first case the one who suffers the action, "feels" on his own blade an externally exerted pressure that induces to defend himself with the parry of second or a ceding parry of fourth.

In the second case the pressure is "felt" in the opposite direction, i.e., internally, which leads to a parry of first (half circle) or ceding parry of third.

We believe it is sufficient to give this example to understand that defending against a left-handed fencer presents not minor difficulties and as many, if not greater, are presented to the latter defending against another left-handed fencer and is dependent on the fact of the rarer chances of being able to do exercise between them.

However, these difficulties do not arise because they change, albeit to a small extent, the various forms of application of the fencing technique, but for the different way with whose right hand must develop offense, defense and counteroffensive on the target of the left-handed fencer and these on that on another left-handed person, a target who both presents exactly inverse to the usual target.

Here are the main variants as far as concerns the target:
- *Glide in first*, half circle, instead of above to the chest, the hit ends at the inner target of the chest.
- *Glide in third*, instead of the external target of the chest, hit ends on the side, flank.
- *The glide in fourth* (*fianconata esterna*), instead of the hit arriving at the flank, it ends at the lower chest.
- *Internal Flanconade* (false glide in fourth), instead of arriving to the inside low target it arrives in the flank.
- *The beat in first* (*mezzocerchio*), the thrust instead of reaching the inside chest, it ends in the flank.
- *The beat in second and straight thrust*, instead of arriving at the side or above to the chest, end above the chest.
- *The beat in third and straight thrust,* instead of the target of the outside chest or at the flank, the hit ends inside chest.
- *The beat in fourth and straight thrust*, instead of the target of the inside chest, ends at the flank or outside chest.
- *The "copertino" and straight thrust*, rather than ending in the internal target of the chest, hit in the flank.

Also, regarding the carrying out the arrest, the following target variants occur:

- From one's own invitation or engagement *of first*, the thrust of the arrest is directed to the internal target, rather than above to the chest.
- From the invitation or engagement *of third*, the thrust is directed to the flank instead of the inside chest.
- From the invitation or engagement *of fourth*, direct the hit to the low line, instead of the flank.
- Another variant is the *inquartata* that is directed to the flank rather than the internal target.

FIRST SYNOPTIC FRAMEWORK *(Primo quadro sinottico)*

The synoptic framework of all actions, offensive and defensive in relationship to simple parries, with the related counter actions that each action may be opposed to the first, second and third tempo.

It is also indicated the number of movements in every single fencing action, from which proper placement or from the opponent's placement it originates; which parry, or parries are eluded; to which part of the target ends as well as what the answers may be later at the final parry.

OFFENSIVE ACTIONS	How many movements the action	From which invitation or engagement is executable	Which parries elude	To which targets it performs	What could be the most suitable final parry	What are the riposte in relation to the final parry	Which exit on time can be opposed?		
							First time	*Second time*	*Third time*
STRAIGHT THRUST TO THE FLANK	One	From opponent's invitation in first	-	To the flank	Of the second	Above to the chest or by glide to the flank	-	-	-
FEINT OF STRAIGHT THRUST TO THE FLANK	Two	»	Of second	Above to the chest	Of first, or third or fourth	Inside, or by glide above to the flank, or by glide above inside, or by glide (flanconade	Arrest to the chest	Time thrust or passed under	-
DOUBLE FEINT OF STRAIGHT THRUST TO THE FLANK	Three	»	Of second and first	To the flank	Of second or circular first	Above to the chest or by glide to the flank inside or by glide above	Arrest to the chest	Arrest to the flank	Time thrust
STRAIGHT THRUST ABOVE TO THE CHEST	One	From opponent's invitation in second	–	Above to the chest	Of first, or third or fourth	Inside, or by glide above to the flank, or by glide above inside or by glide (flanconade)	–	–	–
FEINT OF STRAIGHT THRUST ABOVE TO THE CHEST	Two	»	Of first	To the flank	Of second or circular first	Above to the chest or by glide to the flank inside, or by glide above	Arrest to the flank	Time thrust	–
DOUBLE FEINT OF STRAIGHT THRUST ABOVE TO THE CHEST	Three	»	Of first and second or of third and second	Above to the chest	Of first, or third or fourth	Inside, or by glide above, to the flank, or by glide above inside or by glide (flanconade)	Arrest to the flank	Arrest to the chest	Time thrust or passed under
STRAIGHT THRUST INSIDE	One	From opponent's invitation in third	–	Inside to the chest	Of fourth or circular third	Inside or by glide (flanconade) to the flank, or by glide above	–	–	–
FEINT OF STRAIGHT THRUST INSIDE	Two	»	Of fourth	Outside to the chest	Of third or circular fourth	To the flank, or by glide above inside or by glide (flanconade)	Arrest to the chest	Time thrust or passata sotto	–
DOUBLE FEINT OF STRAIGHT THRUST INSIDE	Three	»	Of fourth and third	Inside to the chest	Of fourth or circular third	Inside or by glide (flanconade) to the flank, or by glide above	Arrest to the chest	Arrest to the flank	Time thrust or inquartata
STRAIGHT THRUST OUTSIDE	One	From opponent's invitation in fourth	–	Outside to the chest	Of third or circular fourth	To the flank, or by glide above inside or by glide (flanconade)	–	–	–
FEINT OF STRAIGHT THRUST OUTSIDE	Two	»	Of third	Inside to the chest	Of fourth or circular third	Inside or by glide (flanconade) to the flank, or by glide above	Arrest to the flank	Time thrust or inquartata	–

OFFENSIVE ACTIONS	How many movements the action	From which invitation or engagement is executable	Which parries elude	To which targets it performs	What could be the most suitable final parry	What are the riposte in relation to the final parry	Which exit on time can be opposed?		
							First time	*Second time*	*Third time*
DOUBLE FEINT OF STRAIGHT THRUST OUTSIDE	Three	From opponent's invitation in fourth	Of third and fourth	Outside to the chest	Of third or circular fourth	To the flank, or by glide above inside or by glide (flanconade	Arrest to the flank	Arrest to the chest	Time thrust or passata sotto
DISENGAGE BELOW TO THE FLANK	One	From opponent's engagement in first	–	To the flank	Of second or circular first	Above to the chest, or by glide to flank, to the chest, by glide above	–	–	–
FEINT OF DISENGAGE BELOW TO THE FLANK	Two	»	Of second	To the chest	Of first, or third, or fourth	To the chest or by glide above to the flank, or by glide above to the chest or by glide (flanconade)	Arrest to the chest	Passata sotto or time thrust	Time thrust
DOUBLE FEINT OF DISENGAGE BELOW TO THE FLANK	Three	»	Of second and first or second and third	To the flank inside to the chest	Of second or circular first of fourth or circular third	Above to the chest, or by glide to flank, to the chest, by glide above to the chest or by glide (flanconade) to the flank to the chest, or by glide above	Arrest to the chest »	Arrest to the flank »	Time thrust » Or inquartata
DISENGAGE ABOVE TO THE CHEST	One	From opponent's engagement in second	–	Above to the chest	Of first, or third, or fourth	To the chest or by glide above to the flank, or by glide above to the chest or by glide (flanconade)	–	–	–
FEINT OF DISENGAGE ABOVE TO THE CHEST	Two	»	Of first or third	To the flank inside to the chest	Of second or circular first of fourth or circular third	By glide to flank, to the chest, by glide above to the chest or by glide (flanconade) to the flank to the chest, or by glide above	Arrest to the chest » »	Time thrust or quartered	–
DOUBLE FEINT OF DISENGAGE ABOVE TO THE CHEST	Three	»	Of first or of second	Above to the chest	Of first	To the chest or by glide above	Arrest to the flank	Arrest to the chest	Time thrust or passata sotto
DISENGAGE INSIDE	One	From opponent's engagement in third	–	Inside to the chest	Of fourth or circular third	To the chest or by glide (flanconade) to the flank to the chest, or by glide above	–	–	–

ACTIONS IN RELATION TO SIMPLE SAVES
(AZIONI IN RAPPORTO ALLE PARATE SEMPLICI)

OFFENSIVE ACTION	How many movemnts the action	From which invitation or ligament is executable	What saves does it evade	To which targets or is it carried out	What will be the m2ost suitable final save	What will be the answers following the final parade	Which exits in time can be opposed?		
							First time	*Second time*	*Third time*
FEINT OF HOLLO WING INSIDE	Two	From the ligament of the third opponent	Fourth grade	Out to the chest	Of third or against fourth	To the side or of thread over the chest, or of thread (flanked)	Chest arrest	Contraction or passed under	–
DOUBLE HOLLOW FEINT INSIDE	Three	» »	Fourth and third	Inside the chest	Of the fourth or against of the third or	To the chest, or of thread (flanked), to the side or of thread above	Chest arrest	Flank arrest	Quartering or contractio n
EXTRACTION OUTSIDE	One	From the ligament of the fourth opponent	–	Out to chest	Third or fourth	Flanked or of thread over the chest, or of thread (flanked)	–	–	–
FEINT OF HOLLOWING OUT	Two	» »	Third	Inside the chest	Fourth or third	On the chest, either of thread (side), on the side or of thread above	Flank Arrest	Quartering or contraction	–
DOUBLE HOLLOW FEINT OUT	Three	» »	Third and fourth	Out to chest	Third or fourth	Flanked or of thread over the chest, or of thread (flanked)	Flank arrest	Chest arrest blow	Passed under or twitching
FIRST THREAD	One	From the ligament of the person who performs it	–	Above the chest	First or third	On the chest or of thread over the hip or of thread over	Twitch or pass under	–	–
	Two	On the enemy's weapon in line	–	»	»	»	Extraction in time	Twitch or pass under	–
FEINT OF THE FIRST THREAD	Two	From the ligament of the person performing it	Third	Inside the chest	Fourth or first	To the chest, or of thread (flanked) to the chest, or of thread above	Hollow stop stroke under	Contraction or quartering	–
	Three	On the enemy's weapon in line	»	»	»	»	On-time excavation	Hollow stop stroke under	Contraction or quartering
DOUBLE FEINT OF THE FIRST THREAD	Three	From the ligament of the person who performs it	Third and fourth	Out to chest	Third or Fourth Against	Flanked or of thread over the chest, or of thread (flanked)	Caving stop stroke under	Chest arrest blow	Twitch or pass under
SECOND THREAD	One	From the second ligament of the person performing it	–	Alongside	Second or fourth grade	Above the chest, or of thread at the side of the chest, or of thread (flanked)	Contraction	–	–
	Two	On the enemy's weapon in line	–	»	»	»	Extraction in time	Contraction	–

ACTIONS IN RELATION TO SIMPLE SAVES
(AZIONI IN RAPPORTO ALLE PARATE SEMPLICI)

OFFENSIVE ACTION	How many movements the action	From which invitation or ligament is executable	What saves does it evade	To which targets or is it carried out	What will be the most suitable final save	What will be the answers following the final parade	Which exits in time can be opposed?		
							First time	Second time	Third time
SECOND THREAD FEINT	Two	From the second ligament of the person performing it	Second or fourth grade	Above the chest	Third or fourth	Flanked or of thread over the chest, or of thread (flanked)	Hollow arrest blow to the chest	Passed under or twitching	
	Three	on the enemy's weapon in line	»	»	»	»»»	Extraction in time	Hollow arrest blow to the chest	–
DOUBLE SECOND THREAD FEINT	Three	From the second ligament of the person performing it	Second and first or second and third	Alongside	Second or first	Above the chest, or by thread at the side to the chest or by thread above	Hollow stop stroke over chest	Flank Arrest	Contraction or Quartering
THIRD THREAD	One	From the third ligament of the person performing it	–	Above the chest	First or third or against fourth	To the chest, or of thread above the side or of thread above the chest, or of thread (flanked)	Quartered by digging in	–	–
	Two	On the enemy's weapon in line	–	»	»	»»»	On-time excavation	Quartered by digging in	–
THIRD THREAD FEINT	Two	From the third ligament of the person performing it	First or third	Alongside	Second or Against First	On the chest, or by thread at the side to the hip or by thread above	Flank Arrest	Contraction or Quartering	–
	Three	On the enemy's weapon in line	»	»	»	»»»	On-time excavation	Flank Arrest	Contraction or quartering
DOUBLE THIRD THREAD FEINT	Three	From the third ligament of the person performing it	First and second or third and second	Above the chest	First or third or fourth	To the chest, or of thread above the side, or of thread above the chest, or of thread (flanked)	Flank hollow arrest stroke	Chest arrest blow	Twitch or pass under

OFFENSIVE ACTION	How many movemnts the action	From which invitation or ligament is executable	What saves does it evade	To which targets or is it carried out	What will be the most suitable final save	What will be the answers following the final parade	Which exits in time can be opposed?		
							First time	*Second time*	*Third time*
FOURTH THREAD (external sidewall)	One	From the fourth ligament of the person performing it	–	Alongside	Second or fourth grade	Above the chest, or of thread at the side of the chest, or of thread (flanked)	Stumbling	–	–
	Two	On the enemy's weapon in line	–	»	»	»»»	On-time excavation	Stubborn	–
FEINT OF THE FOURTH THREAD	Two	From the fourth ligament of the person performing it	Second or fourth grade	Above the chest	First or third or fourth	On the chest, or of thread above the side or of thread outside the chest, or of thread (flanked)	Hollow stop stroke on	Twitch or pass under	–
	Three	On the enemy's weapon in line	»	Out to chest	Third or Fourth Against	Flanked or with thread outside the chest, or with thread (flanked)	»	»	–
DOUBLE FOURTH THREAD FEINT	Three	From the fourth ligament of the person performing it	Second and first Second and third	Alongside Inside the chest	First or third or against fourth »	Flanked or with thread outside the chest, or with thread (flanked) »»	Quartered by digging in	– Quartered by digging in	– –
SECOND SIDE	Two	From the fourth ligament of the person performing it	–	Alongside	Second or Against First »	On the chest, or by thread at the side to the hip or by thread above » »	Flank Arrest On-time excavation	Contraction or Quartering Flank Arrest	– Contraction or Quartering
SECOND SIDE FEINT	Three	» »	Second or fourth grade	Above the chest out to the chest	First or third or fourth	To the chest, or of thread above the side, or of thread above the chest, or of thread (flanked)	Flank hollow arrest stroke	Chest arrest blow	Twitch or Pass Under
SIDEWALL INTERNAL (false fourth thread)	Two	From the third ligament of the person performing it	–	On the inner side mind	First or third party	Inside, either of thread over the side, or of thread over	Quartered	–	–

ACTIONS IN RELATION TO SIMPLE SAVES
(AZIONI IN RAPPORTO ALLE PARATE SEMPLICI)

							Which exits in time can be opposed?

OFFENSIVE ACTION	How many movemnts the action	From which invitation or ligament is executable	What saves does it evade	To which targets or is it carried out	What will be the most suitable final save	What will be the answers following the final parade	First time	Second time	Third time
FEINT OF INTERNAL FLANCONADE	Three	From your own engagement in third	Of first	To the flank	Second or ceding fourth »	Above to the chest, or by glide to the flank inside, or by glide above	Arrest by disengage to the flank	Time Thrust	–
BEAT IN FIRST AND STRAIGHT THRUST	Two	On opponent's blade in line, or from your own engagement in first	–	Inside to the chest	Fourth or first	Inside or by glide (flaconade) inside, or by glide above	Disengage in the to the flank	Quartered	– –
BEAT IN FIRST AND FEINT DIRECT	Three	» »	Of fourth	Outside To the chest	Third or circular fourth	To the flank or by glide outside, inside, or by glide (flanconade)	»	Arrest inside	Passed under
BEAT IN SECOND AND STRAIGHT THRUST TO THE FLANK	Two	On opponnt's blade in line of the flank of from your own engagement in third	–	To the flank	Second or circular first	Above to the chest, or by glide to the flank inside, or by glide above	Disengage in time above to the chest	–	–
BEAT IN SECOND AND STRAIGHT THRUST TO THE CHEST	Two	» »	–	Above the chest	Third or fourth	To the flank or by glide outside, inside, or by glide (flanconade)	»	Time thrust or passed under	–
BEAT IN SECOND AND FEINT DIRECT TO THE FLANK	Three	» »	Of second	Above to the chest	Third or fourth	To the flank or by glide outside to the chest inside, or by glide (flanconade)	»	Arrest above	Time thrust or passed under
BEAT IN SECOND AND FEINT DIRECT TO THE CHEST	Three	» »	Of first	To the flank	Second or circular first	Above to the chest, or by glide to the flank inside, or by glide above	»	Arrest to the flank	Time thrust
BEAT IN THIRD AND STRAIGHT THRUST TO THE FLANK	Two	On opponent's blade in line, or from your own engagement in third	–	To the flank	Second	Above to the chest, or by glide to the flank	Disengage in time inside	Time thrust	–
BEAT IN THIRD AND STRAIGHT THRUST TO THE CHEST	Two	» »	–	Outside to the chest	Third or circular fourth	To the flank or by glide outside to the chest inside, or by glide (flaconande)	»	Time thrust or passed under	–
BEAT IN THIRD AND FEINT DIRECT TO THE FLANK	Three	» »	Of second	Above to the chest	Third or fourth	To the flank or by glide to the chest outside inside, or by glide (flaconade)	»	Arrest to the chest	Time thrust or passed under

ACTIONS IN RELATION TO SIMPLE SAVES
(AZIONI IN RAPPORTO ALLE PARATE SEMPLICI)

OFFENSIVE ACTION	How many movemnts the action	From which invitation or ligament is executable	What saves does it evade	To which targets or is it carried out	What will be the most suitable final save	What will be the answers following the final parade	Which exits in time can be opposed?		
							First time	*Second time*	*Third time*
BEAT IN THIRD AND FEINT DIRECT TO THE CHEST	Three	On opponent's blade in line, or from your own engagement in third	Third	Inside to the chest	Fourth or first	Inside, or by glide (flaconade) inside, or by glide above	Disengage in time inside	Arrest to the flank	Time thrust or quartered
BEAT IN FOURTH AND STRAIGHT THRUST	Two	On opponent's blade in line, or from your own engagement in fourth	–	Inside to the chest	Fourth, first or circular third	Inside or by glide (flaconade) inside, or by glide above to the flank, or by glide to the chest outside	Disengage in the outside	Time thrust or quartered	–
BEAT IN FOURTH AND FEINT DIRECT	Three	» »	Fourth	Outside to the chest	Third or circular fourth	To the flank or by glide to the chest outside, inside, or by glide (flaconade)	»	Disengage in time inside	Time thrust or passed under
COPERTINO AND STRAIGHT THRUST	Two	On opponnt's blade in line	–	Inside to the chest	Fourth, first or circular third	To the chest, or by glide (flanconade)	Disengage in time outside	Quartered	–
COPERTINO WITH FEINT DIRECT	Three	» »	Fourth	Outside to the chest	Third or circular fourth	To the flank or by glide filo above to the chest or by glide (flanconade)	»	Disengage in time inside	Time thrust or passed under
FORCED GLIDE OF FIRST	One	On opponent's engagement in first	–	Inside to the chest	First	To the chest, or by glide (flaconade)	Quartered	–	–
FEINT OF FORCED GLIDE OF SECOND	Two	» »	First	To the flank	Second or circular first	Above to the chest or by glide to the flank to the chest or by glide above	Arrest by disengage to the flank	Time thrust	–
DOUBLE FEINT OF FORCED GLIDE OF FIRST	Three	» »	First and second	Above to the chest	Third, first or fourth	To the flank or by glide filo above to the chest or by glide (flanconade)	»	Arrest by disengage to the chest	Time thrust or passed under
FORCED GLIDE OF SECOND	One	On opponent's engagement in second	–	To the flank	Second or ceding fourth	Above to the chest or by glide to the flank to the chest or by glide (flanconade)	Stubborn	–	–
FEINT OF FORCED GLIDE OF SECOND	Two	» »	Second	Above to the chest	Third or fourth	To the flank or by glide filo above to the chest or by glide (flanconade)	Arrest by disengage to the chest	Time thrust or passed under	–

ACTIONS IN RELATION TO SIMPLE SAVES
(AZIONI IN RAPPORTO ALLE PARATE SEMPLICI)

OFFENSIVE ACTION	How many movemnts the action	From which invitation or ligament is executable	What saves does it evade	To which targets or is it carried out	What will be the most suitable final save	What will be the answers following the final parade	Which exits in time can be opposed?		
							First time	Second time	Third time
DOUBLE FEINT OF FORCED GLIDE OF SECOND	Three	On opponent's engagement of second	Of second and third or second and first	To the flank	Second or first	Above to the chestor by glide to the flank to the chest or by glide above	»	Arrest to the flank	Time thrust
FORCED GLIDE OF THIRD	One	On opponent's engagement of third	–	Outside to the chest	Third or circular fourth	To the flank or by glide above to the chest or by glide (flanconade)	Time thrust or passed under	–	–
FEINT OF FORCED GLIDE OF THIRD	Two	» »	Third	Inside to the chest	Fourth or first	To the or by glide (flanconade) to the chest or by glide above	Arrest to the flank	Time thrust or quartered	–
DOUBLE FEINT OF FORCED GLIDE OF THIRD	Three	» »	Third and fourth	Outside to the chest	Third or circular fourth	To the flank or by glide above to the chest or by glide (flanconade)	»	Arrest to the chest	Time thrust or passed under
FORCED GLIDE OF FOURTH	One	On opponent's engagement of fourth	–	Inside to the chest	Fourth or circular third	Inside or by glide (flanconade) to the flank or by glide above	Quartered	–	–
FEINT OF FORCED GLIDE OF FOURTH	Two	» »	Fourth	Outside to the chest	Third or circular fourth	To the flank or by glide above, inside or by glide (flanconade)	Arrest to the chest	Time thrust or passed under	–
FEINT OF FORCED GLIDE OF SECOND	Two	» »	First	To the flank	Second or circular first	Above to the chest or by glide to the flank to the chest or by glide above	Arrest by disengage to the flank	Time thrust	–
DOUBLE FEINT OF FORCED GLIDE OF FOURTH	Three	» »	Fourth and third	Inside to the chest	Fourth or first	Inside or by glide (flanconade) inside or by glide above	Arrest to the chest	Arrest to the flank	Time thrust or quartered
CHANGE BEAT OF THIRD AND STRAIGHT THRUST TO THE FLANK	Two	On opponent's engagement in fourth, or from your own engagement in fourth	–	To the flank	Second or first	Above to the chest or by glide to the flank inside or by glide above	Disengage on time inside	Time thrust	–
CHANGE BEAT OF THIRD AND STRAIGHT THRUST TO THE CHEST	Two	» »	–	Outside to the chest	Third or circular fourth	To the flank or by glide above inside or by, glide (flanconade)	»	Time thrust or passed under	–
CHANGE BEAT OF THIRD AND FEINT TO THE FLANK	Three	» »	Second	Above to the chest	Third or fourth	To the flank or by glide above to the flank, or by glide above	»	Arrest to the chest	Time or passed under

ACTIONS IN RELATION TO SIMPLE SAVES
(AZIONI IN RAPPORTO ALLE PARATE SEMPLICI)

OFFENSIVE ACTION	How many movemnts the action	From which invitation or ligament is executable	What saves does it evade	To which targets or is it carried out	What will be the most suitable final save	What will be the answers following the final parade	Which exits in time can be opposed?		
							First time	*Second time*	*Third time*
CHANGE BEAT OF THIRD AND FEINT TO THE CHEST	Three	On opponent's engagement in fourth, or from your own engagement in fourth	Third	Inside to the the chest	Fourth or first	Inside or by glide (flanconade), inside or by glide above	Disengage in time inside	Arrest to the flank	Time thrust or quartered
CHANGE BEAT OF FOURTH	Two	On opponent's engagement in third or from your own engagement in third	–	Inside to the chest	Fourth or first or third	Inside or by glide (flanconade), inside or by glide to the flank or by glide above	Disengage in time outside	Time thrust or quartered	–
CHANGE BEAT OF FOURTH WITH FEINT	Three	» »	Fourth	Outside to the chest	Third or circular fourth	To the flank or by glide above, or inside or by glide (flanconade)	»	Arrest inside	Time thrust or passed under
EXPULSION AND STRAIGHT THRUST	Two	From your own engagement in first	–	Inside to the chest	Fourth or first	To the chest or by glide (flanconade) to chest or by glide above	–	Quartered	–
	Two	From your own engagement in second	–	To the flank	Second or circular first	Above to the chest, or by glide to the flank to the chest, or by glide above	–	–	–
	Two	From your own engagement in third	–	Outside to the chest	Third or circular fourth	To the flank or by glide above to the chest or by glide (flanconade)	–	Passed under	–
	Two	From your own engagement in fourth	–	Inside to the chest	Fourth or first or third	To the chest or by glide (flanconade) to the chest or by glide above to the flank, or by glide above	–	Quartered	–
DISARM SPIRAL TO THE LEFT AND STRAIGHT THRUST	Two	On opponent's blade in line or from your own engagement in third	–	Inside to the chest	Fourth or first	To the chest or by glide (flanconade) to the chest or by glide above	Disengage in time inside (I)	–	–
DISARM SPIRAL TO THE RIGHT AND STRAIGHT THRUST	Two	On opponent's blade in line or from your own engagement in fourth	–	To the flank	Second or circular first	To the chest or by glide (flanconade) to the chest or by glide above	Disengage in time outside (I)	Time thrust or passed under	–

(I)   It is possibile to perform this exit in time only when the disarming action is performed on the opponent's weapon in line,

SECOND SYNOPTIC FRAMEWORK
(Secondo quadro sinottico)

The synoptic framework of all actions, offensive and defensive in relationship to circular parries, with the related counter actions that each action may be opposed to the first, second and third tempo.

It is also indicated the number of movements in every single fencing action, from which proper placement or from the opponent's placement it originates; which parry, or parries are eluded; to which part of the target ends as well as what the answers may be later at the final parry.

ACTIONS IN RELATION TO CIRCULAR PARRIES
(AZIONI IN RAPPORTO ALLE PARATE DI CONTRO)

OFFENSIVE ACTION	How many movemnts the action	From which invitation or ligament is executable	Which parries elude	To which targets it perform	What could be the most suitable final parry	What are the ripostes in relation to the final parry?	Which exits in time can be opposed?		
							First time	*Second time*	*Third time*
FEINT DIRECT AND CIRCULAR DISENGAGEMENT	Two	On opponent's invitation in first	Circular first	To the flank	Second or circular first	To the chest or by glide above to the chest, or by glide (flanconade)	Arrest to the chest	Time thrust	–
	Two	On opponent's invitation in second	Circular second or fourth	Above to the chest	First or fourth	To the flank, or by glide above to the chest, or by glide (flanconade)	Arrest to the flank »	Time thrust or passed under »	–
	Two	On opponent's invitation in third	Circular third	Outside to the chest	Third or circular fourth	To the chest or by glide (flanconade) to the chest or by glide above	Arrest to the chest	Time thurst or quartered	–
	Two	On opponent's invitation in fourth	Circular forth	Inside to the chest	Fourth or first	To the flank, or by glide above to the chest or by glide (flanconade)	Arrest to the flank	Time thrust or passed under	–
FEINT OF DISENGAGE CIRCULAR DISENGAGEMENT (COUNTER-CAVATION)	Two	On opponent's engagement in first	Circular first	To the flank	Second or circular first	Above to the chest or by glide to the flank to the chest or by glide above	Arrest to the chest	Time thrust	–
	Two	On opponent's engagement in second	Circular second or fourth	Above to the chest or outside to the chest	First, third or circular fourth	To the chest or by glide above to the flank, or by glide above to the chest or by glide (flaconade)	Arrest to the flank	Time thrust or passed under	–
	Two	On opponent's engagement in third	Circular third	Inside to the chest	Fourth or first	Above to the chest or by glide (flaconade) to the chest or by glide above	Arrest to the chest	Time thrust or quartered	–
	Two	On opponent's engagement in fourth	Circular fourth	Outside to the chest	Third or circular fourth	To the flank, or by glide above to the chest by glide (flaconade)	Arrest to the flank	Time thrust or passed under	–

ACTIONS IN RELATION TO CIRCULAR PARRIES
(AZIONI IN RAPPORTO ALLE PARATE DI CONTRO)

OFFENSIVE ACTION	How many movemnts the action	From which invitation or ligament is executable	Which parries elude	To which targets it perform	What could be the most suitable final parry	What are the ripostes in relation to the final parry?	Which exits in time can be opposed?		
							First time	Second time	Third time
DOUBLE FEINT DIRECT CIRCULAR DISENGAGEMENT	Three	On opponent's invitation in first	Second and circular second	Above to the chest	First or fourth	To the chest or by glide above to the chest, or by glide (flanconade)	Arrest to the chest	Arrest to the flank	Time thrust or passed under
	Three	On opponent's invitation in second	First and circular first	To the flank	Second	Above to the chest or by glide to the flank	Arrest to the flank	Arrest to the chest	Time thrust
	Three	On opponent's invitation in third	Fourth and circular fourth	Outside to the chest	Third or circular fourth	To the flank, or by glide above to the chest, or by glide (flanconade)	Arrest to the chest	Arrest to the flank	Time thrust or passed under
	Three	On opponent's invitation in fourth	Third and circular third	Inside to the chest	Fourth or first	To the chest, or by glide (flanconade) to the chest or by glide above	Arrest to the flank	Arrest to the chest	Time thrust or quartered
DOUBLE FEINT OF DISENGAGE CIRCULAR DISENGAGEMENT	Three	On opponent's engagement in first	Second and circular second	Above to the chest	First or fourth	To the chest, or by glide above to the chest or by glide (flanconade)	Arrest to the chest	Arrest to the flank	Time thrust or passed under
	Three	On opponent's engagement in second	First and circular first	To the flank	Second	Above to the chest or by glide to the flank	Arrest to the flank	Arrest to the chest	Time thrust
	Three	On opponent's engagement in third	Fourth and circular fourth	Outside to the chest	Third	To the flank, or by glide above	Arrest to the chest	Arrest to the flank	Time thrust or passed under
	Three	On opponent's engagement in fourth	Third and circular third	Inside to the chest	Fourth or first	To the chest or by glide (flanconade) to the chest or by glide above	Arrest to the flank	Arrest to the chest	Time thrust or quartered

ACTIONS IN RELATION TO CIRCULAR PARRIES
(AZIONI IN RAPPORTO ALLE PARATE DI CONTRO)

OFFENSIVE ACTION	How many movemnts the action	From which invitation or ligament is executable	Which parries elude	To which targets it perform	What could be the most suitable final parry	What are the ripostes in relation to the final parry?	Which exits in time can be opposed?		
							First time	*Second time*	*Third time*
FEINT DIRECT AND DOUBLE CIRCULAR DISENGAGEMENT	Three	On opponent's invitation in first	Double circular first	To the flank	Second	Above to the chest or by glide to the flank	Arrest to the chest	Arrest to the chest	Time thrust
	Three	On opponent's invitation in second	Double circular second	Above to the chest	Fourth or first	To the chest, or by glide (flanconade) to the chest, or by glide above	Arrest to the flank	Arrest to the flank	Time thrust or passed under
	Three	On opponent's invitation in third	Double circular third	Inside to the chest	Fourth	To the chest or by glide (flanconade)	Arrest to the chest	Arrest to the chest	Time thrust or quartered
	Three	On opponent's invitation in fourth	Double circular fourth	Outside to the chest	Third	To the flank or by glide above	Arrest to the flank	Arrest to the flank	Time thrust or passed under
FEINT OF DISENGAGE AND DOUBLE CIRCULAR DISENGAGEMENT	Three	On opponent's engagement in first	Double circular first	To the flank	Second	Above to the chest or by glide to the flank	Arrest to the chest	Arrest to the chest	Time thrust
	Three	On opponent's engagement in second	Double circular second	Above to the chest	Fourth	To the chest, or by glide (flanconade)	Arrest to the flank	Arrest to the flank	Time thrust or passed under
	Three	On opponent's engagement in third	Double circular third	Inside to the chest	Fourth	To the chest or by glide (flanconade)	Arrest to the chest	Arrest to the chest	Time thrust or quartered
	Three	On opponent's engagement in fourth	Double circular fourth	Outside to the chest	Third	To the flank or by glide above	Arrest to the flank	Arrest to the flank	Time thrust or passed under
FEINT OF GLIDE AND CIRCULAR DISENGAGEMENT IN FIRST	Two	From your own engagement in first	Circular fourth	Outside to the chest	Third or circular fourth	To the flank or by glide above to the chest or by glide (flanconade)	Arrest by disengage below	Time thrust or passed under	–
	Three	On the opponent's blade in line	"	"	"	"	Disengage in time	Arrest to the flank	Time thrust or passed under

ACTIONS IN RELATION TO CIRCULAR PARRIES
(AZIONI IN RAPPORTO ALLE PARATE DI CONTRO)

OFFENSIVE ACTION	How many movemnts the action	From which invitation or ligament is executable	Which parries elude	To which targets it perform	What could be the most suitable final parry	What are the ripostes in relation to the final parry?	Which exits in time can be opposed?		
							First time	*Second time*	*Third time*
FEINT DIRECT AND DOUBLE CIRCULAR DISENGAGEMENT	Three	From your own engagement in first	Third and circular third or third and first	Inside to the chest to the flank	Fourth or first Second or circular first	To the chest or by glide (flanconade) to the chest or by glide above Above to the chest or by glide to the flank to the chest or by glide above	Arrest by disengage below "	Arrest to the chest "	Time thrust or quartered Time thrust
FEINT OF GLIDE AND CIRCULAR DISENGAGEMENT IN SECOND	Two Three	From your own engagement in second On opponent's blade in line	Circular first "	To the flank "	Second or circular first "	Above to the chest or by glide to the flank to the chest or by glide above "	Arrest by disengage to the chest Disengage in time	Time thrust or Arrest by disengage to the chest	– Time thrust
DOUBLE FEINT OF GLIDE AND CIRCULAR DISENGAGEMENT IN SECOND	Three	From your own engagement in second	Second and fourth	Outside to the chest	Third or circular fourth	To the flank or by glide above to the chest or by glide (flanconade)	Arrest by disengage to the chest	Arrest to the flank	Time thrust or passed under
FEINT OF GLIDE AND CIRCULAR DISENGAGEMENT IN THIRD	Two Three	From your own engagement in third On opponent's blade in line	Circular fourth "	Outside to the chest "	Third or circular fourth "	To the flank or by glide above to the chest or by glide (flannconade) "	Arrest by disengage to the flank Disengage in time	Time thrust or passed under Arrest to the flank	– Time thrust or passed under
DOUBLE FEINT OF GLIDE AND CIRCULAR DISENGAGEMENT IN THIRD	Three	From your own engagement in third	First and circular first	To the flank	Second	Above to the chest or by glide to the flank	Arrest by disengage to the flank	Arrest to the chest	Time thrust

ACTIONS IN RELATION TO CIRCULAR PARRIES
(AZIONI IN RAPPORTO ALLE PARATE DI CONTRO)

OFFENSIVE ACTION	How many movemnts the action	From which invitation or ligament is executable	Which parries elude	To which targets it perform	What could be the most suitable final parry	What are the ripostes in relation to the final parry?	Which exits in time can be opposed?		
							First time	*Second time*	*Third time*
FEINT DIRECT AND DOUBLE CIRCULAR DISENGAGEMENT	Three	From your own engagement in first	Third and circular third or third and first	Inside to the chest to the flank	Fourth or first Second or circular first	To the chest or by glide (flanconade) to the chest or by glide above Above to the chest or by glide to the flank to the chest or by glide above	Arrest by disengage below "	Arrest to the chest "	Time thrust or quartered Time thrust
FEINT OF GLIDE AND CIRCULAR DISENGAGEMENT IN SECOND	Two Three	From your own engagement in second On opponent's blade in line	Circular first "	To the flank "	Second or circular first "	Above to the chest or by glide to the flank to the chest or by glide above "	Arrest by disengage to the chest Disengage in time	Time thrust or Arrest by disengage to the chest	– Time thrust
DOUBLE FEINT OF GLIDE AND CIRCULAR DISENGAGEMENT IN SECOND	Three	From your own engagement in second	Second and fourth	Outside to the chest	Third or circular fourth	To the flank or by glide above to the chest or by glide (flanconade)	Arrest by disengage to the chest	Arrest to the flank	Time thrust or passed under
FEINT OF GLIDE AND CIRCULAR DISENGAGEMENT IN THIRD	Two Three	From your own engagement in third On opponent's blade in line	Circular fourth "	Outside to the chest "	Third or circular fourth "	To the flank or by glide above to the chest or by glide (flannconade) "	Arrest by disengage to the flank Disengage in time	Time thrust or passed under Arrest to the flank	– Time thrust or passed under
DOUBLE FEINT OF GLIDE AND CIRCULAR DISENGAGEMENT IN THIRD	Three	From your own engagement in third	First and circular first	To the flank	Second	Above to the chest or by glide to the flank	Arrest by disengage to the flank	Arrest to the chest	Time thrust

OFFENSIVE ACTION	How many movemnts the action	From which invitation or ligament is executable	Which parries elude	To which targets it perform	What could be the most suitable final parry	What are the ripostes in relation to the final parry?	Which exits in time can be opposed?		
							First time	Second time	Third time
FEINT OF GLIDE AND CIRCULAR DISENGAGEMENT IN FOURTH (EXTERNAL FLANCONADE)	Two	From your own engagement in fourth	Circular first	To the flank	Second or circular first	Above to the chest or by glide to the flank to the chest or by glide above	Arrest by disengage above	Time thrust	–
	Three	On opponent's blade in line	"	"	"	"	Disengage in time	Arrest above	Time thrust
DOUBLE FEINT OF GLIDE AND CIRCULAR DISENGAGEMENT OF FOURTH	Three	From your own engagement in fourth	Second and fourth	Outside to the chest	Third or circular chest	To the flank or by glide above to the chest or by glide (flanconade)	Arrest by disengage above	Arrest to the flank	Time thrust or under passed
FEINT OF FLANCONADE OF SECOND AND CIRCULAR DISENGAGEMENT	Three	From your own engagement in fourth	Circular first	To the flank	Second	Above to the chest, or by glide to the flank	"	Time thrust or passed under	–
FEINT OF INTERNAL FLANCONADE AND CIRCULAR DISENGAGEMENT (FALSE GLIDE IN FOURTH)	Three	From your own engagement in third	Circular second	Above to the chest	Third or fourth	To the flank or by glide above to the chest or by glide (flannconade)	Arrest by disengage to the flank	Time thrust or passed under	–
FEINT OF GLIDE AND CIRCULAR DISENGAGEMENT	Three	From your own engagement in first	Circular fourth and third	Inside to the chest	Fourth or first	Inside or by glide (flanconade) inside, or by glide above	Arrest to the flank	Arrest to the flank	Time thrust or quartered
	Three	From your own engagement in second	Circular first and second	Above to the chest	Fourth or first	Inside or by glide (flanconade) inside, or by glide above	Arrest to the chest	Arrest to the chest	Time thrust or passed under
	Three	From your own engagement in third	Circular fourth and third	Inside to the chest	Fourth or first	Inside or by glide (flanconade) inside, or by glide above	Arrest to the flank	Arrest to the flank	Time thrust or quartered
	Three	From your own engagement in fourth	Circular first and second	Above to the chest	First or fourth	Inside or by glide (flanconade) inside, or by glide above	Arrest to the chest	Arrest to the chest	Time thrust or passed under

ACTIONS IN RELATION TO CIRCULAR PARRIES
(AZIONI IN RAPPORTO ALLE PARATE DI CONTRO)

OFFENSIVE ACTION	How many movemnts the action	From which invitation or ligament is executable	Which parries elude	To which targets it perform	What could be the most suitable final parry	What are the ripostes in relation to the final parry?	Which exits in time can be opposed?		
							First time	*Second time*	*Third time*
FEINT OF GLIDE AND DOUBLE CIRCULAR DISENGAGEMENT	Three	From your own engagement in first	Double circular fourth	Outside to the chest	Third	To the flank or by glide above	Arrest by disengage below	Arrest below	Time thrust or passed under
	Three	From your own engagement in second	Double circular first	To the flank	Second	Above to the chest or by glide to the flank	Arrest with disengage above	Arrest above	Time thrust
	Three	From your own engagement in third	Double circular fourth	Outside to the chest	Third	To the flank or by glide above	Arrest with disengage below	Arrest below	Time thrust or passed under
	Three	From your own engagement in fourth	Double circular first	To the flank	Second	Above to the chest or by glide to the flank	Arrest with disengage above	Arrest above	Time thrust
BEAT IN FIRST WITH FEINT DIRECT AND CIRCULAR DISENGAGEMENT	Three	On opponent's blade in line	First or circular third	To the flank inside to the chest	Second or circular first	Above to the chest or by glide to the flank or by glide above	Disengage in time to the flank	Arrest inside	Time thrust
BEAT IN SECOND WITH FEINT DIRECT AND CIRCULAR DISENGAGEMENT TO THE FLANK	Three	"	Circular first	To the flank	Second or circular first	Above to the chest, or by glide to the flank	Disengage in time above to the chest	Arrest to the chest	Time thrust
BEAT IN SECOND WITH FEINT DIRECT AND CIRCULAR DISENGAGEMENT TO THE CHEST	Three	"	Fourth	Outside to the chest	Second or circular fourth	To the flank or by glide above to the chest or by glide (flannconade)	Disengage in time above to the chest	Arrest to the flank	Time thrust or passed under
BEAT IN THIRD WITH FEINT DIRECT AND CIRCULAR DISENGAGEMENT TO THE FLANK	Three	"	Circular first	To the flank	Second or circular first	Above to the chest or by glide to the flank or by glide above	Disengage in time inside	Arrest to the chest	Time thrust
BEAT IN THIRD WITH FEINT DIRECT AND CIRCULAR DISENGAGEMENT OUTSIDE	Three	"	Circular fourth	Outside to the chest	Second or circular fourth	To the flank, or by glide above to the chest or by glide (flaconade)	Disengage in time inside	Arrest to the flank	Time thrust or passed under
BEAT IN FOURTH WITH FEINT DIRECT AND CIRCULAR DISENGAGEMENT	Three	"	Circular third	Inside to the chest	Fourth or first	To the chest, or by glide (flaconade) to the chest or by glide above	Disengage in time outside	Arrest inside	Time thrust or quartered

OFFENSIVE ACTION	How many movemnts the action	From which invitation or ligament is executable	Which parries elude	To which targets it perform	What could be the most suitable final parry	What are the ripostes in relation to the final parry?	Which exits in time can be opposed?		
							First time	*Second time*	*Third time*
COPERTINO WITH FEINT DIRECT AND CIRCULAR DISENGAGEMENT	Three	On opponent's blade in line	Circular third	Inside to the chest	Fourth or first	To the chest or by glide (flaconade) to the chest or by glide above	Disengage in time outside	Arrest inside	Time thrust or quartered
FEINT OF CIRCULAR FORCED GLIDE	Two	On opponent's engagement in first	Circular second	Above to the chest	Third or fourth	To the flank or by glide above to the chest or by glide (flaconade)	Arrest inside	Time thrust or passed under	–
	Two	On opponent's engagement in second	Circular first	To the flank	Second or circular first	Above to the chest or by glide to the flank to the chest or by glide above	Arrest to the chest	Time thrust	–
	Two	On opponent's engagement in third	Circular fourth	Outside to the chest	Third or circular fourth	To the flank or by glide above to the chest or by glide (flaconade)	Arrest to the flank	Time thrust or passed under	–
	Two	On opponent's engagement in fourth	Circular third	Inside to the chest	Fourth or first	To the chest or by glide (flaconade) to the chest or by glide above	Arrest to the chest	Time thrust or quartered	–
DOUBLE FEINT OF CIRCULAR FORCED GLIDE	Three	On opponent's engagement in first	First or circular first	To the flank	Second	Above to the chest, or by glide to the flank	Arrest inside	Arrest to the chest	Time thrust
	Three	On opponent's engagement in second	Second or circular second	Above to the chest	Third or fourth	To the flank or by glide above to the chest or by glide (flanconade)	Arrest to the chest	Arrest to the flank	Time thrust or passed under
	Three	On opponent's engagement third	Third or circular third	Inside to the chest	Fourth or first	To the chest or by glide (flaconade) to the chest or by glide above	Arrest to the flank	Arrest to the chest	Time thrust or quartered
	Three	On opponent's engagement fourth	Fourth or circular fourth	Outside to the chest	Third	To the flank or by glide	Arrest to the chest	Arrest to the flank	Time thrust or passed under

ACTIONS IN RELATION TO CIRCULAR PARRIES
(AZIONI IN RAPPORTO ALLE PARATE DI CONTRO)

OFFENSIVE ACTION	How many movemnts the action	From which invitation or ligament is executable	Which parries elude	To which targets it perform	What could be the most suitable final parry	What are the ripostes in relation to the final parry?	Which exits in time can be opposed?		
							First time	Second time	Third time
FEINT OF CIRCULAR FORCED GLIDE AND DISENGAGE	Three	From opponent's engagement in first	Circular second and third	Inside to the chest	Fourth or circular third	To the chest or by glide(flanconade) to the flank or by glide above	Arrest to the flank	Arrest to the flank	Time thrust or quartered
	Three	From opponent's engagement in second	Circular first and second	Above to the chest	Fourth or first	To the chest or by glide(flanconade) to the flank or by glide above	Arrest to the chest	Arrest to the chest	Time thrust or passed under
	Three	From opponent's engagement in third	Circular fourth and third	Inside to the chest	Fourth or circular third	To the chest or by glide(flanconade) to the flank or by glide above	Arrest to the flank	Arrest to the flank	Time thrust or quartered
	Three	From opponent's engagement in fourth	Circular third and fourth	Outside to the chest	Third or circular fourth	To the chest or by glide(flanconade)	Arrest to the chest	Arrest to the chest	Time thrust or passed under
FEINT OF FORCED GLIDE AND DOUBLE CIRCULAR DISENGAGEMENT	Three	From opponent's engagement in first	Circular second and fourth	Outside to the chest	Third or circular fourth	To the flank or by glide above to the chest or by glide (flaconade)	Arrest to the flank	Arrest to the flank	Time thrust or passed under
	Three	From opponent's engagement in second	Double circular first	To the flank	Second	Above to the chest or by glide to the flank	Arrest to the chest	Arrest to the chest	Time thrust
	Three	From opponent's engagement third	Double circular fourth	Outside to the chest	Third	To the flank or by glide above	Arrest to the flank	Arrest to the flank	Time thrust or passed under
	Three	From opponent's engagement fourth	Double circular third	Inside to the chest	Fourth	To the flank or by glide (flaconade)	Arrest to the chest	Arrest to the chest	Time thrust or quartered
			or						
			Circular third and first	To the flank	Second	Above to the chest or by glide to the flank	"	"	

THE SABER

LA SCIABOLA

originally printed

ITALIAN FENCING FEDERATION - SCUOLA CENTRALE DELLO SPORT

ROME 1970

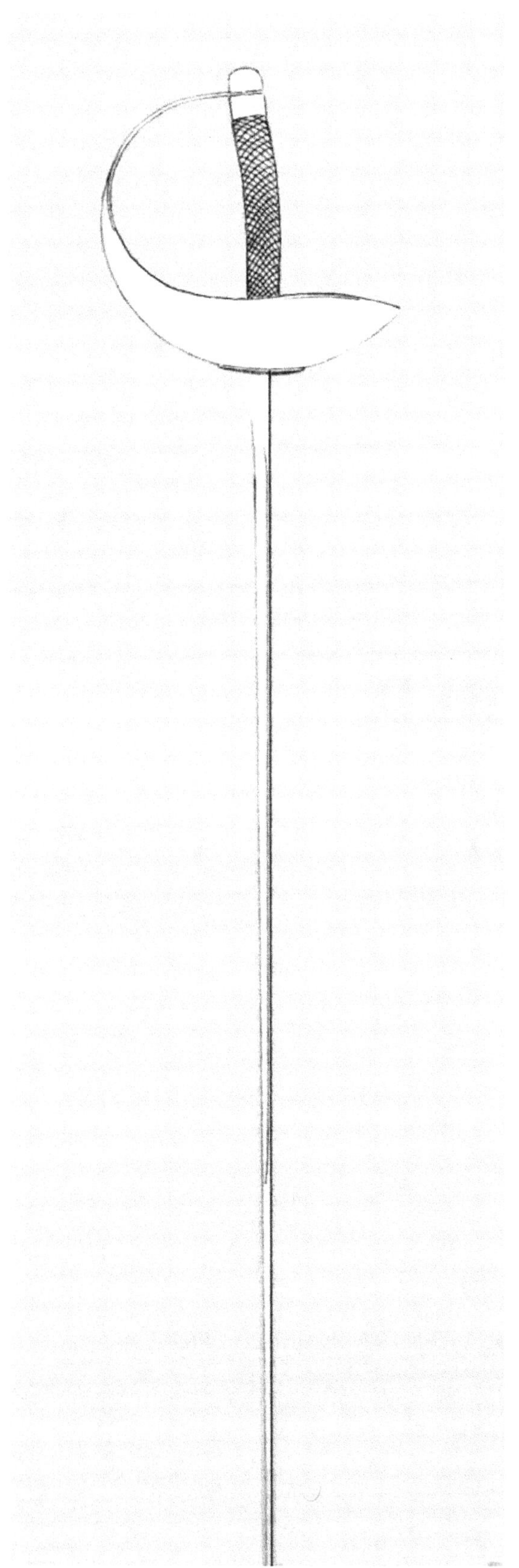

la sciabola

PREFACE

La "Sciabola" complete with "Il Fioretto" and "la Spada" the program that the Fencing Federation had established since 1960. We cannot therefore certainly speak of the execution and speed we have been employed to make the three volumes for over ten years.

However, the case has been made that this delay matches the volume output to finish saber in the same year as the Munich Olympics where we scored and redeemed ourselves from a long period of drought. And that just one of the two gold medals have been awarded to the Italian saber team and is a fortuitous coincidence that renders even more "current" the output of this volume.

In fact, the Olympic victory confirmed once more that the Italian school is always among the most valid in its forms that have been transmitted to us by our old maestri (Radaelli, Masaniello Parise and Carlo Pessina). The Italian school, widespread in the whole world and particularly in Budapest from maestro Santelli (one of the favorite students of Maestro Carlo Pessina), after having given Hungary the chance to win so many victories that they have allowed to maintain absolute dominance in the world for over thirty years, expresses after the not short Russian parenthesis- the best of his content with our five saberist's who Monaco outclass the Soviet heirs of the Hungarians.

The evolution of the weapon appeared clearly during the last Olympics Games, but only with regard to the conduct of the assault, while it seems to have changed in the aspect of mechanics, both in the actions of attack and in those of defense.

The modern saber therefore confirms the validity of our school that had seen its last victory at the Paris Olympics in 1924. The master swordmen are the sons of the Olympic masters of '24: the same fencing language, the same approach, and the same execution.

The present treaty has its roots in teachings that have been handed down from these old masters and, not surprisingly, the task of writing this treaty has been entrusted to the masters Ugo Pignotti and Giorgio Pessina, heirs of a tradition of central-southern fencing from which the saber has drawn most of its lifeblood over the years. To the two masters Pessina and Pignotti we say our most sincere thanks, confident that the work from them completed will be of great help to the training of the new Italian magisterial class.

RENZO NOSTINI

CHAPTER I.

Considerations on Saber Fencing (*Considerazioni sulla scherma di sciabola*) — The Fundamental Elements of Fencing (*Gli elementi fondamentali della scherma*) — Saber Nomenclature (*Nomenclatura della sciabola*) — Balance, Weight, and Total Length of the Saber (Equilibrio, peso e lunghezza totale della sciabola) — Mode of Holding the Saber (Modo di impugnare la sciabola) — Fist (Hand) Position (Posizione del pugno) — The First Position (La prima posizione) — Saber

Online (Sciabola in linea) — The Salute (Il saluto) — The Line of Direction (La linea direttrice) — The Guard (La guardia) — The Measure (La misura) — The Step Forward and Step Back (Il passo avanti e passo indietro) — The Jump Back (Il salto indietro) — The Lunge (L'affondo) — The Return to Guard (Il ritorno in guardia) — The Step Forward and Lunge (Il passo avanti e affondo) — Gain on the Lunge (Il raddoppio) — The Frecciata (La frecciata) (Flèche <FR>, arrow <EN>) — Exercises for the Legs (Esercizi per le gambe).

Considerations for fencing with the saber *(Considerazioni sulla scherma di Sciabola)*

The saber is a typical Italian weapon. In fact, Italian masters brought saber fencing to every country in the world, including and in particular, Hungary. Which for decades and until a few years ago managed to excel in almost all major international competitions.

Even if saber fencing uses the same principles of offense, defense and counter offense and the same fundamental elements of time, measure, and velocity, it is still significantly different than the two other disciplines.

In fact, while the foil and the epee are weapons exclusively using the tip, with the saber the touch can be made with both the tip, the cut, and the counter cut.

Consequently, this possibility of offense and counter-offense requires a particular defense adaptation for which it is the game that the technique of such weapon, assuming, in most cases, the characteristics are different from those of the other weapons. In comparison with the latter perhaps the fencing of saber is more accessible and therefore easier to learn, but it is the handling and the bearing of the weapon that presents great difficulties, both for the offensive use than for the defensive one.

In saber fencing, being reduced to minimum if not completely eliminated, the counter parries as opposed to the cut. It remains easier to design and plan an offensive action as one can almost certainly predict what will be the parry that the opponent will use to oppose our own attack or feint by starting with certain security to avoid the parry which is not the same or with frequent ease as in foil fencing where the attacker is always in the alternative if the opponent resolves to answer with a simple parry or counter.

Example: if in contrast to the invitation of third we want to cut the head we are sure that the opponent will only be able to parry fifth, and if we want to create the feint to the head, we will be just as safe as pretending to hit the head (always means having the ability to understand the opponents defense) and then changing to a second target to evade the parry as assumed. While in fencing foil, carrying out the hit in opposition from the invitation of third, the opponent can make use of the parry of fourth, or counter of third or first, (mezza contro), therefore if desired to perform the feint direct movement we will have the relative data, suggested by the intuition, for evading one of three parries, but not evading the absolute parry as in the case of the feint to the head in saber.

It is clear from this example that to organize a saber attack is less difficult than what must be organized by foil. But, while the foil is like to the epee, the direction of the hit is only one (that followed by the tip), in the fencing of saber we have the direction of the cut, tip and counter-cut. Therefore, very remarkable the difference in the defense, both in contrasting the attack to the various directions that it can travel through the hits of the antagonist, the greater resistance is needed to oppose the blade due to the power of the cut. And it is precisely what they are found in those serious difficulties in the use of the weapon which we have previously mentioned. Indeed, for the greater amplitude of the movements of the weapon and per flattening and smoothing of its blade towards the cutting and counter-cutting, it follows that easily they can generate the swerving of the weapon if this is not guided with care and balance.

It is essential that the direction of the hits that the parry is carried out with the cut (from the back or spine of the blade in some cases) and never from the flat of the blade. That being said, it is easy to understand which device and which adaptation to pass from the hint of a hit to another hit, or from the hit to the parry or vice versa, of from the parry to another parry, waves made to avoid these.

The fundamental elements of saber *(Gli elementi fondamentali della scherma)*

We have said that fencing for achievement of its objectives is based on the three fundamental elements: time, speed, and measure.

The "Time" in fencing has many meanings well distinct from one another, but when we say that a fencer has a good choice of time we mean that he has the gift to perform a certain offensive action in the instant it is prosperous, as if he, reading the thoughts of the opponent or driven by a kind of inspiration, could have guessed that right at that moment the antagonist was in the most unfavorable conditions to render its determination ineffective, or in any case to validly oppose it. In other words, the choice of time consists of knowing how to take advantage of that moment in which he comes to the activity and concentration of the opponent must be reduced.

"Speed" is the minimum time spent to employ any offensive, defensive or counteroffensive action. It springs from muscular work but is also enhanced by the choice of time.

The "measure" properly means distance useful to be able to reach the target in the touch. The good connoisseur of measure is therefore the one who, when attacking, perceived that the distance that separates the tip or cut of the weapon from the opponents' target can be overcome by his offensive action, which, as we shall see, may be competed by using the lunge, step and lunge or frecciata.

Nomenclature of the saber *(Nomenclatura della Sciabola)*

Like the foil and the epee, even the saber itself is composed of the blade and the guard.

In the blade, which is made of tempered steel and whose length must be less than 880mm, are distinguished:

1. The tang *(codolo)* that is the raw, quadrangular part which remains after the blade, having the threaded end.
2. The heel *(tallone)* is the most robust part, not grooved, which gives rise to the blade.
3. The groove *(la scanalatura)* is that which runs in a longitudinal direction down the middle of the blade for two thirds of it, in order to reduce its weight.
4. The cut *(taglio)* is the thinner part of the blade starting from the guard, which begins at the end of the first third of the blade with respect to the heal and goes up to the tip.
5. The back *(dorso)* i.e., is the thickest part opposite the cut.
6. The counter-cut *(contro-taglio)* is the sharpened part that includes the last third of the blade opposite the cut that begins exactly where the groves end and continues to the tip.
7. The tip, *(punta)* the end of the blade with respect to the heel, which is flattened and rounded.

The blade, has been said not to exceed the length of 880mm, must have at its end (the tip) a minimum width of 4mm, and the minimum thickness, likewise at the end, of 1.2mm.

Moreover, it must be neither too rigid nor too flexible and above all it must not bend laterally along the cut.

Fig. 1 - La lama

The guard is comprised of:

A) The guard (*coccia*)- which serves to protect the hand. It is smooth and built with a single piece of metal, either iron or aluminum. It presents one convex shape with a continuous curve without edges or holes in which the point of the opposing weapon can get caught in. Its length, measured in the same cutting direction of the blade, must be less than 150mm, and its width, measured perpendicularly on this

125

same direction, less than, 140mm. In other terms the coccia must be able to pass in a caliber of control measuring 150mm. For 140, with the flat of the blade held parallel to the sides of 150mm.

B) The handle (*l'impugnatura o manico*) generally of knurled wood and with two reinforced metal rings at the extremities- it has a form almost of a flattened cylindrical form that corresponding to that of the back of the blade, and slightly curved at the lower end for the adaptation of the concavity of the hand.

C) The nut or button (*pomolo*) that is screwed to the end of the tang, allowing to keep joined solidly the various parts of the weapon.

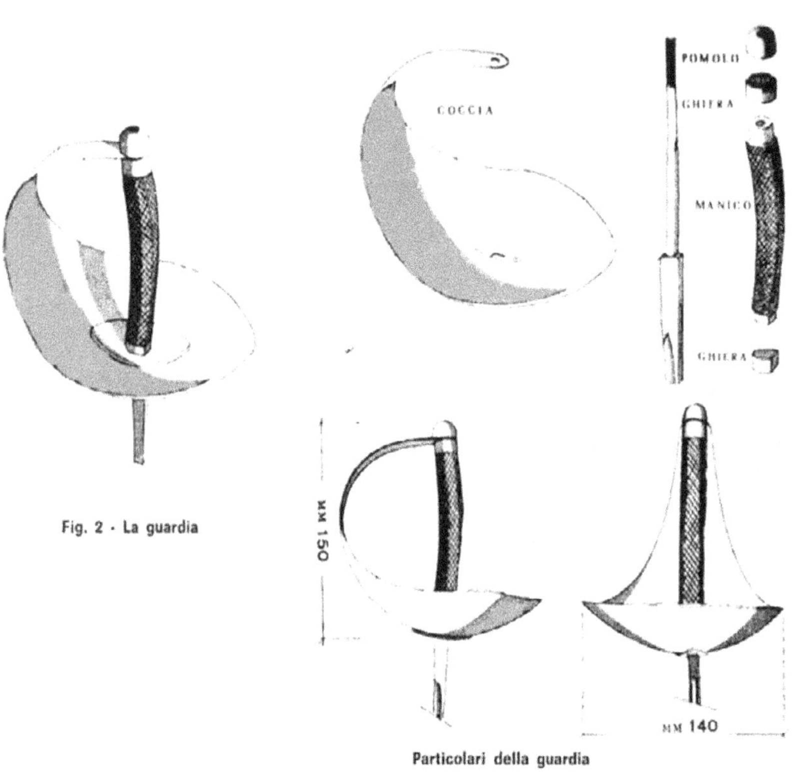

Fig. 2 - La guardia

Particolari della guardia

Balance, weight, and total length of the saber *(Equilibrio, peso e lunghezza totale della Sciabola)*

A properly mounted saber should be well balanced, that is allowing to be able to direct it easily in any direction and perform any movement without it dragging the hand to involuntary fluctuations.

Practically, because a saber is well balanced, requiring that its center of gravity to be about 5 cm from the bell. The total weight of the saber must be less than 500grams and its total length less than 1050mm.

Way to hold the saber *(Modo di impugnare la Sciabola)*

The manner of holding the saber is of the utmost importance. When it is well handled, it is the fencer, who through a particular study of the arm and hand movements, you can buy an irreproachable precision in the handling of the weapon, that is to obtain that set of equilibrium, direction, and gradual tightening of the hand on the handle that in the common fencing language is called «poise of blade».

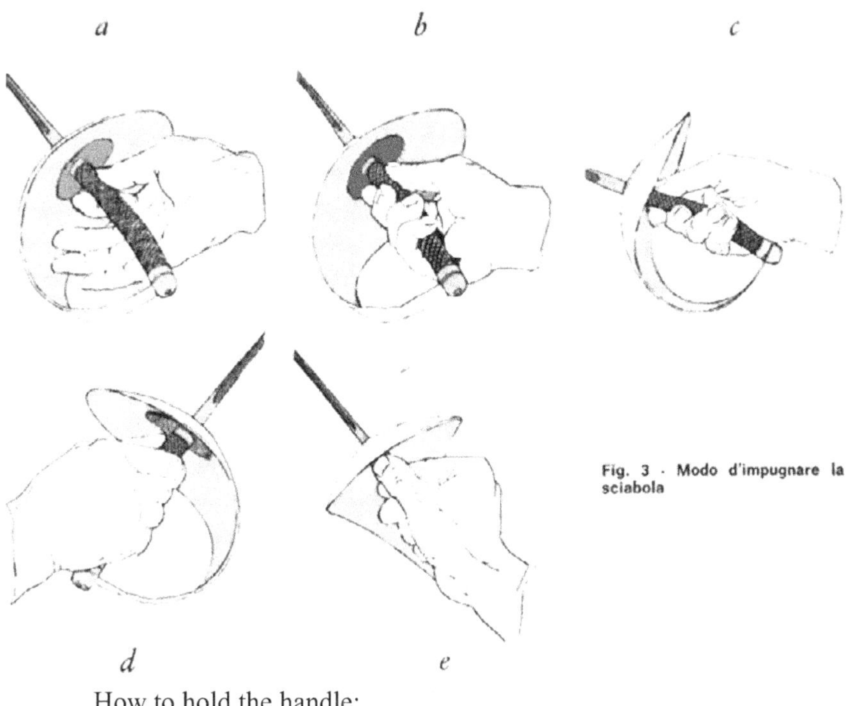

How to hold the handle:

The last four fingers of the hand are introduced between the coccia and the handle that is placed crosswise in the longitudinal direction of the palm of the hand, so that, closing it, the last phalanx of the index finger rests on the rounded part of the handle itself as opposed to the thumb being placed on the flat side and at least one centimeter away from the guard. The other fingers curve around the handle whose lower part must rest on the eminence hypothesize «midline of the palm» of the hand, in order to have a secure point of support in the hit of the cut and cutting actions resisting parries. (FIG.3)

The position of the hand *(Le posizione di pugno)*

The different positions in which the fencer's weapon hand can be, in various contingencies, are referred to as « fist positions ».

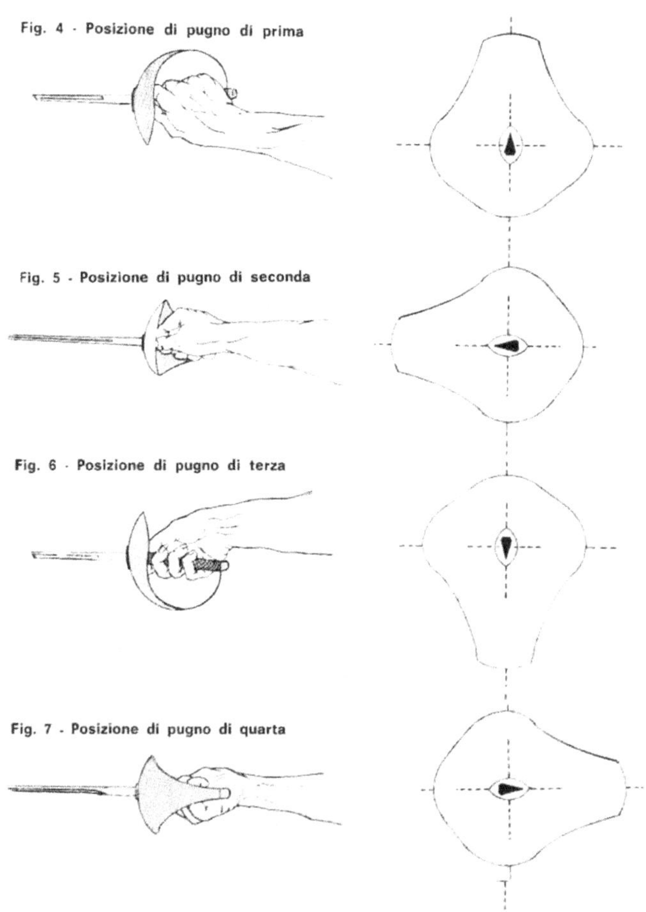

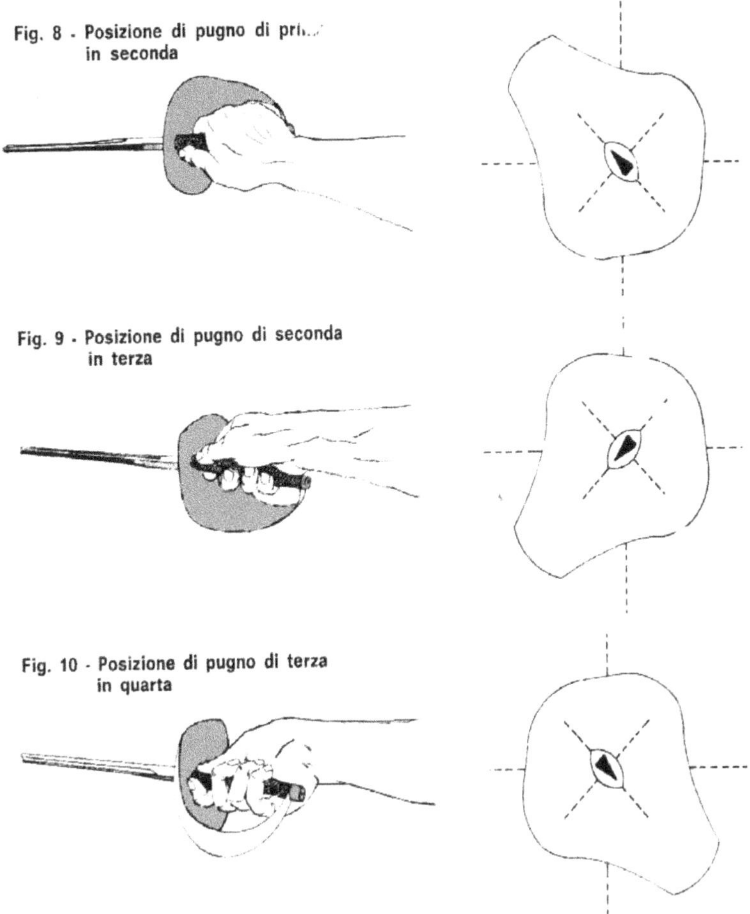

These positions, which are achieved by rotating the hand along the longitudinal axis of the forearm, are seven in total, of which four are normal and three are intermediate: «first» fist position, «second» fist position, «third» fist position, «fourth» fist position, «first in second» fist position, «second in third» fist position, and «third in fourth» fist position.

When the sabre is gripped in the manner described above, the blade's cutting edge, in relation to each of the seven fist positions, should be as follows (see figs. 4, 5, 6, 7, 8, 9, 10):

first fist position: upward cut (back of the hand facing left);

second fist position: rightward cut (back of the hand facing up);

third fist position: downward cut (back of the hand facing right);

fourth fist position: leftward cut (back of the hand facing down);

first in second fist position: diagonal upward cut to the right;

second in third fist position: diagonal downward cut to the right;

third in fourth fist position: diagonal downward cut to the left.

First position *(la prima Posizione)*

Holding the saber in the manner described position the feet at right angle with the heals in contact so that the front foot appears in a longitudinal direction to the fencing strip: hold the body perpendicular with the shoulders open and at the same height between them: with the weapon arm being slightly flexed and the hand in front near the back leg: the blade tilted diagonally back so that the tip appears behind the rear foot just a few centimeters from the earth, with the cut facing down. The unarmed hand rests on the top of the hip (flank) in the shape of a fork between the index finger and the thumb.

Fig. 11 - La prima posizione

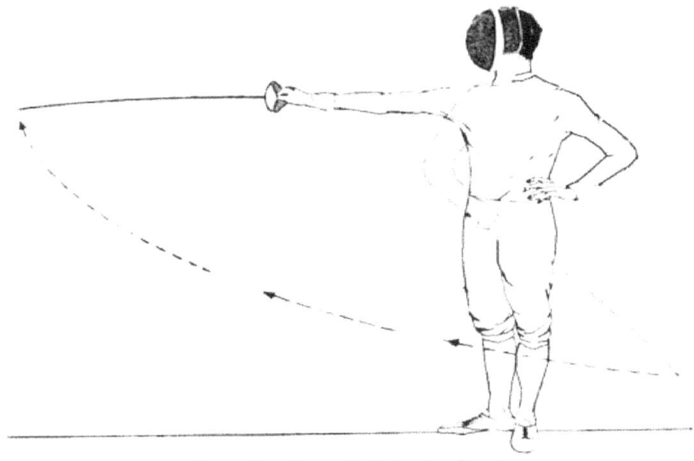
Fig. 12 - La sciabola in linea

The saber in line *(la Sciabola in linea)*

From the first position one passes the saber in line in a single movement, that is by bringing the saber in line with the weapon arm stretched out at shoulder height, cut facing right, with having the shoulder, hand, and the tip of the saber on the same line.

The salute *(Il saluto)*

The salute is a dutiful gesture of courtesy towards the adversary and the bystanders, a gesture that the fencer must not ever fail to perform both at the beginning and at the end of the assault or lesson.

This is performed as follows:

Standing in first position, in front of the opponent, the saber is drawn in line and then the arm is flexed at the elbow so that the hand is at chin level, the tip of the weapon pointing up, elbow close to the body and the fingernails facing your chest, forming a single line between the tip, hand and elbow.

From this position, the arm is stretched so that the saber is in line with the hand in fourth hand position and then returns to where it just came from, thus saluting the opponent. Then, by flexing the arm again it stretches not completely with the hand in third and fourth position to give respect all those on their left, then return the hand back with the tip pointing up and finally with the same movement, but with the hand in second and third position, salute the bystanders to the right.

Naturally the head must be rotated from the neck as one salutes, looking at those present.

The line of direction *(La linea direttrice)*

Assuming two fencers are facing each other in first position. The line of direction is the imaginary line that, starting from the center of the heel of the back foot and passing through the axis of the front foot and extends forward to meet the same points of the other fencer. (see fig. 13)

This line serves to indicate the path that normally the feet should follow during the lesson, exercises, or the assault.

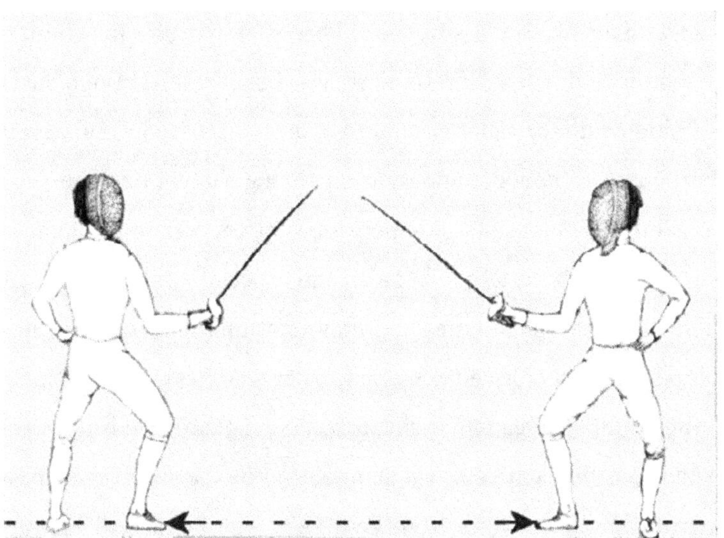

Fig. 13 - La linea direttrice

The guard *(La guardia)*

The position that the fencer takes with the body and with the weapon to be ready both in offensive and defensive actions is called « guard».

From first position we go on guard in the following way:

First bring the saber in line; then the advanced foot is brought forward about one- and one-half foot length bending at the same time the legs so that the back knee is perpendicular to the tip of the foot, and the front knee is instead perpendicular in the middle of the corresponding foot.

In the guard position the weight of the body must be balanced between the two legs equally, the axis of the torso and the head be in a normal position turned forward so to be able to look at the opponent.

The resting arm remains bent with the hand resting on the side as in first position (see fig. 14). The guard position can be named based on the stance that the fencer adopts, with the weapon free from any contact with the opponent's weapon. Therefore, we have the "third guard," if that is the name given to the adopted stance, and similarly in other cases. Although the characteristics of each individual position with the sabre have not yet been discussed, we find it appropriate to mention that the third guard — now commonly used among sabre fencers in every country — is to be preferred over others. This is not only because it offers certain advantages for the arm, which represents the most advanced target, but also and especially because the natural position of the arm in the third guard — facilitating the important disengagement of the shoulder — allows for the development of any movement with greater readiness and speed.

From the guard position with the weapon in line, assume the guard in third by turning the hand in second and third hand position and at the same time bending the arm at the elbow joint so that the elbow appears around a palm length from your side. The blade will line up with the tip slightly outside of respect to the target of the opponent's left cheek.

Fig. 14 - La guardia

The measure *(la misura)*

By measure we mean the distance between two fencers on guard, facing each other, this distance can be: medium, long, or short.

These three different distances are respectively called: *«right measure or extension measure»,*
«measure by walking or marching» and *«close measure»*.

Because the valid target in saber fencing is not limited, as in foil, being the trunk only, it
follows that:

a) From the «right measure » *(giusta misura)* you can hit the opponent in the torso
with a lunge, and you can hit the arm with an extension.

b) The «walking measure » *(misura camminando)* the opponents' torso can be hit
by taking a step and lunge or hit the forward target, the arm by use of the lunge.

c) By «close measure » *(stretta misura)* one can hit any valid target area without
lunging.

Step forward and step back (advance and retreat) *(Il passo avanti e passo indietro)*

No fencing action is performed or even conceived without taking the «measure» factor
into account.

Therefore, knowing how to advance and retreat properly is very important, as this is the
only means by which the fencer can control the measure and the appropriate distances for both
attacking and defending. The advance step (see fig. 15) serves both to decrease the distance from
the opponent and to bring oneself into range to perform the lunge. It is executed from the «guard»
position as follows:

by raising the right foot just a few centimeters off the ground, it is brought forward along
the guiding line by a foot's length at most, and then the same movement is made with the left
foot so that, at the end of the step, the distance between the two feet is the same as the one used
for the normal «guard».

Fig. 15 · **Il passo avanti**

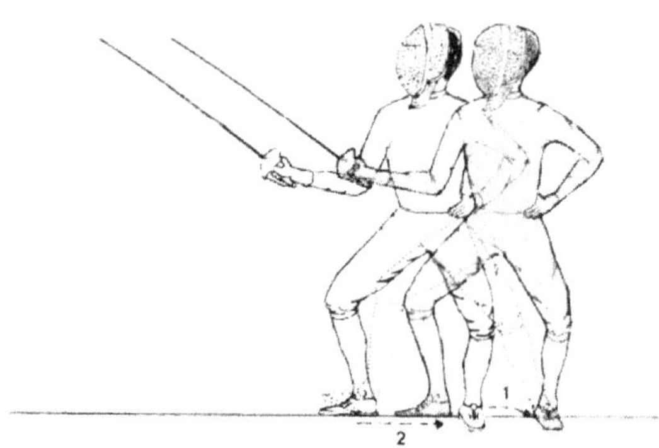

Fig. 16 · **Il passo indietro**

The retreat step (see fig. 16), on the other hand, serves to regain a greater distance from the opponent when they are too close. It is executed by first stepping back with the left foot as far as necessary, and then immediately following with the right foot.

Note — Whether advancing or retreating, it is essential to ensure that the body remains unaffected by the movement and always well-profiled and perfectly balanced on the legs; that the feet stay aligned on the guiding line; that the distance between the heels, after completing the movement, remains the same as it was initially; that the movement is carried out without rising from the «guard»; and that the feet, while moving, are lifted just enough to avoid dragging.

In common fencing terminology, advancing is also referred to as «closing or shortening the measure, » while retreating is referred to as «breaking or opening the measure».

The jump back *(Il salto indietro)*

The jump back is used to quickly get out from the range of action from the opposing offense.

Its execution begins with the passage of the right (front) foot moving backwards from the outside. The right foot must pass closely to the left foot and be thrown as far back as possible from the left foot. The left foot moves backwards passing the right foot and then regains the normal guard position.

The Lunge *(L'affondo)*

The lunge is the position the fencer's body assumes at the end of an offensive action, starting from the guard (see fig. 17). The sequence of movements, which translates the transition from guard to lunge in an instant, must be coordinated so that the execution occurs without the slightest discontinuity and, above all, in perfect harmony.

It is performed as follows:

gradually — with absolute precedence given to the weapon and without causing jerks or contractions — the extension of the armed arm is completed, and without any interruption, the right foot is brought forward, gliding just above the ground, as much as the simultaneous extension of the left leg allows (see fig. 18).

The head must remain unaffected by the movement, as well as the shoulders, which should stay relaxed and at the same level. The unarmed arm remains with the hand resting on the hip. In the lunge position, the torso is kept almost upright, and the right knee is slightly ahead of the corresponding foot's toe.

The return on guard *(Il ritorno in guardia)*

Returning on guard is primarily a work of the legs, although the balance of the torso, being supported by the back and abdomen muscles, performs an important function. The movement must be performed with rapidity and composure of the body. To achieve this it is essential that, as has been said for the lunge, the elements that contribute to it work without minimal discontinuity and in perfect harmony with each other.

That is how:

Pushing off from the right foot and simultaneously with a rapid bending at the knee of the left leg it recovers the weight of the body by pulling it towards itself, it brings back the right foot to its exact starting point lifting it as much as necessary from the ground. (see fig.19)

Fig. 17 - L'affondo

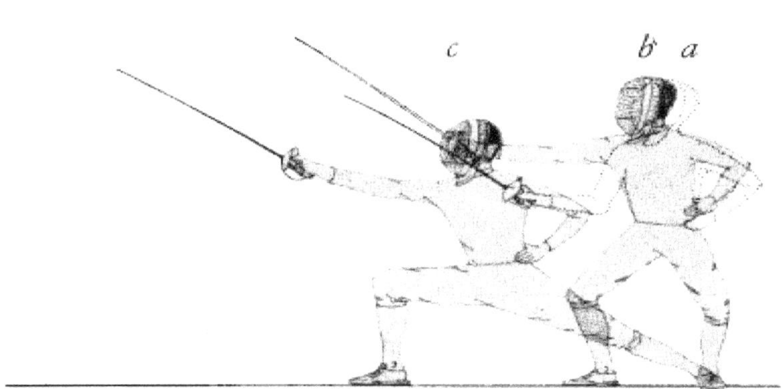

Fig. 18 - Esecuzione dell'affondo

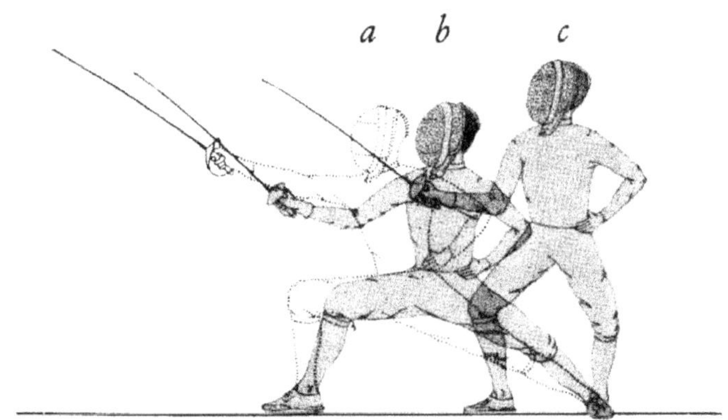

Fig. 19 - Il ritorno in guardia

The step and lunge *(passo Avanti-affondo)*

The step forward and lunge is the unbroken succession of the step forward followed by the lunge and serves to develop the tempo of the attack by walking or marching. It occurs when you want to perform an action of remote offence considered to be such as to require, first a step, in order to reach the correct distance to lunge.

It consists of three stages: first the advance of the right foot, second the advance of the left foot and third the lunge.

Therefore, the execution of the actions marching, all made up of more than one movement of the weapon, it comes set on the rhythm of the three aforementioned times to obtain a harmonious and effective movement, coordinated wholly and fluent, to allow, once the action has begun, to continue with uniformly and accelerated motion, without the slightest discontinuity until its end.

The Doubling *(Il raddoppio)*

The attack of the doubling occurs when, from the guard position — remaining bent on the legs — the left foot is brought forward until the heel makes contact with the heel of the right foot, and then the fencer goes into the «lunge» (see fig. 20).

With the doubling, therefore, a distance equal to or even greater than that covered with the «advance-lunge» can be overcome.

The doubling can also be executed from the «lunge», in which case it is called the «recovery or re-engagement of the doubling attack».

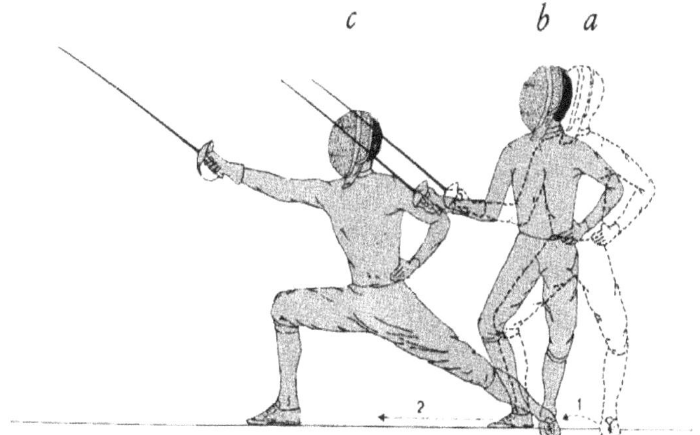

Fig. 20 - Il raddoppio

The fleche « Flèche » *(la frecciata)*

This is a particular attack that, especially in the fencing of saber, as long as it is used sparingly, can be very effective.

Performing the fleche (see fig 21) always requires the maximum decision, since the slightest mention of hesitancy can be enough to make it void and counterproductive.

Here is how it works:

The weapon arm is stretched from the guard position, and at the same time, pivoting on the right (front) foot, keeping the body profiled, the left (rear) leg is tensed as you push your balance over the front leg till you feel that you are about to lose balance. Meanwhile, the left (rear) arm is extended and brought to shoulder level to counterbalance the move. Then, without discontinuity, flowing forward over the right foot, at this moment with the bent right knee, explosively spring forward, propelling the weapon and the body quickly forward. In that instant the left leg (rear) is brought forward to overtake the right (front) foot in order to bring the body back into balance and then being able to dampen the inertia of the fleche with a running forward and sideways trajectory to sidestep the opponent. (1)

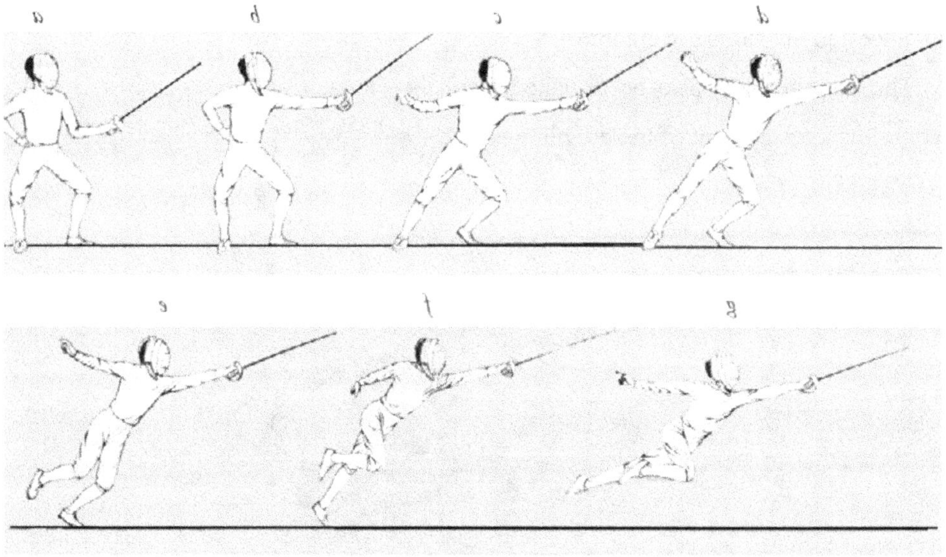

Fig. 21 - Progressione per l'attacco in frecciata

(1) It will be good that the Master, after having explained in detail the various movements in sequence, exercise the pupil to perform the free bout until the student will have acquired accuracy and mastery in the execution, as well as the indispensable snap that the arrow (fleche) requires

Long exercises *(Esercizi per le gambe)*

A good series of training sessions, composed, for example, of advance and retreat steps, normal lunges and lunges with the left foot, doublings executed from the «guard» and from the «lunge», alternating advance-lunge steps with a return to normal guard and with the left foot, normal flèche starts or those preceded by an advance or retreat step, or from the «lunge», etc., etc., repeated and alternated multiple times, with appropriate rest periods, will allow the student to acquire the ease of movement on the piste, particularly useful in sabre fencing.

CHAPTER II.

Preliminary training exercises for the arm *(Esercizi preliminari per l'addestramento del braccio)* — Description of the preliminary exercises *(Descrizione degli esercizi preliminary)* — Defense *(Della difesa)* — Simple parry *(Parate semplici)* — Linking one parry to another *(Passaggio da una parata all'altra)* — Circular parries *(Parate di contro)* — Half circular parries *(Parate di mezza contro)* — Parry against a glide ceding parry *(Parate di ceduta)* — Exercises referring to the circular actions *(Esercizi riferentisi alle parale)* — Molinelli.

Preliminary exercises for the training of the arm *(Esercizi preliminari per l'addestramento del braccio)*

It has been said that the handling of the weapon or bearing of the blade (a term that sums up the balance, direction, and gradual tightening of the hand on the handle) represents the greatest difficulty in the learning of saber, both as regards to the offense and the defense.

Before moving on to the application and study of the various movements inherent in the employment of actions, we believe that some arm training is necessary to prepare the fencer to overcome these difficulties. To that purpose we indicate some preliminary exercises or preparations, part of which are based on large movements of flexion and distension in order to reach the offensive employment a balanced bearing of the weapon and the perfect direction of the cut; others, instead, by circular movements, tracing broadly the path of the weapon in this particular defensive use and to follow in the various changes to the appropriate direction of the cut and counter cut.

The execution of these exercises, at first slow, then gradually increasing in speed, and repeating the movements several times in the same direction to further refine the muscular sense in the opportune coordination of the movements themselves.nWe will switch between these various exercises to help acquire that sense of balanced readiness with which the weapon must be carried, without extra movement in all directions where and when needed. Finally, we will change the amplitude and speed of the movements both in the single execution and in that movement repeated and combined, proceeding from a maximum to a minimum and inversely.

Such modifications, for which one is required gradual grasp of the hand on the handle of the weapon, develop that sense of security in the bearing of the blade that allows the saberist (*sciabolatore*) to master any offensive or defensive movement and to reduce the movement itself to the strict minimum necessary to complete the action.

Description of the preliminary exercises *(Descrizione degli esercizi preliminary)*

These exercises are six in total, and their execution consists of two phases.

First exercise.

In the first tempo — from the weapon in line — turn the hand to third hand position, raise the arm by flexing it at the elbow, describing with the tip of the saber an arc of a circle from the front to the back, stopping the movement when the hand without lateral bending, it will have reached the height of your temple (inside) and not far from it. In this it follows the direction of the forearm, with the cut facing up, avoiding that the tip does not point downwards and keeping the elbow well raised at shoulder level.

The second tempo, keeping the hand in third hand position, the arm is stretched forward, slashing from the top down, preceding to the inverse or where one started from. The movement is stopped without shock and always with the hand in third hand position, when the weapon has almost reached the horizontal plane, with the arm stretched out on the same line as the shoulder with the point of the saber in line with the hand and shoulder.

The torso, with a slight inclination forward accompanies the movement at the point where it is about to end.

Second exercise

In the first tempo - from the weapon in line – maintaining the hand in second hand position and flexing the arm at the elbow joint, the weapon is carried to the left (inside) by having the tip describe an arc of a circle on the same horizontal plane, stopping the movement when the forearm and the hand are at the height of your chin and not far from it, forming a single line together with the weapon.

The second tempo, performing the same movement in reverse, a horizontal flicking is done with complete distention of the supporting arm movement with slight inclination of the torso forward, stopping the weapon at the same point where it started.

Third exercise

In the first tempo - from the weapon in line – turning the hand to the intermediate position of first and second hand position, bring the saber from the front to the back with rotation movement upwards, raising lightly the arm, pivoting on the shoulder and then bending the hand so that the cut maintains the same position diagonally. In the second tempo - keeping the position constant of the hand, bring the saber from the back forward by a rotation movement at the bottom with increasing speed, until returning to the position that one began in.

Fourth exercise

In the first tempo - from the weapon in line - turning the weapon hand to third hand position, raise the arm naturally stretched out, pivoting at the shoulder so that the tip of the saber reaches the height slightly above that of a supposed head of the opponent.

In the second tempo – lower the armed hand naturally to shoulder level keeping it extended and accentuating the final movement of the hand by squeezing the handle firmly.

Fifth exercise

In the first tempo – from the weapon in line – turning the weapon hand to the intermediate position of third and fourth hand position, raise the arm, flexing it at the elbow joint, describing an arc with the tip of the weapon in a circle as in the first exercise, but somewhat more shortened and more inclined to the right (outside), stopping the movement when the hand, without lateral bending and kept in the intermediate hand position, it will come to the height of ones temple and a close as possible.

In this position the elbow must turn out slightly and higher that the shoulder while the forearm and the saber form a single line diagonally with the tip of the saber back and higher than the hand.

In the second tempo – making the reverse journey to that of where the movement started from, the saber is drawn diagonally from the right to left with the same hand position. The movement must be elastic and accompanied with a slight inclination of the torso forward. Then return to the initial position of the saber in line, or, with rotating the hand movement internally, returning to the guard of third.

Sixth exercise

In the first tempo - turning the hand into the intermediate position of second and third, raise the arm flexing it at the elbow joint, carrying the saber diagonally to the top left with the hand at the height of one's temple so that one's vision passes over the arm.

In the second tempo – with elastic movement and keeping the hand in the same intermediate position of second and third, a diagonal slash from the left to the right, stopping when the arm is in line with the shoulder.

Then return to the initial position of blade in line or by internal rotation of the hand back to the guard in third. (1)

(1) In the first periods the Master will take care to have these exercises performed from a comfortable position to not overly tire the student. Then he will begin to have the exercises executed by the guard, then together with a lunge or with stepping forward and backward (coordinated).

The defense *(Della difesa)*

Defense means any movement performed with one's own weapon, apt to divert the blade of the opponent, in the instant in which the latter is about to arrive to the target; or the subtraction of the target itself from the range of the action emanating from the opposing offense by stepping back.

The first is called: defense of blade difesa col ferro. The second method is called defense of measure difesa di misura.

The latter, defense by measure, does not allow those who use it in turn to be able to pass immediately to the offense and therefore it does not conclude the fight, but prolongs it. (Used more so in saber fencing today 2023).

The defense with the blade, or parry, gives to the possibility for those who perform it to follow immediately one's offense.

The parries can be simple, circular, half circular and cedar.

Note – Given that the defense takes place accordingly and in contrast to that of the offense, it would be logical that the parries were treated after the offensive actions. We consider it appropriate to describe them first due to the fact that the resultant position of each parry serves very well which reference point for certain particular exercises of importance, especially when combined with other movements that we will deal with shortly.

Simple parries *(Parate semplici)*

The simple parries are six in total, and they are called: parry of *first, second, third, fourth, fifth, and sixth*. Each of these six parries serves to defend one or more valid target areas, and can be executed both from the sabre in line position or from an invitation or bind (1). Starting from the sabre in line, the fencer moves, in one motion, to the median position (2) of each of the six aforementioned parries as follows:

For the parry of first — which serves to defend the face (left cheek) and the inner side of the chest and arm — the fencer moves by rotating the fist into the first position and, while simultaneously bending the arm at the elbow, brings the weapon in a rotary movement to the left, with the blade directed diagonally from high to low, with the cut facing upwards and the fist at chin height (see fig. 22);

(1) For the parries to be effective, they must be executed with the blade's edge in such a way that the middle-strong areas of the blade meet the middle-weak areas of the opponent's blade. The parries of third, fourth, and fifth, due to their more relevant use in modern sabre fencing, should be considered as "basic" parries.

(2) Some parries also specified in other treaties are mentioned as "low third" and "low fourth". We have considered it to be simpler and logical not to distinguish or give a different name to the same position only because the hand is lower or higher, bearing in mind that all parries are likely in need of adaption according to the case that requires it. And it's precisely for this reason that in the present description of the six simple parries that it has been said the position of the arm and the saber refer to the "middle position" that the same arm and weapon would come to be in normal defense.

For the parry of second — which serves to defend the flank and the area below the arm — the fencer rotates the forearm until the first reaches the intermediate position of first in second, and, while slightly bending the arm at the elbow, brings the weapon to the right with the fist positioned between the side and the armpit, following the diagonal of the forearm with the blade, slightly inclined upwards with the tip lower and more to the right than the fist (see fig. 23);

For the parry of third — which serves to defend the face (right cheek), the flank, the chest, and the outer arm — the fencer moves by rotating the fist from second to third, simultaneously retracting the arm until the elbow is slightly away from the right side, with the weapon slightly moved outward, the tip directed upward beyond the top of the head, and the cut diagonally downward to the right (see fig. 24);

For the parry of fourth — which serves to defend the same targets indicated for the parry of first — the fencer rotates the fist from third to fourth, and at the same time, retracts the arm until the elbow is slightly away from the side. With an internal rotation of the forearm, the weapon is moved to the left, following the same diagonal of the forearm, with the tip outward and slightly higher than the top of the head, and the fist at the level of the side (see fig. 25);

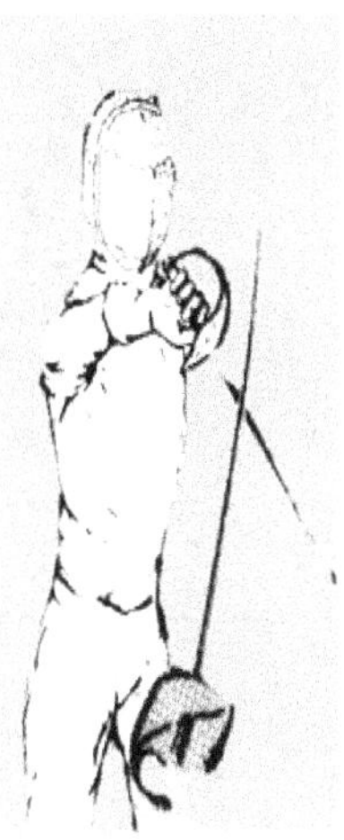

Fig. 22 - Parata di prima

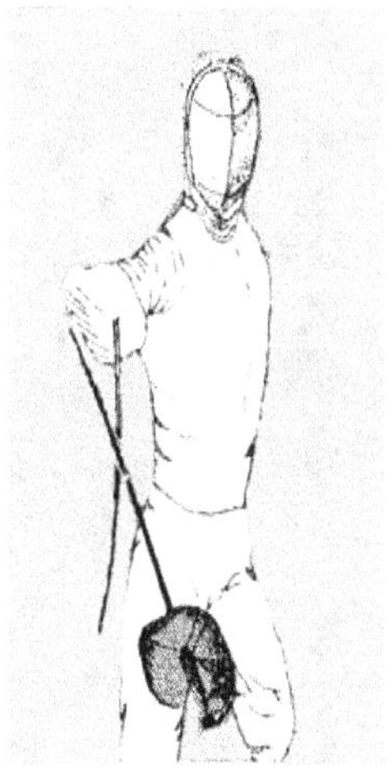

Fig. 23 - Parata di seconda

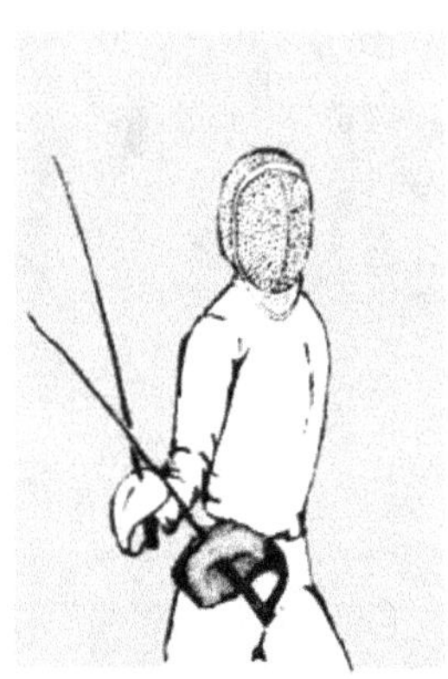

Fig. 24 · Parata di terza

Fig. 25 · Parata di quarta

For the parry of fifth — which serves to defend the head and the upper arm — the fencer rotates the fist from first position, and while bending the elbow, raises the forearm, bringing the fist to the level of the right temple and slightly outward; the blade, with the cut facing upward, is directed diagonally forward from right to left, with the tip just higher than the fist; the gaze passes below the blade (1) (see fig. 26);

For the parry of sixth (2) — which serves to defend the same targets indicated for the parry of fifth, in addition to the face (right cheek) — the fencer assumes a position with the weapon and arm exactly opposite to that of the parry of fifth. Therefore, the fist will be at the level of the left temple, and the blade will be directed diagonally forward from left to right: the gaze passes below the blade (see fig. 2)

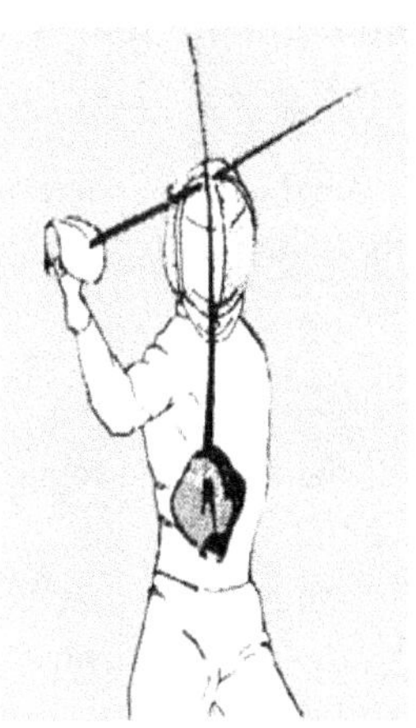

Fig. 26 - Parata di quinta

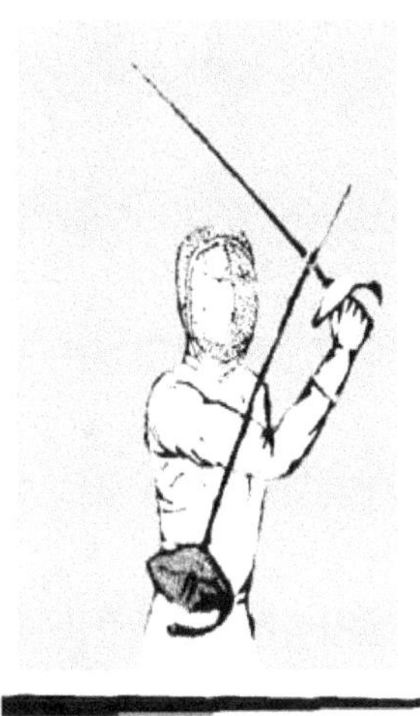

Fig. 27 - Parata di sesta

(1) Some argue that the parry of fifth should be executed by bringing the fist to a position noticeably higher than the one we described, and that the blade, instead of being directed diagonally forward, should be in a perfect horizontal line with the fist, with the tip not further forward than the fist itself. In truth, we cannot understand what the advantages are of executing the parry in this way; instead, we can identify its disadvantages, which are: a wider movement and thus a consequent delay, not only for the parry itself but also for the response, due to the greater distance the blade must travel to reach the opponent's target; delay and greater

exposure of the remaining target in the possible transition to another parry; furthermore, the execution of the point response becomes almost impossible or, at the very least, more difficult due to the positioning of the blade and particularly the tip.

(2) This parry, especially since defense in sabre fencing has generally been centered around the "third-fourth-fifth" triangle, is used very rarely and only in specific cases.

Passing from one parry to another *(Passaggio da una parata all'altra)*

All the parries determined by the wise steps indicated below are «simple parries» as they cover the shortest distance (1).

From the parry of first (or invitation or bind of first), one moves to:

    the parry of second;
    the parry of third;
    the parry of fourth;
    the parry of fifth.

From the parry of second (or invitation or bind of second), one moves to:
    the parry of first (2);
    the parry of third;
    the parry of fifth (2).

From the parry of third (or invitation or bind of third), one moves to:
    the parry of second;
    the parry of fourth;
    the parry of sixth.

From the parry of fourth (or invitation or bind of fourth), one moves to:
    the parry of third;
    the parry of fifth.

From the parry of fifth (or invitation of fifth), one moves to:
    the parry of second; (1)
    the parry of third;
    the parry of fourth.

From the parry of sixth, one moves to:
    the parry of third;
    the parry of fourth.

(1)The passage must take place in a single tempo (time) with a relaxed arm and without the shoulder becoming tight. The hold on the handle of the saber must tighten gradually and become more vigorous in the instant in which one determines a new parry.

(2)For passing from the parry of second to the parry of first or fifth, and vice versa, the movement of the forearm must be adjusted so that the blade describes a path curving thus collecting the opposing blade and diverting it and gaining the proper degrees of relationship between blades.

Counter parries *(Parate di contro)*

A counter parry occurs when, from one of the described parry positions (first, second, third, and fourth) — or from the corresponding invitation or bind, which we will address later — a circular motion is made with the tip of the weapon and the fist, assisted by the forearm, passing either above or below the opponent's blade depending on the situation, and returning exactly to the starting position. (1)

The movement for the «counter of first» is performed from top to bottom, from right to left; for the «counter of second» from bottom to top, from left to right; for the «counter of third» from top to bottom, from left to right; for the «counter of fourth» from bottom to top, from right to left.

The «counter of fifth» and even more so the «counter of sixth» are not commonly practiced.

Counter parries, except for the third, are not easily applied in sabre fencing. However, it is preferable to use them only in opposition to thrust actions and, even better, in opposition to a feint of thrust.

---

(1) The transfer of the blade must occur with the utmost fluidity of the arm, without any involvement from the shoulder. The grip on the hilt, especially in the counter parry, should be light initially and vigorous at the moment when the blade meets the opponents.

Half counter parries *(Parate di mezza contro)*

A half counter parry occurs when, from certain parries or their corresponding invitations or binds, one moves to another parry without covering the shorter distance, but following only the first part of the path indicated for counter parries. The transitions that determine these parries are as follows:

From the parry of second to that of fourth;

From the parry of third to that of first and fifth;

From the parry of fifth to that of first.

Ceding parry *(Parate di ceduta)*

Discussing the execution of the ceding parry whose action happens without resisting the glide of the opposing blade but, on the contrary, favoring the movement itself by giving way at the wrist so that at the last moment establishes the favorable relationship between the two blades without losing contact with the opponents' blade, giving to the defensive attitude of the parry.

The true parries of concession, those that possess the aforementioned characteristics, are only two: the concession of first and the concession of fourth, applied respectively in opposition to the third's edge and the second's edge, both in attack and in response. (1)

---

(1) In some treaties these are included in the ceding parries those performed in oppotitions to a hit with the position or cut preceded by a beat with the back of the blade

---

Exercises relating to parries *(Esercizi riferentisi alle parate)*

Such exercises can be considered of two types: «flexion-extension» and «circumduction».

Flexion-Extension Exercise: Starting from the on-guard position, assume the stance corresponding to a parry (except for the sixth position), and, pivoting at the elbow, bring the forearm closer to the chest, following the direction imposed by the weapon when taking the parry position. Then, with a reverse motion, return the weapon to the starting point, i.e., to the same parry position.

Example: Assuming the position corresponding to the fifth parry, flex the arm by articulating only the elbow while maintaining the same diagonal of the fifth parry, which moves from high to low, retracting the weapon toward the body. Then, extend the arm, directing the weapon diagonally upward and stopping the movement at the starting point, i.e., in the position corresponding to the fifth parry. The same process applies to the other positions.

Circumduction Exercise: Starting from the position corresponding to one of the five parries, preferably the first, second, or fifth, instead of flexing and then extending the arm as in the previous exercise, perform one of the described counter-parries, but align the movement of the first and fifth parries with the standard motion of the second counter-parry, i.e., counterclockwise.

However, this does not exclude the possibility that the movement of the exercise related to the first and fifth parries may also be performed in the standard direction.

Note. — Once the precise delimitation of flexion and extension, as well as the direction of the cut and the gradual tightening of the hand on the grip, has been learned, both exercises should be performed without interruption and repeated multiple times in succession, with increasing speed during the final movement, as would occur in the execution of an actual parry.

Subsequently, the two exercises can be combined, first from a single position, then from all other positions in sequence and progression, and then alternated freely at will.

Finally, it will also be useful for these exercises to be performed with alternating adjustments to their amplitude and speed, gradually transitioning from a wide and slow movement to one that is increasingly narrower and faster, and then vice versa.

Circular cuts *(Molinelli)*

The term *molinelli* refers to all those circular movements that, as we will see below, are performed with the sabre to deliver specific cutting strikes in various directions.

These movements are based on the articulation of the elbow, with the slight involvement of the wrist, achieved solely through the extension and lateral flexion of the hand.

In addition to their direct purpose — namely, disengaging the blade from the opponent's through the characteristic circular motion — *molinelli* also serve to strengthen the arm and, together with the previously described parry exercises, to develop fluidity and flexibility in handling the weapon, as well as to guide it in a well-balanced manner when delivering a strike.

Molinelli are classified into vertical (to the head), horizontal (to the face, both from the left and the right), and rising (to the side and abdomen).

Without exception, all *molinelli*—to ensure the correct direction of the cut and to avoid both rigidity and excessive relaxation of the hand, which instead should tighten its grip on the hilt at the end of the movement—should initially be performed in two distinct stages, as follows:

Head Molinello (Molinello alla testa) (1) :

1°) — From the weapon in line or guard of third, move the weapon to the left into a position similar to the parry of first, but with the arm slightly more bent and the hand at temple height rather than at the chin, so that the gaze passes beneath the arm.

2°) — With a rotational motion from back to front and upward, during which the blade passes close to the left shoulder, deliver a saber strike in a vertical direction with an elastic extension of the arm, stopping the motion when the hand reaches chin height and the blade is aligned vertically with the edge perfectly downward.

---

(1) The head molinello can also be performed from the right, but as it is not practically applicable, its description has been omitted.

Horizontal Molinello from the Left (Molinello orizzontale da sinistra):

1°) — From the weapon in line, rotate the hand into the intermediate position between first and second. Raise the arm slightly, bending at the elbow to bring the weapon to the left. The blade's tip traces a semicircle upward and from front to back, stopping when the hand is at chin level and slightly away from it, with the forearm and weapon forming a single line and the tip pointing backward to the left.

2°) — With an elastic extension of the arm, deliver a sabre strike in a horizontal direction toward the right cheek of a hypothetical opponent, with the hand at chin level and the blade edge angled diagonally upward to the right.

Horizontal Molinello from the Right (Molinello orizzontale da destra):

1°) — From the weapon in line, rotate the hand into the fourth position. Raise the arm slightly and, with a pronounced elbow bend, bring the weapon backward, tracing a semicircle with the tip in a horizontal direction. End with the hand behind the head at temple height on the right, while the forearm and weapon form a single horizontal line with the blade edge to the left.

2°) — With an elastic arm extension, pivoting at the elbow, deliver a horizontal sabre strike toward the left cheek of a hypothetical opponent.

Rising Molinello from the Left (Molinello montante da sinistra):

1°) — From the weapon in line, perform the same movement described for the first stage of the horizontal molinello from the left.

2°) — With a downward and forward rotation, deliver a sabre strike along the flank line of a hypothetical opponent, with the blade edge angled diagonally upward to the right.

Rising Molinello from the Right (Molinello montante da destra):

1°) — From the weapon in line, perform the same movement described for the first stage of the horizontal molinello from the right.

2°) — With a rotation on a diagonal plane downward and forward, deliver a sabre strike along the abdominal line of a hypothetical opponent, with the blade edge angled diagonally upward to the left.

Note — Once all the described *molinelli* have been performed accurately in two stages, proceed to executing them in a single stage. The rotational movement, instead of being wide as previously described, should gradually be reduced to the minimum necessary, performed with a simple turn of the wrist accompanied by a slight flexion of the hand and the subsequent immediate elastic extension of the arm. They may then be performed alternately, varied at will, and combined with forward and backward steps, followed by a lunge and then returning to guard, preferably and simultaneously with the parries of third, fourth, and fifth. When lunging, always ensure that the weapon's tip takes precedence over the body.

Chapter III.

Targets and lines (Bersagli e linee)– Placements of the weapon (Gli atteggiamenti con l'arma)– Invitations (Inviti)– Engagements (Legamenti)– Simple and fundamental offensive actions (Azioni di offesa semplici e fondamentali)– the riposte (Della risposta)– Simple riposte (Risposte semplici) – Inherent exercises to the first attacks and related parries and responses (Esercizi inerenti alle prime azioni di attacco e relative parate e risposte)

Targets and Lines *(Bersagli e linee)*

The valid target in saber fencing consists of the entire portion of the body located above the horizontal line that passes through the top of the folds formed by the thighs and the torso of the fencer in guard position (see fig. 28).

However, due to the position of the arm and the weapon, only a part of the surface that constitutes this valid target will remain exposed, a portion more or less extensive depending on the various positions in which the arm and weapon of the fencer are placed.

Generally, on the high line, the head is considered situated; on the low line, the flank; on the inside line, the near side (left cheek), the chest, and the abdomen; on the outside line, the far side (right cheek).

But in relation to the position of the armed arm, other parts of the valid target, in addition to those mentioned above, may respectively fall on the said four lines, namely:

on the high line (see invitation or engagement in second position) also the chest, the face (right and left cheek), and the upper arm;

on the low line (see invitation in fifth position) also the abdomen and the chest;

on the inside line (see invitation or engagement in third position) also the chest, the abdomen, the inside of the arm, and the head;

on the outside line (see invitations or engagements in first and fourth positions) also the chest, the flank, the arm, and the head

.

Placements of the weapon *(Gli atteggiamenti con l'arma)*

By placements of the weapon, you understand those positions that the fencer can take with his weapon arm, standing on guard in front of the opponent. These placements are three and they are called: *invitation* (invito), *engagement* (legamento) and *blade in line* (arma o ferro in linea).

Each of these placements offers the possibility to develop the contrary, given by the fundamental offensive actions, so that all three could be considered as invitations.

Their distinction is made both to avoid with generic name of invitation can be understood differently with each of them, without reference, a specific one, and to facilitate the study of the various offensive actions.

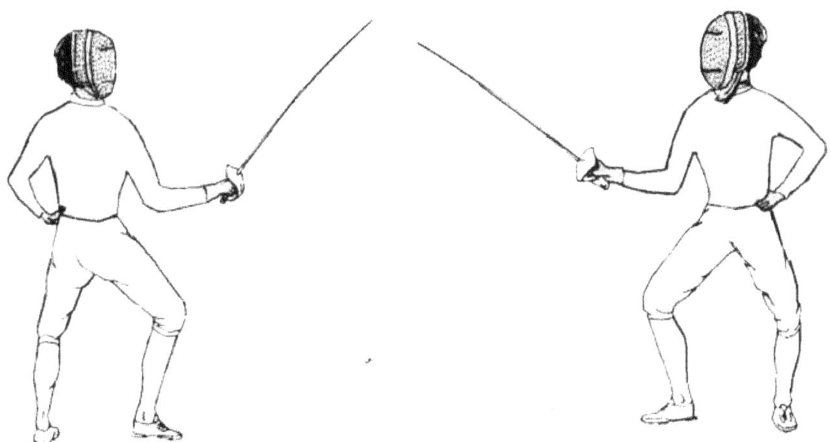

Fig. 28 - Il bersaglio valido

The Invitations *(Gli inviti)*

When the positions described for the parries are not adopted for defensive purposes but assumed in open space, independently of the opponent's weapon, they are called «invitations».

An exception is the position corresponding to the parry of sixth, which can never be assumed for this purpose. Therefore, saber invitations are five, namely: invitation of first, second, third, fourth, and fifth (see figs. 29, 30, 31, 32, 33).

With the invitation, a portion of the valid target is intentionally exposed, and it is generally assumed to provoke the opponent into attacking or to disguise the preparation of an offensive or counteroffensive action.

The engagement *(I legamenti)*

Instead of taking the same determined placement as described in the parries, these are taken to divert the weapon of the opponent from the line whether in line or not, are called «engagements».

Their purpose is more or less the same as that of the invitations; only that contact is established with the engagement of the opponent's weapon, while the invitation, the opponent's weapon is left in the preferred position of the antagonist himself. (1)

(1) In practice, given the habit of fighting from out of distance (misura camminando) and also given the generalization of taking the guard of third, which, as previously mentioned, is the guard preferred, less often the possibility is presented today in saber fencing to be able to engage the opponent's blade in any line and especially in fifth.

Simple offensive actions *(Azione di offesa semplici)*

All offensive actions are defined as those performed without evading the opponent's parry.

When hitting with the point, called «puntata» it is normally directed to the torso: the action made with a slashing motion, which is called the saber cut «sciabolata» can be directed to the head, face, (right or left cheek) chest, abdomen, flank and arm: of the counter-cut, to the face (left cheek), chest, abdomen and arm (internally or bottom).

The *puntata* (point thrust) is classified as: direct, disengagement (*cavazione*), and glide (*filo*).

The *sciabolata* (sabre cut) is classified as: direct, circular cut (*molinello*), and overcut (*fendente*, or *coupé*).

In contrapposizione agli inviti (In response to invitations), any strike (*puntata* or *sciabolata*) is always direct.

In contrapposizione ai legamenti (In response to engagements), the *puntata* is performed as a disengagement (*cavazione*); the *sciabolata* can be a circular cut (*molinello*) or an overcut (*fendente*) if the engagement assumed by the opponent is in the third or fourth position.

In contrapposizione all'arma in linea (In response to a weapon in line), the puntata is executed as a glide (filo) when sliding along the opponent's blade, edge against edge; it is direct if preceded by a beat or any deflection of the opponent's blade. Similarly, the sciabolata, logically preceded by a beat or deflection of the opponent's blade, is direct.

Puntata diretta (Point thrust)

As mentioned, it is applicable in response to any opponent's invitation and is executed in one motion as follows: from the third guard or another position, the arm is extended while simultaneously rotating the fist into the second position. The point of the weapon is directed toward the chest, and a quick lunge is made.

Puntata di Cavazione (Disengagement Thrust)

It is applicable in response to any engagement and is executed in one motion as follows: by making the point of the weapon describe a helical movement through the rotation of the fist at the wrist, assisted by the forearm, the blade disengages from the opponent's engagement. Then, with the arm fully extended, the thrust is directed toward the target with a quick lunge.

In response to the engagements in the first, second, third, fourth, and fifth positions, the disengagement thrust ends respectively at the flank, upper chest, inner chest, outer chest, and flank.

Puntata di Filo (Glide thrust)

There are only two types of glide thrusts: one from the third position and the other from the second position. When executed directly from one's own engagement in the third or second position, they are performed in a single motion; however, when executed in response to the opponent's weapon in line, they require two motions. In the latter case, the engagement occurs gradually and continuously as the distance is gained, accompanied by the rapid extension of the arm and the lunge.

The glide thrust from the third position, known simply as «glide of third» (*filo di terza*), is executed as follows:

by rotating the fist into the second position, the weapon is made to slide along the opponent's blade while the arm extends rapidly, guiding the point of the weapon toward the outer chest target. Without interruption, the thrust is completed by a lunge, maintaining contact between the two blades, with the fist high and the outward opposition in place.

For the execution of the glide thrust from the second position, known as «glide of second» (*filo di seconda*) the same rules apply as for the glide of third, except that the thrust is directed toward the flank.

Sciabolata alla Testa Diretta (Direct Head Cut)

From the third or second guard, or from one's own invitation, the fist is rotated into the third position, and while extending the arm, the weapon is guided toward the head. With a tight and forceful wrist motion from top to bottom, the cut is delivered with a lunge.

Once the action is completed, the weapon should reach nearly horizontal, with the arm fully extended forward along the shoulder line, and the point slightly higher than the fist.

This action can be executed in response to the opponent's invitations from the second, third, and fourth positions, as well as from one's own engagements in the third or fourth positions.

Sciabolata alla faccia (guancia destra) diretta. (Direct Face Cut - Right Cheek)

From the third or second guard, or from one's own invitation, by rotating or maintaining the fist in the second position and quickly extending the arm, the weapon is guided towards the opponent's right cheek. Then, without any interruption, with a tight and forceful wrist movement from left to right, the cut is delivered horizontally to the target, so that once the action is completed, the fist is at the height of the chin.

This action can be executed in response to the opponent's invitations from the second and fourth positions, as well as from one's own engagements in the second and fourth positions.

Sciabolata alla faccia (guancia sinistra) diretta. (Direct Face Cut - Left Cheek)

From the third or second guard, or from one's own invitation, the fist is rotated into the fourth position, and while quickly extending the arm, the weapon is guided towards the opponent's left cheek. Then, without any interruption, with a tight and forceful wrist movement from left to right, the cut is delivered horizontally to the target, so that once the action is completed, the fist is at the level of the chin.

This action can be executed in response to the opponent's invitations from the second, third, and fifth positions, as well as from one's own engagement in the fourth position.

Sciabolata al petto e all'addome diretta (Direct Cut to the Chest and Abdomen) (1)

For the execution of these two actions, proceed in a similar manner to the cut to the left cheek, directing the horizontal cut towards the abdomen with the fist in the fourth position. The cut to the chest, on the other hand, is directed diagonally from high to low, with the fist in the intermediate position between third and fourth.

These actions can be performed in response to the same opponent's invitations as those for the left cheek, namely from second, third, and fifth positions, as well as from your own fourth guard.

(1) In general, the movement of the saber in the execution of these two cuts, rather than being limited to what is essential to reach the target, is continued on the target itself in the sense from right to left and from front to back, by circling of the wrist together with the flexion of the elbow which allows one to move without interruption from the starting position or to another position with a defensive purpose, generally to that of third or fifth.

Sciabolata al fianco diretta. (Direct cut to the flank)

For the execution of this action, proceed in a manner similar to that of the cut to the face (right cheek), but guide the weapon logically lower to strike the flank.

This action can be performed in response to the opponent's invitations from first, fourth, and fifth positions, as well as from your own first, third, and fifth guards.

Sciabolata al braccio diretta. (Direct cut to the arm)

For the execution of this cut, with necessary adjustments, it proceeds in a manner similar to the direct cuts aimed at other targets. However, since the arm is the most advanced target, the cut can be delivered not only when the opponent is stationary in any guard but also when they are in the midst of an attacking movement. In the first case, the cut can be delivered even without a lunge or, in any case, with a limited lunge depending on the distance to the opponent; in the second case, it must always be delivered while remaining in guard, but in the manner we will explain in due time.

Saber strikes directed at the arm can be performed: *Indentro* both cutting and counter-cutting, respectively with the fist in the third to fourth and second to third position; *Infuori*, cutting, with the fist from first to second; *Sopra*, cutting, with the fist of third or third in fourth; *Sotto*, cutting and counter-cutting, respectively with the fist from first to second and from second to third.

Sciabolate di molinello. (Molinello cuts)

These cuts can originate both from one's own guard and from the opponent's, a condition that, in practice, rarely occurs in modern saber fencing, where, generally, the two opponents are not only quite far apart but both in third guard with the point of the weapon much higher than the fist. Therefore, as we will see later, molinello cuts are more commonly applied as responses rather than as attacking actions.

However, it is worth noting that it is not always necessary to use the molinello to launch an attacking cut from one's own guard or from the opponent's. (1)

For example, the cut to the head executed by one's own third guard is a direct cut, whereas from one's own first or fifth guard, it is essential to perform it with a molinello.

(1) The Master will point out, from time to time, the necessity or otherwise of the molinello, as well as the greater risk that the molinello cut may present compared to the direct cut.

Sciabolate di fendente (coupé). (Fendente (Coupé) Cuts)

The application of these cuts is possible only in opposition to the opponent's third or fourth parry, as follows: by flexing the wrist and simultaneously rotating the fist into third position, the tip of the sword is lifted in such a way as to disengage from the parry. Then, by forcefully extending the arm, a cut to the head is delivered.

It is easily understood that the elevation of the tip must be limited to the strictly necessary, and it is equally clear that the fendente, in addition to the head, can also be performed to the advanced target, either internal or external, depending on whether the opponent's parry is third or fourth.

The riposte *(Della risposta)*

The riposte is the offensive action that immediately follows the defense, that is, the hit that is directed to any part of the opponent's valid target after parrying his attack.

In saber fencing, the riposte can be like that of the attack; by direct cut, point, counter cut, and, as in fencing in general, the riposte can be simple or compound.

The riposte can be simple if it consists of one movement (cut or with the point) instead we say the riposte is compound (feint or double feint) when it consists of two or three movements. (1)

(1) It is essential for ripostes like the parries that the student is gradually exercised to control the movement of the arm and not only to acquire ever more rapidity and accuracy in the bearning of the weapon, but also and above all getting used to directing the weapon itself immediately to anyone part of the valid target which, depending on the case, will be more favorable and not to direct it to that suggersted by instinct.

From the parry of second the riposte is directed to: *(Della parata di seconda si puo' rispondere)*

Direct cut to the right cheek *(di sciabolata alla guancia destra dritta)*

Glide with the point to the flank *(di puntata al fianco filo)*

Direct cut to the top of the arm *(di sciabolata sopra al braccio dritta)*

Direct to the chest with the point *(di puntata sopra al petto diretta)*

Direct or circular cut to the head *(di sciabolata alla testa diretta o di molinello)*

Circular cut to the left cheek *(di sciabolata alla guancia sinistra molinello)*

Direct cut to the abdomen, with the cut or counter cut under the adversary's weapon *(di sciabolata all'addome, di taglio o controtaglio sotto l'arma avversaria diretta)*

From the parry of third the riposte can be directed to: *(Dalla parata di terza si puo' rispondere)*

Direct cut to the head *(di sciabolata alla testa diretta)*

Direct cut to the flank *(di sciabolata al fianco diretta)*

Glide with the point to the chest *(di puntata al petto filo)*

Direct with the point to the flank *(di puntata sotto al fianco diretta)*

Circular cut to the inside arm *(di sciabolata sopra al braccio molinello)*

Circular cut to the abdomen *(di sciabolata all'abbome molinello)*

Direct cut to the left cheek with the cut or counter cut (di sciabolata all guancia sinistra di taglio o controtaglio diretta)

Circular cut to the chest (di sciabolata al petto molinello)

Under the front arm with upward cut (di sciabolata sotto al braccio di montante)

From the parry of fourth the riposte is directed to (Dalla parata di quarta si puo' rispondere)

Direct cut to the face (right or left cheek) (di sciabolata alla facia guancia destra o sinistra)

Direct cut to the head (di sciabolata alla testa diretta)

Direct cut to the abdomen (di sciabolata all'abbome diretta)

Direct cut to the inside or outside arm (di sciabolata sopra o indentro al braccio diretta)

Circular cut to the flank (di sciabolata al fianco molinello)

Direct point thrust to the chest (di puntata al petto diretta)

From the parry of fifth the riposte is directed to (Dall parata di quinta si puo' rispondere)

Direct cut to the flank (di sciabolata al fianco diretta)

Direct point thrust to the chest (di puntata al petto diretta)

Direct cut to the outside arm (di sciabolata sotto al braccio diretta)

Circular cut to the head (di sciabolata alla testa molinello)

Circular cut to the left cheek (di sciabolata alla guancia sinistra molinello)

Circular cut to the chest (di sciabolata al petto molinello)

Circular cut to the abdomen (di sciabolata all'addome molinello)

Circular cut to the inside arm (di sciabolata indentro al braccio molinello)

From the parry of sixth the riposte is directed to (Dalla parata di sesta si puo' rispondere)

Direct cut to the inside cheek (di sciabolata alla guancia sinistra diretta)

Direct cut to the chest (di sciabolata al petto diretta)

Direct cut to the abdomen (di sciabolata all'addome diretta)

Circular cut to the flank (di sciabolata al fianco molinello)

Direct point thrust low (di puntata sotto diretta)

Direct cut to the inside arm (di sciabolata indentro al braccio diretta)

Circular cut to the head (di sciabolata all testa molinello)

Exercises related to the first attack actions and the related parries and ripostes.
(Esercizi inerenti alle prime azioni di attacco e relative parate e risposte)

Learned sufficiently the execution of the former offensive and defensive actions will pass the application through the following exercises:

Without prior indication, and in contrast to each invitation or engagement, these will be performed to the corresponding targets that are exposed. By using either the point or the cut studied so far, setting the maximum care in maintaining correct measure and giving care to the direction of the cut or point action and its desired direction.

Example – Put yourself on guard along with a partner at lunging distance. One of the two students will invite in third; the other will perform, at will, direct cut to the head, or direct point thrust to the chest and so on. After these have been done it will be the companion fencers turn to execute as many actions as possible, at will, to the same invitation of third.

Subsequently, to the same actions of offense, the corresponding defense will be applied followed by the simple ripostes to the different targets making use of both the point and the cut.

In the second exercise, in addition to performing the offensive action as perfectly as possible to help with the accuracy of the corresponding parry, its degree of resistance, as well as the balanced bearing of the weapon must be taken care of as well as the direction of the riposte.

Example – the offensive action point thrust to the chest or direct cut to the head, the opponent answers with the parry of fourth or fifth and ripostes respectively with a cut to the right cheek or head.

When the parry and riposte hit the mark with increasing accuracy and speed, the attacker will attempt to parry the riposte (counter parry) and riposte himself (counter riposte)

Note – These exercises, at least on the first period of practice will be performed under the direction of the maestro, which, among other things, will take care to alternate the attack and defense functions so that the two students can develop on both functions.

Chapter IV.

Of the feint in general *(Della finta in genere)* – actions of simple feints with correct distance *(Azioni di finta semplice a misura di Allungo)*- simple feints at step and lunge measure *(Azioni di finta semplice a misura camminando)*– feints as used in the riposte *(Della risposta di finta)* – conventional exercises related to feints *(Esercizi convenzionali inerenti alle azioni di finta)* - of double feints in general *(Della doppia finta in genere)* – actions using the double feints from correct distance *(Azioni di doppia finta a misura di allungo)*– double feints from step and lunge distance *(Azioni di doppia finta a misura camminando)* -- conventional exercises relating to double feints *(Esercizi convenzionali inerenti alle azioni di doppia finta)*

The feints in general *(Della finta in genere)*

The feint is nothing more than the simulation of the attack, as a threat, in order to reach its goal, that is to be able to move against those who are equipped to parry, it must have all the characteristics of the true attack, including the choice of time (see figs. 34, 35, 36, 37, 38, 39).

Typically, one resorts to feint when one is not able to overcome the defense with a simple action, or when, despite having it previously succeeded, it is considered appropriate not to repeat the simple action.

The purpose of feinting, therefore, is to draw in and deceive the opponent on the evaluation of our offensive intentions, skillfully simulating an attack aimed at a particular target in order to provoke a defensive reaction, while it has already been conceived to evade the parry and hit the target which, following the parry itself, will be discovered.

The success of the feint is closely linked to the veracity with which the threat is brought, to appropriate observation of particular trends in the defense of the opponent and also knowing how to exploit the impression exercised on the antagonist with the previous one performing simple attacks to the target on which, however, the feint is then performed.

Feints can be "simple" or "double" depending on whether you feint with one or two hits. Therefore, the feint actions consist of two movements: those of double feints, three movements. Both one and the same as others, can be performed both from lunging distance, step and lunge distance or with the fleche' (This action was disabled by the FIE with the ruling of not allowing the rear foot cross over the front).

And since the feint is nothing but the simulation of a simple attack, the choice of using the point, cut or counter-cut can be employed.

By starting the feinting action with the point, you can conclude the action with the cut or, as well one can feint with the cut and end with the point or cut.

Fig. 34 - Finta alla testa

Fig. 35 - Finta di puntata

Simple feint actions at lunging distance *(Azioni di finta a misura di allungo)*

In opposition to the invitation of first (In contrapposizione all'invito di prima):

First tempo, from the most common and indicated guard in third, with rapid extension of the arm, pretend to point attack below (direct) or cut at the hip (direct);

Second tempo, eluding the parry of second, disengage above with the point to the chest, or cut to the face (right or left cheek), head, chest or arm.

If the opponent has the engagement and not inviting as noted before, the same feint is performed to the side with the cut, which however will no longer be direct, but disengagement.

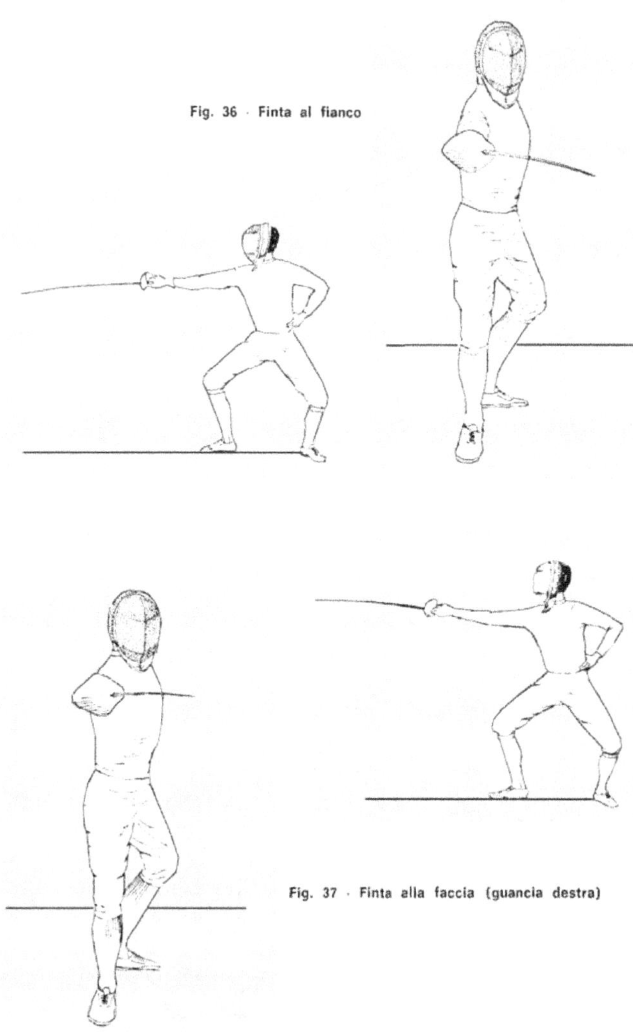

In opposition to the invitation of second (In contrapposizione all'invito di seconda):

First tempo, with energetic extension of the arm, feint with the point above to the chest or with the cut direct to the face (right cheek), or to the arm or the head.

Second tempo, the relative parry (first, third or fifth) is evaded according to the feint, weather with the point or cut to the flank or inside arm; disengage with the point or the cut to the chest and disengage with the point or cut to the inside chest or the arm, or by executing the cut by circular action to the left cheek, chest, abdomen, or arm.

If the opponent has you engaged instead of in invitation, the same feint by point or cut will instead of being direct will be by disengagement.

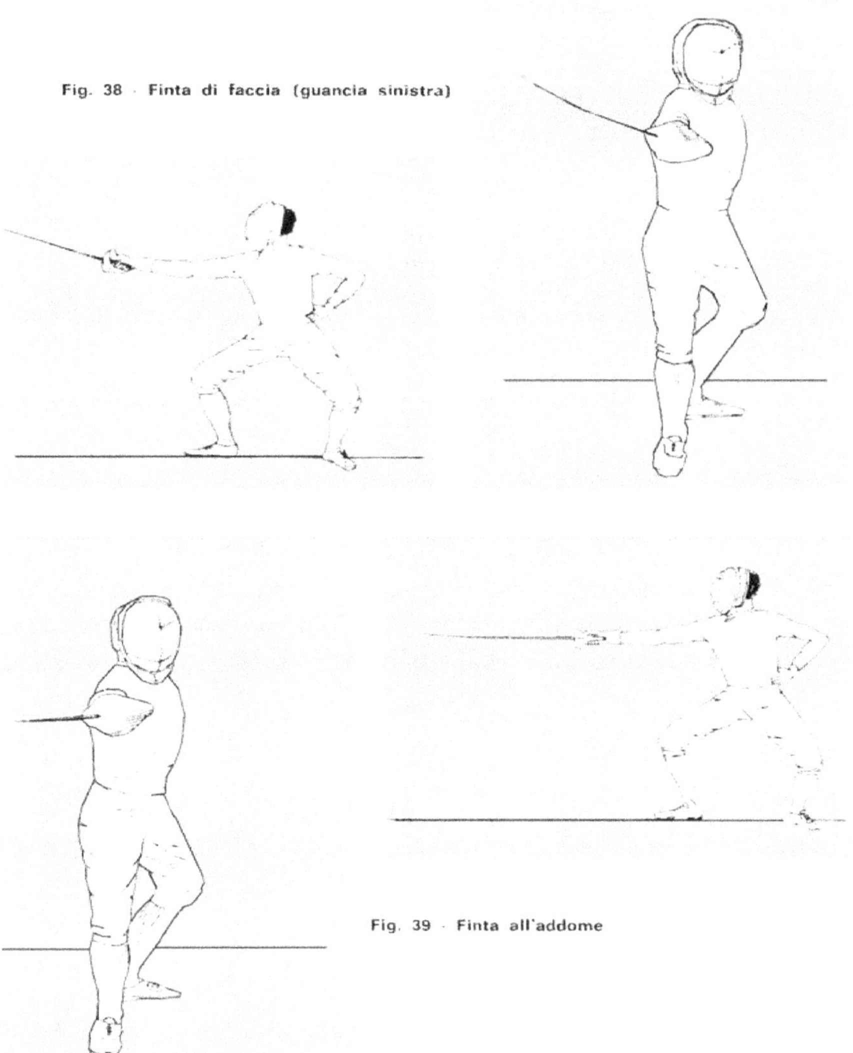

In opposition to the invitation of third (In contrapposizione all'invito di terza):

First tempo, with a rapid extension of the weapon arm, direct the point feint to the inside chest or with the cut feint to the left cheek, chest, abdomen, inside arm or head.

Second tempo, in relation to the parry evaded (either first, fourth, or fifth) depending on where the feint was directed, disengage to the flank with the point or cut to the flank or arm;

disengage to the chest or cut to the right cheek or head (also by cut over); by disengaging with the point or by cut to the flank or by circular cut to the left cheek, chest, abdomen or inside arm.

Finding the opponent has the engagement in third rather than invitation, the same actions are executed in the same manner except the first part of the action will be done by disengagement.

In opposition to the opponent's invitation of fourth (In contrapposizione all'invito di quatra):

First tempo, with rapid extension of the weapon arm, feint with the point to the outside chest or with the cut direct to the right cheek, arm, or head.

Second tempo, the parry of third is evaded by disengaging with the point or circular cut to the abdomen, arm (with cutting edge or counter-cut), left cheek, chest, or head (also by cut or counter cut)

The parry of fifth is evaded by disengaging with the point or cut to the flank, or by circular cut to the left cheek, abdomen, chest, or arm (cut or counter-cut).

If the opponent has the engagement rather than invitation of fourth, the same feint by point or cut will begin with a disengagement rather than direct.

In opposition to the opponent's invitation of fifth (In contrapposizione all'invito di quinta):

First tempo, with rapid extension of the arm, feint direct low with the point or cut to the flank, or direct to the left cheek, chest, or abdomen.

Second tempo, the parry of second is eluded by disengaging with the point to the chest, or by cut to the face (right of left cheek), to the arm, head, chest, or abdomen; the parry of fourth is eluded by disengaging with the point or cut to the right cheek (also by circular cut) arm or head (also by cut over)

(There is no engagement of fifth.)
(The parry of sixth is only a parry, there is no invitation or engagement.)

Simple feints at step and lunge distance *(Azione di finta semplice a misura camminando)*

To perform the same feints as described above by use of the step and lunge, coordinate the first tempo with the step whether using the point or the cut, and without discontinuity, the second tempo is executed as following the same procedure indicated above when in lunging distance.

Feinting with the riposte *(Della risposta di finta)*

As in the attack, the feint is used when not successful or in any case find excessive difficulty overcoming the opponent's defense with simple actions, as for the same reason, after the parry, you can answer by feinting, thus eluding the counter parry to which the opponent may resort to following the negative outcome of his attack.

After performing the ensuing parry to the offensive action of the opponent, the feint by simple riposte (either by point or cut) and evading with a second movement, the counterpart to which the opponent will appeal, the hit is finalized to one of the valid target that is discovered.

Conventional exercises related to feinting actions *(Esercizi convenzionali inerenti alle azione di finta)*

Conventional exercises consist of pre-established actions between two fencers that they will carry out in relation to the offensive and defensive movements, scrupulously followed during the execution of the transaction as established by the maestro.

These exercises, in addition to giving greater sense of truth to the offensive and defensive actions learned in lessons, serve to arouse in the student the first reflections and considerations about the importance the three elements of fencing have in forming the whole basis of the sport, that is: measurement, choice of time and velocity.

First these exercises are done form lunging distance, then from step and lunge distance, simple actions and then feints will alternate as they derive from which ones to alternate from as the one who suffers the attack, i.e., consisting in having to perform one or two parries to defend oneself, learn to simulate the hit well when you want to evade the parry.

Example - as opposed to the invitation of second, it is agreed that the attacker will have to perform direct cut, to the head or feint cut to the head followed by the disengagement to the flank with the point or cut. The opponent will have to consequently oppose either using the parry of fifth alone or followed by the parry of second.

We will proceed in opposition to either invitations or engagements, establishing the hit from time to time as simple (with the point or cut) or by feint used against the single or double parries as needed to defend. (1)

(1) The maestro, at least for the first few times, will supervise the students during the execution of these exercises, providing the students with appropriate suggestions based on the inaccuracies found, and making sure that the students themselves take regular turns in the attack and defense.

Double feints in general *(Della doppia finta in genere)*

When the opposing defense cannot be overcome with a feint or you consider it appropriate not to repeat the action, you can resort to executing a double feint. This is done by not carrying out the movement as described before but simulating a second attack as a feint and eluding the second parry with the point or cut and then carrying out the attack to a valid target which will be discovered following the second parry.

The double feint, therefore, is an action of three movements evading two parries, and that, like that of the simple feint, it can be performed both from lunging and step and lunge distance.

Double feints from lunging distance *(Azioni di doppia finta a misura di allungo)*

For the execution of the double feint from lunging distance proceed as follows:

From the guard, simulate an attack with either the point or cut to one of the uncovered targets, then still from the guard, the opponents parry is eluded by simulating another attack (continuing form the previous movement) using either the point or cut, which can be executed by either a disengagement, circular cut or cut over according to the parry that will be evaded; finally the third movement is carried out, either by point or cut, and always in relation to the parry evaded, the movement may be of disengagement, circular cut or cut over.

Double feints from step and lunge distance *(Azioni di doppia finta a misura di allungo)*

For the execution of the double feint by step and lunge we proceed in the way indicated for the execution of the same action form lunging distance, however, coordinating the two feints with two movements of the step forward, then carrying out the third and last movement together with the lunge. (fig. 40)

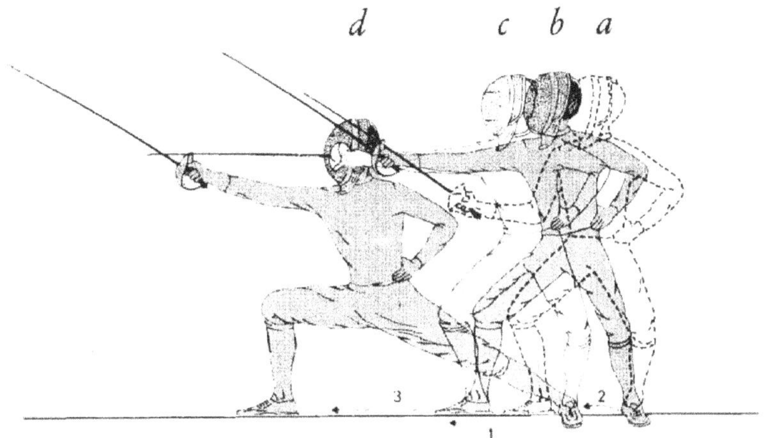

Fig. 40 · Esempio di doppia finta a misura camminando:

    a) guardia di terza
    b) finta alla testa
    c) finta di puntata
    d) sciabolata alla testa

Conventional exercises related to the double feint *(Esercizi convenzionali inerenti alle azioni di doppia finta)*

Established that the actions of the single feint with those of the double feint, these exercises, especially for those who suffer the attack, present greater difficulties than those indicated for simple feints, coming to the alternative of having to perform two or three parries.

To succeed in this, in addition to an immediate answer to the feint, you have to be careful in the movement between the parries, keeping them tight and quick, and not just pass through the motions.

As for the attacker, he will have to pay particular attention not to be caught by the opposing blade and give the necessary expression to the feints, coordinating the feints with the movement of the legs during the performance of the action when at step and lunge distance.

Other essential requirements for the utility and effectiveness of these exercises are of course keeping the compliance of measure (distance), knowing how to simulate (feint) the attack with emphasis of the right choice of time, and in particular, a keen perspective of the alternatives.

CHAPTER V

Offensive actions as opposed to the weapon in line *(Azioni di offesa in contrapposizione all'arma in linea)* — Beats in general *(Delle battute in genere)* — Beat direct from lunging distance *(Battute e colpo a misura di allungo)* — Beat direct from step and lunge distance *(Battute e colpo a misura camminando)* — Blade seizure in general *(Delle prese di ferro in genere)* — Blade seizure and hit from lunging distance *(Prese di ferro e colpo a misura di allungo)* — Blade seizure and hit from step and lunge distance *(Prese di ferro e colpo a misura camminando)* — Feint by glide in general *(Della finta dei fili on genere)* — Feint by glide from lunging distance *(Finta dei fili a misura di allungo)* — Feint by glide with step and lunge distance *(Finta dei fili a misura camminando)* — Double feint by glide *(Della doppia finta dei fili)* — Exercises with the feint and double feint by glide *(Esercizi inerenti alle azioni di finta e doppia finta dei fili)* — Exercises with Beats followed by feints *(Battute seguite da finta)* — Exercises with Blade seizures followed by feints *(Prese di ferro seguite da finta)* — Exercises with the beat or blade seizure followed by feints *(Esercizi inerenti alle battute e alle prese di ferro seguite da finta)*.

Offensive actions in opposition to the blade in line *(Azione di offesa in contrapposizione all'arma in linea)*

So far, the offensive actions have been described are fundamental and are executable from the opposition's invitation and or engagement; now let's see which movements can be executed as opposed to the blade in line.

Of course, to begin with any offensive action to any part of the valid target of the opponent when they are with blade in line, it is essential above all to remove this obstacle. This can be achieved through using one's own weapon in various ways, in which, the more commonly known in fencing language, they are defined by the generic name of <actions on the blade, or «azioni sul ferro». These actions, in addition to the previously mentioned glides in second and third, are the beats « *battute*» and blade seizures «*prese di ferro*».

With the beat, the deflection of the opposing blade takes place by means of a violent blow between the two blades, while the blade seizure is executed by a gradual deviation with accentuated pressure by the blade of the attacker.

Beats in general *(Delle battute in genere)*

By beats we mean the more or less powerful impact that is imprinted with one's own blade on the opponent's blade in order to divert the latter from the offensive line.

Therefore, the beat does not in itself constitute an action of offense which is determined only by the hit that follows the beat itself. The beat, so much so that it is performed at lunging distance or step and lunge, it consists of two movements, the beat, and the hit.

As a rule, the beat is executed with the cut and the stronger degrees, striking the opponents blade on their weaker degrees; only in certain cases, which we will see afterwards, it is preferable to perform it with the back of one's own blade.

The beats, which follow the same direction as the engagements,(1) and there are as many beats as there are engagements themselves, with the modern saber fencing it is not useful to perform then with the stronger degrees of the blade in order to obtain the maximum removal of the opponents weapon, but is better to perform the impact strongly, albeit a dry and energetic strike on a single point of the blade, thus avoiding a wider movement of the blade and arm in order to limit the exposure as little as possible to a potential counter-offensive action by the antagonist. (2)

---

(1) The easiest lines to apply the beats are in order, fourth, second and third.

(2) While we consider it appropriate to repeat that the beat, like the glide and blade seizure, it is indispensable when the weapon of the opponent is placed in the line of offense. We believe the same as it should be noted that the beat itself, as we will see in subsequent actions, finds its practical application also in contrast to a different placement of the weapon. In this case, the beat will be the sole aid to directly access a possible target without having to elude the opponent's parry.

Beat direct from lunging distance *(Battute e colpo a misura di allungo)*

Beat in first (Battuta di prima)

In addition to your weapon on line, this can be performed starting from the guard of second or third in the following way:

    1)   by turning the hand in first position, as you would for the parry of first, with rapid movement of the arm without flexing the wrist, the beat is energetically impacting the opposing blade diagonally left and from bottom to top;

    2)   without any discontinuity, quickly extend your arm, either direct with the point to the chest, lunging with a direct cut to the flank or bottom of the arm, or with a circular cut to the head, top of the arm, left cheek, chest or abdomen.

Beat in second (Battuta di seconda)

This beat is easier to perform from either one's own weapon in line or from the guard in second or third when the opponent's weapon is pointing in the direction of the flank; by the guard in fifth, however when the opponent's weapon is placed on the line of the chest, for this execution, proceed as follows:

1)   keeping the wrist in line with the forearm, make an energetic impact on the opposing blade, keeping the hand in the intermediate position of first and second, as to divert the opposing blade to the bottom right (outside) as in the parry of second;

2)   without discontinuity extend the arm rapidly, taking place together with the lunge with the point or cut to the flank or external arm or direct with the point to the chest or cut the top arm or to the face (right or outside cheek) or to the head, or by circular cut to the face (left, inside cheek) or lastly internal arm.

Beat in third (Battuta di terza)

This can be executed from either your weapon in line or from the guard in third, second or fourth in the following manner.

1)   Turning the hand to the intermediate hand position of second and third, make an energetic impact of the opponent's blade in order to deflect it diagonally to your right (outside);

2)   Without discontinuity, quickly extend the arm coordinated with the lunge direct with the point to the chest or flank or cut direct to the face (right, outside cheek), or flank, head, or external arm, or to the face (left, inside cheek), or to the abdomen with a circular cut. (1)

---

(1) Wanting to follow the beat of third with a direct cut externally to the arm or circular cut to the abdomen, such cut will be easier to apply if the beat is performed respectively to the targets with the hand in second hand position and the intermediate hand position of first and second.

Beat in fourth (Battuta di quarta)

This action can be executed from either your weapon in line or from the guard of third, second or fifth in the manner following:

1)   Turning your fist to the intermediate hand position of third and fourth, energetically impact the blade of the opponent in order to deflect the blade diagonally down and to the left (outside);

2) Without discontinuity, extending the arm quickly with the lunge cut direct to the head, or arm or face (right or left *inside or outside* cheek) or chest both by cut or point. (1)

---

(1) If after the beat in fourth, you will want to hit in the chest with the point or cut to the face (right cheek) this beat it is preferable to strike the opponents blade farther up the grade and on the back side (counter cut) by making the beat with the spine (dorso) of your own blade and not the cut. In this way the movement of the opposing weapon will certainly be more limited, but on the other hand the benefit is that the extension to reach the opposing target will be shorter and therefore faster. The execution of the beat will also result from the fact that the hand position remains unchanged in the execution of the beat.

Beat in fifth (Battuta di quinta)

In addition to your own blade in line, you can execute the action from the guard in third or second when the opponent is with the weapon in line of offense, as follows:

1) Turning the hand to first hand position as you would in the parry of fifth, the rapid movement of the arm and without flexing the wrist, impress itself with the strong degree of the blade, make an energetic impact on the blade of the opponent from bottom to top;

2) Without discontinuity extend the arm quickly, while carrying out the lunge to the chest with the point or cut to the flank, bottom of the arm, to the face (left cheek) chest or abdomen.

Beat direct from step and lunge distance *(Battuta e colpo a misura camminando)*

To perform the described action of the beat with the step and lunge, the beat must be joined with the step forward and then, without discontinuity complete the attack, either with the point or cut with the lunge or fleche' (Arrow)

The blade seizure in general *(Delle prese di ferro in genere)*

The common usage the action called blade seizure *«prese di ferro»* is when the deviation of the opposing weapon from the line of offense occurs by means of a gradual accentuated pressure of the strong degrees of your blade sliding on the grade of the opponents weak of the blade, that is to say this action ends with an perfect engagement that perfectly dominates that of the opponents weapon.

Once the deviation is obtained, the strike will take place by use of the point or cut to one of the valid targets which will be discovered. (1)

---

(1) In carrying out this action – which, among other things, calls for finesse and firmness of the hand to have the right pressure against the opposing blade. The main difficulties are represented by the continuity and progressive rhythm of speed that it must have in the development of the action itself from the moment the opposing blade is contacted.

Blade seizure and hit from lunging distance *(Prese di ferro e colpo a misura di allungo)*

Blade seizure in second (Presa di ferro in seconda)

This can be performed from either one's own guard in third or invitation, or from one's own blade in line as follows:

1)	Binds in second, placing the strong grade of your blade on the weaker grade of the opponent's blade, and without discontinuity, scrolling up to the medium degree of the blade, as it is gradually transported to the bottom right (outside).

2)	While maintaining contact between the two blades and always with dominant of degrees, hit the flank with the point; instead of keeping contact with the blade detach from that of the opponent and hit the chest with the point, or cut to the side of the face (right or left cheek) or at the head or top of arm.

It is also possible to cut the abdomen with the counter-cut remaining below the opponent's weapon.

Blade seizure in third (Presa di ferro in terza)

This can be performed from the guard in third or by invitation, or from one's own blade in line in the following way:

1)	Blade seizure in third (bind), placing the strong degrees (forte) of your own blade on the weak of the opponent's blade, without discontinuity, flowing over their blade until the medium is reached, gradually the opponent's blade is shifted to the right;

2)	Maintaining contact between the two blades while keeping the strong of your blade dominant over the opponents, glide to the chest with the point, or detach your blade from that of the opponents to hit with the point or cut to the flank, cut to head, top of arm or face (left or right cheek) or by circular cut to the abdomen or bottom arm.

Blade seizure in fourth (Presa di ferro in quarta)

This can be performed by your guard in third, invitation or from one's own blade in line is the following manner:

1) The blade seizure in fourth, placing the strong degrees on your own blade on the weak of the opponent's, gradually extending the arm without stiffness and for only what is necessary to slide up their blade till equal to the middle grade and gradually carrying it to the left;

2) Detach the blade from the opposing one to cut direct to the head or face (left or right cheek) or top of the arm or chest, or with the point to the chest, or circular cut to the flank or bottom of arm.

Note- in some treaties it is mentioned that the blade seizure can be executed both in first and fifth, in modern saber fencing it is particularly difficult and risky to implement such actions thus, it was deemed appropriate to omit these descriptions.

However, the Maestro can have the student perform them following the same standards indicated.

Blade seizure and direct hit with the step and lunge *(Prese di ferro e colpo a misura camminando)*

The blade seizure and hit described above are supposed to be executed at step and lunge distance, specifying them on the three engagements from which they can originate and distinguishing the two tempo that make them up. Their practicality and implementation are more effective from step and lunge distance.

For the execution of this measure, it is necessary to establish domination of the opposing blade together with the step forward, then following immediately the completion of the touch (either with the point or cut) with the lunge or fleche.

It is essential that everything is done with absolute priority of the weapon in order to reduce and minimize the opponent's chances of disengaging in time upon the attempted possession of the others blade.

Feints by glide in general *(Della finta dei fili in genere)*

Like the feints with the point or cut, these are respectively the derivatives of the fundamental feints with the point or cut and take place to evade the parry of the opponent. Thus, the feint by glide is nothing more than the derivative of the glide itself, and in this case is a feinting action by use of the glide when you find it difficult to find success with a simple attack by glide. And since as it has already been said, there are only two glides in the application of saber (second and third), it follows that the feint by glide will be only in these two same lines.

Their execution, both on lunging and step and lunge distance, it can originate directly from one's own engagement as well as in opposition to the advisories blade in line. In the second case, the engagement will occur gradually and without discontinuity during the gaining of degrees together with the arm extending to feint the touch by glide.

Feint by glide from lunging distance *(Finta dei fili a misura di allungo)*

Feint by glide in second (Finta del filo di seconda)

From one's own engagement of second, proceeding as described above, the glide is feinted by directing the point of the weapon to the flank simulating the simple attack by glide, then, in contract to the advisories parry of second or the ceding parry of fourth, with rapid movement of the disengagement, complete the attack above with the point or cut.

If the parry of second has been avoided, the touch with the point will be above to the chest, if the touch is decided to arrive by cut, it can be to the face (right, outside cheek) or arm or by circular cut to the head, chest, or abdomen.

If, on the other hand the ceding parry of fourth has been circumvented, the touch will be directed to the outside chest with the point, or by the cut the face (right cheek), arm or head by cut over.

Feint by glide in third (Finta del filo di terza)

We proceed in the same way as described for the execution of the glide in second, bearing in mind that in this case the parry of third or the ceding parry of first will always end with a disengagement with the point or cut.

Avoiding the parry of third, the point thrust will finish to the outside chest, if using the cut, the touch can end direct or by cutover or circular cut to the head, or circular cut to the face (left cheek), abdomen or internal arm.

When avoiding the ceding parry of first, the touch with the point will be directed to the flank, while the cut may also be directed to the flank or outside arm.

Feint by glide from step and lunge distance *(Finta dei fili a misura camminando)*

For the execution of the two aforementioned actions, to be done at step and lunge distance, the feint by glide is made in perfect coordination with the step forward; then without discontinuity, the second movement takes place of any of the proceeding to any of the valid targets indicated above with the lunge.

The initial movement of the weapon must take absolute precedence to that of the legs and in particular so when the action is not performed directly from one's own engagement but as opposed to the adversary's blade in line.

The double feint by glide (Della doppia finta dei fili)

The purpose of the double feint by glide has commonality to all of the double feints, that being the avoidance of two parries of the opponent; and almost always, as for the double feint actions in general, it is used when it is not possible to overcome the opposing defense with a single feint.

The double feint by glide, in use from the distance of lunge or step and lunge, consists of three tempo, or movements: the first tempo is constituted by the feint by glide, the second tempo is a feint by point or cut, and the third movement is the final of the attack by either point or cut which is carried out with the lunge to one of the valid targets discovered following the opponents second parry.

From lunging distance, the two feints will be performed remaining on guard while the step and lunge, the first two feints will be harmonized with the two movements of the step forward. (1)

(1) The double feint by glide, like any other action of double feints, it is practically easier to implement and more effective if made from step and lunge distance.

Exercises related to the feint and double feint by glide (*Esercizi inerenti alle azione di finta e doppia finta dei fili)*

As soon as the exact execution has been learned and perfectly understood the purpose to which the action is aimed with the feint and double feint by glide, it will be very useful to alternate between them as an exercise of application. And in order to make the exercise practical and more effective, it would be good if the attacker is left to their own faculty of being able to perform without the knowledge of what defense the other person is going to employ, this being either a single or double parry.

This alternative will be beneficial to both the practice of defense than to that of the offense, imposing a mutual study of the action to be applied and developed that instinct that allows you to adapt your own concept of attack, of the defense and vice versa.

Beats followed by feints (Battute seguite da finta)

With the beat and feint (either with point or cut), when the touch is followed by the beat, instead of completing the attack, the movement is only mentioned (feinted) in order to induce the opponent to parry and then, with a third movement evade the parry itself, the touch will be carried out (point or cut) elsewhere on the valid target which will be discovered.

The beat and feint, despite being made up of three tempos like the double feinting actions, evading one parry instead of two, since as it has been previously said, at least theoretically, the beat is does not constitute an offensive action, is its function is limited to deviating the point of the opposing weapon from the line of offense. (1)

(1) In practice, especially in lunging distance, it often occurs that making a dry strike of, measured violence using the beat must above all be made at the appropriate time, the one who suffers the beat instinctively parries without the attacker having started the final movement. In this case, instead of mentioning the feint, you will have to evade the parry immediately, carrying out the touch with an instant disengagement eluding their parry and carrying out the attack with the point or cut to the parts of the valid target that will be discovered following the parry itself.

Blade seizure followed by feints *(Prese di ferro seguite da finta)*

The procedure for performing these actions is similar to that described for the beats followed by feints, because what distinguishes and characterizes these two offensive actions, both of which tend to be achieving the same goal, it is only the first tempo in which the different way of deviating the weapon on line.

So, the same rules and considerations apply for the expressed execution of the beat followed the feint, logically keeping in mind whether using the blade seizure or beat.

Exercises related to beats and blade seizures followed by feints *(Esercizi inerenti alle battute e alle prese di ferro seguite da finta)*

Similarly, to what has been said for the feint and double feints by glide, also for these exercises will come established the beat or blade seizure, following each of them the touch or feint, in order to generate in the opponent, the uncertainty of having to resort to one or two parries to defend.

Then adding difficulty to the exercise, the attacker will alternate freely between the beat or the blade seizure, as well as to follow directly with the attack or feint, varying the target.

CHAPTER VI.

Auxiliary offensive actions *(Azioni di offesa ausiliarie)* — Flanconade in second *(Fianconata di seconda)* — False beat *(Battute false)* — Beat from one's own engagement (Battute dai propri legamenti e battute di sforzo) — Beat in the opposite direction of the engagement (change beat) *(Battute in senso opposto ai legamenti Intrecciata)* — Beat and pass over the blade (grazing beat) *(Battute di passaggio)*

Auxiliary offensive actions *(Azioni di offesa ausiliarie)*

So far, the basic actions have been described of offense in close relevance and in opposition to the three attitudes (placements) of the weapon (invitations, engagements and point in line) as well as deriving how to conquer the defense of the adversary.

We will now deal with the auxiliary offensive actions, these actions are although not indispensable, are of great help in achieving the touch, being selective with them to distract the attention of the opponent from the fundamental action or, in any case, to create uncertainty in the defensive or counteroffensive decision.

These actions can be carried out in both lunging and step and lunge distance and some even by the fleche to be followed by feints with the point or cut.

Flanconade in second *(Fianconata di seconda)*

When from one's engagement in fourth, exercising very light pressure on the opponent's blade, there he realizes that they do not offer much resistance, you can carry out the flanconade in second in the following way:

By turning the hand to almost firsthand position, transport the opponent's weapon from left to right in a spiral motion with gradual extension of the arm, while directing the point of the weapon to the direction of the flank in which, without any discontinuity the touch arrives.

False beat *(Battute false)*

The false beat is used in opposition to the weak engagement of the opponent in either second, third or fourth. Giving the impact with either the cut or spine (dorso) of the blade according to the case, and with the same hand position and same general direction of the normal beats.

Sliding Beats from one's own engagement *(expulsion, sforzo) (Battute dai propri legamenti e battute di sforzo)*

These beats are performed from the engagement following the same rules described for the respective beats of first, second, etc. but preceding the impact by first detaching from the blade.

When the above beats are played without the detachment of the blade but with an accentuated gaining in the degrees, they are called expulsion.

Beats in the opposite direction to the engagement (change beat) *(Battute in senso opposto ai legamenti Intrecciata)*

These beats are performed both from your own engagement or that of your opponent's, from either first, second, third or fourth, preceding the beat by a movement of release.

They can be carried out, as appropriate, both by cutting with the cut or with back of one's blade, bearing in mind that when the beat originates from one's own engagement to use the cut, as well as using the strong degree of the blade.

Grazing beat *(Battute di passaggio)*

This beat is made by striking with a sliding action on the opponent's blade with one movement from front to back and continuing the return high or low (passing over the opponent's blade), obtaining the effect similar to that of a simple beat fused together with the feint, but with the gaining of a tempo, with one movement less. (1)

(1) The grazing beat is particularly useful and of easy implementation to bring the offense to the arm.

Therefore, against the invitation or engagement of second, make the beat on the back of the opponents blade with a rapid movement from front to back and starting from the bottom of the opponents blade to the top deviating to the left (inside) by means of a slight flexion at the elbow and wrist, it will be possible to pass directly to the completion of the cut to the head, face, chest or arm.

Against the invitation or engagement in third, make the beat against the back of the opponent's blade with one rapid movement from front to back and from the bottom to the top of the opponent's blade deviating the tip to the left (outside), it will be possible to pass directly to the completion of the point to the flank or cut to the flank or arm.

Against the invitation or engagement in fourth, making the beat against the back of the blade rapidly moving from front to back and from bottom to top deviating the point to the right, it will be possible to pass directly to the completion of the cut to the abdomen. (1)

---

(1) The grazing beat can also be performed from your weapon in line, as well as opposed to the opponent's blade in line.

CHAPTER VII.

The counter attacks or exits in time - The arrest *(Il colpo d'arresto)* - The disengagement in time *(La cavazione in tempo)* - The stop cut to the arm *(Il tempo al braccio)*– Appuntata *(L'appuntata)* - Time thrust *(La contrazione)* – Inquartata *(L'inquartata)* - Fencing time *(Il tempo schermistico).*

Of the counterattacks or exits in time *(Della controffesa ossia uscite in tempo)*

Counter attacks or going out in time means canceling the opposing offensive action, not availing oneself to the parry and riposte, but still making the touch as opposed to that of the attacker. In other words, the counterattack or exit on time is no other than an offensive action on the offensive action of the opponent, with the aim of hitting the latter and preventing them from hitting in turn or otherwise arriving late.

In saber fencing the counterattack can be made with the point, the cut and albeit rarely, the countercut.

The counterattacks or exits on time are: *«the arrest»*, *«disengagement on time»*, *«stop cut to the arm»*, *«appuntata»*, *« time thrust»* and *«inquartata».*

The exits on time, which preferably come applied against attacks made from step and lunge distance, must be considered in relation to the action of offense that the opponent carries out, namely: those of disengagement that are carried out at the beginning of an attack or an attack on the blade (beat or blade seizure) while the rest are implemented on the attacks that do not originate from any deviation of the blade. (1)

(1) Generally, exits on time find practice or usefulness in implementation against opponents who often fall into repetitious actions or make their offensive intentions clear.

The arrest *(Il colpo d'arresto)*

This exit on time is used in opposition to the compound attack and allows you to hit without being hit.

In contrast to the attack of only one feint, the arresting action must be implemented on the first half of the movement, that is when the pretense begins; in as opposed to the attack of double feint, one can implement the arrest at the beginning of the second tempo after moving accordingly, feinting the parry of the first tempo of the compound attack.

The execution of the arrest can take place as much on the low line as on the high line, and in both cases, if well executed, preclude the passage of the opposite blade from one line to the other in the opposite direction.

Therefore, the arrest is carried out on the flank when the feint of the opponent's attack is directed to the internal or high target and disengaging to the external target; it is performed instead to the chest when the feint of the attack is directed low (flank) and disengaging to the head or internal target. (1)

(1) It is not advisable to implement the arrest in contrast to the attack feinting to the high line and disengaging to the internal target or vice versa, because the arrest (for example, feint head and cut abdomen or inversely) as this exit on time does not prevent the continuation of the attack itself.

The disengagement in time *(La cavazione in tempo)*

This exit on time is applicable in contrast to any offensive action that begins on the opposite blade by beats or blade seizure. It is done by subtracting your blade from the impact of that of the attacker, and so as to prepare it in the direction of the target which consequently will result in the touch being discovered by the point or cut.

Example – suppose we are with the blade in line or inviting in third, and to have sensed that the opponent wants to attack us with a beat or blade seizure. In the precise moment that he is starting the action on the blade, we subtract out blade first, so as to not be met by the opposing steel, and without any discontinuity, we touch with the point to the inside or with the cut to the head, right cheek, etc.

Stop hit to the arm *(Il tempo al braccio)*

The stop hit to the arm is considered the counteroffensive par excellence in saber fencing, being possible against all the actions of offense of both cut and counter cut (rarely with the point) on all four lines of the arm (external, internal, above, and below) in reference to the direction of the attacker's line.

The application of the stop hit to the arm can take place as opposed to each of the movement that constitutes the offense and therefore can take place on the first, second or third tempo, respectively implemented on the first, second or third tempo of the offensive action itself. (1)

(1) Normally the stop cut to the arm should never be applied as opposed to a simple attack, in some cases that the action itself is performed with uncertainty or with excessive exposure of the advanced target. It should also not be applied in contrast to the attacks by fleche, if not in cases where the attack itself is performed by a measure excessively long or the attacker withdraws their arm at the time of departure.

As has been said for exits on time in general, the time cut to the arm is easier to apply against the step and lunge, but if having a good choice of time and knowing well to coordinate the counter-attacking action with the withdrawal of the body (step back or jump back) it is also possible to execute the counter action from lunging distance.

In this case, however, for greater guarantee and success in the event that the stop cut to the arm does not have a favorable outcome, it will be useful to associate with the withdrawal of the body to parry in the most suitable manner to avoid the incoming hit. (fig. 41)

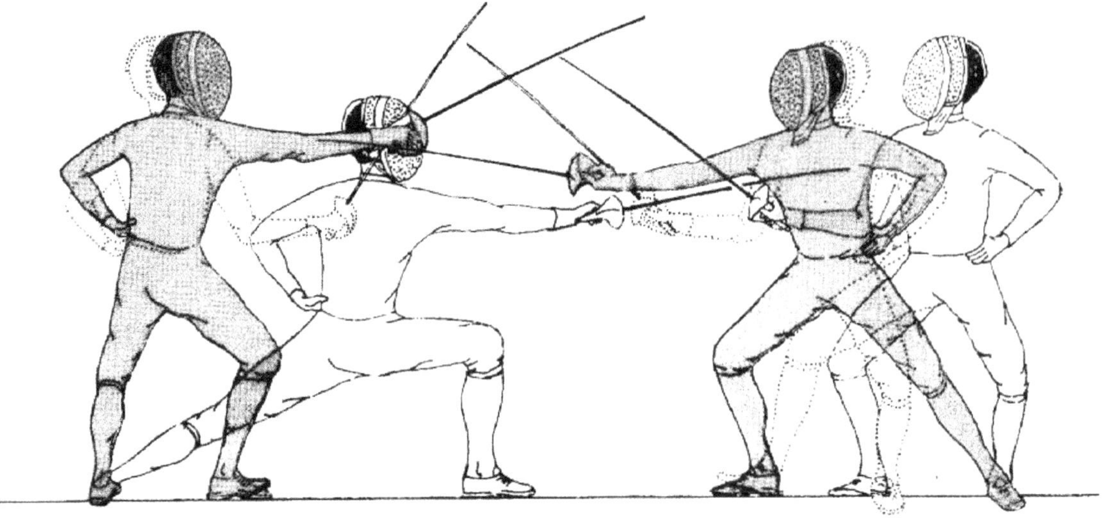

Fig. 41 - Esempio di tempo al braccio su attacco a misura di allungo:

1 { **A** - esegue la finta alla testa
  { **B** - tira il tempo al braccio retrocedendo col piede sinistro

2 { **A** - termina l'attacco con sciabolata al fianco
  { **B** - conclude il passo indietro e para terza

When applied to the offensive action form step and lunge distance, the stop cut will be made when the adversary has stepped into useful distance (to be reached) and always following the retreat of the body after the stop cut with a parry to stop the follow through of the attack.

Appuntata *(L'appuntata)*

The appuntata is the counterattack used in opposition to a compound riposte. It is executed in the following manner:

Our offensive action is parried by the opponent, while they begin the feint by riposte, a new hit is given with the point, remaining in the lunge and on the same line as the original offensive action.

Example – suppose that to our action of feint head and cut side, the opponent parries second and responds with a feint to the right cheek then disengage below. At the instant they are performing the feint to the right cheek, replace the point to the flank remaining in the lunge.

This will occupy in advance the final line that the opponent would have wanted to arrive with his second movement, thus completing the compound riposte.

The time thrust *(La contrazione)*

This counterattack is a point action that is accomplished in one tempo, on the final movement of the opponent, directing the point to the outside or above to the chest or flank.

Therefore, this counterattack takes place only on the external line and on the flank. The time thrust external or in third is performed as follows:

Without lunging, raise and vigorously extend the arm, the touch is directed to the chest of the opponent in order to meet and earn the grade of his blade in the last moments of his attack, and closing the line on which the final movement is executed on. (fig. 42)

Similarly, we proceed for the execution of the time thrust to the flank or second, with the variant that the point strike is delivered to the flank instead of above to the chest. (fig. 43)

Inquartata *(L'inquartata)*

The inquartata arrives in time to the face (left cheek) opposing the attack the opponent carries out on the same target of the face, head with the cut or to the inside chest with the point.

The touch must be made with great determination from the guard position and accompanied by the retraction of the left (rear) foot moving it to the right (outside) and back, keeping the weapon towards the internal line in order to have opposition to that of the opponent. (fig.44)

Fig. 42 - Contrazione esterna o contrazione di terza

Fig. 43 - Contrazione al fianco o ccntrazione di seconda

Fig. 44 - L'inquartata

Fig. 44 - L'inquartata

Fencing time *(Il tempo schermistico)*

By «fencing time» we mean appreciation of time that must elapse between the stroke of offense and that of counter offense so that the latter can be considered valid.

A simple action such as the point thrust or cut, always consists of one movement whatever the target is and where it is carried out; the feint of the same point thrust or cut, consists of two movements, the feint and the second movement is the touch that follow the feint.

To perform the double feint action, there will be three movements (tempo) one is the first feint, one is the second feint, and the last tempo is the touch that follows. Each of these movements take time, therefore, three movements, performed successively without discontinuity or slowdowns corresponds to three tempos.

However, in the event that the attacker slows down his action or stops themself, undergoing a moment of perplexity, they, in effect, wastes that tempo in the current movement, and loses "a tempo" meaning fencing tempo, compared to the opponent, who, although leaving after him, can score with a single tempo of fencing time in advance of the other.

In common practice, as long as it is a compound action, each movement of the action is considered same or equal to a time (tempo) and he who counterattacks, to see his coup validated and cancel that attack of the opponent, must reach the target before the antagonist starts his last movement.

That is: if the attack is composed of three movements, the counterattack must arrive before the third movement begins; if instead the action consists of two movements, the counterattack must arrive before the second movement begins.

Where it is a simple attack of one movement, he who counterattacked may have reason, when the attacker fell, as has been said, in a faulty or slowed execution of the attack and has lost time, this however has to be considered as a case of absolute exception, while the rule wants that against the simple action of a single movement does not exist as the counteroffensive action is based on the appreciation of time.

CHAPTER VIII.

Counter-time *(Controtempo)*- Offensive actions of first and second intention *(Azioni di offesa di prima e di seconda Intenzione)*- Distinction between counter-time and second intention *(Distinzione fra controtempo e seconda intenzione)*- Probing actions *(Lo scandaglio)*- Actions of concealment (*Il traccheggio)* - Distinction between offensive actions performed at one's own choice of time and actions of offense carried out in time *(Distinzione fra azioni di offesa eseguite a propria scelta di tempo e azioni di offesa eseguite in tempo)* - Renewed attacks *(Ripigliata o ripresa d'attacco)*.

Counter time *(Il controtempo)*

There is no fencing action to which there is not its opposite, i.e., another action that can be applied to oppose or cancel. So also, the counter attacks (exit on time) as previously described, can come to in turn be neutralized by the respective contrary, consisting of the parry and riposte, or a counterattack on time against the opponent's counterattack.

Such contrary, in either of the two ways in comes as applied, it takes the generic name of counter time (contretemps)

Counter-time is an action with which you can neutralize the exit in time (counter attack) in opposing time.

Generally, one acts in counter time after having intuition, especially through a probing action, finding that the opponent's tendency is to counterattack. Rather than hinder them, their implementation is facilitated by showing with clarity the attacking action so that it gives rise to their counterattack.

Example - realized that the opponent, in opposition to our attack of feint head, cut flank, is postponed by the opponent applying the counterattack by a stop cut to the flank when the feint is performed.

Keeping a short step with the feint to facilitate the opponent's application of the stop cut, quickly and without discontinuity, pass instead to the parry of second while stopping in the guard.

If you have instead have the intuition that as opposed to the same feint attack of feint head cut flank, the opponent intends to counter attack by applying a stop cut to the arm on the feint, we will perform this together with a short step, then pass quickly and without discontinuity to the parry of third and carrying out the riposte by not remaining in the guard, but with a lunge or fleche, following the backward movement made by the opponent after the implementation of the counter offensive action to the arm.

Realized that the opponent, as opposed to our attack of beat in fourth and cut face, it is proposed to counter attack by applying the disengagement in time (with the cut or point) to the target external, together with a short step forward and with absolute precedence of the weapon, the stop hit will be performed in so as to facilitate his disengagement in time, then passing quickly without interruption to the parry of third and riposte while remaining on guard.

Assuming instead that as opposed to the same beat in fourth, it is understood that the opponent wants to counterattack not with the disengagement in time but with the feint in time and finish to the target inside rather than outside, its counter-offensive can be neutralized both with the two relative parries, also, and without lunging, either with the arrest with the point to the flank carried out immediately after the simulation of the beat, can stop cut the arm as carried out as soon the opponent has disengaged in time as opposed to our beat.

Offensive actions of first and second intention *(Azioni d'offesa di prima e di seconda intenzione)*

Any offensive action, simple or compound, can be performed of first or second intention.

It is said to be *the first intention* when the attack is performed with the intention of directly overcoming the opposing defense or reaching the target with the execution of the attack itself. They say *the second intention* is when the attack is performed not already for the purpose of passing directly the defense, but to promote it, indulging skillfully the intuited tendencies of the opponent and then to parry and riposte. (1)

In the development of primary actions, the attacker must employ all the skill of time and mechanics available, while in the development of those of second intention-while giving the attack all the characteristics of truthfulness so that the opponent's reaction is natural and spontaneous. They will have to use it in a contained way not to be found in the material impossibility of accomplishing what it is was prefixed.

(1) The second intension is very effective against those who from a particular parry they usually riposte to the same target.

The distinction between counter time and second intention *(Distinzione fra controtempo e seconda intenzione)*

As we have seen, even with the counter-time there is a tendency to achieve the touch not directly with the attack (first intention) but after one has provoked and expected reaction of the opponent; therefore, even the counter-time is certainly to be considered a secondary action. But since the counter-time is the action specifically designed to neutralize the exit in time reaction (counterattack) *hence its name* the action cannot be called counter-time neutralizing an opponent's (riposte) whether by simple or compound because of the non-existence of the counterattack.

However, in order not to cause confusion, it is customary to note the following distinction:

The counter-time provokes the counterattack, applying, as contrary, the parry and riposte, or another counterattack; with the second intention, this causes the parry and riposte, applying, which different from the counterattack, the counter parry and riposte. (1)

(1) Both the counter-time and the second intention constitute the most complex and highest sector of all fencing knowledge. The field that is, where, despite having an excellent technical foundation it is easy to get lost if they do not have the ability of observation and lively intelligence; the plane on which the most brilliant, most acute fencer can have opportunity and possibility to entangle a far more powerful and fast opponent if they lack the spark of improvisation and reasoning.

Probing actions *(Lo scandaglio)*

By probing actions, we mean the investigation taken to study the tendencies of the opponent and to reveal the defensive and counter-offensive actions of the opponent, a particularly important investigation for the development of the compound attack.

There are various forms of probing actions of which each fencer can avail himself, also because almost always to attitudes, temperament, and other completely subjective elements. However, it is not wrong to say that the probing is generally represented by the simulation of attacks tending, as we said, to reveal the defensive or counteroffensive tendencies of the opponent, in the hope that these are repeated when we decide to develop the planned attacking action or (like we will see later) counter time, or by second intention.

Actions of concealment *(Il traccheggio)*

By actions of concealment, we mean that complex set of movements deemed to be of value to help in preparing one's own fencing determination or to stimulate that of the antagonist, making one's own intentions masked.

Concealing can develop with the transition from one attitude to another, with beats, or simple presses or contacts, etc. practiced on the opposing blade, and all this, more often than not, done in union with small steps back and forward.

The execution, albeit spontaneous, of these movements does not have to be simply mechanical, but implemented with intelligence and shrewdness, otherwise such concealment would benefit the opponent.

Offensive actions performed at your own choice of time and actions performed on time. *(Azioni di offesa eseguite a propria scelta di tempo e azioni di offesa eseguite in tempo)*

Any offensive action, from the simplest to the more complex considered from the initial aspect of its implementation, is divided into *offense action from own's choice of time* or *offense action performed in time*.

When the moment of departure of the attack takes place from one's own determination and as opposed to an attitude already specified by the opponent, the attack itself is said to have been carried out at one's own choice of time.

When that attack does not start, however as opposed to an attitude already previously defined and accomplished, but in the same instant when the attitude is about to emerge, such attack said to be done in time.

What characterizes the distinction between the two ways of performing the same offense action is determined by the instant of departure, since the development is identical and the "time" factor, in one and in the other case, it is always indispensable for the possible hit.

Example: if we perform the beat in fourth and cut the head on the opponent's weapon already placed on line at the time of departure, we will have performed the beat at your choice of tempo; if instead using the same action we make the beat in fourth in the same instant that the opponent releases his blade from our engagement of third to put it online at the beginning of their own offensive action or as a simple movement of probing action, we will have made the beat in time. (1)

(1) Since very rarely, especially with today's saber fencing, it is possible to surprise the opponent in the attitude of static expectation, it becomes indispensable that the master practice the student as soon as possible to perform the offensive action on time.

The renewed attack *(La ripigliata o ripresa d'attacco)*

The renewed attack is a second offensive action that starts from the negative outcome from the first attack where the opponent fails to react after having defended himself, either parrying and staying on guard, or by parrying with steel or by dissolving the measure.

The new offensive action must therefore be carried out as opposed to the attitude he will have kept or differently assumed the opponent in to defend oneself, and in relation to the distance that he will come to be after suffering the first attack.

Therefore, there are several ways to do the renewed attack, each of them has a specific name:

In the event that the opponent, despite having parried regularly the attack, does not respond, the attacker will be able to take a new thrust from the lunge position on the line opposite the one where parried.

This action is called **second thrust** *(secondo colpo)*

In the event that the opponent still proceeds in the manner above but also supporting the parry with a retreat, it will be appropriate to return to the guard with your left (rear)foot and complete the lunge as a new action that can also be by feint or double feint, or even an action on the blade if, in receding the opponent will have placed the weapon online.

This coordinated attack recovering forward is called **renewed attack recovering forward** *(Ripresa d'attacco di allungo)*

If instead the opponent parries and retreats much more than is necessary to defend oneself, you will be recovering with the left (rear) foot forward, and the new offensive action, compliant to the attitude taken by the adversary, will be found this time by the step forward and lunge.

This coordinated renewed attack is called **renewed attack by step and lunge** *(ripresa d'attacco camminando)*

The renewed attack can also be performed by gaining on the lunge or by fleche directly from the lunge, both after returning on guard with the left (back) foot.

CHAPTER XI.

Preparatory exercises for starting the assault *(Esercizi preparatori per l'avviamento all'assalto)*- Free fencing - *(Lo spraticod'assalto)* – Prolonged friction exercises *(Esercizi di attrito protungato)*- Conduct during the assault *(L'assalto e condotta d'assalto).*

Preparatory exercises for starting the assault *(Esercizi preparatori per l'avviamento all'assalto)*

This is a detailed study of everything that is related to saber fencing and assimilated sufficiently the mechanism of the various offense, defense, and counter-offensive actions you would want to instruct the student on in preparation for the assault.

Done so in a manner so that the student will not become confused with what is essential built through lessons and exercises to show the indicative movements and answers that can be applied. In the initial period, it will be good to only fence the master, who will adapt himself in alternating between the attacker and defender.

In these exercises the teacher will not indicate the action to be developed in opposition to any placement of the weapon but will limit himself to prospecting simple themes to the student and adjusting themselves so that he can find ease on his own application.

More complex topics will be gradually presented until the student, having acquired sufficient autonomy in conception and execution, will be considered mature to move on to the exercise of free fencing.

Here are what the exercises for the above purpose are, in progressive order of development:

1. **Simple action exercises** (Esercizio su azione semplici)

This exercise aims to draw attention of the student of the different offensive actions that they may apply respectively in opposition to the three placements of the weapon.

Example – the master will take on the invitation or engagement in third and the student, without the master having to ask orally, will apply the various simple actions with the point or cut that have been studied in contract to said invitation or engagement. The student will proceed by his own decision to also use beats or blade seizures. The master will let himself be hit and occasionally apply the parry and riposte.

Similarly, we will proceed with the other invitations or engagements as well as opposed to the blade in line.

When the attacker's function will be up to the teacher, to exercise the student in defense, he must always adjust his attack to the possibilities of time and speed of the student, so that in these readiness skills can gradually develop intuition and trust.

Exercises with compound actions *(Esercizio sulle azioni composte)*

This exercise aims to draw attention of the student on how to build the action of compound attack, the execution of which is subordinated to parry or parries that the opponent will oppose.

Therefore, before devoting himself to attack it is almost always indispensable, especially for the development of the double feint, to form a more exact idea possible, through probing actions, of the defense of the opponent.

Example – as opposed to the invitation of third by the master from step and lunge distance, the student before deciding on the attack, he will test the attack with the point to the internal target together with a short step. The master will in turn defend himself with the parry of fourth or with a half circular parry of first. The pupil, having returned to the measure of step and lunge, they will next definitely attack with a feint and disengage with the cut to the outside arm or face or head if he must evade the parry of fourth; instead, he will attack with a feint with the cut or point to the flank if they are to avoid the parry of first.

In a similar way we will proceed for the development of all other compound actions inherent in the three placements, bearing in mind that the preparation of a double feint attack toe hint of the touch from the parry of the student, rather than being limited to the single movement, must be two, and as many the many parries must mention the master. When, to exercise the student in defense, the function of attacker will pass to the master, these will have to be careful in always adapting the choice of time as the speed to the degree of development of the student himself.

Exercise on counter-parry and riposte actions *second intention*) *(Esercizio sulle azioni di controparata e risposta seconda intenzione)*

The master- after having reminded the student what has been said in the discussion of intention, namely that which the counter parry and riposte finds practical implementation of the opponent's usual response following a certain second parry.

Establishing a certain attack (simple or compound) reserving the defense function with the commitment to always answer on the same target.

The student, after experiencing fruitlessness several times of his attack because of the master's parry, instead of increasing his speed or adding a movement to his offensive action, will carry out the attack in a more contained way, and following the masters reply, he will parry in turn (counter parry) and will respond to the most appropriate target.

Example – established which attacking action the feint to the flank and cut head in contrast to the invitation of fifth of the teacher, the student will perform the attack itself, trying to overcome the defense, but the master will parry the final action with a parry of fifth and riposte to the abdomen. The student will repeat the same attack in a more contained way while being prepared to counter the action with the counter parry of fourth, also riposting to the abdomen or to another part of the valid target that will be discovered.

Exercise action of counter time *(Esercizio sull azione in controtempo)*

First of all, the teacher will have to remind the student that this exercise presupposes intention on the part of the opponent to neutralize the attack with a counterattack, rather than opposing with a parry and riposte. It should also be pointed out the importance of the probing action to learn how it is possible to counterattack how the opponent will oppose, this is certainly making use of the probing action, as we have seen, to set up the counterattack using the preparation of the compound attack.

That being said, in opposition to the placement of the blade adopted by the teacher, the student will investigate as indicated in the second exercise: if the teacher instead of parries or multiple parries, rather counter attacks, the student will advance his action of attack in counter-time.

Example – on the probing action of the feint head from the invitation of second, the master arrests with point thrust to the flank, the pupil then upon returning to the step and lunge distance, will compose the attack in the following way: giving great priority to the weapon, will perform the feint head together with a short step forward, and instead of continuing the attack, which is this case would give way to the arrest from the master, the student will stop in the guard and parry second and riposte to the most appropriate target.

If instead of the stop hit, the master applies on the same feint to the head, a stop cut to the arm followed by a retreat, the student will also conduct the attack in the same manner above, however, replacing the easier parry of third rather than second. Should the master dissolve quickly and abundantly to measure, the student will be able to respond either with the lunge or fleche.

Another example: in contrast to the invitation of third or the blade online, the student executes a beat or blade seizure in fourth, whereupon the master hints that he wants to get away to the outside target by disengagement in time with the point or cut. The student then, giving absolute priority to the weapon, will compose the attack by simulating the beat or blade seizure together with a short step forward, and, without discontinuity, will parry quickly third when the disengagement in time is completing by the master, the student remaining in the guard will either cut head or other target discovered.

Free exercise *(Esercizio libero)*

In this exercise, which represents the summary of the previous four, no indication comes pre-established, except that of designating to whom it belongs, among the two fencers, the function of the attacker, and to whom to face the attack.

So, both fencers are reserved full freedom of application: the attacker will be able to carry out the action he prefers and which, however, he believes best suited to surprise the opponent; these, in his time, he can avail himself of the parry at his leisure appropriate.

Both functions present no slight difficulties: for those facing the attack, the difficulties are represented by the vastness of the target to defend from the initiative and from the choice of the attacker's action; for the latter, however, develop the attack in relationship to the opposing defense.

Therefore, we believe it appropriate to repeat the exercise free can be addressed only when the student is sufficiently in possession of all the elements and technique.

The practice assault *(Lo spratico d'assalto)*

This form of the assault is nothing more that the continuation of the free exercise. But, while the latter the function of the attacker and that of facing the attack is carried out by agreement, separated and distinct from each other, in this form the latter is suppressed by convention, whereby the two fencers can indifferently and freely perform on or the other function, according to one's degree of readiness and intuition.

This full freedom of action represents the period more delicate and more difficult to overcome.

Especially in saber fencing- for the greater difficulties of application that the defense against the offense- predisposes the practice assaulting more to attack than to parry, and most of the time, determining to attack more is only for the purpose of preventing the opponent's attack, so that they do not feel secure in facing the attack, therefore, performed in an unconscious way, without that is, a clear concept, with no choice of time and appropriate measure.

Therefore, it is good practice not to entrust to spontaneity or the intuition of the student the beginning of the first assaults: the master must be the first opponent that will have to meet and until the student has acquired sufficient familiarity in orientation, especially with regard to the rapid passage of the concept of offense to that of defense and counter-offense.

The master, always adapting himself to the skills of the student, will facilitate it by playing a game somewhat schematic, using simple attacks or a maximum of one feint, so that the student does not become lost in building defense; he will use moderation in the riposte that will almost always be simple to facilitate and get used to the counterpart, and will refrain from going out in time (counter attack) because the student, without the worry about being stopped, develop the plans of offense with decision and confidence.

The master will progressively attack the student with compound actions and, only when the progress appears remarkable, every now and then he will also apply the exit in time, especially to the arm, specifically for the purpose of inducing the student to limit his offensive impulse, and not to widen the movements.

In addition, the master, with great care, will have to call the student back whenever the craving for hitting begins to draw them to deform the execution of the movements, which occasionally degenerates with ease in habit, difficult to correct when the student will no longer have the teacher as an opponent, but other fencers.

We consider this summary sufficient nod to make people understand how important it is, and how delicate the work of the master in this period is.

This period can be more or less long, depending on that of the individual: for some it will only last some weeks, for others a few months. However, it is always better that it is extended beyond what is necessary since, as we said, it is very easy for the new to assaulting to have defects, while it is very difficult, if not actually impossible, to be able to take them off their defects, if they are not abandoned to himself altogether.

Prolonged friction exercise *(Esercizio di attrito prolungato)*

These exercises are very useful for buying the necessary fluency and independence of the arm and therefore greater speed and lightness in bearing of the weapon, they should always be inserted in the lesson, especially when the young fencer is to be initiated into the assault.

These exercises consist of performing short distance a series of parry and riposte with exchanges reciprocal between teacher and pupil, on any part of the valid target and from all positions, changing each parry or counter parry and riposte allowing to keep developing a fencing phrase that becomes very complex and prolonged, without the movement initial (which provokes a defense and must be logically offensive action) proposing to reach the target.

At the beginning it would be good for the friction phrase to come pre-established and that the teacher, so that the student can well locate and without skidding the various movements, both parry and riposte, moderate your speed gradually increasing it in relation to the progress of the student.

Then, when the execution will take place with due speed and fluidity, the exercise will be performed without predetermining the development of the sentence, and so on with various attack, parry, riposte, counter parry sequences, counterattack etc., in addition to the specific purpose above, they will also have to develop reflexes.

For orientation purposes, we set out below, in progressive order, a group of five exercises on the basis of which, according to the master and according to the student's possibilities, they can be combined with many others and even more complex to create those particular abilities bordering on virtuosity and which then in the assault they become truly precious.

1)   Short friction and always from the position of guard, on pre-established phrases, varied from time to time and with gradually longer sequences.

2)   Repetition of exercise no.1, but each parry or counter parry will be excluded by the student together with a step back on the marching of the master, who will have to take care to constantly keep the short measure initial.

3)   Repetition of exercise no.2, but the first parry of the student will be preceded by a stop cut to the arm together with the step back, and continuation immediate of the predetermined parry-riposte phrase.

4)   Repetition of exercise no.3 but following some response an immediate riposte to the arm, then immediately resuming the sentence of contact.

5)   Repetition of exercise no.4, but the student, on the last counter parry will have to dissolve the measure more abundantly, in a way that is to be forced to carry out the counter riposte with the lunge or fleche.

The assault and the conduct of the assault *(L'assalto e Condotta d'asssalto)*

The free and reasoned application of any offensive, defensive, and counter offensive action through which two fencers try to prevail one on the other, it is called "the assault".

Each assault always presents new characteristics and different, infinite possibilities of play, reasoning, and applications that find their implementation from time to time at a time and depending on the intelligence and sensitivity of individual fencers.

Therefore, it often occurs that an excellent performer mechanically is overcome in the assault by the least technically gifted but smarter and more intelligent in applying its concepts with opportunities. This means that, regardless of any consideration of physical aptitudes, the indispensable basis of technique is not enough to supply the elements by itself to make everyone a strong fencer.

Given, as we said, that the conduct of the assault or combat, varies with the differences between that of the opponents, being that the fencing concepts are all subjective, it would be absurd to want to establish some fixed rules to achieve the best result in an assault whatever the weapon to which it refers. However, experience allows us to provide some indications which, if applied, of course, on a case-by-case basis, can be of great use:

1)   Bear in mind that in fencing everything must be based on maximum naturalness and spontaneity.

2)   Use with caution only those elements learned and perfected in the detailed study from the lesson.

3)   Pay the utmost attention and respect to the measure.

4)   Search through appropriate probing actions to sense the offensive, defensive and or counter offensive intentions of the opponent to apply the related and more suitable contrary.

5)   Do not lose your temper, but always stay present to yourself against impetuous opponents, since the frustration and being upset not only do not allow for the necessary choice of time and measure, that is always appropriate to remember, they represent the factors key to success, but do not allow as well to be able to conceive what is most appropriate to do.

6)   Do not resolve to attack or counterattack without first having sufficiently investigated the intentions of the opponent.

7)   Be quick and decisive in responding to avoid the opponents remise of the attack, and vary the parries and ripostes in order to not allow the opponent himself a easy orientation in the conception of opposites.

8)   Do not systematically suffer the opponent's initiative in the attack but limit it by surprising them with actions performed on their time or with timely and appropriate counter attacks.

9)   Using counter time and second intention respectively against opponents' proclivity to exits in time and to the uniformity of the responses, taking present that in fencing habits constitute a defect and therefore avoid incurring the same.

Note - through exercising with multiple opponents weak, against whom worries are limited, not only do you gain confidence in making the shot, either it carried out an attack or response, but it makes itself also easier to study for the development and refinement of the various fencing concepts.

Exercising instead with opponents the same strength develops the sense of emulation resulting in strengthening of volitional faculties, given the natural desire that each of us must overcome the antagonist.

Against the stronger fencer you measure your degree of progress in relation to endurance and contrast that you are able to oppose them.

THE EPEE

LA SPADA

METODO DEL MAESTRO CAPOSCUOLA

GIUSEPPE MANGIARO

Originally printed

ITALIAN FENCING FEDERATION – SCUOLA CENTRALE DELLO SPORT

MILANO 1071

Maestro Giuseppe Mangiarotti

« The Epee » is part of the series of treatises that the F.I.S. is completing. To "Il Fioretto", therefore, it is added today this treatise by Giuseppe Mangiarotti in care of his son Edoardo.

The disappearance of the great Master and Head of the school Italian epee Giuseppe Mangiarotti induced his son Edoardo, great interpreter of his Father's ideas, if desired rearrange for the Federation all the material he owns that his father had been preparing for some time. If then the publication of the treaty on the epee has lost the great signature paternal, we must however recognize that ideas and beliefs in fencing, which were the great heritage of the Lombard master, were lovingly cared for and expressed.
Edoardo, for his part, undoubtedly gave to this publication a practical and easy-going sense, which was already a great prerogative of his father, who found in his son a very valid exemplifier.

The F.I.S., through me and with this preface, once again to demonstrate the widest liberality of ideas and principles.

It is undoubtedly symptomatic that I am the one presenting this volume as the differences in approach are known to fencing between my school and that of Edward. Mine is a dutiful act of recognition of unforgettable merits acquired by Maestro Giuseppe Mangiarotti, merits that have been given to Italy by many if the greatest champions of this weapon.

We will therefore find some terminologies in this treatise and concepts that differ from those expressed in the foil treatise, even if they reflect the same topics of fencing. But fencing also through different statements can only remain the same.
Undoubtedly the Mangiarotti school represented, not only in Italy, but in old Europe and therefore all over the world, an advanced tip of the most modern orientations of the triangular weapon and is an example of perfect fusion between the classical Italian and French schools and a third concept, the fundamental, perhaps, determinate by the genius of a modern view of combat, in the reflexes of a weapon completely different from that one that the swordsmen of fifty years ago wielded.

Maestro Giuseppe Mangiarotti undoubtedly, with a sense of foresight and practicality, absorbing how much better in foreign schools and in the Italian one, partly through a study on the purposes that he re-proposed the same weapon and partly out of his own instinct, he created a school of swordsmanship that he knew in short order of time to achieve the greatest successes in the national field and international. And from the rosary of his students, the Olympic and world champions gradually rattled off:

Allocchio, Marrazzi, Cuccia, Minoli Renzo, Cornaggia, Riccardi, Agostoni, Bertolaia, Brusati, Mangiarotti Edoardo and Dario, Mandruzzato. Marini Renzo, Dellantonio, Colombetti, Predaroli, Breda.

But Giuseppe Mangiarotti doesn't just create a school, he also creates a family of fencers. And as in oldest Italian tradition that is lost in past centuries, he also convinces his wife Rosa to transform into suitable fencer, one of the few worthy of her time of this name. Also, the three sons Dario, Edoardo and Mario they soon reach the "national" and with it the majority of great results in the world field. Olympic titles do beautiful display among the decorations of Edoardo and Dario. Edoardo then collected 19 gold medals alone, among others.

Olympics and World Championships and makes the name shine of the Mangiarotti school of the greatest splendor.

We can consider this treatise as a work posthumously and a fair recognition from Italian fencing of fencing-masterful and human values which animated Giuseppe Mangiarotti throughout his life, caught by death still working for Italian fencing.

Renzo Nostini

THE EPEE COMPETITIVE WEAPON

The epee, as a competitive weapon, was born in France, Paris at the beginning of the 20th century, in the Hall of Arms of Master Baudry, at least fifteen years before he came known in Italy.

In France they were pioneers, as well as very expert and excellent examples, Joseph Renaud, Bruneau de Labori, Sulzbacher, all journalists and students of the Headmaster Baudry.

In Italy the initiators were Maestro Luigi Colombetti in Turin, and Maestro Giuseppe Mangiarotti in Milan. The first learned the sword from Joseph Renaud who in at that time he was in Turin to further his studies in the Royal Armory; the second by Maestro Lancia di Brolo, which he had received in Paris, returning from Buenos Ayres from Baudry himself the guiding principles of the new one weapon.

The epee, like the foil, the point leads the weapon, but from this differs in the practical concepts of its technique and its regulatory principles.

While in foil and saber the right to touch is subordinated to academic rules and conventions, in the epee the aim is to touch before being touched and the twentieth of a second establishes the time limit for the double hit that in this weapon, unlike the others, it is counted to the detriment of the two shooters.

In epee the whole body is a valid target including the foreparts (hands, arms, legs, head) which makes it stand out to complete his offense and defense technique with respect to that of foil and saber which have limited targets.

The epee that was taught to the current levies of swordsmen it is extremely incomplete and too in conformity with that of foil. In Italy, then, the real epee is known by few master's and for this reason it is not taught with sufficient fervor and talent. For this state of affairs, the result is that our epeeists are technically limited; they disdain actions at the foreparts and almost attack always directly to the body, while they are precisely the foreparts the most easily vulnerable both in relation to measure, both at the execution time of each individual action and then similarly to the recording speed from part of the electrical scoring apparatus.

The opinion has been generated that, due to the flattened tip, it is no longer possible to stop the thrusts on the arm. It is certain that the executive difficulties have increased in comparison to the aggressiveness of the knurled tip, but the only one the difference lies in the need to "put it in your hands". aim with appropriate exercises.

In fact, the real strength of the Soviets and the Hungarians, which in recent years have also prevailed in arms triangular, lies in their general technical completeness and in the particularity of being precise and capable of shooting both first, and of second intention, as of counterattack and of counteroffensive considering first of all the foreparts Teaching the epee with almost identical methodology of foil, leading to the standardization of fencing of flagship weapons, it is a big and obvious mistake. The foil and the epee are completely different weapons and on the plane of technical, tactical, and specialization is therefore necessary, even if it is always possible for a fencer, expert and knowledgeable in successfully practicing the two weapons.

With specific reference to the lesson, so that the student can achieve satisfactory goals, it is necessary for the teacher to combine appropriate skills, technical in nature, others of psychological and didactic capacity. It follows that the lesson, considering different degrees of learning, must be formative, theoretical-technical, executive, tactical, competitive.

Muscular and mental maturity of the student must be achieved through a gradual process. and coordinated methodology, to confer their agility, precision, elasticity, speed, endurance and confidence; equally with will and determination, indispensable qualities. to emerge and assert themselves.

CHAPTER I

THE ESSENTIAL ELEMENTS OF THE EPEE MOVEMENTS AND ACTIONS

(GLI ELEMENTI ESSENZIALI DELLA SPADA

I MOVIMENTI, LE AZIONI)

Nomenclature of the Epee *(Nomemclatura della spada)*

The Epee, like the foil is a point weapon and is made up of the *guard* and the *blade* The guard defends the hand and part of the wrist, we present the following elements:

1- **The Guard**. *(la coccia)* This is made of aluminum or similar material. It has the shape of a half sphere with a maximum diameter of 135mm and carries in the center to slightly off center a rectangular hole through which the blade shank passes. In the Italian epee, the hole is wider to allow the ricasso to pass through as like the Italian Foil.
2- **The Handle**. *(Il manico)* This can be either wooden, aluminum or plastic. It is internally drilled to allow the passage of the tang. The shape of the handle changes depending on whether it is an Italian, model, orthopedic or French.

3- **The Pommel**. *(Il pomolo)* Being conical, cylindrical, nut, etc. *see model type* made of iron, aluminum, steel etc. this is screwed onto the end of the tang, and it holds the blade, guard, and handle together.

4- **Accessories**. *(Gli accessori)* Usually a cushion made of leather, fabric, rubber is placed in the concave part of the guard. Furthermore, that part of the electrical equipment will be mentioned later.

The blade in turn has the following characteristics:

It is made of tempered steel, has a triangular cross section, and a button on the tip made of the steel itself is standard. For electrical, the blade ends at the tip with a threaded screw of 3.5mm and threading allowing for the point to be attached.

A. There is the "ricasso" on the classic Italian model, therefore the shank *(codolo)*, which passes through the handle (however the latter is done) and the end of the tang is threaded to which the pommel is threaded. In the main recess of the blade is the channel in which the wire is glued for the electrical scoring apparatus.

B. The length if the blade cannot exceed 900mm measured from the upper spherical part of the guard-including the very tip of the signal button.

The blade of the epee, like that of the foil, is ideologically divided into three equal parts called degrees according to ancient terminology. The sector near the guard takes the name of strong *forte* and is equal to one third the length of the blade, the middle part is called middle *medio* and the sector near the tip is called the weak, *debole.*

The most used epee handle in Italy and abroad is called 'orthopedic', however some prefer the French model.

The classic Italian model epee, which is held like the foil, has lost many followers, especially after the use of the electric signaling of the hits.

Balance, weight, and length of the epee *(Equilibrio, peso e lunghezza della spada)*

As with other weapons, there is a standard balance for the epee, which is felt by holding the weapon. Usually, the center of gravity is placed 3.5 or 4 cm from the convex side of the guard, but this is not to be taken as an absolute: there are fencers who, for their game, prefer to have a greater weight towards the tip of the epee and others toward the handle.

The total weight of the epee should not exceed 770 grams: the total length must not in any way exceed 110cm measured from the ends of the tip to the last point of the pommel or handle depending on the type.

Way to hold the epee *(Modo di impugnare la spada)*

The French model with a straight handle is held in full hand, with the index finger extended along the handle and holding the weapon by the pomolo or nut.

In the case of the orthopedic handle, the shape itself forces the hand and fingers into the special housing.

The classic Italian model holds itself like that of the Italian Foil.

To hold the epee well, forcefully and at the same time without any rigidity is of utmost importance. The fencing of epee theoretically includes all actions that can be performed in the theory and, in addition, those characteristics of the weapon, of which are aimed at targets (hand, arm, mask, legs and feet) that are difficult to reach if you are unable to apply particular techniques and tactics: to this, therefore, very careful attention must be paid to how one holds the epee.

First position *(La prima posizione)*

This is the position the fencer takes as soon as they get on the fencing strip.

One turns the body to the side, with the heels in contact so as to form a ninety-degree angle. The tip of the front foot is directed towards the adversary, the legs stretched effortlessly, and the torso erect, shoulders open and level, head high, gaze turned to the opponent, the unarmed hand rests on the back hip, with the thumb and index finger forked resting on the top of the hip and the elbow bent.

The epee, grasped in the prescribed way, is placed by the back side (hip) with the arm naturally at rest on the hip, the blade is inclined backwards, so that the tip is behind the rear foot and a few centimeters from the ground.

The line of offense *(La linea di offesa)*

The epee is in line of offense when the weapon is held with the hand in fourth hand position and the arm is naturally stretched without contracting the muscles of the hand it rises to the height of the shoulder. The armed arm forms a single line from the tip of the weapon to the shoulder.

This position constantly threatens the opponent and, at the same time, guarantees one's arm from the opposing hits on the same line, but not from angulations of the line.

The line of direction *(La linea direttrice)*

This is the imaginary line for movement drawn on the middle of the fencing strip:

Passing through the right foot and the heel of the left foot of the fencer who is on the fencing strip and on guard. (vice versa if left-handed).

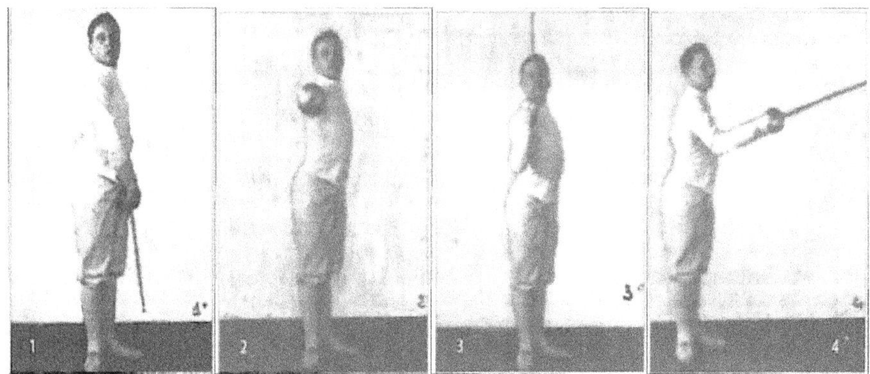

1. First postizion – 2. Blade in line – 3. The salute – 4. The salute

The salute *(Il saluto)*

The salute is a mandatory curtsey both to the adversary and to the people present, both in didactic exercises and in assaults, it is done as follows:

1- From first position, in front of the opponent, the sword is brought into the line of offense describing an arc close to the body so that the hand is at the height of the right shoulder and the tip, hand and shoulder form a single line: then the arm is flexed in so that the hand is as the height of the chin, the tip pointed up, the elbow tightened to the body and the nails facing the chest, forming a single line between the tip, the hand and the elbow.

2- From this position, he stretches out his arm and puts his epee back in the line of offense, with the hand in fourth position, in doing so he greets the opponent.

3- To greet the bystanders who are on the left, facing the head towards that side, the arm is flexed again, as in the first movement, and it is extended to the left, with the hand turned to third and fourth position.

4- The greeting to those on the right side is similarly rendered. With the hand turned from second and third hand position, after which he takes first position again.

The guard *(La Guardia)*

This is the position that the fencer takes with the body and weapon to be ready for offense, defense, and counter offensive actions.

From first position one goes on guard as follows:

1- The epee is brought into the offensive line describing an arc from bottom up and, at the same time, the non-weapon arm is extended, thus forming a single straight line with the other arm and the weapon (parallel to the floor).

2- Bringing the front foot forward about a foot and a half by while at the same time bending the legs so that the back knee is perpendicular to the tip of the corresponding foot, and the front knee is perpendicular to the tip of the front foot. At the same time, fold the defenseless arm into an arch, with the elbow slightly higher than the shoulder and with the hand is a semi-abandonment towards the head.

In the guard position the weight of the body must be distributed equally on the two legs, the head in a normal position, rotated with the gaze turned to the front toward the adversary. The body is more erect and with less leg opening than in the foil guard and this is to offer fewer advanced targets to the adversary. The arm that holds the weapon must be kept almost in the line of offense: the bend of the elbow must be minimal. The hand in fourth hand position and the conical shape of the guard slightly in opposition from the adversary to obtain continuous coverage of the arm. Returning to the first position from the guard keeping the order of movements in reverse.

Measure *(La misura)*

It is called the measure as it refers to the space between the valid target of the two fencers in a given moment of the fight.

For the executive educational purposes, consider the five measures on which the student will have to repeatedly practice the execution of appropriate actions.

- **Tight measure** - (stretta misura) when two fencers are close enough to hit each other in the torso without extending.

- **Stationary**- (da fermo) when two fencers can touch each other, by extending their arms without going into the lunge.

- **Lunging**- (D'allungo) when the lunge is necessary to touch the opponent.

- **Step and lunge** (camminando)- when to be able to touch the adversary one must first move forward a step before lunging.

- **Long measure** (lunga misura)- to perform actions on the forward target and on the arm, for the application of second and third intention.

In particular to epee, the step and lunge it is preferred to apply with the step the arrow running attack (la frecciata) rather than the step forward and lunge because with a step and lunge a response could be the arrest would be easy to perform against this.

Blade online offense

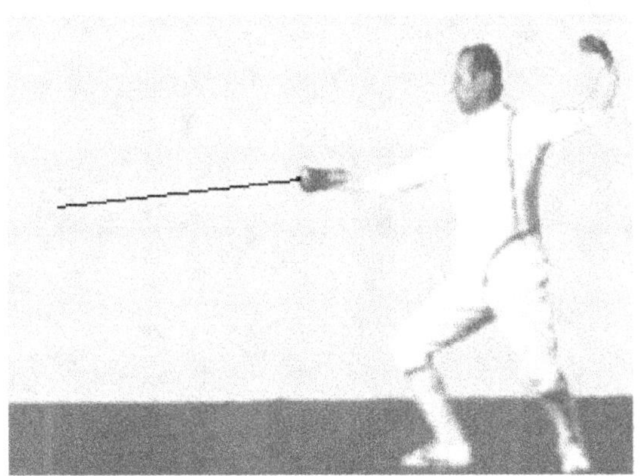

Classic guard with slight bend at the elbow

Blade in line

Blade in line, front view   Guard with invitation

Correct measure to hit the weist

Note: in the assault the appropriate and prudential measure to thrust at the opponent's wrist with a lunge. Note the armored arm covers their target with appropriate opposition. In the depth the armed arm is raised to the level of the face.

The lunge *(L'a-fondo)*

The lunge is the position in which the fencer finds themselves after the attack on the adversary.

This is done as follows: With absolute priority of the point of the epee and without giving rise or undulations, extension of the arm is completed, followed by the forward movement of the torso; then without the slightest interruption, the front foot is brought forward, touching the ground, as far as possible, while a simultaneous and rapid extension of the back leg is performed.

Simultaneously, the defenseless arm extends energetically backwards, but naturally stopping it parallel to the leg. The head must remain extraneous to the movement, as well as the shoulders must remain relaxed and at the same level.

In the lunge position the torso must be kept erect and the knee of the front leg must be perpendicular to the toe of the foot.

The bell guard must be exploited, and this is only possible if the hand is brought to a high horizontal offensive plane.

The longest extension of the lunge must be achieved by trying to break the flank as far as possible by moving the pelvis forward: which is easily achieved with the appropriate springing exercise. Balancing the trunk of the body on the two legs and from the maximum split between the feet.

The epeeist performing the lunge must maintain their torso erect and bringing the armed arm to face level. The rationality of the movement consists precisely in not exposing to the adversary's arrest to one's advanced target and , at the same time, be able to have the muscles of the lower limbs in the most suitable condition to develop immediately and promptly the counter offensive or defensive movements.

Step forward and step backward *(Il passo avanti e il passo indietro)*

These forward and backward movements are carried out to vary the measurement by moving the front foot forward by one foot and a half and bringing the other foot under the same space, respectively, in the forward step. Vice versa in the backward step.

The step forward and back must be elastic and decisive.

You do not drag your foot, let alone hit it on the piste, on the other hand, the movement must be performed with a regular and loose walk: the step must be relaxed, prompt and, by remaining in the guard position with completed movements, one must avoid remaining in muscle contraction.

Keep in mind that in fencing all expressions of strength and contraction delay the execution of even simple movements.

Step and lunge *(Il passo avanti a-fondo)*

This is an advance movement to hit the opponent consisting of a step forward immediately followed by the luge.

Jump back *(Il salto indietro)*

This is a defensive, backward movement which allows you to quickly get out of distance. It is carried out from both the guard and the lunge. In the first case it can advantageously replace the double step back, in the second it replaces the return of guard and step back.

It is carried out by leveraging off the front leg, shooting backwards so as to remain in suspension on the back leg, coming to rest on the other when returning to the guard position. (see defense chapter)

Return on guard *(Il retorno in guardia)*

This is a movement that brings the attacker back to the guard after the lunge. For the purpose of a prompt defense, it must be as quick as possible and must therefore be particularly exercised, in order to pass from the exhaustion of the offensive action, on guard, ready again for the offense and defense.

Renewed attack *(ripresa d'attacco)*

This is an offensive movement preformed after an attack and returning to the guard by recovering forward being ready for a new offensive action on the opponent who parries without responding, with the blade, by measure or with blade and measure.

Gain on the lunge or renewed attack *(Il raddoppio o ripresa dell'a-fondo)*

It is a movement to bring an offensive action that is carried out from the lunge after the attack has taken place on the opponent who defends by measure or by blade and measurement and does not respond with a riposte.

The fleche / Arrow *(frecciata)*

This is an explosive forward movement that is executed from either lunge or the step forward and lunge distance, one must give a higher precedence of the tip than any other attacking movement. Exploit at the same time the athletic principles of the arms throwing to aid in the movement, the rush of the fast launch and the momentum of the jump forward. It is performed by throwing the armed arm into the offensive line with the appropriate hand opposition.

How this is executed, at the same time the profiled body leans far forward, pivoting on the front leg until the loss of balance. Meanwhile the unarmed arm descends backwards to counterbalance the movement. Reaching the diagonal, the arm armed in line, left leg stretched out, shot forward by levering on the front leg and the back leg is brought forward to regain the balance of the body. (For left handers vice versa)

Stop the inertia of the arrow with the legs having moved forward and to the opposite side of the armed arm of the opponent. It is performed both in attack, riposte, counter-offensive, or renewed attack. It is particularly effective if performed with a preordained intention.

The arrow is preformed not only from the guard, but also from the lunge.

Compared to the foil, the line of attack is higher and is of fundamental detail and importance. The advanced targets must be covered with the appropriate opposition whether it is attacked in a free blade or whether it is attacked on the blade. As a principle, the arrow off the blade is directed to the forward target. If you want to touch the body, it is advisable to take the blade to avoid the arrest of the opponent and in any case the occurrence of the double touch.

For these reasons the safest shot in the arrow is the one taken with one's own choice of time in the third line and appropriate hand opposition. The free arrow attack intentionally performed on the attacker who stops, or attacks can facilitate the success of the double touch by pulling on the hit when this is advantageous for the purposes of scoring or to conclude a match in your favor.

The counter-offensive actions performed in the arrow represent, on the tactical level, the most radical and realizing evolution of the fencing bout. From a defensive-offensive tactic we moved on to the diametrically opposed offensive-defensive tactic, that is, of the counterattack tactic which in fencing terms means to counterattack in second and third intention arrows after having brought the opponent to a reactive action.

The attacks using the arrow can be made to the body or arm, with all the attack variations possible on the four lines and precisely:

- Counteroffensive (direct or indirect riposte)
- Continuation of the attack following the lunge
- In counterattack (pulling in anticipation of the opponent's attack)
- By glide
- By blade seizure
- Transports
- Beats
- Change beat
- Counter time
- The remise of the attack or renewed attack

The renewed attack from the lunge

From the lunge, bring the back foot into contact with the front heel while keeping the knees well be

Followed by driving the front foot forward keeping the knee over the foot in the lunge.

The arrow (fleche)

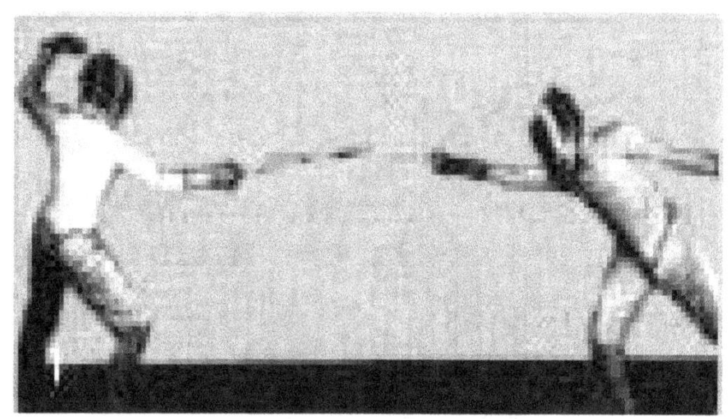

Armed hand shoots out first

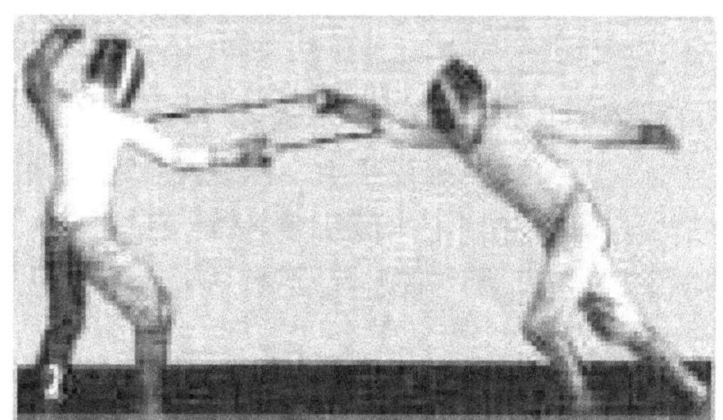

Touch arrives

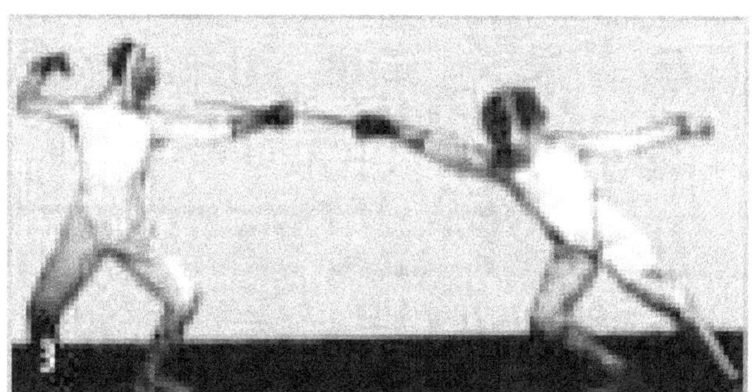

Against the left-handed opponent

Touch arrives with opposition

The arrow in counterattack

This is performed on the backward imbalance of the opponent following a jump back, that is, with preordained counteroffensive action

The arrow with ceding parry

Against the opponent who parries with the blade and measure, without riposting, at the end of the arrow, use a ceding movement under the blade and continue the attack touching the opponent with clear precedence on the following riposte.

Coordination exercises *(Esercizi di coordinamento)*

In order to achieve absolute mastery of the movements, coordination and stability; to increase the speed of execution or to suitably vary the rhythm, the following exercises must be performed and repeated over and over again: step forward with arm extension in the offensive line-step backwards bringing the arm back to the guard in the line of offense with precedence of the extension of the arm- return to guard (like a spring that recharges)- step forward to lunge with progressive speed (like a spring that discharges)- recover from the lunge keeping the knees

231

flexed and the upper body erect-jump backwards falling on the front leg, standing with the back arm in line with the armed arm in the line of offense reasemblement.

Exercise with the legs *(Esercizi per le gambe*

If you want from the beginning to give perfect stability (balance) and ease of movement to the student, it is necessary that they work daily on the following exercises in which all possible movements on movements related to the execution of fencing in general are combined with a logical sequence:

- Step forward
- Step backward
- Step and lunge
- Raddoppio (back foot step and lunge)
- From the lunge, jump backward or recover
- Lunge recover and lunge again
- Spring forward from the lunge
- Form the lunge bring the weight of the body forward leaning on the front knee and arrow.

Springing *(molleggio)*

The springing is carried out from the lunge position, moving the pelvis forward, breaking the flank to the maximum with a continuous movement of pressure of the weight of the body from top to bottom and vice versa, so as to bring during the movement the knee of the front leg perpendicular to the toe. The rear arm raises and lowers following the movement of the body: it lowers in relaxation and rises in the return movement.

The positions of the armed hand

The bell guard (coccia) is the shield protecting the arm. The most logical position is that the blade is in line, with the hand in fourth position with opposition in third.

Naturally the opposition does not have to imply a total displacement of the forearm in third, otherwise we would find ourselves inviting in third and in doing so, exposing the internal targets. Even if the tip of the epee remains threatening the forward target of the opponent, constitutes sufficient guarantee for an immediate arrest (counterattack).

The positions of the weapon arm and the lines relative to the targets

2nd external low target, 1st or mezzo chio: inside low target

The lines and targets *(Le linee ed I bersagli)*

The offense lines are closely related to the target you want to hit. In epee the valid target is divided into four sectors in relation to the body of the fencer in the guard position. These targets are:

- High inside (chest) to which the fourth line corresponds
- External top (chest, back) which corresponds to the third line
- Internal lower part (abdomen) to which first or mezzocherchio
- External low (flank) to which second or octave line corresponds

Similarly, the targets can be considered: high, low, internal, and external.

Since the whole body is a valid target, the epeeist must keep the fact in mind and practice applying all the actions (being offensive or defensive) on the different targets, with particular attention to the hand, arm, legs, and mask foreparts. If the opponent's guard position is exposed, with obvious disclosure.

The positions of the arm *(Le Posizioni del braccio armato)*

When the arm moves from the normal or guard position to perform offensive or defensive actions, it assumes four fundamental positions:

- Fourth, relating to the line and the internal high target
- Third, relating to the line and external high target.
- First, (mezzocerchio) relative to the line and the lower internal target (abdomen)
- Second (or eighth) relative to the line and the low external target (flank)

The positions of the armed hand *(Le Posizione del pugno armato)*

The fundamental position for an epeeist is: in the third line with the hand in fourth position, accentuating the advanced position of the arm that holds the weapon (elbow slightly bent) and maintaining an appropriate opposition. From this basic attitude it is easy to move to any other position in the four lines. The armed hand can take different positions. The fundamental hand positions are:

- **The guard-** *(la guardia)* hand in fourth position with opposition in the third line
- **Fourth-** *(di quarta)* thumb up and nails of the other fingers inside
- **Third- (di terza)** thumb on the outside and nails on the other fingers upwards
- **Second- (di seconda)** thumb down and nails of the other fingers on the outside
- **Octave-** (di ottava) with the hand in fourth and second-hand position
- **First-** *(di prima)* thumb down and nails from the other fingers outwards, completely turned upwards
- **Half circle- (mezzocerchio)** with the hand in fourth position in the first line.

The invitation *(L'invito)*

This is an attitude of second intention that serves to uncover a target, so that the opponent is induced to hit it. There are four invitations which correspond to as many targets:

- Invitation of fourth, which uncovers the external target
- Invitation of third, which uncovers the internal target
- Invitation of second or eighth, which uncovers the upper target
- Invitation of first or mezzocerchio which uncovers the lower target

The invitation of fourth *(invito di quarta)* is made by folding the arm and turning the hand to third and fourth hand position which, at the same time is lowered almost to the height of the abdomen with the tip somewhat higher than the hand.

This attitude uncovers the arm from the outside, the chest, the mask, the flank, the leg and foot.

The invitation of third *(invito di terza)* is made by folding the arm and bringing the hand to the chest height, hand kept in fourth hand position or held in second and third position The tip must be a little higher than the hand.

This invitation uncovers the arm, the chest from the inside, the mask, the abdomen, the leg, and foot.

The invitation of second *(invito di seconda o ottava)* is made by lowering the hand in fourth position to the height of the flank while slightly bending the arm. The weapon must be almost horizontal and the tip not too far from the opposing side.

In this invitation exposes the upper arm, chest, and mask.

The invitation of first or mezzocerchio *(invito di prima o mezzocerchio)* is carried out by moving the epee to your left (to the right if left-handed) remaining the hand in fourth hand position, thus forming a single line between the arm and tip, so that it is at the height of the flank of the opponent.

This attitude uncovers the arm, the side and mask, it is advisable to keep at step and lunge distance.

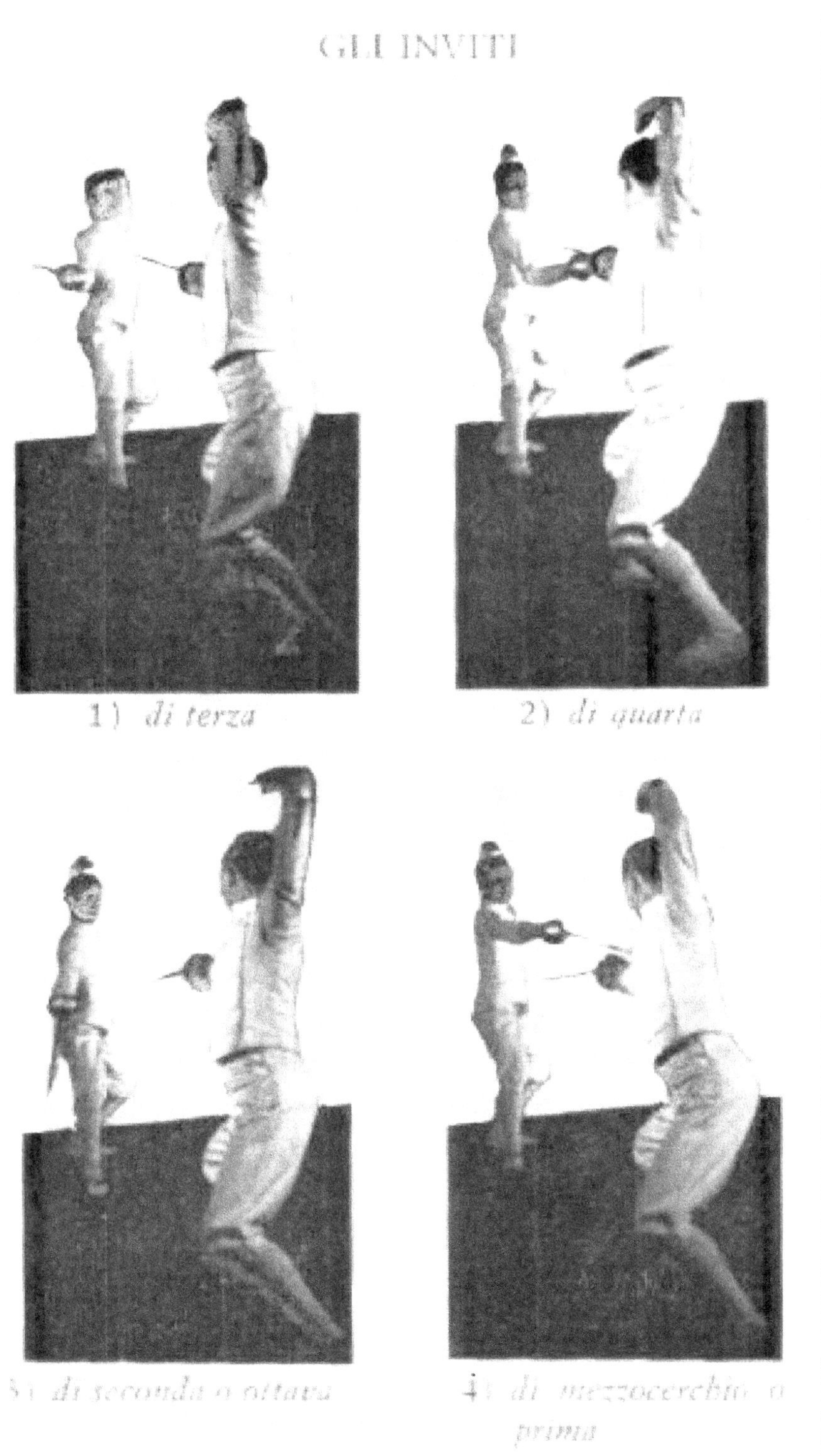

1) *di terza* 2) *di quarta*

3) *di seconda o ottava* 4) *di mezzocerchio o prima*

The engagement *(Il legamento)*

This is the movement of the blade where as it comes into contact with the opponent's blade who is in a certain position or line.

By engagement we also mean that contact that is established between the two blades, so that one's own dominates the opposing one by deviating it from the line and thus discovering an opposing target.

In order to accomplish this at correct distance (misura di allungo), it is necessary that your own strong of the epee is opposite to the weak of the opposing blade; if by step and lunge measure, the contact must be middle to weak.

The engagements, like the invitations, are four:

- Fourth
- Third
- Second
- First or mezzocerchio

These are performed with the same hand positions held for the invitations.

Engagements can be performed as much from the attitude of blade in line as well from the invitation. Note that the engagements described above may vary due to size.

Change of engagement *(I cambiamenti di legamento)*

238

From one engagement it is possible to pass to another by means of a suitable hand movement, accompanied by the forearm so that the opposing blade comes to be tied in the new position. These changes can be made:

- From fourth to third or inversely by passing the point under the opponent's blade
- From second to first and inversely by passing the point above the blade
- From second to fourth and inversely
- From third to first and inversely

In the first two cases the blade must be detached for an instant from the opponent's iron, losing its contact with the movement similar to that of a circular parry, in the second two cases the contact must be constantly maintained, carrying out a movement similar to that of a half circular parry. (in this case they are called transports)

During the attack, these movements can be particularly useful both to disturb the opponent in the moment in which he meditated an attack, and to surprise him with an unexpected attack by the new engagement. They can be performed both lunge or step and lunge distance.

The envelopment *(Il riporto)*

This is an action exercised in contact with the opponent's blade. It is carried out by making a circular movement with the weapon hand, without detaching the weapon from your strong of the blade, all accompanied by the forearm as if you wanted to parry counter and returning to the same placement as before.

There are four envelopments: for mezzocerchio and second you pass the point of your weapon over the opposing blade, and for third and fourth one passes below the blade.

The implementation must be balanced, without sudden movements that would make the blade escape and, therefore, betray the purpose of the action. They can be performed both from

Mancino su destro: in linea di terza alta e colpo alla maschera

Mancino su destro: in linea di mezzocerchio (prima) e colpo al ginocchio

lunging distance and by step forward and lunge distance, always preceding with the blade. In the envelopments the same rules as for the engagement are observed.

Pressures *(La pressione)*

Once the engagement has occurred, pressure is made on the opposing blade, imparting a decisive movement of the opponents weak made in the same direction of the engagement.

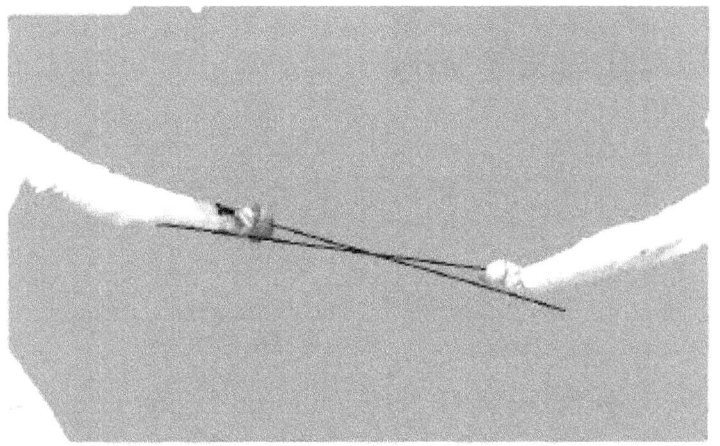

Destra su mancino, presa di ferro in seconda (pugno di seconda) e filo al braccio sotto

Destro su mancino, presa di ferro in mezzocerchio (pugno di quarta) e filo al ginocchio

Mancino su destro in linea di terza

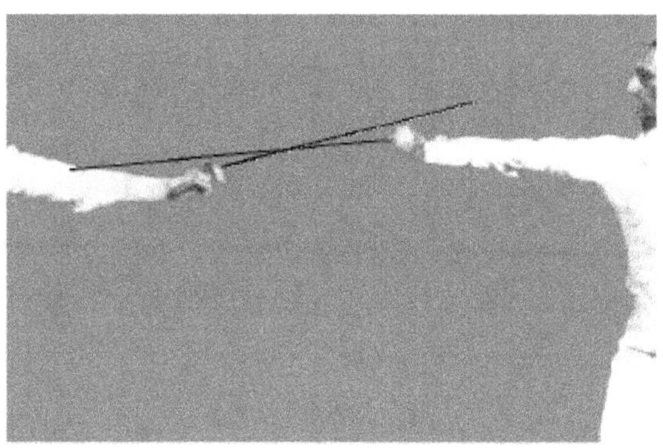

Destro su mancino in linea di terza e colpo al braccio sopra

Blade seizure or change beat *(La presa di ferro o intrecciata)*

The focus of this action is to take possession of the opponent's blade and can be performed in all four lines, both starting with the blade from the guard or from another placement of the weapon.

In the first case, the movement to pick up the blade (in a simple or compound rotational sense) starts from the position of the guard and ends in the position on which one went to take possession of the opponent's blade. In the second case, a blade transport must be implicitly carried out from the line making the movement to the ending in the same line as started.

It is carried out with an accentuated intrusion of one's own blade towards that of the opponent, preferably with a step forward, and this is to ensure the domination of the opposing blade and to prevent direct arrest or disengagement in time. The blade is taken with the strong degree of the blade, exploiting the triangulation between the strong of your blade, the bell guard and the weak of the opponent's blade, a device which accentuates the effectiveness of the position of the hand and therefore, of the covering of the attack.

Simple or compound transports *(I transporti semplici e composti)*

These actions are carried out by taking the opponent's blade with the strength of your own blade, taking a long step forward: from the engagement in fourth, without leaving the blade, a counter of fourth is performed in a close and continuous contact with the opponent's' blade, returning then to the starting point.

This is done similarly in the other three lines.

In the case of double or compound transports, the same movement must be performed twice consecutively.

Transport of the opponent's blade, simple and compound, can be carried out in the four simple lines, while for the half circular passages a change in the line is required.

Direct transports are:

- From fourth to fourth
- From third to third
- From eight to eight
- From first (mezzocerchio) to first (m) and so it is with compounds.

The ceding *(La ceduta)*

This is an offensive and defensive action, applied in time and carried out when one's blade is subjected to the opponent's engagement, pressure, glide, blade seizure or change beat and it consists in avoiding the displacement of the opposing blade in reaching the target with appropriate angulated yielding of your blade with respect to the opponent's.

In addition to the opponent's initiative, the cede can be applied simultaneously on the parrying movement of the attacker in the high lines, thus anticipating the immediate response (see defense chapter).

THE ELEMENTS ESSENTIAL TO EPEE
GLI ELEMENTI ESSENZIALI DELLA SPADA

THE MOVEMENTS AND ACTIONS
I MOVIMENTI, LE AZIONE

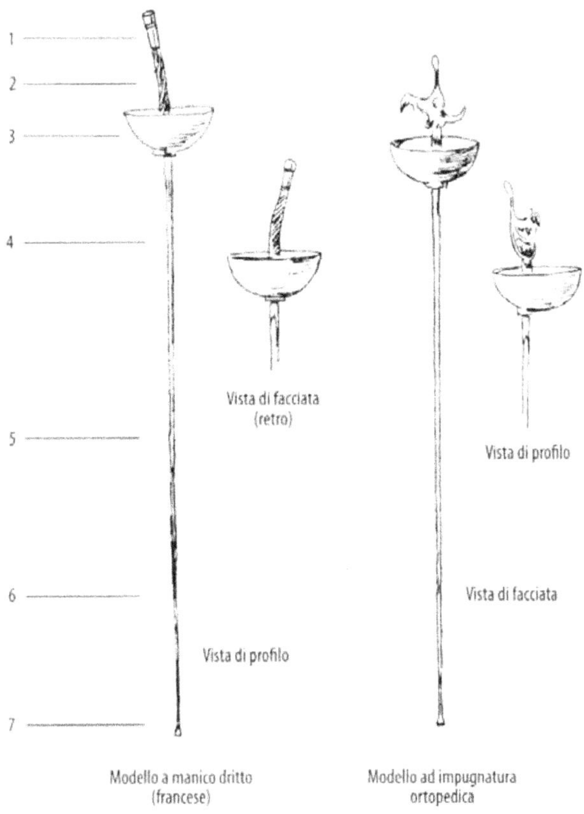

1. Il pomolo (filettato passo metrico 6 mm)
2. Il manico
3. La coccia
4. Il forte della lama o tallone
5. Il medio della lama o parte centrale
6. Il debole della lama o parte terminale
7. La punta (vi è avvitato il bossolo della punta elettrica, passo metrico 4 mm)

1. The pommel (6mm)

2. The handle

3. The bell guard

4. The strong of the blade

5. The medium of the blade, central

6. The weak of the blade

7. The point, (electric point thread is 4mm)

General characteristics of the epee *(Caratteristiche generali della spada)*

Weight *(Peso)*

The total weight of the epee ready to be used is to be less than 770 grams.

Length *(Lunghezza)*

The maximum total length of the epee is 110cm.

Blade *(Lama)*

The blade is made of tempered steel, its section is triangular, without sharp edges. It must be as straight as possible and mounted with the largest flare facing upwards. The width of the triangle must however be less than 1 cm; it is only permitted in the vertical direction.

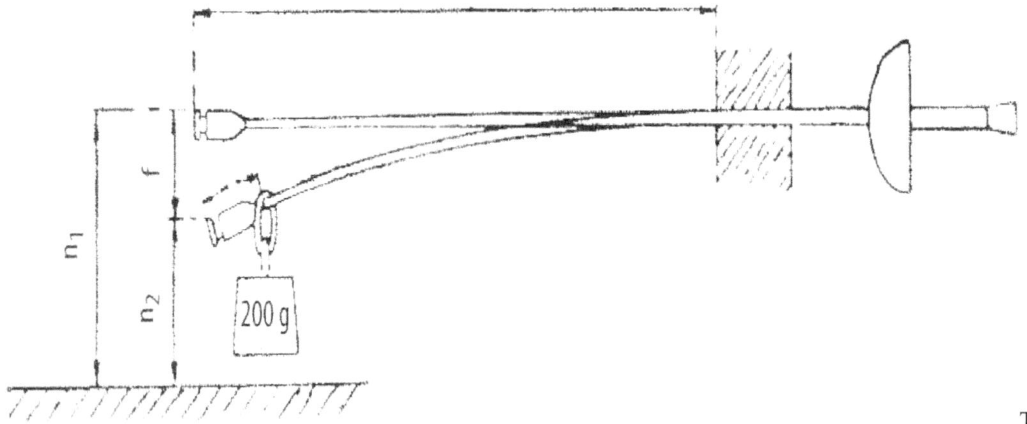

The maximum length of the blade is 90 cm.
The maximum width of any one face of the triangular blade to be the no more than 2.4mm

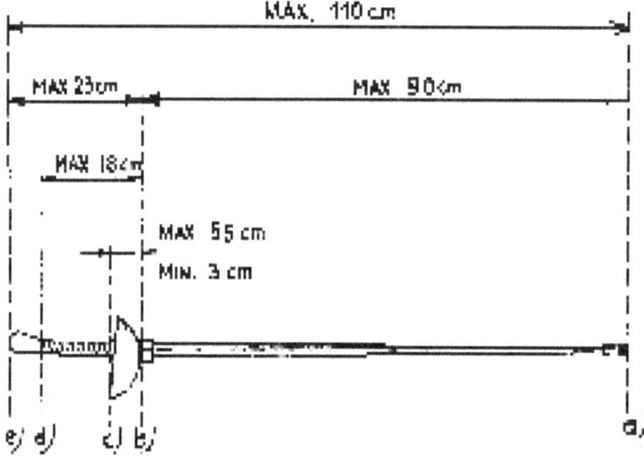

246

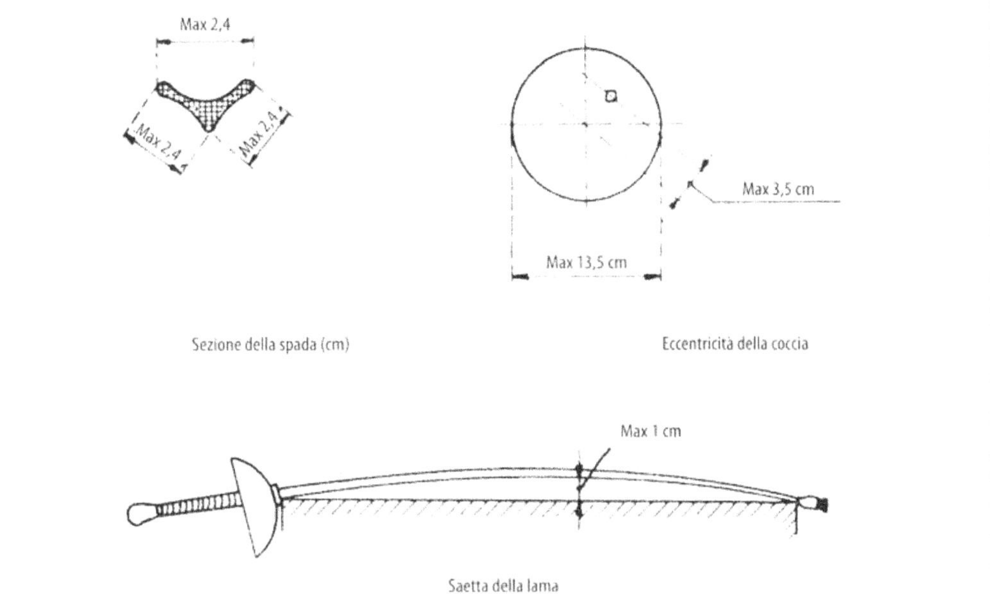

The flexibility of the blade must have a corresponding minimum bend of 4.5cm and a maximum bend of 7cm measured in the following conditions:

1. The blade is fixed horizontally 70cm from the end of the tip;

2. A weight of 200grams suspended 3 cm from the end of the tip;

3. Flexibility is measured at the tip end in the unloaded and loaded position.

Martingale *wrist strap*

If the epee is not joined to the hand of the fencer by an attachment system or electric loop, the use of a martingale is mandatory. (old rule)

Bell Guard *(la coccia)*

The bell guard whose edge must be circular, must pass through a cylinder with a diameter of

13.5 cm and 15 cm in length (gabarit) the depth of the guard is between 3 and 5.5 cm. the eccentricity (distance between the center of the guard and the point where the blade passes through it) is permitted if it does not exceed 3.5 cm. the total length- blade plus guard cannot exceed 95.5 cm.

The Point *(Punta d'arresto)* *international*

a. Per electric point for epee.

1. The tip of the epee blade ends with a point, an electrical switch.
2. It is forbidden to sharpen the corners of the tip.
3. The tip must be fixed securely to the tip of the blade.

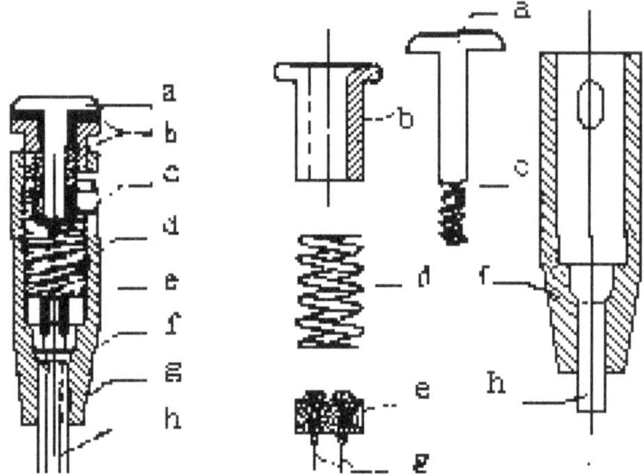

a) crown - b) compass with insulators - c) contact clip - d) weight-repelling spring - e) insulating capsule containing contact pins - f) bushing - g) wires (two) with flat-headed contact pins - h) threaded blade terminal.

4. The pressure from the spring necessary to obtain the release of the point must be higher than 750 grams to push back on the test weight.
5. The travel distance of the tip necessary to make contact for the closing of the circuit to the signaling device cannot be less than 1 mm nor greater than 1 mm.

The additional travel of the stop tip cannot exceed half a millimeter.

b. standard epee

1. If the epee is not wired (standard), then the point must still be the same.
2. Otherwise, the point if not electric must be fixed to the threaded part of the pint of the blade having a minimum diameter of 6mm, fast secured and parallel with the blade and protrude no mare than 2mm past the thread.

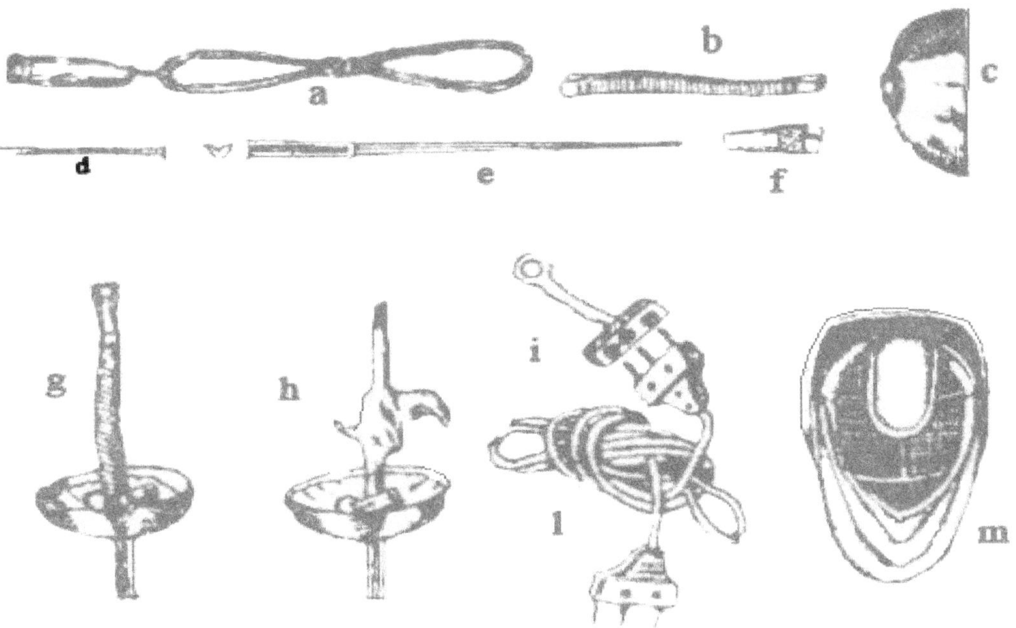

a) tip with wire - b) handle - c) guard - d) threaded blade terminal with tip - e) blade and threaded tang - f) pommel - g) eisa assembly with pin inside guard, French model - guard - h) hilt and pin, orthopedic model - i) internal pin - l) body-through wire - m) mask.

Equipment *(Attrezzatura)*

Mask *(Maschera)*

The mask must not be covered in whole or in part material susceptible to cause the tip to slip when touched. The thread of the mesh, made of steel, must have a minimum section of 1mm. It must also be reinforced by a frame.

Body wire *(Filo di corpo)*

The corde (passing through the fencer's weapon arm) has two ends both with 3 pins. One end for the spool floor cable and the other for the receiver found inside the guard.

1. Have at least double the thickness
2. Move with the body
3. Present the best guarantee of solidness

It can be attached to the vest without entirely being sewn.

Method of holding the epee *(Modi di impugnare la spada)*

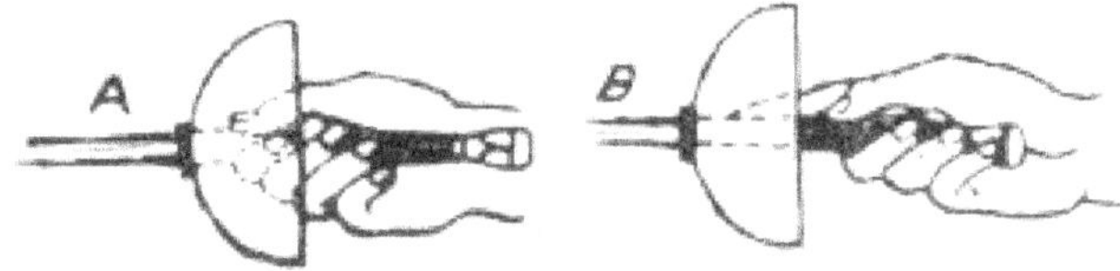

A) Normal   *B)* with extended finger of the straight or French handle sword

C) of the anatomical grip

The target *(Il bersaglio)*

The entire body is valid target

Attitudes of the fencer before going on guard *(Atteggiamenti dello spadista prima di scendere in guardia)*

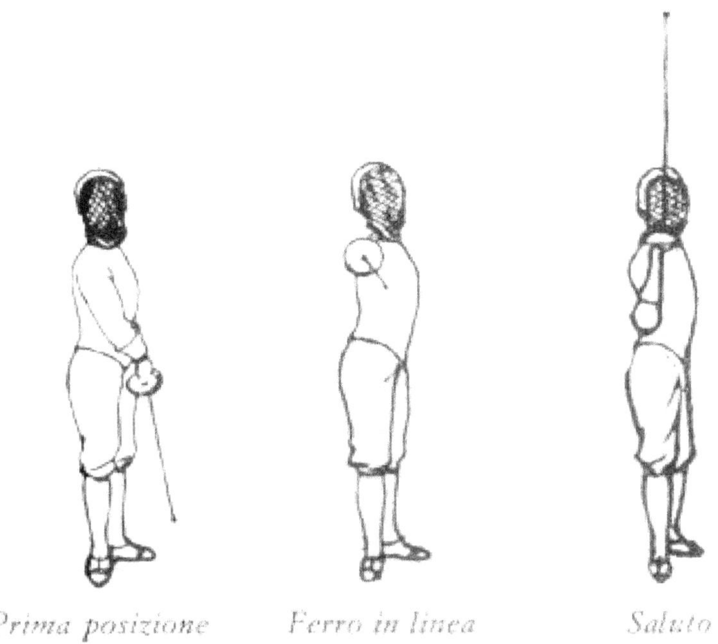

First Position – Blade in line – Salute

The line of offense and line of direction *(La linea di offesa e la linea direttrice)*

a) The line of offense is established by extending the armed arm in a straight line, with the elbow fully extended, at shoulder level of the fencers in the guard position.

A) The guiding line is the line of movement: it runs, imaginatively, between the feet of the fencers

The Guard *(La guardia)*

The guard is higher in relation to that of foil. The tip held a little below the offensive line, arm slightly bent. The feet are orthogonal to each other.

The different degrees of the legs in the guard *(Il compasso della guardia)*

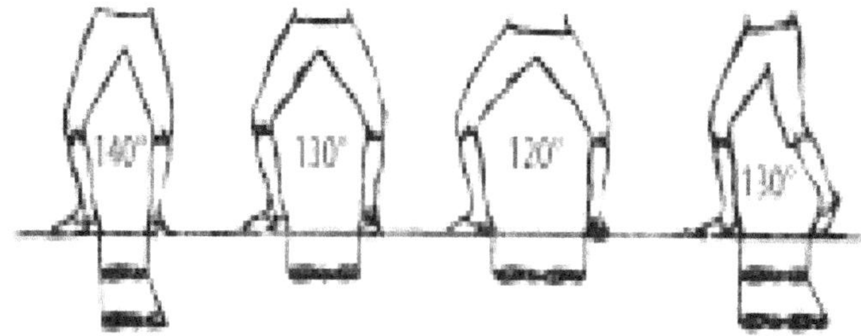

At **140°**, too high; at **130°**, correct and balanced; at **120°**, too wide; at **130°** with the left foot turned inward resting on the sole: competitive position.

Positions of the feet in relation to the line of direction *(Le positure dei piedi rispetto alla linea direttrice)*

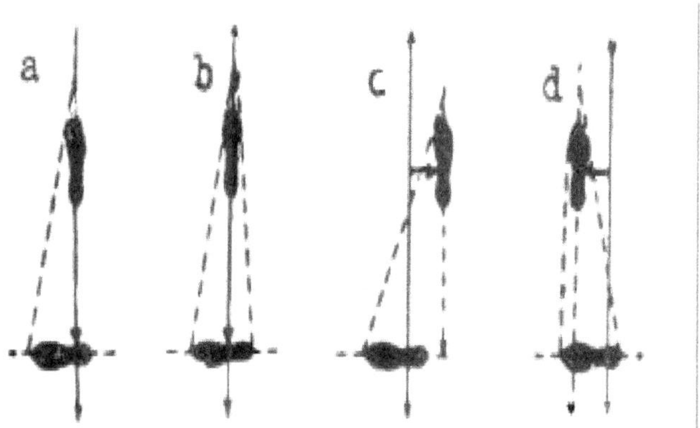

a) Feet orthogonal: right foot aligned with the left heel; - b) Right foot on the same line passing through the center of the left foot; - c) Right foot shifted outward toward the back; - d) Left foot shifted inward toward the abdomen. The most rational and balanced stance is a). (For left-handers, the opposite applies).

Rationality of the guard *(Razionalità della guardia)*

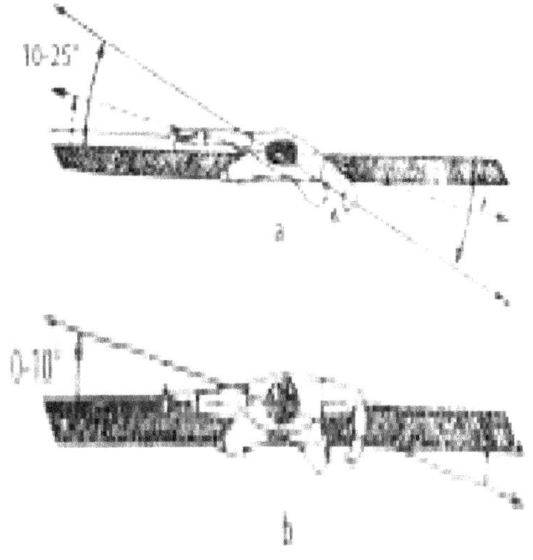

A) The most natural stance is when, relative to the guiding line, the armed arm is positioned at an angle of about 10°, and in relation to the axis passing through the shoulders, it is situated at about 25°.

B) Holding the armed arm on the same guiding line and the axis of the shoulders about 10° off this line creates an artificial position, contradictory to the naturalness and rationality of the movement.

The Measure *(La misura)*

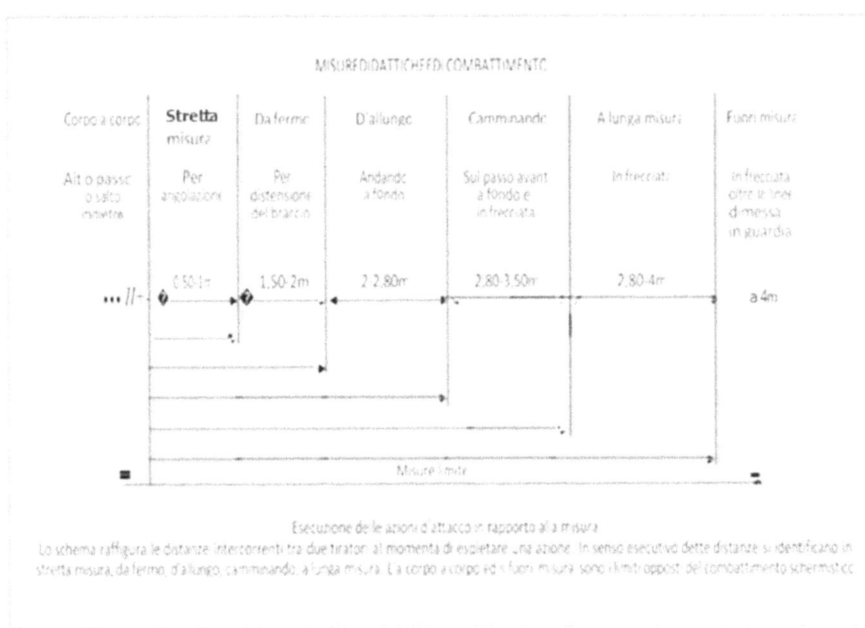

The execution of attacking actions in relation to the measure.

The diagram depicts the distances between two fencers when carrying out an action. In an executive sense these distances are closely identified, from close distance *(stretta misura)* arm's length, *(da fermo)* lunging *(d'allungo)* step and lunge *(camminando)* and long distance *(a lunga misura)*. The corpo a corpo are the opposite limit of combat fencing.

The lunge *(L'a-fondo)*

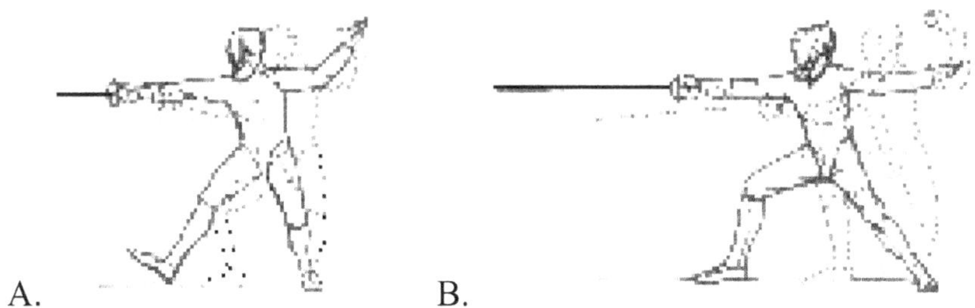

A) Iron in line and start of front leg movement   B) A-short lunge, back knee semi-extended.

C) A-canonical lunge, maximum extension, forward thrust generated by the extension of the back knee. Armed fist with extended arm held at face height. Front knee and foot on the same vertical line.

The return on guard *(Il retorno in guardia)*

1) Keeping the armed arm extended, pivot on the heel of the front foot and push backward, without any contraction.
2) Return to the guard position.

Movements to vary the measure *(Movimenti per variare la misura)*

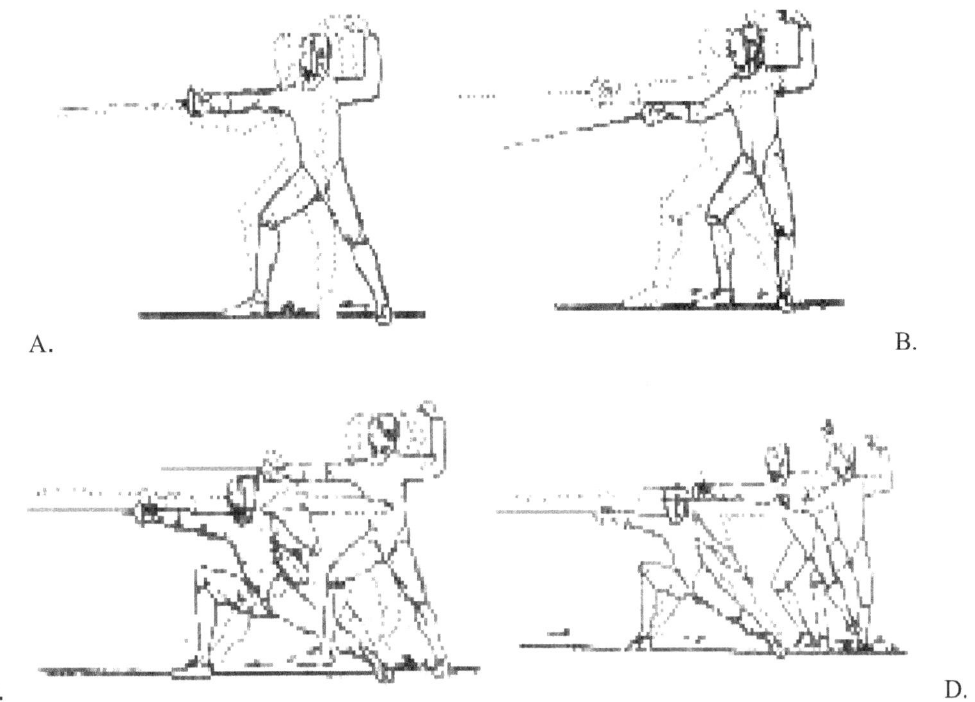

A.   B.

C.   D.

A. Step forward *(Il passo avanti)* - B. step backward *(Il passo indientro)* - C. The step forward and lunge *(Il passo avanti a-fondo)* - D. The jump back from the lunge *(il salto indietro)*

The renewed attack from the lunge *(Dall'affondo portare il piede dietro, ripiegando il ginocchio)*

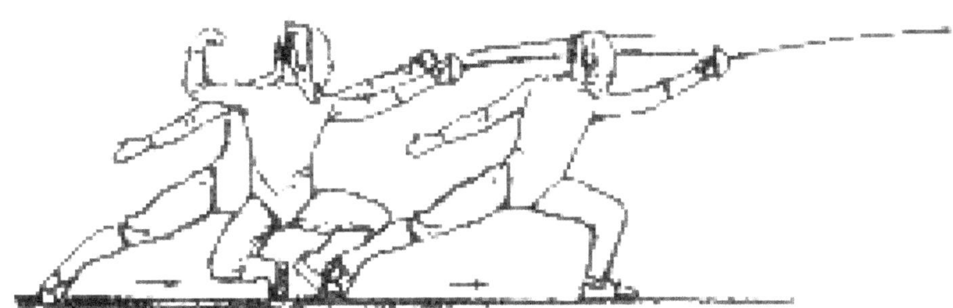

From the lunge, bring the back foot, bending at the knee while remaining on the same plane, not rising, touching the forward target, the lunge again keeping the armed hand remaining at face level.

The arrow *fleche (La frecciata)*

Starting from the guard, extend the armed arm and at the same time protract the body forward until you lose your balance. Passing the back foot over the front one suddenly rushing forward with the weapon extended towards the opponent.

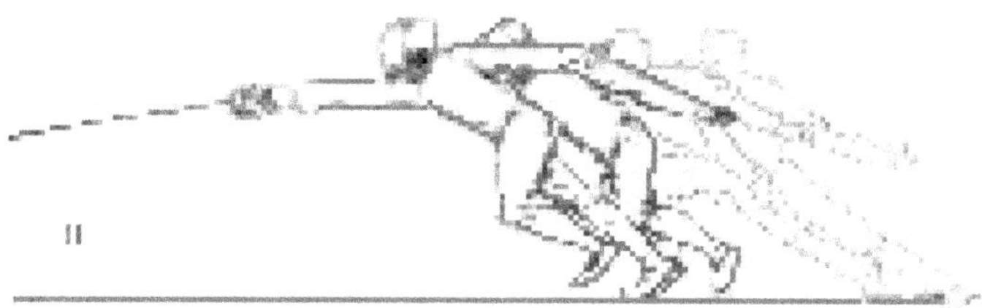

Starting from the lunge, the arrow is performed similarly as starting from the guard. This is particularly effective as a decisive action in the attack phase, counter attack or renewed attack, especially if applied against the foot. The body must be catapulted forward in a directed diagonal towards the opponent.

The thrust in relation to the opponent *(La frecciata in rapporto all'avversario)*

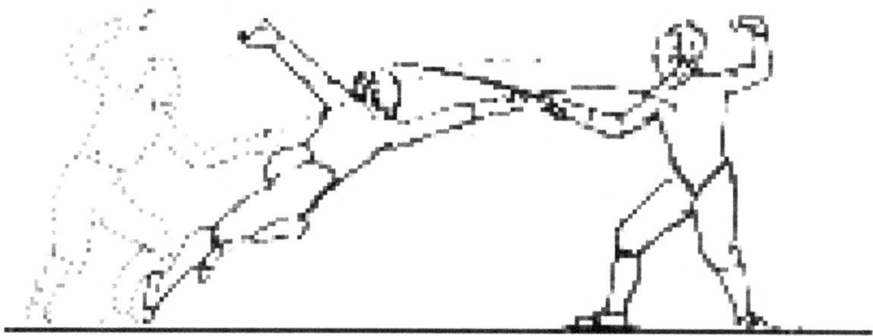

From the guard, the arrow to the body of the opponent. (note: the touch occurs before the back foot touches the ground, from lunging distance)

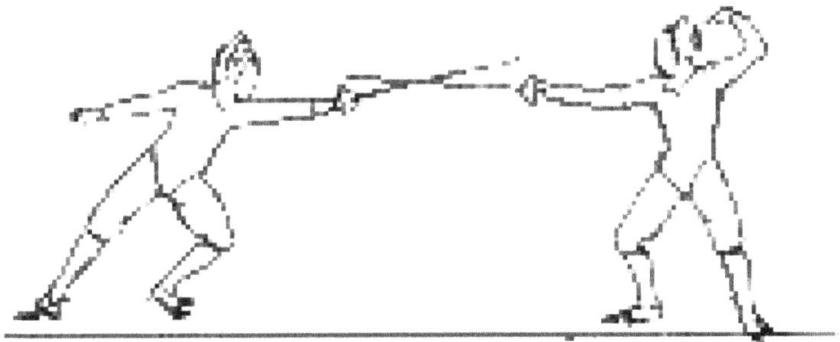

For the left-handed fencer on the right. Moving the body forward in the first tempo. It is appropriate, in epee, to take possession of the opponent's blade, decisively in order to avoid the arrest.

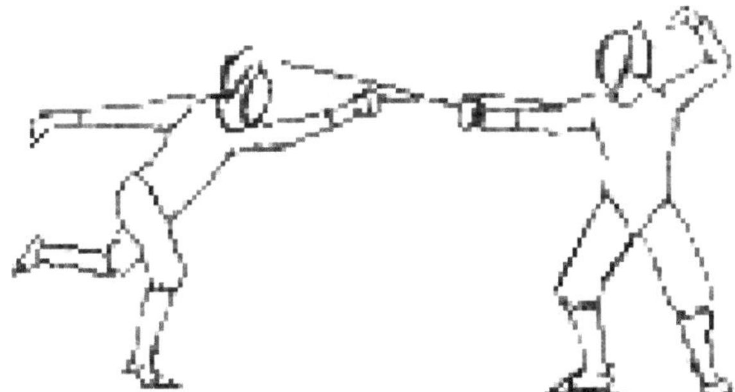

The arrival phase. The back foot having passed with momentum the one in front and the armed arm being well extended the tip is directed to the opponent's forearm. The forward targets (hand, forearm, mask in the high line, know and foot in the low lines) are easily reachable with actions using the arrow.

The thrust in counterattack *(La frecciata in contropiede)*

On the opponent's backward imbalance.

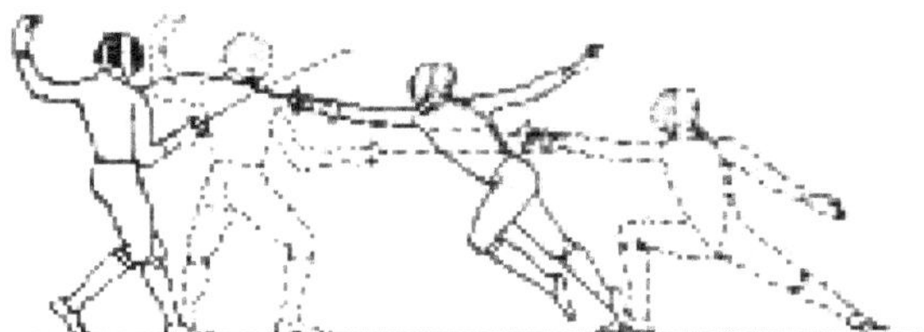

From the lunge on the opponent's step back *retreat*

Exercises for the legs: the bouncing *(Esercizi per le gambe: il molleggio)*

From the lunge, leveraging the heel of the front foot, stand up and then descend again with momentum, forcing the bending of the knee. The pelvis must "break" while the torso remains erect.

Angel of the torso *(angolo gambe tronco)*

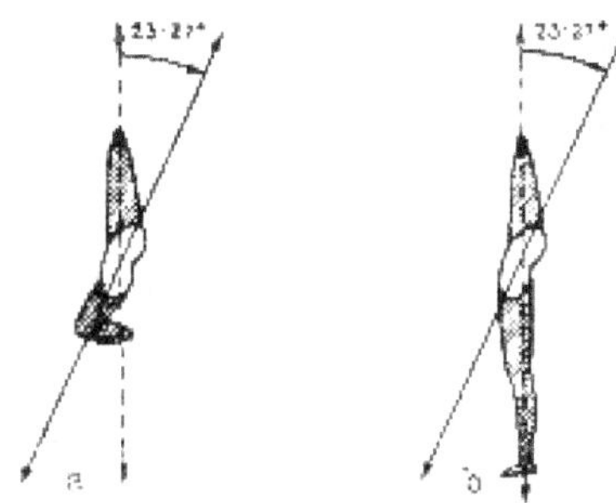

a) The torso, relative to the legs positioned in the direction of movement, should not rotate more than 23-27° to promote a natural stance.

b) Even in the lunge, the same angle must be maintained to favor motor coordination and the most rational movement.

The measurements for exercises for the upper bodies *(Le misure per esercizi agli avancorpi)*

Between two fencers in guard: left-handed vs right-handed
One fencer in lunge and the other in guard: right-handed vs right-handed.

The lines of offense - the quadrants of the target *(Le linee di offesa - i quadranti del bersaglio)*

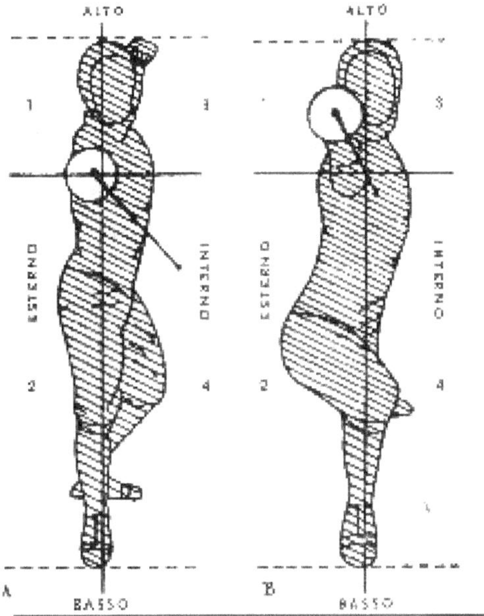

The entire body is a target; the lines of penetration are relative to four quadrants: high, low, inner, outer.
Parries are also relative to the lines and quadrants.
A) The portions of the target of the fencer in the guard position.
B) The same portions presented by the fencer in the lunge.

The positions of the armed fist *(Le posizioni del pugno armato)*

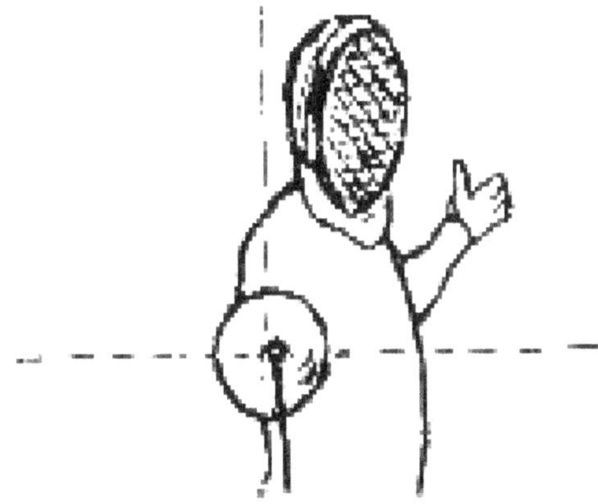

The position of the armed hand is a epeeists classic guard is in the third line, hand in fourth position,
arm outstretched, point inside the offensive line, constantly threatening the opponents' arm.

In the positions: 1) first or half-circle; 2) second or eighth; 3) third; 4) fourth.

Similarly, the same positions are assumed when aiming at a target. The resulting action is called an invitation. If, in one of these positions, the blade is brought to meet the opponent's, the action is considered a bind. The fundamental stances of the fencer with a sword are similar to those of the foil fencer, specifically: blade in the line of offense; invitation; bind. Naturally, the swordsman will perform each movement ensuring maximum coverage of the armed arm, keeping the tip of their weapon always directed at the opponent's arm, and to achieve this, they must execute movements from one line to another, from one position to a different position, making use of fist opposition and appropriate forearm rotations.

The invitation (Gli inviti)

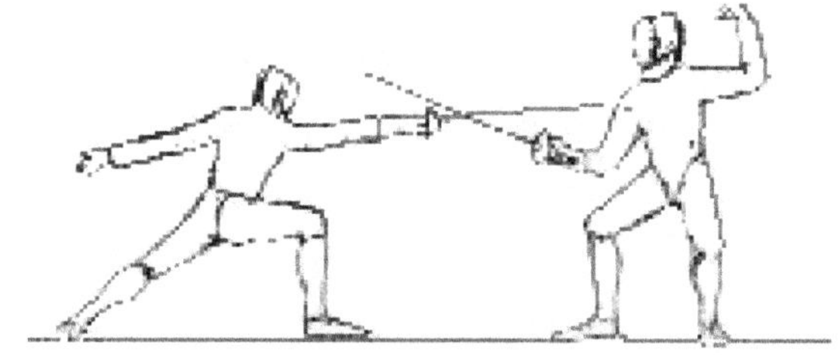

From the invitation in fourth, straight thrust to the outside arm or chest.

From the invitation in third, straight thrust to the inside arm or below or to the chest.

From the invitation of first, straight thrust to the arm, external or above.

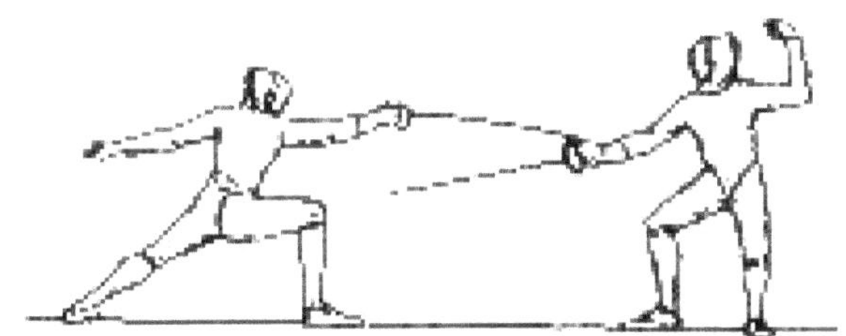

From the invitation in second, straight thrust to the wrist, above.

Graphing of the paths followed by the tip of the weapon in the execution of fundamental actions in relation to the quadrants of the target and the related passages, engagements, invitations, and parries.

Simple or direct (semplici e diretti):

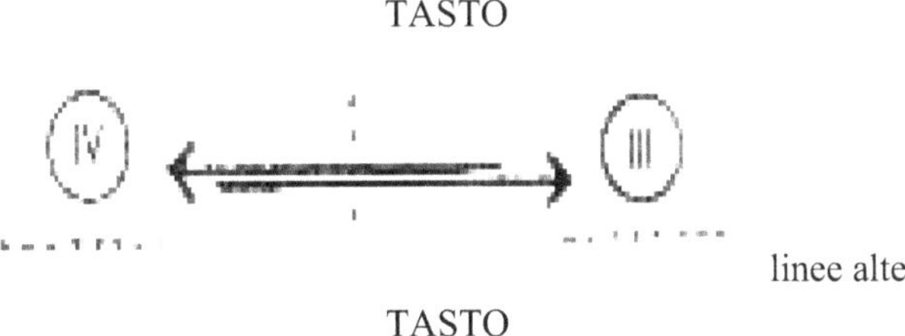

261

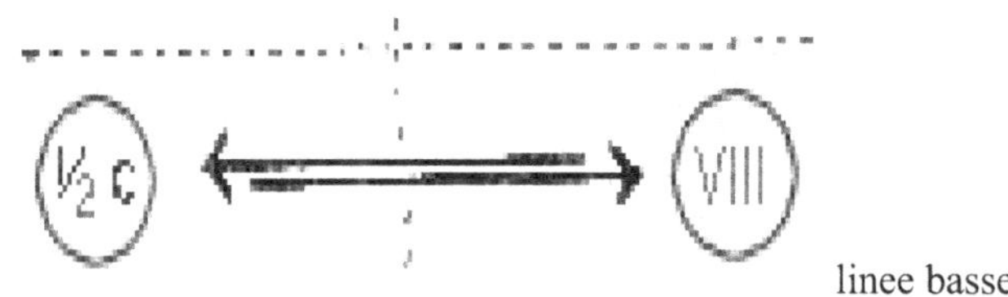

linee basse

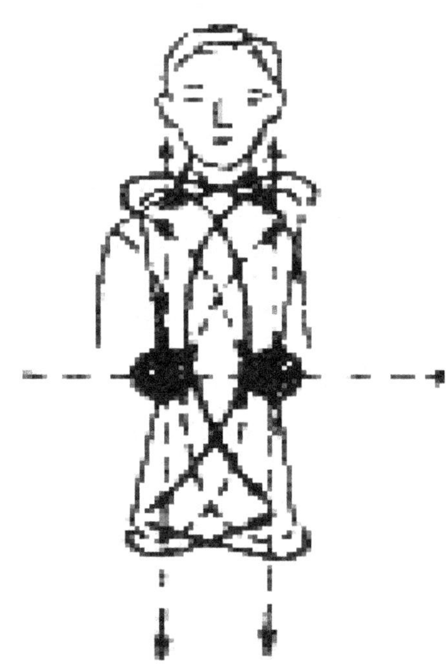

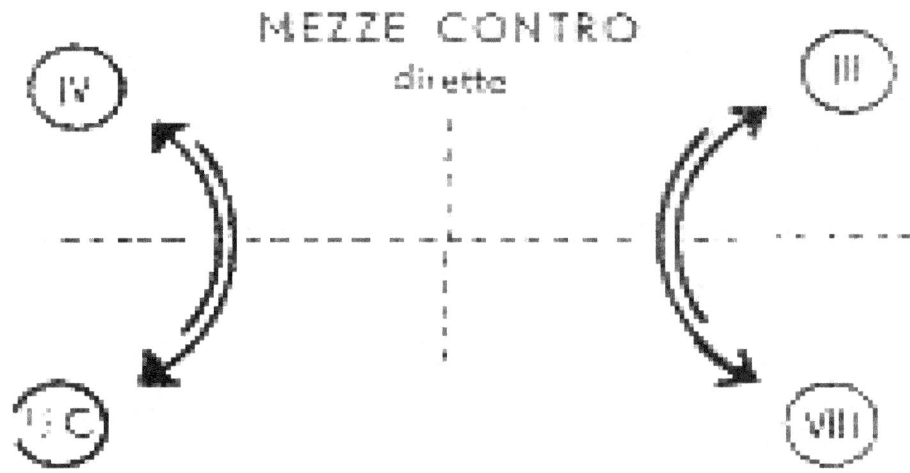

Half circular (first) from high to low and vice versa.

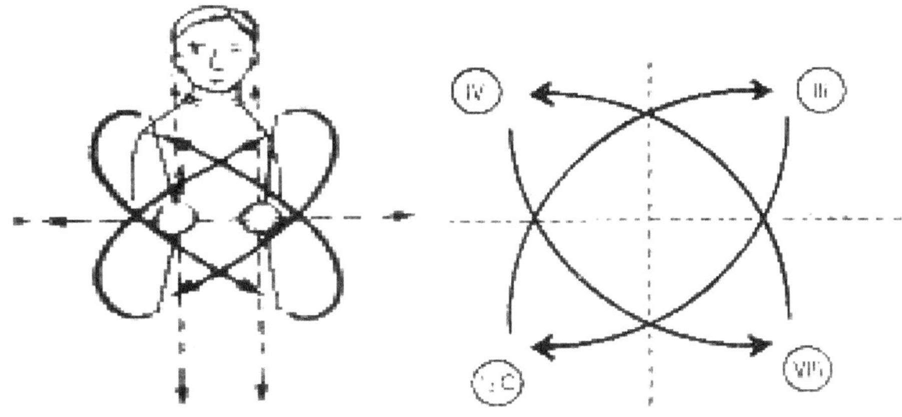

Summary synthesis *(Sintesi riassuntiva)*

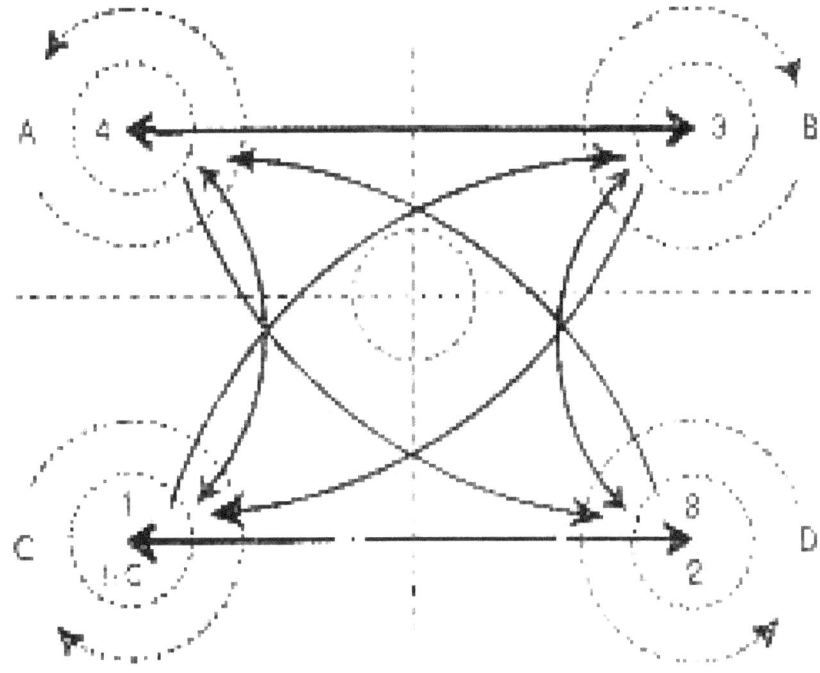

Key: high line from A-B to B-A; low line C-D and D-C half circle: direct line A-C to C-A and from B-D to B-D, transversal line from A-D to D-A and from B-C to C-B. Circular on all four lines A-B-C-D. According to the scheme all the actions consisting in the key, half performed as composite and as counter.

The engagement *(I legamenti)*

The engagement in fourth: in the high internal line

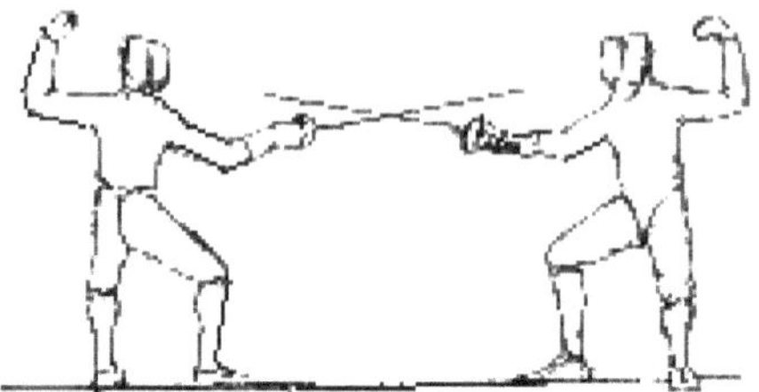

Engagement in third: in the high external line

Engagement in first or half circle: in the low internal line

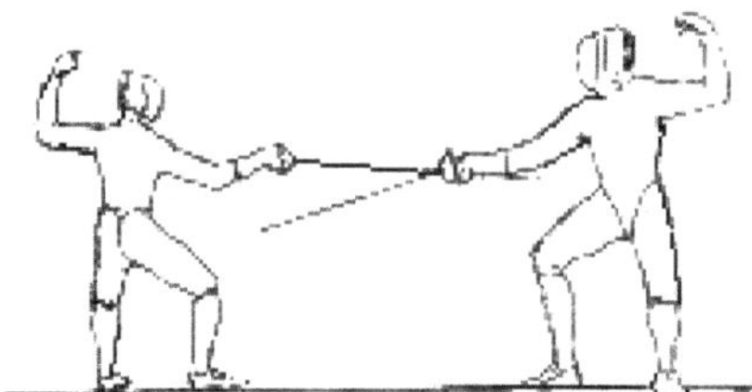

Engagement in eighth or second: in the outside low line.

The transport *(I trasporti)*

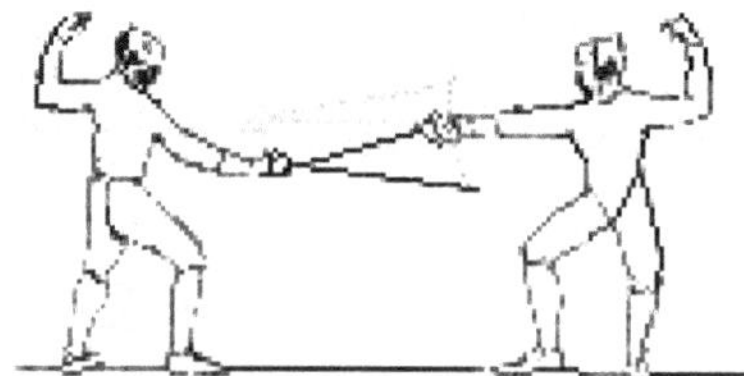

From the engagement in fourth, transport to second

From the engagement of third, transport to first

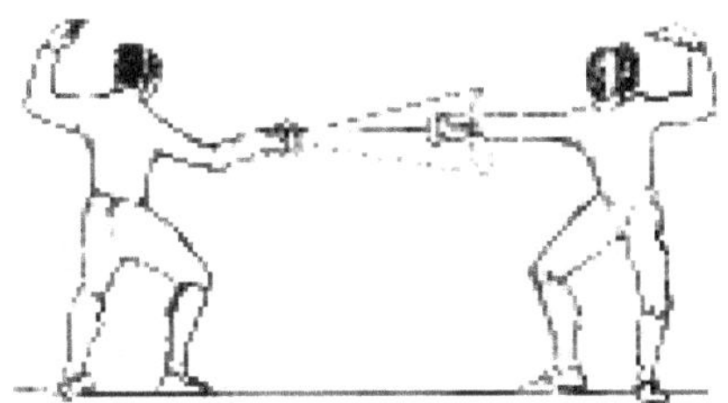

From the engagement of first, transport to third

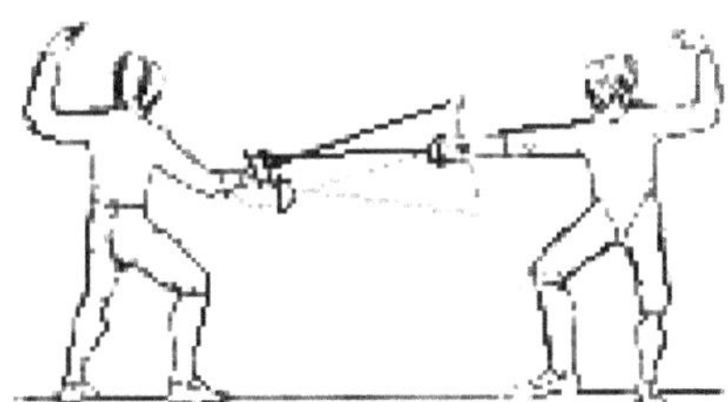

From the engagement of second, transport to third. (Note it is transport to first)

Transports are carried out by keeping one's blade constantly in contact with that of the opponents and gradually forward propulsion.

THE BASIC ACTIONS IN EPEE
LE AZIONI BASILARI DELLA SPADA

THE OFFESE
L'OFFESA

Offensive actions *(Azione di offesa)*

All actions that bring the tip to the target are offensive actions, both on attack and in response. These actions, of carried out correctly, must bring the tip of the weapon, by stretching the armed arm, on to the target, with clear precedence on the movement of the legs (step forward, step backward, lunge and arrow.)

The only exemption allowed for this fundamental concept refers to actions carried out in *lost time* performed with second intention, in two or more times. Whoever executes them, however, hoes so at his own risk since the immediate counterattack will come first.

The straight thrust *(Il colpo dritto)*

The simple and direct action brought to the target by the various measures, geometrically in a straight line.

The straight thrust, in its simplicity, is the most difficult, but it is of utmost importance because all the fencing actions end with it.

Its execution requires choice of time, rapidity, and coordination of movements so as to overcome the speed of the opposing defense.

The straight thrust with a lunge *(La botta dritta)*

The straight thrust going to the lunge: it must be hit with a choice of time and distance to the target, preferably on the forward target and in executed from lunging distance.

Direct thrust to the mask

Direct thrust to the leg

Direct thrust to the foot

The straight thrust with opposition *(Il colpo dritto eseguito con apposizione)*

If the opponent is with blade in line, ready to perform a counterattack (stop hit) on the arm because they expect an angulation to his advanced target, or insists on threatening with the blade in line, it is performed to maintain a suitable cover to hit with the straight thrust with opposition.

This action only takes one tempo: it can be performed from your own blade in line, or from an invitation. In the first case, it is sufficient to exercise the opposition in the act in which they hit the chest from the inside. In the second case the hit strikes with opposition, turning the hand completely in fourth. This caution is also performed in the low line, with the hand in fourth against the opposite side.

Exact knowledge of the measure is essential for the hit to be effective.

The action requirements are length, power, direction and line. It is performed from the four invitations or, when the opponent moves from high to low, to the right or left, bringing the epee into the offensive line. It can be performed from close range, step and lunge or arrow. The straight thrust can be directed to the arm chest, mask, leg or foot.

The disengagement *(la cavazione)*

This is a simple and indirect action that brings your blade from the starting line to the opposite line by passing below the opponent's blade when it is performed in the high lines and over or above the blade if performed in the low lines.

It is considered <in time> if performed without having been found by the opponent's blade in an engagement, and "released" if from the opponent's engagement.

The disengagement can be applied with the same concepts in a counterattack, on the stop hit on the pressure and on the blade seizure. It is called <touch by disengagement> *(cavazione a toccare)* if the tip is brought to the target. Geometrically, it is a matter of making a half turn.

As in the foil, the execution of the movement pivots in the wrist or the person who allies it: on must take particular care that one's tip does not differ from the opponent's guard, continually eluding the latter's search for the blade.

The disengagement must always follow with the straight thrust and therefore the expression of the movement must be forward, if not even in the perfect line of offense.

If this Is used as a feint, the disengagement must not change in the expression of movement, because the feint must also express intention of offense; therefore, it would be illogical to perform lateral pretensions or, on any case to wide.

As a release action, the disengagement must ensure that the passage of the tip from the part of the uncovered target preceded the opponent's engagement. This movement must be performed in such a way as to describe a spiral, insinuating the tip of the epee as much as possible, supported by the natural movement of the arm, and ending with a final grasp of the hand at the movement when the hit to the target must strike.

The disengagement can be directed to the arm, chest, mask, or leg.

For the implementation all the rules already described for the execution of the straight thrust must be observed; the same applies to the measure to be taken during execution.

It is very useful to know how to apply them with safety and precision on order to quickly move from one line to another, deceiving the opponent and avoiding his arrest.

The circle *(La circolata)*

The release action that opposes the circular parry: composed and direct, it brings its blade from the starting line to the same line after having made a complete turn around the opposing blade. It excludes a simple action and counter action.

The counter disengagement *(La controcavazione)*

This is a composed and indirect action that brings the blade from the starting line to the opposite line, eluding the opponent's engagement and counter parry (circular movement to collect the blade).

Geometrically it takes a circle and a half.

Being a compound action, given by the subsequent execution of two disengagements, the same precautions described for the disengagement also apply to this. It is essential that the movement be carried out with the maximum coverage of the arm and therefore with the use of only the wrist; in this regard it must be exercised particularly.

The angulation *(L'angolazione)*

This offensive free blade action builds on the final extension of the arm, the angle intentionally formed by the forearm and blade with appropriate hand opposition.

The angle is even more effective the faster and more sudden the final hand opposition movement.

In epee the angle is one of the fundamental actions to hit the arm placed in the offensive line and, therefore, covered; moreover, carried to the body, it is intended to enter under the parry.

The angulation is applied advantageously as in the attack and in the counterattack, in short distance.

The angulation follows the four guard positions:

- Angulation to the bottom of the arm *(angolazione al braccio sotto)*
- Angulation to the external arm *(angolazione al braccio esterno)*
- Angulation to the internal arm *(angolazione al braccio interno)*
- Angulation to the top of arm *(angolazione al braccio sopra)*

The angulation to the bottom of the arm is performed with the hand in second position.

The angulation to the external arm is done with the hand in fourth position, and to the internal angulation the hand in third position, with an internal opposition.

The angulation above is performed with the hand in fourth position and opposition at the top.

It should, however, be born in mind that the joint of the wrist is somewhat dangerous for the fact that in the offense plan, the broken line is shorter that the straight line opposite the forearm and the blade stretched in the same direction.

Therefore, the defense opposed to these hits, it is not a real parry, but a moving the arm out, in, above or below always following with the tip of your own weapon in the direction of the opponent's arm, so as to oppose the opponent's strike the arm to stop or hit with a counter action where this is advantageous. This is precisely the system to defend oneself by offending.

Angulation directed to the arm must be performed by surprise, with the maximum speed and with the choice of time so to always manage to escape the tip of the opposing sword, although not following the line of offense. They must also be performed form the long Angulation directed to the arm must be performed by surprise, with the maximum speed and with the choice of time so to always manage to escape the tip of the opposing sword, although not following the line of offense. They must also be performed from the long distance *(fuori misure)* to avoid the arrest.

The angulation, for use of a useful exercise and for the appropriate tactics, should always be followed from an arrest, whether going to the renewed attack or jumping back after the touch.

The angulation (Le angolazioni)

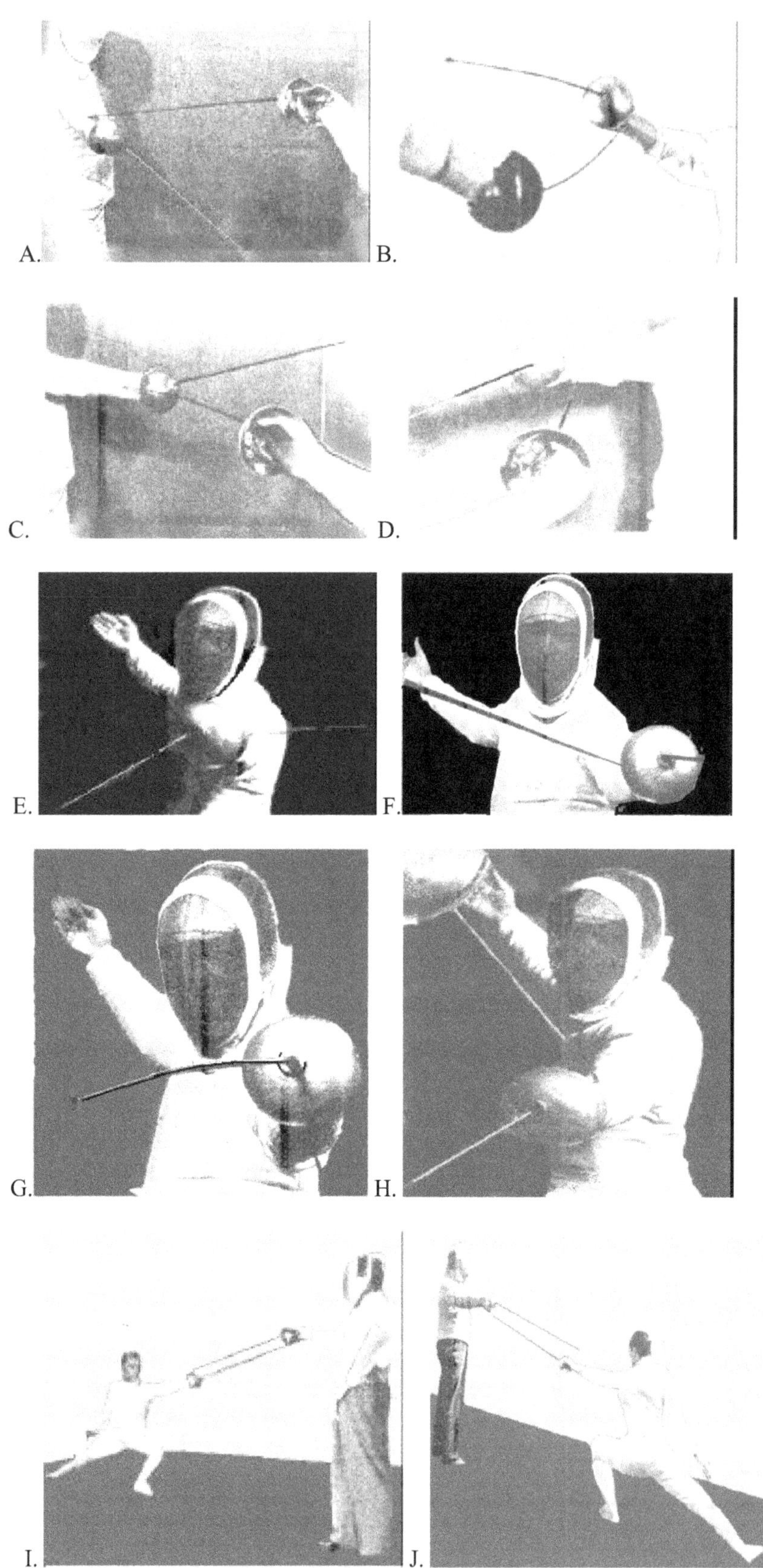

The disengagement and the counter disengagement and angulation *(La cavazione e la controcavazione angolata)*

To perform them, he attacks by disengagement *(cavazione)* or by counter disengagement, avoiding the parry of fourth and counter of fourth, and at the end of the action, angle underneath, with the hand in second position. The same action can be performed in all four lines and must always end at the angulation below, with the hand in second, an immediate arrest direct to the crook of the arm can be added with the reasemblement (jump back).

The glide *(Il Filo)*

It is the action that leads to hitting the target (keeping one's own iron in contact with the opponent's iron) from the engagement in the attacking action, in response, after the parry has taken place.

The actions are six:

1.   **Glide in Fourth** *(Filo di quarta)*: from the position of fourth, stitching along the opponent's blade to the target, keeping the hand in fourth hand position.

2.   **Glide in third** *(Filo di terza)***:** from third position, stitching along the opponent's blade to the target, with marked opposition in third.

3.   **Glide in second** *(Filo di seconda)*: from second position (hand in turned with the thumb down and the nails of the fingers out) stitching on the opposing blade with a marked angulation *pugno-spada* or pointed upwards to the target.

4.   **Glide in eight** *(Filo di ottava)***:** like the glide in second, but with the hand in fourth position, the point of the epee is conveniently angled by breaking the wrist.

5.   **Glide in first** *(Filo do prima)***:** with the hand in first, stitch up the opponent's blade and thus bringing the tip of your epee in the direction of the abdomen, or of the lower part of the opponent's side, at an appropriate angle.

6.   **Glide by half circle** *(Filo di mezzocerchio)*: like the glide in first, but with the hand in third and fourth position, stitch on the opponent's blade until it hits the flank (side) or the abdomen.

The correct angle in the application of the glides must be calculated and exercised repeatedly in relation to the measure.

THE GLIDE *(I fili)*

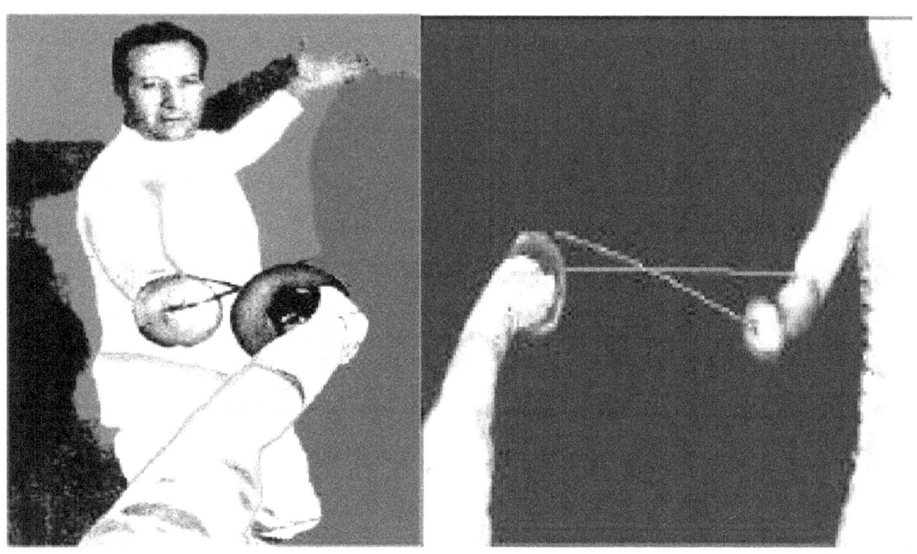

In the third line · In the fourth line

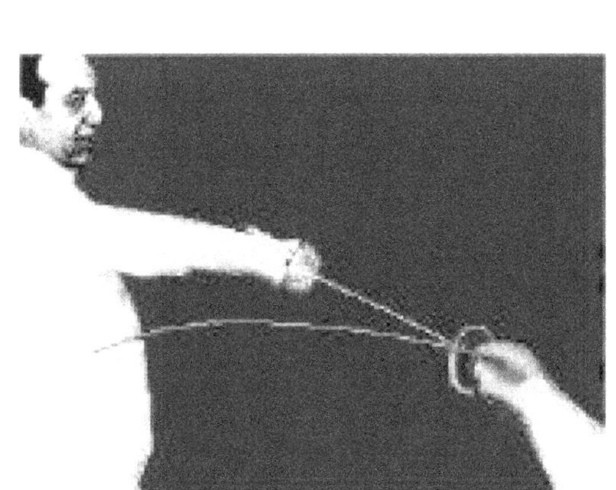

In the line of eighth

Half-circular to the knee

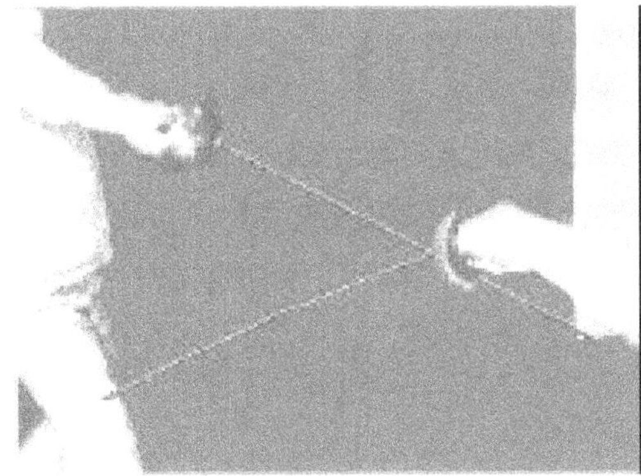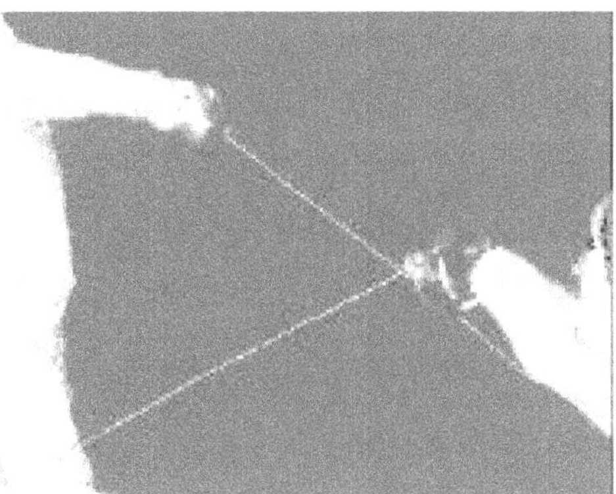

Line of eighth hand in second   line in eighth, hand in fourth to the knee

Glide in third to the mask with opposition in third (outside)

Forced glide *(Il filo sottomesso)*

Being in front of fencers who habitually engage the blade without opposing too much are often advantageous to the implementation of the forced glide *(filo sottomesso)* since in this way they are surprised.

These glides are activated when one's blade is subject to one of the four opposing engagements or even when the two blades in line are in contact. They are performed by giving the maximum hold of the hand at the moment of intruding the epee in the direction of the chest or flank, gaining the degrees of the blade, and then going to the lunge.

These glides are said to be made with pretense or feint, when instead of carrying them out, they are only mentioned and, evading the parry, they hit the uncovered target. They can be directed to the arm, chest, mask, or leg.

When at step and lunge measure it is preferable to use the feint of forced glide, since easily the pressure exerted on the opposing blade instinctively sends the message to parry.

Finding yourself at step and lunge distance and wanting to perform the forced glide, it is good to exert the necessary pressure on the opponent's blade at the same moment with the step forward ending at the correct distance to lunge.

Flanconade in second *(La fianconata di seconda)*

This is an action capable of harnessing the opposing blade with the strength of one's own. A movement like the transport in second with the hand in either second - or fourth-hand position, the hit is carried out and the tip of the epee is directed to the opponent's side, with the touch arriving from wither lunging or step and lunge distance.

The flanconade in fourth *(La fianconata di quarta)*

This is performed similarly to the flanconade in second using the strength of one's own blade against the weak of the opponents with the hand in fourth hand position and keeping in the fourth line. The point Is then directed to the opponent's flank, immediately striking the opponent while maintaining contact with the opposing blade. This can be performed from either lunging or step and lunge distance.

The beat *(la Battuta)*

Is epee fencing it is particularly effective, because, as a result of the impact it impresses on the opponent's blade, it makes it deviate from the possibility of an attack and also prevents it from being put back online promptly. Beats can be performed from all measures according to the target chosen. The beats are four types: beat proper, the touch, the expulsion (sforzo) and disarmament.

The beat itself is when it slides (***testo***) on the opponent's blade along the grads.

The sharp beat *(**pico**)* of the beat strikes the opposing blade in one place, with one dry strike, without crawling on it.

The expulsion *(**sforzo**)* is performed exclusively from one's own engagement without detaching the blade as for in the beat, but by crawling on the opponent's blade gaining on the grade. This offers the advantage of preventing disengagement in time.

Disarmament *(**disarmo**)* is an energetic strike on the opposing blade in the opposite direction to the opening of the hand to make it no longer able to hold. Even if you fail in disarming your opponent with the line, you still have succeeded in making the defense almost impossible.

The beat in third *(la Battuta di terza)*

This action can be performed from one's own engagement in third or from the invitation in fourth or second, or by keeping one's blade in line, when the opponent is with their blade in the outside high line.

Stretching the arm energetically forward, with the initial movement of the wrist supported by the forearm, the beat is made in the third line so that the force of his blade, starting from the weak of the opponent's blade, crawls us, thus gaining the degrees in a diagonal direction downward, until the tip of the epee is at the level of the opponent's shoulder.

This action can also be performed horizontally with the hand turned in the second position.

Following the beat in third (diagonally) the blow is directed to the arm above (below???), the chest, the mask, the leg can also be hit. With the same beat performed horizontally can end at the mask (keeping the hand position unchanged) also arriving at the arm below, the hip or leg.

The beat in fourth *(La Battuta di quarta)*

This action can be performed against either an invitation, engagement or blade in line if presented to the inside high line.

To accomplish this action, keeping the arm bent, then energetically flexing it to the inside without flexing the wrist, make the beat with the hand in fourth hand position so that the strong of your blade crawls from the weak of the opponents toward the medium, gaining degrees as the tip is lowered to the level of the opponents' right shoulder. The thrust is delivered to the upper arm, chest, mask, or leg. For greater security, this beat should be performing by *inquatando. (inquartanding, v- beat in fourth, with the wrist well broken, keeping the point on the adversary, as if performing an inquartata, and not throwing the rear leg back)*

Half circular beat *(la Battuta di mezzocerchio)*

This action can be performed from one's own engagement, from their invitation or by your own blade in line or when they present their blade in the lowline.

Bending the arm at the elbow and energetically flexing without aid of the wrist, make the beat with the hand in third- and fourth-hand position so that the strong of the blade starts on the weak of that of the opponent's blade, crawling up gaining on the degrees from weak to medium in an ascending direction, until the tip rises to the level of the opponent's right shoulder. The touch is directed to the arm, chest, or mask.

The beat in second *(La Battuta di seconda)*

This action can be performed from one's own engagement, from the invitation of the opponent, or from the blade in line when the opponent is with the blade in line with the flank.

Bending the arm energetically with light aid of the wrist make the beat with the hand in the intermediate position of second and third or second, so that your own strong of the blade, starting from the weak of the opposing blade is met, crawling diagonally down or horizontally, gaining the degrees until the tip is at the height of the opponent's side. The touch is directed to the arm, chest, or mask.

The fencer, in performing the beat, must try to graduate the power of the beat by reason of the target he has set himself to hit; however, depending on the effect obtained by the beat, the target is easier to arrive at and less risky.

Variations flowing the beat *(variazioni sulle battute)*

- Beat direct to the body in any of the four lines
- Beat and disengagement to the body in any four lines
- Beat and counter disengagement to the body in any of the four lines
- Beat and feint by disengagement to the body in any of the four lines
- Beat and double feint by disengagement to the body in any of the four lines
- Beat and feint by counter disengagement to the body
- Beat and feint by double counter disengagement in the opposite line to the body in any of the four lines
- Beat and double counter disengagement in the opposite line with double feint to the body in any of the four lines.

These exercises can be performed at lunging distance or step and lunge distance or arrow *(frecciata)* To these attacks you can add all the beats to the body or arm in the aforementioned unit or with the jump back, except when the arrow is done as the final movement.

Expulsion *(lo sforzo)*

The expulsion has the same purpose and result as the beat and is performed in the same manner, with the hand in the same hand positions as the beats and executed in the same four engagements. But one must not separate the contact of the blades from that of the opponent, rather forcefully swipe the blade down the opponent's blade, following the degrees.

Once the expulsion has been made, the touch can be directed to the arm or other target.

Cut over *(L'intagliata (buttuta di tocco) o coupe (French)*

There are two ways two release your tip:

1. Disengagement under

2. Overtaking the opponent's blade by passing above, in the different lines, with the tip moving backwards. This second way of releasing the blade is called *cut over*

intagliata is performed with a light smear backwards while you pass the opponent's blade to go from one side to the opposite side of the engagement, a simple or compound parry is performed in opposition to the opponent using this action.

The releasing movement must be carried out with the wrist since making it with the forearm it is too slow and therefore liable to the stop hit.

Simple and direct cut overs are performed:

1. From the engagement or counter parry, the cut over is directed outwards, overtaking the opponent's blade from the inside to the outside with a final on the opponent's high external target. During the passage it is advisable to apply a slight back pressure on the opponent's blade to provoke the counter-pressure which frees the target to be hit.

2. From the engagement or counter parry of third, execute the same movement in the opposite direction ending on the internal target.

3. From the engagement or counter parry of fourth, cut over arriving to the flank, executable with the hand in fourth hand position or second hand position. To oppose such action, use the ceding parry of second.

Reverse cut over *(L'intagliata di rovescio)*

This action is best carried out at close range.

Out: from either the engagement or from the circular parry, an immediate transfer of the wrist is performed, turning the hand to first position, loosening the grip of the hand on the handle and immediately letting the tip of the epee to fall towards the ground. Then the blade is made to describe a complete circle from bottom to top, passing by a pendulum close to the body; after this movement is carried out with extreme lightness his blade is brought back in line, recovering the strong possession of the epee in order to hit the opponent's high external target.

Inside: the same is true for the inside reverse cut over, only that following the simple parry or circular parry, the movement of the wrist transfer takes place in reverse. The rotation of the blade takes place from the opposite side to that of the first one, that is, outwards to then resume and put the iron back in line and hit the opponent's internal target.

Feint by reverse cut over (*L'intagliata di rovescio con finta*)

You can also perform the feint by reverse cut over outward and subsequent reverse coupe inward and the pretense of reverse cut over inward and subsequent reverse cut over outward.

In the first case, on the extension of the arm after the feint, the opponent's simple parry of third is evaded and in the second case the simple parry of fourth is evaded.

The Feint (*La finta*)

The Feint is the hit mentioned in order to induce the opponent to defend, then to strike him where the new target is discovered.

Feints must be done with art, energy, expression, and choice of time in order to give all the appearance of truth. As the instinct for the defense is inherent in human nature, the simulated attack undoubtedly achieves the intended purpose. On the contrary, if it is poorly executed, in addition to not reaching its purpose, it can be harmful since it offers to the opponent the possibility of opposing you with and exit on time. (counterattack)

The feint must also be proportionate to the sensitivity of the opponent, in each way and clear that before the feint they are preceded with simple attacks to the target on which you want to feint to.

Even a feint with the body will undoubtedly produce an impression on the soul of the opponent and therefore it is useful in certain cases to harmonize this with the movement of the blade. If it is abused, the movement of the body in a continuous manner that may be harmful since it is the attackers essential base in keeping permanently on guard.

The feint is a simple or compound action, direct or indirect, performed as second intention that simulated, therefore the attack, to induce the opponents to parry and then hit them in the same line or in a different line, both with simple actions or with compound actions.

These identify themselves with a sudden feinted attack direct and direct. *(Si identificano finta di colpo dritto e botta dritta)*

Beat, feint direct and direct (*battuta, finta dritta e botta dritta*)

Beat, feint direct and disengagement (*battuta, finta dritta e cavazione*)

Feint by disengagement and direct (*finta di cavazione e botta dritta*)

Feint by disengagement and disengagement (one two) (*finta di Cavazione e cavazione (uno-due)*)

Feint direct and double disengagement (one two) (*finta di botta dritta, cavazione e cavazione (uno-due)*)

Feint by double disengagement and direct (*finta di uno-due e botta dritta*)

Double feint by disengagement and disengagement (one, two, three) (*finta di uno-due e botta dritta*)

Feint direct as (one two three) (*doppia finta di cavazione e cavazione (uno-due-tre)*)

Counter disengagement with feint (*controcavazione con finta*)

Feint by disengagement and counter disengagement (*finta di cavazione e controcavazione*)

Feint by counter disengagement and counter disengagement (double double) (*finta di controcavazione e controcavazione (fr. doublé – dedoublé)*)

Feint by counter disengagement one two (*finta di controcavazione e uno-due*)

Feint by counter disengagement, one two three (*finta di controcavazione unodue-tre.*)

All feinting actions and final actions can be performed in any of the four lines and from any measure. Finally, they can be performed as a releasing (change) action instead of touching.

Example:

MAESTRO	STUDENT
Invitation or engagement in mezzocherchio	From the guard, extending naturally and energetically, direct the hit to the flank or outside arm, leaving the hand position unchanged to ensure covering the arm above
Parry of second	Evading the parry, disengage to the chest above, or top of arm or mask
The touch arrives	
Invitation or engagement in second	From the guard, extending the arm naturally and energetically, feint the hit direct or by

	disengagement to the chest or arm or mask, leaving the hand position unchanged
Parry of third or mezzocerchio	Evading the parry, the disengagement is directed to the chest, inside arm or low arm or mask
The touch arrives	
Invitation or engagement of third	From the guard, extension of the arm is elastic and energetic, leaving the hand position unchanged and feints a direct thrust or by disengagement to the inside chest or inside arm
Parry fourth or second	Evading the parry, direct the disengagement to the outside chest or above, or to the outside arm, top of arm or mask
The touch is received	
Invitation or engagement of fourth	From the guard, extension of the arm is elastic and energetic, leaving the position of the hand the same feint direct or by disengagement to

Feint by glide *(la finta di filo)*

The simulation of the glide.

This can be performed from all measures and is carried out with two movements: the glide is mentioned as gaining the degrees on the blade of the opponent, then a disengagement to the target of the opponent as they are parrying, thus discovering, from the effect of the threat, the available targets of the arm, chest, mask, and leg.

MAESTRO	**STUDENT**
Presents the blade in line	Engage in third from either the invitations of fourth or second, or being with the blade in line of the chest or flank, hint at the glide of third by turning the hand to second and third position, or fourth and crawl on the opponent's blade gaining degrees, insinuates the tip in that line toward the chest
Parry mezzocerchio or third	Evading the parry of mezzocerchio or third, perform the disengagement to the side of the arm, or evading the parry of

	third, perform the disengagement to the inside chest, mask or leg

The same procedure is followed for the implementation of the other feint by glides.

If the master defends himself with a parry at the same time if the feint, then the pupil does an angulation to the arm, following the same rules as the straight thrust or disengagement.

The feint in time *(la finta in tempo)*

When going out in time (feint in time) one senses that the opponent is to advance in counter time to defend himself, then, instead of carrying out the arrest, he feints in that moment and then eludes the parry and continues to the target.

If the opponent is found advancing in counter time, instead of parrying testo (lay on blade) parry by counter (circular) or half circular parry, you can feint the arrest by a circular or counter disengagement.

When the opponent advances in counter time, to defend against a hit in time to the arm, feint to the arm, and on the final movement the touch can be completed by either staying online or by angulation to oppose the defense.

Particular details of some actions

- **Attack to the body and stop hit to the arm**: to all attacks on the body, except those in the arrow, you can always do the following stop hit both by targeting the arm, or to the body with the reasemblement or jump back.

- **Hits directed to the knee of foot**: performing a pressure from the engagement in third by a feint by glide and upon the natural press back from the opponent, you drop the point of the weapon to the knee or foot. It can also be performed on a pressure and feint by glide in fourth with the same procedure as above and with all arrests by using the reasemblement or jump back on the final of the attack or indirect frecciata.

- **Feint to the knee and direct on the mask**: an expressive feint is made to the opponent's knee then, with a rapid change to the high line pull the direct hit to the mask. The Feint is done with the arm covered by lowering the point of the weapon not the arm, this action is feasible while the opponent is in the lunge of the attack or upon returning on guard. Wanting to do the opposite, we begin with the feint to the mask followed directly with the point to the knee.

The remise *(la rimessa)*

The fencing action that applies to the delayed response (riposte).

In modern fencing this is an action of the utmost importance since, if intentionally preordained, it always reaches the target inverse with considerable advance on the parry and riposte. This is evident from the fact that the remise takes place immediately on the opponent's parry when the attack is already very close to the target you want to hit, while the parry and the counter riposte need a considerable distance from the opposing target for the counter parry to operate, and this implies a normal and evident waste of time.

It can also be explained geometrically by asserting that the straight line joining two specific points is significantly shorter than the curved (disengage) one between these two same points; it follows that an immediate remise (or throwing of the point) is performed with the arm outstretched (in line) has a certain advance in time and measurement on that curve of the same and the riposte or the counter parry riposte.

The rimesse is in this way an important principle of electrified fencing since the electric apparatus records the hit with evident difference of time and this, in epee is decisive because whoever touches first is right.

Variations of the remise *(Variazioni sulla rimessa)*

The remise made on the same target against which the attack was directed.

- Remise by disengagement *(le rimesse di cavazione)*
- Remise by counter disengagement *(le rimesse di controcavazione)*
- Remise by feint *(le rimesse can finta)*
- Remise by cut over *(le rimesse di intagliata)*
- Remise by angulation *(le rimesse angolate)*
- Remise by glide *(le rimesse di filo)*
- Remise by transport and glide *(le rimesse con trasporti del ferro e di filo)*

The above actions can be performed in all four lines.

The double hit *(Il colpo doppio)*

At the end of an attack on the leg with a broken wrist and loss of balance on the lunge, the direct stop to the body with an un-extended arm and in a partial reasemblement.

These two are both incorrectly performed actions

On a fleche attack to the body by blade seizure, ceding parry to the body by the opposition. Note the outreach of the attacker's arm which is counterattacking by the unbalanced guard.

The double hit *(Il colpo doppio)*

This occurs when two attackers touch each other simultaneously. Usually, it is the consequence of an error by one of the two who has not respected the convention (foil and saber), but by Epee this action can be sought to resolve a meeting.

The recording device signals a double hit every time the touches of the two fencers arrive within the time of a twenty-fifth of a second (25/60) and the touches thus recorded are marked on the liabilities of both contenders.

The double hit can be intentionally provoked by the fencer who has the advantage to decide the match in his favor.

For the fencer who is at a disadvantage he must follow a prudent tactic and keep himself on the offensive-defensive (arrests especially to the forward target, brought with decision on pressing the opponent.)

It is only with experience that you can intentionally carry out the double hit by generally applying simple, preordained actions, after having considered the opponent's tactical attitude.

CHAPTER II

GRAPHIC SUMMARY

THE OFFESE
L'OFFESA

The angulation *(Le angolazione)*

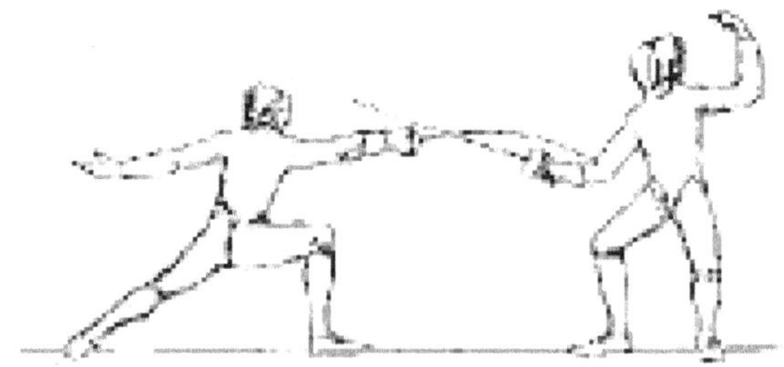

Angulation to the outside high line

Angulation to the inside high line (crook of arm)

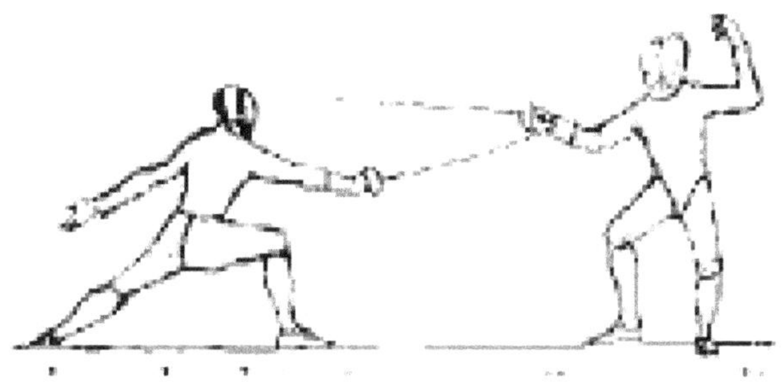

Angulation to under the wrist, hand in fourth position

Angulation to under the wrist, hand in second hand position

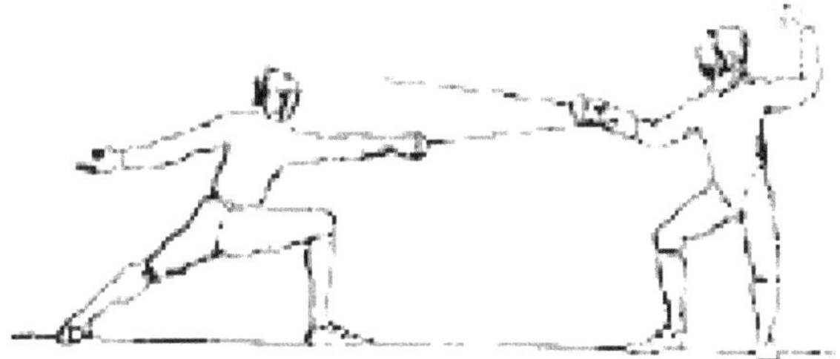

Angulation to the inside arm high line

Angulation above to the arm in the guard, hand in second hand position

Angulation to the arm, outside high line

Angulation to the arm in the lunge, hand in first position

Direct thrust *(I colpi dritti)*

Direct thrust to the mask with a lunge

Direct thrust to the torso with a lunge

Direct thrust to the bottom of the arm with a lunge

Direct thrust to the knee with a lunge (note incorrect picture used in original text)

Direct thrust to the foot with a lunge

The disengagement *(Le cavazione)*

From the engagement in third, disengagement inside to the chest

From the engagement in fourth, disengage to the outside, arriving at the arm

From the engagement of second, disengage above to the arm as the opponent retreats, finish with the arrow

From the engagement of first, disengage to the bottom of the arm, turning the hand to secondhand position

The glide *(I fili)*

From the guard, on the opponent's blade in line, blade seizure in third and glide above to the arm

From the guard, as the opponent places the blade in line, blade seizure in fourth and glide to the chest
with the arrow

From the guard, with the opponents point in the low line, blade seizure in first and glide to the abdomen,
thigh, or knee

From the guard, on the opponents point in the low line, blade seizure in second and glide to the thigh or
abdomen

The beat *(La battute)*

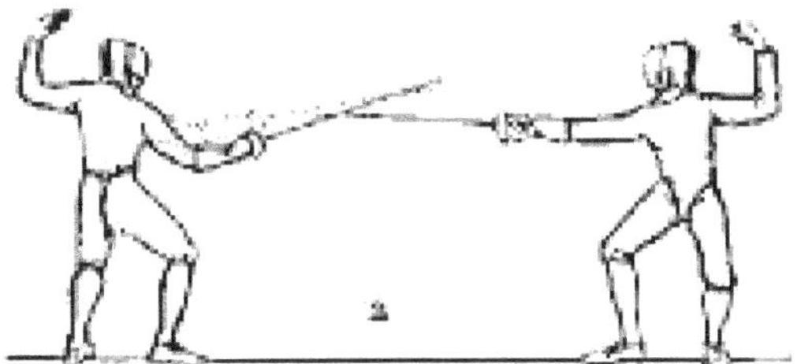

On the opponent's blade in line, beat in fourth (a)

followed by a direct thrust to the inside arm with a lunge (b)

On the opponent's blade in line, beat in fourth and direct thrust with the arrow on the opponent who retreats, lowering his armed arm. The attack is thus brought on opposed to a counterattack

On the opponent's blade in line, beat with a counter of third and with the arrow hit the abdomen or to the thigh or knee of the opponent who retreats. The offensive action is compound, indirect and performed on the counterattack. (a+b)

Beat with a counter of third, at the same time as the step forward b. disengaging inside with the arrow, on the step backward of the opponent

On the opponent's point in the low lone, beat by half circle (a) and direct thrust to the abdomen (b). the same thrust can be directed to the thigh, knee or foot.

In epee the beat and the thrust performed going forward, the hand must be kept in opposition to the beat. The detachment of the blade from that of the opponent can favor the reaction of the opponent and cause, at a minimum, a double hit.

The grazing beat *(Le intagliata "battute di tocco" o coupes)*

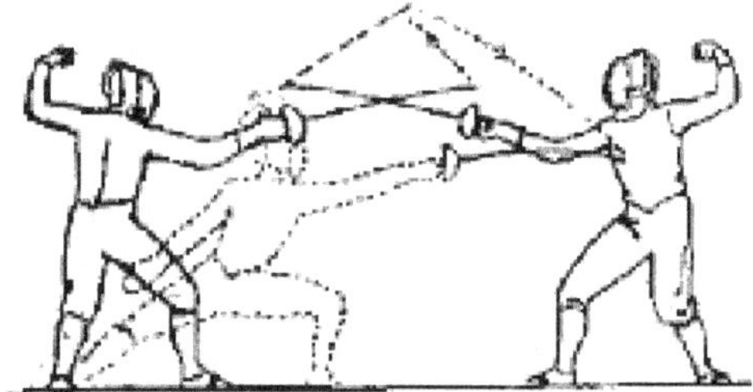

From the engagement or beat in fourth, crawling on the opponent's blade until clear of the tip, flexing at the wrist (not at the elbow) cut over to the outside chest

Cut over *(La intagliata e coupe)*

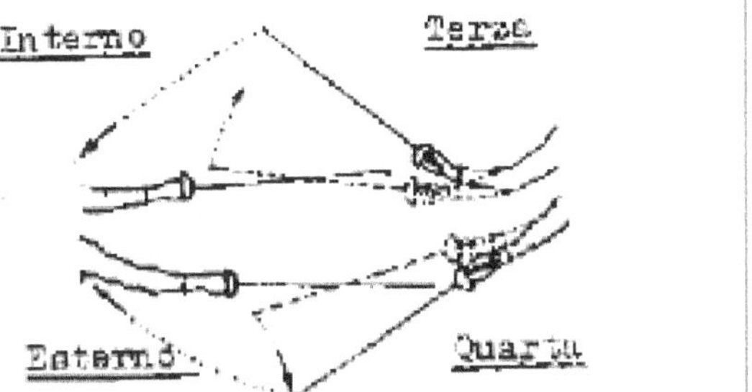

From the position of the armed arm outside of the opponent's blade: cut over to the inside. From the position of the armed hand inside with respect to the blade of the opponent: cut over outwards.

On the opponent's straight thrust, first parry and riposte by reverse cut over (under) inside turning your point from the bottom upwards finding the attackers bottom arm. The same action can be performed advantageously in close combat or intentionally closing the measure.

The Feint *(La finta)*

The simulation of a thrust by means of an action defines the action itself in its executive concept. The feint performed in the offensive and counter-offensive phases it determines compound actions, direct and indirect executable in the lines accessible to the targets.

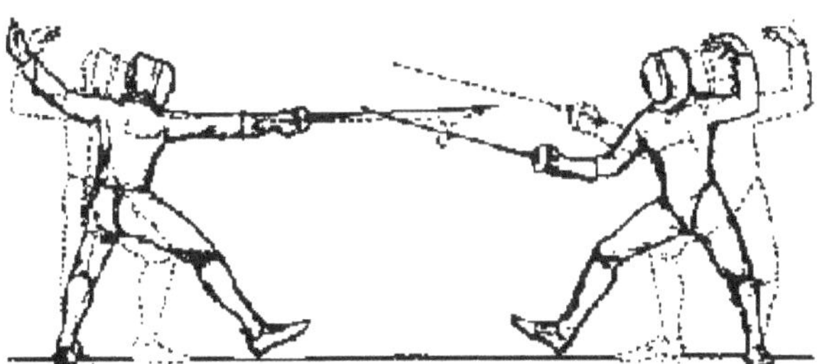

Feint direct to the inside chest and when the adversary parries fourth, disengage to the outside

Feint direct to the outside high line (shoulder), on the opponent's parry of third, disengage inside. The feints can be carried out with simple and direct actions (in all four lines) feint by disengagement and direct thrust: double feint by disengagement (feint by disengagement and disengagement) feint by circular (deceive): counter disengagement: feint by counter disengagement: feint by double counter disengagement, (two circular deceives) circular disengagement and disengagement, one, two, three. Actions consisting of three or more feints are called "disordered".

The double hit *(Il colpo doppio)*

a)   Hit to the knee and stop hit to the arm
b)   Thrust to the chest and stop hit to the mask

The double hit in epee is recorded when the two fencers are touching at the same time, within $20/25^{th}$ of a second. Contrary to foil and sabre, weapons of convention, so in the event of a double hit you have to seek the "reason" for touching and then attribute the scoring according to the agreement; the double blow of epee determines the assignment of a hit to both shooters. It follows that this possibility is exploited tactically in order to complete, without rushing and taking unnecessary risks, a meeting that turns in clear favor. Usually looking for the double shot means pre-ordering an action within the opponent's action: on the attacker, stop; on whoever arrests, attack; but one is needed reasoned determination.

CHAPTER III

THE BASIC

ACTIONS IN EPEE

(LE AZIONI BASILARI DELLA SPADA)

PREMISE

The best defense action for the epee is the arrest, both direct and counter.

On the opponent's attack, especially if prolonged arrest is the most logical reaction to apply; in any case, however, it must be followed by an immediate remise, going to the parry only as an extreme defensive possibility. We must keep in mind that one must be ready to break measure (step back, reasemblement or jump back) constitutes the most rational means to be able to stop touch and dissolve distance, thus intentionally preparing the right measure for the counter-offense, with a precise defensive understanding as an offense.

Parries with the epee are however to be performed going forward, with minimal displacement of the offensive line and conquering the dominion of the opponent's weapon with the strong degree of your blade.

In the fencing phrase of epee, going to the classic counterpart of foil constitutes a contradiction that must be avoided in order to remain in the real terms of the fight conceived in accordance with the principle of striking before being struck, on contrast with the academic royals and conventions that govern the foil and sabre.

The arrest *(L'arresto)*

The counterattack of the epeeist is the arrest that touches with time precedence on the attack of the opponent. Unlike in foil and sabre, being conventional weapons, the epeeist who pursues only the principle of touching before being touched, in by making a stop hit in counterattack generally does not care to precede the opponent's strike of an appreciable or *fencing* time but try only to avoid the double hit or to seek a double hit according to convenience. The recording time of the double hit is fixed at 20/25 of a second which is a chronometric time which is not related to the speed of execution of the actions by the fencers, to their executive capacity – relative to each fencer – as per counter that occurs in foil and sabre in order to establish the fencing time.

The arrest of the epeeist can therefore be considered of two orders:

The time thrust *(di contrazione)* If touching by closing the line when the opposing blade enters deviating the point while precluding the touch from occurring in turn.

Direct or indirect *(diretto, indirette)* with simple or compound action, if touching first neutralizes the subsequent blow of the weapon.

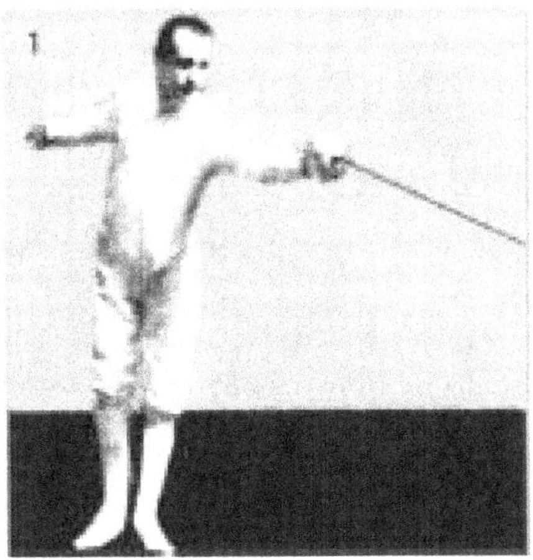

Reassembling, with opposition in third to make direct arrest to the foreparts while dissolving the latter.

Jumping backwards to quickly get out of distance after seeking the arrest to the arm and being able to go to the counter offensive by resuming an offensive initiative of the frecciata.

Reasemblement to the arm on the unbalanced lunge of the opponent.

The arresting actions are more effective if you quickly pass from the guard or lunge to the reasemblement (*riunita*) in which the shoulder and the arm are stretched in an offensive line, while the body is removed from the opponent's attack by gathering backwards with feet together and extending the weapon arm forward.

The reasemblement is preferably applied on the opponent standing still or in the lunge, while if they attack with step and lunge or frecciata it is preferable to arrest with jumping backwards.

The arrest to the arm *(L'arresto al braccio)*

That straight or angled thrust quickly delivered to the opponent's arm in the act in which they perform any offensive action, whether simple or compound. Said hit is performed from the guard or by stepping back or by joining the heel of the front foot with the one behind *(riunita)*.

In opposition to the angulation from the opponent, the stop hit (arrest) must always be taken straight and directed to the most advanced target, i.e., to the wrist.

The arrest to the body *(L'arresto al corpo)*

It is a strike that arrives on the opposing action, made up of at least two movements.

If the threat is directed upwards or to the outside chest, the arresting thrust is carried out to the flank; if feinting low and, arrive high, it is performed to the chest, high; if the threat is inside to outside to the chest, the arrest is directed to the inside chest.

Appuntata *(L'appuntata)*

An immediate remittance on the opponent's indirect response. Instead of defending himself by returning to his guard, a straight thrust is delivered from the lunge to the target which is discovered after the parry and as soon as the opponent detaches his iron to respond. If the attack is directed to the arm, then the appuntata is performed from the guard to the arm, chest, or mask.

Inquartata *(L'inquartata)*

The thrust that is directed in the opponent's internal quadrant, discarding the guard with the left foot to the right (for left handers the reverse) to taking a step to the right on the side. This action is opposed to the opponent ending in the internal high line and the thrust can be directed to the chest, mask or by angulation to the arm.

A lateral dodge, performed by opposing the opponent's blade in the fourth line. It is a counterattacking action that must be performed on time at the end of the opponents attack at the precise moment that his blade is placed in the offensive line.

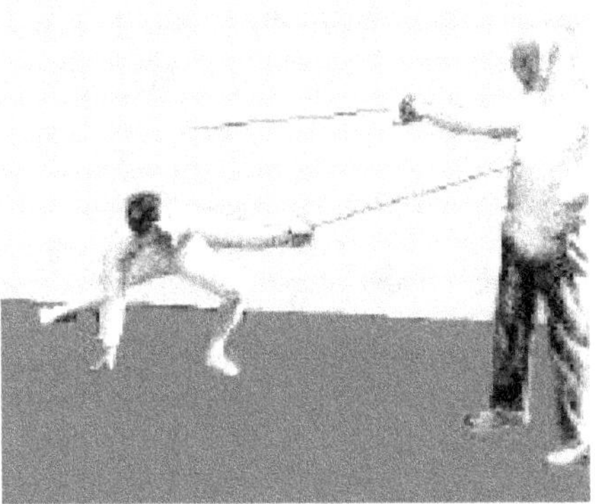

The passata sotto *(La passata sotto)*

This counterattack is done in time and with the displacement of the target, by ducking below the threat. The unarmed hand is used on the ground as support for the unbalanced body in a forward movement.

This thrust is performed by the guard or by retreat or by bringing the heel of the front foot to touch the back foot before performing the action. In opposition to an angulation from the opponent, the thrust must always be delivered direct and aimed at the forward target, for example the wrist.

Variations of the arrest *(Variasioni di arresto)*

The arrest actions to be exercised are:

- Direct stop on the arm by simple attack *(arresto diretto al braccio su attacco semplice)*

- From a disengagement of the four lines, blade seizure, glide, or soft parries *(parate di tasto) (di cavazione sui quattro legamenti, prese di ferro, fili o parate di tasto)*

- From a disengagement or the attempted engagement or counter *parry (di controcavazione sul legamento e parata di contro)*

- From a feint from the soft parry *(con finta su una parata di tasto)*

- From a double feint on two parries *(con doppia finta su due parate di tasto)*

- From a counter disengagement and feint *(con controcavazione e finta su contro e tasto)*

- On two counter parries in the opposite line *(su due parate di contro in linee opposte)*

- From a counter disengagement and double feint in opposite lines followed by two hits *(con controcavazione e doppia finta su due contro in linee opposte seguite da due tasto)*

They are performed on any opponent's attack:

- When stationary *(da fermi)*

- In a reasemblement *(in riunita (rassemblé))*

- In jumping back *(nel salto indietro)*

With the following variations:

- Direct *(diretti)*

- Disengagement *(con cavazione)*

- *Counter disengagement (con controcavazione)*

- *Feint (con finta)*
- *Double feint (con doppia finta)*
- *Counter disengagement and feint (con controcavazione e con finta)*
- *Double-debouble (deceive or circular action) (con doublé-dedoublé)*
- *Double-debouble and double feint (con doublé-dedoublé e doppia finta)*

The arrest by time thrust *(L'arresto di contrazione)*

It is the most typical offensive-defensive counterattack of the epeeist, because it closes the opponent's attack in the end. It is more effective and safer if intentionally pulled, opposing the blade to that of the opponent or, better, collecting it in the high lines (third or fourth) preferably in third which, naturally, brings the action of the attacker.

The arrest by contraction can be performed in the four lines with a decisive and progressive movement of the armed hand and at the same time using the guard to oppose and meet the line that the opponent's blade is to be.

The arrest on time, on feint *(L'arresto in tempo, sulla finta)*

Realizing that the opponent is tending to stop or repeatedly evade, rather than parrying and riposting, you can perform the stop hot on the feint.

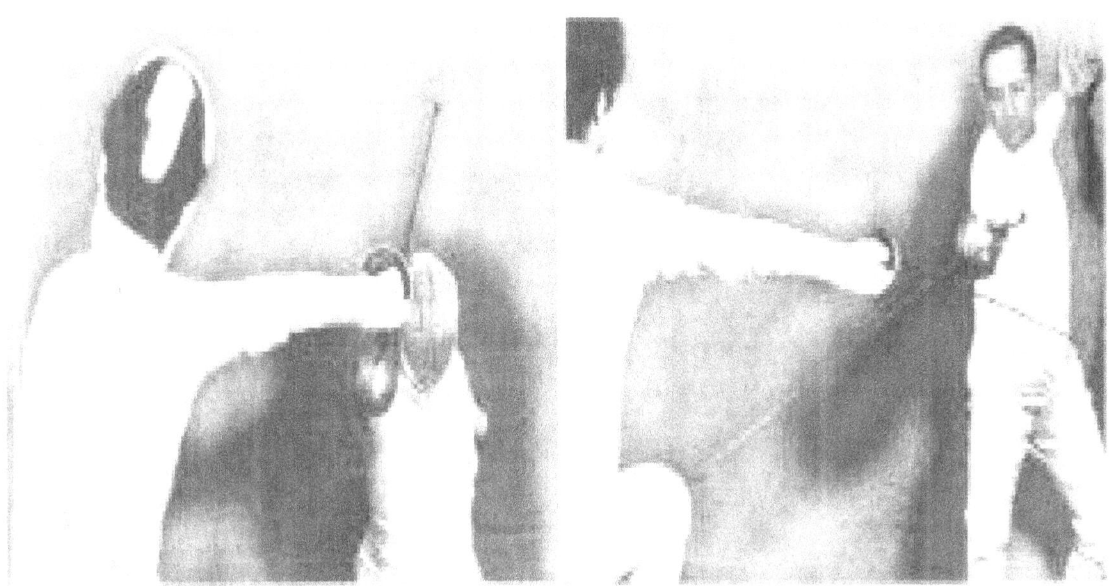

With third position opposition and the blade to the mask - With half-circle opposition and the blade to the knee

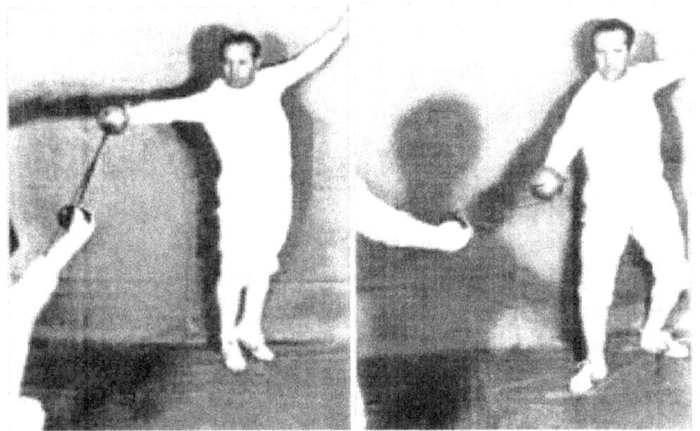

With third position opposition and the blade to the arm, in meeting - With fourth position opposition in the low line

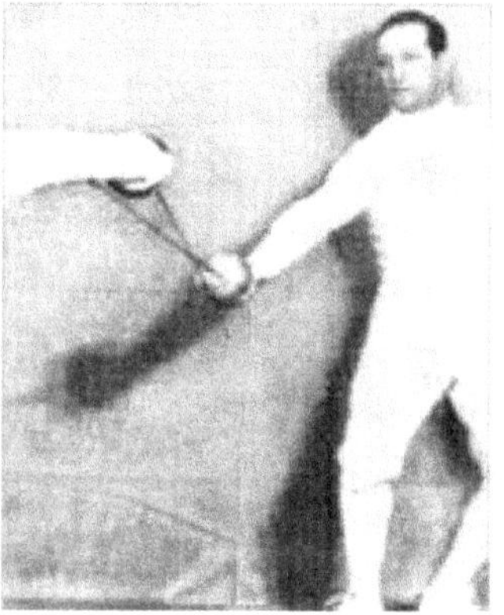

With second position opposition, half-turn, and the blade to the knee - With second position opposition and the blade angled to the lower arm

The parry *(la parata)*

This is a defensive action performed with the blade to deflect the opponents iron aimed at a target. The parries can be simple, half circular, circular, compound or by ceding.

The parry, ultimately, and the position of the weapon with which it is opposed to the advisories attack, defending oneself, it can also be avoided by retracting or retreating thus removing the target sought while threatening the attacking opponent with your own weapon Parrying with the blade requires rapid arm movement and contained and secure movements to promptly close the lines the opponent's attack is attempting to access.

Parry with the blade *(Le parate col ferro)*

In execution and practice, there are four fundamental parries to consider in relation to the four sectors of the target: internal and external high lines, internal and external low lines.

Considering, in fact, the target from a geometric point of view, we find ourselves in front of a surface ideally divided into four quadrants.

This division conceptually frames the choice and execution of attack and defense actions in the correlation and rationality in the fourth (internal high line), third (external high line), first or half circle (internal low line) or octave (external low line).

The parries, with the exception of those of the ceding, can be performed in two different ways, that is: soft or supported *(di tasto)* and the beat or strike *(di picco)*. They are called soft when the deviation of the opposing weapon is obtained by opposition of its own so that, at the end of the parry, the two blades are in contact with each other; the parry is called by beat, when the opposition on the opposing blade, for the purpose of a greater deviation of the same, ends with a real impact following which the two blades are clearly separated.

The simple parry *(Le parate semplici)*

They are called soft or simple parries and in them the blade moves with a linear movement directly from one line to the opposite one. The soft simple parries are four: in the high lines from fourth to third and from third to fourth; in the low lines from first or half circle to second (octave) and that from second (octave) to first or half circle.

The parry of fourth *(Le parata di quarta)* is carried out in one time (tempo) only by deflecting the opposing blade in the act that he strikes the steel, by turning the hand to third- and fourth-hand position and lowering it almost to the height of the abdomen, while the tip is kept a little higher than the hand.

The parry of third *(Le parata di terza)* is carried out in one time, deflecting the opponent's blade outside and in the high line the act that this action strikes. It starts with a slight movement of the hand accompanied immediately by the forearm: keeping the hand din fourth position or turning it to second and third, it is lowered to the height of the chest, while the tip of the epee is a little higher than the hand.

The parry of half-circle or first *(La parata di mezzocerchio)*, is performed in one time, deflecting, and picking up the opposing blade inward against the thrust, pivoting the shoulder-humeral joint without stiffening the arm. The position of the hand must remain unchanged, a single line must be formed with the arm and the tip of the epee, which must be at shoulder height and not far from the opponent.

The parry of second *(La parata di seconda)* is performed in one time, deflecting the opposing blade out and down in the act that is hit, pivoting the shoulder with a natural movement, without stiffening the muscles and turning the hand to second hand position or keeping it in fourth, lowered almost to the height of the side (flank), forming a single line with epee whose tip must be kept slightly away from the opponent's side.

Half circular parry *(La parata di mezza contro)*

In half circular parries, the movement describes a semicircle moving from one line to another. There are eight: four in a direct line. Direct: from fourth to first *(mezzocerchio)* and vice versa; from third to eighth (second) and vice versa; transverse line: from third to first *(mezzocerchio)* and vice versa; from fourth to eighth (second) and vice versa.

Circular parry *(La parata di contro)*

In the counter parries, you make your iron perform a complete turnaround the opponent's blade to seize it. In soft or simple parries, one starts at the opposite line: in counter (circular) parries one starts from a line and return to it. The circular parries aim in particular to collect the advisories blade in the starting line. There are four: fourth, third, first *(mezzocerchio)* and eighth (second).

Compound parries *(Le parate composte)*

They are made up of the alternation of simple parries, half circular, circular, double circular, double circular, and simple, simple and double circular, simple and half circle, half circle and simple, half circle, circular and half circle.

Compound parries are the opposites in defense of all compound offensive actions. Each offensive action therefore corresponds to a relative defense action that can be developed in the same line as the attack or by bringing the opponent's iron to another line.

Ceding parry *(la parata di ceduta)*

This is performed under correct measure and can be done in any of the four lines by transposing the blade from the guard line, giving the hand so that the blade is on a vertical plane, with the tip pointing upwards to parry the attack aimed at the high targets and the hand pointing diametrically opposite (point down) to block the low targets. There are four ceding parries. Fourth ceding parry is in response to the glide to the internal chest; the ceding parry of third is in response to the glide by angulation to the back the ceding parry of eighth is in response to the glide to the abdomen; the half circular ceding parry is in response to the cut over *(intagliata)* in reverse *(di rovescio)* to the external high target.

Parry of measure *(La parata di misura)*

This is a defensive action that eludes the opponent's attack by simply breaking measure, subtracting, that is, the target from the opponent's offense with an appropriate backward movement of the limb or body. To be effective the measurement parry must be performed in relation to the starting distance and the speed of execution of the opponent's attack, to pass from a defense condition to that of an immediate possibility of offense. From a point of view of competitive logic, in fact, any parry made with the blade must be followed by the immediate response and, similarly, to the measurement parry, must immediately follow a counter offensive action, thus removing the initiative from the opponent.

System of defense-offense *(Il Sistema defensive-offensivo)*

The most effective defensive actions consist of parries with the blade and measure deliberately applied as a second intention.

They tactically constitute the dynamically most rational expression and give the possibility to vary the fighting rhythm to one's advantage by increasing or decreasing it in contract with the opponent's rhythm.

Another defensive-offensive system is to anticipate the end of the opponent's attack by subtracting the target from the adverse offence by going forward by entering in a short measure.

Actions of concealment *(Il traccheggio)*

Concealing your intentions by changing several times between invitation or engagement and vice versa, practicing light beats insinuating the tip or threatening with very fast disengagements, in order to hide from the opponent, the moment of attack, or to entice him to attack to take advantage then the parry and riposte or counter attack *(uscita in tempo)*.

Body evasion *(La schivata)*

The opponent's offensive action can be neutralized by dodging. The dodge is therefore an action intended to subtract one's target from the attack brought by the attacker and you can perform:

- By profiling the chest;
- Passing momentum from the guard to the reasemblement;
- Abandoning the line of direction with a lateral movement (sidestep).

Passata sotto *(La passata sotto)*

This is a dodge, performed on the spot, which subtracts its target from the attack of the opponent carried on the external high line. It is performed by lowering and bending the body forward and to the side, while the armed hand extends the blade directing it to the attacker's hand, trunk, leg, or foot. If necessary, the unarmed hand comes to rest on the ground.

Closing the line *(La chiusura)*

It is performed with a rapid step forward, from the guard or meeting position, up to the marrow measure, avoiding the hand-to-hand combat, an action allowed by the regulation and conceptually applies to hinder the opponent's offensive initiative.

The dodge *(La giravolta)*

Carried out within the terms of the regulation, that is, without exceeding the opponent, and a counter-offensive action that allows you to hit the attacker who 'closes' to tight closely. It is performed by abandoning the opponent's blade and turning themselves on to touch the opposite side.

Jump back *(Il salto indietro)*

A defensive action and a type of parry by measure, you subtract your target promptly from the opposing offense. The execution keeps the blade In line to apply a counter attacking action.

The jump backwards, contrary to custom writings described in some treaties who see him leaving and arriving on the balls of the feet, determined by joined movements of the two feet, it must represent a propulsive springing backwards from the heel of the front foot, whether it comes from the guard position, or that from the lunge, to fall back on the legs with an accentuated movement (timed to arrest) and immediately step back out on the back leg to recover into the guard for balance and stability.

Even the jump back, rationally performed, is part of the defensive-offensive system.

Counter-time *(Il controtempo)*

The opposite of arrests are counter attacks. These apply against the attacker where one is ready to thrust into the last part of the opponent's tempo, giving the thrust all the semblance of truth, simple, counter, or half circular movement of the exit in time of the opponent and responding quickly to the uncovered target. These can be accomplished in counter-time as all actions, both on their own choice of time, same time or by offering the opponent an invitation or engagement or by feint of angulation. You can advance in counter time by exiting on the opponent's time.

CHAPTER III

GRAPHIC SUMMARY

THEDEFENSE
LA DIFESA

Counterattacks or arrests *(I controattacchi o arresti)*

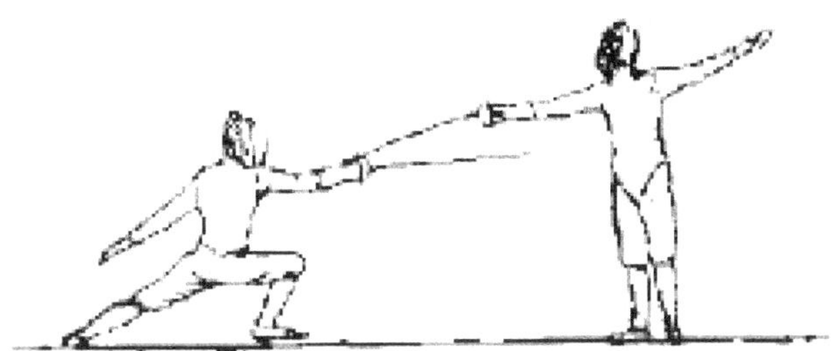

Arrest to the top of the wrist by reasemblement

Arrest to the mask by reasemblement

a. Arrest to the top of the arm by angulation from the guard against the opponent who attacks the bottom of the arm. **b.** arrest on the top of the arm against the opponent who attacks the foot.

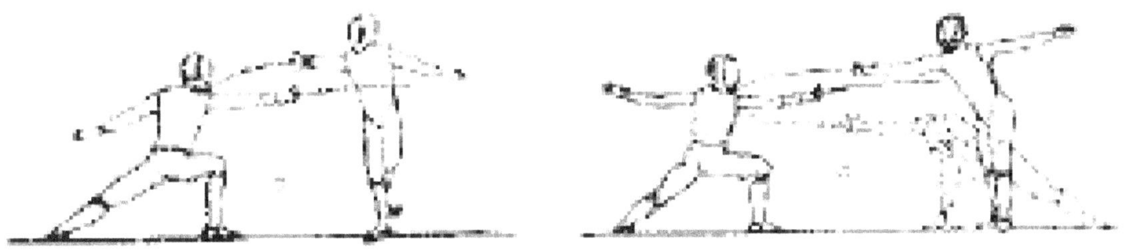

c. Arrest to the chest by inquartata against the opponent who attacks straight: **d.** arrest above by reasemblement or by passata sotto directing the thrust to the flank.

The arrest by time thrust *(Gli arresti di contrazione)*

Time thrust to the top of the arm. The arrester's weapon must be brought decisively forward to contact the forward movement of the opponent's blade, with marked opposition of the hand below.

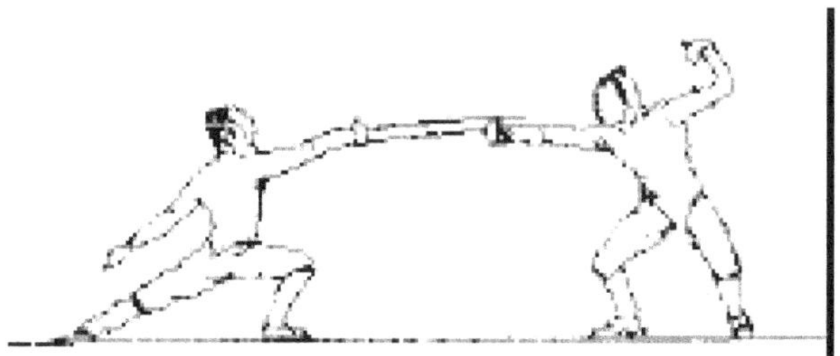

Time thrust to the bottom of the arm. The arrester's weapon must be brought decisively forward to contact the penetration of the opponent's blade, with marked opposition of the hand upwards while directing the tip of the epee to the arm of the opponent.

Arrest by time thrust of a left-handed fencer on right-handed (or vice versa) Carried out in first and directing the point to the adversary's knee.

The parry *(Le parate)*

Against the straight thrust from the opponent to the inside high line: parry of fourth.

Against the straight thrust to the outside high line: parry of third

Against the straight thrust to the inside low line: parry of half circle, or first.

Against the straight thrust to the outside low line: parry of eighth.

Against the straight thrust to the outside low line: parry of second. The hand is turned 180 degrees from the parry of eight.

From the invitation of eight or second, if the opponent thrusts to the internal target, parry with half circle or first. The half circle with the and in fourth hand position, for first by turning the hand 180 degrees, nails facing upward.

Against the direct thrust to the inside line: parry by first advancing, thus closing the distance on the attacker's action thrusting to the arm and close distance. The same action can be performed with a turn, while still facing the opponent.

Against the attackers straight thrust, while advancing parry fourth and riposte to the mask by glide while maintaining accentuated opposition.

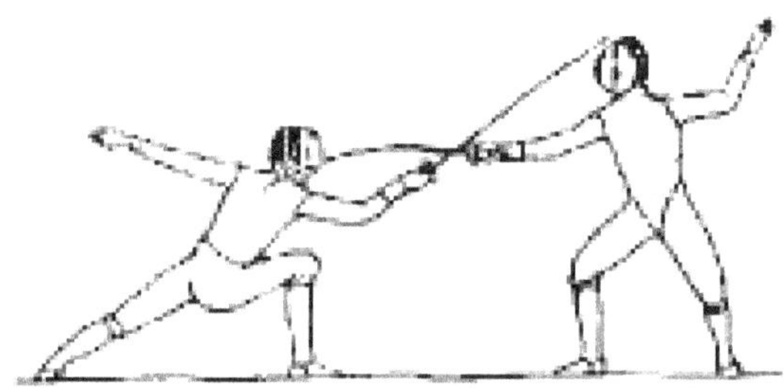

Right hand to right hand, parry of third and riposte to the back.

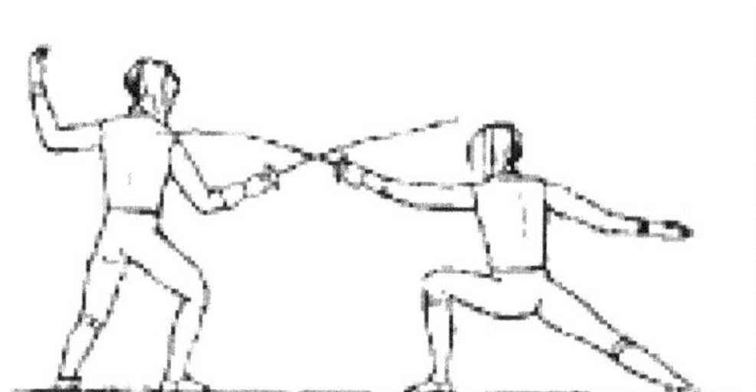

Left-handed to right-handed, parry of third against the straight thrust to the back.

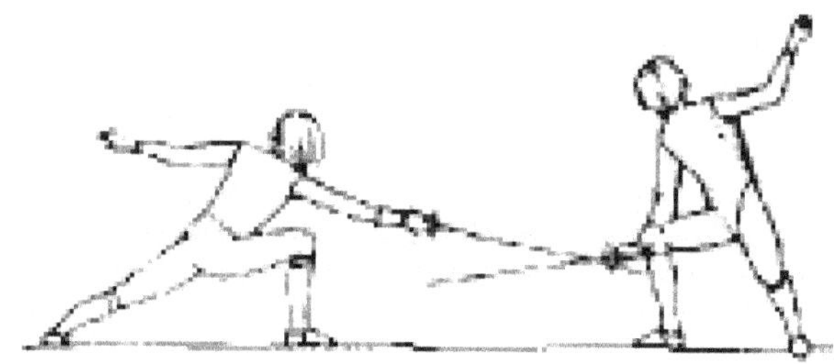

Parry of low fourth, simple or ceding. It must be performed with strong opposition of the armed hand to avoid possible continuations or rimessa by the attacker.

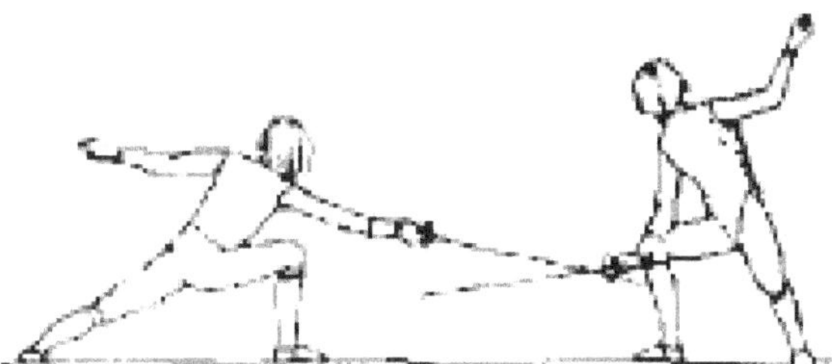

Parry of low fourth from close range. The armed arm is strongly bent at the elbow and the riposte will have to be brought without releasing the blade, preferably to the opponent's chest.

Counter Time *(Il controtempo)*

From the guard position, out of measure the attacker b, advances one step, decisively taking on the invitation of half circle. The opponent a. threatens the flank with a lunge b. who premeditated the action, responds in second with a glide to the flank and closing the measure.

The counter time us an applied concept understood and executed with various actions and on different targets, also varying the measure as "contrary" to the arresting actions (counterattacks).

CHAPTER IV

COUNTER-OFFENSE
LA CONTROFFESA

Counter offense *(La controffesa)*

It is expressed with actions aimed at causing offense to the opponent after scoring a hit during the defense. It follows that the response actions (riposte) and those brought with resumption of offensive initiative, respectively after having defended with the blade, or of measurement, with iron and of measurement, they are to be defined with a tactical and applicative concept: the counter offense. It should be underlined that the counter offense is something else than the counterattack. In fact, it is now an established norm that every action is defined as a counterattack which is opposed to the attack, i.e. the arrests, which does not define the same for the three weapons. The convention that holds foil and saber combat requires to classify arrests by giving the right or wrong to those who arrest depending on whether the arrest action nips the bud the offensive initiative - time after time - that precludes to the attacking action every possibility of reaching the target – time thrust or dodge, or that, on a compound action, arrives to touch with an advantage in fencing time, that is preceding the final movement by one full tempo of the attacking action. For the epeeist, arrest only means arrive first, touch before being touched, avoiding so that the device cannot record the double hit.

Having said this, it should be noted that the most canonical counter offence is the riposte that for all intents and purposes must be performed immediacy and with maximum coverage keeping in mind what was clearly stated in defining the actions of attack.

The riposte *(La risposta)*

The action that strikes as an answer immediately after the opponent has been parried, thus following the action defensive as counteroffensive.

Simple riposte is done both as detached, by glide as appropriate, staying perfectly on spot, or tightening the measure by a step forward, or dissolving with a step or jump back or getting up in the reasemblement.

From the parry of fourth the riposte can be:

- By detachment to the chest, mask or arm
- By glide to the chest or hip
- Both by glide or detached to the leg.

From the parry of third the riposte can be:

- By glide to the mask, chest, top of arm

- By detachment bottom of arm, hand in second and third or fourth.

It is dangerous to riposte to the flank or to the leg but not excluded. From the parry of second you can riposte:

- By glide to the flank or top of leg
- Or detached to top of arm, chest, or mask

From the half circle parry (mezzocerchio) you can respond:

- By glide: flank, chest, or leg
- By detachment: the arm, under or below, chest, or mask.

The answer by glide gives more warranty and safety. From the above parries you can respond by angulation to the arm, however, the angle opposite to the line where it was parried.

Simple riposte direct *(le risposte semplice e dirette)*

- Direct: when touching the opponent without leaving the line where the parry was made.
- By glide: when touching the adversary by crawling on his blade after the parry.

The riposte simple indirect *(Le risposte semplice e indirette)*

- Riposte by disengagement: when touching the opponent in the opposite line to that in which the parry was made, after having passed under the blade of the opponent when performed in the high line and above the blade if the parry was made in the low line.
- Riposte by cut over (risposta di intagliata) when touching the adversary in the line opposite to the one in which the parry was made but done after passing over and in front of the opponent's blade going over the tip.

The compound riposte *(le risposte composte)*
Counter disengagement (or double disengagement) *(Risposta di controcavazione o doppia cavazione)*

- when touching the opponent in the opposite line to that which the parry was made, after describing around the opponent's blade one whole circumference.
- Riposte by one two: when touching the opponent in the same line on which it is parries, but after having brought the blade in the opposite line passing below that of the opposing blade.

- Riposte by cut over or feint by cut over: when you touch your opponent in the same line as the parry after having passed in the opposite line by going above the tip of the opponent's blade.

CHAPTER V

THE FIGHT
IL COMBATTIMENTO

The combat *(Il Combattimento)*

Before being able to get on the piste for the fight it is essential that the student has assimilated with sufficient security and coordination the execution of the fundamental actions of attack, defense, offense in the defense, arrests in counterattack, of response in immediate counter offense and in fast break *(contropiede)*

The fencer then must have a precise idea of the meaning and the applicative possibilities of the simple actions conditioned by time, speed and measure. Finally, the various initiatives must be determined by fencing reasoning, that is, by a logical offensive-defensive tactical plan of actions and reactions based on the possibilities and conditions of their own and those of the adversary.

SIGNIFICANT TECHNICAL TERMINOLOGY *(Significato dei termini tecnici)*

- **Time (*tempo*)**: the duration of a single action
- **The attack** *(L'attacco)* is the initial offensive action, extending the threatening arm continuously threatening the valid surface of the opponent.
- **Angulation** *(L'angolazione)* is the action to hit mainly the forward target, taking advantage of an appropriate angled penetration of one's blade into the opponent's defensive cover.
- **The arrest or stop hit** *(L'arresto)* is a shot taken with precedence of time on the attack of the opponent. If brought into contact with the blade and with appropriate opposition and cover to prevent the opponent's attack from touching, it is called **time thrust** *(definisce contrazione)*
- **The remise** *(La rinessa)* is the action that the attacker makes following his offensive action when the opponent after having parried does not respond, responds late or by compound. In epee, the remise is thrown intentionally following the attack or stop hit (arrest), preferably taken to the forward target and without withdrawing the arm. Only in close proximity or in a melee, in epee fighting is allowed, it may be necessary to fold the arm.
- **The parry** *(La parata)* is the action performed with the blade that prevents the attack form touching.
- **The riposte** *(La risposta)* and offensive action of the fencer who after parrying the attack is therefore counterattacking.
- **Counter parry** *(La controparata)* is the second parry executed on the opponent's riposte.
- **The counter-riposte** *(La controisposta)* is the offensive action of the fencer who parried a second time.
- **Gain on the lunge** *(Il raddoppio)* whether simple action or compound, which is executed by bringing the back foot to touch the front heel and then lunging used against the opponent who has dodged, moved to the side or back.

- **Renewed attack** *(La ripresa d'attacco)* is the restart of the original attack performed immediately after returning to the guard position, on the opponent who parries without responding.
- **Fencing phrase** *(Frase schermistica)* is thus defined as the sequence of offensive and defensive actions of the two fencers, that follows fencing reasoning without pauses.
- **The counterattack** *(Il contropiede)* the application of the concept of bringing counter-offensive actions and responses or new offensive initiatives. At the end of an offensive action by the opponent or immediately upon their return on guard, arrest with reasemblement or jump back.

WAYS TO CONDUCT THE ASSAULT *(Modo di condurre l'assalto)*

You cannot give precise rules, if you have to change how you conduct the assault depending on the opponent in front of you and your training and the respective resistance. Not always, for example, it is possible to tire the adversary. However, a few can be given suggestions on the method to follow in the study of the assault and on the way to behave in general.

It is very useful to often be faced with irregular and incorrect adversaries and to learn how to dominate them by opposing them with suitable opposition, not to let themselves be broken down by their game, to keep one's own approach to avoid being surprised.

One of the main factors of success if perfect serenity of mind and the way of fencing it must be inspired by a great activity on the brain: do not rush the actions for the purpose of wanting to immediately touch the opponent, but rather wait, patiently, for the favorable moment, varying considerably the measure and preform all those actions aimed at attracting the adversary to your own design, to have the possibility of the choice of time to take the attack.

Against opponents of tall and harmful stature insist on the high line, as the adversary of shorter stature, to produce effective threats, and easily forced to find out more the arm and to use of forward measure is not convenient for him, exposing himself at the risk of being hit in turn with ease, especially in the arm.

It is instead advisable to threaten to the arm and to the low line, especially to the leg, holding on the ready, when the adversary on such movements pulls as the mask or chest, to strike the arm below with a counterattack. Of course, this does not detract from the fact that, if the favorable opportunity presents itself, yes it can also threaten the chest or mask.

When the fencer sets out to touch the adversary's chest it is useful for him to draw his deceptively, pretending to want them to strike the arm, just to distract their attention and then surprise him with a beat or glide in the opposite direction, or even better with second intention.

It is very profitable to hold the epee in line, always following the adversary's bell guard with the point, to be ready to hit at every moment that they uncover a target, disengaging the tip as they attempt to engage it or beat, and procuring to never let oneself be dominated by the blade, in order to avoid or at least make difficult gliding actions.

However, given that you have to keep the blade constantly in line produces, in the long run, tiredness and stiffening of the arm, it is useful to alternate this game with invitations or engagements, evaluating the measure in the way that prudence advises.

Against the opponent who insists on tightening the measure, the actions appropriate offense are performed in time.

It should be noted that by dissolving the measure continually loses ground and it can be a good tactic against backtrackers system, they attach to the limit and force them to develop an attacking action.

These considerations are enough to confirm more obviously than a fencer of epee cannot be complete if one is not used to performing actions from a ling hand of attack with suitable choice of time and if they can't have all those means that they can buy only with a patient and diligent study.

Preordained actions *(Le azioni preordinate)*

Moving on then to consider the various possibilities to hit the opponent according to a pre- established tactically, a thrust can be scored first, second and third intention.

The first intention and the one that realizes the hit by preventing the initiative from passing to the opponent, that is, when the opponent fails to find the blade, to parry, to release or to stop in time.

The second intention is the one that causes the opposing initiative to neutralize it promptly. Example: walking in reverse – initiative attack on the invitation of third – counterattack of high internal straight thrust of the opponent – parry of fourth (beating) and riposte in counterattack response.

The third intention is the one that intentionally eludes the opponent's second intention. Example: direct attack on the line of the invitation of third (first intention) – counter attack of the opponents straight thrust – parry fourth of the attacker in the attack phase (second intention) – counter parry of fourth and riposte by retreating from the opponent – counter- parry and riposte direct from the attacker which concludes the attack (third intention).

The first and second intention are possible to apply to all measures; the third intention is applied from step and lunge measure on the opponent who retreats and for a long measure.

It is clear that the second intention, and even more so third intention, they require one to special study and training.

The contraries (opposites) *(Le contrarie)*

The fencer must have a precise idea and certain of the "contraries" to be opposed to the opponent's actions.

ACTION	CONTRARY
Straight thrust	Simple parry keeping contact, time thrust, defensive measure with parry
Beat direct	Simple parry soft, disengagement, defensive measure, misura with parry
Disengagement	Circular parry in the same line or going in the opposite line, defensive measure, measure and circular parry, defensive measure with parry
Counter disengagement	Double circular parry in the same line, double counter parry in the opposite line, defensive measure with double circular parry, defensive measure, with parry
Deceive	Counter disengagement (see #4)
Feint	Parry in relation to the feint that simulates the attacking action (see cases above, 1 -5)
Grazing beat (Intagliata)	Same as disengagement (#2)
Angulation	Breaking half circular parry collect the blade as time thrust
Forced Glide or Pressure	Disengagement avoiding contact with the blade
Glide	With counterpressure or disengagement or defensive measure with counter pressure or disengaging
Blade seizure, change beat, transport	Counter pressure, disengagement, counter disengagement, defensive measure with counter pressure,

	disengagement or counter disengagement
Ceding	Half circular parry
Continuation of the attack, second touch or renewed attack	Breaking the measure by retreating or withdrawing and applying the contrary to the attacking action
Remise	Applying the appropriate opposition to the renewed attack or parry by measure

Defense in the four lines

ACTION	CONTRARY
Beating parry	Disengagement or cut over
Half circular parry	Simple parry soft, disengagement, defensive measure, misura with parry
Circular parry	Counter disengagement or deceive
Double circular parry	Feint by Counter disengagement
Counter parry by beat	Counter disengagement one two
Counter parry with a beat in the opposite line	Counter disengagement one, two three
Counter parry two opposite lines	Counter disengagement on opposite lines (double-double) i.e. counter disengagement in one direction then counter disengagement in the other direction
Time thrust	Counter time
Ceding parry	Counter with ceding parry in opposite line
Defensive measure, retreat	Continuation of the attack, replacement of thrust or renewed attack

Executive details of some contrary (opposites) *(Particolari esecutivi di alcune contrarie)*

Against the angulation

In response to direct attackers performed with appropriate guard opposition, there are only parries "against" by advancing with the blade in order to close with adequate concentration of the enemy's offensive.

In the usual parry of *fourth* with accentuated hand opposition (*inquartando*) from the part of the adversary, the opposite to be applied and to secure the blade at the start; transport the opponent's blade in 'counter of third' and follow the edge (glide) to the body, to the external high target.

Against the rimesse *(Contro le rimesse)*

Against the rimesse 'replacement' the parry must be performed pressing forward and with much opposition.

Against the renewed attack 'continuation' *(continuazione d'attacco)*

Continuation of the attack constitutes a whole chapter unto itself. After the parry, one must never detach the blade, and one always answers with a glide. In such this will prevent the continuation of the attack taking away their "touch"

Against the cut over *(L'intagliata)*

The cut over can be parried effectively following the counter parry, that the opponent must necessarily evade, a spanking parry *parata di tasto* in the opposite low line (eight or second) if the attack ends in the flank, half circle if in the abdomen.

However, these immediate changed of line on the parry of counter beating parry *contra e tasto* they need to be practiced a lot because they must be made with remarkable speed.

CHAPTER V

THE FIGHT
IL COMBATTIMENTO

The combat (assault) *(Il combattimento)*

The set of offensive and defensive, offensive-defensive actions (arrests), defensive-offensive (time thrusts) performed conditioning them on executive (the best) time, speed, and measure which determine the fencing phrase.

The various initiatives, based on one's own and the opponent's possibilities, must be determined by a logical plan of offensive-defensive tactics, i.e. being guided by precise fencing reasoning.

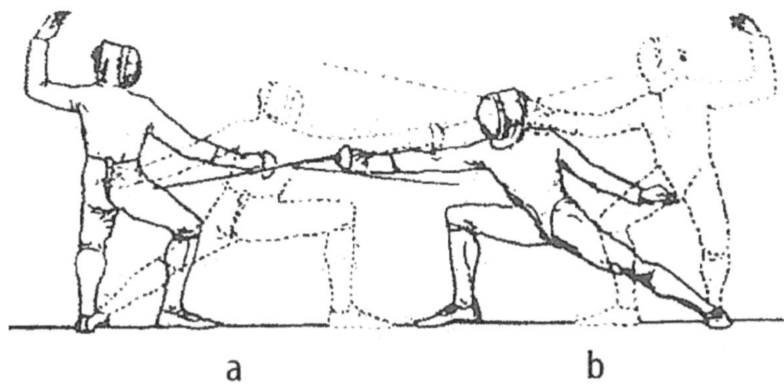

Straight thrust by **a.** parried by **b.** followed by the riposte by lunge and this is counter parried by **a.** Lines of third and second used.

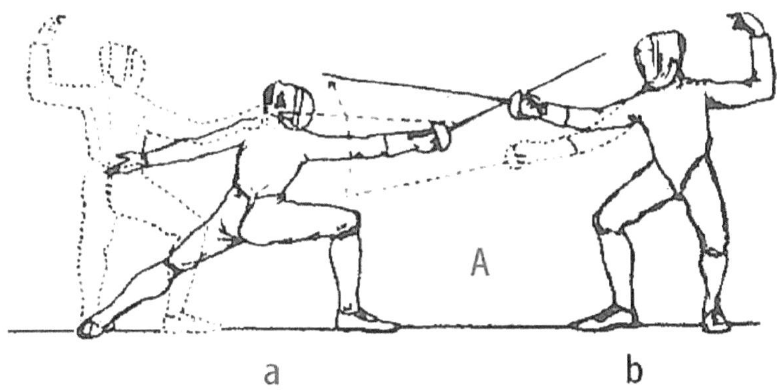

From the invitation of second **b.** straight thrust to the outside high line, half circular parry of third.

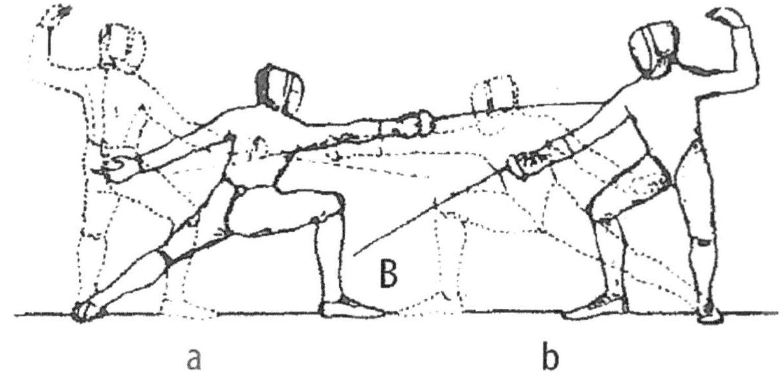

From third, b. responds to the flank of a. they respond with a parry of second and ripostes above with a lunge while b. returns to the guard with the armed arm lowered.

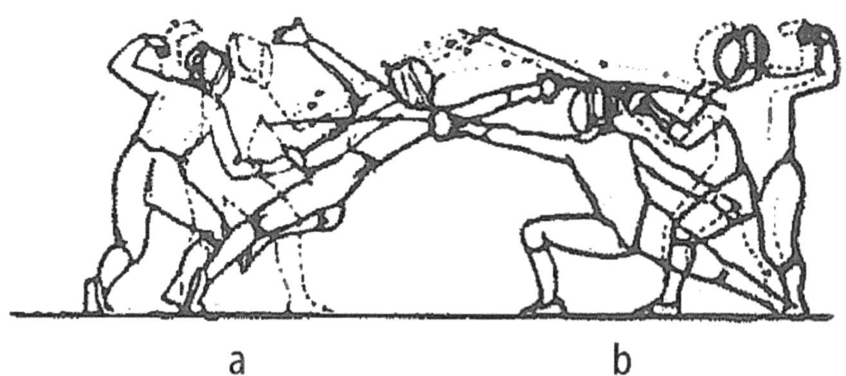

Attacking fencing phrase b. parries a. and the subsequent response (counter-offensive) is the arrow pulled by the return on guard of b.

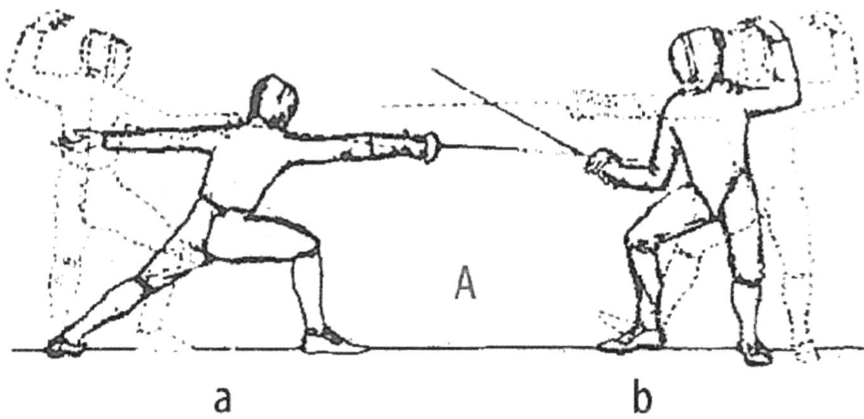

From the blade in line of the attacker b. the opponent a. directs a straight thrust to the abdomen b. parries fourth and ripostes.

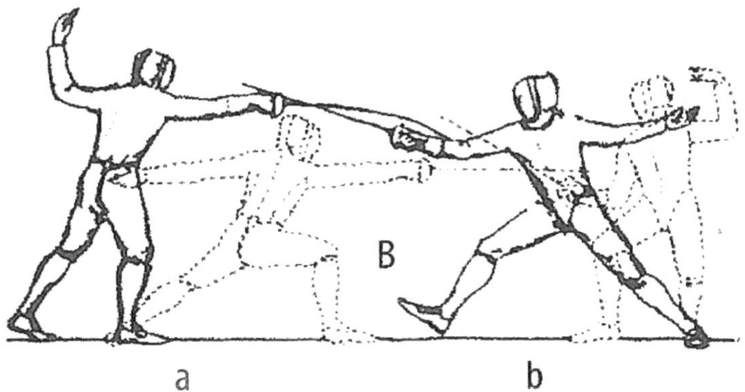

a   b

On the direct riposte to the bottom of the arm b. the opponent a. arrests with an reasemblement from the retreat (offense in defense) addressing the tip of the weapon to the top of the forearm with marked opposition of the hand in third.

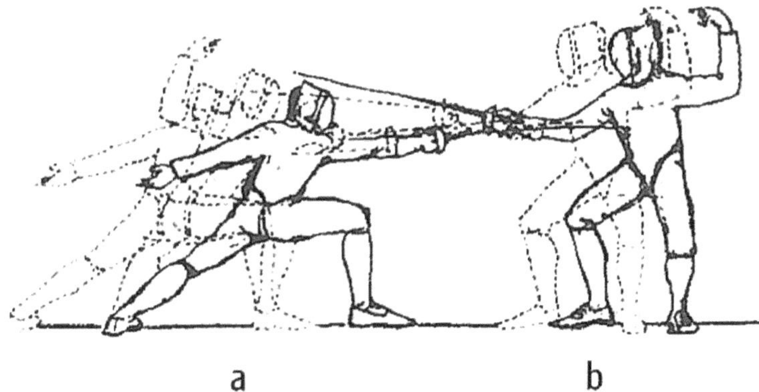

a   b

Lunge and forward recover and lunge again of a. on b., with a straight thrust, b. responds with a parry of measure with no other reaction.

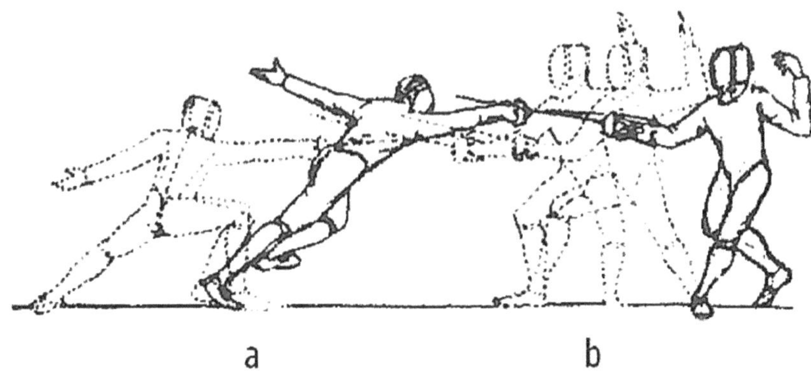

a   b

From the lunge, recover forward with the arrow a. b. retreats from correct distance taking a step back followed by a cross step back, always backwards.

The executive concepts of actions in epee are attack, arrest, replacement, parry (by blade, measure or blade and measure), counter parry and riposte, counter riposte, renewed attack, reasemblement, jump back, on the opposite foot, in phase of offense, defense and offensive-defensive.

The Second intention *(La second intenzione)*

This opposes the actions carried out by the first intention of the adversary. With second intention one provokes the opponent's initiative to neutralize it promptly with actions contrary to those that have occurred.

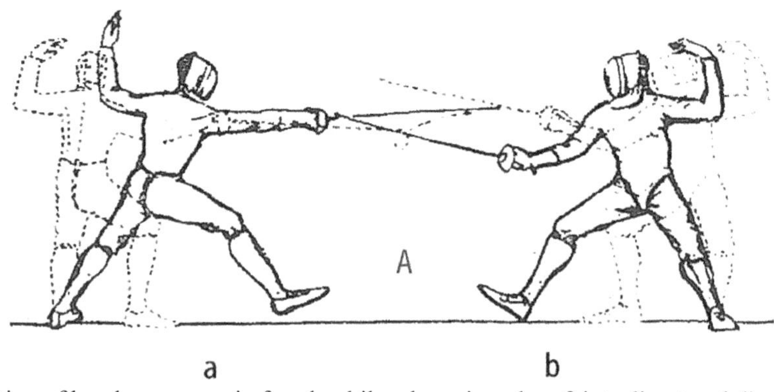

On the initiative of b. who engages in fourth while advancing, then feints direct and disengagement, a. advances to attack

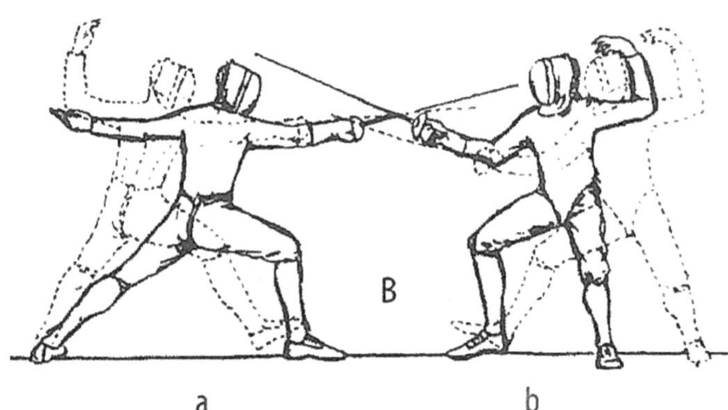

On the lunge of a. b. parries picking up the blade in third while at the same time stepping forward.

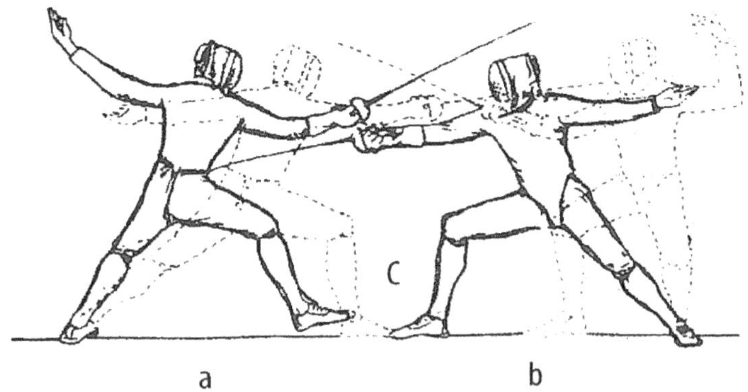

The riposte is brought by b. going into the lunge thrusting to the flank of a. as they begin to return to the guard.

THE CONVENTIONS OF EPEE COMBAT

The way of making a hit *(Modo di tirare le stoccata)*

The epee is a point only weapon. The offensive action of the epee is therefore practiced with the tip and the tip only. Fencers are prohibited from dragging their tip of their own weapon on for any amount of time on the fencing platform.

Valid target *(Bersaglio valido)*

In epee, the valid target includes the entire body of the fencer, including the equipment. Therefore, every hit that arrives counts, regardless of the part of the body (torso, limbs, or head), clothing or equipment hit.

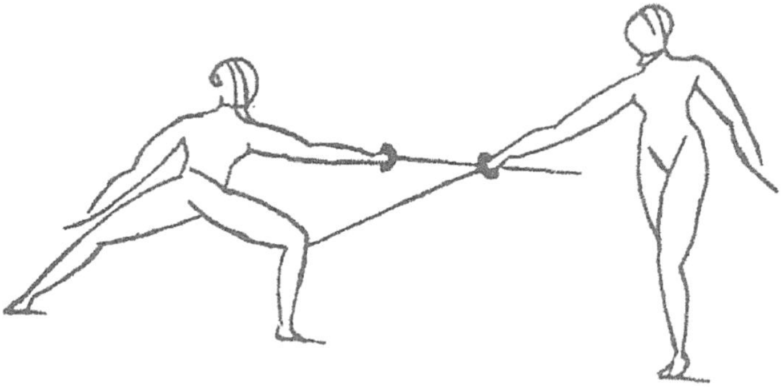

Valid targets in epee

The melee *(L'a corpo a corpo)*

In epee, the fencer who, both in arrow and in carrying himself decidedly forward, gives rise, even several times in a row, to hand-to-hand combat (without brutality or violence). transgresses the fundamental conventions of fencing and does not commit any irregularity.

The "arrow that ends systematically should not be confused as the melee" with the "arrow that ends with a blow that causes the opponent to lose balance » and which, in all three weapons, is considered an act of voluntary brutality and therefore punished.

On the contrary, 'it is the arrow delivered with momentum and which overcomes the movement the opponent' is not prohibited: the President must not give the "Stop" too soon so as not to cancel the possible riposte; if executing a arrow the fencer does not touch the opponent, but systematically goes out of bounds to the side of the platform, he will have to be penalized as expected.)

The number of touches and duration of the match *(durata dell'incontro)*

Epee matches take place in 3 periods, with one duration of 6 minutes per meeting: in the direct elimination, two meetings with 3 periods and possible beautiful (one deciding touch, La Belle) or meetings with a given number of hits.

If, following a double touch, the two fencers reach the number of hits expected, they must throw one or more additional phrases, up to the time limit. Every new double shot will be canceled (and the shooters will therefore be left in place).

The result, in this case, will always be scored at the maximum of hits for each fencer (e.g., at 5 hits, the result marked on the board will be S5 and V-5).

If time expires before the match ends:

a)   at a hit, the opponents are both considered touched, and each has a defeat;

b)   with multiple hits:

If one of the opponents received more hits than the other, the number of hits necessary is added to it reach the maximum, and the same number is added to the other fencer;

If the opponents have the same number of hits (or they have no hits), they are supposed to have received the maximum hits and they are both defeated

Judgement of the hit in epee: *(Giudizio della stoccata alla spada)*

The épée tests are judged with the aid of apparatus electric signaling device that records hits (mandatory measure for official F.I.E. tests).

To judge the materiality of the touch, only the indication of the device is authentic. Under no circumstances should the President declare a shooter touched, without the device having registered the hit regularly (except in cases penalties provided for by the regulation).

Annulling the touch *(Annullamento dei colpi)*

1.   *In judging the President does not validate the resulting signals from touches:*

a.   Touches made before the command of 'fence' or after the 'halt'

b.   caused by a meeting between the tips or by a blow to the ground (if there is no metal platform or outside it) or they touched objects that are outside of the opponent, including his own equipment.

The shooter who intentionally provokes a hit placing its tip on any surface outside of his opponent, he will be penalized with one touch, after a warning during the same group or team match or in knockout bouts. (direct elimination)

2.	*Furthermore, the President must take into account any faults in the* electrical equipment and cancel the last hit registered, in the following cases:

a.	if a shot landed on the guard of the shooter and reported as if touched or on the metal platform, it causes ignition of the scoring apparatus;

b.	if a regulated thrust carried by the reported fencer touched, and it does not cause the scoring apparatus to turn on.

c.	if the appliance turns on unexpectedly from that of the reported shooter touched, for example, following a concussion of the iron, of any movement of the opponent. Of vibrations of the platform transmitted to the device or following of any other cause other than a regular thrust;

d.	If the signal for a hit made by the fencer indicated touched:

I)	does not prevent the signal for further signaling a hit after a time longer than that of the double shot;

II)	or it is canceled out by a further thrust of the adversary.

3. *The   President   must   also   apply   the   following   rules   for   canceling   hits:*

a.	only the last thrust that precedes the observation of the fault can be canceled and only if it is the fencer given as touched that he is disadvantaged by such failure;

b.	the fault must be confirmed by tests carried out immediately after the fight stopped, below the surveillance of the President and without changing the used material

c.	in such examinations, one should not attempt to reconstruct what actually happened during the assault, but it must only ascertain whether there is a material possibility of an error in judgment due to a fault. The determination of this fault in the entire appliance electrical equipment, including one's personal equipment or of the other fencer, is of no importance for the judgment of annulment;

d.	the shooter who, without being invited by the President, proceeds to modify or change its material before the judgment is rendered, he loses his right to annulment.

I)	After warning and effective resumption of combat (1), a shooter can no longer claim the cancellation of a touch on him reported before such recovery;

e.	it is not necessary, to cancel a hit, that the reported fault repeats with each shot, but it must be established, without any doubt, at least once by the President;

f.	if accidents occur following detachment of the shooter's cord contact sockets (both at the hand, or on the back of the shooter), they cannot give rise to the cancellation of the reported hit.

I)	However, if the prescribed safety device, not working or does not exist, annulment must be granted in the event of detachment of the pin on the shooter's back;

II)	The fact that the President pronounced 'fence' the fact that a certain amount of time has passed does not mean "stop" the effective combat if the shooters remained in passive attitude without crossing irons. Because we must believe that there has been a resumption of combat the two opponents must actually have had one exchange of actions by engaging in a fencing phrase, what could have changed the state of the material used.

g. the fact that a fencers sword presents, on the guard, on the blade or elsewhere, more or less insulating stains diffuse, formed by oxide, glue, paint or other material, on which opponent's moves can cause a signal, cannot constitute a reason for cancellation of annulling a touch of that fencer;

h. the fact that the fencer reported as touched is found having broken his own blade, motivates the cancellation of the touch on him brought by the opponent;

i. in the event that, due to a hit to the platform, a fencer tears the metal of the platform, and at the same time the signal lights up from opponent's side, the touch must be annulled.

(1) The President will also have to supervise the state of the metal platform; he will not allow the assault to be carried out or continue if the platform has tears susceptible to alter the recording. (The organizers will have to take the measures necessary to allow the repair or rapid replacement of metal platforms).

Judging the double touch *(Giudizio del colpo doppio)*

In épée, if the two fencers are touched, it will be admitted a precedence only if it will be possible to ascertain an appreciable time difference between touches; where it misses, you will have a "double hit", i.e. one hit per each.

Electrical devices signal double strike, if the time difference between the two hits is less than an interval between one twentieth and one twenty-fifth of second.

In judging without the electrical device, the President decides whether there is a time difference or no priority place, or whether it is a double hit.

If there is a double touch for two valid hits, the two fencers are considered touched.

If there is a double hit for a valid hit and an invalid hit, the valid (hit outside the opponent, hit after having stepped off the platform), only the valid hit is considered valid.

If there is a double touch for a certain hit and a doubtful one (electrical appliance failure, disagreement, or indecision of the judges), the fencer who delivered the certain hit has the right to accept the double strike or have it annulled.

The fencing strip, Piste *(terreno – Pedana)*

All epee competitions can be held either in the fencing hall, both in the open air. The official tests of the F.I.E. they cannot be disputed than in the hall.

The width of the pedana is 1.80 to 2 m. with a length of 18 m. For practical reasons, the length of the platform is expected to be 14 m; the distance will be given to each fencer so that, being placed at 2 m. from the line of center, has a length available to retreat total of 7 m., without exceeding the limit with both feet.

7 lines are clearly drawn on the platform perpendicular to the length of the platform, i.e.:

-1 center line (which can be replaced by a point central or by a special sign on the edge of the platform);

2 warning lines (guard lines), 2 m. on each side of the center line and which must be drawn across the entire platform

2 rear limit lines, which must be drawn on the platform at 7 m. from the midline, distance that it can be less if you do not have sufficient land; this ground, in any case, cannot be less than 5 m

-2 warning lines, drawn at 2 m. with extreme limits and which can only be traced for 30 cm. on each side of the platform.

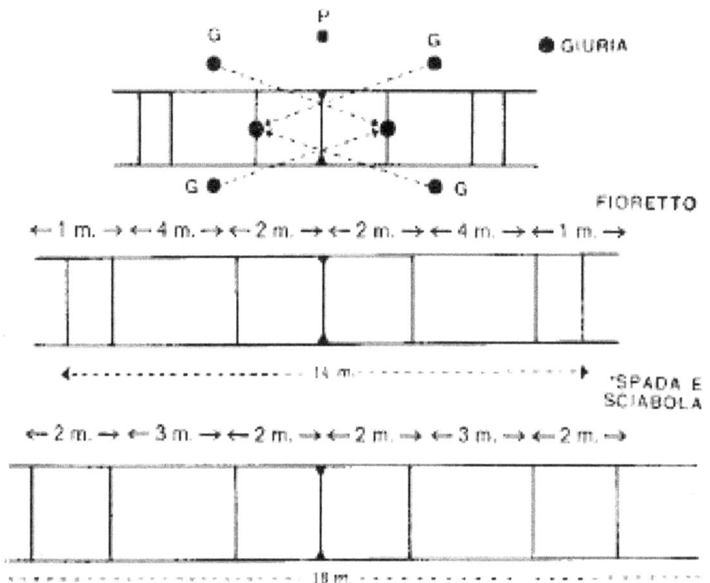

For competitions judged using the electric apparatus, the platform and its extensions are entirely covered with a metal platform, in order to obtain the neutralization of shots landed (mandatory for official tests of the F.I.E.).

The table on which the signaling device is placed must be placed at least at 1 m. from the platform, in front of the center line and the President must oversee why isolation is respected as much by the auxiliary people as much as by fencers and spectators. In principle, the same table must not be used by poster artists, timekeepers, etc.

CHAPTER VI

APPLICATION LEARNING AND EXERCISES
APPRENDIMENTO APPLICATO ED ESERCIZI

The conventional exercises *(Gli esercizi convenzionali)*

The purpose of the conventional exercises is that of training the student in prompt and sure defense and offense and, therefore, in all actions of attack and counter-offense and in all counterattacks (uscite in tempo). It is therefore necessary that one gets used to observing, to knowing how to scrutinize and discern the opponents intention, to know how to choose the time and decide resolutely to carry out his action with confidence and conscience in his own strength, without, however, never to forget, in the various succession of fencing actions, the severe correctness and elegance that make fencing an art that is also aesthetically beautiful.

There is no doubt that these exercises are useful for the development of the attack, and it is advisable for the master to have the foresight to know how to graduate them, so that one passes from the easiest to the least easy, finally to the most difficult. Furthermore, care must be taken that the pupils are matched with opponents of equal strength, because if this does not happen, the weakest can be influenced, remaining perplexed in the game of the exercises to be employed and losing that mastery and calm so necessary in the art of fencing. To enumerate the exercises that can be performed based on all the steps contemplated in the present treatise would be too long. Therefore, we limit ourselves to exposing a part of it, starting with some very easy and simple and moving to more complex ones. The difficulty of the latter arises from the variety of actions that can be carried out at one's own choice of time, or at the choice of the opponent, while the latter, in turn opposes the appropriate defense or executes an counterattack, or applies the counteroffensive, which, given the size of the target, is difficult to achieve.

By simple directive from the Master, we exemplify some exercise, then leaving the faculty of establishing others to the intelligence, imagination, and ability of the teacher, coordinating them and adapting them to the personality, progress and executive mastery of the student, not forgetting, however, in the composition of them the basic principles of fencing, referred to in the present treatise.

Exercise 1

STUDENT A	STUDENT B
From blade in line, at lunging distance, one must defend themselves or counterattack with the arm	From the blade in line, deliver an angulation to the bottom of the arm at ones won time, avoiding being counter-attacked

Exercise 2

STUDENT A	STUDENT B

From the invitation or engagement at lunging distance, defend themselves and counter-attack the arm or the mask, avoiding the counter against them	From the blade in line, deliver a straight thrust at ones own choice of time or disengage to the arm or chest, avoiding being counter attacked

Exercise 3

STUDENT A	STUDENT B
From blade in line at lunging distance, must defend oneself with a counterattack to the arm, chest, or mask avoiding the counterattack	From the blade in line, or invitation or engagement, thrust by angulation to the bottom of the arm, or execute a beat in fourth or half circular beat ending in the chest and avoiding the counterattack

Exercise 4

STUDENT A	STUDENT B
From the blade in line at step and lunge distance, defend or counterattack to the chest, to the mask, or disengagement in time to the arm, avoiding the counter	From blade in line or from an invitation, performs any action on the blade at their choice of time ending in the chest, mask or arm, avoiding the counterattack or the disengagement in time

Exercise 5

STUDENT A	STUDENT B
From the blade in line, either invitation or engagement at lunging distance, they must defend themselves or counter attack or counter offense to the arm, mask, or chest avoiding the counter	From the blade in line, one has the freedom to implement at his own choice of time, an action ending in the arm, chest or the mask or leg, avoiding the counterattack or the counter time

Exercise 6

Same as exercies 5, but performed at step and lunge distance and varying speed

Exercise 7

STUDENT A	STUDENT B
From the blade in line, at lunging distance, executes a disengagement to the arm, chest or mask avoiding the counter time	From a blade in line or invitation, perform an action on the blade of your choice or time preventing the disengagement in time

Exercise 8

STUDENT A	STUDENT B
From the invitation or engagement, at lunging distance, presents the blade Inline and must defend or counter attack avoiding the close fight (corp e corp)	From blade in line or invitation, as soon as the opponent puts their blade in line, performs an action on the blade ending to the arm, chest, or mask avoiding the counterattack

Exercise

The 8th exercise is repeated, from step and lunge distance with simple actions performed by disinterment, with the addition that student A can also counterattack to the arm, chest or mask. It can be done from either the guard or a small step forward immediately followed by a step backwards and always while in step and lunge distance.

Renewed attack from the lunge *(Esercizi di ripresa dell'a-fondo)*

The student performs a lunge to the body or the arm of the master who moves away gradually and continuously, letting himself be touched as he retreats. The student performs the renewed lunge (attack) without standing up, keeping the blade at eye level and the arm extended, bringing the back foot forward till it touches the heel of the front foot, without changing the position of the torso. To give impetus to the movement, the rear arm goes up and throws down with impetus at the right time.

These actions must be performed with and performed in all four lines unless noted:

- Renewed attack with straight thrust *(Ripresa di botta dritta, nelle quattro linee)*
- Renewed attack by disengagement *(Ripresa di cavazione, nelle quattro linee)*
- Renewed attack by counter-disengagement *(Ripresa di controcavazione, nelle quattro linee)*
- Renewed attack with a feint *(Ripresa di botta con finta, nelle quattro linee)*
- Renewed attack with double feint *(Ripresa di botta con doppia finta, nelle quattro linee)*
- Renewed attack by counter-deceive as a feint *(Ripresa di botta di controcavazione con finta, nelle quattro linee)*
- Renewed attack with a double deceive *(Ripresa di botta con doublé-dedoublé, nelle quattro linee)*

- Renewed attack by double deceive as a feint *(Ripresa di botta con doublé-dedoublé e doppia finta, nelle quattro linee)*

Resuming from the lunge it is necessary to always precede with the movements of the toes on those of the legs and to maintain perfect coverage of the arm with the adequate oppositions.

Counter parry exercises and touch and touch against *(Esercizi di parate di contro e tasto e tasto e contro)*

Special exercises on counter parries in all lines and with all variations of ripostes (direct, half circular, circular, vertical as indicated in the drawing of the graphic summary in the first chapter).

These exercises are performed:

- From counter of fourth to the simple parry of third *(Dalla contro di quarta alla parata semplice di terza)*
- Counter of third to the simple parry of fourth *(Dalla contro di terza alla parata semplice di quarta)*
- From the counter parry of third to simple parry of eight *(Dalla parata di contro di terza alla parata semplice d'ottava)*
- From the counter parry of eight to the simple parry of third *(Dalla parata di contro d'ottava alla parata semplice di terza)*
- From the counter parry of fourth to the half circular parry of mezzocerchio *(Dalla parata di contro di quarta alla parata semplice di mezzocerchio)*
- From double half circular parry to simple parry of fourth *(Dalla parata di contro di mezzocerchio alla parata semplice di quarta)*
- From a counter of fourth to simple parry of eight *(Dalla parata di contro di quarta alla parata semplice d'ottava)*
- From counter parry of eight to simple parry of fourth *(Dalla parata di contro d'ottava alla parata semplice di quarta)*
- *From double circular parry of third to half circular parry of first (mezzocerchio)*
- *(Dalla parata di contro di terza alla parata semplice di mezzocerchio)*
- *From the double circular parry of first to simple parry of third (Dalla parata di contro di mezzocerchio alla parata semplice di terza.)*
- *From the double circular parry of eight to simple half circular parry of first (Dalla parata di contro d'ottava alla parata semplice di mezzocerchio)*
- *From the counter of first to simple parry of eight (Dalla parata di contro di mezzocerchio alla parata semplice d'ottava)*

The ripostes performed from on spot (guard) or by lunging or arrow (fleche or running attack).

Special exercises for the counter (circular) parry *(Esercizi speciali per contenere le parate)*

Circular attacks to the body double circular parry while returning to the guard and subsequent retreat are used to learn to contain the double circular parry and spanking parry and are practiced with tightening on time on the final of the parry itself

Example

The student attacks the body with a counter disengagement, then on the return to guard and subsequent retreat, they parry the double counter of third, without finding the blade, stopping the final with tightening on time so as to get used to excessively widening the parries

The following exercises will be performed:

- Attack to the body by counter disengagement to the outside, parries double counter of third not finding the blade.*(Attacco di controcavazione in fuori, al corpo, parate di doppia contro di terza a vuoto)*
- Attack to the body by counter disengagement inwards, parries double counter of fourth.*(Attacco di controcavazione in dentro, al corpo, parate di doppia contro di quarta a vuoto)*
- Attack the body with counter disengagement, parry of double counter of eight *(Attacco di controcavazione sopra, al corpo, parata di doppia contro d'ottava a vuoto)*
- Attack the body by counter disengagement to the flank, double counter of first not finding the blade *(Attacco di controcavazione al fianco, parata di doppia contro di mezzocerchio a vuoto)*

It should be noted that upon the return to the guard and subsequent retreat, they must harmonize with the movements of the hand in such a way that when one finishes, the others finish too, that is to say synchronized. After each exercise one must return to guard.

Exercise to feel the touch *(Esercizio di tasto)*

This exercise is of great use as it is the only one that can improve the knowledge of time and exercise the sensitivity of touch, and of the immediate visual reaction; represents the basis of fencing. Later it can also be performed with eyes closed by increasing the sensitivity of the hand and starting time.

Fencing as a whole is made up of deviations of the opponent's blade necessary for a copertino (blade cover) in the different lines.

It is obvious that the uncovered part, the one on which the thrust can be struck immediately, will be at the opposite of any engagement, of the beat and of the glides, pressures exerted by the opponent on the blade, of the blade seizure, of the feint by glide and simple transports.

Example:

The master binds the pupil's blade with a light contact in fourth. On the detachment of the blade towards the invitation of third, the student will immediately throw a straight thrust to the chest of the teacher and on the pressure in fourth the student will free himself with a solicitous disengagement (high line). This exercise can be performed in all four lines.

From the engagement of third, by detachment, direct thrust to the chest, high line, and on the pressure of third, disengage to the internal target.

From the engagement in first, on the detachment, the thrust is directed to the internal low line and on the pressure the disengagement is directed above to the body.

Similarly in tall these exercises, in the four lines, the thrust can be directed to the arm.

Releasing the point on all lines from the guard position *(Esercizi di svincolo della punta su tutte le linee dalla posizione di guardia)*

These exercises must be performed with the arm extended and covered (in line) and only with the wrist. Their importance is basic since they teach the pupil the release of the point in the different engagements of the master, in the beats, glides, blade seizures, transports, etc. On the performance of all these actions the student disengages in time. These can be performed with all possible variations:

- Disengagement-counter disengagement *(cavazioni – controcavazione)*
- Feint by disengagement *(finta di cavazione)*
- Double feint- feint by counter disengagement *(doppia finta - controcavazione con finta)*
- Feint by deceive and double deceive *(finta - doublé – dedoublé)*
- Feint by double deceive *(doublé - dedoublé con doppia finta)*

It should be noted that the pupil on the half circular parry of first will thrust for the bottom of the arm with hand in second position.

All the above actions can also be performed in time.

In addition to the hand, the rotator muscles in the forearm are also exercised.

Arrest exercises, angulations, and parries and riposte while backing off (*Esercizi di arresti, angolazioni e parate e risposte indietreggiando*)

On the master who advances with the blade in an angular line, threatening the top, bottom, inside and outside of the student's arm, they parry and riposte from all lines while continuous retreating.

Arrest exercises with subsequent rimesse and final parry (*Esercizio di arresto con susseguente rimessa e parata finale*)

When an arrest is made on the opponent's attack, missing the target, one must always have a remise of the attack (continuation) striking further (deeper) on the target, ultimately executing a parry. Thus, it appears evident that after the arrest it is always necessary to secure oneself with a remise followed by a final parry.

Exercise of counter parries and riposte *(Esercizio di controparate e risposte)*

The counter parry and second parry against the opponent's riposte. The adversary's parries and direct and indirect riposte (response) can be counter-parried and riposted with direct and indirect actions on all lines and on all targets, including the disengagements.

Exercise for the guard (on spot) of time thrust and transport (*Esercizio dalla guardia (da fermi) di contrazione e trasporti*)

The pupil parries a thrust to the internal high line with a double counter of third and ripostes direct to the arm. The master parries this in third and ripostes to the bottom of the arm. On this riposte the pupil contracts the arm, and then advances the point while yielding (ceding) the bell guard low and forward to cover themselves.

This stopping movement is called a time thrust (contraction). Following the time thrust, one can also add a transport of the opponent's blade in double third and riposte direct by glide to the arm.

Gliding exercises *(Esercizi di filo)*

These exercises are performed with lunges, step and lunge and arrows (fleche) to the body or arm.

- From the engagement of fourth, glide direct to the inside high line, with opposition of the guard in fourth *(Dal legamento di quarta filo diretto in dentro, sopra, con opposizione della coccia in quarta)*

- From the engagement of fourth, flanconade with opposition in fourth *(Dal legamento di quarta fianconata con opposizione di quarta.)*
- From the engagement of third, glide above to the outside highline with opposition in third *(Dal legamento di terza filo diretto sopra, in fuori, con opposizione in terza)*
- From the engagement of octave or second, glide direct to the outside low line with opposition above *(Dal legamento d'ottava o di seconda filo diretto sotto, in fuori, con opposizione sopra)*
- From the engagement of first, glide direct to the inside low line with opposition in first *(Dal legamento di mezzocerchio filo diretto in dentro, sotto, con l'opposizione di mezzocerchio)*
- From the engagement of first, transport to the outside high line, and glide with opposition to the outside *(Dal legamento di mezzocerchio trasporto sopra, in fuori, e filo con opposizione di mezzocerchio)*

The feints by glide will be performed with a previous feint to the body in order to make the point advance giving it the maximum forward expression so as to cause counter-pressure from the opponent so that they uncover themselves and then perform all the compound actions, such as disengagement, counter disengagement, double feint, etc. up to double deceive with a double feint.

One can add all the arrests with a reasemblement or jump backward, on the final of the attack or even with the fleche (arrow) direct or indirect.

Exercises with simple and compound transports *(Esercizi di transporti semplici e composti)*

Take the opponent's blade with the strong of your own blade executing a long step forward and from the engagement in fourth perform a circular movement with a tight and continuous contact with the opponent's blade returning to the starting point.

To perform double transport's, the same movement will be performed twice consecutively. Simple and compound transports of the opponent's blade can be performed in the four lines. The direct ones are:

- From fourth to fourth *(dalla quarta alla quarta)*
- From third to third *(dalla terza alla terza)*
- From eight to eight *(dall'ottava all'ottava)*
- From first to first *(dal mezzocerchio al mezzocerchio)*
  For half transports or passages no line changes are necessary, for all remaining compound transports a line change is necessary.

Exercises in opposition to pressures *(Esercizi di contrarie alle pressione)*

By simulating a phase of the fight, on the pressure exerted by the adversary on all the lines and on the blade, apply release actions with immediate reaction-disengaging, cuy over, counter disengagement, feints and disengage etc.- performed from on spot, with a lunge, step and lunge or arrow (fleche) aimed at the resulting uncovered target. The same can be performed on counter-offense (response) after having parries the opponent's attack and on his consequent counter-pressure in the opposite line.

Marching exercises in counter-time *(Esercizi di marcia in controtempo)*

Example:

On the arrest in time made by the master on the arm of the attacking student, the latter will parry with a counter of third and riposte by glide *all'avancorpo*. With the same attack and arrest in time, the student will by pivoting the wrist, strike the maestro by angulation directed to the arm.

It is understood that the parry must be executed with remarkable speed and precision, the same parry can be performed, retreating on the master's attack, always with a double of third, riposting by glide to the arm with a reasemblement or leap backwards.

Exercises against continues advance by blade cover by the maestro *(Esercizi contro l'avanzata continuative e coperta dal Maestro)*

The maestro, keeping his blade in a covered line, advances quickly while always directing his point towards the bell guard of the opponent who, retreating, defends himself with appropriate and immediate defensive and offensive changes such as: arrests, parries and ripostes, angulations, beats, transports, glides etc. without letting oneself be touched.

Second intention exercises *(Esercizi sulla seconda intenzione)*

Example

- The pupil engages the master's blade in fourth with a long step forward. The master disengages in time. The pupil stays on the engagement and directs a thrust to the arm in the inside high line.
- The pupil tries to engage the maestro's blade in fourth with and advance, on the attempted engagement the master disengages in time above. The student parries the counterattack and ripostes with a lunge to the outside arm high.

- The pupil, with a step and lunge, engages the maestro's blade in fourth on the internal high line and on this engagement the maestro executes a disengagement in time. The pupil parries third and reposts to the arm, either above, outside, with a lunge.

These exercises can be performed in all lines with counter parry ripostes and simple compound ripostes.

Knee strike exercise *(Esercizio di colpo al ginocchio)*

The student performs a pressure followed by a feint by glide in third upon the opponent's natural counter-pressure they let the point fall to the knee.

This can also be performed from the pressure and feint by glide in fourth with the same procedure.

Exercise with feint to the knee and thrust to the mask *(Esercizio di finta al ginocchio e colpo alla Maschera)*

An expressive feint direct executed towards the opponent's knee then, with a quick change to the high line, a direct thrust to the mask is made. The feint is performed with the arm covered and with the lowering of the point only. This action can also be performed when the opponent is deep in the attack phase or in their return to guard.

Conversely, a feint to the mask and thrust to the knee can also be performed.

Disarming exercises *(Esercizi di disarmo)*

There are two disarmaments, and they are performed:

- From the engagement in fourth, gaining grade on the blade performing a transport of the opponent's blade from fourth to second turning the hand to second hand position, moving from top to bottom transversing (expelling the blade, called expulsion), followed by a thrust on the exposed target, i.e., on the hand on the outside high line.
- From the engagement in third, crawl on the iron carrying the opponent's blade from third in a half circular motion to first, from top to bottom moving forward with the hand, then performing a angulated thrust to the arm which is uncovered, i.e. inside.

These exercises can be performed standing (on spot) the lunge, step and lunge or fleche (arrow). Then one can also apply the arrests with the reasemblement, jump back, and following with a counterattack as a fleche. (This action when done properly will throw the opponent's blade in the final direction of the violent transport.)

Exercises on all lines *(Esercizi su tutte le linee)*

- From the engagement of fourth, on the disengagement, parry counter of fourth and riposte direct, parry fourth and riposte by disengagement, parry third and riposte above, parry octave and riposte above, parry half circle (first) and riposte by detachment, parry in first, and riposte by disengagement to the flank.

- Parry of double counter on all lines and riposte by deceive.

- From the engagement of fourth, parry double counter and riposte by feint on all lines. And consecutively from all the double parries, respond with a double feint, a feint by deceive and double deceive.

- All direct ripostes by glide, direct, and counter parries.

  o **A)** from the double of fourth, riposte in opposition with the hand in fourth position.

  o **B)** From the counter of fourth, riposte by glide to the flank (fianconata)

  o **C)** from the counter of third, riposte by glide above with opposition in third.

  o **D)** From the double counter of eight, riposte by glide to the low line with opposition of the hand outside.

  o **E)** From the double counter of first, riposte by glide with opposition in first, and again from the double circular parry in first, riposte by glide with opposition in first

- From the engagement in fourth, parry against the counter of fourth and transport the adversaries' blade twice consecutively, on the same side, making your point perform two complete circles, thus returning to the starting point. Then carry out the glide in fourth direct high line and , always making use of the same procedure, carry out the double transport and glide in third, octave and first and glide above. The final of the transports will be performed with the hand in opposition.

- The double counter parry in opposite lines with passaggio followed by counter-riposte in the high lines (fourth and third) and from top to bottom in the passages of half double and transversal double (third-octave and octave-third, fourth-first, first-fourth, fourth-octave, octave-fourth, third-first, first-third).

- Have the student perform on all lines consecutively beats with subsequent double circular and double feint.

- From the double counter of fourth, riposte by cut over, from the double counter of third, cut over to the inside, from the double counter of fourth, cut over to the flank

- From the double parry of forth, backhand cut over to the outside, from the double counter of third, the cut over of reverse inside; from the double fourth, backhand cut over feint to the outside, backhand cut over inside and from back third double backhand cut over by feint inside, backhand cut over outside.

- Remaining in the lunge, perform three or four replacements until the Maestro is touched who will remain out of measure. Pause for a moment in the lunge, then return directly to first position and salute.

Special exercise in renewed attacks with step and lunge with counter parry and riposte with all the possible variations of defense and offense *(Esercizio speciale in ripresa d'attacco camminando in controparata e risposta con tutte le variazioni possibili di difesa e di offesa)*

This exercise is used to accustom the student to the renewed attack by step and lunge in counter parry with successive arrests and fleche responses.

On the disengagement to the outside performed by the master, the pupil will parry fourth and riposte direct with a lunge. In turn, the opponent-master will parry fourth and will also riposte direct, trying to hit the student who, promptly returning to the guard, will counter parry fourth and resume with an attack by feinting direct and direct touching the master on the arm or chest. Then he will execute an immediate arrest by reasemblement to the arm or chest or with a jump back and from this same position they will start again with direct fleche (arrow) to the master's arm or chest. The Maestro will have the exercises repeated in all four lines with the same procedure, after which they will have it performed by counter-parry and riposte by disengagement, with a renewed attack from step and lunge distance with the disengagement and successive arrest by disengagement, followed by a final thrust by disengagement with the arrow. The exercise will be repeated in all four lines and with all the variations, namely: with counter disengagement, with feint, double feint, feint by counter disengagement, double disengagement, and double feint.

Summary exercise based on all offensive actions and defensive *(Esercizio riepilogativo basato su tutte le azioni offensive e defensive)*

1.   The student will perform a straight thrust with a lunge to the hand, with a renewed attack from the lunge, hit direct to the body immediately followed by a arrest to the top of the arm, followed by an angulation to the bottom of the arm from the lunge followed by an arrest by reasemblement or jump back at the same time parry third and riposte to the arm. Subsequently with a direct glide followed by a transport, they will counterattack with an arrow to the arm or chest.

2.   Have the same exercise performed applying the disengagement. It is preferable to carry out this exercise on the high lines of third and fourth. Initially disengage with the hand, resume with the arm in and so on in all the movements that follow one another, ending with the transport of the blade in double third or double fourth, riposting sharply with accentuated opposition of the guard to cover and avoid the double hit.

3.	Have the same sequence of movements performed starting with the hand inward or outward; repeating all the movements of attack, renewed attack, angulation, arrest, parry riposte, double transport and glide in thrusting lines to the arm or body in either third or fourth, taking care to always maintain with the double movements of the bell guard the exact oppositions to cover themselves both in the attack and ripostes and subsequent arrows. The same exercise can also be performed with an initial double deceive or double transports in the two opposite lines to finish in the opposite line with an arrow or by glide.

Preparation for the assault with the method of fencing from the ground Duel

The simplest method to cover oneself from the opponent's thrusts and the best way to strike without being touched is that of directing one's point towards the opponent's guard with an outstretched arm, following it continuously in all its movements. This was also in the duel the simplest method of guaranteeing oneself.

The master uses this elementary game to initiate the student early in the practice of the assault.

It is exercises in the following way: the Maestro keeps the blade in line, with his arm stretched out and covered, and continuously directs his point towards the pupil's bell guard, carefully following him in all his possible movements and movements of the arm, preventing him from hitting. The student tries in every way to find the masters arm with all possible actions: engagements, pressures, beats, disengagements, angulations, feints, double feints, transports followed with glides, without widening the execution of the action so as not to touch himself by falling on the opposing point of the master.

This exercise will serve to prepare the student for an immediate reaction and to start disengaging in time.

QUESTIONS AND ANSWERS
DOMANDE E RISPOSTE

Questions and answers *(Domande e risposte)*

Question: What is the epee?

Answer: It is the most rational weapon (once used for the duel) as whoever touches first is right and everything the body constitutes a valid target. The guard is larger of that of the foil; the blade, with a triangular section, is longer, heavier, and more rigid than that of the foil.

Question: How many parts is the weapon divided into?

Answer: The blade, the guard, the handle ending in the pommel. Question: As for the blade, in turn, in how many parts is it divided into?

Answer: Threaded tang (inner part of the handle). to screw the pommel onto its end and blade properly said which is broken down into: forte (first close third to the bell guard); medium (second third); weak (top third), part at the end of which there is the tip.

Question: What is the offensive line?

Answer: The offensive line is the armed arm position: elbow, hand, and tip on a single line, threatening the opponent's valid target.

Question: What is the line of direction?

Answer: It is the imaginary line of movement of the fencer on the platform. Question: What are the fundamental movements of advance and retreat?

Answer: Forward: extension of the arm; lunge; step forward; step and lunge; renewed attack with a lunge; arrow (fleche). retreat: return to guard; step back; jump backwards.

Question: What is measurement?

Answer: The space between the valid target of the two fencers. Question: What is the fundamental principle of the sword?

Answer: Whoever touches first is right. Question: How is this precedence registered?

Answer: By preceding the opponent's hit by 20-25th of a second, otherwise it's a double shot.

Question: What is the classic sword guard like?

Answer: High, with the body erect, with the blade in line, guard with minimal bending of the elbow and hand of third in fourth with slight opposition in third; the tip constantly facing the opponent's arm, legs slightly flexed ready for offense and defense.

Question: Define the lunge?

Answer: Trunk erect, head back, pelvis in forward so as to break the side as much as possible, armed arm extended and at face level, arm behind shoulder-leg on the same line.

Question: How to do step forward and step backwards?

Answer: Without crawling or stomping, executing the movement lightly, naturally and without muscle contraction.

Question: What are the epee measures?

Answer: The same as the foil except made to measure step and double step and lunge instead of stepping forward is preferable the arrow.

Question: What is the logical sequence of the sentence in epee fencing?

Answer: Offensive actions are countered by time thrusts, arrests, renewed attacks and only as a last resort the parry and riposte.

Question: How should the parry be performed?

Answer: Forward to gain dominance of the opponent's iron and with minimal movement from the offensive line, while keeping the tip on the target in so that the response to touch has to travel the minimum distance possible.

Question: How many fundamental angles are there to the arm? Answer: Four: below, above, inside, outside.

Question: How are the four angles performed?

Answer: The one below with the hand in second, the inside one with the hand in third and the other two with the hand in fourth with appropriate oppositions.

Question: How are arrests made?

Answer: From a standstill, reasemblement or jumping backwards.

Question: When is rimesse performed?

Answer: After the attack, at arm's length.

Question: What are the remise's?

Answer: Direct on the same line; indirect on the line opposite, applying release actions.

Question: How are blade seizures performed?

Answer: Bringing the blade forward, with the forte of blade and taking advantage of the guard-blade angle.

Question: When can you throw an arrow?

Answer: In attack and in counter offence: in response and in counterattack.

Question: From what measurements?

Answer: In attack by advance lunge or long-distance measure; on the counterattack also from lunging distance.

Question: How do you carry the blade during execution of the direct thrust by arrow?

Answer: Forward and with appropriate opposition from the hand to ensure arm coverage.

Question: In principle, when can you perform the arrow with no blade contact?

Answer: By targeting the foreparts.

Question: And wanting to thrust to the body?

Answer: As a principle, with a blade seizure and glide.

Question: What is the safest attack using the arrow?

Answer: The blade seizure in third and glide performed by second intention.

Question: How can one deliberately carry out the double touch?

Answer: By provoking the attack or arrest of the opponent and thrusting on the free-iron thrust with the arrow.

Question: To the epee, what is the safest action of defense?

Answer: The arrest by time thrust.

Question: How do you defend yourself against a sustained attack from the opponent?

Answer: By following the arrest attempt with rimesse, breaking the measure and resorting to the parry only as a last resort.

Question: How many measures are considered didactically?

Answer: Five: from the guard; lunging; step and lunge; narrow measure; long measure.

Question: What is the handle?

Answer: In the nomenclature of weapons, it is understood everything that is beyond the bell guard, that is, the handle and its members annexes. The various types are defined with the same term armed hand positions that must be distinguished from positions of the armed arm.

Question: How many fundamental positions of iron are there?

Answer: Four: of fourth, relative to the internal target high; of third, high outside; octave, low outer; Of half circle, low inside.

Question: What is the valid target in fencing epee?

Answer: The whole body.

Question: How many main targets are there?

Answer: There are four.

Question: What are the names of the invitations?

Answer: In relation to the invitation of fourth: external chest high; in relation to the invitation of third: high internal chest; in invitation of second: abdomen; in relation to the invitation of half circle: flank.

Question: What are the attitudes (placements) that a fencer can take while on guard?

Answer: There are three: weapon inline, invitation, engagement.

Question: What are the fundamental actions that one can execute in opposition to the opponent's line weapon?

Answer: There are three: beats, engagements, and glides.

Question: And in opposition to the invitations?

Answer: Straight thrust.

Question: And in opposition to the ligaments?

Answer: The disengagements.

Question: What is the invitation?

Answer: The invitation is the attitude of second intention which the fencer takes on discovering voluntarily a target to induce the opponent to hit it.

Question: How many invitations are there and what are they?

Answer: There are four: half circle (first), second, third and fourth.

Question: What is engagement?

Answer: Moving your blade to bring it into contact with that of the opponent.

Question: How many and what are the engagements?

Answer: There are four: half circle (first), second, third, fourth.

Question: What are the main offensive actions?

Answer: Straight thrust, beat, disengagement, counter-disengagement, deceive, feint and cut over.

Question: What are the substantial differences?

Answer: The straight thrust go straight to the target; the beat moves the opponent's iron from his offensive line; disengagement eludes a ligament, an blade seizure or a parry.

Question: What is the difference between counter disengagement and deceive?

Answer: Counter disengagement bypasses an engagement and counter (circular) parry starting from one position; the deceive evades the same actions as opposed to an invitation. The first requires one and a half turns, the second one.

Question: What is a feint?

Answer: Action to induce the opponent to reveal a target. It can be simple or compound, direct or indirect.

Question: What is the intagliata (cut over) (fr. coupé)?

Answer: Release action from the opponent's blade performed by wrist flexion, withdrawing your weapon with swiping pressure, subsequently bringing it to the opposite line, passing over the opponent's iron.

Question: What is angulation?

Answer: Direct offensive action on a line for finish with the hand in opposition.

Question: What are the expulsions and pressures on the blade?

Answer: Once the engagement has taken place, moving the opponent's blade, performed with accentuated force on one certain line.

Question: What are glides?

Answer: Glides are offensive actions aimed at the target direct and with constant contact of your iron with the opponent's.

Question: What is a blade seizure?

Answer: Offensive action that brings one's weapon to seize, with the forte, the opponent's blade in each line (example: blade seizure in third; blade seizure in fourth).

Question: What is transport?

Answer: Offensive action that leads to taking over with the strength of his own weapon the opponent's blade, deflecting it forcefully from one line to another.

Question: What is the ceduta?

Answer: Counterattack carried out in good time with one's own blade subjected to that of the opponent. (Similar to a force glide on the opponent's attack.)

Question: What are the continuing actions? the offensive action?

Answer: The continuation of the attack, the gain on the lunge, renewed attack, and replacement (rimessa). The first during the attack when you are forced to change the offensive plan; the second due to a lack of response from the opponent who defends by measure; the third with the attack exhausted returning to guard and taking back the initiative; the fourth from short measure on delayed response or on the response that does not hit.

Question: What are the defense actions?

Answer: Parries with the blade and defensive measure.

Question: What and how many parries are there with the blade?

Answer: Four beating parries: two in line high and two in line low; eight half circle: four straight (simple) and four in transverse line; four circular in the four lines.

Question: What are compound parries?

Answer: All those performed by alternating saves of beat, half circle and circle and vice versa.

Question: What is contraction (time thrust)?

Answer: Defensive action on the blade that closes, meeting with appropriate opposition, on the line of the opponent's attack

Question: When is the defensive measure used?

Answer: When it is done in a timely and convenient manner to be able to move from a defense condition to an offensive action.

Question: What is meant by defensive-offensive system?

Answer: Intentional tactic to be able to switch between one defense condition to immediate offensive action e vice versa by counteracting the opponent's pace or by retreating both advancing.

Question: When is jumping backwards rational?

Answer: When it allows the application of immediate counteroffensive actions.

Question: How can execution vary in combat? of an action?

Answer: Based on measure, speed and time.

Question: What is attack?

Answer: The initial action of a fencing phrase continuously threatening the opponent's valid surface.

Question: What is the riposte?

Answer: Offensive action of the fencer who parried the attack.

Question: What is counter-parry?

Answer: The offensive action of the fencer who parried the riposte. (of the opponent)

Question: How can the attacks and parries be delivered?

Answer: Direct and indirect, simple, and compound.

Question: An example of a simple and direct attack.

Answer: The straight thrust.

Question: An example of a simple, indirect attack.

Answer: The disengagement and the cut over.

Question: An example of a direct and compound attack.

Answer: Beat direct, one-two.

Question: Give an example of an indirect and compound attack.

Answer: The counter disengagement; the one-two-three; the beat and the disengagement.

Question: What are counterattacks?

Answer: Simple actions coordinated with precedence of time on the opponent's attack.

Question: What are they?

Answer: Time thrust, disengagement in time, arrest.

Question: What is meant by counter time?

Answer: All intentionally preordained actions by the attacker to neutralize counterattacks.

Question: What is meant by counter offense?

Answer: Generic term to designate the renewing of offensive initiative of the fencer who suffered the attack (e.g. response, counter-response, attack on returning to guard, etc.).

Question: What is meant by "fencing phrase"

Answer: Completed sequence of actions in combat.

Question: What is meant by "opposites" (contraries)?

Answer: The opposite is the action that is rationally opposed to the opponent's offensive or defensive action, or when the actions are performed in transit and release.

Question: How should an attack be countered?

Answer: By arresting, parrying, or sharply dodging.

Question: When is an attack considered correctly executed?

Answer: When the tip is carried with harmonious coordination directly to the target.

Question: What are the key elements to hit the target?

Answer: Time-measure-velocity.

Question: How do you rationally execute a parry?

Answer: Without abandoning the direction of offense, gaining space forward.

Question: How can you reach the target?

Answer: In relation to the measurement: by angulation of the blade, stretching out the arm, lunging, step and lunge, or arrow.

Question: How can it be simulated with expressive effectiveness the thrust?

Answer: By moving the guard line from bottom to top or vice versa, inviting, beating, engaging, or pressing on the opponent's blade or alternating these attitudes and movements (probing actions).

Question: What other means exist to maintain the initiative?

Answer: By coordinately varying the expression and the speed of advancement and retreat of the body, of blade, of the hand.

Question: How can you hit your opponent by applying a preordained tactical plan

Answer: Of first, second, third intention.

Question: When does one strike with first intention?

Answer: When the initiative is prevented from passing to the opponent.

Question: And second intention?

Answer: When the initiative is intentionally provoked opponent to neutralize it by scoring one's own thrust.

Question: And third intention?

Answer: When you intentionally evade the second intention of the opponent, concluding to one's advantage.

CHAPTER VIII

ELETRICAL SIGNALING OF THE HITS
SEGNALAZIONE ELETTRICA DEI COLPI

Equipment and materials *(Apparecchiatura e materiali)*

- – The appliance (score box)
- – The repeaters
- – The rollers (floor reels)
- – The connection cables
- – The platform
- – The passerby
- – The internal guard plug
- – The conductive threads in the blade (blade wire)
- – The tip

The electric epee *(Spada elettrica)*

Background. First attempts in 1919. First device battery-powered created by the Swiss engineer Perin di Geneva in 1932 and made by the Souzv company of Paris. First mains powered device created by the engineer from Milan street for the Sala Mangiarotti in 1933. Adopted in Italy by the FIS on an experimental basis for training for the Los Angeles Olympics. Adoption definitive international in 1933 (European Championships of Budapest).

The wapon (Arma)

Weight ....770 gr. Max

Total leght 110cm

Blade leght .... 90cm max

Blade width 24mm

Arrow: with a notch at 70 cm
from the tip and a weight of
200 g applied 3 cm from the tip .... 4,5 to 7 cm

Guard: with a circular edge,
it must fit into a cylindrical
gauge with a diameter of .... 13 cm in diameter and 15 cm in length

Depth .... From 3 cm to 5.5 cm

Length from the edge of the
guard to the tip .... 95,5 cm. Max

Eccentricity .... 3,5 cm

Electric tip:

    Operating pressure .... over 750gr
    Ignition stroke .... 1mm min
    Additional stroke .... 0,5mm max
    Diameter 8nm
    Electrical resistance .... 3,5-ohm max

Signaling device *(Apparecchio segnalatore)*

Operating conditions: in the case of storage from both parts the appliance signals a double hit if the interval is less than 40 milliseconds. If the interval is superior must signal only the first hit. Between 40 and 50 milliseconds the "tolerance zone" (or uncertainty) exists.

With external resistance in series with the tip of 10 ohms hits lasting 10 milliseconds must be reported milliseconds. With an external resistance of 30 ohm the hits must be reported without duration limit.

The neutralization of blows against the guard (or platform) must be ensured with resistance up to 30 ohm placed in series on the plate.

The signals must be red on one side and on green or orange on the other.

SECTION OF THE ITALIAN PUNTA MOD. E.M.

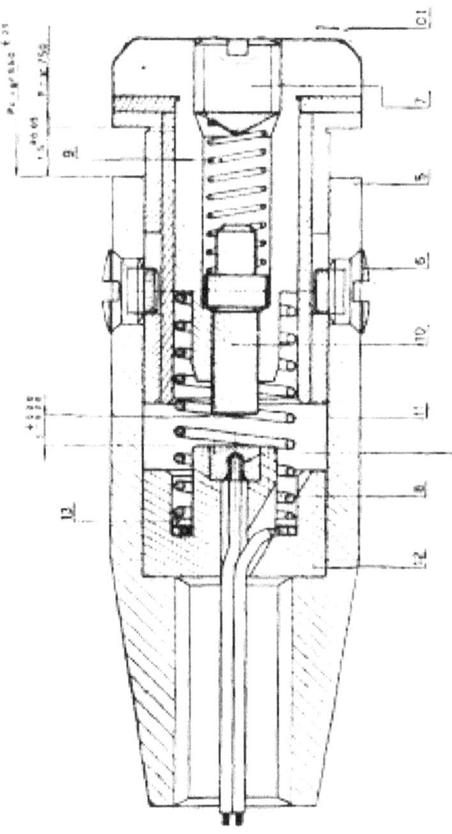

Legend

5) Shell. — **6)** Lateral stop screw. — **7)** Closing screw on the contact cylinder spring. — **8)** Weight-repelling Spring (750 g). — **9)** Contact cylinder spring. — **10)** Contact cylinder (polarity +). — **11)** Contact terminal (polarity —). — **12)** Lower insulator. — **13)** Wire ring, polarity +, which carries current to the contact cylinder through the weight-repelling spring.

The E.M. tip has been adopted by Italian manufacturers; in this system, contact occurs when the cylinder (polarity -+~) touches the terminal (polarity —), unlike the "international" system, illustrated in the summary of the first chapter, where the circuit closes when the contact spring (small on the tip pin) rests on two pins of different polarity located in the lower insulator.

The advantages of the Italian model are:

a. impossibility to vary the contact travel (mm 1)

b. no heeling to the side of the spring contact resulting in "mass" that cancel out reporting hits;

c. safety and stability of contact.

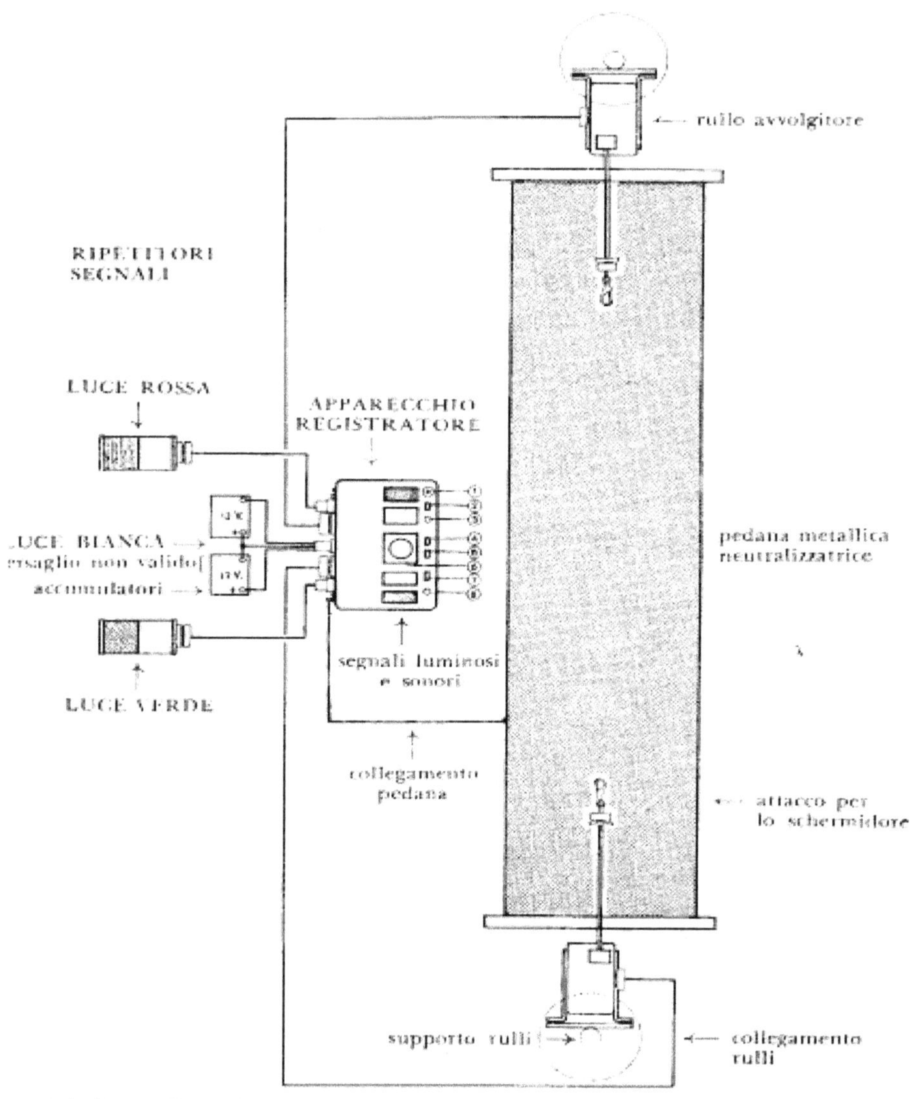

1 Pulsante di ricarica 2 Inseritore ricarica automatica 3 Regolatore ricarica automatica 4 Pulsante fioretto 5 Pulsante spada 6 Suoneria 7 Interruttore generale 8 Lampadina spia

VOCABULARY

TERMINOLOGY IN

ITALIAN — FRENCH — ENGLISH — GERMAN

ITALIAN	FRENCH	ENGLISH	GERMAN
A-fondo	Fente (se fendre)	Lunge	Ausfall
Angolazione	Angolazione	Angolazione	eine Aktion in abgewinkelter Faustlage
Apparecchio Signalgerät	Appareil électriquc	Electrical apparatus	Signalgerät
Appuntata	Appuntata (Remise)	Remise	Rimesse
Arresto	Coup d'arrét	Stop hit	Zwischenstoss
Assalto	Assaut	Bout	Kampf, gefecht
Attacco	Attaque	Attack	Angriff
Attacco diretto	Attaque directe	Direct attack	Direckter Angriff
Attacco in tempo	Attaque d'à propos	Attack in time	Tempoangriff
Attacco sul ferro	Attaque au fer	Attack on the blade	Klingenangriff
Avancorpo	Avancés	Nearest part of the target	der vorderste Teil der Treffläche
Battuta	Battement	Beat	Eisenaufschlag
Bersaglio (valido)	Surface (valable)	Target	Giíltige Treffläche
Botta dritta	Coup droit	Straight thrust	Gerader Stoss
Braccio in linea	Entre en ligne	Be in line	Gestreckter arm
Cambiamento	Changement	Change of line	Wechsel
Camminare	Marcher	Advance (to)	Vorgehen
Cavazione	Dégagement	Disengagement	Umgehung
Cavazione in tempo	Dérobement	Disengagement in time	Umgehung in Tempo
Ceduta	Cedé	Ceding	Nachgebung
Chiusura	Fermer la ligne	Close the line	Abstand schliessen
Circolata	Doublé	Deceive	Kreisstoss
Coccia	Garde	Bell Guard	Glocke
Codolo	Queue de la lame	Tang of the blade	Stiel
Colpo di taglio	Coup de tranchant direct	Cut	Direckter Hieb
Colpo doppio	Coup double	Double-hit	Doppelstoss
Combattimento	Combat	Assault	Kampf
Composto	Composé	Compound	Gesemtaktion
Contraria	Contraire	Opposite	entgegengesetzte Aktion
Contrattacco	Contre-attaque	Counter-attack	Gegenangriff
Contrazione	Coup di temps	Time thrust	Gegenaktion
Contro cavazione	Contre dègagé (doublé)	Counter disengage	Umgehungskreisstoss
Controffesa	Contre-offense	Counter offensive	Gegenangriff
Controparata	Contre-parade	Counter-Parry	Gegenparade
Contro risposta	Contre risposte	Counter risposte	Gegenstoss oder Hieb

Controtempo	Contretemps	Counter time	Gegenzeitangriff
Corpo a corpo	Corps-à-corps	Corps-à-corps	Köeper en Köeper
Dare il ferro	Donner le fer	Give the blade	die Klinge geben
Debole	Foible	Foible (weak)	Schwäche (schwach)
Difesa	Defense	Defense	Verteidigung
Direttorio tecnico	Directoire tecnique	Direct technique	Technisches Direktorium
Disarmo	Désarmement	Disarm	Disarm
Duello	Duel	Duel	Duell
Eisa	Garde	Hilt	Parierstange, Korb
Eludere il ferro	Tromper le fer	Deceive the blade (to)	der Klinge ausweichen
Esercizio	Esercizio	Exercise	Ubung
Essere in vantaggio	Mener	Lead in a bout (to)	Fuehren
Ferro in linea	Fer en ligne	Blade in line	gestreckte Klinge
Fianconata	Liement au flanc, crois~	Flaconade	Sturzangnff mit Flankengleitstoss
Filo	Coulé	Glide	Gleitstoss
Finale	Finale	Final	Endrunde
Finta	Feinte	Feint	Finte
Fioretto	Fleuret	Foil	Florett
Forte	Fort	Strong	Stäerke (Stark)
Frase schermistica	Phrase d'armes	Fencing phrase	Gefechtsabschnitt
Frecciata	Flèche	Flèche (arrow)	Struzangriff
Giravolta	Volte	Ducking	Umdrehung
Girone di Eliminazione	Poule de élimination	Elimination Round	Vorrunde
Girone di semifinale	Poule de Demifinale	Semi-final Round	Zwischenrunde
Girone finale	Poule finale	Final	Endrunde
Giurato	Assesseur	Judge	Kampfrichter
Gradi del ferro	Degrés du fer	Parts of the Blade	Klingenaufteilung
Guardia	Garde	Guard	Stellung
Impressione	Impression	Impression	Eindruck
In guardia	En garde	On guard	in Stellung
Inquartata	Estocade avec écart de côté	Inquartata	Ausweichen mit Innenstoss
Intagliata	Coupé	Cut over	Wurfstoss
Intenzione	Intention	Intention	Absicht
Intrecciata	Enveloppement	Envelopment	W'echselglei tstoss
Invito	Invite	Invitation	Einladung
invito aperto	Absence du fer	Absence of Blade	Offene Einladung
Lama	Lame	Blade	Klinge
Legamento	Engagement	Engagement	Bindung
Legamento d'invito	Liement	Bind	Einladungsbindung

Linea di attacco	Ligne d'attaque	Line of attack	Angriffslinie
Linea di offesa	Ligne d'offense	Line of attack	Drohungslinie
Linea direttrice	Ligne directrice	Line of direction	Führungsl mie
Manico	Manche	Handle	Griff
Martingala	Martingale	Martinglale (wrist strap)	Martingal
Maschera	Masque	Mask	Maske
Mezzocerchio	Demi-cercle	Demi-cercle (half-circle)	Halbkreis
Mezzo giro	Demi-vol te	Side-step	Flalbumdrehung
Misura	Mesure	Fencing Measure	Fechtabstand
Molleggio	Faire ressort	Springing	federnde Bewegung
Mulinello	Moulinet	Reel	Kreishieb
Offesa	Offense	Offensive	Angrff, Offensive
Opposizione	Opposition	Opposition	Widerstand
Parare bene	Avoir de la main	Secure parry	Gui parieren
Parata	Parade	Parry	Parade
Parata di tasto	Parade de tac au Tac	Parry by detachment	Tastparade
Parata semplice	Parade simple	Simple parry	Einfache Parade
Parata di prima	Parade de prime	Parry of first	Ente Parade
Parata di seconda	Parade de Seconde	Parry of Second	Z\veite Parade
Parata di terza	Parade de tierce	Parry of tierce	Dritte Parade
Parata di quarta	Parade de quarte	Parry of fourth	Vierte Parade
Parata di quinta	Parade de quinte	Parry of fifth	Fiicnfte Parade
Parata di sesta	Parade de sixte	Parry of sixte	Sechste Parade
Parata di settima	Parade de septime	Parry of Septime	Siebente Parade
Parata di ottava	Parade de octave	Parry of octave	Achte Parade
Parata di ceduta	Céder	Ceding parry	Nachgebungsparade
Parata di contro	Parade de contre	Counter parry	Kreisparade
Passante	Fu du corp	Body wire	Körperschnur
Passata sotto	Passata sotto	Passata sotto	Ausweichen mit tiefen Stoss
Passo	Pas	Step forward	Schritt
Passo avanti	Pas en avant	Advance	Schritt vorviirts
Passo indietro	Pas en arrière	Retreat	Schritt niìchrviirts
Pié fermo	De pied ferme	From immobility	In nahem Fechtabstand
Pedana	Piste, planchet	Platform (piste)	Fechtbahn
Pomolo	Pommeau	Pommel	Knopf
Posizione	Position	Position	Stellung
Presa di ferro	Prise de fer	Blade seizure	die Klinge nehmen
Presidente di giuria	Président	President	Obmann

Pressione	Pression	Pressure	Druck
Prima posizione	Position de base	First position	Grundstellung
Pugno in seconda	Pronation	Pronation	Zweite Faustlage
Pugno in quarta	Supination	Supination	vierte Faustlage
Punta elettrica	Pointe electrique	Electrical point	die Spitze einer elektrischen Waffe
Punteggio	Score	Score	Wertung- Trefferstand
Raccogliere	Envelopper	Envelopment	Wechselgleitstoss
Raddoppio	Redoublement	Redoublement	Wiederholter Ausfall
Retrocedere	Rompre	Retreat	Zurùeckgehen
Ricasso	Ricasso	Ricasso	Ricasso
Rifiutare il ferro	Refuser le fer	Refuse the blade	der gegnerischen Klinge Ausweichen
Rimessa	Remise	Remise	Rimesse
Riporto	Reporter le fer	Taking the blade	Klingenbindung
Ripresa	Reprise	Reprise	Wiederholter Angriff
Risposta	Risposte	Risposte	Nachstoss Riposte
Ritornare in guardia	Revenir en garde	Recover to Guard	Wiedereinahme der Fechtstellung
Riunita	Rassemblé	Reasemblement	Rassemblé
Rompere il gioco	Briser le jeu	Cut the line	Das gegnerische Spiel sti5eren
Salto indietro	Saute en arrière	Leap backwards	Riicksprung
Saluto	Salut	Salute	Gruss
Sciabola	Sabre	Sabre	Saebel
Schivata	Esquive	Displacement of Target	Entziehung der Trefflaeche
Serrare la misura	Serrer la mesure	Close the measure (to)	Fechtabstand Vermindern
Spada	Epée	Epée	Degen
Stoccata	Touche	Hit	Treffer
Strisciare sul ferro	Fròlement	Graze	angelegter Stoss
Striscio	Froissement	Froissement	Streich-battuta
Tasteggio	Doitgté	Finger-play	Abtasten
Tempo	Coup de temps	Time	Vahl zur Aùsfuehrung eines erfolgreichen Angriffs
Tempo commune	Coup simultané	Simultaneous Hits	Gleiche Zeitwahl
Terreno guadagnato	Terrain gagné	Ground gained	Gewonnener Boden
Terreno perduto	Terrain perdu	Ground lost	Verlorener Boden
Traccheggio	Trainer le fer	Drag the blade (to)	Klingenspiel
Transporto	Prise de fer (maitriser le fer)	Transport	Uebertraguno

Trovare il ferro	Trouver le fer	Find the blade	die Klinge finden
Turno	Tour	Round	Runde
Uno, due (tre)	Un, deux (trois)	One, two (three)	Eins, zwei, (drei)

The educational photographs that illustrate this volume are original and kindly provided by personal collections of Maestro Giuseppe MangiarottiI and of sons Dario and Edoardo; from photo agencies Giancolombo and Coppini of Milan.

The cover and photographs of the text are by Irene Lopez.

The line drawings were created with graphic collaboration of Prof. G. Cappadonia reworking elements taken from the texts:

« La vera scherma » -edizione Longanesi 1965

« Fechtavanie» -arti grafiche sovietiche 1967

« Degenfechten » -arti grafiche ungheresi 1969

COMPLEMENTARY NOTES FOR TEACHING

For aspiring Maestro di scherma Written by Maestro Giancarlo Toran

Introduction Definitions of initial positions

Targets and lines Offensive actions Defensive actions

Tactical notes and readings How to give the blade Teaching

Italian and French fencing

INTRODUCTION

More than fifteen years after the first version, and perhaps the case to explain why these handouts were written and approved as an exam text: alternative to the Mangiarotti text (Giuseppe and Edoardo, who wrote it) but for free choice of the student, who has been able to opt for one or the other text, without preclusions.

The Epee from the time of Giuseppe Mangiarotti having won titles in numerous championships in the field, and the many champions produced after his brilliant competitive career, was a very different game from the classic teaching of the Masaniello Parise School. Giuseppe had studied it, and then perfected it in Turin with Maestro Colombetti, but he was soon convinced of the need to change the method, turning his gaze to the French School, which excelled in the weapon. The facts proved him right. However, from the systematic and terminological point of view, the two schools were and are very different. In addition, it is not that Giuseppe attributed excessive importance to terminological questions: hence a notable difference between the treaties which continued, without departing too much, along the Parise line and the Military Magistral School, and that of the Mangiarotti School, Mangiarotti focused on how and not so much the pedagogy.

The latter, however, has the great advantage of being much more open to the competitive innovations also made by the emerging Eastern European Schools.

Differences in Italy have always been a resource rather than an obstacle in the long run. But for a student, aspiring teacher, or instructor, being the natural recipient of these treatises, the primary need has always been to have a clear and simple enough text, suitable for a study with eminently practical purposes. From this point of view, also because most of the teachers and examiners came from the similar books of foil and saber, and therefore from the Magistrale culture, the Mangiarotti text presented many problems: definitions in contrast with those of the other two treatises, different development of material, and also some internal contradiction, deriving from the breadth of the sources from which he had drawn.

Thus, was born the idea of these epee handouts, which never had the pretense of being considered a treatise, and which aimed to mitigate the frictions between the different conceptions: ultimately, in order to make the study of aspiring technicians easier. Lecture notes which, rather than replacing, have integrated the Mangiarotti treaty, the reading of which is still highly recommended today.

The first version of these handouts on the epee was prepared for the courses for the instructors of Madonna di Campiglio, in 1995. Some changes were made for the courses of

Misano Adriatico, in 1996, up to the current version, which finally includes also and iconographic part.

As mentioned, the aim remains to offer a teaching aid to aspiring Masters or Instructors, for the study of the most technically complex and difficult weapon: the epee.

The approach remains to refer the terminology of the epee to the consolidated one of foil: which also seems to me to need a thorough revision, which goes beyond the technical comments reported in the first volume of these Fencing Notebooks.

When it was not possible for me to do otherwise, I introduced new but coherent terms and concepts (at least I hope), abundantly explaining the reasons.

The qualifying and, in my opinion, important part of these handouts are the chapters on the way of giving the blade and teaching, with the main aspects absent from the treatises. In the courses it is the most requested part, it is most useful.

For the need to close my job in time, I fear that there will be errors or oversights in this latest revision, and I apologize in advance.

Giancarlo Toran

December 2012

CHAPTER 1 DEFINITIONS AND INITIAL POSITIONS

The first chapter "Initial Definitions and Positions" includes some definitions that are missing in other treatises: the definition of modern sports fencing, the technique, and fencing actions. The main positions of the body and of the armed hand are then described. It explains how to hold the weapon, with the two grips in use today. The new hand positions are described and discussed, no longer referring to the crossbar of the Italian sword. To the three attitudes with the weapon described in the foil treatise is added a fourth attitude, called the normal guard position. (central)

At the end of this chapter, you should be able to:

—   Define modern Olympic sport fencing
—   Briefly indicate the difference between strategy, tactics, and technique
—   Know how to hold the two main types of weapons
—   Describe the new hand positions
—   Describe the guard position, even in its modern variants
—   Describe traditional and normal attitudes of the guard position

If you are able to answer these questions, then proceed to the next chapter
—   How can modern fencing be defined?
—   What is the difference between strategy, tactics, and technique?
—   What is a fencing action. What are its purposes?
—   In epee, what are the main positions of the legs, of the body and the weapon arm?
—   How is the French grip held? How is the atomical grip held?
—   What are the new hand positions and why?
—   What are attitudes?
—   What is the classic guard position and why can it be different in modern competitive fencing?
—   How is the arm placed in the normal guard position and why?

Key words
—   Weapons specialty of fencing (armi, o specialità della scherma)
—   Strategy (strategia)

- Tactics (tattica)

- Technique (tecnia)

- fencing actions (azione schermistiche)

- handgrips, and ways of contesting them (impugnature o modo di impugnarie)

- positions, and attitudes (posizione e atteggiamenti)

Definition of fencing *(definizione della scherma)*

Fencing is, today, an opposition sport deriving from the martial art of the same name. It includes the three Olympic disciplines' (also called weapons), which take their names from the sports equipment used and reproduce the weapons that bear their name: epee, saber, and foil.

Fencing, governed by regulations issued by the FIE, and by the national sports federations, consists of offense (hitting the opponent's target) and defense (avoiding being hit) according to modalities, rules of valid target, method of hitting, right of way, priority, is different for each discipline.

In Epee, some of the most significant differences in the International egulations (IR) compared to foil and saber, are the extension of the target, (forward target) the recording of time of the double hit, the timing clock nulling a late double hit and different teaching of technique and tactics.

Learning and study of fencing *(L'apprendimento e lo studio della scherma)*

The learning of fencing, for cultural, technical-didactic, competitive purposes, together or separately, takes place both theoretically and practically (training).

The numerous fencing treatises that have come down to us, from the Middle Ages onwards, allow us to understand the deep history and evolution of the subject.

The constantly evolving theory of fencing makes use of the terminology and classification of fencing actions: the study and research of the executive model of these actions, taken together, constitutes the field of fencing technique.

The study of the situations and intentions that precede and accompany the application of the technique constitutes the field of fencing strategy (programming one's actions) and tactics (programming the opponent through one's actions)

Tactics, therefore, are part of the strategy.

Technique *(La tecnica)*

The fencing **technique** includes the whole set of fencing actions. A single action can be understood as a fencing technique.

Actions *(Azione)*: all the movements (of legs, of body and of the armed hand) from a starting position to an arrival position, with certain modalities, done for a specific purpose.

Fencing *(Schermistiche)*: as the purpose of the actions and among those specific to fencing, namely, to offend (strike) and defend one's target. The investigation of the opponent's offensive and defensive intentions, and therefore the preparation and simulation of offensive and defensive actions.

In the following we will describe the main positions of the various parts of the body, then of the armed hand, and the meaning in terms of the target and protecting, the guard position, the main movements of the legs and the measure, the way to carry the hit. We will then deal with the various simple offensive actions, dividing them into fundamental and auxiliary actions, and we will give particular emphasis to the actions on the blade, and the way to perform them. We will then examine defensive actions, including parries. Finally, the compound offensive actions, and the counter-offense.

The significant positions in epee are:

- Position of the legs;
- Positions of the torso, head, and unarmed hand
- Positions of the weapon arm

Position of the legs *(Posizioni delle gambe)*

Here are the most common.

- **First position** *(prima posizione)* (feet at right angles, heel square to opposite heel, front foot with axis on the line of direction: this is found in the greeting and in the end of the reasemblement (reunite).
- **The guard** *(guardia)* (ankles bent, and one foot and a half distance apart between the heels)
- **Lunge** *(affondo)* (rear leg extended, heel of front foot at least three feet away from the rear foot, front knee plumb on the front foot, 90 degrees bent)
- **Cross step** *(incrociate)* (generally an intermediate position passing over the other foot) as normally crosses over the other foot either going forward or backward.
- **Reasemblement** *(riuniti)* (stance with feet together at the heels, made by drawing the front leg back) with slightly bent knees

- Front foot advanced or rear foot back one foot more that in the guard for provocations or feints

- **Squatting** (sitting) position *(posizione accovacciata)* (intermediate for the pass under *passata sotto* or for the doubling the attack from the lunge, *raddoppio*.)

Positions of the torso, head, and unarmed hand *(Posizioni del busto, della testa e del braccio non armato)*

- The torso, normally erect and aligned with the vertical, can be tilted forward or backward.

- The head, normally erect, may be, in some circumstances, inclined decidedly forward or backward.

- The unarmed arm can be flexed, backwards, at various heights, lying, always towards the back, horizontally, or parallel to the rear leg, as in the lunge; abandoned along the side.

Arm positions include: *(Posizioni del braccio armato)*

- The way to hold the weapon
- The positions of the hand
- The positions of the blade

Ways of holding the weapon and handles *(Modi di impugnare l'arma e tipi di impugnature)*

There are two main handles in use today: the anatomical (pistol grip) and smooth (French). In the first, the position is obligatory, and in the second can be held by subtle variations during the bout.

There are two handles used today *(come impugnare l'arma)*

- The anatomical, or orthopedic one, in its numerous variants.
- Or the one with a smooth handle, called the French.

The anatomical handle adapts to the shape of the hand, so it does not present any particular difficulties. This does not mean that we must neglect to train the student to a soft, non-spasmodic grip, variable with the type of action: paying particular attention to the right juxtaposition of the thumb and forefinger, for the control and sensitivity of the tip.

The smooth handle allows, contrary to the anatomical one, different ways of holding it; it also allows you to vary the grip during the assault (but not during the execution of the blow, by regulation)

The handle, with a rectangular section, has the wide sides of the rectangle (near the inside of the guard) parallel to the widest part of the blade (the upper, fluted one), this lines up with the triangular section (isosceles triangle).

The thumb, elongated, rests on the upper part of the handle (for some, adhering to the guard from the inside; for others, more than a centimeter away), and is opposed to the junction between the two first phalanges of the index finger (according to some, to the second phalanx), which support the lower part. The opposite end, on the pommel side, is kept by the other fingers adhering the handle to the hollow of the hand, between the thenar and hypothenar eminence. This is the most solid grip, the most suitable for the complete and powerful use of the weapon, which does not exploit the possibility of a greater reach offered by the other modes.

A second way is with the extended index finger, in which the hand is further back, and the index finger on the lateral face of the handle.

A third way is obtained by gripping the weapon by the pommel, with the index finger (point between the first and second phalanx) opposed to the thumb or elongated (lateral face of the handle).

The last two ways are less suitable for parries, but advantageous for the greater reach. Other variants, less used, which are not described, are obtained by rotating the handle in the hand, for angles, or other.

The hand positions *(Le posizioni de pugno)*

There are four main hand positions and three intermediates. The four main ones, limiting ourselves to consider the weapon in line, starting with one complete rotation (palm out and thumb down) and proceeding clockwise 90 degrees at a time, they are: firsthand position, second, third and fourth.

The intermediate positions are between first and second, second and third, and third and fourth.

In the in-line or guard position the hand is normally in third hand position (thumbs up)

Hand position *(posizioni de pugno)*

There are thrusts, angulations, and flicks and or certain contractions and glides in which this does not apply.

To establish, therefore, what name to give to a position of the hand, in all circumstances, we should refer to two independent variables: it is not enough to verify, in case of doubt, how much is still possible to rotate the hand and arm in one sense or the other.

Too complex, however our current goals: we will limit ourselves to consider positions relating to the line, and we will describe the others, when necessary, without coining new terms.

Our starting position, (using the right hand) we can call it, respecting tradition, fourth hand position: even if, on closer inspection, correctly holding an Italian weapon with the crossbar *(gavigliano)* horizontal, fingernails up, there is still room for a residual clockwise rotation. In fact, if the hand was fully rotated outwards, it could not be held with the thumb on top as it would appear on the side.

Rotating, starting from the fourth position (thumb out), the fist in the sense counterclockwise, after 90 degrees turn, we will have the hand position of third (with open hand, thumb up and palm in); after another 90 degrees the hand will be in second (palm down and thumb to the side); and, finally, hand in first, thumb down and palm out.

From this position, we wanted to use the weapon with the crossbar, we would see that it is still missing a little to bring it to the vertical: to succeed, we must force the movement, also curving the torso to the inside.

And indeed, if we consult Masaniello Parise, we find that this position, already then abandoned, for the use of the mask, was used "by ancients" pulling to the side, to ensure the face: which suggests, in fact, the torso contraction. This position of the hand in first, because that is the position you would assume in drawing the sword from its sheath, ending in first position.

Traditional hand positions do not match today when using modern handles with anatomic or smooth-handled weapons.

The normal position of the hand, with the weapon in line or in the position of the guard (thumb up, palm facing inside), and that of third, and no longer that of fourth, at least in Italian fencing, in which the rotation towards the outside is not used for any particular thrusts, but in the parries. We will then see the reasons later.

Positions of the blade or placements *(Posizioni del ferro, o atteggiamenti)*

As in foil, we will consider teaching the three classic placements of the weapon hand.

- In line (*linea*)
- Invitation (*invito*)
- Engagement (*legamento*)

To these we add one more, which is the <normal guard> placement, which we will examine after the guard position.

We will then define the target, the line of offense, the opposition, and the cone of protection.

The position of the guard *(La posizione di guardia)*

The guard position is the most rational for the execution of the various fencing actions. It is the result of a compromise between the need to offer a limited target (profiled position) and the need for fluid and rapid movements.

The classic guard and the one recommended for setting the guard position: feet at right angles, heels and front foot on the line of direction, space between the feet of about one and a half shoes (we use shoes here so as to not be confused with the imperial measurement of feet); torso erect and well profiled, shoulders at the same height; knees well apart and plumb on the respective toes; unarmed hand arm raised in an arch, elbow lower than shoulder, or to the same height; armed forearm parallel to the platform, elbow of the armed arm about a palm width from the hip, tip of the weapon towards the origin of the opponent's blade, in the guard, if in a normal position.

The position of the guard (*Le posizione di guardia*)

In fact, it is often seen, at a high level, very different guard positions. The Guard position can in effects vary, according to the modalities that we will clarify later, with the speed of displacements and the type of fencing.

The reasons should be briefly discussed for the observable variants.

As the speed of travel increases the tendency to wear the weight of the body on the forefoot (toes), instead of the heels, which are replaced as the origin of the push or lunge.

Consequently, they bring the toes on the line of direction turning them inward, which tend to become almost parallel. This decreases the spread of the knees, and the torso becomes less contoured assuming a position slightly facing more front.

The unarmed arm lowers, sometimes quite a bit, the step forward tends to lengthen, and the center of gravity is higher.

To a greater need for control, instead, it accompanies the return to a more classic position, a lowered center of gravity, more support on the heels, steps shorter and therefore less displacements. Sometimes the non-arm comes back into play as an aid to balance and to add to the velocity.

The position of the armed arm, rather advanced in the setting phase (but not so much as to cause stiffening of the shoulder) you can move back later when the pupil will base his fencing more on time and measure than that on the opponent's blade, its initial point of reference.

Another consideration is related to the age of the students, and therefore to the possibilities.

An advanced and well-covered armed arm is certainly to be recommended for beginners, for the youngest and in any case for the first years of activity. Later, when the technique and experience will have grown, and when even the adversaries will be more able, it will be necessary to pass to one more armed arm setting back in position, to avoid quick blows, or flicks, more difficult to counter.

The attention of the student, and that of the Maestro, will gradually shift away from the pure mechanics of the hand, to move on to the choice of time, to control the measure, to the tactics.

Arm in normal position on guard *(Braccio in posizione normale di guardia)*

In Foil there is the line, in compliance with the convention it must be performed with the arm completely stretched out. In Epee, with absence of convention, for reasons of geometry they can induce you to stretch out completely the arm, to get as close as possible to the target.

For tactical reasons, or didactic, may make us consider a more useful arm being flexed, but more or less elongated, always keeping the tip pointed towards the target, and therefore the threat.

We will thus have a placement which is not an invitation (at least, none of the traditional four) in line: the recommended placement for the guard, with the point pointing towards the center of the guard of the opponent, when his arm is in normal position (line or invitation not excessively decentralized).

CHAPTER 2 **TARGETS AND LINES**

In the second chapter "Targets and Lines" it is emphasized the need to adopt, for the epee, a different and more complete way of describing the targets, which include the whole body, are at different depths, and sometimes require particular angles of the blade and of the armed arm to hit or defend them. The concepts of the line of offense, cone of protection and opposition are described. The variants of invitations and engagements are briefly discussed, with respect to those of the foil. The main movements of the body and legs are then described, and the concept of measurement is expanded. Finally, the manner of carrying the blows is described, including the modern lashing or flicking blows.

At the end of chapter II, you should be able to:

- Know the relationship between invitations and targets
- Describe the various lines of offense
- Know the difference between the five didactic measures, and the real distance to go through
- Describe the different ways of delivering shots

If you are able to answer these questions:

- What are the different epee targets called?
- What are the lines of offence? What is the difference with respect to the foil?
- What is the protective cone? Can you describe it and specify its meaning?
- What is the opposition and how do you name it?
- What is the difference between the invitations and the engagements in foil and the epee?
- What are the main movements in the body and in the legs?
- Why can the observed measurement be different from the real one?
- How many and what ways of striking do you know?

Key words

- Target *(bersaglio)*
- Offense line *(linea di offesa)*

- Protection cone *(cono di prptezione)*

- Opposition *(opposizione)*

- Blade contact *(contatto di ferro)*

- movements of the body and legs *(movimenti del corpo e delle gambe)*

- Measure *(misura)*

- Hits delivered by with blade *(portati)* direct *(lanciati)* and flicking blows *(sferrati)*

The target *(I bersagli)*

In epee, the target takes the name of the anatomical part of which it is made. Some targets are classified as advanced. For example, the armed arm, at various depths: wrist, forearm, arm (meaning in this case, the relative part bicep) shoulder, etc., thigh and leg front, mask. With reference to the only armed arm, the target can be divided in relation to the blade that defends it: high, low, internal, external, and intermediate positions (inside high, outside high, inside low outside low).

In traditionally foil the denomination of the target and related to the position of the blade: low target (flank), high, internal, external, offered by those who engage or invite, respectively, first, second, third or fourth. This simplification was justified at the time of Masaniello Parise, from the fact that the correct target was reduced, to the chest (one point, more than a surface) and to the side. Saying, for example, hit the target straight external, more information was summarized: straight shot, taken to the chest, opponent on the invitation in fourth.

In modern foil fencing, that really uses everything, and frequently the target (including back), reachable from the most varied angles, and with the thrusts of foil, the simplification and excessive, and now unjustified. In modern epee it is even impossible: as in the saber, the target has the same name as the anatomical part intended. It would be of no use to consider as internal, for example, the foot target, just because the opponent is on the invitation of third. Furthermore, also the line, in epee, offers further targets, as in advanced, without precluding those more arrears.

The simplification of use, in the epee, was the subdivision of the target into quadrants, making the center in the guard. Also here, we had an internal, external target high or low, with their possible combinations. But to give an example, as opposed to an invitation in third possible to thrust to the foot, or on the mask or at the wrist below, inside, above, and so on. It makes sense to consider all targets internally.

It makes sense, however, to say that the invitation or engagement of third, for example, covers targets external high (relative to the blade), leaving all the other targets open; that of fourth covers the high inside line, that of second low outside, first low inside. But it is a very limited clarification useful: being able to be the targets, of the same quadrant, numerous and different in depth.

Another consideration, for targets, has considerable importance. Each target, where he is hit, shows up with a different characteristic: consistency, impact angle, shape.

Characteristics of which will necessarily land well, in the more advanced stages of learning.

Offensive line *(Linea d'offesa)*

The blade, directed towards a target, indicates a direction, a line of offense, which takes the name of the threatened target. If greater precision is needed, the target position is added to the threatened target, compared to the blade that defends it (inside, outside, top, bottom); the opposition of the threatening fencer's bell guard and/or the angle of their blade; the position of the hand.

The line, arm outstretched, weapon on the extension, pointing to the valid target, which is ideally the chest: the segment of the line is a straight line from the tip of the weapon to the shoulder that is parallel to the ground, and in the vertical plane that the floor. This has two functions, in foil: threatens and covers (in theory) all targets, obliging (by convention) the adversary to move it, before striking.

In epee, the line also offers target, and so it also has an invitation function. The target offered by the arm, when and in line, and can only be reached with angles (and with flicks, what are they as the modern variant), if the line is covered, i.e., if initially it is directed to the center of the adversary's guard, is also online.

But if the line threatens decentralized targets, such as the foot or mask, the target offered is also reachable by straight thrusts. The target threatened by the line (from offense) can name the line itself (e.g., "weapon on the line of the wrist") by adding, if desired, information relative to the advisories blade. (Externally e.g.).

If the line also involves angels to the wrist, it takes the name from any opposition relating to the iron, (with external opposition high) and from any relative angle to the threatened target (in case of the example reported, in which the adversary on the invitation of fourth, there is no angle).

For the sake of completeness, it will also be indicated the first position of whoever has the weapon in an offensive line. Another example: weapon on the line of the mask, inward, with opposition inward and angle to the lower outside of the mask, hand in second and third. The adversary could be imperfect line, or external, or on the invitation of third. The definitions of opposition and angle are given later: they are both obtained with an angle in the wrist, and sometimes coexist, but the first angles the defense with the guard, the second is necessary or useful angle to offend the target.

However, the student does not necessarily have to be burdened by so many notions, that instead they are necessary for those who teach the matter. Often, but not always, a simplified description suffices. It can, for example, in many cases it is best not to keep singing of the position taken by the adversary. Therefore, keeping in mind all the possible angles resulting from the position of the guard and the blade, in threatening a target, we can observe that the lines will resemble engagements or invitations very advanced.

We can also, by analogy, and simplifying, describe the line, say: weapon on the line of fourth, or third, second, first. We could say, for example: "weapon on fourth line", meaning a line with the guard moved inward, and the tip slightly higher than the guard itself.

It should be noted that this classification differs from those previously used. Confusion was born from wanting to use the target together absolute (chest, side, etc.) and relative (internal, external, high, or low target) of the opponent and, in addition, the position of one's guard, in relation to one's target (see the book of the FIS on the epee on lines and targets, in which it also confuses left and right, in the photo).

For example, the weapon on the fourth line covers the internal high target of who is in line, but is it not accurate enough to say that it threatens the internal (or external for the left-handed) target? It threatens a target that can be internal, if the adversary is on the invitation of third, or external, of and on the invitation of fourth.

Protection cone *(Cono di protezione)*

Excluding the flicks, which use the flexibility of the blade, you can fix with accuracy the coverage effect of the line; and, more generally, of the system it comprises, tip, blade, guard, and target.

Imagine a cone, with the vertex on the guard of who brings the offense, at the point where the blade comes out, and with the tangent surface to the external profile of the other guard, extending indefinitely up to meet the target, and beyond. If the weapon travels to the target in the direction of your blade, all internal targets the surface of the cone will be covered. Given maximum mutual coverage of the two lines of offense that meet, lying on the same line. The line also brings the bell guard (*cocce*) close in the moment of striking the target, increases the amplitude of the protection cone.

The protection cone shown in these images, with a dotted line. The targets contained within the cone are protected. The fencer who stops at the forearm, above, protects himself with an opposition below. The one who gets hit attempted the angulation below, but the target cannot be reached, because it is inside the protection cone

Opposition *(opposizione)*

Opposition of the line, or the normal attitude of guard, can be slightly modified, creating an angle in the wrist, approximately at the height of the guard, in part, by modifying the protection cone, by some blows to the arm or body. When the vertex of the angle approaches the adversary's blade (cover), we have an opposition. More generally:

Opposition, being a defensive action, and in relation to one's target (mainly the closest to the opposing tip: the forearm). Which is covered. It will take the name of its corresponding target(relative to the blade), in the various possible combinations. So, in addition to high, or low, or internal or external opposition, we will also have high internal, or low external.

> The movement of the guard (from position of weapon in line, or of attitude normal guard) vertically and or lateral, for defensive purposes (towards the adversary's blade), it will be called opposition

In the two images above, the fencer has his arm extended, with strong movement of the guard in an external position, and a low internal one. We cannot, however, define these two positions (exemplifying all the others) as oppositions or angles, in the absence of the opponent's blade and target

The four invitations and engagements of the foil can be hired, as well as in the traditional way: by moving the tip and, much more limitedly, the guard, in the direction corresponding (angular movement that hits the wrist; the traditional engagement and approximately, a translation of the forearm and of the iron, making center in the elbow). In fact, the target offered, to be covered quickly, with little displacement, it can be articulated by use of the wrist.

The engagement can be done from several measures and, as we have said, can be executed with movement of the point, accompanied by a lighter movement of the guard. In these conditions, the engagement is weaker, and can more easily be forced (forced glide, *filo sottomesso*): or it is possible to threaten the target by sliding on the blade (glide) (*coule* in French) although subject to the engagement: it will be more correct to call these: contact of the blade (*contactto di ferro*).

In the final position of the invitation or engagement (first, second, third or furth), and the movement necessary to reach it, they take the same name as the matching parries, (simple, counter, half circular). We will see later which, for the study of the glides, of each engagement we will have to consider the version high or low.

Invitations and engagements, in the epee, we can more rightly say they cover a target (or a few targets, to different depths), discovering all others: in Foil, simplifying the targets after all, there are only two, chest and flank, it was said that they only discover one target.

The French call our engagement (and also the simple contact of the irons) engagement (same as English) and our disengagement (the movement to release the iron from the others engagement that a feint can follow) degagement; but then more precisely, they call "trompement" the action of removing the iron in an adverse defensive action (parry); and "derobment" the action of subtracting the iron from an attacking opponent (who attacks the iron pressing forward as *presa di ferro*, or blade seizure.

Body movements and legs *(Movimenti del corpo e delle gambe)*

The movements of the body and legs can be forward, backward, sideways, vertical and involve the passage from one to the other in all the directions described for various purposes. They include:

- **The steps** (forward and backward <*avanti e indietro*>), normal, crossed, and inverted rear foot advance before the front foot or *raddoppio*: or the front foot retracting before the rear foot;

- **The lunge,** *(l'affondo)* normal and or crossed (*incrociato*)

- **Lateral displacements** *(gli spostamenti laterali)* (to occupy different areas of the fencing platform, used for tactical purposes);

- **Side dodge** (*schivate*) subtracting the target of the body and head;

- **Vertical dodge** (*passata sotto*) under attacking iron;

- **Reasemblement** *(la riunita)* subtracting the lower target and legs.

- Some movements among those indicated can be accomplished by detaching, at the same time, both feet off the fencing platform. Thus, we have jumps, or various leaps, including;

- The leap forward (*la balestra*) and leap backward (*salto indietro*) (the swinging of the front leg behind and then landing in the guard);

- The cross step back or cross step jump *(I salti indietro incrociati)*

- The arrow (fleche FR. Frecciata IT) is the more dynamic version of crossing forward;

- The renewed attack *(la riunita in sospensione)*

The measure *(la misura)*

Fundamental for the success of every action in fencing is finding the so-called measure, generally it is understood as the distance separating the two fencers. It is an erroneous concept, or rather insufficient, which we will discuss later in the section dedicated to tactics. The distances to consider are two; the apparent one, and the one that must be overcome to deliver the thrust to an opponent who moves.

In Epee, due to the presence of the advanced target, and for the importance of the actions of renewed attacks, at very close range it is well to consider, for the teaching of actions, five measures instead of the three found in foil. In Epee we add a closer (narrow between fencers) range that found in foil and a longer range (wide) about an extra step when at step and lunge distance *(camminando)*.

The normal distance of the measure, which allows the touch to the chest with a lunge, also allows the touch to the wrist by only extending the weapon hand, without any movement of the legs. In the section dedicated to tactics we will see instead, how it is appropriate to consider, from the point of sight of the coming mental mechanisms activated, two measures, the long and the short, and the border area between the two, which we will call the critical point.

Methods of making the hit *(Modo di portare i colpi)*

- **Thrusts delivered** *(Colpi portati)*: the arm is outstretched first so that the hit reaches the target. This type of blow (straight or angled with various hand positions) are more controlled and allows for easier recovery of the weapon and readiness for a counterattack or a new action. This is healthy to learn first.

- **Thrusts thrown** *(Colpi lanciati)*: the arm is in the phase of distension (stretch out) when the thrust reaches the target. These are part of the group that includes *fuetto* (flicks) described in the auxiliary actions. They require a squeeze of the handle in a more determined (earlier) time. The coupe *(cavare angolata)* or *molinillo* can be carried or thrown. Among the advantages of the thrown thrust is that of greater speed of impact to the target, with increased probability to record the hit with all other things being equal.

The direction of movement from the guard, in carrying the hit, can be deferent from the direction of the blade (angles, coupe, *molinelli lanciati*) or its terminal use of the flick *(fuetto)*.

Shots and ways of carrying them *(Colpi e modo di postarli)*

The extension of the arm is faster than that of the distension of the rear leg, or the inclination of the torso in the lunge. The maximum final speed of the hit is secured by the sum, being perfectly coordinated, of the three movements. But maximum speed is not always required, except in the final phase of the action in offense: for example, in feints, speed and synchronization in relation to that of the opponent's parries.

The energy transmitted to the spring in the point required for registering the hit depends on many factors: speed of impact, impact angle, impact duration, friction, virtual mass. The work accomplished in the bending of the blade and the depression of the spring are due to the transformation of kinetic energy to potential energy of the spring itself.

The kinetic energy is proportional to the mass and to the square of the velocity. A small increase in speed of the hit makes, therefore, a grater increase in mass: the latter, however, is only virtual, depending in when the tightening in time occurs (tightening of the armed hand) (which also allows you to better resist lateral displacement) and of the flexibility of the blade, and not just the mass of the epee.

The duration of the impact also depends on the quality of the surface stricken: it is minimal on the hard surfaces such as the mask, and longer on softer parts of the body. There is a real risk that a blow on the mask, due to the rebound being too fast, does not give rise to the signals, even though the tip has completely retracted (there is a minimum time, below which the blow is not registered by the apparatus, because the tip can, in bouncing, detach itself from the target before the head is pushed back by the spring): so the blows on the mask must be carried with particular precautions (when both move in the same direction, and the speeds are subtracted), and without excessive speed.

The best condition to prevent the blow from sliding on the target is to arrive perpendicularly between the tip and the target: a condition rarely achievable. Approaching this condition in practice improves the odds that the blow will be signaled.

CHAPTER III **OFFENSIVE ACTIONS**

In the third chapter "Offensive Actions" the offensive actions are defined and classified, postponing the description of the counter-offense, which is part of the offensive actions, till the next chapter. Some differences considered on the concepts of attack and the renewed attack, riposte and the rimesse. As in foil and saber treatises, a distinction is made between the fundamental and auxiliary actions, always considering the particularities of the epee. It describes the choice on time (stretta in tempo)

Given the greater importance in the epee, of a realistic control of the adversaries' iron, the various types of hits are described in detail, then the engagements, transports and the half transports, the understanding of which is necessary to introduce the complex technique of the glides. For the need in epee, to protect oneself while taking offense, the various blows with opposition are described, being useful in all offensive actions, and in particular those described below, the counter-offense, and specifically the counter-offenses described below with-in the counter-offense the counter-variants of the forced glide. The chapter closes with a discussion on the varieties of auxiliary actions.

Variants of the force glide. The chapter closes with a discussion on the varieties of auxiliary actions

- Define and classify the various offensive actions
- Know the difference between basic and auxiliary offensive actions
- Describe the opposite and fundamental action to various attitudes
- Explain the difference between the various beats
- Describe the technique for the glide
- Describe the hits with opposition
- Describe angulations
- Know the auxiliary actions

If you can answer these questions you can proceed to the next chapter

- What are offensive actions and how are they classified?
- What is the initiative?
- What is the counter-offense?
- What is the epee fencing time?

- When does the stretta in tempo take place?

- What are the main beats?

- What does it mean to transport?

- What is the difference between the basic glides and the other glides?

- What are hits in opposition?

- How are angulations performed?

- What are the forced glides and how are the executed?

KEYWORDS:

Offense (*Offesa*)

Attack (*Attacco*)

Initiative (*Iniziativa*)

Riposte (*Risposta*)

Replacement (*Rimesse*)

Counter offense (*Controffesa*)

Counterattack (*Uscita in tempo*)

Simple actions (*Azione semplici*)

Fundamental, auxiliary actions (*Fondamentali, ausiliarie azione*)

Fencing time (*Tempo schermistico*)

Tight in time (*Stretta in tempo*) Beats (*Battute*)

Expulsion (*Sforzi*) Pressures (*Pressioni*)

Transports and half transporting (*Trasporti e mezzi trasporti*)

Glides (*Fili*)

Opposition (*Opposizione*) Angulation (*Angolazione*)

The offensive actions *(Le azione di offesa)*

Offensive actions are all those tending to determine the hit. Therefore, they are offensive actions, regardless of their success:

- Attack and renewing of the attack
- Ripostes
- Counter-offensive actions
- Replacement of the attack

Attack *(Attacco)*

The attack is any offensive action that takes precedence (or contemporaneity in the case of a simultaneous attack) of the initiative, without solution of continuity until the blow is completed, regardless of the success.

The proposed definition of attack is substantially different from that of the conventional weapons timing (already insufficient for conventional weapons) in which the priority of the threat is the only factor in identifying the attack. It is necessary to classify many blows brought backwards on an opponent who advances without threatening a target and that has the priority of the threat, but it is not possible to call attacks. And calling them attacks in preparation, without being able to make them fall into any of the categories indicated for the offense, means, it unnecessarily complicates things: it is preferable to include them in the counter-offense section.

It is said whoever has the initiative and starting from the last interruption, or from the last pause in the action, first advances towards the opponent, until the hit of one of the two, or both arrives or until the pause or next break. The initiative and the threat (real or simulated) together configure the beginning of an attack, which can be carried out or stopped. The initiative alone is part of the preparation.

The introduction of the concept of "initiative" is necessary because, from the treaties and from the international regulation (RI) it is not clear enough that an attack can take place only be advancing. And, because in the epee it is more easily possible to strike going backwards, during a preparation: as an advance without threat. These blows although the attack has not started, we will still have to call the counter-defense blows.

The resuming of the attack *(La ripresa di attacco)*

A resumption or renewing of the attack is defined as any new attacking action carried out by the same attacker immediately after the first failed attacking action, because of a parry not followed with a riposte or the subtraction of the target or an error made by the adversary.

The definition includes all the actions included in foil: second strike (on another line or better, on another target by advancing) and all the varieties (simple or compound, with the various movements of the legs) of new attacking actions. Given the definition of the attack given above, it is understood that the second strike implies the initiative and therefore the advancement of the person making it.

Riposte *(Risposta)*

Any offensive action simple or compound, carried out by the person who has made the parry, immediately after the parry itself is call a riposte.

Counter offense or counter time *(Controffesa, o uscita in tempo)*

Counter-offense or exit on time is any offensive action that is intentionally carried out during the offensive action of the opponent's initiative.

The term "counterattack" often used as a synonym for counteroffensive or exit in time, has a different more restrictive nuance: offensive action during the opponent's attack, and not during any offensive action. The treatise on the epee from the FIS (as opposed to those of foil and saber) intends however by counter-offense, the recovery by the one who has suffered the attack, or the riposte. We will not follow this definition which has no parallel with the other treaties.

Remise *(Rimessa)*

Any offensive action carried out, without further advance, is called remise, as immediately after one's own offensive action failed, because of a parry, subtraction of the target or error on the opponent's accord.

The amplitude of the epee target leads in common use, to call remises' even a few seconds (in the sense of subsequent blows) Remise's play an important role in epee. Therefore, they deserve a more accurate definition. We distinguish them from the so-called second blows because the latter are attacking blows: they presuppose a new and immediate initiative (advancement) which may have been premeditated. Remise's on the other hand, are generally remedial actions for an unforeseen event, to a strict extent, and must be automated, because their effectiveness depends on their maximum speed.

Since we are talking about technique, and not about tactics, we ignore the intention that preceded and accompanies the thrust: therefore, it is certainly possible that apparently identical actions can be classified in a different way. Therefore, we will be able to have the same executive modalities for an action that we will classify, from time to time, as a second strike, remise or counter offense.

Definition of simple offensive actions, fundamental and auxiliary actions
(Definizione delle azioni di offesa semplici, fondamentali e ausiliarie)

The definition of simple, fundamental, and auxiliary offensive actions.

Offensive actions that evade one or more parries, or searches for the blade, or that intentionally lead the offense to a target other than the one threatened at the start, are called compound actions.

Each simple offense action can be simulated, constituting a part of the compound action (feint) which will take its name from the simulated action.

Simple actions can therefore involve even more than a movement, such as hitting and banging; and they can end on the opposite line, like disengagement, starting from the engagement.

Simple actions are divided into fundamental and auxiliary. The fundamentals are those that reach the target by the shortest route, or in the most immediate and linear way.

The auxiliary actions, less immediate, and often more difficult to execute, increase the variety of actions available and make it possible to organize a more diversified, less predictable, and therefore more effective offense.

Simple actions and fencing time *(Azione semplici e tempo schermistico)*

The fencing time according to the definition of the RI and the duration of the execution of a simple action. It could be deduced therefore, that a simple action consisting of a single unit of time, and that the fencing time is subjective, being able to have, for two opponents with different speeds, two different fencing times in the same real time interval.

This definition, already inadequate for foil, is wrong for the epee, in which the fencing time is determined (by the RI which establishes the margin of delay so that a double touch can be signaled) between the twentieth and the twenty-fifth of a second, i.e., between fifty and forty hundredths of a second: in practice less than half of a tenth of a second.

The Italian school and the French school agree in calling "composite" offensive actions that elude one or more parries. It would follow that the others are "simple", which do not elude parries, as the Italian school defines even if the action includes more than one movement.

Wanting to attribute the definition to offensive actions in a single time, involves two problems: the inadequate definition of "fencing time" for the epee, because it is too short to perform the action; the need to consider then, as part of the preparation, and not the actual attack, actions such as the beats, when they immediately precede the thrust. This would entail the logical consequence of classifying, for example, the disengagement in time (which can also be performed by reversing direction) not as a counter-offensive action, but as an attack on the preparation. And we do not think it is the case.

Simple offensive fundamental actions as opposed to the attitude of the opponent's invitation (*Azioni di offesa semplici e fondamentali in contrapposizione all'atteggiamento di invito dell'avversario*)

In contrast to the opponent's attitude of invitation, starting, therefore, from one's attitude of invitation, or of a weapon in line, the simple offensive action is fundamental and the straight thrust to the various uncovered targets (carried blows).

The pupil must be trained to deliver a straight thrust to all the targets, identifying the size and movement of the legs suitable for each of them. Then the blow to the mask, the flank, on the wrist, forearm, crook of the elbow, arm, shoulder, thigh, knee, leg, and foot. Particular attention should be paid to the various possibilities of hitting advanced targets, and the arm in the first place. The blows must be carried out, according to possibility, from stationary, extending only the arm; also extending the torso; with the step, with lunges of various lengths, with the crossed step, with the arrow. The action, subsequently, will be performed "in time" that is, when the Maestro changed attitude, with the Maestro still advancing and or retreating.

Simple offensive fundamental actions as opposed to the attitude of the opponent's engagement (*Azioni di offesa semplici e fondamentali in contrapposizione all'atteggiamento di legamento dell'avversario*)

In contrast to the engagement, the simple action of the fundamental offense and the disengagement, to the various targets. By disengaging we mean a blow that immediately follows a releasing movement: freeing the iron from the engagement or avoiding a parry or a search for the blade.

The disengagement *(La cavazione)*

The definition of disengagement that comes from foil is rather contradictory: first, disengagement is defined as the action of freeing one's iron from the others engagement; then it is defined as a blow (i.e., a straight thrust preceded by a *svincolo* or disengagement). After defining the term, it is used, however in a different way, even with feints. The disengagement after a feint direct and *altra cosa*, is different because it does not start from the engagement.

The definitions, however accurate, are models, approximations, or simplifications of reality. For the epee, less simple, more accurate and purposeful models are required.

One disengagement understood as a thrust, consists of three parts: the releasing action, (or evasion from a free blade) the extension of the arm and the thrust. The release action has three main types or attitudes: from the engagement, during the glide executed by the adversary and eluding or avoiding the blade when it is free.

The arm stretch may not be there (to simply steal the blade, without taking any action, or to parry after the release or avoidance, or to hit the advanced target) or be aimed at a feint or a thrust.

The shot can be taken on a large variety of targets, as well as in various ways (straight, angled, with opposition, etc.) and therefore it can no longer be said that it ends in the opposite line to the starting line. We will come back to this later.

As for the straight thrust, the student will have to practice bringing the disengagement first to the chest, then to various targets uncovered by the engagements with different leg movements, and different sizes, always taking care of the absolute precedence of the toe movement, and absence of unnecessary contractions, especially in the shoulder.

Simple offensive fundamental actions in opposition to the opponent's placement of blade in line *(Azioni di offesa semplici e fondamentali in contrapposizione all'atteggiamento di arma in linea dell'avversario)*

In contrast to the opponent's weapon in-line there are various possibilities of delivering a blow. Among the fundamental ones, in accordance with the foil theory, we consider only two. The beat direct and the engagement followed by the glide.

We do not inset, as in foil, the straight thrust by detachment following the engagement, because as an epeeist will preferably keep control of the blade by using various precautions, which we will see later. It will first be necessary, however, to describe the beats and glides: two important groups of actions, mainly for the epeeist. For a better understanding, we will first delve into the concepts of *stretta in tempo* and *trasporto* (envelopments)

The tightening on time *(La stretta in tempo)*

With the smooth handle or with the anatomic, the grip on the weapon is not constant. It is minimal when in the guard position, or in line; in increases when the fingers direct the tip for the interchanges; and still greater in the carrying of the thrust, and in the contact with the opponent's blade. Since the squeeze occurs at the instant the action is performed, it is called tighten in time.

Pressures, variable *(La presa variabile)*

Education to a variable grip, and to rest the hand when the control is obtained with the measure, allow to avoid the easy tiredness, harmful muscular contractions or even damage to the joints and tendons. And it helps, in the initial phase of learning, not to insist too much on complete extension of the arm, requiring soft, free movements.

The variable pressure allows to have and seek different effects in dealing with the opponent's weapon. A beat is most effective when the opposing hand in not gripping the weapon strongly. A gliding action or a time thrust, on the contrary, to fully maintain contact and control of the iron (avoiding *svincoli* or *rimessa*) are preferable when the opponent squeezes the weapon, to strike (for example in counter time) or when induced to attempt a release in the wrong direction. For example, search for the blade in third, to cause an inward release, to then perform the engagement is second and glide.

The beat *(Le battute)*

The main purpose of the beat is to obtain the maximum distance from the starting position of the opponent's weapon. It is performed with a firm squeeze in time, preferably between the edges of the two blades. There are three principal types of beats: Simple beat, in which the contact between the blades is limited to single point; the Expulsion, in which the degrees of the opposing blade are pressed with a forceful sliding action; Grazing beat, spanking the iron in the opposite direction while passing over the tip of the opponent's blade.

The path of the iron in executing the beats allows us to classify them, similar to the parries, being simple, half circular and circular.

Beats, expulsions, and pressures *(Battute, sforzi e pressione)*

Particular attention should be paid to the technique of the beats and to their real effectiveness. The beat can have tactical purposes, to induce a reaction that you want to take advantage of; or the purpose of discovering a target to hit, before or at most together with the arrest of the adversary. In this case, he must transmit the maximum energy to the iron and hand of the other, possibly with the minimum expenditure and movement, to avoid a disengagement in time and maintain good control of your weapon. The beats of ancient fencing, foil or epee, aimed at the purpose: but for some strange reason at a certain point a mistake was made, most likely which has been handed down over time.

The real beat, as it once was is now called an expulsion (*di Potenza*) a diagonal forward movement along the blade from wither third or fourth (high lines) with a rotation of the hand (so that to hit with the edge and to add energy from the rotation and strength due to the position of the hand) which runs through the degrees of the opposing blade, starting from the meeting point of the strong of the antagonist on the weak of the receiver. The direction of the beat, and the time of application of the force applied along the blade is to transmit the considerable energy hidden in the movement. The same result is obtained with the pressure, which is exercised in the same way, but starting from one's own engagement.

The beats once called sharp (*tocchi*) become habitual, in foil in which the realism of the fight is lacking due to the convention, should be performed with a lateral impact towards the other blade strong on weak (per Masaniello Parise) or somewhat improving the effectiveness but loosing realism due to the too close of measure (the chest being reached with an extension of the armed arm) strong over medium.

This need to strike with the strong on the weak probably derives from the study of levers: they are used for something else. In the case of engagements, or pressures on the iron, having the advantage of degrees is decisive. For our case, the study of collisions is much more useful. The transmitted energy, as we have witnessed for it repels the tip away, increases much more with the increase in the speed of the impact. And since the collision occurs between two points, it is important to make the point of the blade hitting the other one travel at maximum speed. Pivoting in the wrist, or from the elbow, the point that moves at the greatest speed is the farthest and corresponds to the terminal part of the blade: which is also the most flexible and absorbs, by bending, a larger part of the energy delivered.

Furthermore, the measure of reach (points that just go beyond the guard with the weapon in line from the guard position) allows you to overlap in the contact between the blades, strong on weak, or medium on medium: and not strong on medium or strong on strong.

The only concrete possibility remains, therefore, to obtain the desired effect (discover the target for the necessary time) that of striking the medium with the medium. We discard the beat of the strong over the weak, because the movement of the hand of the one who makes the movement too wide; and because the energy transmitted is minimal. Let's consider instead the beat of the weak on the strong (medium weak on medium strong) as useful for hitting the wrist, if the beat is made, even lightly, when the others hand is relaxed. The medium-to-medium strike on the other hand can be used for all targets. Another trick to improve the effectiveness of the beat is to hit the opposing blade with the edge of the blade. Since the epee has a triangular cross section (the foil is square at the strong and tapers to a rectangle) the edges are three.

The edge corresponding to the lower vertex of the isosceles triangle should not be considered, as the blade flexes more in that direction. The optimal conditions are given by a collision with the remaining two edges, so the position of the hand must vary accordingly: or if you want to also use the rotation of the hand, this must be less accentuated than for the foil.

The beat requires on the part of the performer a decisive choice of time; vice versa to obtain the maximum deviation, one must hit when the opponent does not tighten strongly. Unless you want to get a defensive or offensive reaction from the adversary, take advantage of it in another way. Furthermore, the beats are easier if the opposing point is far from the center of the guard: otherwise, this decentralized condition must be created with diversionary actions.

Finally, some considerations on the pressure on the opponent's blade. The aim of moving the opposing blade away from the line, to strike the uncovered target at the detachment, is certainly achieved more effectively with the beat. Pressure is more useful for tactical purposes, that is to provoke a reaction to take advantage of how the opponent reacts (say a parry in the same direction as the pressure or counter disengage to evade it).

It is generally inadvisable in the epee, to strike following a detachment or pressure or from an engagement. It is therefore logical to try and obtain the maximum effect from this provocation. The purpose is achieved by carrying out the pressure with a disadvantage of the degrees: medium weak against medium strong. In this way, a strong displacement of the opposing blade is obtained with a small displacement of his own, and it is natural that the adversary, feeling that he has an advantage, reinforces his engagement, opening the opposite line.

Transports, half transport and varieties of engagements *(I trasporti, i mezzi trasporti e le varieta di legamenti)*

There are four traditional transports considered in foil. From first to third, from third to first, from second to fourth and fourth to second.

There are four half transports: the transition from low first (seventh if French or false fourth from traditional foil) to high first; from low second to high second; from high third to low third and from high fourth to low fourth.

For each of the four engagements we will have the high version and the low, for a total of eight. We define the lower first lower second, upper third upper fourth engagements as fundamental for epee.

Envelopments, transports, and engagements *(Riporti, transporti and legamenti)*

From the technique of foil, we know the difference between changes of engagement, transport and envelopments. For the latter, now no longer used in foil, it should be noted that it is easier execute and control them (such as a transport) when the adversaries blade rests on two points of our weapon: the blade and edge of the guard. Furthermore, for the same reasons it is good to reduce the width of the cone described by the weapon of the person carrying out the envelopment, placing the vertex of the cone in the joint of the elbow, rather than in that of the wrist.

The transport considerations in foil are only those that go from the fourth to second engagement, and vice versa, and from first to third engagement and vice versa, Healthy transports starting on one side (internal or external) and ending on the other side. Transports that begin and end on the same side are not mentioned, inverting only the top with the bottom and vice versa, and which also have an importance of the glide. Since, in carrying them out, they are very similar to the first part of normal transport, it is appropriate to call them means of transport.

Let's clarify with an example, for the most common case: from the engagement in fourth, right hand to right hand, having the tip of the epee above the point of contact. To execute the glide to the flank, as we will see better later, the guard is lowered, and then the tip until immediately before the hit, with the tip below the contact point, which is always inside the blade. A means of transport was thus called a part of half transport.

Continuing the movement, and shifting the contact point outwards, we would end up on the second engagement, having performed a complete transport (fully going from one engagement to another without losing contact of the blade) initial and final position of a means of transport determine two different engagements, in a high or low version, bringing the number/types of significant engagements to eight. We consider fundamental those from which the glide not preceded by means of a transport start, as we will see later.

The glide *(I fili)*

There are four fundamental glides in epee. First, to the low internal target, second, to the external low target, third, to the high external target and fourth, to the high internal target.

Glides can be preceded by envelopments, transport, half transports. Essential for a correct choice and execution of the glide, and to consider the position of the guard and the opponent's blade.

The technique of the glide *(La tecnica dei fili)*

The technique of the glide is particularly complex in epee, and unfortunately written in treatises, it is not sufficiently explained in depth. A glide starts from one's own engagement. The optimal starting condition, to overcome any resistance and that of strong grade over the weak grade. Better yet, to have the opponent's blade be resting on the guard and blade (forming triangulation) of the line that is not too distant so that the tip of the opponents blade does not reach or go beyond the guard is easily doomed to fail, being easily defeated by releasing off the blade even in an involuntary manner.

The same effect is very likely going to be realized even if resistance offered by the opponent is lacking. Therefore, the glide is an action to be taken against opponents who tend to stiffen the arm: or after having caused, with appropriate preparation, a greater grip than the opponent, or a releasing movement in the wrong direction. With a very soft hand being found more so with those who use the smooth grip the glide is preferable than using a beat.

The guard is of fundamental importance as well. As a result of the cone of protection, it needs to be absolutely avoided when directing the hit to the opponents' target. To be more precise, since the guard of the one who glides can move in a different direction from that of the point, (angulation) it is necessary that the guard of the fencer who glides does not go in the same direction of the opposing guard.

It is therefore necessary to observe the position of the guard of the person who is subjected to the glide (and to foresee their movements during the action) to select the suitable glide. The general rule for orientation for the glide is based on the opponents' bell guard.

Assuming a "perfect' line (without angles of the blade or any opposition) any movement of the guard from this position or line (assuming the tip is close to one's own guard) will tend to the line diametrically opposite of the plane perpendicular to the line of offense. We will keep in mind as well the fact that the opponent's tip, after passing the edge of your own guard, will be offline to the center of the opponent's guard.

To execute the glide, it is done so by going through the degrees as previously noted in the definition of the forced glide. The manner to perform this is different: the point of contact moves from the point of contact at one's own strong against the opponents weak and slides along the degrees of the blade (length) toward their strong always keeping contact with the opponents' blade with the strong of your own as the tip is directed towards the target.

The optimal condition to execute the glide in first (the fundamental one) is that the guard of the opponent is to their inside and the point is below their hand. The engagement between the blades presses to the inside (inside of both blades touching, executors strong against opponents weak) as if one wanted to pass underneath their guard. The guard of the executer of the glide pushes towards the inside with the point low. The target can be the thigh, flank or armpit depending on the height of the opposite guard.

For the glide in second, contact is between the outside of each blade pushing towards the outside, point lower than the hand targeting the thigh or flank of the opponent.

The glide in third, contact between the blades each touching the outside edge, tip above the hand targeting the chest or mask.

The glide in fourth, contact between blades is on the inside, tip above the hand targeting the shoulder or mask.

Conditions of the adversaries' blade being slightly different from what is already described can make a glide preceded by a transport more convenient: this action is classified as auxiliary as discussed below. Having a slightly lower hand compared to the tip than described for the first fundamental glide to the flank, can make the glide above to the shoulder or mask preferable, always with opposition to the inside following a transport from the engagement of first low to high.

The glide in high second to the chest is preferred if the opposing hand is lower; the glide in low third to the abdomen is preferable when the opposing guard is higher; the glide in fourth to the flank is appropriate against a higher guard or hand.

Let us take the latter case as an example: glide in fourth (right to right). If the opponent has their weapon approximately in line or in line with slight opposition and has their guard (hand) low and to the inside with the point slightly high (weapon on the fourth line) it will be easier to glide to his high line target and or inside, shoulder, chest or mask, performed with opposition to the inside.

If, on the other hand the guard is higher and the tip slightly below the hand, the glide is just described, because of the protection cone will be deflected in the final part of the thrust. It will be more useful in this case to direct the hit to the flank which will be carried out by lowering one's guard (before the tip) and then directing the shot to the target discovered.

In this case, it will be observed the blades which previously (in the engagement) crossed with a point of contact upwards (with respect to the bell guard) find themselves due to an action very similar to a transport (from high to low and vice versa staying on the same side of the blade) with the contact point down. The French call this type of action with this type of transport (as also others) "*croise*". As mentioned above we will call it a means of transport.

To a "perfect" line (however unusual) on the other hand we can oppose any glide, as in the foil theory, by moving the guard conveniently and avoiding moving it in the direction of the adversary's guard.

A specific case with glides to the arm, which can be performed from all lines, keeping in mind what has been noted above. In the normal guard position, with the arm flexed, a glide to the forearm will be like an action against the line, while being able to find the target further from the elbow onwards.

For completeness in the case of glides to the arm, we must also consider the high line glides, from the engagements in third and fourth. And the low glides from the engagement of second and first. All with the bell guard on the same vertical plane.

And finally, the internal glides, executable from both third and second engagements; and the external glides from the engagement of fourth or first, all with the bell guard at the same height.

The latter start from engagements neither high nor low, for which we have no specific names.

We will manage in any case identifying each glide from the starting engagement and the target acquired. For example, glide in second to the arm; glide in third to the abdomen; glide in first to the outer bottom of the arm and so on.

Simple and auxiliary offensive actions (*Azione di offesa semplice e ausiliarie*)

Simple offensive actions (which do not evade parries or end at a target other than the one initially threatened) are accompanied by other fundamental actions, which are simple by definitions, and that are known as auxiliary: knowing how to perform them increases the repertoire, helps to be less predictable and allows one to better exploit some technical errors of the opponent. But it is necessary to know these actions, although numerous, to know how to defend them.

They are:

- Hits with opposition, direct, crossing and collection.

- Angulations to the arm or body

- Flicks

- The cut over

- The forced glide

Some of the previous hits may be preceded by releases, beats, pressures, envelopments, transports, changes of engagement.

Thrusts with opposition, direct, crossing and collecting *(I colpi con opposizione, diretta, incrociando, raccogliendo)*

There is direct opposition when the offender moves the guard in the direction of the opposing guard and blade, thus closing the threatened line, due to the cone of protection. At the end of the action the bell guards are on the same line.

Opposition occurs when the offender moves his guard in the direction of the opponent's blade, with a movement similar to that of direct parries, and thus moving it out of the target line. At the end of the action the bell guards are on opposite lines.

There is the opposition to picking up *(raccogliere)* when the offender, with a movement of the blade similar to that of a parry against or with the middle of the blade, collects in carrying the hit the opposing blade, pushing it to the outside of the offensive line. The bell guard at the end of the action, can be found on the same line (more or less) or on different lines or even opposite lines giving one maximum guarantee.

In all cases, opposition is carried out during the advancement of the arm, with precedence over the distension of the arm, moving the point as little as possible from the target, so as to make the action appear as a single movement.

Thrust with opposition *(I colpi con opposizione)*

In epee there is need to protect oneself from being hit while making the offensive. One of the most effective means is by opposition using displacement from the cone of protection and therefore of the bell guard and the blade itself making a triangle between the points which supports better than two points of contact. By moving directly toward the adversaries' guard and blade while performing the shot. This type of opposition we will call "direct opposition".

Even more effective if done well is the opposition that will be called "crossed" or "crossing" which resembles a glide executed "on the fly" without a preliminary engagement, and to be effective it must observe the same precautions described above for glides.

Slightly more difficult and equally effective, making sure to follow the same precautions as the glides, the hit with opposition by "picking up" the opposing blade by use of a circular or semicircular movement.

Some examples for clarification. Right against right, the one in line with external opposition, point slightly high. The other from the invitation of third, executed a straight thrust to the shoulder or mask with opposition inside on the fourth line, while moving the guard to the inside toward the blade. If the adversary modifies their position slightly, were to bring themselves to the high external line with the tip slightly lower that the hand directing the hit to the armpit and with direct opposition, the high internal would be safer.

In contrast to the same line, the other starts from the invitation of fourth (with the blade on the outside of the adversaries) and pulls to the chest, crossing the blade and keeping it on the outside as like the glide in third (but as a result of the hit is done in a single movement) it ends with opposition.

In opposition to the line in third (external with the tip slightly above the hand) the opponent starts from either invitation of third, or from the invitation of second, one pulls a shot to the chest and picking up the blade as it gets close to the chest, wrap around the blade and bring it to the outside line as like the glide in third (always done with a single movement forward from the guard) and end the strike with opposition.

These same actions can be performed on the arm or other targets. For actions using the cross oppositions and collecting the blade it is important for expedient movements. That is to execute them when the adversaries tip is close to our own bell guard. Hits with opposition are easier to execute when the tip of the opponent is further away; in these cases, a viable alternative is the direct thrust or angulation to the uncovered target.

The analogy of these actions by use of glides were used so frequently that they can be called by someone in the past "flying glides". We can add to the indications already explained, these are reserved for the more experienced.

We must avoid at first meeting the enemies guard as we would meet their own protection cone. It would seem, however, in the attacks ending with direct opposition, to do exactly the opposite. When one wants to pull or call the shot on a line slightly different. looking for a target just outside of the protection cone.

Exploiting the effect of the wedge, due to the fact that in the final phase of the hit, the points of support on the opposing blade become two, the guard and the blade itself.

For shots that cross and collect it is possible without arranging the guard in a diametrically opposite direction to the opponent. It will be easier to lose control of the opponent's blade during the execution of the action.

In these cases, a finer and more sensitive execution will be required, and the preparation taken more carefully and more so than what already noted by choosing to provoke the moment of the opponents closing in time of the adversary or of a retraction movement in the wrong direction.

For example, in contrast to the same starting in the line of third as in previous examples, the strike with opposition above to the arm, shoulder, mask or chest is also possible starting from the invitation of first or fourth and will end with direct opposition.

Finally, we consider that direct opposition can also take place without contact of the blades, and that paradoxically, in the case of an angulation or the thrust by glide, the attack with *ancraciata* or *raccogliere* can end with a line with no angles but covered and therefore without opposition! A paradox that we except for convenience and simplicity of classification.

Angulations to the arm or to the body *(Le angolazione al braccio e al corpo)*

Angulations are offensive actions that are performed by creating an angle in one's own line, generally only at the wrist, but as needed in the elbow and shoulder.

These are done more frequently to the arm. To reach a covered target, but also to strike any other part of the body by improving the angle of impact on the chosen target or to frustrate the opponent's parry.

The thrust by angulation *(I colpi angolati)*

Angulations are used in reference to attacks delivered to the forward target of the wrist or forearm when the opponent's weapon is in line. For this purpose, the offender's arm is flexed in the wrist and or elbow and the guard moved off center, while the point is directed at the target.

We have already said that the arm online is not always covered, per se, and can be reached in many cases without angulation: it is enough that the opponent's line threatens a somewhat decentralized target as compared to our guard.

Furthermore, it is possible and useful to use an angulation to the uncovered target in order to improve the angle of impact and for the same reason or to make a planned parry more difficult. Angled attacks can also be delivered to other, more rearward targets.

The angulation, which is an offensive action, and is in relation to the opponent's target from which it takes its name. "External angulation" therefore, is an attack delivered to the opponent's external target; "external opposition" on the other hand is a displacement of one's own bell guard to cover one's external target.

The most common angulation is those to the wrist and forearm. It is therefore used to mean that we are talking about these targets, if we say, for example, internal angulation, without specifying anything else. Otherwise, all the necessary information will be given.

Generally, but not always (for example in the glides to the arm or body, cases in which the opposition, defensive action of the guard and the angle, and offensive action of the tip coexist), in the angulation the guard moves away from the blade of the opponent or tends to move away from in (for example in an angulation of a yielding *imbroccata* the opponents parry).

Already said about the angulations or "*attaque en cavant*" per the French, that allow one to hit a covered target (line); if the target is uncovered but presents itself with a difficult angle of impact, or being far from the perpendicular, these allow us to improve the angle of the hit; these are also applicable in making the adversary's parries more difficult and broader exposing all the consequences.

The angulation almost always uncovers (except for some glides and *imbroccata contractions*, the target of the one who performs these: it is important that it is not foreseen and that the tip of the opponent's weapon threatens a different target. A common mistake for example, an angle under the arm is in contempt to an angulation above, thus exposing oneself even more.

Much better the line (without corners) directing the tip where the arm of the other makes an angle; or an adequate opposition between those already described.

The positions of the hand, in the angles, vary according to the preferences and according to the type of handle.

It has more value, for the success of the hit, to have naturalness and unpredictability in the attack. However, for the smooth grip and for attacks carried out to the wrist, the most rational position is: third (thumb on top) for the above and external angulation; secondhand position for the strikes below and or internal.

With the anatomical grip, even the internal angulation can be easily performed with the hand in third position. For both a variant for the external angulation and the second hit (used more for thrown strikes). We described only four angles to the wrist for oversimplification: in reality the strike to the arm can be carried out from all possible angles.

The flick *(fuetto)*

The strikes using the flick or lashes, are carried out by exploiting the flexibility of the blade, in the sense of its widest side and downwards. They are similar to angulations in that they allow one to reach covered targets, improve the angle of the impact and make parries more difficult. They are not possible from all directions.

Strikes using the flick *(colpire di fuetto)*

The so-called *fuetto* hits (Italianizing as lashing blows or flicks) are today widely used especially in epee: which preferably is used for the target the top of side of the arm.

These allow one to reach the target even when covered, with better results than angulation. But, having to load the movement with a certain force, they slow it down in the initial phase, thus exposing the wrist of the one performing the action to considerable risks: to reduce them, they are often preceded by grazing beats.

The flick exploits the natural flexibility of the blade downwards, whereby the position of the hand changes with the target (we always refer to right to right for orientation): secondhand position for the external target; third hand position for high targets; fourth for internal target. All intermediate positions are used as well to reach the target.

It is possible to pull this shot, with some difficulty, even when directed to the low external direction by raising the elbow somewhat. The way to start these blows is by the following: move the point slightly backwards, with the use of the wrist and forearm, flexing in the same direction as the thumb and the edge of the hand, doing so in the same vertical, horizontal, or intermediate plane. The attack is then launched with a quick extension of the arm, which is stopped with a firm squeeze in time just before its completion. The blade thus stressed continues to flex bringing the point to the target. For a good result, it is necessary that the whole arm collaborates, so that the point reaches the target with the forward thrust, as well as that towards the cut of the hand, due to the lashing movement: a good technique allows to obtain the effect with less force and flexion of the blade and with less risk for the person who performs it.

Another necessary observation: the flicks, if often carried by an insufficiently and not progressively trained hand can lead to annoying ailments in the wrist and elbow that are slow and difficult to heal.

The cut over *(Il coupe)*

This action was once called an angled disengagement (*cavazione angolata*). The coupe differs from the normal disengagement as it takes place by climbing over the top of the opponent's blade from above rather than under. But there are also those who accept it with the passage from below, as opposed to the lower engagements of first and second. Those who accompany these disengagements from their engagements in the low line by using movements similar to the *molinillo*, typical of saberist's, calling them a backhand coupe. As with the flick, these movements make the parry more difficult but expose much target to those who execute it.

The forced glide *(Il filo sottomesso)*

More aptly called a submissive glide, we need some clarification. In foil, this action the line is regained by a strong opposition to the subtle engagement. The final part of the action is identical to that of the basic glides. In epee, having also inserted simple contact between the engagements, we will have to consider its variant (*coule* in French) which consists by inserting the point by sliding against the blade without forcing the line: to strike or more frequently, used to provoke a reaction.

Variety of auxiliary actions, releases, and actions of the blade *(varieta di azione ausiliarie, svincolie azione sul ferro)*

The auxiliary offensive actions above are combined in various ways using releases and actions on the opponent's blade.

They can be preceded by *svincoli* (subtracting ones blade from the opponents engagement, already in place): hits with opposition crossing and collecting but not those with direct opposition, even if they end in the same manner: it will first be necessary to free ones blade, with a counter movement the attacks with opposition by crossing are possible (preceded by a releasing of the blade) if we also consider the engagements (already described) obtained with only the displacement of the point.

Angulations and flicks can be preceded by a release. Disengagements and cut overs are attacks that already include the release, and we must make the distinction between the engagement (and the cut over) that starts from an engagement, and the one that follows a feint, therefore with the blade free, which we find in compound attacks.

Various attacks can be preceded by beats (either false beats that start from the opponent's engagement or *battuta di potenza*) the expulsion is not a real beat in the part that the actions starts from one's own engagement without first detaching ones blade; the touch or simple beat); beats preceded or followed by a release (envelopment, by one's own or opponents engagement, cut over, or grazing beat, which ends as a cut over); by change of engagement or contact of the blades.

The last type of action can also precede the attacks that begin with transports or an envelopment (easier to execute when the point of the opponent is close to one's guard) which are called by the French liement and envelopment.

These start or are preceded by an engagement and then undergo, without loss of contact, simultaneously by advancing the tip forward slightly on the grade of the opponent's blade, the transport (on another line) or the envelopment (on the same line) until the final thrust is delivered.

In epee there are provided four fundamental engagements and must be performed with the same precautions required by the glides. We also consider the four auxiliary glides, receded by a means of transport. In foil, limiting ourselves to transports, only some of these actions are a variation of the final action, and they go by flanconade (fianconata) these are from the glide in fourth arriving in the flank, hence the name.

In the theory of foil, we distinguish the action of transport from the glide; while for the French the envelopment (which in Italian one must be careful not to be confused with the engagement *ligament* which can happen with a slight imperfection of pronunciation) we include both.

These actions on the blade are reduced to a minimum in foil, they are very useful in epee against opponents who willingly give the blade and are skilled in the release and yielding parries (ceding parry).

As an exercise, improve the feel of the blade and the precedence of the point moving first before the legs.

CHAPTER 4 DEFENSIVE ACTIONS

The fourth chapter "Defensive Actions" begins dealing exclusively with defensive actions: parries, oppositions, and subtraction of target, which includes defensive measure and body evasions. The terminology of parries is discussed, proposing some corrections. The counter-offensive is then examined with the practical and terminological differences as compared to foil. The field of compound actions is clarified and, when dealing with feints, the circular parry is redefined.

AT THE END OF THIS CHAPTER, YOU SHOULD BE ABLE TO:

- Define the concept of defense, and the means to achieve it.
- Explain the difference between the defense of blade and measure, defensive measure, and target subtraction
- Know the various types of parries, and the difference from those used in foil
- Indicate the various types of ripostes
- Describe the variety of arrests used in epee
- Understand compound actions and the different definition of the circular action (circolata)

IF YOU ARE ABLE TO ANSWER THESE QUESTIONS YOU CAN PROCEED TO THE NEXT CHAPTER

- What is the difference between body evasion and actual target stealing?
- How many types of parries do we have? On the basis of which elements are they classified?
- How many half circular parries are there? And of ceding parries? And counter glides?
- Define the counter-offense?
- What is the difference between the disengagement in time used in foil to that used in epee?
- What is the difference between a compound action in foil and epee?
- What is a feint? What is a circolata?

TERMS

Parry (*Parate*)

Defense of measure (*Difesa di misura*) Body evasion (*Schivete*)

Target subtraction (*sottrazione di bersaglio*) Riposte (*Risposta*)

Counter-offense (*Controffesa*) Arrest (*Arresto*)

Compound actions (*Azione composte*) Disengagements (*Cavazione*) Circular actions (*Circolata*)

Defensive actions *(Azione defensive)*

There are only three types of defensive actions

- Target subtraction (*le sottrazioni di bersaglio*)
- Oppositions (*le opposizione)*
- Parries (*le parate*)

Target subtractions are then divided into two groups:

- Dodging (*le schivate*) lateral right or left or vertical, lowering to avoid strikes to the body

- True target subtraction (*la sottrazioni di bersaglio propriameente dette*) used to avoid hits to the advanced target or to the body by moving backwards are called defense of measure.

The dodges, if combined with the strike at the target, take the name of the foil counter attacks: *inquartata* (by movement to the outside) and *passata sotto*.

The movement to the inside has no name, perhaps because it is rarely used (once, for some, this was called *l'intagliata*). These body evasions give name to the offensive action they as: arrest by *passata sotto* and arrest by *inquartata*, etc.

The target subtraction is the retreat (to avoid the hit); reasemblement and its variants are used to subtract the low targets and is generally connected to a counter-offensive action); the movements of the armed arm (generally moving backwards to avoid the hit or moving from one line to another thus countering with offense with angulations).

Already mentioned previously, oppositions are rarely alone as we find them more often associated with actions of counter-offense (arrests) or in offensive actions such as glides, and attacks with opposition.

Parries are movements of the blade, starting from a position to a finishing position in order to deflect the attack by the opponent.

- The name of the parry is given by its final position

- The type of parry is given by the movement: direct, half circular, circular, ceding and *controfilo*

- There are two ways in which to contact the opponent's blade in the parry; keep contact with the blade or to neatly and sharply beat it away.

Parry *(Parate)*

The parries, lacking convention, must truthfully correspond to the purpose. It is not enough to simply touch the opponent's blade to deflect it completely if you also want to riposte. It is necessary to ensure control of the blade (with the lines and related variants) during the necessarily rapid response, or to divert it enough for the time needed to arrive with a singular touch or at most together as a double touch. This is achieved by using beating parries and careful management of the measure.

The greatest effectiveness is realized by the speed and the timing of the hand and in the point in which the two blades meet.

For beating parries and riposte by detachment, with or without opposition, the optimal point is the center of the blades: which often involves a decentralization of the guard from the opposing line. Before the parry, which must be performed to create the maximum effectiveness diagonally forward. For the glides, a contact is indicated as close as possible to the guard of the one making the parry, guiding the hand back, if necessary, in the final phase of the parry for the correct relationship.

The classification of the parries is quite close to the classic titles. It is possible to simplify by indicating only the final position of the parry.

We will give only the final position of the parry to designate the name. For a more complete description we will have to indicate the path of the blade and guard to denote if the movement is a simple parry, circular, or half circular or, if contact is maintained between blades such as in a glide, a ceding parry by changing the relationship between strengths or *controfilo* (counter glide); the methods of contact between the blades, distinguishing between sharp parries or soft (the first the riposte can only be by detachment, the soft parry the riposte can be either glide or detachment).

Let's avoid the misunderstanding of the sharp parries. As intended as a synonym for a simple parry in foil, which we will call direct. We remind that simple, counter, and half circular parries can be performed either with a sharp or spanking or a soft parry. They are still both performed with rapidity with one beating the blade away and the other keeping in contact.

There are four main parries, as in foil. As in the treatise, FIS on epee, there are eight noted, unlike foil. From the same side, from high to low, and vice versa: fourth to first internal and third t second external. And four transversals (crossing) same as in foil and in reverse.

These classifications are to be preferred: for reasons of simplicity. In fact, in foil, for reasons that are not the case here we go into depth.

The parry of third to second are considered simple; fourth to first double. But it must be considered that the parry of first in foil is described in its variant called half-circular, which is not recommended in epee, because the target is uncovered. The parry of first in epee has the lowest guard and aims to protect the abdomen. In the ceding parry, used in a narrower measure, it resembles the parry of first in saber.

The two ceding parries found in foil, in epee there are four: adding to the two in foil (ceding parry of third and fourth) we must add that of first (in opposition to the glide in third) and that of second (in opposition to the glide in fourth). It will be verified that, due to the position of the guard, the ceding parry of first is easier (possible against both glides in third to the chest or abdomen) and the glide in fourth (possible against the glide in high second and the more difficult against the glide in low second); the ceding parry of second is easy as well, only possible against the glide in fourth, but not against the chest, except for particular virtuosities; less easy the ceding parry of third, easier against the glide in high first, and more difficult or impossible according to the target for the low lines.

Not covered by recent treaties and seems to be a gap in information, the parries which are opposed to the fundamental glides that do not yield as the yielding parries of the classical definition but done so by regaining the degrees of the blade and in the line as in the forced glide and without the loss of contact between the blades. We will call these counter glide parries. Useful and of practical use, and as exercise, because they improve the feel on the blade. Used in all four lines as with the basic glides, they end in the position of the starting engagement of each line.

Finally, as for use against offensive actions, the parries can be simple or compound. The latter are a succession of more than one parry movements in contrast to compound offensive actions. And this is why it is more appropriate, to avoid overlapping of names, to call a simple parry direct rather than simple, these parries being from third to fourth, from first to second and vice versa. Another consideration to be made for the movement of the legs that accompany the parry, which can be done standing still, by retreating or advancing. It is necessary to practice in the different directions in relation to the different parries and methods of execution and also to the various targets for the riposte.

For the French school of fencing, parries (dependent of the final position) are eight in count, and they correspond approximately two per quadrant, compared to our school: the hand is placed so that the nails are facing down (as is first, second, third and fifth, the names match except for fifth, which corresponds to our fourth) or nails facing upwards (seventh, eight, sixth and fourth, corresponding respectively to our first, second, third and fourth.)

The riposte *(La risposta)*

The riposte is an offensive action which follows the parry without pause. Like all offensive actions, the riposte can be simple if not evading a counter parry (a parry of the riposte); or compound, if at least one parry is eluded. It can be direct, angled, with opposition, by glide, by transport, cut over or flick to any target and from any measure.

Frequently used in epee are blocking parries, purely defensive or with tactical purpose that a riposte does not follow.

Counter offense *(La controffesa)*

Counter-offense actions, or exit in time, is the name given to any offensive action intentionally carried out during the offensive action of the opponent's initiative and is subordinate to it. Any counter-offensive action is called an arrest; therefore, we have:

- **Direct arrest** *(arresti diretti)*
- **Contractions arrest <Time thrust>** (by direct opposition, crossing or gathering) *(arresti di contrazione (con opposizione) diretta, incrociando, raccogliendo)*
- **Arrest by angulation** *(arresti con angolazione)*
- **Arrest by disengagement** (by disengagement in time, with or without opposition or angulation) *(arresti di cavazione (cavazione in tempo, cioe a ferro libero, o cavazione durante ii filo), con o senza opposizione o angolazione)*
- **Arrest while subtracting the target** (with or without opposition or angulation) *(arresti con schivata (con o senza opposizione) o sottrazione di bersaglio (con o senza opposizione o angolazione)*

The arrests in epee *(Gli arresti nella spada)*

The classification of counter-offensive actions in epee presents some difficulties due to the use of grouping them under generic denomination of the arrest. Additionally in foil the term arrest has a somewhat different meaning because the concert of fencing time is different: it is linked to the unspecified duration of a simple action, and to the sensitivity of the director; and in the timing and strict rule of forty-five hundredths of a second of the scoring box. In foil, the definition of the arrest and any counter-offensive action is that it precedes the final of the attack by at least one unit of fencing time, closing the line through which the attack would pass in the succeeding tempo. Thus we are witnessing an arrest that anticipates the final tempo and effectively closing the line (the arrest outwards, both starting from the invitation of third in opposition to the feint direct and disengagement) and to arrests correctly executed, which precede by two tempos and do not close the line at all are not judged valid (same arrest, but with anticipating the same with two tempos ahead from the same situation would allow for a double feint direct).

To help interpret timing in epee, the signaling device takes care of it, after the set time window. Hence, in epee, each counter offensive action executed during the offensive action of the attacker is called an arrest. We will therefore have different type of arrests; a direct arrest; contraction arrest (with direct opposition, crossing, gathering); arrest with angulation, disengaging arrests (disengagement in time, i.e., with free iron, or disengaging during a glide) with or without opposition or angulation; stops with dodging or removing target. All these varieties of arrests are executable while staying on spot, retreating, or advancing to various targets.

The counter offense is not limited to strikes during the adversary's attack. We must also consider the strikes taken during the opposing initiative, which we have agreed to call a counter-offensive, and not an attack because it is in preparation. We will classify them, generically, as strikes or actions in time: because, in any case, they are subordinated to the initiative of others. And we will also give these the somewhat improper name of arrests.

Next, we must consider the thrusts delivered after one's attack has been parried, which are to be considered as counter-offensive only if there is a riposte and the counter-offensive action is timed on this: in this case we will also call these, generically, arrests, distinguishing them from renewed attacks, second thrusts.

Finally, we have the counter-offensive thrusts on the counterattack which, in foil, are traditionally homologated to counter-time, but which we, for simplicity, will continue to call an arrest as above.

To avoid conflicts, let us new briefly examine the exits on time or better known as counter attacks. looking for the application and denomination in the epee with the following criteria set out. As one will remember the FIS treaty in foil there are seven counter attacks. The disengagement in time among these is the only one that has right of way even when arriving together or even later. In the epee this does not make sense: this is the reason why the disengagement in time performed without contact of the blades, or from the glide with an angulation or opposition is preferable to catalog it among the arrests.

We have already talked about the arrest in foil. The *L'appuntata* is nothing more than a second thrust used against the opponent who habitually ripostes with a feint. The time thrust, which is executed on the last tempo of the opponent's action (for epee it may be enough to delay it sufficiently to touch alone or for a double), is a close relative to the *imbroccata*: particular to the time thrust used against the glide in fourth that terminates in the flank. Relatives of the time thrust, to which they add, is the body evasions of dodge, they are the *inquartata* and the passata sotto: which are carried out at the end of the action but can also work without use of opposition of the blade.

Anticipating (or arriving together) in counterattacks the opponent, who has the initiative, it is possible in three ways: hitting on the preparation (looking for the blade; moving forward without threat), striking at the more forward targets, deflecting his blade while countering. In all cases, it is a question of the timing of the action because the timing of the action depends on the movement of the opponent, who has the initiative or attacks. The most difficult actions are, perhaps, the counter attacks: due to the great variety of possibilities, to the different ways of presenting the blade and the opposing target; and because they add up the difficulties when adding the offense and defense options.

We have already dealt with the attacks with opposition, which also includes time thrusts. With the latter we limit ourselves to counter-offensive actions, as we referred to earlier substantially with touches brought in attack. The main difference is the fact that many counter attacks take place planned forward, while the adversary who attacks launches the hit: the speed of impact and the sum of the two, and the difficulty of controlling together the target and the adversaries blade increases remarkably. It becomes essential, therefore, the ability to master one difficult and complex technique. To teach this effectively the Maestro must know how to imitate realism; to know in depth the geometric aspects (the cone of protection and the disposition of the targets plans) and the tactical (such as preparing the action) of the problem the adversary presents.

Compound offensive actions *(Le azione di offesa composte)*

Offensive actions that evade one or more parries or searches for the blade or carrying the offense, intentionally, on a target different from the one threatened at the start, these area all called compound actions. These noted above are valid for the attack as well as an answer to the counter-offense.

Any simple offensive action can be simulated, constituting a part of the action compound, called a feint, which will take the mane from the simulated action.

The feint *(Le finte)*

A simple offensive action can provoke a defensive reaction (parry, or removal of target) or a counter-offensive reaction (arrest) which in turn may be associated with target abduction, or even no reaction.

In foil an action is composed which eludes at least one parry; in epee they are, necessarily, also those that end on a target, after having threatened another, and having provoked one of the reactions described above, other than parrying. For example, an action is composed of angulation to the top of the wrist and striking the foot, when the opponent does not parry, but merely retracts the arm, or a feint direct to the arm and continuation to the body, and so on.

To evade the parries, the actions used are disengagements or deceives or the cut over. In foil the name of deceive is given to the action that avoids the circular parry, hence the name: and not because the tip describes a circle. And, to the one that avoids the half circle parry or search, because they say, it is the goal of a counter parry. In epee, having included among the half circular parries considered, in foil, simple we will call disengagement the action that eludes them.

The offensive action is defined as circular, which eludes the circular parry, passing the point around the opposing guard, and ending at the same target threatened at the start.

The deceive can follow a feint or evade (deceive in time) a search for the blade.

Therefore, we will also have the deceive in time, as well as the disengagement in time, while relegating it, too, to arrests. The clarification that the deceive, to be defined as such (and not generically disengagement) must end at the same target and necessary. For example, opponent on the invitation of third, feint to the inside and disengage (better than deceive) to the foot to evade the parry of counter third.

Finally, while the term disengagement is also used for the thrust (or the feint) that starts from the opposite engagement, the same is not possible for the deceive, which is always preceded by a feint, or by an angulation. On the contrary, the deceive in time can also start from an engagement of the adversary, which performs a change of engagement.

The feints discussed so far are all simulations of offensive actions, and do not exhaust the meaning of the term, which from a tactical point of view has a broader meaning.

CHAPTER 5 TACTICAL NOTES AND READINGS

The fifth chapter "tactical notes and readings" begins with some considerations on tactics and strategy, and on the classic trinomial that includes speed, measure, and timing. This is followed by a reading on the process of strategic elaboration in fencing, and a review on the typical actions found in epee.

At the end of this chapter, you should be able to:

- Know the difference between strategy and tactics
- Know the difference between reaction time and choice of time
- Describe the main themes of epee fencing

If you are able to answer these questions you can proceed to the next chapter

- What is the difference between tactics and strategy?
- What is meant by opponent programming?
- What is the choice of time?
- What is the critical point?
- Why is cover in epee important and how is it achieved?
- Can you explain why the double touch is important, to whom it Is convenient and how to get it?
- Can you describe the advantages and disadvantages of the different handles?

KEY WORDS

Strategy (*Stretegia*)

Tactics (*Tattica*)

Time (*Tempo*)

Speed (*Velocita*)

Measure (*Misura*)

Feint (*Finte*)

Features of fencing epee (*Caratteristiche della scherma di spada*)

Notes on strategy, attention, time, measure, speed, tactics, and feints *(Note su strategia, attenzione, tempo, misura, velocita, tattica e finte)*

The strategy and rational planning of one's actions, according to the situation, to achieve a predetermined goal, possibly with the minimum cost.

In preparing or elaborating a strategy, we must possess or obtain the necessary information on the existing situation (circumstances, knowledge of one's own means and of the opponent). We will have to take into account the variability of the situation, trying to modify it in our favor, and modifying the strategy as circumstances change strategic activity, or programming, continuations, as far as possible, in parallel with motor activity.

The aim of the strategy is subordinated to the aims of fencing: to defend and offend, and therefore the simulation, the investigation, the preparation, subordinated to them. A strategy can be defined as a program, which contains various subroutines. Among the subordinate programs, one of the most important is the programming of the opponent's actions: tactics.

The opponent's programming takes place by intervening on his data processing process: firstly, by providing him with false information, through use of feints, and by hiding and limiting the real ones; secondly, placing him in the position of having to decide in the presence of insufficient or false information, and in conditions of high space-time pressure; thirdly, by exploiting the limits of his attention span. Let's start with this last factor.

Attention is, first, a filter that selects the objects or events on which the senses are focused. The advanced athlete is able, much more than the inexperienced one, to select the significant stimuli, ignoring the others: in this way they are able to limit the costs (time taken, number of errors, load of the processing system) of mental work. In learning the technique, and even more than tactics, it is therefore important to help the student early on to recognize and reproduce or hide these stimuli. Secondly, attention has a limited capacity, both in the sense of the quantity or events that it can simultaneously deal with, and in the intensity of its activation. One can remain very attentive only for brief moments, and these are inevitably followed by short periods in which the attention relaxes. Hence the importance of knowing how to provoke moments of tension, to take advantage of subsequent moments of relaxation, in which reflexes appear to be slowed down. From this data we can also understand the importance of an active rather than passive role: who is active, and therefore provokes, chooses the moments of their maximum attention, because they know their real intentions.

Who is passive, except in cases of evident technical-tactical disparity, is forced to a greater expenditure of mental energy, because he does not know whether the attack will follow the provocation or will have to take more action, and for longer time. Reacting, or predicting and therefore anticipating, are therefore two different paths, which involve different costs, and therefore present a waste of mental and physical energy. In fencing, fundamental importance has always been attributed to the factor of time, in particular to the choice of time, which requires particular attention.

Information processing leads to making the choice of a motor act that requires time and information. In fencing, the time to decide is limited, and the information is, by and large in part, voluntarily falsified. The risk of error is therefore high, and increases strongly with the decrease, even minimally, of the time available. Below a certain limit, the processing system must default to automatisms, because it is not more capable of making decisions without unacceptable delays, in the face of speed of the action to be countered. Let's see, now from what depends on the passage from one to the other modality, and the relationships between time and measure.

Reaction time and choice of time are two factors of extreme importance in fencing, and it is necessary to understand the fundamental difference between the two. Given an unexpected stimulus, and a single reaction (or response) required at the appearance of the stimulus (simple reaction time) there exists a time between the first (the stimulus) and the second (the reaction) which cannot descend beyond a certain physiological limit: let's say as an order of magnitude, around the tenth and one half second, or one hundred and fifty milliseconds. The variability of this time and due to many factors, including the sensory channel chosen (visual, tactile, acoustic stimulus) and the intensity of attention (given by extreme importance, for the reasons exposed above). As the number of stimuli and possible responses increases so does the time and the accuracy of the response decreases.

There is only one way and possibility to go beyond the physiological threshold of reaction time: knowing in advance and therefore foreseeing the moment in which the expected stimulus will present itself. In this case it will also be possible to reduce to zero, or even negative numbers the delay between stimulus and response.

We will talk, in this case, about choice of time. We will find abundant possibilities of examples in all cyclical events, which have their own rhythm (games with the rope, with the ball, etc.,). The fencing rhythms are less evident, but equally identifiable and exploitable.

Choosing time therefore means fencing, identifying, and predicting the exact moment to start your own motor response, which entails, their choice of time and not a negligible execution of time. It is therefore also necessary to synchronize one's motor response with rhythm of the other, to make the two motor acts interact in the desired way. And since the motion occurs in a space, which in fencing a measure, we will deal with this key factor, *essential in the study of all fencing actions.*

Distance, or measure, that is established between opponents at the beginning of an assault, when still the offensive strategies are not well delineated, and measure is wide enough to allow for everyone to react (reaction time) to unexpected initiative of the other, by retreating. However, this distance is limited from the need to carry out an effective action only investigation can be conducted. So, during the processing phase, distance from the opponent (control measure), as a rule, just above that necessary for an effective action (attacking measure). The preparation phase tends to minimize the difference between the two measures, determinizing when the measure is changing between the two, which we can define as a critical point. Beyond this point (larger measure) one can check the movements of the other, exploiting the reaction time mechanisms (before the stimulus, then the response).

On the attacking side of the critical point (closing measure) the reaction time is to high: who has foreseen acts in time, who has not foreseen reacts to the action, resorting to automatic reactions, which are the fastest answers among those available, thus suspending the processing system. When the critical point is reached, there are two possibilities to choose from in as little time possible: go back outside of the critical measure or launch the resolving action. The first choice is taken when the conditions found are not those expected, and when the voluntary programming activity of the other is in progress. The second choice is taken when the conditions found are those required. The shortness of the passage of time into the critical point therefore requires that it be reached having foreseen it: the choice of time is required in advance in predicting the occurrence of the favorable measurement condition.

The assault begins in conditions of long duration: for an offensive action to be possible, it is necessary that at least one of the two takes the initiative to shorten it. the following cases can occur.

- Fencer A wants to shorten the measure, B does not want this to happen. A can succeed thanks to a greater acceleration, or by taking advantage of the (casual or induced) inattention of the other, or by taking them to the bottom of the fencing platform, or by taking advantage of B's need to recover, in the pauses of A's initiative, the lost ground. B on the other hand, can succeed in his intent, but for limited periods, by backing off; placing the other in as unexpected situation (attitudes, counter-initiative) every time he reaches the critical point. This is the typical situation of containment trolling against the attack initiative. Attempts to overcome the control of B's measure, which in turn tries to nullify the conditions required and prepared by A to launch the decisive action.

- A and B want to shorten the measure, each one, however, on his own terms (measure, time, and placement of the blade). In this case perhaps the most common initiative and counter-initiative are balanced, alternating until at least one of the two fails.

- A and B want to shorten measure, under the same conditions of time and attitude. In this case the shorter measure is accepted because both are convinced that they have identified the correct answer, or that they have successfully programmed the opponent. Upon entry into close measure, both planned actions start and compared.

In all cases, the resolutive action can result in a failure of both: then generally automated actions (rimesse, second thrusts or counter parries) not foreseen follow, up till the director halts action or the signaling of a touch, or even when returning to the longer measure.

Velocity has always been considered the foundation of fencing together with the choice of time and measure. We can now better define its meaning. Check the other while preventing them from checking ourselves are the two fundamental operations of the fencer: for an action to be successful, both are necessary.

The control follows the stimulus-response mechanism: from a starting situation (long measure) to the attempt to reduce the measure follows (because there is time to do it, given the measure) the choice to lengthen it again, or to accept the exchange. In this second case, the sequel to the action from a shorter measure, is in time: the two motor programs confront each other automatically, and the best wins.

Whoever has the initiative and whoever suffers it both control, until one of the two manages to overcome the control of the other, preventing them from being able to maintain the desired measure, and preventing synchronization. Synchronizing with the other, only mentally or even from a motor point of view, is an effective way to get to the actions preformed in time, always preceded by a control phase, in which the movement follows, and therefore does not accompany that of the other.

Think, for example, of an attack while marching, countered by an affective parry and riposte: already in the preparation movement you can observe a certain synchronization of the movements of the two opponents, which becomes perfect at the moment of the parry, in which the two blades meet just in time for the attack to be deflected. To be successful, the attacker must avoid a successful synchronization process. The main means of achieving this purpose is found in the variation and rhythm of the action.

Varying the rhythm means varying the speed (increasing or decreasing or by more or less frequently) of the forward or backward movement (by use of the legs) or of the armed arm alone, or both.

Maximum speed has a high cost, and cannot be sustained for long; more ever, it makes It more difficult to coordinate the movement of the arms with that of the legs and leads in a short time to a decline in accuracy. In fencing it is more appropriate and exact to speak of acceleration, which gives the passing from one measure to another from the change of speed (acceleration) the change of pace. A high base rhythm causes a considerable waste of energy and favors those with greater resistance. A slow pace makes greater acceleration possible and favors the more technical and thoughtful fencer.

Finally, sudden accelerations lend themselves to alarming the other, overloading his attention span; slowdowns, on the other hand lend themselves to relaxing the alertness of the other, in particular immediately after an overload phase.

Tactics and the study and application of actions that aim to program the opponent's actions, so that they are predictable and are to our advantage. It is not possible to obtain such a result at a reasonable limited cost without an involuntary collaboration of the adversary, who will provide it only if deceived; or without benefiting from a considerable technical and physical advantage, over an opponent somewhat inexperienced on a tactical level.

The main actions that are used in order to deceive the other and provide him with false information, are the feints, simulations of actions that require, in order to be effective, precise choice of time and measure conditions: they must be performed when passing into the critical point.

The feints are of two types:

- Technical feints (*finte tecniche*)
- Tactical feints (*finte tattiche*)

The technical techniques include simulations of thrusts and provocations but immediately precede the conclusive action of offense (eg: feint direct, feint by disengagement, feint by parry or feint by arrest) or defensive feints (eg: feint by arrest and parry; feint by searching for the blade and parry). These are called fake or mock techniques because they are performed when the expected reaction of an automatic type is highly probable (by observation or previous programming) while the technique used as the opposite includes the feint and conclusive action of offense.

The fake tactics are precisely those that aim at the acquisition of information and not at concluding with the offensive action; and to the opponent's programming through a double mechanism: clear and repeated feints, to obtain that the other prepares a specific action, chosen from amount those he prefers or is able to perform (preparation tracing); unclear and varied feints, to disturb and prevent the programming of the other (containment tracing). In this type of feint, even the variations in size lend themselves to being simulated, together with variations in body attitude which have the specific purpose of affecting the adversary's attention skills.

The process of strategic processing in fencing (*Il processo dell'elaborazione strategica nella scherma*)

We have already said that in order to elaborate a strategy we will have to possess or obtain the necessary information on the existing situation (circumstances, knowledge of our own means and that of the adversary); and to take into account the variability of the situation, trying to modify it in our favor, and modifying the strategy as the circumstances change.

Let us now specify the sequence of the necessary operations.

The strategy of an assault is subordinate to that of the tournament; that of a single touch, to that of the assault; and so on. The athlete is not always aware of this work of elaboration: the automatisms, even mental ones, acquired through years of competitions and lessons, tend to keep it below the level of consciousness.

A strategy is elaborated at the beginning of each assault, and must be updated frequently, possibly at each pause and, when the pace of the assault allows it, even during the assault itself: each new information acquired allows to refine or vary the strategy itself.

Before the assault begins, we already have some information about our means and those of the adversary, which it will be necessary to compare, to evaluate the points in our favor or against us and try to conduct the comparison on the ground that is most favorable to us. We will therefore evaluate if we are stronger or weaker:

- On the **psychological level**: aggression, impressionability, calm, held in moments of pressure (intensity, running out of time, situations at the bottom of the platform), ability to wait, various superstitions, ability to adapt, and so on;

- On a **strategic and tactical level**: predictability, ability to act as a second intention, capacity for initiative, flexibility in changing strategy:

- On the **technical level**: available techniques, coordination skills, precision, preferences in terms of measurement, left-handedness:

- On the **physical plane**: endurance, speed, height.

Some characteristics of the opponent will already be known and in memory, or obtainable from teammates and technicians; others can be guessed from his appearance, from his serene or nervous attitude, from the way he is on guard.

The initial information on the opponent will then be integrated, during the attack, with sounding work (scandaglio) and with the results of the first touches given or received which, let us remember, have a strong programming effect on the processing of both fencers: as the lowest level it is possible that one will tend to repeat the action that has proven successful (often, especially for the younger fencer, who has great difficulty in changing even when the action no longer works) and to avoid other actions.

We will then evaluate the circumstances, which vary during the assault:

- Advantage or disadvantage in the situation;
- Remaining time;
- Position on the platform;
- Conduct of the director and the public;
- Variations in one's own psycho-physical condition, and in that of the adversary.

There are many aspects to consider and evaluate, so we can only give very general indications. Each athlete, with his specificity and experience, will have his own way of setting up his assault, learning from experience.

However, even just training the young athlete to ask himself questions (by asking them often, during the pauses of the bout and in training) and to give himself answers, on each of the points indicated above, will help to build his strategic and tactical skills more quickly, and to be aware of it: which means that it will be possible for him, when natural inspiration, as often happens, is not present, to have good and rational starting point to favor its return.

Characteristics of epee fencing, and tactical annotations *(Caratteristiche particolari della scherma di spada, e annotazioni tattiche)*

The R.I. among the most significant differences with other weapons provides:

- The extension of the target (which can only be hit with the point) to the whole body;
- A wide bell guard, to protect the hand;
- The absence of right of way (convention or agreements of precedence) for the judgement in the event of a double touch;
- The interdiction time of the second touch, in the event of a double (from 40 to 50 hundredths of a second or between 25-20 tenths of a second less than one half of a tenth of a second.

These features lead to significant practical differences:

- In attack, during the initiative, and in general during any offensive action, the absence of convention and the amplitude of the target make the range of possible counter- offenses wider; the offender must also worry about the defense at the same time; the percentage of compound and marching actions decreases, and the actions by lunging and arrow (frecciata) increase; counter time attacks increase; it is preferable to attack on advanced targets, to reduce the risk; the attack does not end in the first shot, but often includes remise's or second thrusts while advancing; low target thrusts of the leg, thigh and front foot are frequent, the greater risks of the attack lead, on average, to longer and more thoughtful assaults, with a longer duration of the preparation phase;

- In defense, increases the risk that the response is preceded by a rimesse, or anticipated by an arrest, or leads to a double touch; the most suitable responses are those of gliding, or the detachment following a beating parry (picco) these are rapid and are often followed by one or more rimesse; to reduce the possibility of another rimesse (on the riposte) they increase the parry by advancing on the opponent's advance;

- The counterattacks increase considerably in number and variety, and constitute, on average, as a whole, the thrusts that most frequently arrive, and the greatest resource of the epeeist.

Consequently, it is necessary that the epeeist practices in a particular way on some typical actions of the arms and of frequent application:

- All thrusts taken while maintaining cover;
- All thrusts to forward targets, and in particular angulations to the arm;
- Multiple thrusts and counter-time actions;
- Remises, pre-meditated and reaction;
- Arrests against various offensive actions;
- Searching for the double touch.

Furthermore, the epeeist will have to develop, according to his settings and characteristics, the game on the blade or absent of the blade, the actions to be preferred against the opponent who uses the anatomical handle or with a smooth handle; he will have to pay particular attention to the precedence of the point in the development of an offensive action or preparation of the action; must pay the utmost attention to the situation and advantage and or disadvantage, perfecting the necessary actions in the two cases, and avoiding the others, with assaults with an obligatory theme, and or reduced times; for this purpose he must consider the specificity of the parrying techniques and ripostes, and to delve into the study of second intentions. Finally, they will have to consider the different behaviors in the different areas of the platform, and in conditions when pressured with time; and he will also have to take note of the differences in accuracy and performance at the beginning and at the end of the bout, and of the tournament, which is longer that other specialties.

Thrusts carried while maintaining coverage *(Colpi portati mantenendo la copertura)*

By covering we mean adequate thrusting on the same line as the opponent to decrease the chances of being hit during an offensive action. Absolute coverage does not exist, due to the impossibility of predicting with certainty the adversary's blade movement. In carrying out any fencing action, the fencer must assume the risk of failure.

It is necessary to accept a high risk in conditions of disadvantage and high space-time pressure, or when the other imposes it on us with their initiative; and it is reasonable to accept it even when the advantage is great, for the possibility of concluding the attack first and saving energy for the next, while obtaining useful information.

In Epee, for the considerations already made, it is statistically riskier to attack, or parry and riposte: an action that requires more than the others, in fact, a cover, to reduce the risk.

Opposition as we have previously specified, can be directed, by going towards the opponent's blade with the guard (example: strike with opposition on the fourth line, starting from the invitation of third, with an opposing blade in third, keeping it inside); or it can be preceded by a circular or semicircular movement to collect the blade (examples: from the invitation of second, opponent is in third, strike with opposition to collect the blade in third, keeping the opposing blade on the outside; same position of the opponent and same final position, but starting from the invitation of third; or it can be crossed going towards the opponent's blade, as in the first case, but moving it to the opposite line (example: from the invitation of fourth, with the opponent in third, strike with opposition crossing over ending in third with the adversary on the outside).

In addition to the rear target, these opposing thrusts can also be taken, but not all, and with greater difficulty, to the other advanced targets, especially to the arm and wrist, the most important of the latter being those with slight direct opposition, when the opponent also directs the thrust to the toe or to the wrist (example: the opponent threatening the bottom of the wrist by angulation, direct the thrust low as well in opposition).

Hits with opposition if they improve coverage, often worsen the angle of impact on the target.

The fencer will therefore evaluate whether the certainty of the thrust is more convenient (because for example, in a specific situation a double hit is also useful) or to avoid the thrust from the other. Angulations to the wrist can also be effectively countered with a direct line where the opposing wrist makes a corner. It is useful in these cases, to train the student to moderate opposition by leaving the arm slightly flexed and therefore more relaxed and ready for the next action.

Thrusts to the forward target and angulations to the arm *(Colpi ai bersagli avanzati, e angolazioni al braccio)*

Blame the mask. For mechanical and electronic reasons, explained in the technical section (way of carrying the thrust) very fast thrusts to the mask may not be reported.

To this difficulty is added that there is low friction between the point and the mask, for which it is necessary to have the conditions close to perpendicular (square) (for example, on the external side with an external angle, low in the lower part, high is the upper one; on the internal side with internal angle). Another expedient, to facilitate the signaling of the thrust, is to pull it when the two speeds are subtracted (one advances, while the other retreats) and with blows carried and not launched. For the physical characteristics of the subjects, naturally slower, it is a thrust not to be overlooked for the youngest and for women. Although classified as advanced, the target of the mask is less than others. As with all thrusts to the rearmost or off-center targets, the thrust to the mask is favored to a shot or threat to the arm, preferably accompanied by the appropriate opposition. It is also useful as a riposte, especially on the internal line; or as a stop on the riposte, with opposition, when the opponent's guard is high and covers the target of the arm, shoulder, or chest.

The thrust to the mask Is also useful with ripostes, generally on the glide, after the parry of third or fourth. It is also excellent as an arrest, or reasemblement when the high position of the opposing guard makes it difficult to target the shoulder, arm or chest.

Thrusts to the thigh, leg, and the foot *(Colpi alla coscia, alla gamba ed al piede)*

These thrusts are particularly effective against opponents who have a habit of parrying in the high lines of third and fourth. On the other hand, they are dangerous against opponents who are ready to arrest. It is good therefore to have them preceded by a feint high to the advanced targets, or by a first thrust on the same target, by beat or by pressure. The conclusion can take place with the blade free or with opposition to collecting the blade, from the high to low lines, always keeping in mind the opportunity to foresee a renewed attack to the body, or an arrest by reasemblement in case of an error.

They can be brought in attack, or even in response if the opponent tends to counter in the high line. The most effective use is against those who advance in counter time.

The thrust to the foot is one that can be brought from the greatest measure, or by starting the movement backwards, because the front foot of the one who suffers it advances first (for example, in the search for the blade while marching) and backs up last marching normally.

The angulations to the arm *(Le angolazioni al braccio)*

We have already mentioned the thrusts to the arms with opposition. When the opponent's blade is directed to the body, or at least to the rear most target, angulations to the arm or wrist are frequent. Angulation is not always necessary, and sometimes only serves to improve the tip-to-target angle.

These same thrusts are also used to counter, after the subtraction of the target of the arm and changing the line, direct adverse thrusts to the arm. They are also useful as a preparation for other strikes, with free blade or taking the blade usually by glide: the angulation to the arm easily leads the opponents to bring his tip closer to our guard and to squeeze the fingers (tight in time) optimal conditions for binding the opposing blade and performing the glide.

The multiple thrusts and actions in counter time *(I colpi multipli e le azioniin controtempo)*

We have already noted that in epee there is the need to be ready for a possible rimesse, intended as a backup to the original thrust and not as second intention. Multiple thrusts are usually delivered intentionally, and we could classify them among the attack, even if the rhythm is similar to that and is to be replaced or changed following the first thrust directed to the advanced targets. The first shot on the wrist can cause the arm to withdraw, opening the path for a second shot to the leg, foot, body and so on: always with the possibility of a rimesse. A second possibility is that the first shot to the wrist causes a parry, opening the way for a second shot by disengagement below with good chances of preceding the riposte. A third possibility is that the first thrust causes an arrest, then you can continue with the taking of the blade (or parry, in the case of arresting while advancing) and the thrust (preferably by glide, except in the case of a beat or beating parry) or the feint by glide: a classic action in counter time. In this case, and in the previous ones, we will have to predict that the opponent's reaction may take place moving forward, stationary, or backward and adjust accordingly.

The rimesse, premeditated or unforeseen *(Le rimesse, preordinate o impreviste)*

A rimesse, (second thrust) if the action was automated, has a good chance of preceding or arriving together with the opponent's response. Optimal, if the action has been premeditated, knowing in advance the parry of the opponent. Rimesse are possible for any type of parry, and it is appropriate to automate them while maintaining coverage on the most likely or habitual line of the riposte.

Even in teaching this, it is necessary to distinguish the two types. One precedes normally for those actions pre-meditated or varying them with the various situations studied. The rimesse not premeditated must be made automatically by learning the most common parries used and entering them suddenly in the course of actions: the Maestro, instead of allowing the touch, suddenly parries, and the pupil will soon have to get used to how to react with the appropriate action, without hesitation, and abolishing the reflex of the counter parry, typical of foilists.

In training it should be held that the target reachable by the rimesse varies with measure as well as the parry. The most common occurrences to the arm either outstretched or withdrawn, done direct, by angulation or with opposition.

The usefulness of a rapid rimesse evident in other cases: (after the offense, counter-offense at close distance or corp a corp) in which the first offensive action yields no touch and there is no time to observe the situation and decide on a new action.

Arrests on various actions of offense *(Gli arresti sulle varie azioni di offesa)*

The arrest is the most frequent action in epee. We basically call the arrest an exit on time: actions that can be performed during the offensive action of the opponent or even during the initiative of a simple action. The most effective arrests are those provoked (as when one is passing into the critical point) on their own initiative or counter initiative: moving backwards or forwards on the action of offense provoked, the latter to be preferred when the thrust is called for to make a double touch.

The most common arrests are angulation to the arm, and those of time thrust to the body. Arrests are frequent on the riposte, to be distinguished from a rimesse and from second thrusts. They are generally preformed going back and following the response. The target of the arrest is often more executed going back than threatening with the attack.

One example among many possibilities: attack top of the wrist, direct or preceded by a beat; parry of third and riposte by glide to the chest; arrest the riposte by disengaging above to the top of the wrist, from the lunge, or in the crook of the arm, returning on guard, or on the shoulder or by time thrust to the inside chest, by reasemblement, with or without jumping: the movement of the legs will depend on the speed and reach of the opponent.

Other effective provocations to arrest are the engagement and the invitation, carried out during his own initiative, or during that of the adversary. They lend themselves well to arrests, angulations, the disengagement of the adversary while they are moving back and those of time thrusts (from an engagement) while advancing.

The search for the double touch *(La ricerca del colpo doppio)*

The most typical action of the epee fencer is when in the lead to double touch. He is not, however, like someone seems to think (justified, perhaps by the idiom "to pull a double") that you are looking for to get the double touch. Indeed, whoever makes the "double touch" has the advantage of choosing among a wider variety of actions or possibilities, denied to the other, which he must avoid the double hit. They who seek to double touch will be much happier if they touch alone!

The preparation for the double touch, in the sense just explained, can be done in many ways, according to individual preferences, and those of the opponent.

Conversely, we will have on the part of the other, preparation to make up for the disadvantage, avoiding the double touch. It is therefore assumed that, sooner or later, he is forced to take the initiative, to make up for the disadvantage. They will have to avoid the double, limit to very advanced targets (wrist, foot) the action must be free of the blade, or resort to time thrusts as the attack, rather risky. Will make extensive recourse to counter-time actions, and they will try to force the adversary to the bottom of the platform, to force them to come forward, shortening the measure.

Consequently, who can afford the double will have the arrest as their main weapon, alternating targets, so as not to be predictable, and with less concern for the opposition (improving the target angle); the position of their weapon arm will be further back, not to offer the wrist as target; will make little use of parries and extensive use of rimesse or second arrest; will be ready for the counter-initiative, to recover the lost platform. On the other part, the burden and the risk of the initiative fall to their opponent, who risks defeat when time runs out: it is reckless to launch into risky attacks, except that the advantage is large. In this case, there are also effective attacks similar to those ones would see in foil, without giving the blade, that they end with the touch on the arrest of the other.

Grips (handles) and fighting styles *(Impugnature e stili di Combattimento)*

Smooth handles (also called French) and anatomical are widespread enough equally in the world of epee, while foil the former have almost disappeared, following the fate of the Italian ones.

In epee, the disadvantage of a smaller grip, and a more difficult and prolonged learning of the way to use the smooth handle, are widely compensated by the greater versatility of use and the greater extension.

On the other hand, a strong hand will have less difficulty in adopting a complete fencing on the blade, typical of those who use the anatomical handle; while the younger students, and those who have a wrist less robust, they will adapt to a fencing of releases and ceding, based on time or measure more than on the blade and on the friction.

This way of pulling usually causes noticeable difficulty for those who use the anatomical handle, who finds themselves forced, against whom he does not use the blade, to improve (time and measure) fencing that gives fewer points of reference, than what one is used to, even in lessons. Contrary to who gives it, the difficulty in the control of the blade, soft, yielding, and elusive. The actions of the glide become ineffective, if not performed with finesse and great speed, better on the counterattack: in these cases, will execute beats are more useful, and the time between the beat and the touch is reduced to a minimum.

Those who use the smooth handle have more difficulties, on average, in performing actions in counter time, and therefore in recovering the disadvantage: a strategy to acquire an advantage, or to avoid the disadvantage, becomes even more important from the beginning.

Of the assault; hence a greater recourse to the search for the double, even in conditions of equality.

The precedence of the point *(La precedenza della punta)*

The modern development of conventional weapons (foil and saber) and mainly the way of judging the fencing phrase, has made the precedence of the tip, or hand as they say, less important in them. In saber it seems that we are returning to the archaic and the foil benefits consequently from greater severity. The epee, not depending on the judgement and sensitivity of the referee, has not undergone this type of degeneration. The precedence of the tip has remained an essential condition to precede the other, and to make one's movement less visible and predictable: it must therefore be cultivated with care.

The advancement of the tip brings with it the advancement of the guard, and therefore the widening of the protection cone.

Peak precedence also means delay in bringing your target forward, exposing it. The precedence is not limited to thrusts but also applies to all maneuvers on the blade (beats, pressures, engagements, transports, envelopments) in which the work of the arm must be perfectly coordinated preceding and accompanying it, with the work of the legs.

Practice is, of course, essential to acquiring this skill, for this purpose, even compound and complex exercises are useful, to perform actions that do not find current application in the assault.

The parry and riposte *(La parata e risposta)*

We have already noted that preferred parries followed by glides, or beating parries followed by lightning-fast ripostes are to be preferred. The saberist and even more the foilist can often afford to choose the target, after having parried. For the epeeist, this luxury rarely allowed, due to the very high risk of being anticipated by a renewed attack: for them it is easier to organize the defense, given the greater predictability of the thrusts (the opponent must be more cautious). The epeeist will resolve to parry after having programmed the other not to expect it (or to expect it in a different extent), and must nevertheless be quick in responding, already knowing the target, the way to carry it, and the opponent's subsequent reaction.

Beating parries, from a technical point of view, resemble beats; the difference is in the fact that the opposing blade is not stationary, but travels in the opposite direction, while the opposing hand (tight on time) immediately prior to the touch. Therefore, powerful collisions are possible and frequent which, added to a more evident wedge effect (diagonal parry forward, rather that backward or sideways), lead to greater effectiveness: especially on the external lines (third and second, for two right handers), less suitable for close range angulations (typically, low fourth).

Second intention *(La seconda intenzione)*

Known definitions do not clearly delimit the field. Action of the first intention is defined as any offensive action that aims to directly overcome the opponent's defense (therefore, even compound actions, with feints): the action of second intention is defined as any action that aims to obtain an offensive reaction from the opponent to be used to carry out the planned thrust. In foil, established that even counter-time (and its variant of counterattacks) is a second intention, it is customary to give this name only to offensive actions that voluntarily fall under a habitual block of the opponent, to take advantage of the equally usual response, counter-parrying, and riposting. So also, is the exit in time, if the offensive action is opposed and provoked is classified among the second intentions.

We have also seen the many probing and concealing actions used to provoke offensive reactions which it is intended to take advantage of at a later time: and the same goes for the actions that aim to program the other. You can choose not to include them among the second intentions (and, in this case, we should refine the definition by requiring that the reaction be immediate); or we can opportunely, consider these as actions of second intention: in epee, we have seen the programming of the adversary has particular importance.

Among the second intentions and little used, due to the risks already exposed, the counter- parry and riposte. On the other hand, there is a frequent counter-time, which responds very well to the need to make up for the disadvantage. But the most used, taking into account the previous classification, is the arrest: both in the variant that can be defined as counter time (arrest on the arrest: pretending to attack to cause the arrest, and arrest); and in the variant opposed to other offensive actions, however provoked (invitations, engagements, searches) always with the aim of arresting them.

CHAPTER 6 **HOW TO GIVE THE BLADE**

Chapter six, "how to give the blade" deals with a rather neglected topic in fencing texts: how to give the blade in various circumstances. Engagements, parries, beats, glides, disengagements in time, and other useful suggestions to the teacher who has to give the individual lesson. Here are some simple or complex exercises for some typical epee actions.

AT THE END OF CHAPTER 6 YOU SHOULD BE ABLE TO:

- Know how the blade is given for the different actions required of the students
- Know some typical epee exercises

IF YOU ARE ABEL TO ANSWER THESE QUESTIONS YOU CAN GO TO THE NEXT CHAPTER

- How is the blade given for the different engagements?
- What are the elements to watch out for when giving the blade for a glide?
- How do you give the blade for the soft parry? And how for the beating parry?
- How is the blade used for beats? What is the difference between beats and parries?
- What measure should be used for the disengagement in time?

KEY WORDS:

- Giving the blade during the lesson (*Dare il ferro in lezione*)
- Engagements (*Legamenti*)
- Beats (*Battute*)
- Parries (*Parate*)
- Glides (*Fili*)
- Angulation (*Angolazioni*)
- Disengagement in time (*Cavazione in tempo*)

PREMISE

The giving of the blade is fundamental: one must know how to offer it, know how to oppose the right resistance to lateral displacements, know how to vary the opposition or the angle of the guard. In this way it is possible to make it easier or more difficult to perform each fencing action. One also learns, by perfecting one's own way of giving the blade, to make one's actions more effective, proper action significant as it imitates the opponent.

These notes presuppose that the ability in the instructor to be able to correctly execute the various actions, and to recognize the correct execution from the pupil. These are intended to give some useful hints in the area where experience or theory does not help, as hitting and not being hit have been practiced so far. It is important now to place oneself from the point of view of the other: not to hinder them, but to help them improve.

Giving the blade for engagements *(Dare il ferro per i legamenti)*

The Maestro places the guard in a central position (at the height of his stomach) points to one of the four vertices of an ideal rectangle: anterior shoulder (for third engagement) posterior shoulder (fourth engagement) anterior iliac crest (second) posterior iliac (first). The point is always on a target, never outside.

A slight resistance in the opposite direction to the engagements must be constantly opposed. The Maestros arm, to a narrow extent, must be bent; to a greater extent it can be flexed, but more or less stretched forward. The arm of the student who performs the engagement must always be forward, rather than in the normal position of invitation.

Engagement exercises *(Esercizi per i legamenti)*

For each engagement assumed by the pupil, the blade given as described; then you can vary the position of one's weapon, lowering the tip so that the blade touches the guard (a position favorable for a glide) by raising the tip so that the blades meet in the center (position favorable to a pressure); moving the guard from the side opposite to the of the pupil (position favorable to the glide if the blade is on or near the guard); or on the same side (position favorable to thrusts by detachment, or to transport followed by a glide, if the blade is on the guard). Verify that the point of the pupil, in executing the engagement is not too far from the guard of the Maestro (line of direction) and that the angle between the wrist and forearm is minimal.

For each engagement of the student, check the coverage by stretching the arm, under the engagement, as if to touch; to accentuate the engagement, add to the previous movement a displacement of the guard from the same side of the engagement.

Check from time to time, the solidity of the engagement with an increase in pressure in the opposite direction.

Without saying the name of the engagement, the Maestro presents the blade to the pupil and asks him to hold the engagement, then he releases and presents the blade to the pupil in the same or different line, again asking to engage and hold; and so on, taking care that the pupil executed the engagement suggested by the position of the blade, and taking care of the resistance to any displacement. For no reason should lateral displacement be favored or anticipated.

Giving the blade for glides *(Dare il ferro per i fili)*

A glide is preceded by an engagement or a parry.

In the first case, except at a close distance, it is good that the Maestros arm is almost extended. A fundamental point during the glide, the guard of the Maestro is maintained for the entire time from the opposite side (on a hypothetical plane perpendicular to the line of offense) to that required for the guard of the student, always providing the appropriate resistance with the blade. Another important point is that of the position of the Maestro's blade: close to the guard to help facilitate the glide, further, away to make it difficult. Finally, it is essential to maintain adequate pressure on the student's blade for the entire duration of the glide.

The same principles are valid for the glide executed as a riposte. The difference is in the way of presenting the blade, as we will see in the paragraph reserved for parries. Another difference is for the glides preceded by a transport, which are inadvisable as a response, due to the risk of bringing the opponent's tip to the target.

For example, right to right: in the glide in third, which starts from the engagement of third, the pupils guard must have opposition to their outside, and high. The Master will bring their guard slightly downwards and to their right (left for the pupil): easier, but less correct, to facilitate the glide by bending the arm. Better to keep the arm extended and give at the wrist. In the event that the student does not use the right opposition (or to increase the difficulty), they can be forced to do so (otherwise they will not be able to touch, due to the action of the Maestros guard) by reducing their own opposition, or putting it, very slightly, on the contrary.

Exercises for the glide *(Esercizi per i fili)*

From each engagement of the pupil to execute the two possible glides (high and low) by varying the position of one's blade (near or far from the pupil's guard) and of one's own guard (moving it away or bringing it closer to the path of the pupil's guard).

Subsequently, from time to time, the Maestro deliberately mistakes the position of the blade and or that of the guard, verifying the effect of his voluntary error on the execution of the pupil.

For each glide, ask the pupil to perform the engagement: the pupil must observe the position of the Maestro's guard and decide to either glide above or below. For example, for the glide in fourth, the Maestro presents the blade for the engagement, and while the pupil engages, he moves the guard, always slightly towards his inside, and upwards for the glide on his flank, shift downwards for the glide to the chest.

Precede the glide with a transport on the opposite line, each time the Maestro presents the guard on the same side of the engagement. For example, give the blade for the student's engagement in fourth: while the pupil engages, the Maestro moves the guard to their outside; the pupil will then perform a transport in second and glide.

With the student's eyes closed. The Maestro detaches from the pupil's engagement. When the Maestro releases his blade from the student's engagement, the pupil attempts to feel for the Maestros blade to find if it has been placed near the guard, in which case they will make the glide, or far, in which case they will thrust detached.

Engagements and glides without pause. The maestro gives the blade for each engagement, the student executes the glide and immediately the Maestro gives the blade for a second engagement. Start with only two engagements (third and second) and them move to the succession of the four engagements: for example, first and above, second to flank, fourth to flank and third to chest. The Maestro must avoid that the student makes confusion between the exercise performed with parries and ripostes (two distinct movements) and the same exercise performed with contractions (one movement). It is an excellent exercise for training in how to vary the opposition.

Giving the blade for parries *(Dare il ferro per le parate)*

Two points are essential to train the student to parry: not to widen the movement of the tip, following the direction of the parry; bring the tip with decision and with the necessary change of speed to the target. One can stop immediately before the touch, if the case requires it (pupil does not make the parry sufficiently. Neglecting these two points leads to various negative consequences. The pupil widens the parries beyond what is necessary and tends to lean on the opponent's blade; if the shot is not delivered, the parry becomes ineffective. The way to strike is different if a beating parry is requested from the student, for the response to the riposte, or a soft parry, for a response that can also be detached, but which is generally by glide.

For a beating parry the Maestros blade must be presented in such a way that the contact of the blades takes place at the center of the blades or, in any case, away from the guard of the beater (greater energy transmitted in the impact). There are two cases for the soft parry. If you want the answer by glide, the blade should be given near the guard of the pupil. If, on the other hand you want a response of detachment, or a feint by glide (pressure to obtain the opposite reaction), the blade can be given as for the beating parries. Other considerations can be made in relation to the type of parry that the student wants (simple or circular). Circular parries are made difficult or impossible if the Maestros point is aimed at a target far from the pupil's guard. In fact, in this case, the pupil is forced to widen the parry movement by pivoting mainly in the elbow, rather in the wrist: otherwise, they would meet the Maestros blade on their weak.

The ceding parries present further difficulties, as they require the student to strike the blade in the right way, from the glide of the Maestro. A useful trick described in the exercises.

Exercises on parries *(Esercizi sulle parate)*

Once a parry has been established, have it performed on a straight thrust (invitation of the student) or on a disengagement that starts from the pupil's engagement on the opposite line. Strike the blade alternately on the manner indicated for the beat or soft parries, demanding from the student the response to the detachment or that of the glide. In the case of a riposte by glide, enter the variants described in the paragraph on glides.

From an invitation or engagement, direct the thrust at a nearby target near or far from their guard, demanding the counter or simple parry respectively. Next, add the variants related to beating or soft parries, and those related to reposts by glide.

For the ceding parries, start from the student's engagement. The Maestro looks for the ceding parry (see below: how to look for the blade) and the pupil disengages in time, with opposition from the side requested by the teacher, who executes a direct parry and riposte by glide, immediately or after a transport (if necessary) for the parry of the student. Examples: from the engagement of third by the student, the maestro looks for the blade by counter of fourth, the pupil disengages to the external chest with opposition to the outside (from the third line), the Maestro parries third and ripostes by glide, the pupil cedes in first and reposts:

The pupil engages in second, the Maestro looks for the blade in counter of first (half circle), the student deceives in time to the flank with opposition to the outside. The Maestro parries second and ripostes by glide, the student cedes in fourth and ripostes;

from his engagement of fourth the student deceives inside, maintaining the same opposition on the search for the blade in counter of third the Maestro parries fourth and ripostes by glide to the flank while the student cedes in second and reposts;

From the students engagement of first, (tip threatening the flank of the Maestro) the Maestro searches for the blade in second and on the pupils deceive in time (who maintains the starting position) he parries first high and reposts.

Turing the hand in first position, on the outside, for the ceding parry of third and riposte of the pupil: or for the same ceding parry, the pupil engages in third, the Maestro looks for the blade in counter of fourth:

The pupil deceives in time with opposition to the inside, the Maestro parries third and ripostes to the flank (transport in first by glide, or false fourth to the flank) the pupil cedes in third and reposts.

Giving the blade for beats *(Dare il ferro per le battute)*

The difference between a beat and a beating parry is due to the fact that in the first case there is not an attack on the target. The beats are therefore made on contract to a presentation: the blade in line (a fundamental action) or on invitation or engagement (an auxiliary action). If the Maestro directs the tip towards the center of the guard, he will make it difficult for the student to beat and will be forced to decentralize their guard before beating. For grazing beats, it is advisable for the Maestro to move the tip further away than for normal beats.

Exercises for beats and glides *(Esercizi su battute e fili)*

Presenting the blade for the beat for three different reactions: simple beats direct (tip and guard away from the pupil's guard); circular beats (tip close guard); engagement and glides (tip close with the variants already described). For near or far guard we mean opposition from the same side (high or low, external, or internal) or from the opposite side.

Disengagement in time against the search for the blade *(Cercare ii ferro per far cavare in tempo)*

To train the student to disengage in time, the Maestro searches for the blade as an engagement or a beat. The movement must be quick, but at the same time allowing the student time to disengage. Therefore, the blade movement must be done with the right pace, but it must stop just before the impact to allow time for even the slowest disengagement.

Various exercises - Some exercises for the four angles *(Alcuni esercizi per le quattro Angolazione)*

Initial measure being able to hit the arm without lunging, intermediate distance is between the step and lunge distance in foil and the previous, this favors the angulation to the arm without having total arm extension by the teacher, so that they get less tired, and the student does not stiffen.

Always starting from the engagement, making it easier for the student to find the measure, and to have the opportunity to check the way of giving the blade from the maestro.

From the pupil's engagement, the teacher disengages and direct the point towards the appropriate target, taking care to move the forearm forward while the student strikes to facilitate the success of the thrust and to stop the tip. The Maestro is covered, that is almost in line (does not bend the wrist, and the tip is always on a target) and can facilitate the pupil by moving the guard out or in, up or down, or aiming at a target more peripheral than the guard of the student.

From the student's engagement of third, maestro disengages towards the back shoulder, angling towards the armed hand.

From the student's engagement in third or first, maestro disengages towards the flank (then to make more difficult, towards higher targets) angle above.

Students' engagement if fourth, maestro disengages to the shoulder of the armed hand, angled outside or inside depending on the weapon hand.

From the student's engagement in second, maestro disengages above to the mask and then lower to increase difficulty, angulation below.

When the four angles are done well enough, one can tie them together in one exercise that includes multiple thrusts:

The student engages in third (fourth if left-handed) the Maestro searches for the blade counter of fourth, the pupil deceives and angles outwards, then the Maestro searches in third, the student disengages inside, then the Maestro searches for the blade in second, the pupil disengages above, finally the Maestro searches for the blade in high first and the pupil disengages and angles below.

Initially the Maestro will make a movement that is not too tight, to facilitate the student and allow them to learn the sequence; then they will tighten the movements more and more, and will demand more marked displacements, in the four directions (quadrants) of the student's guard.

When these exercises are successful, one can make it even more complicated by adding on the part of the maestro; a second search for the blade: so always starting from the students engagement of third (fourth if left handed) the Maestro will attempt to engage with double counter of fourth, then with double counter of second, followed by third and ending with first, while the student after the necessary interchanges, will end angling to the outside, indie, above and below.

All the exercises described must be performed from on spot, then to mobility, taking a step forward or a step back for each thrust, taking care of the timing. The Maestro will especially pay attention to the precedence of the arm moving first with respect to the legs.

Some exercises for giving the blade for angulations from engagements and glides
(Alcuni esercizi per dare il ferro per angolazioni seguite da legamenti e fili)

The following exercise (one will be described, can be used on all lines with numerous variations) and very useful to learn how to strike the blade and target, varying the position of both during the action: we start as for the angulation below, as first described.

From the student's engagement in second, Maestro disengages and threatens the mask while lifting the guard and remaining in line:

The pupil angles below, as the Maestro breaks the touch (advancing slightly to the target as explained above) then lower only the point towards the student's wrist, beyond their guard, as if they wanted to touch above:

The student binds in third and glides to the chest raising the hand with opposition to the outside, while the Maestro, at the same time and without bending their arm, or flexing it, lowers their guard and holds it on the opposite side to that of the pupil, offering with the blade some resistance to the glide.

Start by performing these actions slowly at first, taking care the synchronization of movements, then quicker, until it results in a smooth execution. At this point the exercise can per performed with movement in both directions.

Some exercises suitable for oppositions *(Alcuni esercizi suite opposizione)*

Having defined the meaning and usefulness of opposition, and the first exercises for thrusts to the body with opposition (straight thrust with opposition to the invitation of third; feint direct and deceive in opposition to the invitation of third with final opposition (closure) to the inside, etc., some exercises are directed to the wrist and are completely analogous to those proposed for angulations: the difference consists in the fact that the Maestro will pull an angulation to the wrist, as opposed to the line of the student, than to his arrests with slight opposition on the same side. The students' arm is to be soft, slightly flexed and the final movement forward.

One can propose the same exercise as the four angulations for the four arrests to the wrist with opposition:

In this case the Maestro after every search for the blade will direct the tip, angling towards the target and the student will arrest with opposition.

Then (right to right) from the student's engagement of third, the Maestro will search of the blade with a counter of fourth and then angulation to the outside or in third if angulation to the inside, in second for the angulation below and first to the high line:

The pupil will evade any search for the blade by arresting by time thrust, (terminology typically *spadistica*) with opposition inside, outside, above, or below.

Some exercises for thrusts to the arm followed by thrusts to the body *(Alcuni esercizi per colpi al braccio seguiti da colpi al corpo)*

A thrust to the wrist carried out effectively and with realism may not touch but provoke a reaction. Three possible reactions are: the opponent withdraws the arm; they may parry or arrest. This gives opportunity for numerous exercises and interesting considerations for tactics.

Maestro withdraws the arm: *(Maestro che ritira il braccio)*

From the student's engagement in third, when the Maestro wants, they open in second invitation, the pupil touches the wrist and the teacher withdraws the first target, (the arm) and the student continues to the body as the Maestro moves the tip away from the target. This can be done by the guard, with a lunge, or with a step and lunge or even retreat, following the movement of the coach. Initially the action is performed with the first thrust pulled from the guard, or with a step and the second thrust with a lunge. More realistic, and more difficult, the same action performed with the two shots taken during the lunge.

Greater difficulty is presented with the same action using three thrusts, to be coordinated with a single step and lunge, directing the thrust to the wrist, crook of the arm and final to the body, coordinating the thrusts with the first foot, then second foot and final with the lunge.

When the Maestro parries: *(Maestro che para)*

From the student's engagement of third; the Maestro looks for the blade with a counter of fourth and the student disengages, touching the wrist on the outside; The Maestro parries third and the student disengages to the inside chest with opposition to their inside to avoid the possible arrest of the Maestro after the parry fails to find the blade. The Maestros parry of third, to avoid the touch to the wrist can be real or delayed, so as to ensure that the student continues to the body regardless of the first thrust, which must be pulled in order to touch the body.

A more complex variant of the same exercise is the following: same beginning, but after the thrust to the wrist the pupil continues to the thigh and them immediately returns to the body, avoiding the parry of second of the Maestro. Also in this case, exercise performed while in spot, or with forward or backward movement or with the step and lunge.

Maestro arrests: *(Maestro che arresta)*

From the students engagement of second, on the Maestro disengagement for the angulation below the student immediately after the Coach lowers the tip as if to stop as the wrist above, the pupil parries (if the Maestro advances') or engages in third and glides to the chest; the Maestro performs a ceding parry of first (parrying late and receiving the touch) and the pupil executes a second touch to the flank with opposition to the outside. It is also useful as an alternative, for the Maestro to ask the student to add a second thrust in the event of a parry, to condition them to react quickly with the rimesse and not with a counter parry, in the event of an unexpected parry by the opponent thrust to the body.

Another exercise on the same theme: *(Un altro esercizio, sullo stesso tema)*

From the students engagement of third, the Maestro disengages and aims the point towards the pupils chest, not too high; the student angles above and the Maestro immediately threatens the wrist below; the pupil takes the blade in second and executes a glide to the foot; the maestro immediately after the shot withdraws his foot and reassembles to the mask, the pupil does a beating parry of third (diagonal forward beat, away from their guard) and ripostes to the flank detached, immediately on the double (the Maestro goes to second). Even these actions like the others can be performed stationary or with movement.

A complex exercise ending with the arrow *(Un esercizio complesso terminante con la frecciata)*

We now describe a more complex exercise with many thrusts to be performed with movement.

It starts in the same way as the four angles exercise done in a row. After the last thrust, the pupil engages in third, and after a very short pause the same exercise (already described) with two interchanges. Another engagement in third and short pause, then the exercise described with a thrust to the wrist, continuation to the leg and last thrust ending to the chest.

Short pause (always in order to synchronize) then the teacher looks for the blade and thrusts to the body of the student who goes into a reasemblement arresting to the shoulder and, continuing the same movement, bring the rear foot back while returning to the guard at the same time as the second parry. Followed by a riposte to the thigh and immediate rimesse to the chest.

After a very brief pause, then the maestro takes a step back looking for the blade, the pupil disengages and lunges to the chest.

Another short pause, for synchronization and balance, then the Maestro steps back again looking for the blade twice, while the student begins the one-two, coordinating with the push of the rear foot which rapidly advances just enough to facilitate and speed up the arrow while the body begins the forward unbalance for the arrow.

CAPITOL 7 **TEACHING**

Chapter seven "teaching" completes the previous chapter, which had introduced some elements of teaching.

The didactic sequence is a rather neglected topic in fencing treatises, as well as topic such as tactics and the psychological aspects of fencing.

Here are some useful suggestions to the teacher who gives individual lessons.

AT THE END OF CHAPTER 7 ONE SHOULD BE ABLE TO:

- Knowing how to evaluate and control the measure in the lesson, especially for the different actions required of the student
- Manage a group lesson, leg work or paired exercises
- Learn about different types of lessons and set up didactic sequence

IF YOU ARE ABLE TO ANSWER THESE QUESTIONS YOU CAN PROCEEDED TO THE NEXT CHAPTER

- What are the elements to pay attention to when evaluating and checking the measure in the lesson?
- How does a group lesson take place?
- How are the mechanical (technical) and the coordinative (tactical) lessons different?
- What are the related techniques?
- And for those alternatives (choice) or with a study of the opposites (contraries')?
- What precautions should the Maestro use in a tactical lesson?
- And what is the role of the pupil?

TERMINOLOGY

- Measure (*Misura*)
- Time (*Tempo*)
- Rhythm (*Ritmo*)
- Training (*Addestramento*)

Types of lessons:

- Collective (group) (*Collettiva*)
- Individual (*Individuale*)
  o *Mechanics' (Meccanica)*
  o Coordination (*Coordinative*)
  o Tactical (*Tattica*)
  o Training (*Allenante*)

INTRODUCTION

The fencer, from the moment they step into a fencing hall for the first time, has the opportunity to learn a great many things. From teammates, opponents, from the many professional figures they may meet: physical trainer, doctor, instructors, notational analysis and relationship experts, managers and secretarial staff. The fencing master of all these people is certainly the most influential and decisive for their progress. Because they have the specific knowledge required and knows how to use the most important tool for a sure technical and tactical growth of the student: the individual lesson. The time and attention dedicated to this instrument means that a bond is gradually established between teacher and student that allows one to have a profound influence on the phycology of the fencer in training, increasing self-esteem, motivating them, helping them to solve the numerous problems in training, as a way of technical and moral development.

For the student, the availability of a good teacher is a great opportunity. For the teacher, it is a great responsibility, which must induce them to never stop learning, updating, perfecting, and understanding themselves.

The psychological structure of each pupil differs from that of the others and teaching must adapt to be effective. Some pupils especially want to know the "why" of everything they have to do, otherwise they do not perform as well as they could. Others just want to know "what" they have to do, and the explanations are more often than not downright harmful. The former want "analytical" teaching, with many explanations, while the latter want "formal: teaching. The former mainly want to 'understand' and the second want to 'do' and a lot of effort can be saved by understanding and following their attitudes.

Taking this into account, the lesson topic can be addressed.

The lesson, we have already said, can be collective or individual. In any case, before starting, you need to be clear about the goals you want to achieve learning, improvement, training. In general, or specific. Technique or tactical.

A lesson can contain many themes, although often one will be prevailing one.

We leave aside an important part of the athlete's preparation, pertaining, when there is, to the physical preparation expert: who will have to subordinate their work to that of the fencing master, responsible for general programming.

We also ignore the educational component (behavior) implicit in all the activities of the fencer as such, in the gym and outside.

The conditions in which fencing companies and masters operate are too different to have claim to give precise rules for the organization on the room or work, collective or individual.

There are also different conditions in which the students present themselves in the room, which could suggest a more or less long preliminary period of general physical preparation, learning patterns and non-specific motor skills.

Let us refer, for the following, only to the specific preparation: what is most closely recalls the movements and actions typical of fencing.

The collective (group) lesson *(La lezione collettiva)*

Society around us changes rapidly, and consequently the strategies of sports clubs have to change as well in order to survive and thrive. The individual lesson is a tool that allows you to reach a higher quality but limits the ability of the teacher to deal with more students, with obvious repercussions on the economy of the whole.

The collective lesson, the group work, represent a possible solution for the sustainability of the system. It is necessary to know how to find the right balance between the two types of lessons, constantly striving to improve the quality of both.

The collective lesson fits the group, but not the individual. The individual lesson, on the other hand, can and must adapt to the characteristics of the student. In this-also in this- lies the skill of the maestro: that he cannot draw his knowledge only from the manuals, but from his personal training, and sensitivity, to be continually refined.

For some years the number of teachers who take charge, in addition to the technical part, also of the management of the association in which they operate, and of which it may happen are also founders and presidents has been increasing. Especially if the legal form of the Limited Liability Corporation amateur sports club has been chosen. The growing commitment and greater responsibilities make the task of effectively combining quality of results and quantity of members more difficult. The collective lesson, even with its limitations can give valuable help in this direction.

We add that this type of lesson stimulates, especially in the younger ones, the spirit of emulation, and favors socialization.

Group lessons can be used for warming up large muscle groups, before assaults or individual lessons: a job that has spread in Italy under the name of "legs-fencing" by some Hungarian and Polish Masters (Bela Bagolgh, Janos Kevey, Richard Zub) since competition from Eastern European professionals made it essential to pay more attention to the physical preparation of athletes.

This type of lesson usually takes place frontally (the teacher in front of the group lined up on one or more lines, according to the number of participants and the space available) and focuses mainly on the movements of the legs. Variety of steps, lunges, return to guard, arrows with the inclusion of various other gymnastic movements at the discretion of the teacher.

Progressive muscle engagement and possibly homogeneity of the group are important to avoid damage. The teacher will briefly point out any errors in posture or execution, slowing down the rhythm of the session as little as possible.

If the level of the participants allows it, they can continue with arm-leg coordination exercises, suggesting fencing actions of increasing complexity, for a real ideomotor training, conducted without the weapon and without an opponent.

We can also consider the exercises in pairs with supervision by the teacher as a collective lesson. They are very useful because they force the student to realize the importance and the differences in the way of giving and receiving the blade.

In the individual lesson, the teacher avoids or grades the difficulties: in the exercises in pairs, the exercise partner makes numerous mistakes, which over time lead to greater awareness and precision of the technical gesture. The maestro will point out the importance of the correct guard position, of narrow and rational movements, of the position of the iron, of the depth of the feints, of the precision of the parries, of the position of the targets.

The teacher will have to explain the exercises in a clear and concise way using the correct terms: in this way the students will familiarize themselves with the right terminology and will learn to connect correctly and quickly words and mental images with increasing complexity and with evident improvement of communication and understanding of the necessary concepts.

In this type of lesson, the teacher will always assume position external to the group: that is he must always be able to have a control and overview of the entire group, which is under his responsibility. They will have to limit as much as possible the interventions in which he replaces an element of the couple unless they use this possibility to demonstrate an action to the whole group.

Particularly useful will be, in this phase, the exercise on measure:

• the evaluation of the various distances, to be checked frequently by extending the armed arm from the guard position.

• The maintaining of a predetermined distance, taking turns guiding the movement on both directions and stopping often for verification.

It is important that the teacher does not neglect to point out the errors of posture and movement which, if repeated, lead to the establishment of defects that are difficult to correct later on. Among these, unbalanced positions of the guard and feet; the dragging of the rear leg, which is for pushing, and must be recalled with vivacity; the lunge with the sole of the front foot, rather than on the heel; too long of steps forward; swinging of the back arm delayed in relation to the thrust of the rear leg and more. Finally, it is worth noting the possibility and the usefulness of the exercises in pairs with the plastic weapon: which allows one to work without complete protection and does not develop the aversion to exercises typical in young athletes. Aversion caused more often than not by painful and repeated blows in inadequately protected targets, such as those of the maestro with his plastron. Not to mention the accessory and indispensable protections, in the epee and saber, for advanced targets.

The individual lesson *(La lezione individuale)*

Many teaching objectives are possible, the Maestro should decide before starting what they intend to achieve or improve in the student. During the lesson they can then adjust the thrust, orienting themselves more on certain aspects than on others, according to the student's response, or also to the needs of the situation: Let's not forget in the fencing hall, all the factors must be taken into account, so that the overall activity proceeds smoothly. Note that the Maestros plan may not be able to proceed as easily as planned.

The teacher does not always have to share the objective with the student, nor the fact that he modulates the difficulty of the exercises on the ability of the student: it is important to keep motivation and satisfaction high, that the required task is quite difficult, but not higher that the possibilities of whomever must carry it out.

The Maestro can propose to develop:

- First the technique or also called the mechanics
- Hand and leg coordination
- The rhythm and speed, and therefore time
- The study of the contrary
- The study of measure
- Tactics (provocation and deception)
- Resistance
- Confidence in one's own means
- Feedback from notational analysis
- And so on

The themes can overlap and be modified during the lesson, according to the judgement of the teacher and the student's response.

Wishing to classify the different types of lessons we could divide them as follows:

- Mechanical lesson
- Coordinative lesson
- Tactical lesson
- Training lesson

The mechanical and coordinative lessons train the student to react quickly to certain stimuli, but in an automatic way: they are in fact lessons that aim to crate automatisms. There is no provocation, no elaboration, of the meaning of the stimulus received.

Other types of lessons make it possible to compensate for this negative effect, while presenting, in turn, contraindications.

There is no lesson that totally corresponds to the reality of combat. The Maestro, whatever the type of lesson, one ends up getting hit, perhaps grading the difficulty, collaborate do not oppose.

And they could not, with the strongest athletes, compete in terms of speed and endurance. In the long run, they cannot even with the weak ones, if they have to do a good number of lessons.

It is always the maestro who proposes the stimulus or the exercise. The student is limited to the development of a more or less complex theme that is assigned to them.

The final synthesis, in the assault is up to the student, who must be helped by the maestro to see the various aspects and to link them together in a harmonious way.

It should be emphasized that different masters have achieved great results with very different lessons. This probably means that the result can be achieved in many ways: the personality of a student and teacher, the collaborating of an intern environment (training or team mates, technical staff as a whole) but above all the intense commitment and regular, eventually bear the desired fruit. No matter how hard we try, however we have not found a sure model of reference, neither for the winning athlete, nor for the lesson. Art or science then? Surely both, as Masaniello Parise already wrote in 1884; and he was certainly not the only one, nor the first.

Before examining the first two types of lessons, some observations on the type of communication that is established since the first lesson. The maestro explains and demonstrates by example. Then they stand in front of the student and asks them to perform certain actions:

initially the simplest ones, such as direct thrust, or by disengagement, beat or glide, at your choice of time, that is, when you feel ready and sure you understand.

It is useless to underline the importance, for the teacher, knowing how to give the blade correctly and expressively, as already explained in a previous chapter.

Once this phase is over, the teacher will pass on to have the so-called actions performed "in time" a way of saying fixed by tradition, but to be rejected, so as not to confuse them with real actions in time: executed, that is simultaneously with a certain movement of the opponent.

In the case of the lesson, it is instead a reaction of the "stimulus-response" type: the teacher changes attitude or performs a given movement and the student must immediately (but always after the stimulus) perform the set task.

Over time the maestros' gestures become more and more standardized and customary, and the student learns to recognize in the desired way.

By changing students, or by changing teachers, the problem immediately arises in an evident way, and it is necessary to patiently re-establish a shared "language".

A good lesson generally follows a certain didactic progression, ranging from easy to difficult, simple to complex, slow to fast.

Each maestro develops their own method, but some advice can be given. Before the lesson, a decent warm-up should be expected, especially for the legs. It is advisable to start from close measure, with exercises that gradually engage the armed arm.

The required measure must be found by the pupil, not by the maestro.

Start with the engagement of the student, who still may not be able to hold the blade correctly for the teacher to engage the student's blade. A short pause between the request for a movement (action) and its execution is always necessary, to allow the student to mentally calculate the task and to make the mental image of it before executing.

Always asking the student to keep the measure tight, begin to make the student move with steps forward and backward, to thrust from a standstill and stepping froward (without lunging) taking care of the desired precedence of the tip and the coordination. Then increase the distance so that the student is required to do the actions with a lunge or a step and lunge, progressively increasing the speed and frequency of the actions, as well as their technical difficulty. The maestro is always very attentive to signs of physical and mental fatigue, and adjusts themselves, accordingly, allowing breaks, and taking advantage of them for their observations and explanations.

Never forget the necessary feedback, on good or bad execution: remembering however that a compliment is much more motivating than a reprimand.

You may wish to teach the student all fencing knowledge but, more realistically, you will end up teaching them a more limited range of actions, what can the guiding criterion be?

For the beginner, one can start by teaching a few simple offensive and defensive actions, to enable them to quickly start sparing, thus overcoming the boredom and impatience of the long preliminary learning periods; and also, to make it autonomous as soon as possible. In modern times, an apprenticeship that is too long is no longer feasible: you risk losing the pupil, one has to take this into account.

Subsequently, observation will give us an idea of their aptitudes and defects: they will learn with greater speed and pleasure the actions they will understand and need, thanks to the experience they have on the platform. For this reason, it will be useful to stimulate them to ask questions. It is also very useful to force them to judge the attacks of their companions, to force them to observe and understand.

The mechanical lesson *(technical) (La lezione meccanica)*

This is the oldest lesson. With this term (mechanical or technical) we refer to the hand and leg technique, perfected through accurate and repeated descriptions and executions: the handling of the weapon, the correctness of the attitudes or placements of the weapon and of the movements of the legs, the acquisition of the necessary automatisms of the arm and hand. The necessary notions will derive from the treatises of from the schematic practice of the maestro, and it is not necessary to return to them now.

It is necessary that the maestro has given precise points of reference to the student, that they check with them frequently and that they make the movements repeated sufficiently a high number of times (repetition). Any difficulty in performance can be overcome by breaking down the movement into its finer components, practicing them separately and them recomposing the action a s a whole and with the original rhythm.

It is good to start with a visual example, relying on the pupil's imitation, and proposing a position, or a movement, without exceeding with explanations: only if the student reveals the difficulties they will go into details. In correcting the difficulty, work on one part at a time, neglecting for the moment the other errors, and focusing their attention on the singular established point. The maestro is stationary, and askes the student to perform the particular action from a set distance. The maestro carefully corrects the mistakes, and has each action repeated a good number of times until they are satisfied with the execution.

It is the lesson found in treaties of the past. Perhaps it is the least suitable for modern fencers, but nevertheless it is still liked by many: both teachers and students. From apparently solid points of reference, and therefore the safety of things long experienced. **It tends to give the pupil a predetermined shape, rather than adapting the shape to the characteristics of the pupil.** Ultimately it derives from military teaching, which necessarily had to be standardized.

An evolution of this type of mechanical work and that of multiple thrusts, and continuous friction: such as a prolonged series of parries and replies, with or without the Maestros counterparts. Having to thrust more shots in succession, the student will be forced to maintain control of the weapon for a longer period of time (while modulating the tight in time of the hand so as to not get too tired) and will not exhaust his attention after taking the first thrust, as happened to beginners.

As a practical example, for point only weapons. Other examples are at the end of chapter VI. For each parry, without interruption, the first riposte is detached and again by glide. From the students invitation or engagement of third, at close measure, the Maestro thrusts to the chest and the student responds with the parry of fourth and riposte, then returns to parry fourth (Maestro can counter parry or withdraw their arm allowing themselves to be hit, and thrust again: the student must not vary in their task for this reason) and ripostes by glide to the flank or chest (the maestro varies the position of the guard to elicit either of the two responses).

After the exercise has been performed for the individual parries, it can be merged into a single overall exercise (and also performed with movement: see coordinative lesson): for example, passing from fourth to third (following the glide in fourth to the flank, the Maestro directs their thrust to the front shoulder, forcing a parry of third and riposte detached) then to the second and first for a total of eight thrusts.

Then there is the movement of the legs to execute with a step forward, or backward and also with the lunge and return to guard.

The coordinated lesson *(La lezione coordinative)*

The purpose of the coordinative lesson is, in fact, to obtain the coordination of both hands and leg movements, in the shortest possible time, and with the greatest effectiveness: coordination and rhythm of the required action.

A high number of repetitions is required for a motor pattern to become fixed (that is to become an automation, executable with great speed and low cost) a high number of repetitions is required. Too many explanations at this stage can have the opposite effect. This type of lesson minimizes the need for explanations and allows one to develop many actions quickly. By simply changing actions, pace, speed, and amount of work, one gets an excellent exercise for the development of endurance (training lesson). The remarkable possibilities of variation of themes, of the measure, forces the student to always keep the attention alive. Its limit, as for the mechanical lesson, and in the lack of realism, as regards to the search for measure and tactics: to be developed in other types of lessons, when coordination problems are less urgent.

In this type of lesson, the first point to observe is that the signal always comes from the maestro. The pupil follows the movement according to two rules: they move the blade in immediate response to the stimulus given, with the blade, by the Maestro; moves the legs following the movements of the legs of the Maestro.

Let's take for example a simple action that lends itself well to the purpose: the beat in fourth and straight thrust. The action can be proposed starting from the student's invitation in third and the Maestros invitation in second.

At first, the maestro at close measure, raises the point exposing themselves to the students beat in fourth. The students must immediately beat and thrust. The Maestro does not proceed if the reaction time is not immediate.

When the action is done with satisfaction it can be done with a lunge. At this point the synchronization of the leg movements begins.

The Maestro moves, back and forth, taking great care in insert short pauses, sometimes after one step, sometimes after two or more steps, and checking that the student performs the movements and pauses in the same way. When they are satisfied with the execution and with the synchronization, the coach inserts the action prepared previously, but initially only with the munge.

Then if all goes well, begin presenting the blade for the beat together at the beginning of your step back: that is, it will automatically lead to the students beat coordinated with the beginning of the step forward.

Without saying anything to the pupil, the Maestro will vary the moment of the beat, presenting the blade sometimes together with the movement of the front foot and other times with the movement of the second (back) foot: thus, obtaining the beat in the first or second tempo. The step and lunge action are often alternated with that of the lunge, so that the student does not foresee the movement he will have to do with their legs.

At this point it will also be possible to insert the parry and riposte of the student, again as an alternative to the previous actions, in the same exercise: the Maestro, from time to time, will not only raise the tip, but will direct with decision advancing a direct thrust to the internal target of the student who will parry and riposte. The Maestro must, in this case, pay the utmost attention to the precedence of the point, if they want the pupil to parry without first starting to retreat.

The same procedure can be applied to other more complex actions of two or three movements. The student's synchronization will lead to coordinated actions and with the rhythm set by the Maestro, who must be careful not to make a mistake with his own coordination if he does not want to inevitably transmit the error to the student.

Consideration should be given to the differences in coordinating a beginner or an experienced athlete. The Maestro will have to vary the advance in presenting the stimulus, adjusting to the speed of the student's arm: in fact, beginners have greater difficulty with the movements of the blade, which tends to be delayed compared to the faster legs.

For example, for the beat in fourth and disengagement, performed by marching by a beginner, it might be advisable to present the blade for the beat before starting the step back, instead of on the first foot, because the time required for the disengagement is longer.

Example beginner lessons *(Esempio di lezione ad un pricipiante)*

Let us now give an example of the principles of the mechanical and coordinative lesson, supposing that the lesson is given to a child with a few days or weeks of fencing. We assume that they have already learned the salute, advance, retreat and lunge.

Let's begin with the first exercise with the blade: at the beginning the child must learn and know how to control the reactions of the foil. When the blade bends from the thrust to the target, the hand receives unusual stresses, and one must learn to tighten in time and hold the hand steady.

From close measure, we make them perform an engagement, initially in third. It is preferable that the student does the engagement, not the Maestro: because the student still does not know how to move the blade, and because in this way he can always keep the line closed (the Maestro touches them on the outside if line is not closed) for the measure (the Maestro can touch him on the inside for example, if he lets themselves get too close when they should keep lunging distance.

At this point the Maestro removes the blade from the engagement and invites in fourth (the Maestro arm moves back so that the pupil does not feel this variation as a threat): the pupil touches while extending the arm.

This exercise aways remaining to a strict extent, can involve three levels of difficulty: the student touches without fully extending the arm (useful to avoid shoulder stiffening) extending the arm fully; stretching the trunk forward as well.

The Maestro checks the following points: the student does not rise from their guard, on the contrary they tend to drop more for the distant thrusts; the hand is able to maintain the direction of the blade and the initial opposition of the guard even with the blade bent, with the concavity downwards (taking care to explain that the grip of the fingers is done at the moment of the touch, and not continuously, it is painful and causes the shoulder to stiffen); the movement of the front toe precedes that of the torso, which is necessary only in the third case; the shot is accompanied by the throwing of the rear arm.

When these difficulties are well overcome, the student is pushed back to the extent of the extension, and the coordinative lesson is started with the same simple action, alternating the straight thrust with a lunge with that of the step and lunge (inviting at the end of the step).

Subsequently, always following the principles of the coordinative lesson, we continue with more difficult actions: the disengagement in time, when the Maestro looks for the blade in counter of fourth, the student disengages, when the Maestro lifts the tip and puts pressure on the side opposite the engagement; the feint and disengagement, when the maestro as before, passes from the engagement to the invitation, the student beats direct, when the maestro releases and gives the blade or the line, with the execution in the first or second tempo. This last exercise, being more difficult than that of beating and disengaging, are useful for practicing giving the blade in the right moment (either on the first or second foot); and also to check the differences between a beginner (who must receive the signal more early) and the more experienced athlete.

The tactical lesson *(La lezione tattica)*

It would perhaps be more appropriate to define this as a "strategic-tactical lesson" because it includes both factors. Before continuing, let's define them again, so as to avoid misunderstandings.

On strategy and tactics, we read, when we read numerous "non-definitions", which do not help at all to understand, and therefore distinguish these concepts on a practical level.

According to the writer, **the strategy and planning of one's actions to achieve and objective.** The better the strategy, the lower the cost.

When the programming must take into account an opponent, who obviously does not want to cooperate, one can try to overcome them by force, or induce them to cooperate with deception. **The tactic is to catch decisions useful to us against the opponent and not useful to them**: it can only be obtained by deceit, and therefore fencing with the various types of feints, that constitute an attempt to program the opponent's actions. The tactic, therefore, is part of strategy.

The strategic/tactical lesson aims to make the student understand and master the means necessary to influence decisions of the opponent. It is a higher-level lesson, which is based on the technical skills already acquired (mechanical and coordinative lesson) and on the theoretical and practical knowledge of some contrary. It requires, for each action, an accurate study of time and measure, the observation and memorization of the characteristics and preferences of the opponent, and the correct evaluations of one's means in relation to those.

Tactically effective action starts from observing the opponent's favorite actions.

It must be induced to execute (therefore, programming it) the one for which an adequate opposite is available. If not, then in this case, that in the crucial moment, we do not have the time to make a choice.

The crucial moment is that in which we will enter into measure (critical point, see chapter V), or we will allow, by our choice, to let the other enter into measure, and we will offer them the opportunity the sought, inducing them to act as perceived.

It is decisive, to this end, that the moment of entry into measure is foreseen by us, and not by the adversary: in order to act "in time" while the other will have to "react". The advantage of the initiative, of the driver is to who foresees the action and calls for it on their choice.

As we can see, this is a very broad task, which must be faced step by step. Let's break it down, therefore, into various types of lessons.

Lesson with alternatives *(Lezione can alternative)*

This work is introductory to the study of opposites, with the limits that we will see.

In this type of lesson, the Maestro proposes, at low speed, always different stimuli to the student, who must immediately act with a possible contrary. For example, the Maestro can present the blade for a simple beat direct; a straight thrust or a parry and riposte; he can invite to make the pupil thrust directly.

To each of these reactions they can oppose an opposite, to which the student will have to directly oppose another opposite:

In the first case, for example, the Maestro can evade the beat with a disengagement, and the pupil will have to parry and riposte; similarly, in the second case, the Maestro will be able to attack with a feint, for the parry and riposte or the appropriate counterattack of the student;

In the third case they can try, for example, a parry, or a search for the blade on the preparation step (in the case of a longer measure), and the student will have to evade it by disengagement.

The minimum speed that can be reached in the type of lesson is lower than in the others: having to process a contrary in real time considerably increases the reaction time (which is her the choice reaction time).

The main limitation of this type of lesson is in the way of distorting the reality of the assault, in which the available times are too short to process the response during the action: it is not possible to decide, for example, whether to escape or move while the opponent parries, quickly, simple or counter.

However, the merit of this lesson is in keeping the pupil's attention always awake; in forcing them to think in terms of opposites, and in speeding up the search in their long-term memory.

Furthermore, it is always possible to insert, where it proves necessary, to immediately correct some errors, by using the mechanical lesson or the coordinative lesson.

Lesson with the study of opposites *(Lezione con studio o delle contrarie)*

In this type of lesson, to be performed at a higher speed that the previous one, the Maestro proposes, as a starting stimulus (and starting from a predetermined presentation of the student) one of three attitudes (presentations) or a simple attack. The student must react with the opportune action, previously preordained.

For example, the Maestro can invite, and the pupil will attack direct; it can line up, and the pupil will have to beat and pull; they can hit direct, and the pupil will have to parry and riposte; they can look for the blade, and the pupil will have to disengage. To each of these actions the Maestro can oppose an opposite, taking care to repeat it until the student finds the opposite in turn, which can be discussed and modified.

For example, the Maestro can counter with a parry of their choice and respond to a certain target; the next time (even not immediately after, to exercise the memory that the same situation will be repeated, the student will have to apply the opposite, for example by answering by disengagement, in the proposed case.

From any point of the lesson, if necessary, you can return to the technical or coordinative lesson, to refine poorly executed actions or movements.

The lesson can be complicated as much as one wants (or as much as one can) as long as the student is able to follow and remember. A higher level of difficulty, and a greater adherence to reality, will be found in the lessons in which the initiative passes to the student.

Lessons with probing actions and preparation *(Lezione con scandaglio e preparazione)*

In this type of lesson, the student takes the initiative with a probing action.

The Maestro assumes a presentation, and the pupil proposes, by changing rhythm, a feint or a search for the blade, without concluding the action.

When the Maestro reacts, the pupil dissolves the measure. If the Maestro changes his presentation, the pupil resorts to the probing action again, memorizing the new information.

Subsequently, if or when the Maestro proposes the same starting presentation, the student will start directly with the opposite, to touch. From this moment everything can proceed as in the lesson with the study of the opposites, for the subsequent variants.

Finally, when the previous difficulties are easily overcome, the preparatory actions (concealing) will be introduced: once the Maestros defensive or counter-offensive reaction is known starting from their presentation, the preparatory actions will be tried to induce them to assume that attitude.

For example, if the student, with the previous probing action has ascertained that the Maestro, from the invitation of third, reacts to the straight thrust with the county parry, the problem to be overcome will be that of leaving the Maestro at the required attitude: or with waiting, and concealing of their possible offensive actions; or with initiative consisting of changes in presentations, feints, or various actions on the blade.

Lessons with provocation *(Lezione con provocazione)*

In this type of lesson is to note the reaction (defense or counterattack) that the Maestro opposes a certain type of action from the student, who will have the task of effectively simulating the starting action.

The pupil's reaction will in any case be a conclusive action of offence, defense or counter- offense, while in the previous case the probing action aimed at discovering the defensive or counter-offensive reactions, to use them at a later time.

Typical cases of this type of lesson are counter-times and second intentions, parries and ripostes or counterattacks on provoked attacks, attacks, and defense "to see" with different modalities.

In the second case being second intention, the provocation will consist of a truly carried attack, with all the characteristics of a change of pace and choice of timing. However, the student will have to take care of the measure, slightly longer, and the final measure a little long for an easy counter parry.

In the case of counter-time, the correct provocation is the beginning of an attack, with or without the search for the blade, in practice, for the reasons explained above, even an invitation can have the same function. The effective features of the provocation are: the enter into measure and the sudden acceleration, followed by the parry (stopping or continuing forward) and the riposte.

Similar provocations can precede a counterattack on the Maestro's beginning movement, a parry and riposte, standing on spot, retreating, or advancing: a feint or thrust directed to the forward target (in epee or saber) a search for the blade, an invitation, to be performed when the maestro starts moving his front foot forward. The maestro's reaction may be the conclusion of the attack, with the blade free or with contact, which will be countered by the programmed stop of their initiative, which one can take advantage of with an attack.

The "see" attacks described elsewhere for the other weapons are also possible in epee. In the case of foil and saber they begin with a slow start from a long measure, with an inviting attitude that is at the limit (and beyond) of the correct interpretation of the rules.

The possibility of carrying them out successfully depends to a large extent on the referee's way of seeing, but they offer, if allowed, an undeniable advantage, so it is advisable to learn how to defend against them. They aim to get a "wrong' arrest, in conventional weapons, while the attack generally ends with a straight thrust. In epee, the same action can lead to a double touch, sought by those with the advantage: but a quicker conclusion is necessary, to remain within the narrow time limits of the double touch in epee.

The keystone of the defense against these attacks is in their weak point: waiting for the attacker, to conclude the action, a certain visual stimulus (the search for the blade, the arrest, and the end of the retreat, or the advance, of the defender), they are given exactly (time, measure) the required stimulus, which will cause the launch of the attack, which will be opposed by the opposite, or the dissolution of the measure.

Then, in the lesson, the Maestro will advance as described in one of the previous "calling" attacks. The student, at a certain point of his backward march, when the measure will be sufficiently short (approximately lunging measure), will propose the visual stimulus, which can also be accompanied, to increase effeteness, by a stimulus by sound, either foot stamping

or voice. For example, if the maestro waits for the arrest before concluding, the student will feign the arrest in the way described, and them parry with a jump back.

The training lesson and educational progression (*La ezione allenante e la progression didattica)*

All the previous lessons become training simply by increasing the pace of the lesson, increasing its speed and duration. It can happen to an athlete, overloaded with school and family commitments, that he does not have enough time to devote to physical preparation, even if they do not want to give up their competitive activity. Thanks to the training lesson, dosed according to the Maestros sensitivity, it will be possible to remedy at least in part this deficiency.

The lessons above also represent, in order, a didactic progression. Fencing legs, exercises in pairs, technical lessons, coordination lesson and tactical lesson, and finally the training lesson, can be used to build an athlete physically, technically and tactically.

The complete fencer must know how to express himself by mastering the technical means but supported on the one hand by a sufficient physical condition; for another, form a good knowledge of the dynamics and logic of the game of fencing.

The scheduling of the training session is the task of the instructor, who will have to draw the appropriate indications for the athletes he has to deal with from his knowledge and experience. The division into sectors of the lesson is a mnemonic trick, to be taken with a grain of salt: nothing prevents - indeed it is the best thing to do – to pass within the same lesson, from one modality to another, according to the emergence of needs and problems.

Finally, we can also include the themed assaults controlled by the Maestro among the lessons, who will thus have the possibility to intervene and explain during the composition of the battle phrase. Situations of advantage or disadvantage are to be sought and reproduced in swordsmanship; limitations of allowed targets; space limitations; higher score attributed to previously requested actions; validity of only the actions of attack, or counter-offense, or riposte; and so on.

Knowing how to structure work is positive.

Negative, on the other hand, and letting yourself be caged in by excessive structuring. Flexibility is required also and even more so for the Maestro, not just for students.

In times like these we are experiencing, of rapid change, flexibility, the ability to experiment and to open up to the new is as important as tradition: this must be a starting point, and not a prison.

CHAPTER 8 FENCING ITALIAN AND FRENCH

The Eighth Chapter "Italian and French fencing" briefly examines the main differences in the terminology and classification of actions for the theory of Italian and French fencing. The reference text is the one published on the FFE (Federation Francaise d'Escrime) website.

Tradition is not always helpful, and sometimes it is an obstacle, to understanding the new and governing changes in the most efficient way. The International Regulation (IR) was initially set up following French terminology, and it is therefore useful to know, at least in broad terms, both.

BY THE END OF CHAPTER 8 YOU SHOULD BE ABLE TO:

•Know the translation of some French fencing terms, and the differences with the corresponding Italian terms

- Know the topics of fencing time, simple actions, lines and targets

IF YOU ARE ABLE TO ANSWER THESE QUESTIONS YOU CAN MOVE ON TO THE NEXT CHAPTER:

- How are fencing actions classified according to Italian theory?
- How are fencing actions classified according to French theory?
- Does Gosa mean simple action for the French?
- How is fencing time defined in the Regulations?
- With what terms is disengagement defined, in its varieties, in French fencing?
- What differences are there in the concept of preparation?
- What are the lines and targets for the French?
- What parries do the French consider, and with what hand positions?

TERMINOLOGY

Theory (Theoria)

Terminology (Terminologia)

Classification of preparation (Classificazione preparazione)

Offense (Offesa)

Counter offense (Controffesa)

Defense (Difesa)

Lines and targets (Linee e bersagli)

Simple and compound actions in the two theories of fencing *(Azione semplici e composte nelle due teorie della scherma)*

The fencing time (Il tempo schermistico)

The oldest and most established fencing traditions, from which all the others are derived, are the Italian and the French schools. The other European traditions, the German, and the Spanish, perhaps even more ancient, have had less influence in more recent centuries, especially raegarding modern terminology and classification.

Fencing, yesterday as today, on the ground or within the framework of shared sporting rules, has moments of comparison that allow for verify the effectiveness of theories and means of training. Each School, therefore, gives rise innovations from observation of the results techniques and methodologies that will be then incorporated into an updated educational method . But things are not that simple: the weight of tradition is such as to limit, and sometimes counter, updating fluid and logical systems. It's easy to edit a detail, but it is much more difficult to modify the entire system. And when this logic of progressive adaptations and progress forward for over a century, as it happened in International Regulations, the company seems prohibitive, and few would feel it difficult to get to work.

It follows that the two main theoretical systems of fencing, the Italian and French, would have, in the opinion of the writer, a great need for a major overhaul. Rather than read an exhaustive explanation of causes that led to the choices that characterize the two systems. While waiting, let's be happy to examine, at least superficially, the main differences.

There is already plenty of information about the Italian system written in the official texts, so a very brief summary will be given here. The main reference remains in the terminology of the foil, and its setting didactic, with different adaptations for saber and epee: on the advisability of such a choice it has been discussed and is being discussed, but at the moment and the prevailing one, given the organization of the technical levels, which it provides for the Masters three weapons exam. A terminology and a classification as common as possible to three weapons and therefore a favorable choice for learning, and is appreciated by students, who will later be free to make their own educational choices.

In the Italian system, after a initial description of targets, armed arm positions (attitudes and positions of hand), and leg movements, we proceed with a description of the principle fencing actions, dividing them into offensive and defensive. They define themselves among the principal actions those who do not evade a simple parry, and the others compound actions.

We start from the technical description of the offensive actions, which logically precede those of defense. Simple actions are divided into fundamental and auxiliary and are examined, starting from each of the attitudes taken of the opponent. (Invitation, engagement, or blade in line) Then examined are the defensive actions, especially parries, and the consequent answers (riposte), always in logic of a linear development of actions. The parries can be evaded by actions corresponding as compound. The exits in time (counter attacks) are alternative offensive actions to defense, the counter time and the second intention are opposites described in their executive mode, leaving little space to the description of the tactical part (investigation, preparation, simulation) preceding the application of actions: the scandaglio and traccheggio (probing actions and concealing actions) are the Italian names for this important phase of the assault. It is stated that time, speed, and measurement are fundamental elements of fencing, and here we will not be delving deeper into the topic.

Let's see now in greater detail, but always in summary, the classification French of actions. Reference texts they've changed over the years, as well, in a non-substantial way, for which we will abide, as a reference, to the most recent text "Guide. Les diplomes federaux. Le lexique" published on the Federation French Fencing (FFE) website. For whom, how we Italians, and accustomed to another way of seeing things, certain choices appear questionable.

It would be good to reaffirm, however, that there are also other choices on our side that appear equally criticisable.

After a brief mention of the rules of combat, positions and movements are examined on the platform: the guard, the step forward and step back. A distinction is made between "distance" and "mesure": the first is the space that separates the two fencers, the second is the maximum distance from which it is possible to touch the opponent with a lunge ("developpement" = the lunge, the "fente", plus the extension of the arm armed). Then there is talk of the return to guard, going back, or forward for one new offensive action with the lunge or arrow ('redoublement'), not to be confused with our "doubling".

At this point, we arrive at three groups actions, which include: those offensive, defensive and counter-offensive. Offensive actions include attacking, simple or compound; the riposte, and the counter-riposte (which is still a riposte).

Defensive actions include parries, dodges and defense of measure.

Counter-offensive actions, simple or compound (the Italian feints in time), defined as the set of actions intended to touch, brought on the opposing offensive, they understand the counterattack, which involves arrest with free iron, or on the iron (ours contractions); the remittance ("remise counter offensive') and the recapitulation ('reprise counter offensive", corresponding to our second thrust) counter-offensives, to distinguish them from those that are not; the arrest on the arrest ("contre arret'), what the Italians would call counter time.

The "preparations" follow, which are not equivalent at all to our preparations. According to the most recent definition, it is of "mouvements de la main, du corps et des jambes, qui previous l'offensive, la defensive ou la contre-offensive". It seems that everything that precedes the final action is to be understood as preparation, independently from intentionality, which in Italian fencing makes the actions of investigation (the scandaglio), from preparatory actions (traccheggio). Also, for the final offensive actions (which do not include counteroffensive actions) it seems that the actions on the iron (beats, engagements, and pressures) are to be considered as preparations.

Italians, for example, a fundamental action as opposed to the weapon in line is the beat and straight thrust, or the engagement and straight thrust by detachment, or by glide. According to the French, the beat or the engagement are to be considered part in any case of preparation.

This leads to difficulty in correctly distinguishing between a counter attack and an attack on the preparation, in the case, for example, of disengaging in time.

At this point, it is useful to focus on the concept of attack. Until a few years ago, the International Regulation, in its part technique, did not specify the need for forward movement of the legs, for the attack, defined as: "... the offensive action initially performed by stretching the arm and continuously threatening the valid target of the opponent". The criticisms of this incomplete definition have led the FIE to modify it, adding, in recent times, "movement that must nevertheless precede the beginning of the lunge or fleche": leaving thus understood that lunge or fleche are the normal complement of the attack. The French, in the writing we are dealing with, they go even further, incorporating (without defining it) both the concept of initiative ("offensive: action du tireur qui prend ou reprend /'initiative pour toucher l'adversaire'), *action of the fencer who takes or regains the initiative to hit the opponent* and the need for the "progressive" forward movement of the legs. The initiative, if defined (see the epee handouts by M Toran), finally allows us to give a complete meaning to the word "initial", in the definition of the attack.

The problem of the "simple attack" remains in French fencing and in the International Regulations. The Italians get by relating it to parries: the attack is simple if it does not evade parries and, in the epee, if it threatens only one target. Thus, even attacks made up of multiple movements, such as the change beat, are simple. For the French, however, the attack is simple if performed in a single time (fencing): an ambiguous concept, given that fencing time, in the Rules, is defined as the duration of the execution of a simple action; and the simple action is that performed "in a single movement". Steps for the extraction from the ligament, which for the French are simple and indirect: but it is not clear how it can be considered "simple", i.e. performed "in a single movement", an attack or a coupe, in which the blade must pass in front of the opposing tip (backward movement of the blade and tip) before being brought back to the target. A mess made even more evident by the fact that the same "fencing time", when evaluating precedence, in the case of a double shot, can refer to different durations, depending on the speed of execution of different athletes. The epee, with its fencing time regulated by the chronometer (between 20th and 25th of a second), escapes this logic. While the changes made to the times of the foil and saber doubles attempt to remedy the inconsistency, imitating the logic of the épée.

The attack, therefore, for the French, can be simple or compound, where simple has a different meaning from ours. And the simple attack can be a straight thrust, a "degagement", or a "coupe": the ancient Italian "tagliata", today called "angled cavazione" *cut over*.

Although it may appear that the "degagement" or the "coupe" must necessarily start from an "engagement", like our extraction which starts from the adversary's engagement, this may not be entirely true: and this can be understood by studying the French subdivision of lines and targets.

The line of attack and the portion of the target at which the thrust is directed, in relation to the weapon of the defender. The French, to give a visual representation of the various targets, draw two lines passing through the guard of the fencer, and between them perpendiculars, one vertical and the other horizontal, thus dividing the plane of the target into four quadrants, or "lines". of offense (lignes). Traditionally they are called (from the point of view of those who defend themselves):

• ligne du dedans (inside line), upper left quadrant, protected by the fifth and fourth parries;

• ligne du dessus (high line), upper right quadrant protected by the third and sixth parries;

• ligne du dessous (low line), lower left quadrant protected by the first and seventh parries;

•ligne du dehors (outside line), lower right quadrant protected by the second and octave parries

The parries, as you can see, are two per quadrant, with the hand prone or supinated (nails down or up), in that order. The only two hand positions considered, in relation to our seven, recall the times when the blade was flat, and it was parried with cuts, while the seven theoretical Italian hand positions also refer to the edges of the foil blade, which It has a square section.

For the Italians the targets, and therefore the lines of attack, are in relation to clear positions, determined by the invitations or engagements: for example, the fourth invitation reveals the external target, and only that, with perhaps an excessive didactic simplification . For the French, the position of the blade is less obligatory, as we will also see for the engagements, and therefore does not require starting the threat from a specific target, nor moving from one target to another, necessarily evading a parry.

If we imagine, for example, both opponents with the blades in a more or less central position, but not in contact, it will be possible to attack by directing the tip to the nearest exposed target ("coup droit'), or to another, making it pass around the opponents hand ("degagement"), or in front of the tip ("coupe"). With the blades in contact, which is different from our engagements, in which one blade dominates the other, it will be possible to perform the same actions , or a "coule": which is different from our glide, whether normal or submissive, because with the "coule" contact is maintained, without necessarily "gaining" on the grade of the blade.

Disengagement (*cacation*) with "degagement" and engagement (*legamento*) with "engagement" are therefore not completely comparable in the two systems. And not even with "liement", which is instead equivalent to our transport: action, the latter, which is included among the "prises de fer", a term with different meanings from our "blade seizure". For the French, in fact, it means seizing the opponent's iron by controlling it: opposition, "liement", as already mentioned, "enve/oppement" (carry over), "croise", which should correspond (the definition is not clear) to our means of transport . In Italian fencing, the term "blade seizure" is clearly defined only in the saber text, and consists in the deviation of the opposing blade from the line "by means of a gradual accentuated pressure" of the strong degrees on the weak ones. (Translators note, some confusion in terms as the use of French terms as English have been used).

The compound attack actions are preceded by feints ("feintes"). Keeping in mind what was said above about the "degagement", we can exemplify with the feint direct and disengagement ("feinte de coup droit degager'), the feint of disengagement and disengagement ('Une-deux', i.e. 'la feinte de degagement degager'), the *countercavazione* (deceive or circular disengagement) ('doublement', i.e. 'la teinte de degagement, tramper la parade circulaire').

For Italians, disengaging has several meanings: disengaging out from the engagement ("degager"); disengaging following a feint ("tramper"); to disengage in time ("derober"). In any case, for our teaching, disengaging is considered a thrust, while for the French the corresponding terms simply indicate removing the blade from contact with the opposing iron. To avoid confusion, it should be noted the term "en cavant", which has nothing to do with cavants, and refers, instead, to angled shots (angulations or colpi angolati)

To conclude, a Zen story, which seems to me to illustrate well the concept expressed at the beginning: the tradition followed passively, which from support becomes encumbrance.

THE MEDITATION CAT

The Father L'Abate of monastery had only one weakness: a cat who, sure of the master's affection, he was the true master of the monastery.

The cat even used to walk around the meditation hall while the monks occupied it and, by rubbing and walking near priest Lorn, and it disturbed his concentration. The Father then got into the habit, before practicing meditation, of tying the cat in front of the door of the hall.

Time passed, and tying the cat became a habit that no one noticed anymore. Then, one day, Father Marl, his successor, tied up the cat at the last time.

Then the old cat passes, and immediately message is sent the monastery's successor to buy another cat, so that he can tie it up before the meditation.

TECHNICAL COMMENTS
INTRODUCTION

Among the fencing texts republished today for the press, the "Epee Notes" are certainly the most recent, and therefore, perhaps, they need the least updating. Furthermore, in epee, the changes have been much smaller than in the other weapons, both in regulations and materials, having the basic principles remained unchanged. The new rules on "non-combativeness", rather contested, have, all the more forced to make some new tactical adjustments. Like the other weapons, the epee had to adapt to the now prevailing professionalism, which led to a greater importance of physical preparation: which, however, had a relatively low weight for the epee minor, so much so that it is by far the most widely practiced weapon, even at an advanced age.

a.   We report here the articles of the FIE Regulation on non-combativeness manifest" (t.87). Television needs seem to have the better on screen ones. The new rules push for action who is at a disadvantage and have the opposite effect on those who are at an advantage: like the double touch already. They therefore make the result even more random, reducing time for reflection. It then seems difficult to apply correctly the rules correctly, in the absence of timekeepers dedicated to detecting them 2nd minute without hitting (which isn't too difficult), or 15 seconds without iron contact (which is very difficult to do precisely).

4.   When the two shooters demonstrate manifest non-combativeness, the referee will immediately give the command "Stop!"

Manifest non-combativeness

If one of the two criteria listed below occurs, we will be present of non-combativeness:

1.   Time criterion: about a minute of combat without thrust.

2.   Absence of iron contact or excessive distance (greater than distance of one step forward - lunge) for at least 15 seconds.

5.   Individual test

a)   if during the first two fractions both shooters give evidence of manifest non combativeness during an assault of direct elimination, the referee will move on to the next stage without taking a minute's rest;

b)   when the two shooters demonstrate manifest non-combativeness during the 12th touch of a knockout bout, the referee will automatically proceed to the last minute of the fight. This last minute, which will be drawn in full, will be decisive and will be preceded by a coin toss to determine the winner in case of equal scores at the end of the minute.

1. Team test

a)   When the two teams demonstrate non-combativeness manifested during a team match by the referee to the next assault.

b)   When the two teams demonstrate non-combativeness occurs during the last half, the referee will automatically proceed to the last minute of the fight. This last minute, which will be drawn in full, will be decisive and will be preceded by a coin toss to determine the winner in the event of a tie score at the end of the minute.

b.   Visualizing the cone of protection helps to understand and assimilate the effect of the movements of one's guard. As they say, in football, of the outgoing goalkeeper, who "closes the angle of attack" of his own goal frame, thus carries the guard, pushing forward and towards the opponent's guard, protects your target more; or, decentralizing, and by thus moving his line of attack, he discovers more the opposing target. Furthermore, by leverage effect, who goes first occupies the space with his own guard has a greater chance of deflect the other's blade.

c.   Here "expulsion", which is not a beat, should be replaced with "beat of power" (as stated below).

d.   I only discovered later that the Lambertini had already given this name to the parries described in his "Treatise of sword and saber" of 1870 (page 64, par XXXII, "On the counter- line").

e.   Often, students are asked for a classification of counter attacks in epee, all called "arrests". These are more numerous than in other weapons, also for the greater variety of targets. We can divide them into four groups, which can be combined with each other, each with its variations:

☐   Arrest without blade contact, or flying, (as they used to say): on the attack, and on the riposte (appuntata, if composed); straight, angled, of fuetto (flick), directly or preceded by a beat.

☐   Arrest by disengagement: from the free balde, engagement or glide.

☐   Arrest by time thrust: (arresto di contrazione) on the final of all actions including the imbrocatta.

☐   Arrest by body evasion or dodge (arrresto di schivata) by inquartata, passata sotto, target subtraction.

Of Italian and French parries, you can consult:
http://www.accademiadellascherma.it/booksand-culture/the-french-ed-italian-parades.html

THE BIRTH OF MODERN EPEE

The advent of gunpowder had an effect of a radical social and then technical transformation of the art of fencing. The epee, which is the symbol of fencing, was transformed from a weapon of war into a courtly weapon, which progressively lightened, to remain at the side of the gentlemen, even at cards, as long as it was permitted to be worn. It was used later, above all as a practice and dueling weapon. The practice weapon was the foil; a lighter sword, which in the fencing room had very restrictive rules of use, for safety reasons. The mask with wire mesh came later and was invented in the second half of the 18th century by the French master Texier La Boessiere. Before this fundamental invention, fencing accidents were quite common. To limit them, rules were established, which then turned into the modern convention of foil and Sabre.

The problems, for gentlemen trained for a long time with such an artificial system, probably became more serious after the Revolution: when even the bourgeois conquered the right to compete with equal terms, on the ground, sometimes prevailing thanks to a more realistic technique and practice. Therefore, a new concept of fencing thought took hold, which repudiated the academicism of foil, and developed a new fencing, and a new weapon. The French (Baudry ** in the lead) had the merit, or the historical opportunity, to provide first. And this was the first "revolution" of the modern epee.

In Italy the resistance was greater. Masaniello Parise had won the competition to become the director of the Military Masters School, with a treatise on Epee and Sabre, referring to the glorious but by now ancient Italian traditions.

His epee was actually the Italian foil, and his regulations were those of the convention, as can be easily understood by reading paragraph 166 of his treatise, dedicated to "meetings". But reality imposed itself, inexorably. Athas di San Malato and the Greco brothers became standard bearers, of which the younger, Aurelio, wrote in 1907 the first true Italian treatise on the new dueling epee.

Sport, however, is something else. Giuseppe Mangiarotti was the first to understand it well, who was the first and most prolific architect of the modern Italian sport epee: the author of the second epee "revolution". Let him, from his memoirs, remind us:

After having, for a few years, triumphed in the amateur field in epee and foil, I thought it would be useful to obtain the master's diploma in order to finally be able to profit from the name that my success had earned me.

When my Maestro Baron Lancia di Brola left for America, I thought of going to my cousin Luigi Colombetti for a couple of years to perfect myself in the art of teaching. Every morning, with meticulous scrupulousness, I set myself not only to study the treatise by Masaniello Parise paragraph by paragraph, but to immediately translate it into action making use of mt cousin's consummate expertise. Colombetti introduced me to teaching by becoming his assistant at the Fencing Club of Turin where I thus began my career as a teacher, even before having obtained my diploma.

After two years of work, I took the masters's exam before a commission, as was the custom at the time, for exams for civil masters, presided over by the President of the Fencing Club Turin, Baron di Santagabio and by the masters: Colombetti, Bonioli, Rodolfi and Davoli.

Everything went for the bet but this time I had done my duty because I felt really attracted towards the new profession and I realized I had an innate didactic sense which, later on, over the years, I developed to the fullest, so much to become one of the best teachers.

Profound in my art, strong-willed and patient, I know how to develop absolutely new and precious themes, especially in my favorite weapon, the epee, in which I trained a myriad of excellent champions who I will later enumerate as they were the sure confirmation of my ability in teaching, and of my useful and fruitful work for the benefit of Italian fencing.

Don't think yet that my task was one of the easiest! Having opened my first room in via Chiossetto in Milan, I first had to do my utmost and sweat the proverbial seven shirts to create the first nucleus of epee players who could validate the goodness of my method with their successes. Therefore, this happened sooner than I had really desired and the Basletta, Chiappas, Mantegazzas, Pracchis, Maestro Wejsi, Madinis, Saranas, Baines were the standard bearer of my hall, almost triumphing all epee tournaments of that era.

These unexpected successes aroused a real hornets nest in the fencing environment of the time and we suddenly found ourselves, teacher and student, having to fight against the entire fencing nation which resented the revolutionary action of the newcomers and fought in a compact mass the rise of this new weapon which they dared to denigrate, calling it "the ruin of fencing"; and this only because they did not know her. But I, who didn't need anyone at the time, did not give in and, after a few years of efforts and tenacious and prolonged battles against everyone, I ended up imposing on the admiration of even the most obstinate adversaries and making it triumph.

If, in Italy, the epee was able to be introduced and finally put on a par with the others, foil and saber, it is mainly due to my tenacity. Other masters and amateurs had tried it before me, but at the beginning none of them had the courage to publicly praise it, as I did from the beginning. These masters and amateurs were too tied to conventional weapons and their innate parochialism.

This did not allow them to honestly recognize that the epee was born in France, fifteen years before it was known in Italy. In fact, Master Baudry had dictated the canons of the new weapon, later enriched by his favorite students: Joseph Renaud and Brenau de Labori, both authors, journalists, and incomparable epeeists. There, in Paris, the combat epee was born, the first true enthusiasts of the new weapon, who later became very numerous and very skilled in France.

However, they too had to fight in their country against the supporters of the so-called classic weapon who, at the time, authoritatively directed the fortunes of French fencing and who were called: Louis Merignac, Prevost, Rue, Kichhoffer, Lucien, Merignac, Rossignol: the Rouleau brothers, Mimiague and Haussy, Benneton Filippi and others.

And all these protagonists, masters and amateurs gave life to a very large number of Tomei who lined up the flower of professionalism and amateurism, all together for the good and future of fencing.

In Nice, a grand tournament of masters and amateurs was held annually with over one hundred competitors among the most popular epee fencers in the world; and it was precisely at this important meeting that, seeing the best fight, I learned all the subtleties of the weapon through the personal interpretation of each individual competitor. I returned to myself a truly rich and valuable baggage of knowledge, so much so that I personally created a teaching method that was to give flattering results. As a good observer I have always closely followed all the fencers, from the strongest to the weakest, since even from the latter one can always find something to learn; I tried to correctly detect and evaluate each of their movements and then in turn, put it into practice in combat.

This is the only way to become strong and fierce fencers. Unfortunately, it often happens in the tournament to underestimate certain fencers who at first sight seem mediocre, but who have innate talent for timing and a perfect sense of measure land shots against the strongest of who are not careful observers of their opponents.

It must be known that every fencer not only has his modest talents, but always presents something personal an new in the whole of his game, and herein lies precisely the beauty and interest of the art of fencing. Every action has its opposite, so the study of fencing never ends and is passionate to the point of obsession.

My room via Chiossetto was later baptized "the lions pit" by those who systematically opposed, were the first to have the courage to face the numerous systematic enemies of the epee, routing and defeating them wherever they were. Thus, after a long and exhausting struggle, the road was opened to a new, complete, and very interesting weapon which was to give great satisfaction and subsequently add many laurels to Italian fencing.

The names of the many other students of Giuseppe Mangiarotti, starting with the sons Edoardo, Dario and Mario, are not part of the history of Italian fencing. And since he does not always remember to mention, together with the name of the champion, that of the Maestro who made him such, we want to remind ourselves of those here as well: Allocchio, Marrassi, Cuccua, Minoli, Comaggia, Riccardi, Agostoni, Bertolaja, Brusati, Mandruzzato, Marini, Dellantonio, Predaroli, Breda… and more.

Let us go back to the epee, the sporting one, over which the Italians and the French fought so much at the dawn of the modern Olympics: each wanting to impose their own grip and their own rules. The smooth handle of the French, which could be held almost to the pommel, gave the advantage of a longer weapon, although less powerful that the one tied to the wrist of the Italians.

An agreement was not reached, and the Italian proposals were rejected. Therefore, Italy did not participate in the Stockholm Olympics in 1912 - the first for the newly formed Italian Fencing Federation - in epee competitions: and by this mane we mean the field epee, in the sense that the competitions really took place on the field, outdoors, and with a single touch, while for saber and foil, we measured ourselves indoors, on linoleum or cork platforms, with three touches.

There was also a long discussion about the value of the touch, the different targets, and the time sufficient to guarantee precedence: always inspired by the duel, and the disabling power of a touch. But the reality of the duel, with the fear of dying, and the possibility of continuing to fight and getting more tired, has and has had little to do with the sport of epee. It took time to understand and accept it, and the appearance of the electrical signaling device, official for the first time at the Berlin Olympics in 1936, marked the definitive turning point. Those of Berlin therefore also changed the last rules of the field of epee, which was moved indoors to the gymnasiums, progressively reduced the length of the platforms, which still on 1940, was 34 meters, and also abandoned the single touch. Subsequently, the double touch was also abolished, with the introduction of priority, and the final round was replaced by direct elimination, today at 15 touches.

The timing of the double hit remained to be established: the interdiction of the second lamp, initially set to a tenth of a second, and then to a fifteenth, all definitively brought to the current twentieth/twenty-fifth of a second.

Basically, the divorce from foil had now taken place, the sports epee was born, but the awareness that sport and dueling were two very different arts was slow to establish itself. Dino Rastelli, long-time secretary of the FIS and a great friend of Nado Nadi, explains it very well in the following article, published in 1941 in the official magazine of the federation.

DUELING EPEE AND THE EPEE FOR TOURNAMENT

Not everyone has noticed it yet: but for some time now the three fundamental weapons of fencing have become four. To be more precise, on the contrary, the third weapon, the last born, the terrain epee, split in two, and form the split were born the dueling epee and the tournament epee.

Two sisters who speak a very different language and have completely different characteristics and habits: one, the dueling epee, had holed up in a dark corner, on the edge of the Penal Code and Chivalry Code, with no more cultivators or followers: the other, the tournament epee, has been modernized, has become electrified, lives in the open light of the competition platforms, has countless followers, and finds all the details of its marital status on the Collection of fencing Regulations.

Ultimately, therefore, the weapons of fencing, having become four, return in practice to still be three: foil, saber, and tournament epee. This is not a play on works or an academic suability: this transformation has occurred both in practice and in theory and has caused, as we will see, an immense change in the conception of the weapon.

Born towards the end of the nineteenth century, the tournament epee joined the other two academic weapons existing up to then, the foil and sabre, but wanted to differentiate itself from the latter by basing its game no longer on "artistic" conventions but on reality, i.e., pretending that the match took place on the field and that the two competing swordmen behaved like two duelists.

So here are the first competition tournaments: assaults on a single touch (duels to the first blood); direct elimination (in real duel the wounded and dead are carried away on stretchers); meeting in the open air, preferably on clay or gravel (in imitation of duels in secluded villas).

The fiction, however, could not last: first of all, because it would have been necessary to distinguish the hits according to the target hit, if there had been a hit from both sides, to see if the hit that arrived first would have been able to prevent, in a duel, that the adversary struck at his own turn. (Then the juries should have been composed of doctors and surgeons, who could judge, for example, whether a scratch in the arm could have prevented or not the continuation of the opponent's action, or if instead a decisive jab would have been necessary in full mask and able to switch brains from side to side.)

In addition to this, the one-hit eliminating formula, too hasty and too random, was not suitable for bringing together, at the competitions, many competitors, who would have badly adapted to travel to distant locations to be eliminated after an assault or two, while competitions in the open air were to subject to the whims of the weather, and in any case possible only on the good season, when instead fencing was essentially a winter sport.

So here are the first changes: multi-hit assaults, Italian rounds indoor competitions on a normal platform.

The ground sword that slowly becomes a tournament sword.

And again: the tip of the opponent's epee which, in a duel, sharp and stiff as it is, does not invite you to get too familiar, in a tournament it is covered with a pitched edge and ends in three harmless pins. Moreover, one can look at it through a robust mask and with the arm and body covered by a solid canvas: one can therefore also attempt more risky actions, because one's skin is safe and at the most one can be declared touched.

Thus, here is an essential modification to swordplay: here is that old principle: "to strike without being struck" no longer exists except in the old fencing treatises and in the hurried lessons of "preparations for the duel". (If the opponent takes a step forward, you take a step back. Don't uncover yourself, don't risk it, don't threaten beyond the opponent's arm!).

But in practice who is now studying fencing to prepare for duels? Who thinks anymore, in the twentieth century, of the romantic encounters on the ground, dear to the gentlemen of the nineteenth century? Certainly not those who go to the fencing hall to fence, to rain for tournaments, in short, to devote themselves to a fun, exciting, and educational sport, but nothing more than a sport!

These fencers (100% young people) have no other purpose, in fact, than to carry out healthy athletic exercise, to participate in competitions and tournaments, to win matches, to measure themselves against every new opponent. And in fencing, by natural change of ideas, by modification of collective psychology, what is happening at the same time is all sports, i.e., considering the practice of sport as a practical means and not as an end in itself, occurs.

For some time, therefore, the moment has been propitious for the vastest fencing revolution that has ever occurred: the application of electrical signaling for the judgement of epee thrusts. If fact, here is a system which eliminates the inevitable drawbacks of "human" juries, which avoids partiality, which interests the public, which prevents the protests of the fencers and does not show favoritism in favor of the strongest.

Thus, the principle of "strike without being hit" dies definitively and the more practical "strike with precedence" arises in its place.

In fact, what is the goal to be achieved when you take part in an epee competition? Evidently to win the match, not to train for a duel; to hit, not try not to be hit.

So, all the actions that reach the goal are schismatically correct: and the arrow (fleche) and the thrust, the angulation, and the rimesse, and so on.

It should not be said that they are not fencing correctly because they are not found in the old treatises: fencing has evolved like all other human activities, and experience has shown that all fencing actions must be performed with their correct style, because only the correct style, always and in all cases, offers the best performance. After all, modern fencing obeys, like past and future fencing, the three fundamental factors of fencing: time, speed, and measure.

The electric machine, with the large "double time" currently in use, tends to sharpen the study of these three factors.

If we reflect that in 1/15th of a second a sprinter completes, on foot, about sixty-six centimeters, we can easily understand what study of measure, time and speed it is necessary to apply, to prevent the adversary to apply, to prevent the adversary, in a 1/15th of a second, that 1/15th of a second can make its tip travel the few centimeters required to strike in its turn after being struck, so as to cause at least a double touch!

The style of epee fencing therefore changed accordingly and adapted to the needs of the electric machine; therefore the measures had to be lengthened, and the arm moved away from the line so as not to keep it too exposed and to avoid the opponents actions on the blade while having greater possibility of striking by surprise; the guard is less bent on the legs to have greater mobility, albeit to the detriment of the thrust, but above all the weapon had to transform itself, from an essentially defensive weapon, into an essentially offensive one.

For this reason, the almost absolute totality of the fencers has now adopted the epee without the crossbar as the one that offers the greatest qualities of handling and practicality, as it allows all types of angles and contractions without the need to always keep the line, and it absolutely essential during the phases of combat at close measure.

In this regard, it is appropriate here to mention the erroneous habit of some fencers of calling the epee without a crossbar "French epee", which has always been used by the vast majority of Italian epeeists, and which is manufactured entirely in Italy, by Italian workers, with materials exclusively Italian; that is , in contrast to the so called "Italian" epee with the crossbar which in its classic model should rather be called foil like, while in general it does not have its own defined type, as many Maestro, such as Pini, Greco, San Malato, Eccheri and others, they each made substantial changes.

Both the epee without the crossbar and the one with the crossbar are, by construction, material and use, completely national weapons and differ from each other only for the purposes for which they are intended.

As a practicality of use, the epee with the crossbar, which requires an exclusively online game and generally requires an out of the ordinary physique, has essentially defensive characteristics, and is therefore used without exception in all epee dules, in which it is necessary above all take care of one's own safety, while the epee without the crossbar, thanks to its greater handling and the play outside the line that derives from it, is of particular use in the electric epee competitions, in which it is necessary to strike before the opponent, regardless of your own safety.

The type of epee with a handle in the shape of a hand (Visconti model) deserves a separate mention, which has characteristics somewhere between an epee with a crossbar and that with a smooth handle.

Be that as it may, the tournament epee, which is still erroneously called a field epee, while now it is exclusively a sporting weapon governed by sporting regulations, has not definitively established itself thanks above all electric signaling: the growing success of the first two editions of the Empire Cup and the development of the Nedo Nadi Trophy, the ever-increasing knowledge of the weapon by all epeeists, indicate that by now the epee has its specialized enthusiasts, has its own public of enthusiasts, in short, it has a purely national style.

And that this style is good as demonstrated, in addition to all the international competitions, also by the last Olympics in which the three Italian epeeists admitted to the individual event finished in the first three places of the individual final after winning the team competition.

Even in epee, Italian fencing teaches the world! Dino Rastelli

This article was followed by discussions and technical meetings: and it must be noted that on the opposite side there was an authoritative name such that of Agesilao Greco who, due to his position, put himself at odds with the Federation which he had helped create. But by now the road had been traced, and the CONI, shortly after, imposed its definitive decisions:

AN APPROPRIATE MEASURE OF C.O.N.I.

Rome, 1ˢᵗ of May 1941 XIXII C.O.N.I. communicates:

The technical discussion on Epee fencing has been extensive enough, so that any polemical aftermath must cease. The Italian Fencing Federation has taken its decisions and set the directives, which must be followed by Maestros and fencers. Any arbitrary variation is to be considered harmful to the improvement of this sporting activity and therefore subject to measures.

The revolutions, however, were not over. The signaling apparatus has made it possible to almost eliminate the errors of the juries completely in establishing the materiality and precedence of the touch. But notable technical changes, in the conduct of the assault, occurred when from the sharp trident point, which easily gripped the cloth of the fencing uniforms, and recalled the danger of real dueling points, we moved on to the flat and rounded point: fencing with the weapon strictly in line, so dear to the Grecos and their sworn followers, became counterproductive. The weight that the tip has to bear without causing any warning was soon brought from the initial 100 grams to the current 750. The blades, lighter and more flexible, for safety reasons, had to curve in an arc along their entire length, and the whip or flick strikes appeared. It is easy to understand that these new conditions led to new strategies and new techniques, much more similar to the current ones.

The East wind, with the disguised professionalism of its athletes the increased importance of physical preparation, also influenced the epee, but perhaps less than on other weapons: the lack of convention, and the importance of the counterattack, have always made more cautious and thoughtful then in the other weapons based on the assault behavior of the epeeist.

The last important revolution, so to speak, compared to the past, was the female one: women were authorized to participate in the Olympics in the events of epee starting in 1996 in Atlanta. More recent and less important changes, from new materials to wireless signaling devices, ending with the disputed rules on passivity, show a weapon that is always evolving, even if less radical and tumultuous than that which occurred in the early years, and in the weapons sisters.

PERFORMANCE FENCING

FROM THE SdS-SCHOOL OF SPORT MAGAZINE

THE PERFORMANCE MODEL OF MODERN FENCING MEASUREMENT

MANAGEMENT IN FENCING

Giulio S. Roi

Centro Studi Isokinetic, Bologna

Giancarlo Toran

Pro Patria et Libertate, Busto Arsizio Antonio Fiore, Alberto Bressan Federazione italiana scherma, Roma

Mauro Gatti, Ilaria Pittaluga, Alessandra Maserati Servizio valutazione funzionale, Centro Marathon, Brescia Ermanno Rampinini

Laboratorio di valutazione funzionale, Centro Mapei, Castellanza

Giorges Lariviere

Dipartimento di educazione fisica, Universita di Montreal

INTRODUCTION

Each of us has a conception of the sporting discipline in which we operate, which derives, in part, from practical experience and , in part, from the knowledge acquired through training and refresher courses, as well as through reading more or less specialized publications. In reality, every coach thinks he is the custodian of a performance model which, more often than not, presents a certain hierarchy of values and things to do and not to do in order to obtain the result. Often however, the synthesis of the information acquired in the field and by studying does not allow to have a functioning model available; this causes numerous practical difficulties, which frequently result in errors which could easily have been avoided.

Starting from these considerations, the authors of this article wish to contribute to the discussion on training with two main objectives:

- Highlight the set of factors that have a direct or indirect influence on sports performance;
- Define the type of relationships existing between these factors.

In this work fencing has been taken into consideration, one of the oldest sport disciplines, which has some characteristics that can be found in all other situation sports and which, in Italy, has produced and continues to produce many champions, thanks also to the competence of the various Maestro's and coaches. Furthermore, the heritage of knowledge of the fencing world is unique in its kind and can certainly provide interesting food for thought for all those involved in sports with a high technical-tactical component.

THE PERFORMANCE MODEL

The keyword of the proposed theme is model. This is a very fashionable word, which can be interpreted differently. Actually, a model can be defined as the representation of an object or an idea. This representation can be material or symbolic. A model can be used to explain a whole consisting of several parts, for which a theory is not yet available. Alternatively, a model can be proposed to simplify various aspects of a theory that is difficult to formulate, or to visualize, a model can also be proposed to complete the various missing parts of a theory or system.

The analysis of a model can be carried out in various ways, considering its different characteristics which are: the type of representation, the level of abstraction, the level of metaphor and the type of figure or non-hierarchical illustration. Depending on the type of representation, a model can be:

- Iconographic (use a photo or a scaled image);
- Analog (uses the characteristics of one system to represent another);
- Symbolic (uses often mathematical symbols).

Considering instead the level of abstraction, a model can be represented with simpler elements, which represent a replica, in scale, of the real phenomenon (isomorphic models) and which are mostly descriptive models, up to models with a level of high abstraction, as occurs for example in mathematics.

It is important to underline that there is a difference between a model and a framework, (???) A model, in fact, tends to organize its constituent elements in the most logical way possible.

Table 1 lists the possible relationships between the various factors considered in a model; these relationships can be symmetrical, asymmetrical, causal, probabilistic, temporal, concurrent, sufficient, conditional, or necessary.

Table 2 shows the benefits offered by a model.

There is also a type of model, widely used in pedagogy, which considers a list of factors, which are identified as foremost, context, program, process, and product variables. These factors are all related to a given performance, so this model can be well adapted to sports performance.

symmetrical	If A, then B. If B then A
Asymmetrical	If A, then B; but if not A, no conclusions can be drawn about B
Casual	If A, B always occurs
Probabilistic	If A, then probably B
Temporal Succession	If A then B
Competitor	If A also B

Sufficient	If A, then B, regardless of any other variables
Conditional	If A also B but not C
Necessary	If A, but only if A, then B

Table 1- Relationships between factors or between concepts (Hardy 1973). Each type of relationship is exemplified by three factors named A,B and C.

1. Experiment without risk
2. Predict the behavior of performance of a system
3. Understand in more depth a reality or a system
4. Observe the relative importance of the various components of the system
5. Identify the type and quantity of data needed to understand a phenomenon
6. Define various research hypotheses

Table 2- Main advantages offered by a model

Contact variables are represented by material and human resources: program variables are all parts of the pre-intervention; process variables are represented by training; those of the product are the evaluation of physical form, technique, tactics and performance. By applying these concepts to the performance model, we can see that often in sport we work too much on process variables (training) and too little on prediction variables (characteristics of coaches and athletes.)

Some aspects of fencing performance will be illustrated in the following paragraphs: each aspect, considered individually, has its own importance. However, there are two major difficulties encountered in proposing a performance model:

- Have a global image of sports performance;

- Specify the relative importance of the various factors that determine performance, also considering their development over time.

FAVORING FACTORS AND FACTORS DETERMINING PERFORMANCE

Literature data shows a considerable variability of the many factors that can be considered, in relation to performance, for a group of fencers of the same competitive level. For example, the average values of maximum aerobic power are not particularly high and are similar to those found in active sedentary individuals of a comparable age (di Paramperoet al. 1970; Vander et al. 1984; Roi, Mognoni 1987). Furthermore, there are no significant differences in maximum aerobic power between the various categories, although a certain inter-individual variability is evident: in each category there are athletes with both much higher and much lower than average aerobic power (Roi, Mognoni 1987). So, how important is aerobic power in fencing?

Similar questions can be formulated considering the other physiological factors (anaerobic threshold speed, explosive power of the lower limbs measured on a dynamometric platform or with the Bosco test, etc.) or the anthropometric characteristics of the athlete (mass, stature, body mass index, lean muscle mass of the limbs etc.). these are the easily measurable factors, which, in situational sports, present a considerable inter-individual variability and for which it is practically impossible to detect any relationship with performance (Roi, Mognini 11987; Margonato et al. 11994).

However, this variability is difficult to enclose in a single performance model and the rest that one runs is to give too much or too little importance to one of these factors, depending on preconceptions about the athlete or group of athletes considered. It is well known that in the marathon, maximal aerobic power is certainly an important factor for performance and a positive correlation has been described between maximal aerobic power of a large group of marathon runners and their performance (Sjodin, Svedenhag 1987). When we look at lactate rate, the correlation with performance improves. However, these correlations lose their statistical significance when analyzing a group of high-level marathon runners, with a race time of less than 2 hour 20 minutes. In other words, even in high level marathon runners there is a certain variability in the anaerobic threshold speed, even though this parameter is important for everyone in terms of performance.

It is therefore natural to ask ourselves how each single factor we are going to consider is involved in the performance of a specific athlete who practices a specific sport, or what kind of relationship exists between a certain factor and a certain performance? And, consequently, what are the criteria by which we identify some factors as more important than others? We can distinguish two types of factors that must be considered to formulate a performance model:

- Factors that favor performance
- Factors determining performance

Generally, it is almost impossible to find statistically significant relationships between contributing factors and performance, while we define a determinant when a significant relationship with performance can be demonstrated.

This distinction is not absolute, but dynamic, that is to say that the same factor can be decisive or favorable depending on the movement in which it is considered.

For example, a male athlete who has a percentage of adipose tissue equal to 18%, will certainly not be able to obtain high movement speeds due to being overweight and probably, does not have sufficient physical condition to obtain a stable performance in the time. It is probable that in this situation, the high percentage of adipose tissue could constitute one of the negatively determining factors for the purposes of performance; but it will go on to assume the role of favoring factor once it is reduced, let's say to 10%.

The distinction between performance determinants and performance enhances can also be applied to conditional skills, especially in closed skilled disciplines. For example, one cannot achieve a high-level performance in the marathon if one does not have a high maximum aerobic power and an equally high threshold speed.

In the case of the marathon, these two factors must be considered as determining factors, but we have seen previously that these factors lose their importance when considering marathon runners of the highest competitive level. In fact, these athletes are naturally gifted and have already developed the aerobic and threshold characteristics to the maximum, which therefore assume the role of factors favoring performance, while the determining factors will be other (for example the amount of km traveled weekly, or the psychological characteristics, or others).

On the other hand, in open skilled sports, such as fencing and many team games, it is impossible to find a relationship between conditional skills and performance, even when athletes of different competitive levels are considered. It can already lead the coach to absolutely not consider some conditional abilities (for example, resistance), since there are not obvious relationships with performance, when, in reality, these abilities have a precise role as favoring factors. In this regard, it should be noted that we have often observed high- level athletes, practicing open skilled disciplines with very little physical shape, and who practice incorrect lifestyles. Even so, these athletes sometimes manage to perform at the highest level, however they are often achy and unable to maintain their performance at a high level over time.

A correct approach to the problem relating to physical form, understood as a variable characteristic, and distinguishing the various aspects on the basis of the favoring and determining factors, allows us to understand how unexpected performance can occur and to apply the most appropriate performance model for a given athlete during a certain period of his career.

THE DETERMINING FACTORS PERFORMANCE IN TECHNICAL-TACTICAL SPORTS WITH PARTICULAR REFERENCE TO FENCING

In sporting activities with a high technical-tactical component, we can identify three main factors which we believe come into play, already at a youth level, in determining high level performance and which should be considered in a performance model, especially as regards to the selection of talents and their specialization. These factors are:

- The specific talent
- Early start-up
- The psychological characteristics, with particular reference to the ability to react positively to stressful stimuli. A fourth factor traditionally considered is left- handedness, but its role needs to be reviewed today, at least as regards high-level performance.

THE SPECIFIC TALENT

The specific talent depends, not only in fencing, on coordination skills and on what we define as strategic-tactical competence. These two factors, often considered jointly, must actually be distinguished, since they present peculiar and complementary characteristics, which can be distinctly alienated. In a complex gesture, such as a lunge, the maximum speed depends on the activation of various muscle groups, which must take place in precise periods, in order to maintain the execution speed high and reduce the duration of the movement to the minimum necessary. It is a phenomenon of a coordination type, which can be trained in any case, even if with many difficulties.

Since movement is nothing other than the implementation of a motor scheme, the motor scheme assumes a crucial role, also considering that rapid movements require that all commands have been previously structured (Abernethy et al.1997). Fast movements are performed automatically, as there in no continues solution between the preceptive process and the implementation one, so the ability to make fast movements in situational sports depends, to a large extent, on the level of attention.

Attention is a mental process which, together with the correct image of motor action, motivation, and willingness to perform, constitutes one of the most important prerequisites for sporting success.

The attention is limited in time, since one cannot always remain attentive and it is selective, since it is usually directed towards a single objective. Attention allows the high-level fencer a discriminating activity, in which he limits the stimuli to be analyzed, managing to circumscribe what is truly useful for finalizing the action. In this way, when deciding, the fencer can choose among the various possibilities, the one most suited to the purpose. This already happens in a very short time, thanks to experience. This process, which consist of numerous mental operations, takes place unconsciously and only through selective attention does it become conscious.

There is an important difference between the low-level or novice fencer and the high-level fencer: the former recognizes the situation, chooses the answer, and responds effectively, the latter recognizes and responds more quickly, having already pre-programmed the possible choice. In particular, for the fencer, the ability to process the greatest possible amount of information at the same time takes on a decisive importance, with a procedure that leads to choosing the right information and omitting useless and wrong information. From this point of view, the difference between fencers of different levels consists in the fact that the low- level fencer sees one element at a time, often his attention is not directed to the pertinent stimuli, they are able to read the events after they have occurred and struggles to be attentive and focused when necessary.

On the other hand, the high-level fencer is able to see multiple elements simultaneously, both central and peripheral, selecting and focusing attention on the pertinent stimuli, which allows them to read the situation in advance and predict what they will do next. (These concepts will be developed later, in the paragraph relating to tactics).

The specific coordination skills and strategic tactical competence are already present In young talents and are more developed in high-level athletes. However, what is important to the coach is that these characteristics can be alienated. In fact, the ability to rapidly perform a gesture in fencing (but also in all other dexterity disciplines, including team games), does not seem to depend solely on the predominance of rapid motor skills. This affirmation arises from the elaboration of numerous field tests which show, without fear of contradiction, that there are various muscle types in high-level Italian fencers, just as there is a wide range of muscle types in athletes who practice other technical sports, tactics in both individual and team sports.

The data collected through specific field tests for fencing indicate that the speed of execution of the movement is a peculiar characteristic of high-level fencers (Harmenberg et al. 1991; Bressan, Ranzani 1998), independent of their muscle type. It follows that speed in fencing is the consequence of a functional specialization, which is strictly dependent on the elaboration of motor patterns suited to the situation, which arise from an exact perception of the distance between the two opponents (Toran 1996; see paragraph concerning the tactical aspects and the measure).

THE EARLY START

It is important to underline that both coordination skills and strategic-tactical competence find fertile ground for training in young people, above all of prepubertal age (Caldarone, Berlutti 1983). Hence the need for an early start to sport is justified.

THE PSYCHOLOGICAL CHARACTERISTICS AND THE ABILITY TO REACT POSITIVELY TO STRESSFUL STIMULI

The mental typology of the fencer is particular: they must think a lot before acting, without conditioning their own instinct. The perfect fusion of rationality with instinct is the basis of the fencing action and has a vast emotional resonance. Fencing, in fact, can be considered the metaphor of survival, where one rejoices only if the other succumbs, where each thrust brings back this experience and where each attack involves a considerable expenditure of energy.

The fencer's personality must be solid, compact, and decisive. However, this personality is never granite, since it is always subject to the effects of emotion, which are expressed with fear, doubt, uncertainty, anxiety, etc., all aspects that sometimes contrast with how one should be on the platform during the assault, but which belong to man and, in any case, make them the most evolved being in today's world. The ability to react positively to the stressful stimuli typical of the life of the high-level athlete is an essential characteristic of the winning mentality. Experience leads us to extrapolate the most evident mental aspects of the fencing into three variables: aggression, ambition, and self-esteem.

By aggressiveness we mean that constructive energy which allows to translate the dream into reality.

By ambition we mean the desire that the dream becomes reality.

By self-esteem we mean the willingness not to give up and to continue until the end.

Naturally, the variables of personality are many and more, but in structuring a successful performance, the coach (i.e. the Maestro di Scherma) is called upon to work mainly on these mental aspects, integrating them between men and investigating them, as far as possible, already during the first years of youth activity.

The speed of the fencing action, highlighted by the kinematic analyses, finds its foundations in the speed of the mental processes, which is based on the ability to keep the focus of attention constant.

By focus we mean the ability to become aware of what is happening, restricting the attention field to the specific situation. The focus can be internal, i.e., directed towards oneself, or external, i.e. directed towards what is happening outside. During the competition the focus can switch from internal to external and vice versa, but it must remain flexible, i.e., maintain the ability to focus attention towards the goal. This ability is characteristic of elite athletes and can be trained. When a fencer makes a mistake, they must put in place a procedure which leads them to recover. This happens by shifting the focus inward, to appeal to one's energies and personal abilities, in order to get out of the difficult situation. The ability to keep one's attention active throughout the competition, in such a way that interference (internal and external) does not condition the performance or condition it as little as possible, and is also linked to physical fitness and, therefore, to training aimed at preventing fatigue.

THE LEFT-HANDER

Finally, left-handedness, which entails a neuro-functional advantage (Saibene et al. 1986), no longer seems to be a factor favoring or determining high-level performance today. In fact, if left-handed people can have some advantage among non-high-level fencer, left-handed people do not seem to have a particular advantage among elite fencers. In fact, the percentage of left-handed fencers in the finals of the Olympics or World Championships, as well as in the top ten positions of the Italian rankings has significantly decreased in recent years (generally no more that 20-30%), indicating that the performance of high-level and today independent of the left-handed factor, while the left-handed probably remains at an advantage where technique, understood as simple executive speed, is more important than the tactical components.

TACTICS AND STRATEGY

In all sports disciplines, the mental operations that precede and accompany the motor action can be summarized in:

- Retrieval of information, from the internal or external environment, though sensory channels (sensory input)

- Comparison with the information present in the short-term and long-term memory (processing)

- Programming, choice and execution of the motor act (motor output)

- Evaluation of feedback information on the control and effects of the motor action (feedback)

This complex sequence of operations can be graphically illustrated in figure 1:

In the ambit of open skilled sport disciplines, a distinction must be made between those in which the environment changes independently of the motor response and those in which the environment (the opponent) changes as a function of the response (Toran 1996).

And this is the case of combat sports, and therefore also of fencing. In this case, the graphical representation of figure 1 is completed, as exemplified in figure 2.

The motor response, in fencing practice and in other combat and situational sports, therefore, derives from the processing of information, a part of which is voluntarily provided by the opponent (false information), and a part involuntarily (true information, errors).

This information is provided and/or obtained in the conditions of considerable time pressure typical of combat, which make the occurrence of errors due to fatigue or insufficient mastery of the technique more and more probable. Furthermore, the processing of this information (which is often very scarce) must take place quickly. It follows that, in evaluating the adversary's action and bringing it back to this or that model (and therefore in predicting the adversary's intentions), it is necessary to assume a certain risk of error.

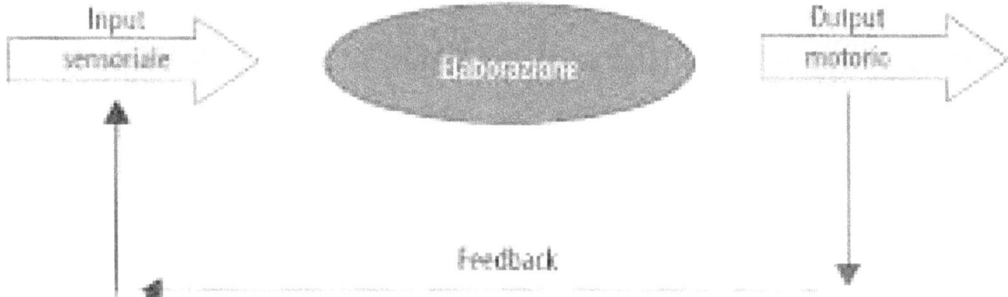

Figure 1 – Diagram of the mental operations that precede and accompany the motor act

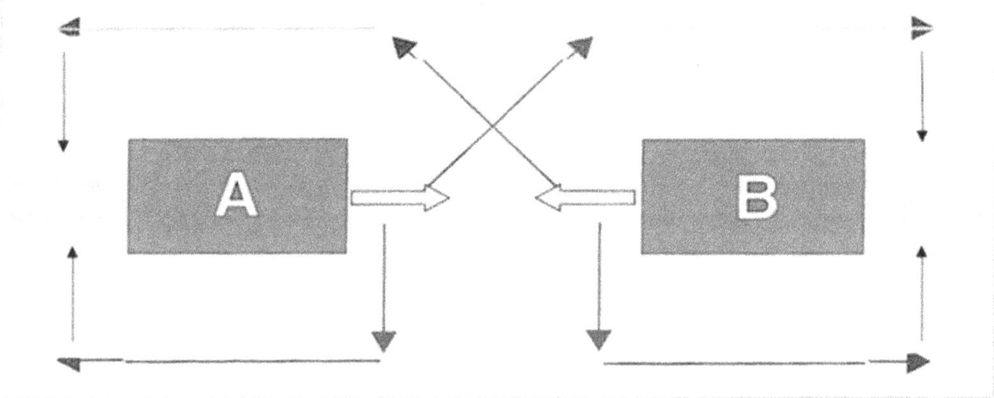

Figure 2 - In open sports (open skills) the scheme illustrated in figure 1 is completed with the introduction of the opponent

THE SPACE BETWEEN THE CONTENDERS

True information about automated or involuntary motor responses (under unforeseen conditions) and information about intentions are not provided spontaneously by the opponent. To obtain them, provocations are used which, to be effective, must be carried out at a precise moment, depending on the space that divided the two opponents. In fencing jargon, this space is called measure.

From a tactical point of view, there are two significant measures: long and short. The first is a distance that allows for control. When the measurement is long, the motor response occurs after the opponent's action, according to the scheme illustrated in figure 1, and with the typical timing of stimulus-responses reactions, because distance allows it.

The short measure does not allow you to react in good time. At this distance, whoever predicted the events acts in time, i.e., with a response synchronized with the opponent's movement. Stimulus and response are contemporary, not successive. In other words, he ling measure allows the necessary time to unexpected stimuli. When this time falls below the reaction time due to the shorting of the distance, the corresponding mental and motor processes are activated. In this way, those who have not foreseen always react late, with automated actions (even very rapid), which tent to always be the same (stereotyped), when the same situation arises again.

PROGRAMMING THE ADVERSARY

It is evident that, in order to program the adversary, false information is voluntarily provided which is all the more credible and effective the more it is gathered in the critical phase of the passage from the long measure to the short measure. Programming the opponent's motor response is something different and more advantageous that simply predicting it, thanks only to the previously collected information. Effective adversary programming required:

- Knowledge of the opponent's habits, preferences, and defects, which is obtained from observations already made, even during previous encounters
- The repeated presentation of false information about one's own reactions or intentions, which must have as a possible opposite (= action capable of neutralizing it) a technique among those requested by the adversary
- Observation of the anticipatory signals provided by the opponent, indicating that the desired motor program has been selected
- The presentation of the stimulus in the situation and in the measurement conditions suitable for the programmed action.

If the programming attempt is successful, it is equally important, after the touch, and before a possible repetition, the de-programming phase, which consists on bringing the opponent's attention to other issues (programming a different action) or in creating confusion (containment trickery) by proposing many different themes. Programming is not only undergone, but also carried out by athletes of even the highest level, often unknowingly.

This happens because the necessary mental operations have now been internalized and automated, thanks to years of lessons with the Maestro and experience in competitions. The data provided by the kinematic analysis show that the difference observed between athletes of different levels and consisting in a considerable increase in the reversals of the direction of march by the high-level fencers, is to be connected to their better tactical strategic skills (Roi, Pittaluga 1997). These indeed require a good number of repetitions and , therefore, a certain amount of time precisely for the success of the opponent's programming operations and for deciphering and canceling the other's programming attempts.

We can therefore define strategy as the process of optimizing one's programming while we define tactics as the set of operations that are implements in order to program the adversary (Toran 1996).

THE TECHNIQUE

It is therefore appropriate to also define the effectively usable technique, as here any motor act or mental process automated: that is, such that it can be carried out without the intervention of attention, conscious, addressed to the constitutive details of the technique itself.

Is it therefore possible to assemble and automate increasingly complex techniques, to leave the fencers attention free to perform higher strategic tasks, which consist in selection and programming the most suitable techniques for the situation.

	SPF	SPM	FM
Total duration (minutes)	47-81	48-98	77-122
Effective duration (minutes)	28-48	22-39	17-34
Duration of breaks (minutes)	19-33	26-59	60-89
Interruptions (count)	126-150	96-180	246-318
Attacks (count)	66-138	96-180	138-210
Change of direction ()	210-582	102-294	120-180

Table 3 - Extrapolation of the minimum and maximum race durations and the minimum and maximum number of events necessary to successfully complete an elimination competition live broadcast of 64 shooters (Pittaluga, personal communication 1998). SPF: female epee; SPM: male epee; FM: men's foil)

FATIGUE AND METABOLIC COMMITMENT

Physical, psychic and intellectual capacities are subject to a deterioration in performance due to fatigue. It follows that training is also important to prevent fatigue. To set up a training program it is necessary to consider the characteristics of the sport practiced and the metabolic commitment required.

The performance model for high-level fencing (direct elimination table of 64 athletes) must take into account that a competition lasts a total of 6 to 10 hours, of which only one or two are spent in bouts, which have a effective combat between 17 and 48 minutes (table 3) (Roi, Pittaluga 1997). During bouts a fencer covers a total distance between 250 and 1000 meters (Lavoie et al. 1985). The duration of each action can be very short, equal to one second, or exceed 60 seconds, and on average it is 5 seconds in foil and 15 seconds in epee, with an average ratio between the duration of the action and the duration of the pause between actions equal to 1:1 in men's epee; 1:3 in men's foil and 2:1 in women's epee.

Monitoring of heart rate and lactate levels in training and in competitions provide important complementary indications on the contribution of energy sources and on the intensity of the competition (Sardella 1982; Bressan, Gambarotto 1999). Heart rate is an individual variable, influenced by various factors, among which age, level of training and the technical-tactical models used in combat are of particular importance. In general, when the technical-tactical skills are better than those of the opponent, the heart rate is high, but always below the maximum and the lactate level is always below 4mM (Hock et al. 1988). As the technical-tactical commitment increases, heart rate increases hand in hand, while lactate levels are always linked to the state of physical fitness and the characteristics of the match, which can lead lactate to even very high levels and above 810mM (Cerizza, Roi 1994).

The lactic anaerobic metabolism is present in the explosive engagements of strength, on the execution of the technical fundamentals of the resolving phase of the thrust.

The anaerobic lactic acid metabolism intervenes continuously in short term hand high intensity actions, which are typical of fencing, and which are proposed intermittently and close together, with incomplete recovery times.

The aerobic metabolism is present in the low intensity phases, in the prolonged phases with high effort and in the phases of payment of the lactic and anaerobic oxygen debts.

Furthermore, the aerobic metabolism also intervenes during the phases of studying the opponent and in the preparation of the thrust.

The data from kinematic research and metabolic analysis during competition bouts allow us to conclude that in foil and sabre, the intensity of the bout is always greater than in epee (table 3). This presupposes a different role of the metabolic aspects in proposing the specific performance model for each single weapon. Consequently, each setting of the training method must be in tune with the combat model practicable by the fencer and with his physiological characteristics (Bressan 1994).

There are various forms of fatigue; here we want to mention only fatigue of metabolic origin.

This fatigue depends on the energy sources used and usable, on any deficiencies of substrates that can be produced in the muscles, on the availability of glycogen in the muscles or in the liver, on dehydration, on alterations in hormonal homeostasis and on nutrition during training and in competition.

It is clear that an appropriate diet and adequate training are the prerequisites for having the physical form that allows you to maintain a high technical-tactical level throughout the match, even in unusual environmental conditions.

Training and nutrition also play a very important role in the prevention of injuries. The fact that functional overload pathologies are on the rise in all sports and also in fencing could indicate that there is a certain inconsistency between training loads and the human body's ability to absorb these loads (i.e., the ability of load): this inconsistency would be more evident when it comes to athletes, even elite ones, with insufficient physical shape.

THE PSYCHOLOGICAL ROLE OF THE COACH

The complex work of the fencing master, who is master and coach, cannot disregard adequate psychological attention, which is not always innate gift.

In the relationship between coach and athlete, emotions, expectations, and conflicts are generated which are constantly evolving, since the fencer grows and matures continuously, and the master must be able to adapt to the ever-new demands of the student. Without a good psychological preparation, the master-coach cannot be able to understand in depth the needs and problems of the student-athlete, who, in their technical and psychological evolution, needs to find in the master a prepared and available interlocutor discuss and evaluate all the situations that gradually arise.

Hence, a psychologically prepared and attentive Maestro-Coach becomes an indispensable prerequisite for high-level performance.

WHAT IS THE PERFORMANCE MODEL FOR MODERN FENCING?

Everything described up to now should in some way enter into an ideal model of fencing performance, with which to format when setting up training, and try to predict if the athlete has the potential to become a champion. The model, the ideal fencer could therefore be the winning athlete. But successful fencers are very different from each other in terms of physical and mental characteristics.

We recall that in fencing, as well as in all sports with a technical-tactical component, it is practically impossible to define a relationship between performance and any of the factors that we have mentioned previously, some of which present intraindividual variations even during the season (Kouterdakis and Coll 1993). The performance in fact consists in successfully facing different adversaries during a tournament, season and even over an entire career. In fact, in this type of competition the opponents (on each of which act all the same factors that act on our athlete) change continuously, and we can therefore say that what distinguishes the high-level athlete, is the ability to adapt continuously and quickly to the new opponent.

Figure 3 illustrates an example of a model in which the two fencers are represented, since all the forms of stimulus we have analyzed so far act on both fencers, in addition to the variable and invariable characteristics of the athlete (Roi, Lariviere 1997).

In fact, fencing, like all other combat sports, cannot be considered an individual sport, since everything we train is based on the opponent and without an opponent there can be no combat sport. This concept can also be extended to all other sports with a technical-tactical component, including team sports.

To further underline this concept, we mention Daniel Revenu (1974), former World Champion in individual men's foil, who in his book Escrime et Education, states that fencing allows you to establish a sort of affective relationship with your opponent, and this aspect is well understandable by anyone who has practiced combat sports and technical-tactical disciplines.

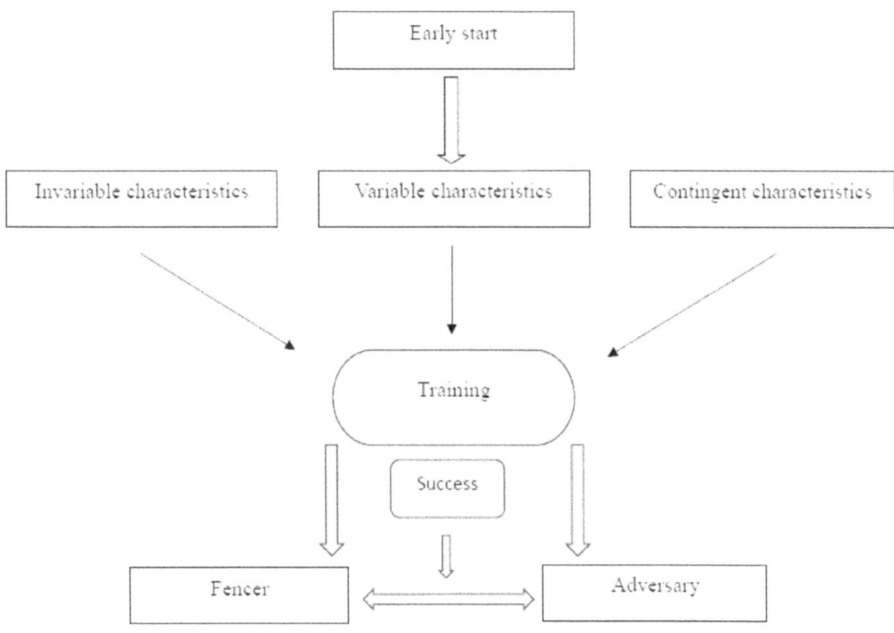

Figure 3 - Performance model for fencing

CONCLUSION

Indicating a performance model for a technical-tactical sport such as fencing is a difficult undertaking. In technical-tactical disciplines, in fact, performance is the result of the amalgamation, even casual, of several factors, so that it becomes practically impossible to establish a hierarchy of conditions that are valid for all athletes. One of the main mistakes that can be made by a coach is thinking that there is one quality that is more important than the others, so that the more that quality is developed and trained, the better the result will be. This is not always true in conditional sports, and it is never true in technical-tactical sports. The high-level fencing performance model must necessarily be a dynamic model, capable of continuously adapting to the evolving situation and which is based on knowledge of the contingent factors and the variable and invariable characteristics of the athlete.

This dynamic conception of the performance model allows us to understand why athletes with inconceivable but highly gifted lifestyles can occasionally achieve exceptional results.

The performance model that guarantees success as a priority does not exist, or at least until now, no one has ever found one. The sample of the champions are always an exception, and the exception cannot be a good point of reference to improve the level of all the other athletes. The performance model, understood in the general sense, should therefore limit itself to indicating the way to initiate as many young people as possible into high-level sport.

In this sense it can be conceived as a means of limiting the damage. On the other hand, the performance, i.e., the victory, needs to be tailor-made for each individual athlete, merging together various elements, many of which have been mentioned in this work, by many of which are still difficult to identify today, as demonstrated by the different typologies of the various champions who populate the competition fields of all the sports disciplines.

BIBLIOGRAFIA

1. Abernethy B., Kippers V., Mackinnon L. T., Neal R. J., Hanrahan S., The biophysical foundations of human movement, Human Kinetics, Champaign, II, 1997.
2. Bressan A., Teoria e metodologia dell'allenamento. Quaderni tecnici di scherma (a cura di Dueci Escrime), Giardini Ed., Pisa 1994.
3. Bressan A., Ranzani P., La valutazione funzionale degli arti inferiori nella scherma, SdS-Scuola dello sport, XVII, 1998, 41-42, 104-119
4. Bressan A., Gambarotto L., La scherma femminile under 20, SdS-Scuola dello sport, XIX, 1999, 45-46, 25-31.
5. Caldarone G., Berlutti G., Aspetti medici della scherma., in: Studi e ricerche di medicina dello sport applicata alla scherma, Giardini Ed. Pisa, 1983.
6. Cerizza C., Roi G. S. Aspetti fisiologici dell'attività sportiva di base, le caratteristichefondamentalidel giovane schermidore, in: Lodetti G., Ravasini C. (a cura di), Sport & educazione giovanile, Ghedini Editore, Milano, 1994, 89-96.
7. di Prampero P. E., Pinera-Limas F., Sassi G., Maximal muscular power aerobic and anaerobic, in 116 athletes performing at the XIXth Olympic Games in Mexico, Ergonomics, 13, 1970, 665-674.
8. Hardy M. E. The nature of theories, New York, MSS information Corporation, 1973,10-22.
9. Harmenberg J., Ceci R., Barvestaa P., Hjerpe K., Nystrom J., Comparison of different tests of fencing performance, Int. J. Sports Med., 12, 1991, 573-576.
10. Hoch F., Werle E., Welcker H., Sympathoadrenergic regulation in elite fencers in training and competition, Int. J. Sports Med., 9, 1988, 141-145.
11. Koutedakis Y., Ridgeon A., Sharp N. C. C., Boreham C., Seasonal variation of selected performance parameters in épée fencers, Br. J. Sp. Med., 1993, 27, 171-174.
12. Lavoie J. M., Leger L., Pitre R., Marini J. F., Compètitions d'escrime. Épée. Analyse des durées et distances de déplacement, Med. du Sport, 59, 1985, 279-283.
13. Margonato V., Roi G. S., Cerizza C., Galdabino G. L., Maximal isometric force and muscle cross-sectional area of the forearm in fencers, J. Sports Sci., 12, 1994, 567-572.
14. Revenu D., Escrime et education, Vrin Ed., Parigi, 1974
15. Roi G. S., Larivière G., La valutazione funzionale dell'atleta Presupposti teorici edimplicazioni pratiche, Coaching & Sport Science Journal, 2, 1997, 1, 37-42.
16. Roi G. S., Mognoni P., Lo spadista modello, SdS-Scuola dello sport, VI, 1987, 9, 51-57.
17. Roi G. S., Pittaluga I., Time-motion analysis in women sword fencing, Proceedings ofthe Fourth I.O.C. Congress on Sport Sciences, Monaco 1997, 66.
18. Saibene F., Rossi B., Cortili G., Fisiologia e psicologia degli sport, Edizioni EST Mondadori, 1986.
19. Sardella F., Risultanze delle ricerche effettuate su schermidori impegnati in esercitazioni di gara nel corso degli allenamenti premondiali 1982, Scherma, 6, 1983, suppl.
20. Toràn G., Introduzione alla tattica schermistica. Società Stampa Sportiva, Roma,1996.
21. Vander L. B., Franklin B. A., Wrisley D., Scherf J., Kogler A. A, Rubenfire M., Physiological profile of national-class collegiate athletic association fencers, JAMA, 252, 1984,500-503.

MANAGEMENT OF THE MEASURE IN FECING

"The variety that nature has placed in things and in the minds is so great that even philosophers themselves, although they seek the same truth, nevertheless because of the very different aspects in which the same proposition presents itself to different minds, are all original, if they didn't read other philosophers, and didn't observe things with other people's eyes.

And it is easy to discover that a very large part of the truths told in our times by those writers who consider themselves original, even if these truths pass for new, have nothing new other than their appearance, and have already been expounded in another world (June 18, 1820).

And you see how all the non-European writers, like the Orientals, Confucius, etc. although they say almost the same things as ours, in any case they seem original, because not having read our European philosophers, they have not been able to imitate or follow them and conform unwillingly, as happens to all of us" (1)

Giacomo Leopardi

INTRODUCTION

In January 1963, the publication of the monthly Coni magazine "Quaderni dello sport" began, with the explicit aim of "giving readers an overview of the institution's activities, its directions, its achievements" (2)

Among the various authors who took part in those first issues, the contributions of Walter Winterbottom appears to us to be of primary importance, as the leitmotifs reflect CONI's ability to certify already in the early 1960's the consolidated creation of national and international networks, as well as connect the various fields of investigation of the scientific disciplines applied to sport, in an interdisciplinary perspective, of rationalization of interventions, of harmonization with the real needs of all sport sectors.

Winterbottom was thus introduced in the box of the article: "former manager" of England's national football team, and one of the best know personalities in the football world.

Born in Oldham (Lancashire) I stated playing football at school and, not neglecting my studies, immediately gave proof of being able to become a capable manager one day. For many years he was coach of the British national team (Director of Coaching). Playing as a professional at Manchester United, he fought the war enlisting in the RAF, reaching the rank of squadron commander (Wing Commander) and was then put in charge of organizing the sporting activity in the air force. He lives in Stanmore with his wife, two daughters and a young son. He is an appreciated scholar, whose books are easily sold and read, due to the clarity of the technical exposition of the game. His perspicacity in judging teams and men is proverbial and the acuity of his observations has prepared and made possible many victories of the English National Football Team". (3)

Of the broad description of the man, what is most striking, in addition to the multifaceted life path not only in sport, is the emphasis on observation skills, especially if read with the current parameters of the analysis of competitive performance. In fact, today the process of therefore the collection and data processing is accessible to all interested parties.

In a conference organized by the Scuola dello Sport in 2008 on Match Analysis, it was remarked that providing an interpretation of the data also helps to better define some specific characteristics of the performance studied, with the aim of "proposing appropriate training processes that aim at improving the same". (4)

Well, these concepts were already present in Winterbottom, who thus began his report, in the aforementioned "Sport Notebook" of 1963: "The condition of the footballer is evaluated on the basis of his ability, compared with that of the other players, to play effectively and meet the demands of the game. Physically, it refers to the elements of endurance, strength, speed, and mobility, and the extent to which these elements are developed relative to the demands of challenging play. One can get some idea of a player's work by carefully observing his activity and playing ability during a game. You can trace a line of a player's movements on the floor by plotting them on a scale plan. On the basis of these it is possible to estimate approximately the distance of his run at speed, moderate pace (jog) and pace (walk).

For example, the total of Robson's movements (inside right of the English Team in the England v Wales test), offers us 660 yards of marching (walk), 3210 yards of trotting (jogging), and 1385 yards at full speed, for a total of 5255 yards. Robson touched the ball 42 times in total during the 90 minutes. This was considered to be quite a sustained game from Robson as a forward. Regardless of the game itself, these 5255 yards of movement in 90 minutes can hardly be considered a very demanding performance. It is therefore important to examine the conditioning in relation to what the player has to do during a football game". (5)

Also on the occasion, we have been shown that observation Is focusing attention on some entity and extracting information from and about that entity. The aspects of observation therefore refer to seeing, measuring, asking, requiring various requisites, such as the ability to discern (sensation), to interpret (perception), to represent (conception), to remember (memorization), of tell (exposition).

Observation and therefore also measuring, i.e., producing "measurements" (sic. Measurable results) by assigning numerical symbols to variables on the basis of fuels: in the England- Wales test, according to what Winterbottom tells us, in 90 minutes the half forward Robson made 5255 yards of movement and he gave a total of 42 touches on the ball.

The history of scientific ideas reports a series of models, of "ways of seeing the world", which are more or less useful for solving problems. Scientific evolution consists in an evolution of the very conception of things and of reality: science develops though paradigmatic revolutions (Kuhn 1962).

The investigation into the possibilities of knowledge of the physical world can be traced back at least to the pre-Socratic philosophers, through theories based on observation of the world rather than on intuition or faith.

It is therefore completely obvious that, even in the sporting field, we can trace at least in contemporary moments the very birth and first development of Decoubertian Olympism – at the turn of the 19th and 20th centuries, when Europe was a great cultural forge, with abundant cultural exchanges between people of various nationalities and between different disciplines – theories capable of giving answers to questions of a technical nature, connected to competitive performance. Theories which, like what Winterbottom has exposed, start from data relating to the positions, actions, time and outcome of the events.

Jacques Revel affirms that societies are historical because they are concerned with the trace they will leave after themselves: "…It is for this reason that they have left testimonies, monuments, inscriptions, archives, then in more elaborate forms, tales, in order to fix in time what they had been: all this has lasted for more that two thousand years"6.

Notational analysis can represent for sport an epochal passage, comparable, with due differences, to that which took place in Greek culture between the formulation of Homeric oral poetry and the codification of the written word in the Platonic Dialogues 7, for the understanding of which a "physical" writing basis? And when to backdate the birth of this performance analysis, albeit in distinct forms, with respect to current modern technologies?

In reality, we have documentary sources well before our century which allow, for specific sport disciplines, a sort of reconstruction of the oral culture-civilization process of writing, interpreted in the light of the evolution of the means of communication.

Since the Middle Ages, in fact, the Fencing Treatises represent an example of protonotational methods. In them, at different levels and with different frequencies, there are descriptions, classifications, explanations, and predictions, in relation to some significant situations, which can occur in the duel and that is in the fencing challenge, which has become an Olympic discipline over time.

In reality, even in this sector of knowledge, orality and writing have mixed and continue to contaminate each other on a daily basis, both due to the ease of meetings and exchanges between the different cultures in which fencing too root, and due to the particular communication relationship between the Fencing Maestro and his pupil.

Writing represents an effective way of organizing man's social life, a system which, in addition to giving a formal aspect to words, makes them reach where the voice cannot. It is important not only because it has made it possible to communicate in a more complete, alternative and often more effective way than oratory, but also because it has made it possible to preserve and better disseminate culture, therefore knowledge and experience.

As previously reported, observation, whether or not it refers to sport, also refers to remembering (memorization). In 1986 Franks and Miller reported that, for all coaches, the overall probability of correctly recalling all observed critical events was about 42% 8.

It is therefore obvious that this availability of information must correspond to an effective management capacity. Treaties have tried to respond to all of this in the past, which - in a complete way, following a scheme which certain principles and a basic method – they allowed the exposition of concepts in the most varied fields of knowledge, often with didactic purposes.

Today, "computer systems which, thanks to the use of modern technologies, organize and manage the information necessary t respond to the technical and sporting needs of coaches and trainers" provide significant support. 9 Technological development affects the world of sport and its professionals in the same way, who find themselves having to choose whether to reject those innovations or instead manage them to obtain better results.

Even in tis Olympic evolution, fencing has seen athletes and technicians, already trained on the Treaties, dedicate themselves to annotating the characteristics of others, so as to be able to subsequently analyze them without any emotional influence. A first evolution of this technique, which was often not adequate at the time of the competition, was represented by the birth of evaluation forms, often handcrafted, which allowed the operator to write down the outcome of various predetermined situations using simple standardized symbols.

Subsequently, the use of the first video cameras to record the performance offered the possibility of reviewing the race several times and, in addition to being able to reduce certain inaccuracies in the observer's evaluation, the detectable parameters multiplied, providing the technicians with an image more complete than performance.

In the last thirty years, Asian fencing organizations have shown a great interest in the use of scientific methods useful for storing information in databases 10, so it was easy to see in their competition venues groups of experts working on a team or on an athlete, managing the new technologies with the coaches, making them and the fencers achieve increasingly effective results. All this can be "the keystone which, on the basis and with the help of new technologies, can evaluate the phenomena involved in the execution of a high-level sporting performance? 11.

However, far from advocating "the inerrancy of technology", we can continue to encounter various "mistakes" in finding measure, which in turn can arise from various factors, such as:

- The appropriateness of the measuring instrument: is the instrument suitable for measuring what it is believed to be able to measure? In fact, the lack of appropriateness leads to systematic errors;
- The reliability of the measuring instrument: is the instrument reliable during the various measurements? In fact, the lack of reliability leads to making random mistakes.

In fact, let us remember that every technological system, however sophisticated, is never perfect and will reveal errors, for example in terms of resolution of the acquired images or of measurement: real, physical, magnification, sampling, distortion of distances, like any other traditional optical instrument.

A further clarification remains necessary: the human eye has immense talents and offers extraordinary performance of visual information, such as the ability to adapt to extreme and contrasting lighting conditions, scientifically defined as dynamic range. The dynamic range indicated the difference between the maximum and minimum light values tolerated by the human eye, which it is good to remember is extremely dynamic and difficult to imitate in the possibility of always seeing what is in front of us, whether it is the strong midday light or twilight. In the world of technology, video cameras have so far tried in vain to copy the characteristics of the human eye. By comparison, the dynamic range of a camcorder is very limited. The difference between the minimum and maximum values of light that can transform into visible video signal is relatively small, even in extremely advanced video cameras.

All this, in our opinion, should not be considered an obstacle to the use of notational analysis experts, who already find strong prejudices among those who believe this use of specialized teams is still very expensive, ineffective and in any case an option only for sports federations rightly or wrongly considered richer.

Indeed, today increasingly cheaper equipment is slowly entering the market, but above all there is a trend reversal in terms of sensitivity of sports institutions towards information technology and the dialog between technology and competition. Our wish is to see technicians and fencers also in Italy benefiting from the large amount of data that Performance Analysis can offer.

Precisely to avoid the overabundance and unmanageability of information, we suggest limiting the observation, collection and processing of data. This work intends to be a contribution to the examination of Fencing, especially for those who want to submit it to performance analysis, suggesting to take into consideration the distance between fencers during bouts (fencing matches), through the study of the Treatises' and of the Regulation of the International Federation.

It starts from an awareness: this distance, defined in the Fencing Treatises as "measure", has a direct influence on the outcome not only of the bout, but above all of the individual fencing actions.

Thus, the analysis of this "parameter" and the time that will be dedicated by the technicians to the construction and improvement of the fencing performance analysis processes, using the data generated by it, will become fundamental.

It will be essential to examine the match taking into consideration the type of match referenced (training, individual competition, team competition, national, international, etc.), also for the purposes of the incidence of the so-called competition invariants.

While waiting for the analytical tool to reach full maturity and sharing, which will allow the technical staff to work in the different temporal domains, from the past to the future, passing through the present, in managing the meeting, the Maestro (technician) and collaborators will be able to make it easier to see some key movements are functional, such as the break between the various fractions of the assault and above all the waiting times between on meeting and another. All of this will certainly require a fencing operator capable of receiving information from the Match Analyst, in real time, directly coding the fundamental information for the match choices of the "Master-coordinator" or rather of the "Technical Commissioner".

The Fencing Treatises from the 19th century to today

Premise

As explained in the Treatises that characterize the study of this noble sporting discipline from the 19th century to the present day, fencing, which: "is both science and art at the same time, teaches, with rational and practical principles, to use white weapons, for defending oneself from the adversary and offend him. and a science, because fencing movement has its rigorous and demonstratable reason for being and art, because its existence cannot be conceived, separating it from its exercise" (Masaniello Parise, 1861).

For the Masters Pignotti and Pessina (who published two Treatises starting from 1970, precisely for the Edixioni della Scuola dello Sport): "fencing, in order to achieve its objectives, is based on three fundamental elements: time, speed and the measure".

All these elements had already been identified in the aforementioned nineteenth-century treatise by Maestro Masaniello Parise, in which we read: "fencing, generally speaking, consists of time, speed and measure, that is, one must choose the right moment to be able to perform an action, joining the choice of tempo to the due speed, and thrusting to the target with sufficiently to touch the opponent. First of all, the measure must be learned deeply". For Masaniello Parise, in fact, a Fencer is the one who brings together all the requisites that art requires, that is, exact knowledge of time and measure, dexterity and speed.

Maestro Mangiarotti, who also authored a treatise in the 1960's, also published by the Scuola dello Sport, mentions the measure in defining combat as: "the set of offensive and defensive actions, offensive-defensive (stops), defensive-offensive (arrest) performed conditioning them to the correct execution of time, speed and measure and which determine the fencing phrase", arguing that: "in combat the execution of an action can vary according to the measure, speed and time".

Measurement definitions and identification of the "measures"

We have remembered that observing and also measuring, that is, producing "measurements" by assigning "numerical symbols" to variables on the basis of rules, but also by offering "definitions".

In the treatise by Pignotti and Pessina, by measure we mean the distance between two fencers on guard, facing each other, which properly means the useful distance to be able to reach the target in carrying out the thrust. The good connoisseur of measure and therefore the one who, when attacking, perceives that the distance that separated the tip (or the cut on saber) of their weapon from the opponent's target can be overcome by his offensive action. This distance can be medium, long and short. These three different distances are respectively called:

- Correct measure, or lunging measure
- Step and lunge measure (also called marching measure in saber)
- And close measure

Since the valid target for foil is limited to the torso only, it is the correct measure when it is possible to reach the opponent's target with only a lunge; for step and lunge, it requires at least one step forward to reach the correct measure in order to lunge; close measure on the other hand, it is possible to hit the opponent without performing a lunge

Measure in saber

Since the valid target in saber fencing is not limited, as in foil fencing, to the trunk alone, it follows that (table 1).

Correct measure	One can hit the torso by lunging and hit the arm while remaining on guard
Step and lunge measure	One can hit the torso by taking a step forward then lunge, and you can hit going to the arm directly with the lunge
Narrow measure	One can hit anywhere on the target without lunging

Identification of the "measures"

The Treaty of Masaniello Parise already distinguished different measures and gave this definition: "By measure we mean the distance at which the fencers must keep when fencing. It will be measured standing still, provided that, by throwing the jab (thrust) only (and or for saber strike with the cut), it will be possible to hit the opponent (in saber, by the cut it will be possible to strike the opponent with the last third of the blade). It will be measured by walking, when, in order to strike the adversary, it is necessary to advance one step. It will be a narrow (close) measure when the adversaries are near to each other to be able to strike each other without advancing the right (front) leg". The definition of this concept is also found in Mangiarotti:

"…The space between the valid target of the two fencers at a specific moment in the fight is called measurement".

For executive didactic purposes, five measures are considered on which the student must repeatedly practice in the execution of the appropriate actions.

- Close range (*Stretta misura*): when the fencers are in close range or corp a corp.
- Standing (*da fermo*): when two fencers can touch each other by extending their arms without lunging.
- Lunging *(D'lungo)*: when the lunge is necessary to touch the opponent.
- Walking (*camminando*) when in order to touch the opponent you have to take a step forward before lunging or arrow (flech).
- Long measure (*lunga misura*): to carry out actions to the forward target or for the application of second or third intention

According to Mangiarotti, in epee, using walking measure, it is preferable to apply "the fleche or arrow" in a decisive way, rather than the step forward and lunge which exposes the attacker to an easy arrest.

Refer to the figure for a better understanding of "the fleche or arrow", i.e., that particular attack which arises from a set of movements which lead the fencer to project themselves forward so that they pass from the guard to a position in which the body is decisively inclined forward with the armed arm slender and the other arm extended backwards (figure 1) 12.

Even Maestro Toran, in his notes, considers 5 measures in epee fencing and deepens the concept: "…fundamental, for the success of every fencing action, is to keep track of the so called "measure". In epee, due to the presence of the forward target, and the importance of the rimesse, at a great distance, it is good to consider, for the teaching of the actions, five measures, instead of the three found in foil: adding a body measure to body <corp e corp> (closer than the close measure in foil) and a long measure (wider, by about one step more than the step and lunge measure). The normal measure of lunge, which allows one to touch the chest with the lunge, also allows the thrust to the wrist by extending the arm only, without any leg movements". Again, according to Toran: "…the measure, generally understood as the distance that separates the two fencers, is an erroneous, or rather insufficient concept. There are two distances to consider: the apparent one, and the one that must be overcome to deliver the thrust, to a moving opponent".

Measure for combat as a teaching point

Corpo e corpo	Tight measure	Close (step)measure	Lunge measure	Step and lunge	Long measure	Grand measure
Either step or jump back	angulation	Extending the arm	With lunge	With step then lunge	Fleche or arrow	Beyond the guard lines
	.5-1m	1.5-2m	2-2.8m	2.8-3.5m	2.8-4m	4m

Execution of attack actions in relation to the measure. The diagram depicts the distances between two fencers when carrying out an action. In an executive sense, these distances are identified in strict measure, from standing still, when reaching out,(d'allungo) walking,(camminando) in long measure. Body-to-body and out-of-measure distances are the opposite limits of fencing combat

The author also considers the measurement from the point of view of the mental mechanisms that are activated, examining two measurements, the long one and the short one, and the border area between the two, which is called the critical point: "…The distance, or measure, which is established between the adversaries at the beginning of an assault, when the offensive strategies are not yet well defined, and wide enough to allow everyone to react (reaction time) to an unexpected initiative by the other, stepping back. However, this distance is limited by the need to carry out effective investigative action, which must be conducted closely.

Thus, during the elaboration phase, the distance from the opponent (measure of control) is, as a rule, just greater than the necessary for an effective action (measure of action). The preparation phase tends to minimize the difference between the two distances, determining a measure of passage between the two, which we can define as a critical point. Beyond this point (larger extent) it is possible to control the movements of the other, exploitation the mechanisms of reaction time (first the stimulus, then the response). On this side of the critical point (minor extent), the reaction time is too high: whoever predicted acts in time; those who have not foreseen reacting, resorting to automatisms, which are the fastest responses among those available, and by suspending the processing system. When the critical point is reached, there are two possibilities to cheese from in the shortest possible time: go back or launch the resolving action. The former is chosen when the conditions found are not those expected, and when the other's voluntary programming activity is in progress. Instead, the second is chosen when the conditions found are required.

Therefore, the brevity of the passage of time for the critical point requires that one arrives there having foreseen it: the choice of time is preliminarily required if foreseeing the occurrence of the favorable measurement condition".

For an evaluation of the measure

In foil fencing according to Pignotti and Pessina, the practical means to evaluate the measure is the following: "… if two fencers are in first position, facing each other with weapons in line, they are: in measure lunging if the points of the respective weapons meet at the point where the medium grade is distinguished from the weak grade in the blade: to the distance of step and lunge if the points just meet where the strong grade is distinguished from the medium grade: if the two fencers are instead on guard, but always with the weapon in line, the find: measure is lunging if the points passed the bell guard by four fingers, step and lunge if the point reach where the medium degree is distinguished from the weak: close if to touch the chest of both fencers.

It is understood that these indications must be considered in a relative sense, i.e., in relation to the stature and also to the physical conformation of the individual.

Previously, precisely in the 19th century, Masaniello Parise in the paragraph dedicated to the practical way of knowing the distance of measure, stated: "…Having put the sword on the offensive line with the arm extended, it will be understood that the distance has been taken when, standing with feet on line and heels together, the tips of the swords are just touching.

This will be called walking measure or out of measure; what matters is that, to strike the adversary, it is necessary to advance one step. It will be a standing measure or the correct (right) measure, when, the two adversaries standing, they reach with their respective sword tips the point that separates the weak grade from the medium grade: and even if, standing on guard with outstretched arms, having the swords on the offensive line, they will go beyond the opposing guard by four fingers. You do not need to go one step further at this measure. Close measure is meant, whenever the two fencers, while on guard, get close enough to strike a blow, without bringing the right leg forward. Correct fencers must never reduce themselves to this measure".

Again Masaniello Parise in the appendix to his treatise, in the paragraph dedicated to the "Measure", identifies the "initial measure for field fencing" (that is, the first dawning of sport fencing), when: "…put the two fencers facing each other, standing with the weapon on the line of offense, the two points of the swords are 40cm away from each other, and having taken the guard position with outstretched arms, the points of the sword barely touch. Thus, it will be necessary to advance one step to find oneself at the normal walking (step and lunge) measure, from which it will be possible to execute the attack either with a step forward and lunge (to hit the opponent's chest), of with a single full blow performed with the right foot if you prefer to strike the opponent's hand or forearm"

Measurement and fencing actions

According to Pignotti and Pessina, no fencing action is performed or even conceived if not as a function of the measurement factor. Therefore: "…knowing how to rightly advance and retreat is a very important thing since this is the means by which the fencer can have control of the measure and the most appropriate distances for offending and defending himself.

The step forward serves to decrease the distance from the opponent and to reach such a size as to be able to strike him by lunging". Mangiarotti previously wrote on the point, who identified in the step forward and step back the movements of advance and retreat which are performed to vary the measure.

In the current language of fencing (for Pignotti and Pessina), advancing is also called tightening the measure" or "shortening the measure" and retrocedere "breaking or loosing the measure".

In the fencing language of Masaniello Parise we also find the definitions referring to the "measurement" factor in the following table.

Steal the measure *Rubare la misura*	Approaching or moving away from the opponent with the left foot, without letting him notice it
Take the measure *Farsi la misura*	It means standing at the right distance while walking, in order not to be surprised by a thrust, which the adversary could throw, at the measure of a firm foot
Dissolve the measure *Sciogliere la misura*	It means going back one or more steps
Corp a corp *Corpo e corpo*	Equivalent to close measure, that is, when both fencers are so close, that they cannot fence, except by throwing blows

The measure as an element of defense

The measure is also a fundamental factor of defense; already in the treatise by Masaniello Parise, there is a paragraph dedicated to the "parry of measure". In particular, it is written that: *it is possible to defend oneself from any fencing action with a measured parry, which is carried out by retreating one step.* And again: "Saber fencing is equally based on time, speed and measure, but each movement will always be based on time, speed and measure. In particular, it will be very important to know how to play with measure, which offers those results that could hardly be obtained with an parry with the blade".

The concept is taken up and reaffirmed also in the Treaty of Pignotti and Pessina, who argue: "Defense means any movement, executed with his own weapon, act to deflect the opposing one in the moment in which the tip of the latter is about to reach the target, or target subtraction itself from the range of action of the offense by retreating.

The first way it is said: defense with the blade; the second is defense of measure. The latter does not allow who if it serves to pass in turn immediately to the offense and therefore it does not conclude but prolong the fight".

Even in Mangiarotti's epee treatise speaks of a parry of measure, more properly: "and a defensive action that evades the attacking opponent by simply breaking the measure, that is, subtracting the target from the offense of the opponent with the appropriate displacement backward with either the limb or body. For this to be effective the defense measure must be performed in relation to the starting distance and the speed of execution of the attacking opponent, in order to pass from one condition of defense to that of an immediate one possibly of offense.

From the point of view of agnostic logic, in fact, any parry with the blade must be followed by an immediate response and, similarly at the measure parry (defensive measure) they must follow immediate counteroffensive action, thus removing the initiative from the adversary".

Toran himself, in his notes, resumes the concept: "The actions exclusively defenses are of three types:

- Target subtractions
- Oppositions
- Parries

Target subtractions are divided into two groups: dodges (lateral, right or left, vertical, ducking) to avoid body shots, and target subtractions properly speaking, to avoid forward target hits; or to the body, withdrawing (the so-called defensive measure). The author adds the "measure" factor as well in mock tactics: "Mock tactics are precisely those aiming at acquisition of information (probing action) and not a conclusion with the offensive action: and to programing the opponent through a double mechanism:

- Clear and repeated feints, to achieve that the other prepares a determined action, choice between the ones you prefer or and, in the ability, to perform actions of concealment in preparation);
- Feints unclear and vary, to disturb and prevent the programming from the other (their probing actions and actions of concealment). In this kind of feints, even the size variations lend themselves to being simulated, together with changes in body attitude that have the express purpose of affecting the attention capacity of the opponent".

After this part dedicated to the definition of the concept of measurement from the point of view of the treatises, in the next issue we will be addressing the related regulatory aspects as well as some hints of fencing tactics and refereeing news.

Space and time: the chronotope in fencing

Among the main features of sports games there are certainly those dedicated to the "game on the terrain" and the "length of the match" the significance in the meanings of space and time, albeit modified several times in human history, are also of particular importance in sports performance analysis processes, especially in those that aim to record in an objective way qualitative feedback and quantities in the management of fencing measure.

In physics, chronotope means the space of four dimensions (the three spatial coordinates, real, plus time, imaginary), introduced by H. Minkowski (1908), to highlight the close link between space and time, established from the special theory of relativity. (14)

As well as in our classical vision of space, its three component dimensions (forward-back, right-left and up-down) are equivalent, homogeneous to each other and relative to the observer (what comes considered ahead or behind by an observer can be considered right or left by another observer arranged otherwise), the relativistic vision assimilates also the time dimension (before or after) to the three spatial dimensions, making it perceived differently by observers under different conditions.

A possible use of fencing interest of the concept of chromotrope and what it is intended to be proposed here to indicate: "the interconnectedness of temporal relationships and spatial within each assault of fencing, depending on the different observers".

According to the well-known linguist of the 20th century Ottorino Pianiggiani, observe comes from Latin observare, composed of *ob*, which has the sense of forward, above, around, and to *serve* that is to guard, save, look too in the sense of keeping an eye on him. So It means to consider, to look diligently so much with the physical eyes, that with those of the mind. 15

So what are the observers for this purpose? Of the interconnection of temporal relationships and spatial within each assault of fencing?

First the actors without whom there could be no fencing assault: the contending fencers and the referee of the bout (with the councilors and video consultants if video-refereeing); subsequently those who are directly interested to sports performance, among which, certainly the technicians and the match analysts.

The concept of "duration of the fight" and "terrain" in the regulations of the international fencing federation (FIE)

The reference to the main rules of sports games, the "length of the match" and "the playing field", also leads us in fencing to analyze the normative data, namely how the international fencing federation (Fencing International Escrime Federation) has regulated the matter.

The FIE regulations define the courtly fight between two fencers as an "assault"; when the result of the fight (competition) is taken into consideration, it is defined as a "match".

The set of matches between fencers from two different teams is called a "match". By combat duration we mean the effective duration, i.e., the sum of the time elapsed between the "fence" and the "halt" commands, which we will discuss later.

The duration of the bout is controlled by the referee or the timekeeper.

For the finals of the official trials of the FIE, as for all phases involving a stopwatch visible to the spectators, the stopwatch must be arranged in such a way that is is also visible by the two fencers on the platform and by the referee.

The duration of the actual fight is: in rounds of 5 hits maximum or 3 minutes (and the formula of the initial phase of individual competitions); in the direct elimination to 15 hits (and the formula of the final phase of the individual competitions), maximum 9 minutes divided into 3-minute periods; in team matches, 3 minutes for each fraction (each single match between the two contending fencers).

A fencer can request the sequence of action every time the fight is stopped, but if they try to abuse or provoke to prolong the stoppage of combat, the referee will sanction them.

At the end of regulation time, if the stopwatch is inserted into the signaling device (compulsory standard for all finals of the official tests of the FOE), this shall automatically cause the emission of a powerful sound signal and block operation automatically of the appliance; however, the scores recorded before locking the unit must remain visible on the same device.

After the perception of the sound signal, the fight is over. When the stopwatch has run its time, the timekeeper must shout "Halt!" or operate a sound signal that stops the fight and also the last thrust thrown is not valid.

In case of the stopwatch malfunctioning or error of the time keeper, the referee will have to independently evaluate the time which remains at the end of the fight.

Therefore, in fencing it is intended to use a stopwatch, which provides us with a measure of time organized as a succession of countable periods, since equivalents, the continuous sum of which indicated to us the passage of the pre-established time.

We have so far noted how concepts and definitions already present in the first treatises of modern fencing have been repeatedly taken up and handed down, to reach the day ours in the more or less original version. And definitely interesting to see that at such texts also refers to the current FOE regulation, for example in the section that it's about the "warning".

In fact, we read in Masaniello Parise "Terrain Fencing Scherma da terreno" (1904) that the adversaries, standing with outstretched arms. They must be with the tips of the blade either epee or saber to be about 40cm apart.

Once on the guard lines, no attack shall be executed until the order "fence" (*A voi*) has been given by the director or combat, which must always have the foresight to ascertain it to be impossible for wither opponent to attack the other unawares. At the "Halt" (*alt*) command given by combat director, who will prevent the continuation of the action even with the intrusion of their own weapon, the tow opponents they will have to stop immediately and take the position of "standing" (in piedi or first position) carrying the weapon in the direction of the opponent's chest. If there was no hit, the opponents will recover on guard.

The FIE regulation takes up the matter of discipline: on the platform, part of the ground destined for combat, is drawn, clearly visible, five lines perpendicular to its length, between which also two warning lines two meters <from the end> and two meters on each side of the midline. The referee places each one of the two opponents so that the front foot of each is behind the guard line.

The warning at the start of the assault renews their guard always carried out in the middle of the pedana width. In the moment of warning, during the assault, the distance between the two fencers must be such that in the "blade in line" the tips cannot touch. After each hit judged valid, the fencers are put back on guard in the center of the platform.

If the thrust was not valid, the fencers are put back on guard in the place the occupied at the interruption of the fight. The thrust that is valid, afterwards the assault or the eventual extra minute, must be performed starting at the center of the platform.

The return to the guard when not for the center, cannot have as a consequence by beyond the end line which the fencer is near when the moment the action was called in the moment of suspension of the fight.

If the fencer has one foot beyond the end line, he remains in that place. The return to guard at the right distance, due to an exit to the side, can place the competitor in defect beyond the end of platform line, assigning them a touch against.

The fencers at the starting line receive the command to "on guard" ("*en garde*" French being the international language of fencing) given by the referee, after which the referee will question: "ready?" (*pronti?*) (French *etes-vous prets?*) after the affirmative answer or in the absence of a negative answer, the referee sahl give the combat signal: "fence!" (*A voi!* IT,

Allez! FR).

Fencers need to be on guard correctly and maintain the immobility complete up to the command of "fence!" Foil and saber the guard position cannot be assumed by placing themselves in the "blade in line" position.

The FIE Regulation thus takes up the concept of "terrano" already outlined by Masaniello: the land must have a surface flat and horizontal. It cannot benefit nor disadvantage one or the other of the two opponents, especially when it comes to lighting.

The platform, (pedana IT, piste FR)

The FIE Regulation introduces an element, which is basic to understand Olympic fencing: the platform. We have seen that the part of the terrain intended for combat it is precisely defined as a "platform". The trials of the three weapons (arm) are disputed on the same platforms.

The width of the platform can be either 1.50 to 2.00 meters. The length of the platform is 14 meters, in such a way that each fencer, standing 2 meters from the midline, has as their disposal the ability to back up without going beyond the end line with both feet, one total length of 5 meters. On the platform is traced, in a manner clearly visible, five lines perpendicular to the length of the platform, i.e.:

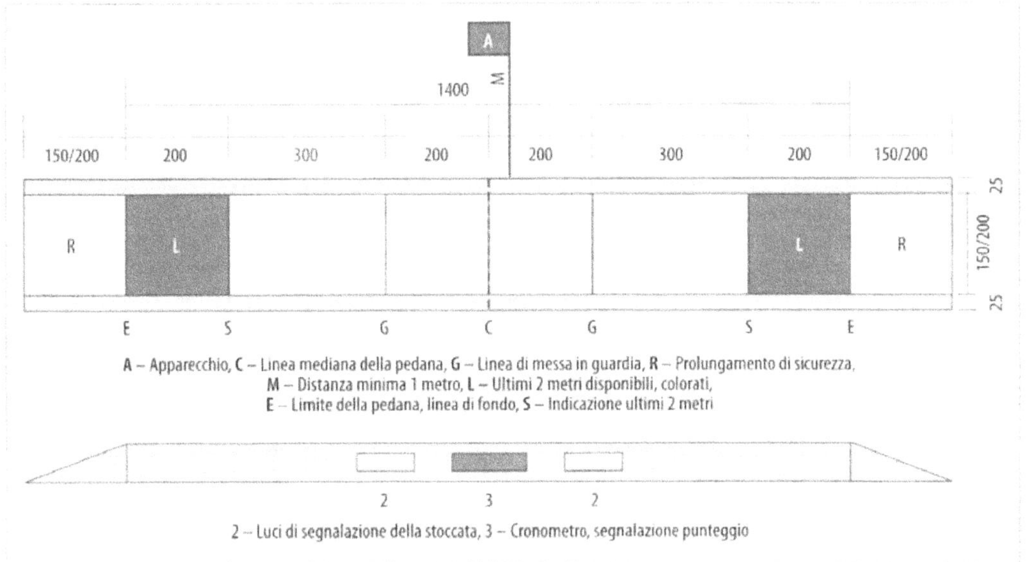

- A median line which must be drawn with a dotted line across the entire width of the platform;
- Two on guard lines drawn two meters from each side of the median line (to be drawn across the whole platform);
- Two end-of-platform lines, which must be drawn across the entire platform, at a distance of seven meters from the midline).

Furthermore, the last two meters, which precede these rear limit lines, must be clearly marked, possibly with a different color from the runway, so that the fencers can easily identify their position on the platform (see figure).

Thus, the terms "Terrain gained or lost" can be better understood, according to the FIE Regulations, which provide that in the order of "Halt" the ground gained remains acquired until a hit has been granted. At the moment of the caution, each fencer must retreat an equal distance, in order to resume the caution (correct) distance.

For the limits of the platform, naturally the FIE Regulations govern both those in the horizontal direction (so-called "rear limits") and those in the vertical direction (so-called "Lateral limits"), under the heading "Overtaking the limits". If a fencer exceeds one of the lateral limits of the platform with one or both feet, the referee must immediately give the "Halt".

If the fencer leaves the platform with both feet, the referee must cancel everything that happened after exceeding the limit, except for the hit received by the fencer who has exceeded the limit, even if after exceeding it, provided that it is of a simple and immediate hit. On the other hand, the hit made by the fencer who leaves the platform with one foot remains valid if the action is launched before the "Halt". When one of the two fencers leaves the platform with both feet, only the hit delivered by the fencer who remained on the platform with at least one foot can be taken into consideration, even in the case of a double hit.

Returning to the "Rear limits", when a fencer completely crosses the rear limit of the platform with both feet, he is declared hit.

For the "Lateral limits", the fencer who crosses a lateral limit of the platform with only one foot will be penalized. At the time of the warning, their opponent will have advanced one meter from the position he occupied a t the time of the overrun and the penalized fencer will have to go back to regain the correct distance. Fi, due to the application of this penalty, one of the fencers finds themselves with both feet beyond the rear limit of the platform, they will be declared hit. The fencer who, in order to avoid being touched, leaves one of the side limits of the platform with both feet – especially by making a fleche – will be penalized.

Corp a corp (melee IT) and excessive distance

In foil and saber, it is forbidden to provoke corp a corp (jostling) (even without brutality and violence). In this case, the referee will inflect some sanctions on the offending fencer and any hit delivered by the offending competitor will be annulled 16. In all three arms it is forbidden to provoke voluntary close combat to avoid a hit, or to bump into the opponent. In the event of such an infringement, the referee will inflict penalties on the guilty fencer and the eventual hot delivered by them.

Nonetheless, if the bout was suspended due to a hand-to-hand combat, the fencers will be warned so that the one who suffered the hand-to-hand combat remained in the place where he was; so too if the opponent has executed a fleche, even without a melee.

The fencer who, either with a fleche or by moving decisively forward, provokes hand-to-hand combat several consecutive times (without brutality or violence) does not transgress the rounded conventions of epee fighting, nor does he commit any irregularity.

The fencer who voluntarily engages in close combat to avoid a hit, or who bumps into the opponent, in instead penalized. We must not confuse the "fleche which systematically ends in a hand-to-hand combat" with the "felche which ends in a clash which hits the opponent".

Which in all three arms is considered a voluntary brutal act and punished as such.

Conversely, the "arrow performed running beyond the opponent" and without a melee it is not prohibited: the referee must not give the "halt" too early as to not cancel any response; if the fencer executes this type of attack without touching the opponent and crossing one of the touch lines of the platform, must be sanctioned.

Finally, the FIE Regulation mentions the excessive distance (greater than that of step-forward and lunge) indicating it as one of the criteria needed to identify the manifest of non-comative.

The "measure" in fencing tactics

In the panorama of Italian fencing sources and international, alongside the Treaties and the FIE Regulations, has developed an interesting literature that he has deepened some concepts or introduced new ones, in light of the evolution of materials, of the spirit of the game, of interpretations, arbitration and various attempts to integrate the existing notions, mostly used for didactic purposes.

Indeed, the definition of "measure" is given by the Treaties and very much anchored to a conception statics of the same. Toran, in his "An Introduction to Fencing Tactics" he underlines the dynamic nature of the measure, assuming the fencers face each other, as the move, react, foresee and strive to cancel the other's attempts to adjust the fit to their liking. 17

Furthermore, Toran states that one must include the forecast factor and then the factor of deception, taking into account the modalities and of the operational possibilities that vary in distance, and speed. He comes then offered a new classification of measure, which is based on movement expected of the opponent and the time to act to that movement. 18

Measurement management

Toran introduces the concept of control that is the operations with which you keep the adversary at a safe distance (it can be avoided the touch is desired), while remaining close enough to impart realism and danger to probing actions. 19

Such safety distance, also defined as a measure of control, and the one that allows whom to check that you react-thinking- to the initiatives of the opponent. To establish, in meters and centimeters, the limit value of the control measurement we should know several variables: reaction times, types of stimuli and of the decisions to make, speed skills and acceleration, physical characteristics, etc. the author points out that, from a certain distance then, the fencers being too close, for those who control it is no longer possible to react by processing in good time, but rely either on automatisms or on predictions.

Such a dangerous situation, i.e., out of the security measure (control) is defined to be "in measure". In our opinion, wanting to give a definition that is added to those existing in the Treaties or in literature, that being in measure it seems more appropriate to say that it is in measure to touch or strike, seen that between two fencers there is always a "measure" a measurable distance and therefore worthy of definition.

We deduce that indeed the control and a part of a more complex whole, defined as "measurement management", that is, those operations that a fencer, processing them or by automation, try to adjust the distance from the opponent profitably.

The distance from the opponent, i.e. the measure, is managed taking into account the operations of the other fencer, but also of the space-time limits given by the platform and the duration of the bout.

The referee: an observable observer

We can, therefore, discuss whether even the activity of the arbitrator can be assessed in this regard: being accustomed (as referee) to stop (or not) contending fencers 20 with a certain advance compared to the practice, in situations, for example, in close combat can constitute a variable appreciable in advance?

Surely arbitration activity has become today even more of absolute interest, for reasons summarized below, and therefore worthy of being considered as well for notational analysis purposes.

Knowledge of key features of a sport (and therefore of the various components) and a basic assumption for proper organization performance analysis.

In fencing, for example, there may be methodologically helpful to use traditional classifications of sports activities, where the same are combined and adapted to this particular discipline: we have characteristics of situation sports, where the behavior of the athlete and a dependent variable from the evolution of the situation itself (open skills: open motor skills, which unfolding and conditioned and modified by the behavior of the opponent, such as we have seen for the "measure"). But we have also the elements of the so-called sports games, with the attribution of a conventional score the execution of variable actions. Finally, as already mentioned above, there is discussion lately, following an orientation questionable arbitration, but now consolidated, if they have not been introduced, in absence of specific regulatory standards, principles of assignment, evaluation of the thrust based on the "methods of execution" of a fencing action, such to assimilate this sport for example to the gymnastics. And this is the case as with sabre, where the arbitration component, second authoritative experts, does not apply the convention provided for by the FIE Regulations.

Measurement, performance and indicators: examples of studies and benchmarks

New technologies are being used in a large variety of situations that are different title referring to evaluation. In this headquarters we are focused on the identification of one of the various indicators to be used as a tool for evaluation performance of individual athletes or a team: the measure.

With performance, we have seen that one may refer to the set of characteristics desirable of the work of an athlete or of a team: the quality of performance; the activity volumes; for performance analysis we can understand, therefore, the effort to make judgements on the various aspects of the work of an athlete or a team, putting who "directs" it or who "participates to management" in the conditions of taking/suggesting better decisions or strategies.

In Anglo-Saxon countries and Northern Europe there is an over thirty-year tradition of construction and use of performance systems for measurement, in order to keep under control and improve the performance of subjects observed, systems developed beyond outside of sports models.

Subject to the necessary prudence clauses for a transposition of these experiences, naturally "decontextualized", to the Italian reality and above all to the sport performance, we believe one can draw some useful universal indications from the experiments within the major US Federal sponsored ct of 1993, titled the Government Performance and Results Act. 21.

Rather than illustrating in detail how the performance analysis system was created, for the obvious reasons of brevity of the present work, our intention is to highlight the philosophy that guided the construction process, where the evaluation of the indicators to be used and it was just an in-between moment.

Before and after this phase, they have in fact dedicated their self-particular attention to other aspects considered equally important:

- Definition of indicators and information that satisfy

- Possible ways to enable this for real use, especially within the decision-making process

- The probable risks of alterations or inexact interpretations of the results within organizations (yes, one thinks in a transposition in the model sport, to the performance analyst report-fencing coach/master athlete- sports club/federation- executives)

- The identification of suitable standards and terms of comparison.

Basically, the recalled US law required the US Federal Governments to redefine, through the development of strategic plans, their institutional missions and to identify long-term goals who could guide the programs of the Agency for the next five to ten years.

No.	Latin	Italian	English	Examples of performance questions
1	Quis	Chi	Who	Who can use this information
2	Quid	Cosa	What	What you want and can measure
3	Quando	Quando	When	In competition and in training
4	Ubi	Dove	Where	The positioning of the technological means (camera to the fencing platform)
5	Cur	Perche	Why	Why analyze the measurement in fencing
6	Quantum	Quanto	How much	The value of what has been measured
7	Quomodo	In che modo	How	What comparisons need to be made in order to express an opinion on the performance sport
8	Quibus Auxilis	Con quali mezzi	By what means	The choice of technological means

Furthermore, they were obliged to submit annual performance plans, programmatic documents that indicate the activities to be carried out and the objectives to be achieved over the next year, the performance reports, reports that contain the results of the analysis carried out and explained whether, and to what extent, the objectives declared had been archived, as well as the reasons for any failures and solutions suggested to improve mediocre or shoddy performance.

With the enactment of this law, they had then, stated a process of experimentation on a large scale, which lasted about six years: production which resulted of reports, articles, comments and reflections on related problems to the implementation for such analytical systems. (Martini, Sisti, 2002) 22 represents a capital of knowledge and experience since which-in our opinion- it is possible to draw with full hands, even for the sports sector and particularly for fencing, at least as a benchmarking method.

Within this experimentation, a role of particular importance was carried out by the General Accounting Office (GAO), the Court of Auditors America, which accompanied the implementation of the law as both critical observers, on behalf of Congress, both as a methodological point of reference in opposition to the federal administrations.

From our point of view, they have therefore notes have appeared of great interest some studies on documents produced by the GAO, which represent a testimony of the spirit that led the performance law and of the difficulties that characterized the implementation. Indeed, they contain analysis and evaluation of recommendations general methodologies addressed to the Agencies, on critical remarks specific to internal experiences of individual administrations, of certain utility also for performance analysts in sports.

In its methodological framework that the GAO 91996) identifies three key steps that should mark the path to take towards performance analysis:

- Mission and desired outcomes
- Measured performance
- Use of performance information

These form the heart of the approach.

As already highlighted in the administrative field, even for our sporting purposes it can be useful to share the healthy realism on what was foundation of the American experience, using extreme caution on the possible use of the results of the analysis, with particular regard for decision-making purposes, in the awareness of probable dangers of alterations or inaccuracies interpretation or these results. 23

Even if the subjects observed were organizations, while in sport there often is reference to the lone athlete, the American strategy took into full consideration the weaknesses and dangers inherent in the application of a method of analysis that aims to judge the success based on simple quantitative measures. Also, there was concern to establish which comparisons carry out with the indicators that are built, in order to identify some criteria general to set up a correct analysis of performance.

The cases taken from the US experience highlight that there is no one unique methodology for construction and the use of performance indicators. However, there are "transversal" awareness's which tend to recur, albeit with different intensities (Martini, Sisti, 2002).

Here, we have deemed appropriate to remember these awareness' that, in our opinion, they are useful to anyone to evaluate sprots performance through new technologies and, therefore, by identifying of indicators, holding song which cannot objectively be found and then, propose an applicable methodology at each contest. We made our own the purpose of identifying a minimum common denominator of precautions to be respected in the cases where the evaluator has the ambition to: "making a judgement on the observed subject using simple measurement operations of their performance, i.e., the indicators" (Hatry 1999).

As already been studied in the administration sciences, anyone preparing to develop performance indicators asks themselves some questions, first of all those relating to the fundamental information needs to which the analysis intends to give answers, as well as to the interested parties and their reactions.

In general, even in sport, the scheme created by St, Thomas Aquinas in his most famous work, the Summa Theologiae, in which, at the end of the 12th century, the theologian identified the fundamental elements that identify the structure of moral action (see table on previous page).

We have referred to the considerable help offered to coaches and athletes by modern technologies for observing technical sports behavior, to evaluate their performance and post-performance. It must also be considered that there are other factors that can contribute to a better observation and feedback process.

These factors can represent in extreme synthesis what fencing masters, coaches, athletes, biomechanics, psychologists, and motor learning experts have been proposing in recent years: a holistic view of the athlete.

This new approach naturally involves challenges, especially when some assessments – think of those of a behavioral nature and the quality of mental engagement – require the construction and implementation of observation models with processes that are not always easy.

The same studies carried out by the Scuola dello Sport, to identify some peculiarities of fencing (Arpino, Aquili, Badolato, Svalduz 2011), have tried to draw inspiration from this lease common denominator of caution. In particular, an investigation was launched to identify the presence of characteristics of the sabre, essentially those referable to the distances, detected through a notational analysis, existing between the two contenders during the assaults.

On the occasion of some training sessions of the Italian National Team, television footage was made and thanks to the positioning of markers and the use of the Dartfish software, data was collects.

Some results have emerged, even if the small size of the sample calls for caution and makes further checks necessary, summarized below.

- The technical-tactical characteristics of the saber show different measures between the actions that take place in the center of the platform (about 75% of the total) and actions outside this area and, therefore would seem to indicate the need for a different approach in the management of the training and automating certain actions.
- The largest extent found in the center-stage actions, mainly due at the "4m start" and therefore to the need to "enter into measure", emphasizes the importance of phase functional preparation for the particular scheduled action.
- In training there appears to be appropriate drills to shuttle up narrow measures, evaluating even if not visual stimuli should be introduced.
- Future studies may be of interest to a larger sample and a comparison with the two more specials.

The resigning the conclusions of the present work, it is worth mentioning that in this fencing year it opened a discussion on referee interpretations which apply, perhaps a little too much "free and extensive" way, the rules written in the FIE Regulations: the same rounds on TV shows amply and confirm what has been said about the discrepancy between codified normative source (FIE Regulations) and arbitration orientation (presidents of the FOE jury).

Maestro Toran called recently due to this deep gap between what is written and what is really applied in matters of arbitrage, above all in saber fencing. In its rubric on the Fencing Academy website, offers us an interesting first diachronic vision of the FIE Regulations, with some ideas and reflections, which in our notice are pregnant not only for the single sustained position. 24

The FIE Regulation was born in 1914, with the International Fencing Federation itself. According to Toran that version, which has remained largely unchanged for the technique part, was already then, the result of a compromise among the schools prevalent at that time: the French, Italian and Hungarian, respectively hegemonic for the epee, foil and saber. Like any compromise, the FIE Regulation had many flaws, and the time has accentuated it. Then as today, referred to the "Treaties", without indicating which. But the definitions on which they are based, according to the author should be taken mainly from French texts.

We report the two examples used by Toran in the table following.

The "fencing time": the "duration of a simple action" (t.1: is reported the numbering followed in the latest version of the FIE Regulations)

> For the French, the simple action is one performed in one movement, while for the Italians it is that who does not evade a parry. From this it follows that: a beat and straight thrust for the French is not simple, but it is for the Italians. Reliefs: for the French, it is simple- that is, performed in one movement- as well as the coupe action (cut over), in which the blade, for example for a riposte, passes in front of the tip of the opponent, with and evident backward movement of the weapon: simple and indirect response, says the FIE Regulations. Furthermore, there is no reference to the movement of the legs that can accompany the movement or the armed arm. So, the "fencing time" is the same for a straight thrust performed in different measures, standing still and in step forward and lunge.

The different offensive actions, the attack, the riposte, and the counter riposte (t.7)

> Remarks: the counter-parry and riposte (otherwise, we would have to include the counter to the counter-riposte as well and so on...), i.e., the offensive action that immediately follows the parry; a few more lines further on "explains" and mentions, among the offensive actions, the counterattack, which did not exist before. A little further we find that there are also others: and in the same family we find the renewed attack, the second thrust (redoublement in French), the resumption of attack, which is nothing more than a new attack by whoever has exhausted the first, and the counter time: complex action, of second intention, which includes a simulation of attack, a parry and riposte, in the most common case

According to Toran, if these are the "definitions" and "explanations" on which the continuation of the FIE Regulation is based, there is nothing to be surprised about and it matters little that the drafters, as if to justify themselves, declare in a note that these "definitions" do not constitute a treatise on fencing, but only serve to "facilitate" the understanding of the text.

We share these criticisms of Toran and also his conclusions on the FIE Regulations: if the foundations are not very solid, the whole edifice is not standing, but ironically this is the strength of the International Regulations, because no one is capable of changing it, or if feels like facing the challenge of changing the foundations of the building. The regulatory system remains unchanged in the written part, but is worn down by arbitral interpretations, which in fact replace the royal ones, even in a burdensome way.

Typical example of interpretation that has replaced the definition and quantity implemented for a long time by the arbitration class in matters of the attack.

Per the FIE Regulation.

Attack

It is the initial action performed by extending the arm and continuously threatening the opponent's valid surface, preceding the execution of the lunge or fleche (t.7)

This outstretched arm action has not been seen for decades, except in epee. Indeed, the forward movement performed by the lower limbs has become, in the current interpretation of the referees, by far the most important factor in foil and saber.

It is necessary at least two aspects that have conditioned the concrete realization, in the life of the fencing community, of what is ordered by the rules that make up the FIE Regulations:

• Fencing has become enormously faster and has adopted materials and instruments, even for arbitration purposes, which did not exist at the time of the first extension of the rules;

• The referee continues to be positioned at an average distance of one to two meters form the two contending fencers, therefore insufficient to ensure a correct vision of the simultaneous development of very rapid actions.

However, one wonders whether it might not be the dusty of the International Federation, through its bodies, to ensure the application of the norms. It almost seems as if we wanted to delegate the application of the Regulation to the arbitration category, as well as to the prudence and common sense of the individual, rather than imposing it, even in an authoritarian way, with an authentic interpretation, i.e. clarifying once and for all the meaning of the rule and imposing uniformity of judgement, thus cutting off any doubt.

Toran argues that fencing with conventional weapons, i.e. foil and saber, changed profoundly around the 1950's and more precisely since the introduction of electric foil, thanks to strong Italian pressure on the FIE. The International Regulations, on the other hand, remained the same, proving to be absolutely inadequate.

How and why did it change? Limiting ourselves to foil, before the advent of the electrical system, the thrust has to be "seen" to give the point. So the fencer's concern was centered, therefore, on the visibility of the touch. Aesthetics has their part. The chest target was the primary, if not the only one. Each touch, as the Treaties we mentioned in the first part of the article said, had to be delivered with due opposition; the weapon had to be well in line and the hit angled towards the body almost did not exist: these situations are very similar to dueling 25.

We therefore agree with Toran that when electric foil took hold, angled thrusts and shots on the edge of the valid target, including the back, became common. In fact, it was enough for the new instrumentation, the so-called "apparatus", to record them. Angled hits require even a partial flexion-extension of the arm. As a result, the parries expanded.

Furthermore, as anticipated above, the new material has had its impact as well: the new blades, more flexible and lighter for safety reasons, have transformed angled shots, cut overs and flicks, which require an even more flexed arm, and parries of the opponent even wider.

Here then, the closures appear, i.e., contractions together with shortening of the measure, up to physical contact with the other fencer, almost always with a flexed arm, as it is considered the only effective solution to counter an attack with a flexed arm. We return, therefore, to the conditioning of the referee on the interpretation of the attack.

The management of the measure involves larger movements on the platform: the referee, in order to sight athletes and apparatus at the same time, should run faster than them and clearly he cannot do so. We share Toran's conclusions: "peripheral vision allows the referee to perceive changes in direction, but not the precedence of both weapon movements. In this situation, it is indeed evident that judging the correctness of an attack is really difficult.

Furthermore, what appears at normal speed, then, is often very different from what is evident from a slow-motion shot".

Returning to the FIE Regulations, it states that the touch must reach its maximum when the front foot touches the ground, in the lunge. But at this point the first differences not codified by the Regulation itself already arise.

In foil, if the thrust was not parried, but the attacker remained in line, the priority would remain his. In sabre, on the other hand, and with the same convention established by the Regulations, while continuing to threaten a target, the attack is considered as concluded; the fencer in defense, while not parrying, is rewarded by the referee if they throw their hit together with the final blow of the opponent (by final thrust we mean the one that follows the feint, performed by the attacker together with the contact with the ground of his front foot).

Rightly, Toran does not understand the reason (and we with him), given that the defending saber does not parry, but above all does not reach the target with an advantage "fending time": the Rules clearly state that only the parry, the one with the iron, from the "right" to respond with the riposte. He then arrives at the conclusion that : "…if we wanted to be consistent, we should judge this action as a simultaneous, a common time, without assigning the point to anyone.

But if we really wanted to judge the action in this way, I.e., agreeing with whoever suffered the first attack, it would be good if the rule were written somewhere. We could believe, as with other actions, that the rule is silly, or wrong: but at least we would have a sure point of reference. Instead, we have to learn that the houses are like this, from a certain point onwards, because that's what was decided in some meeting, before some competition. But, apart from the referees present, and those who learned about it by oral transmission, nobody knows anything about it. It is an indecent situation, but we ended up accepting it.

Who is smarter, who knew or understood before, will be able to teach the "new" action to their pupils, and take advantage of it. For the others, there will be nothing left but the sterile protest, and the liver ache.

Referee orientation on the attack in saber

In conclusion, if a possible use of the concept of chromotrope of fencing interest is the one we intend to propose here to indicate "the interconnection of temporal and spatial relationships within each fencing bout, according to the different observers", we believe that not only the athletes, but also the fencing referee can and should be subjected to notational analysis, in order to allow the fencer and whoever prepares them (Maestro, technicians, video-analyst,…) to adapt the fencing actions to the modus operandi of the one who judges the match.

His right

The fencer who is defensively trying to parry feints, but then ripostes as soon as his attacking opponent touches the ground with his front foot

Motivation

The fencer who in attack touches the ground with his front foot unloads their offensive action

Notes

(ll Leopardi G., Zibaldone di pensieri, vol. 1, Mondadori, 2004, 108.

(1) Cfr. Onesti G., Prefazione, Quaderni dello sport, 1963, Anno I, 1,3.

(2)   Cfr. Winterbottom W. (1963), La messa in condizione dell'atleta, Quaderni dello sport, 1963, Anno I, 2, 24-28.

(3)   Ruscello B., Usi e principi della Match Analysis, Aspetti Metodologici, Atti del convegno Match Analysis, Scuola dello Sport, Roma, 2008.

(4) Cfr. Winterbottom, Op.cit.

(5)   Cfr. lntervista a Jacques Revel: "La memoria e la storia" – San Marino, 11 giugno 1995, pubblicata su http://www.emsf.rai.iVtv_ tematica/trasmissioni.asp?d=303.

(6)   Havelock E. A., Cultura orale e civilta della scrittura. Da Omero a Platone, Laterza, Roma-Bari, 2006.

(7)   Franks I. M., Miller G., Eyewitness testimony in sport, Journal of Sport Behavior, 1986, 9, 39-45.

(8)   Sgro F., L'lnformatica per la valutazione della performance, in Allenare l'Atleta: Manuale di Metodologia dell'Allenamento Sportivo, Edizioni SdS, Roma, 2011 .

(9)   The design and development of databases recall the world of the software industry, which has also developed tools in the sports sector to support performance analysis, such as Focus, ProZone, Dartfish, Quintic, Data Volley, etc.

(10)   Dalla Vedova D., Besi M., Faina M., Nuovi occhi per l'allenatore" SdS-Scuola dello Sport, 2008, -ml, 71.

(11)   the arrow (flech). The Regulations of the International Federation of Fencing allows the execution of the arrow only in foil and spee. In saber it is prohibited, as the fencer cannot advance with the rear legadn/or foot in front of the front leg and/or foot.

(12)   Toran's notes are used by the Italian Fencing Federation for the preparation of its technical tests, with particular regard to the National Instructor and Fencing Master exams, which are held at the National Fencing Academy in Naples.

(13)   Einstein A., The electrodynamics of moving bodies (Zur Elektrodynamik bewegter Korper), in Annalen der Physik, 1905, 17, 891.

(14)   Pianigiani O., Etymological vocabulary of the Italian Language, Dante Alighieri publishing company of Albrighi, Segati, 1907, available for consultation also on the internet www.etimo.it.

(15)   Nature of the sanctions. In fencing there are three types of penalties (in ascending order: yellow card; red card; black card) whose application is governed by a special table contained in the article 120 of the FOE Regulations. In this venue it is sufficient to report that when an director must punish a fencer who commits multiple offenses at the same time, they shall initially punish the least serious offense. The sanctions are cumulative and valid for the match, with exception of those communicated with the black card, which has the meaning of a exclusion from the test, suspension for the rest of the tournament and for the following two months of the current or going season beginning (October 1st for World Junior Championships and January 1st for the Worlds Championships). On the contrary, one team excluded from the tournament due to a black card inflicted on one of its members is by no means excluded, as a team, from subsequent trials, but cannot include the punished fencer. Some infractions may result in the

cancelation of the touch delivered by the fencer who committed it: in the course of the bout only the hits brought in are annulled in relation to the infringement. In general, the warning, expressed with a yellow card, signals to the offending fencer that any new offense committed by him will result in a hit of penalty. The red card signaled by the director to the offending fencer incurs a hit added to the score of their opponent and, in the case of the last hit, the loss of the assault. Furthermore, every red card cannot be followed by another red card or a black card, according to the nature of the new infraction.

(16) Toran G., Introduction to Fencing Tactics, Press Society Sportiva, Rome, 1996, 31.

(17) "…greater distance means more time to process and react; shorter distance, little or insufficient time, and therefore reactions necessary are automated", Toran, Op,cit, page 32.

(18) With the term probing actions (scandaglio), Pessina and Pignotti define in the Treaties the investigative study tending to reveal the defensive way or counteroffensive of the adversary, represented by a simulation of attack executed with truthful expression in a manner to induce the adversary to reveal his reactions.

(19) For the FIE Regulations, close combat is admitted as long as the fencers can use their weapon arms regularly and until the referee can, in foil and sabre, continue to follow the actions.

(20) For the Government Performance and Results Act and later for studies on the activities carried out by General Accounting Office (GAO), see; AA.W., Performance measurement in public administrations, 2009, CNEL.

(21) Martini A., Sisti M., indicators or performance analysis? Implications of the US experience in performance measurement, Rivista Management Science Quarterly, 2002,2.

(22) Martini A., Sisti M., Evaluation the success of public policies, The Mill, 2009

(23) Toran G., "Opinions are opinions, and rules are rules. But the reality and something different, in every field. The real royals of the game not are those written, but those actually applied, and depend on those who apply them, the referees, and by whom It selects. I feel like affirming that one of the conditions for one to be able to speak of advancement of civilization and the narrowing of the gap between quantum and written and how much is actually applied. Apparently, the opinion is widespread that, in fencing, this gap is still too wide. I agree with this opinion, and think I know the reasons why this happens", www.accademiadischerma.it

(24) In reality, the "visibility" of the hit and therefore the awarding of the point has always been a constant of modern fencing, above all in conventional weapons: foil and sabre. In the chronicles of the great rivalries between Italian and French fencers in the latter decade of the nineteenth century, a nice episodic is counted. Protagonist was the great master from Livorno, Eugenio Pini, who engagement with the French masters legendary encounters. Reports William M Gaugler, in his splendid History of Fencing, which in 1889, in the Cirque d'Ete, the Livorno fencer met the Left-handed master Rie, Known as "the invincible". When the Frenchman, after being hit twice in a row not announced of being hit, Eugenio Pini, not seen, removed the protective button from the tip of his blade and directed his blow exactly in the center of the Invincibles' jacket, tearing it apart. Then the Livorno master took off his mask and furiously shouted at Rie, "Is this touch not valid too?" (Gaugler W. M., History of Fencing, Busto Arsizio, Nomos Editions, 2007.

Translators Selected Bibliography *(Bibliografia)*

Barbasetti, Luigi. (1936) "The Art of the Sabre and the Epee" E.P. Dutton & Co., Inc. New York

Barbasetti, Luigi. (1998) "The Art of the Foil" Barns & Nobel Books ISBN 0- 7607-0943-2

Clery, Raoul, Lieutenant (1948) "Traite D'escrime de Pointe" Republique Francaise, Minisere de la Guerre, Etat-Major de L'armee

Commissione Tecnica dell'Accademia Nazionale di Scherma (2015) "Dispensa di Scherma Storica e Artistica" Accademia Nazionale di Scherma ISBN 979- 12-50230-00-3

CONI Scuola Dello Sport-(2014) "Quaderni della Schuola dello Sport, Quaderni di Scherma il fioretto, la schiabola storia della scherma" A cura Arpino, Marco e Gulinelli, Mario. Pessina, Giorgio e Pignotti, Ugo. Coni Servizi S.p.A. ISBN 978-88-97337-06-5

CONI Scuola Dello Sport-(2013) "Quaderni della Scuola dello Sport, Quaderni di Scherma: la spada, complemento per la didattica nascita della moderna spada sportive la prestazione schermistica" A cura Arpino, Marco e Gulinelli, Mario. Mangiarotti, Giuseppe. Toran, Giancarlo. Servizi S.p.A. ISBN 9788897337072 *Gardenti, Stefano*, "Trattato Globale di Scherma" printed by Amazon fulfillment, Poland

Gaugler, William, M. (1997) "The Science of Fencing: A Comprehensive Training Manual for Master and Student; Including Lesson Plans for Foil, Sabre and Epee Instruction" Laureate Press, Main, ISBN 1-884528-05-8 *Gaugler, William, M.* (1998) "The History of Fencing: Foundations of Modern European Swordplay" Laureate Press, Maine, ISBN 1-884528-16-3

Gaugler, William, M. (1993) "A Dictionary of Universally used Fencing Terminology" Laureate Press, Main, ISBN 1-884528-00-7

Mangiarotti, Edoardo. And Cerchiari, Aldo, (1966) "La Vera Scherma" Longanesi & C. Milano

Nadi, Aldo, (1994) "On Fencing" Laureate Press, Florida, ISBN 1-884528-04- X

Orlandi, Giuseppe (1953) "Dizionario Italiano-Inglese, Inglese-Italiano: voci dell'uso corrente e familiar e della lingua classica termino commerciale, scientifici, techini americanismi-voci del gergo" Carlo Signorelli, Milano *Parise, Masaniello,* (1901) Fifth Edition "Trattato Teorico Pratico Scherma di Spada e Sciabola" Roux e Viarengo, Torino-Roma

Pecoraro-Pessina (1910) "La Scherma di Sciabola, Trattato Teorico-Pratico" Giuseppi Romagna, Roma

Pessina, Goirgio e Pignotti, Ugo (1969) "Il Fioretto" Federazione Italiana Scherma, Scuola Centrale Dello Sport, Roma

Rastelli, Giorgio, (1942) "La Scherma" Sperling & Kupeer, Milano (Con l'approvasione tecnica della F.I.S.)

Revenu, Daniel, (1985) "Les Fiches de L'educateur" Federation Francaise D'escrime, Melun

Six, Gerard (2022) "Glossaire de l'escrime sportive" Federation Francaise D'escrime, Paris

546

Extensive use of Google Translate for general sentence translation and correspondence with M' Igor Celli, M' Giancarlo Toran and M' Ralph Sahm.

Six, Gerard (2022) "Glossaire de l'escrime sportive" Federation Francaise D'escrime, Paris

INTRODUCTION 3

THE FOIL 7

PREFACE 8

CHAPTER I. **ESSENTIAL ELEMENTS** 10

(ELEMENTI ESSENZIALI) 10

  The nomenclature of the foil's parts 10

  Balance, weight, and total length of the foil 13

  Holding the foil 13

  CHAPTER II. **THE OFFENSE** *(L'OFFESA)* 31

  CHAPTER III. **THE DEFENSE** *(DELLA DIFESA)* 38

  CHAPTER IV. **COMPOUND ACTIONS** *(AZIONE COMPOSTE)* 44

  CHAPTER V. **AUXILIARY ACTIONS** *(AZIONI AUSILIARE)* 57

  CHAPTER VI. **ABOUT CIRCULAR PARRY AND RELATED CIRCULAR OFFENSIVE ACTIONS** *(DELLE PARATE DI CONTRO E CONSEGUENTI AZIONE DI OFFESA CIRCOLATE)* 64

  CHAPTER VII. **THE FUNDAMENTAL ELEMENTS OF FENCING** *(GLI ELEMENTI FONDAMENTALI DELLA SCHERMA)* 79

  CHAPTER VIII. **APPLICATION** *(APPLICAZIONE)* 92

  FIRST SYNOPTIC FRAMEWORK 99

  SECOND SYNOPTIC FRAMEWORK *(Secondo quadro sinottico)* 109

THE SABER 119

LA SCIABOLA 119

PREFACE 121

CHAPTER I. 121

  Considerations for fencing with the saber *(Considerazioni sulla scherma di Sciabola)* 122

CHAPTER II. 142

Preliminary training exercises for the arm *(Esercizi preliminari per l'addestramento del braccio)* — Description of the preliminary exercises *(Descrizione degli esercizi preliminary)* — Defense *(Della difesa)* — Simple parry *(Parate semplici)* — Linking one parry to another *(Passaggio da una parata all'altra)* — Circular parries *(Parate di contro)* — Half circular parries *(Parate di mezza contro)* — Parry against a glide ceding parry *(Parate di ceduta)* — Exercises referring to the circular actions *(Esercizi riferentisi alle parale)* — Molinelli. 142

    Head Molinello (Molinello alla testa) (1) : 153

    Horizontal Molinello from the Left (Molinello orizzontale da sinistra): 154

    Horizontal Molinello from the Right (Molinello orizzontale da destra): 154

    Rising Molinello from the Left (Molinello montante da sinistra): 155

    Rising Molinello from the Right (Molinello montante da destra): 155

Chapter III. 156

    Chapter IV. 168

    CHAPTER V 176

    CHAPTER VI. 186

    CHAPTER VII. 189

    CHAPTER VIII. 197

    CHAPTER XI. 202

THE EPEE COMPETITIVE WEAPON 215

    CHAPTER I 217

    THE ESSENTIAL ELEMENTS OF THE EPEE 217

    MOVEMENTS AND ACTIONS 217

    (GLI ELEMENTI ESSENZIALI DELLA SPADA 217

    I MOVIMENTI, LE AZIONI) 217

    Way to hold the epee *(Modo di impugnare la spada)* 219

    First position *(La prima posizione)* 219

    The line of offense *(La linea di offesa)* 220

    The line of direction *(La linea direttrice)* 220

    Gain on the lunge or renewed attack *(Il raddoppio o ripresa dell'a-fondo)* 227

    GRAPHIC SECTION FOR CHAPTER I 244

    THE ELEMENTS ESSENTIAL TO EPEE 244

    GLI ELEMENTI ESSENZIALI DELLA SPADA 244

    THE MOVEMENTS AND ACTIONS 244

    I MOVIMENTI, LE AZIONE 244

CHAPTER II 266

THE BASIC ACTIONS IN EPEE 266

LE AZIONI BASILARI DELLA SPADA 266

THE OFFESE 266

L'OFFESA 266

CHAPTER II 287

GRAPHIC SUMMARY 287

THE OFFESE 287

L'OFFESA 287

CHAPTER III 297

THE BASIC 297

ACTIONS IN EPEE 297

(LE AZIONI BASILARI DELLA SPADA) 297

PREMISE 297

CHAPTER III 309

GRAPHIC SUMMARY 310

THEDEFENSE 310

LA DIFESA 310

CHAPTER IV 315

COUNTER-OFFENSE 316

LA CONTROFFESA 316

CHAPTER V 319

THE FIGHT 319

IL COMBATTIMENTO 319

ANALYZED GRAPHICS 326

CHAPTER V 326

THE FIGHT 326

IL COMBATTIMENTO 326

THE CONVENTIONS OF EPEE COMBAT 332

CHAPTER VI 337

APPLICATION LEARNING AND EXERCISES 337

APPRENDIMENTO APPLICATO ED ESERCIZI 337

CHAPTER VII 351

QUESTIONS AND ANSWERS 351

DOMANDE E RISPOSTE 351

CHAPTER VIII 360

ELETRICAL SIGNALING OF THE HITS 360

SEGNALAZIONE ELETTRICA DEI COLPI 360

VOCABULARY 365

TERMINOLOGY IN 365

ITALIAN — FRENCH — ENGLISH — GERMAN 365

INTRODUCTION 372

CHAPTER 1 **DEFINITIONS AND INITIAL POSITIONS** 374

CHAPTER 2 **TARGETS AND LINES** 384

CHAPTER III **OFFENSIVE ACTIONS** 395

CHAPTER 4 **DEFENSIVE ACTIONS** 417

CHAPTER 5 **TACTICAL NOTES AND READINGS** 425

CHAPTER 6 **HOW TO GIVE THE BLADE** 442

PREMISE 443

CAPITOL 7 **TEACHING** 453

INTRODUCTION 455

CHAPTER 8 **FENCING ITALIAN AND FRENCH** 471

TECHNICAL COMMENTS 478

INTRODUCTION 478

THE BIRTH OF MODERN EPEE 480

DUELING EPEE AND THE EPEE FOR TOURNAMENT 484

PERFORMANCE FENCING 490

FROM THE SdS-SCHOOL OF SPORT MAGAZINE 490

INTRODUCTION 492

MANAGEMENT OF THE MEASURE IN FECING 510

The Fencing Treatises from the 19th century to today 517

Premise 517

Measurement definitions and identification of the "measures" 517

Measure in Foil 518

Measure in saber 518

Identification of the "measures" 518

For an evaluation of the measure 521

Measurement and fencing actions 522

The measure as an element of defense 523

Space and time: the chronotope in fencing 524

The concept of "duration of the fight" and "terrain" in the regulations of the international fencing federation (FIE) 525

The platform, (pedana IT, piste FR) 528

Corp a corp (melee IT) and excessive distance 530

The "measure" in fencing tactics 531

Measurement management 531

The referee: an observable observer 532

Measurement, performance and indicators: examples of studies and benchmarks 533

Arbitration news: the observed observer 537

Attack 539

Referee orientation on the attack in saber 541